34946

D1156650

349146

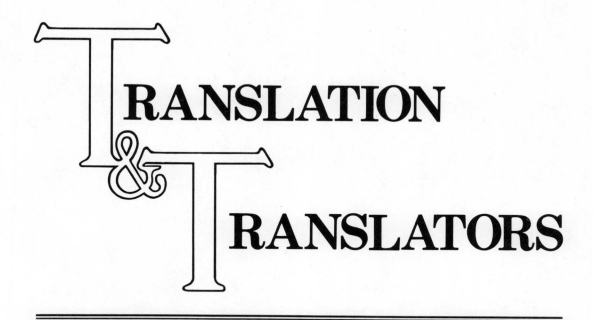

An International Directory and Guide

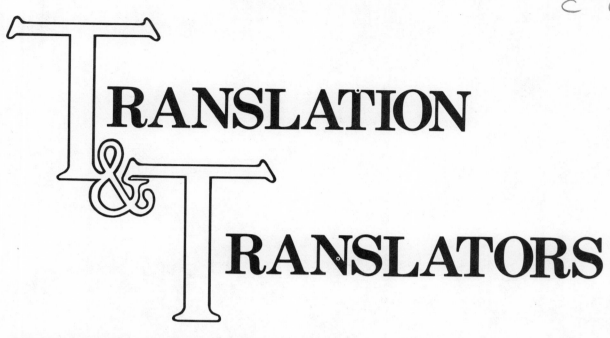

TRANSLATION & TRANSLATORS

An International Directory and Guide

Compiled and Edited by

Stefan Congrat-Butlar

R. R. Bowker Company

New York & London, 1979

Published by R. R. Bowker Company
1180 Avenue of the Americas, New York, N.Y. 10036
Copyright © 1979 by Stefan Congrat-Butlar

Library of Congress Cataloging in Publication Data

Congrat-Butlar, Stefan.
  Translation & translators.
  Includes Index
  1. Translating and interpreting—Handbooks,
manuals, etc. 2. Translators—Directories. I. Title.
P306.A2C6   418′.02   79-6965
ISBN 0-8352-1158-4

CONTENTS

PREFACE

"Translation is, henceforth, a profession. A translator will have rights, protection, decent remuneration, better professional standing, improved working conditions." *Jean-Paul Coty,* VIII World Congress of FIT, Montreal 1977

"Translators—the proletarians of literature with nothing to lose but their chains." The quotation is from Robert Payne, prolific biographer, novelist, organizer and director of the first conference on literary translation ever held in the United States (see Sec 1, 1970). A director of the Columbia University Translation Center, he has been one of this country's—and the globe's—most fervent fighters for what he called "the translator's rights" (and, in fairness to the investing publisher, "the translator's obligations to the publisher"). The characterization is fitting and to the point, for there is a general unawareness in the United States of the art-*cum*-craft-*cum*-skill-*cum*-knack-*cum*-industry of translation that is seemingly inexplicable.

When one considers, as Payne did, that "we are the heirs of all the cultures of the past only because translators have made them available to us," it is surprising to learn that even the relatively educated, literate and sophisticated are still unaware and seemingly unappreciative of the role translation plays in bridging cultures, in promoting understanding between peoples and cooperation between nations, and making international publishing practicable and possible.

We in the English-speaking world could have no Greek epics, no Bible or Cervantes, no Tolstoy or Dostoyevsky, no Flaubert, Balzac, or Proust, no Goethe, Heine, Mann, or Hesse, no Neruda or Beckett (a rare self-translator!)—without translators. Germany could have no Milton or Wordsworth; France, no Edgar Allan Poe or Whitman; the Soviet Union, no Shakespeare or Coleridge; Italy, no Faulkner, or Hemingway, or Bellow—without translators. Foreign readers would remain ignorant of contemporary American, Canadian, British, Irish, and Australasian writers, and American and other English-speaking readers could not read the works of contemporary foreign writers—without translators.

Translation makes possible all foreign news coverage in the press, radio, television, and the weekly news magazines, as well as highly specialized trade publications like *Publishers Weekly* which serve an international polylingual industry. It enables people of all cultures to enjoy foreign films (whether through subtitles or voice dubbing), plays, and television productions. Also, children of all lands learn of other children and other lands through books translated or adapted for them from all the living languages into all the living languages.

Without translators, the writings of persecuted, suppressed, or banned writers (living in countries where the freedom to write, to be published, or to be read is drastically restricted) could not be made known to the rest of the relatively free or freer world.

Yet, it is only during the past few decades, since the establishment of the United Nations and UNESCO and their numerous international governmental and intergovernmental agencies, and the consequent increased need for highly trained linguists, bilingual and multilingual experts, and translators and interpreters in all fields of human activity, that translation has become a recognized profession in its own right.

With the increased need has come a multitude of related support services and facilities for the profession: professional societies for the protection of translators, their work, and their legal, social, and fiscal status; academic translator-training centers offering courses, workshops, and curricula leading to certificates, diplomas, or degrees; guidelines, such as codes of professional ethics and conduct, model contracts and agreements, and national legislation; professional journals; dictionaries, glossaries, and terminology data banks; and national and international conferences, symposiums, colloquiums for the exchange of information and knowledge.

The concept for this directory and guide evolved from the realization that there was a need for those who serve and who are served to know more about each other. There was a need to document and record the global status of a profession that had finally come into its own, and to do justice to the words of Donald Walsh, a long-time translator of Latin American writing, in his evaluation of this project: " . . . it gives great promise of bringing order and reason to a profession that is sadly disorganized and undervalued. The publication of this volume will mark a major advance in the professionalization of our profession."

The volume was designed for the use of (1) editors and publishers; (2) college, university, and special libraries; (3) teachers and students of translation and interpretation; (4) the growing number of international organizations, governmental and intergovernmental agencies, and commercial and industrial enterprises that employ translators and/or interpreters on their staffs, or who use their services regularly on a free-lance basis.

In the compilation of this directory, close to 10,000 individuals, organizations, and institutions, representing more than 90 countries and over 70 languages, were contacted for specific information about their translation activities. Every effort was made to include all information received up to press time. In those cases where a well known organization or institution did not respond, entries were created through the use of printed secondary sources. All material has been organized into eight distinct section categories, each one introduced by an annotation describing the content of the section, its arrangement, and pertinent abbreviations/acronyms used.

To the best of one's knowledge, the diverse data and information contained in this volume pertaining to the translating and interpreting profession is here compiled and published collectively for the first time "since," as an eminent documentarian has put it, "man found it indispensable to translate."

Since the ultimate comprehensiveness of this material depends entirely on the participation of all persons and institutions associated with any aspect of translation and interpretation, the editor welcomes all submissions of data and information, especially from those sources not yet reached, and all suggestions that might contribute to making this compendium as encyclopedic, universal, and all-inclusive as communication permits: the profession's international forum.

Stefan Congrat-Butlar

ACKNOWLEDGMENTS

This landmark volume, the first in a projected multi-volume series entitled *Materials for a History of Translation,* is the product of many minds, many careers, and much collective knowledge and experience. Although there is but one name on the title page, this pioneering compendium with its vast amount of interrelated information could never have been compiled, nor ever realized, without the collaborative efforts of thousands of translators and interpreters, professional associations and their officers, academic training centers and their directors, translation journals and their editors, scholars and teachers of comparative literature and of foreign languages and literatures, editors, publishers, and also friends of translation, all of whom submitted material or indicated diverse sources of information and data on various aspects of the profession.

The overall project was launched in 1976 with the aid of a grant of $2000 from the American PEN Translation Committee (from funds provided by The Merrill Trust of Ithaca, New York) on the initial recommendation of Richard Plant and toward the end of Kirsten Michalski-Kalow's eight-year pro-translation tenure as executive secretary of the writers' association.

The project was kept alive through 1977 by a supportive grant of $1500 from the Columbia University Translation Center on the recommendation of Frank Mac-Shane; by another grant of $500 from The Center for Inter-American Relations through the director of its Literature Program, Ronald Christ of Rutgers University; by the miracle of donations, contributions, and small loans from a score of the same supporters who recommended it, or who contributed material, and who themselves are listed in the Register of Translators & Interpreters; and by the proceeds from the liquidation of the editor's Russian and Slavic philological and linguistic library and a collection of published documents on "the holocaust."

The project was planned and conceived as a collective undertaking and only the enthusiastic and steadfast support and participation of those aware of the profession's long, dismal non-recognition and miserable remuneration enabled it to endure long enough to find an appropriate publisher. Everyone without exception knew in advance that, owing to its nature and its potential audience, the project was destined for R. R. Bowker Company, publisher of essential tools—journals, bibliographies, directories, guides—for the book industry and for libraries.

The project has been recommended and/or evaluated by the following established translators and/or staunch supporters of matters translational:

Mary Jane Anderson, Children's Services Division, American Library Association;

Etilvia Arjona, former chairperson, School of Translation and Interpretation, The Monterey Institute of Foreign Studies;

George D. Astley, The Translators' Association and The Society of Authors, London;

Barbara Bannon, executive editor, *Publishers Weekly;*

Thomas Bauman, president-elect, American Translators Association;

Ben Belitt, Bennington College;

Konrad F. Bieber, The State University of New York at Stony Brook;

Bernard Bierman, Ad-Ex Translations International;

Marguerite Borchardt, American Society of Interpreters;

Eva Bornemann, editor, *Der Übersetzer,* West Germany;

Susan Brownsberger;

Bonnie Carroll, Conference on Latin American Women Writers;

B. J. Chute, American PEN Translation Committee;

Marchette Chute;

Jonathan Cohen, Islands & Continents Translation Award;

Thomas Colchie, Latin Americana Associates;

John Y. Cole, Center for the Book, Library of Congress;

John Alexander Coleman, New York University;

The Council of Communication Societies;

John Donovan, The Children's Book Council, New York;

Arnold Ehrlich, The Atlantic Monthly Press, who submitted the project to the publisher during his editorship of *Publishers Weekly;*

Paul & Hualing Nieh Engle, International Writing Program, The University of Iowa;

Inge Feltrinelli, Italy;

Adrienne Foulke, *The New Yorker;*

Maurice Friedberg, University of Illinois;

Frances Frenaye, Italian Cultural Center, New York;

the late Lewis Galantière;

Serge Gavronsky, Translation Studies, Barnard College;

Mirra Ginsburg;

Talat Sait Halman, Near Eastern Program, Princeton University, and former Minister of Culture, Turkey,

Michael Hamburger;

Brian Harris, School of Interpreters & Translators, University of Ottawa;

the late Max Hayward;

Lars Hellstrom, Swedish Committee of FIT;

Bill Henderson, The Pushcart Press;

Thea Hoekzema, Association of American University Presses;

James S. Holmes, University of Amsterdam, and editor, *Approaches to Translation Studies*;

Edwin Hönig, Brown University;

Indian Scientific Translators Association (ISTA), New Delhi;

Robert M. Ingram, president, American Sign Language Associates;

Ivar Ivask, editor, *World Literature Today* (formerly *Books Abroad*);

Frances Keene, The Mannes College of Music;

Howard Klein, director of the arts, Rockefeller Foundation;

Helen R. Lane, France;

Everette E. Larson, president, The Society of Federal Linguists;

Thomas Lask, poetry editor, *The New York Times*;

François Latortue, president, Inter-American Association of Translators;

Ramón Layera, translation editor, *Latin American Literary Review*;

Isabel A. Leonard, editor, *ATA Chronicle*;

Margaret Levick, president, International Association of Conference Translators (AITC), Geneva;

Jean R. Longland, curator of the library, The Hispanic Society of America;

Marilynn Meeker, former senior editor, Grove Press;

August J. Molnar, American Hungarian Studies Foundation;

Sidney Monas, University of Texas at Austin;

Claude Noël, president, Association of Literary Translators of France (ATLF);

Sidney Offit, The Authors Guild of America;

Joachim Neugroschel;

Ewald Osers, The Translators Guild of The Institute of Linguists, London;

Robert Payne, Columbia University Translation Center;

Margaret Sayers Peden, University of Missouri;

Nidra Poller, Editions Cimarron, France;

Kaca Polackova-Henley;

Gregory Rabassa, Queens College and Graduate Center of The City University of New York;

Burton Raffel, University of Denver;

Charlotte Read, Institute of General Semantics;

Allen Walker Read, The Alfred Korzybski Foundation & The Geolinguistic Society;

the late George Reavey;

Alastair Reid, *The New Yorker*;

Richard B. Rodman, senior translator, *Soviet Astronomy*, Harvard College Observatory;

Marilyn Gaddis Rose, Translation Program, The State University of New York at Binghamton;

Yvon St-Onge, president, Canadian Council of Translators & Interpreters;

Howard E. Sandum, American Scandinavian Foundation;

Edward G. Seidensticker, Columbia University;

Lief Sjöberg, American Swedish Historical Museum;

Roger H. Smith, contributing editor, *Publishers Weekly*;

William Jay Smith, Hollis College, and member of the Board, Columbia University Translation Center;

Judah Stampfer, The State University of New York at Stony Brook;

Frances Steloff, The Gotham Book Mart, New York;

Ben Teague, chairperson, ATA Accreditation Committee;

Josephine Thornton, Mellon Bank, Pittsburgh, and president, American Translators Association;

Royal L. Tinsley, Jr., University of Arizona, and past president, American Translators Association;

Laurence Urdang, editor, *Verbatim*;

Marjorie Mattingly Urquidi, Mexican Institute of Foreign Trade, Mexico

Lisa Valyiova, president, The American Association of Language Specialists (TAALS);

Gerardo Vásquez-Ayora;

Susan Wagner, UNESCO International Copyright Information Center;

Donald D. Walsh;

Helen Weaver;

Daniel Weissbort, director, MFA Degree in Translation, The University of Iowa;

the late Victor Weybright, founder of New American Library and this project's staunchest supporter;

Sophie Wilkins;

Miller Williams, director, Program in Translation, University of Arkansas, and president-elect, ALTA;

L. Leslie Willson, University of Texas at Austin, and president, ALTA;

Richard & Clara Winston;

Helen Wolff;

Harry Zohn, Brandeis University.

The volume is dedicated to all those above and to all of Robert Payne's numberless, unidentified, indispensable, aptly named "proletarians of literature who have nothing to lose but their chains." Without them, knowledge we have of the past would not have come down to us. Without them, mutual cultural borrowings and interpenetrations would have been impossible and would be even more difficult in the linguistically complex future.

Special gratitude goes to these members of the Bowker editorial staff: Judy Garodnick, executive editor, who was instrumental in the acquisition of publishing rights; Olga S. Weber, managing editor, Market Places/Directories, Book Division, who could not have been a more ideal enthusiast, suggester of solutions to unexpected editorial problems arising in a previously untried area, and superb coordinator of material and contents; Kathleen Craig, her assistant, who virtually memorized the project, and controlled all mailings of questionnaires and responses and all outgoing and incoming correspondence; Soni Grossberg, for editorial production; and Terry Croom, for the cover design.

Stefan Congrat-Butlar

1

Recent History & Breakthroughs

Several developments and events within and without the profession during the past few decades indicate that after centuries of being the most neglected and underpaid literary activity, translation as a profession has come into its own. A great impetus to these developments was the founding of the United Nations with its numerous international and intergovernmental cultural and scientific agencies, with the consequent increase in the need for highly trained linguists, bilingual and multilingual experts, and translators and interpreters in all fields of human endeavor. Such needs fostered and continue to foster the establishment of professional protective translators' associations and of translator-training centers at institutions of higher learning.

Following is a chronological survey of the most significant developments since the end of World War II and especially since the founding of the UNESCO-sponsored International Federation of Translators (FIT), with emphasis on:

translation associations/societies/guilds/centers
translation courses/training centers
translation congresses/conferences/symposiums
translation journals/books
translation awards/fellowships/grants/prizes/subsidies
translation guidelines: charters/codes of ethics/model contracts/legislation

Most entries in this section are cross-referred to extensive main entries in other sections.

1945–46

Introduction of simultaneous (in lieu of consecutive) interpretation at the Nuremberg war crimes trials. It was later reintroduced at the United Nations, and although at first challenged by consecutive interpreters soon established itself as an advanced form of oral conference interpretation.

1948

Resumption of publication *Index Translationum* (Translation Index) under UNESCO sponsorship, a bibliographical catalog of translated books published in as many countries each year as respond to requests for information; first issued in 1932 in Old Series and discontinued in 1940 at the outbreak of World War II (see Sec 8, UNESCO, France).

1952

Founding of the Sprachen-und Dolmetscher-Institut, München in Munich, Germany (see Sec 4, Germany, West).

1953

Founding of the International Federation of Translators (FIT, acronym of the French name, Fédération International des Traducteurs), at the I World Congress, held at the University of Sorbonne, Paris (see Sec 2, International).

Founding of the International Association of Conference Interpreters (AIIC, acronym for Association Internationale des Interprètes de Conférence), Geneva, Switzerland, which assesses, determines, and guarantees the qualifications, standards, and linguistic competence of its members, ensures the maintenance of high ethical standards throughout the profession, and seeks to establish rules governing conditions of work binding on its members everywhere (see Sec 2, International).

1954

Establishment of the Foundation for the Promotion of Translation of Dutch Literary Works in Amsterdam, Netherlands, to bring to the attention of the rest of the world literature written in the Dutch language by both Dutch and Flemish authors (see Sec 2, the Netherlands).

1955

First issue of *Mitteilungsblatt für Dolmetscher und Übersetzer*, official *Bulletin* of the Bundesverband der Dolmetscher und Übersetzer e.V. (BDÜ), the Federal Association of Interpreters and Translators, West Germany (see Sec 6, Journals).

Founding of The Monterey Institute of Foreign Studies, Monterey, CA, offering an extensive translation and interpretation program and graduate degrees in Intercultural Communication and in Language and International Studies, with work in Chinese, French, German, Russian, Spanish, and emphasis on language proficiency and on the understanding of other nations and their cultural traditions (see Sec 4, USA).

First issue of *Traduire,* a quarterly journal of the French Society of Translators (see Sec 6, Journals).

Formation of The Translators' Guild of The Institute of Linguists, London, to encourage cooperation between members of the Institute who are regularly engaged in translating and to present the range of services they offer to the public at large as technical, scientific, commercial, or literary translators (see Sec 2, UK).

Founding and first issue of *Babel,* an international journal of translation, published quarterly by the International Federation of Translators (FIT) under the auspices of UNESCO and under the direction of a FIT Editorial Committee (see Sec 6, Journals).

First issue of *Translation Monthly,* published

by the University of Chicago to list translations deposited in the Special Libraries Association Translation Pool.

1956

First issue of *Journal des Traducteurs* (Translators' Journal) of the School of Translation, University of Montreal, published by the University of Montreal Press, edited collaboratively by the Society of Translators (Quebec), the Association of Translators and Interpreters of Ontario, and the Council of Translators and Interpreters of Canada, and considered to be the most distinguished journal in its field. Now known as *Meta* (see Sec 6, Journals).

II World Congress of the International Federation of Translators (FIT), Rome, Italy (see Sec 2, International).

1957

Establishment of The Translators' Association of The Society of Authors (London) to represent members in all matters affecting their interests and to protect and further their interests at home and abroad, to seek to improve both conditions of payment and the status of translators, and to furnish advice on all questions, whether legal or nonlegal, affecting them in their capacity as translators (see Sec 2, UK).

Founding of The American Association of Language Specialists (TAALS), Washington, DC, to represent translators and interpreters working at the international level, either in conferences or in permanent organizations, and to determine their qualifications and standards (see Sec 2, USA).

Publication of *The Art of Translation,* by Theodore H. Savory, London: Jonathan Cape (see Sec 6, Books).

Establishment of École Supérieure d'Interprètes et de Traducteurs (ESIT) at the University of Sorbonne, Paris, offering diplomas for translation and conference interpretation (see Sec 4, France).

1958

Publication of *Vvedeniye v Teoriyu Perevoda* (Introduction to a Theory of Translation), Moscow: Literature in Foreign Languages (see Sec 6, Books).

1959

Founding of the American Translators Association (ATA) as, in the words of its first president, Alexander Gode, a "forum and clearing house to represent and promote the material and intellectual interests of translators and interpreters in the U.S., providing an anonymous collectivity of the profession with an organ of articulate expression" (see Sec 2, USA).

III World Congress of the International Federation of Translators (FIT), Bad Godesberg, West Germany. Theme: "Quality in translation" (see Sec 2, International).

Establishment of a Translation Committee by the American Center of International PEN, the writers organization, to be concerned with literary translation and intended to give the translator at least some measure of dignity and security (see Sec 2, USA).

Publication of *On Translation*, edited by Reuben A. Brower, Cambridge, MA: Harvard Univ. Press. A collection of essays on (1) translators on translation, (2) approaches to the problem, (3) a critical bibliography of works on translation (see Sec 6, Books).

1961

Publication of *The Craft and Context of Translation: A Critical Symposium*, edited by William Arrowsmith and Roger Shattuck, Austin, TX: Univ. of Texas Press. Essays delivered at a symposium on translation held in 1959 at the University of Texas (see Sec 6, Books).

1962

Founding of the Indian Scientific Translators Association in New Delhi to bring scientific and technical translation to the focus of public and government attention and to raise the quality and status of translators in India (see Sec 2, India).

First issue of *The Incorporated Linguist*, the quarterly journal of The Institute of Linguists, London, which devotes much of its space to translation issues and to the activities of The Translators' Guild and its members (see Sec 6, Journals).

1963

Publication of *Quality in Translation*, edited by E. Cary and R.W. Jumpfelt, proceedings of the III World Congress of FIT (see Sec 6, Books).

The first American PEN Translation Prize of $1000, from funds provided by the Book-of-the-Month Club, to be awarded annually for a distinguished translation of a foreign work of literature that has appeared in the preceding year (see Sec 3, USA).

IV World Congress of FIT, Dubrovnik, Yugoslavia, which saw the proclamation of the "Translators' Charter" (see Sec 2, International).

Publication of *Les Problèmes Théoretiques de la Traduction* (Theoretical Problems of Translation), by Georges Mounin (see Sec 6, Books).

First John Florio Translation Prize of £200 for a translation into English of a 20th-century Italian work of literary merit and general interest published by a British publisher during the preceding year, under the auspices of the Italian Institute and the British-Italian Society (see Sec 3, UK).

1964

The Alexander Gode Medal established in honor of ATA's first president and awarded annually to an individual or organization for outstanding achievement in the profession (see Sec 3, USA).

Publication of *Toward a Science of Translating*, by Eugene A. Nida, Leiden: Brill (see Sec 6, Books).

First Scott-Moncrieff Translation Prize of £500 established under the auspices of The Translators' Association, London, and awarded annually for a translation of a French 20th-century work of literary merit and general interest published by a British publisher during the previous year (see Sec 3, UK).

1965

Founding of the National Translation Center at the University of Texas at Austin with a grant from the Ford Foundation of $150,000 annually for five years. Its aim: to support the quality, availability, and financial reward of literary translation into English of texts having cultural and artistic significance—works in the humanities and arts, in the social or natural sciences, or in any other domain of genuine contemporary relevance (see Sec 2, USA).

First issue of *Traduction Automatique* (Machine Translation), an international revue of the Association for the Development of Machine Translation and Applied Linguistics, Paris. Now known as *T A Informations* (see Sec 6, Journals).

First Schlegel-Tieck Prize, established by The Translators' Association of The Society of Authors, London, for a distinguished translation published in the United Kingdom by a British publisher of German 20th-century works of literary merit and general interest (see Sec 3, UK).

Incorporation in the District of Columbia of The American Society of Interpreters. Principal purposes: to foster a higher code of ethics among interpreters in the United States, and to improve working practices and recommend professional standards within the profession (see Sec 2, USA).

1966

V World Congress of FIT, Lahti, Finland. Theme: "Translation as an art and a science" (see Sec 2, International).

Founding of the Swiss Association of Translators and Interpreters in Berne, Switzerland, to defend the moral, social, economic, and legal interests of its members and to promote contacts between them and with similar organizations in other countries (see Sec 2, Switzerland).

First issue of *The Japan Interpreter*, Tokyo, quarterly journal published to acquaint English-speaking readers with current Japanese thinking, published by the Japan Center for International Exchange (JCIE) (see Sec 8, Japan).

1967

First issue of *The Federal Linguist*, official semiannual journal of the Society of Federal Linguists, Washington, DC, the oldest such group in the United States, founded in 1930 to represent the interests of translators working for the U.S. government (see Sec 6, Journals).

Publication of *Ten Years of Translation*, edited by I. J. Citroen, New York: Oxford Univ. Press (see Sec 6, Books), the proceedings of the IV World Congress of FIT, Dubrovnik, 1963.

Presentation of first National Book Award in Translation.

Reorganization of the Translators' Society of Quebec (founded in 1940), with the addition of the Circle of Translators and the Corporation of Professional Translators of Quebec, enlarging its membership to over 1000 and making it one of the largest translators societies in the world (see Sec 2, Canada).

1968

First issue of *DELOS, a journal on and of translation*, published by the National Translation Center at the University of Texas at Austin, referred to by many as the most distinguished journal in its field ever published. Although 12 issues were scheduled, the journal was liquidated with issue no. 6, 1970 (see Sec 6, Journals).

First issue of *Actualité Terminologique*, published by the Terminology Center of Ottawa, Canada (see Sec 6, Journals).

1969

Proclamation of "Manifesto on Translation," drawn up under Robert Payne's chairmanship of the American PEN Translation Committee, and opening with an eloquent statement of the current lack of respect for translators, those "lost children in the enchanted forest of literature," and continuing with specific plans to do something about this state of affairs (see Sec 5).

Publication of *The Theory and Practice of Translation*, by Eugene A. Nida and Charles R. Taber, Leiden: Brill (see Sec 6, Books).

1970

Conference on Literary Translation, the first ever held in New York City, sponsored by American PEN (see Sec 2, USA) with funds from the National Endowment for the Arts. Proceedings of the conference, *The World of Translation* (see Sec 6, Books), were published in 1971.

VI World Congress of FIT, Stuttgart, West Germany, a statutory meeting (see Sec 2, International).

First issue of *Equivalences,* a triquarterly published in Brussels, Belgium, by the State Institute of Translators and Interpreters and the Association for the Promotion of the Study of Modern Languages (see Sec 6, Journals).

Founding of the Brigham Young University Language and Intercultural Research Center (LIRC), Provo, UT, as a specialized research organization within the College of Humanities, designed to serve governmental and educational institutions, private enterprises, and the general public, operating with two major ongoing goals: (1) research, development, service, and training for enhancing communication throughout the world, and (2) sharing with others, on a reciprocal basis, resources to further language and intercultural research (see Sec 4, USA).

Publication of *The Nature of Translation*, edited by James Holmes et al., The Hague: Mouton (see Sec 6, Books).

First issue of *L'Antenne* (The Antenna), the official news bulletin of the Translators' Society of Quebec, published seven or eight times a year (see Sec 6, Journals).

1971

Establishment of a Translation Workshop at the State University of New York at Binghamton, expanded into a Translator Training Program in 1973 with the aid of funding from the U.S. Office of Education (see Sec 4, USA).

Publication of *The Forked Tongue: A Study of Translation*, by Burton Raffel, The Hague: Mouton (see Sec 6, Books).

Founding of Chinese-English Translation Assistance Group (CETA) in the U.S. to meet the needs for aid in translation of modern Chinese language materials with a focus on the current language (see Sec 2, USA).

1972

The American Translators Association makes public a set of "Proposed Guidelines for a College-Level Training Program," prepared by the Committee on Translator Training in response to requests by colleges and universities contemplating the initiation of academic programs designed to prepare students for a career in translation (see Sec 5).

First issue of *Sign Language Studies*, a journal devoted to sign language interpretation and translation (see Sec 6, Journals).

Founding of the Translation Center of Columbia University with a grant from the National Endowment for the Arts and the New York State Council on the Arts, a central organization intended to advance the art of literary translation in the United States and to represent the needs of the literary translator (see Sec 2, USA).

1973

Guild of Professional Translators established in Philadelphia as a professional union to serve the interests of practical translators who share English as a working language. Official bimonthly journal: *Professional Translator*. Both liquidated in 1978.

First issue of *Translation*, a journal devoted to the art of literary translation, published by the Translation Center of Columbia University (see Sec 6, Journals).

Launching of the American PEN exhibit, "Translation and its role in bridging cultures," written, designed, and mounted by S. Congrat-Butlar and directed to college students to deepen their awareness of the importance of translation and the demands of the profession. First exhibited in the main branch of the Brooklyn Public Library and later dispatched across the United States to college libraries.

Carnegie-Mellon University in Pittsburgh announces the establishment of a belletristic translation program with funds from the Pittsburgh Foundation and the National Endowment for the Humanities—funds to be earmarked for "an innovative program in translation that will open new opportunities for students and benefit the business and industrial community" (see Sec 4, USA).

Founding of the Association of Literary Translators of France (ATLF) and of its quarterly *Bulletin d'Information d'ATLF* (Information Bulletin) (see Sec 2, France).

Publication of *Proteus, His Lies, His Truth: Discussions of Literary Translation*, by Robert M. Adams, New York: Norton (see Sec 6, Books).

The Portugal Prize (Prémio Portugal), funded by the International Poetry Association in Rome, Italy, is awarded for the first time to an American, Jean R. Longland, curator of the library of The Hispanic Society of America in New York for her translations of medieval and modern Portuguese poetry (see Sec 3, Portugal).

First issue of *Le Linguiste/De Taalkundige* (The Linguist), official journal of the Belgian Chamber of Translators, Interpreters, and Philologists (see Sec 6, Journals).

1974

VII World Congress of FIT, Nice, France. Theme: "Translation, a bond between nations" (see Sec. 2, International).

Latin American Translation Conference, sponsored by The Center for Inter-American Relations and American PEN, bringing together writers, translators, editors, publishers, reviewers, and agents to discuss esthetic, legal, and economic problems involved in the translation and publication of Latin American writing (see Sec 2, USA).

First annual Goethe House-PEN Translation Prize of $500 for a distinguished translation from the German (see Sec 3, USA).

Founding of the Brazilian Association of Translators (ABRATES) in Rio de Janeiro, Brazil (see Sec 2, Brazil).

Founding of a Translator Training Program (Programa para la formación de traductores) at El Colegio de México, Mexico City, and the publication of Spanish versions of Canadian and European glossaries and terminology banks (see Sec 4, Mexico).

1975

Establishment of the Lockert Library of Poetry in Translation by Princeton University Press, a series intended to publish worthy translation of significant poetry that is in itself poetic, rather than literal (see Sec 3, USA).

The first Canada Council Translation Prizes, one in English and one in French, awarded annually in recognition of the increasingly important role played by this discipline in communications, arts, and culture in Canada (see Sec 3, Canada).

Establishment of the Master of Fine Arts Degree in Translation by the University of Arkansas under the direction of Miller Williams, president-elect of the newly founded American Literary Translators Association (ALTA) (see Sec 4, USA).

Publication of *After Babel: Aspects of Language and Translation*, by George Steiner, New York: Oxford Univ. Press (see Sec 6, Books).

The American Academy of Arts and Sciences in Boston sponsors a conference on the problems of translation and the theoretical and practical questions relating to the translation of literary and scholarly texts, and announces that a grant from the National Endowment for the Humanities will enable it to explore a single aspect of the larger problem of translation availability and to conduct a survey of "translation needs" of a single field, the history of architecture, to (1) identify and produce a complete list of primary and secondary materials in need of translation, and (2) provide a methodological model for similar surveys and the production of further lists in other fields of the humanities and humanistic social sciences.

Publication of *Jerome: His Life, Writings, and Controversies*, by John N. D. Kelly, London: Duckworth.

New York State Supreme Court reverses the New York State Tax Commission's ruling, affirming that a translator, engaged in the practice of a profession, is thus entitled to exemption from assessment of unincorporated business taxes (see Sec 5).

1976

The Society of Federal Linguists embarks on a series of programs, "Bicentennial Panel Series," to underscore the importance of the linguistic aspects of the U.S. Federal Service and the inability of the major part of this Service to (1) function on its present level without utilizing, directly or indirectly, a broad variety of foreign language sources, and (2) satisfy the current demand for access to materials published in foreign languages by the existing Federal translating services (see Sec 2, USA).

Near Eastern Literature Conference, held in New York at the Graduate Center of the City University of New York and at The New York Public Library, sponsored by Princeton University and American PEN and bringing together for the first time major Near Eastern scholars, critics, writers, and translators from Iran, Israel, Turkey, and the Arab countries to meet each other on neutral ground and to meet with U.S. writers to discuss matters of mutual concern (see Sec 2, USA, PEN American Center).

The first Harold Morton Landon Translation Award of $1000, to be awarded biennially by The American Academy of Poets, New York, to living citizens of the U.S. for published translations of poetry—book-length poems, collections of poems, or verse dramas translated into verse—from any language into English (see Sec 3, USA).

Approval by the General Conference of UNESCO at its 19th session in Nairobi, Kenya, of the "Recommendation on the legal protection of translators and translations and the practical means to improve the status of translators" (see Sec 5).

Translation in the Humanities, a forum on translation problems and practice organized by the Translation Research and Instruction Program of the State University of New York at Binghamton (see Sec 4, USA).

Launching of the Inter-American Association of Translators (AIT), Washington, DC, to provide a professional forum for the translators of the Americas (see Sec 2, USA).

First issue of *The Concordiat*, a quarterly journal of Concordiat (see Sec 2, USA), the association of students and alumni of the Translation and Interpretation Department of The Monterey Institute of Foreign Studies, Monterey, CA, intended to serve as a link between students and the growing number of alumni now working professionally in the fields of translation and interpretation (see Sec 6, Journals).

Publication of *Translation: Applications and Research*, edited by Richard W. Brislin, New York: Gardner (see Sec 6, Books).

Establishment of the *Denver Quarterly* annual translation award of $500, funded by readers of the journal, for the most important publishable translations into English of an essay-length work of literary or esthetic theory or criticism, the work to be published or accepted for publication in the quarterly during the year of award (see Sec 3, USA).

1977

Announcement by the National Endowment for the Humanities of an experimental program to fund translations into English of major works in foreign languages and an invitation to submit proposals for that purpose (see Sec 3, USA).

First issue of *The Word Guild Magazine* in Cambridge, MA, featuring articles on various aspects of translation by Harry Zohn of Brandeis University (see Sec 6, Journals).

VIII World Congress of FIT, Montreal, Canada, the first ever held in the Western Hemisphere. Theme: "Now, as never before, translation is a profession" (see Sec 2, International).

Exploratory meeting between a group of translators and officers of The Authors League of America to discuss the problems and complexities of founding a professional nationwide translators guild, patterned after The Authors Guild and The Dramatists League.

The first Islands and Continents Translation Award for an outstanding book of poetry translated from another language and published in the United States in the current year, poets-translators rewarding their fellow translators for work that merits special praise (see Sec 3, USA).

The University of Texas at Dallas established a Translation Center as part of the Arts and Humanities School in order to be of service to translators, publishers, teachers, writers, and students through a variety of functions (see Sec 2, USA).

Appearance on the front page of the Sept 15 issue of *The Wall Street Journal* of an extensive report on literary translation, "The Translator's Role Is Crucial and Delicate, and Widely Unnoticed."

First Encounter with Brazilian Literature in São Paulo, Brazil, designed to introduce foreign editors, publishers, translators, and literary agents to their Brazilian counterparts. Organized by the Brazilian Book Chamber, a vast nationwide association of trade editors, writers, and bookstores, and sponsored by the municipal Secretariat of Culture and Science.

International Symposium on Fernando Pessôa, organized by the Portuguese Center of Brown University with the participation of several principals, ranging from readers of his poetry to lectures on Pessôa's work and on the art of his day.

Senator Dennis DeConcini (D), Chairman of the Judicial Improvement Committee, introduces the Bilingual Courts Act, legislation sponsored by Senators Allen of Alabama, Bayh of Indiana, and Kennedy of Massachusetts and designed to guarantee the services of a competent interpreter in federal court proceedings to every citizen who is not fluent in English, singling out "citizens of Spanish, Puerto Rican, Chinese, native American, and other heritages, as well as deaf citizens who must communicate by sign language," all of whom "are in effect denied real justice under the law without this guarantee" (see Sec 5).

Publication by the American PEN Translation Committee of "The Rights of the Translator," a list of urgent recommendations for the attention of translators and publishers intended to serve as guidelines for negotiations between translators and publishers (see Sec 5).

Inauguration by Brooklyn College of the City University of New York of the first in a series of "Summer Translation Workshops," sponsored by the Department of Comparative Literature and of Modern Languages and Literatures in cooperation with The Center for Inter-American Relations and to be held at the Graduate Center of CUNY (see Sec 2, USA).

Announcement that a large-scale project surveying the linguistic problems of translation between Hindi and other major languages of the world is being established by Dr. G. Gopinathan at Calicut University in Kerala, India. Planned as "an international symposium through correspondence," the project should eventually result in a book surveying the general issues to be studied: the role of translation as a cultural bridge, the national and international role of Hindi as a translation medium, the general theory of investigating linguistic problems of translation, and the language-pair problems involved in translating between Hindi and some 30 languages.

Founding of a translation workshop, El Taller Xochiquetzal, at the Instituto Allende in Guanajuato, Mexico (see Sec 4, Mexico).

Founding of the Center for the Book in the Library of Congress, its purpose to stimulate appreciation of the essential role of the book and the printed word in our society (see Sec 2, USA).

1978

The International Board on Books for Young People (IBBY) announces it will include translators of children's books on its Honor List for the first time. IBBY honor lists are prepared every two years. They include books that each of the 40 IBBY national sections considers worthy of worldwide attention and international publication (see Sec 3, International).

Barnard College initiates a pilot project, "Translation: Access to Cultural Communication," supported by a grant from the National Endowment for the Humanities, and designed to explore the multiple processes of translation and to allow undergraduate students to develop through a rigorous practice in textual analysis and the complex ways in which humanistic activity involves the translation of ideas (see Sec 4, USA).

Establishment of the Pacific Northwest Translation Award by Mr. Cogito Press of Pacific University, Oregon, to consist of a $100 cash award plus publication of a chapbook for

the best poem or group of poems in translation submitted to *Mr. Cogito Magazine* (see Sec 3, USA).

Announcement by the Japan United States Friendship Commission in Washington, DC, of the Japanese Literary Translation "Friendship Fund" Prize of $1000 to be awarded for the first time in 1979 to a translator whose previously unpublished or newly published first translation of a Japanese literary work—book-length fiction, literary essays and memoirs, drama, or poetry—is judged best by a jury of editors, writers, and established translators (see Sec 3, USA).

The first issue of *Translation Review*, official journal of the Translation Center of the University of Texas at Dallas (see Sec 2, USA) and of the American Literary Translators Association (see Sec 2, USA), intended to serve as a national and international forum for all matters relating to literary translation (see Sec 6, Journals).

Initial organizing meeting of the American Literary Translators Association (ALTA) at the University of Texas at Dallas with a charter membership of 300. First president: A. Leslie Willson; president-elect, Miller Williams (see Sec 2, USA).

American PEN announces that beginning in 1979 and every alternate year thereafter, it will administer the Calouste Gulbenkian Foundation Prize of $500 for a distinguished translation from the Portuguese (see Sec 3, USA).

"Symposium on Translation Theory and Intercultural Relations," organized in Tel Aviv by the Porter Israeli Institute on Central Issues in Poetica and the Semiotics of Culture, together with the Tel Aviv University Chair of Translation Theory, bringing together leading scholars from Europe and North America to present a synoptic view of the achievements of translation studies in recent years.

Latin American Women Writers' Conference held at Instituto Allende, University of Guanajuato, Mexico, including a translation workshop for discussion of women writers in Latin American literature and women writers in English translation (see Sec 4, Mexico, Instituto Allende).

Inauguration of the Europäisches Übersetzungs Kollegium (European Translators' College) in Straelen/Niederrhein, West Germany, near the Dutch border (see Sec 4, Germany, West).

First Columbia University Translation Center "Gold Medal" awarded to Willard R. Trask "for a lifetime of excellence" in the field of literary translation (see Sec 3, USA).

Creation of the Translation Service Center in Tokyo, Japan, a binational project of The Asia Foundation with basic support from the Japan-United Friendship Commission, intended to provide intercultural communication by broadening the American and European readership of recent and current Japanese writing on all subjects (see Sec 2, Japan).

Publication of *Interpreting for International Conferences*, by Danica Seleskovitch, Washington: Pen & Booth. A translation and adaptation of the original French edition (see Sec 6, Books).

International Symposium: Literary Translation and Ethnic Community, sponsored by The Maryland Committee for the Humanities, the state granting agency of The National Endowment for the Humanities, in conjunction with the University of Maryland, and held during the last week of February. Participants: major writers in, and translators of Spanish, Russian, Yiddish, Greek, and the Slavic languages, with the conference featuring discussions of translations, poetry readings, poet-translator dialogues, and panel discussions on bringing to the ethnic communities of the US a better understanding of the conditions under which their own literatures are translated into English.

1979

Summer Translation Institute of the University of California at Santa Cruz, designed to introduce students to the art of translating foreign literature into English, and to allow advanced students an opportunity to sharpen their skills (see Sec 4, USA).

"Japanese Literature in Translation," a symposium held at the Library of Congress, co-sponsored by the library's Asian Division and the newly founded Center for the Book. Symposium discussions focused on linguistic aspects of translation, translating modern fiction and poetry, translating from the literature of the social sciences, translating in the medium of film, and the publishing of translations (see Sec 2, USA, Center for the Book).

Conference on General and Jewish Lexicography, held in July under the auspices of the University of Delaware and the Yiddish Studies Program, University of Haifa, Israel, with a special session devoted to dictionaries of Jewish languages and entries of Jewish interest in dictionaries of non-Jewish languages.

First Annual International Conference on automated translation and publication systems, held in Bermuda, hosted by the International Computer Translation Corporation of America, attended by representatives of governments and corporations involved with SYSTRAN, and covering the evaluation of machine translation systems, automated document production, the integration of translation with document production, the present status of SYSTRAN, multilingual technical documentation, word processing (automated dictionaries), and formalized technical writing.

2

Associations/Centers

Unions of practitioners of the same business, craft, trade, or profession, engaged in kindred pursuits and having common purposes and interests, first appeared in Western Europe in the Middle Ages. Their primary functions were to establish some form of organized control over an occupation within a community, to promote the welfare of their members, to establish and uphold standards of workmanship and price, and to offer their members a respectful and recognized status in the community and protection against unfair practices.

Of the numerous professions requiring a relatively extensive and diverse education and training, the knowledge of foreign languages and cultures, acquaintance with at least one—frequently, more than one—discipline, subject field, or area of specialization, and at times intellectual equipment of one degree or another, translation is probably the most recent newcomer on the scene.

Although the oldest professional association of translators in the United States, the Society of Federal Linguists, was formed as early as 1930 and continues to represent government-employed translators, it was the American Translators Association, founded in 1959, that first attempted to satisfy on a national scale the need for an organization sufficiently broad in both scope and membership to meet the professional demands of the profession and to merit international recognition. Today, translators associations, centers, guilds, and societies are to be found throughout the world.

In this section national translation associations and centers have been listed under alphabetically arranged country headings. International groups appear under the heading "International" within the alphabetic arrangement. Wherever available, information on officers, founding date, type of membership, aims, activities/programs, publications, and membership in other associations appears within an entry.

Argentina

COLEGIO DE TRADUCTORES PUB-LICOS DE LA CIUDAD DE BUENOS AIRES (Society of Certified Translators of the City of Buenos Aires)
Corrientes 1250, 3 L, 1043 Capital Federal *Tel* 35-9403 *Pres* Gustavo Leon Evrard *Founded* 1973.
Membership Public translators graduated from private and national universities with jurisdiction in the law courts of Buenos Aires, National Territory of Tierra del Fuego, Argentine Antarctica, South Atlantic Islands.

Australia

AUSTRALIAN TRANSLATORS' ASSOCIATION LTD
381 Pitt St, Sidney NSW.
Member of FIT.

Austria

ÖSTERREICHISCHER ÜBERSETZER-UND DOLMETSCHER-VERBAND "UNIVERSITAS" (Austrian Society of Translators and Interpreters "Universitas")
Dr Karl-Lueger-Ring 1, Universitätsgebäude, A-1010 Vienna 1 *Tel* 42 76 11. *Secy* Liese Katschinka, Institut für Dolmetschausbildung an der Universität Wien.
Member of FIT.

Belgium

CHAMBRE BELGE DES TRADUCTEURS, INTERPRÈTES ET PHILOLOGUES (CBTIP) (Belgian Chamber of Translators, Interpreters, and Philologists)
De Haynlaan 110, B-1090 Brussels *Secy Gen* Freddy Lepeer.
Member of FIT.

Brazil

ASSOCIAÇÃO BRASILEIRA DE TRADU-TORES (ABRATES) (Brazilian Association of Translators)
Rua Almirante Barroso 97, 3 andar, Rio de Janeiro *Tel* 221-4486, 4844 *Pres* Daniel da Silva Rocha *Secy* Maria da Gloría de Sousa Reis *Founded* 1974.
Membership About 200.
Aims To better conditions of work and to increase the quality of translation.
Publications *ABRATES* (see Sec 6, Journals).
Member of FIT.

Bulgaria

UNION DES TRADUCTEURS ET INTER-PRÈTES DE BULGARIE (Union of Translators and Interpreters of Bulgaria)
Rue Neofit Rilski 5, Sofia *Contact* Elena Nikolova, Str San Stefano 8, Sofia.
Member of FIT.

Canada

ASSOCIATION OF TRANSLATORS AND INTERPRETERS OF ONTARIO (ATIO) (Association des traducteurs et interprètes de l'Ontario)
260 Dalhousie St #202, Ottawa, ON K1N 7E4 *Tel* 613-233-6395 *Founded* 1920.
Established under the name "Association technologique de langue française d'Ottawa," the group was given legal status in 1921 by letters patent from the Government of Ontario, and it assumed its present name by supplementary letters patent in 1962. It is affiliated with the Canadian Translators & Interpreters Council (CTIC), which is affiliated with the International Federation of Translators (FIT) (see under International).
Membership 451 members in the following categories: (1) Full Members (400): individual members who meet all the requirements in the by-laws concerning admission and professional work and who are entitled to cast a vote at general meetings; (2) Trainee Members (50): individual members who pledge to seek full membership within three years of becoming trainee members, and full-time students enrolled in an academic translating or interpreting program who are given five years to seek full membership; (3) Retired Members (20): who are no longer practicing translators or interpreters; (4) Honorary Members: persons to whom the Association, prompted by Council, are granted the title in recognition of their contribution to the profession; (5) Corporate Members: companies or institutions interested in the translating or interpreting profession, and whose staff includes one or more full members of ATIO; (6) Associate Members: whose profes-

sional activities share common traits wih translating or interpreting.

Aims To bring together translators and interpreters of all categories—literary, technical, commercial, administrative, others—in the province of Ontario with a view to (1) defend the professional interests of Ontario translators and interpreters; (2) promote the training of qualified translators and interpreters; (3) improve the quality of translating and interpreting; (4) maintain friendly relations and professional ties with corresponding groups in Canada and abroad.

Admission requirements Only those persons who are working or have worked as translators or interpreters may become full members of ATIO. Applicants must have received university training in translation, interpretation, or a similar field, or the equivalent experience, and meet ATIO's proficiency requirements. Applicants may become full members of ATIO by simple screening if they hold equivalent membership credentials granted them by an organization deemed to have status comparable to that of ATIO.

Proficiency requirements As determined by Council, these refer to methods of evaluating professional expertise, and are aimed at safeguarding public interest. There are two avenues of entry into full membership, and in both cases the target language must be French or English: (1) The traditional two-hour written exam is held once a year (usually on the last Saturday in October) in Ottawa, Toronto, and Sudbury. The passing mark is 70 percent (average based on two evaluations), and the results are announced in February; only those candidates whose mark lies between 50 and 70 percent have the right to appeal. The exam fee was $25 in 1978. (2) There is also the review process. Applicants for review by a proficiency board must meet the following conditions: five years of competent translating experience, attested by employers or clients; submission of 5000 words of their own translation, supported by references corroborating the authorship of the translation; payment of the same fee as for the traditional examination. Candidates for the review process should realize that, while entitling them to full membership in ATIO, this process may not qualify them for reciprocal status in the other Canadian translators' associations.

Activities/Programs Professional development courses (Ottawa and Toronto); an annual two-day convention; symposiums; luncheons; receptions, get-togethers; job opportunities.

Publications Annual directory of members; glossaries, minutes of meetings; *InformATIO,* monthly bulletin (see Sec 6, Journals).

BUSINESS LINGUISTIC CENTER (BLC) (Centre de Linguistique de L'Enterprise)
Bureau 2403, 1103 rue Sherbrooke W, Montreal H3A 1G8 *Founded* 1972.

Aims A private, nonprofit organization established to help member firms to formulate language policy, to develop and manage language training and translation programs, to study the development and application of public linguistic policy, and to pool the experience and resources of its member firms in order to strengthen the individual member's capabilities of solving language-related problems.

CONSEIL DE TRADUCTEURS ET INTER-PRÊTES DU CANADA (CTIC) (Canadian Council of Translators and Interpreters)
Case postale 452, Succursale A, Ottawa K1N 8V5 *Pres* Yvon St-Onge.
Member of FIT.

TRANSLATORS' SOCIETY OF QUEBEC (Société des traducteurs du Québec)
1010 rue Sainte-Catherine W #841, Montreal H3B 3R5 *Tel* 514-866-9101 *Pres* René Deschamps *Founded* 1940.

Membership Reorganized in 1967 with the addition of the Circle of Translators and the Corporation of Professional Translators of Quebec, it now has a membership of well over 1000 (125 in the Quebec city section alone), and is among the largest translators' societies in the world. It is directed by a 14-member board and supported by a full-time secretariat. Membership is open to those who pass the Admission Examination, permits students, recent graduates and other translators to share in and contribute to the life of the group while they acquire the skill and experience necessary to pass the more difficult Certification Examination, held annually under the aegis of the Canadian Translators and Interpreters Council. Success in this examination confers the status of Certified membership.

Activities/Programs The society sponsors luncheon meetings which are educational in the broad sense of the term and which give members an opportunity to strengthen relationships and to hear qualified speakers on some aspect related to language or to the translating function. Formal educational activities, such as training courses and seminars, are offered periodically.

Publications *L'Antenne* (The Antenna) (see Sec 6, Journals); membership directory.
Member of FIT.

Czechoslovakia

SVÄZ SLOVENSKÝCH SPISOVATELOU (Commission for Literary Translation, Union of Slovak Writers)
Ulica Obrancov Mieru 8a, Bratislava *Contact* Joseph Kot, Suvorovova 16, Bratislava.

Aims One of four translators' groups in the Slovak Socialist Republic. Since translations of scientific literature and translations into the languages of the minority groups are not included in the activities of the Union, these groups come under the Slovak Literary Fund, which provides the necessary financial means, grants, and bonuses for the activities of all translators' organizations. The Fund embraces about 1,200 translators, of which 480 are literary translators.

Activities/Programs 1973, a postgraduate course for young translators in Nitra; 1974, the first Conference on the Criticism of Literary Translations, Bañska Bystrica; 1975, the first Summer School for the Interpretation of Original and Translated Texts; 1976, II Summer School for the Interpretation of Original and Translated Texts; 1976, seminar on the theme "The Standard of Slovak in Contemporary Translation Work;" 1977, a seminar on the theme of "The Present State of Translation of

Dramatic Works," with the participation of literary editors and theatrical producers, television, radio, and film studios, translators of dramatic literature.

Among the works of several members of the organization are: *The Theory of Literary Translation* by Anton Popovic (Tatran, 1975). *Literary Translation in Czechoslovakia* (Matica slovenská, Martin, 1975). *Text and Style* by F Miko (Smena, 1975). *On the Interpretation of Literary Texts,* vols 1–5 (Slovak Pedagogical Publications, Bratislava, 1968–76).
Member of FIT.

Denmark

TRANSLATØRFORENINGENS
Bornholmsgade 1, DK-1266 Copenhagen **Contact** Ellen M Andersen.

Finland

SUOMEN KÄÄNTÄJÄIN YHDISTYS—FINLANDS ÖVERSÄTTARFÖRENING r y (Society of Finnish Translators)
Erottaja 5 B 10, SF-001 30 Helsinki 13.
Member of FIT.

France

ASSOCIATION DES TRADUCTEURS LIT-TÉRAIRES DE FRANCE (ATLF) (Association of Literary Translators of France)
80 blvd Pasteur, F-75015 Paris *Pres* Claude Noël *Founded* 1973 in accordance with French law, following a separation from the French Society of Translators (SFT). *Founding sponsors* Miguel-Angel Asturias, Marcel Bataillon, Maurice-Edgar Coindreau, Etiemble, Max-Pol Fouchet, Pierre Leyris, Pierre Moinot, Maurice Nadeau, Claude Roy, and Claude Simon.

Membership 231 as of September 1978; only highly qualified literary translators are considered by a special commission, which studies the work of each applying translator and bases its decision on a thorough analysis of one published translation in comparison with the original text.

Aims To improve the quality of literary translation and of published translations in France; to protect the interests of its members with respect to copyright, remuneration, conditions of work. The group is strictly apolitical.

Activities/Programs The Association has been influential in the passage of legislation affecting the artist's rights, and has been responsible for the appearance of numerous articles on the subject of translation in such prestigious journals and periodicals as *Le Monde, Les Nouvelles Littéraires, Figaro, Femmes en mouvement,* and for radio interviews devoted to translation. It protests against the omission of translators' names from reviews of published translations and against publishers who violate contractual agreements.

During the past few years ATLF has organized and sponsored a number of conferences and lectures with the participation of prominent French translators and writers: "Translation of a haiku by Basho," by Etiemble, (1974); "Translation and linguistics," by Michel Pernier and Monique Nemer (1974); "Translation of poetry," by Yves Bonnefoy (1975).

Publications *Directory of Members of ATLF; Bulletin d'information,* quarterly (see Sec 6, Journals).

Member of FIT.

SOCIÉTÉ FRANÇAISE DES TRADUCTEURS (SFT) (French Society of Translators)
1 rue de Courcelles, F-75008 Paris.
Member of FIT.

Germany, West (Federal Republic)

BUNDESVERBAND DER DOLMETSCHER UND ÜBERSETZER e V (BDÜ) (Federal Union of Interpreters and Translators)
Pestalozzistrasse 26, D-7100 Heilbronn, West Germany.
Member of FIT. (Hans Schwarz, pres, Olbrichstrasse 53, D-6000 Frankfurt/Main; Hans-Jürgen Pfisterer, member of FIT Council, Rohrbacher Str 138, D-6900 Heidelberg).

VERBAND DEUTSCHSPRACHIGER ÜBERSETZER LITERARISCHER UND WISSENSCHAFTLICHER Werke e V (VDÜ) (Association of German-Speaking Literary and Scientific Translators)
Fürststrasse 17, D-7400 Tübingen.
Publications *Der Übersetzer* (see Sec 6, Journals).

Greece

PANHELLENIC ASSOCIATION OF TRANSLATORS (PAT)
26 Tsimiski St, Salonika.

Guatemala

ASOCIACIÓN GUATEMALTECA DE INTÉRPRETES Y TRADUCTORES (Guatemalan Association of Interpreters and Translators) (GAIT)
6a Avenida 14–17, Zona 9 *Contact* M E Falla.
Member of FIT.

Hong Kong

THE CHINESE UNIVERSITY OF HONG KONG
Comparative Literature and Translation Ctr, Inst of Chinese Studies, The Chinese Univ of Hong Kong, Shatin, NT *Tel* 12-612211 *Cable* Sino-university *Dir* Stephen C Soong.

Aims Originally called the Center for Translation Projects and founded in 1971, the Center concerns itself with research and publication involving English-Chinese and Chinese-English translation. Its translations from Chinese into English are mainly in the areas of literature, history, and philosophy, while its English into Chinese work concentrates on the social sciences and the humanities.
Publications *Renditions: A Chinese-English Translation Magazine* (see Sec 6, Journals).

THE HONG KONG TRANSLATION SOCIETY
PO Box 335, Kowloon Central PO, Kowloon *Tel* 12-612211 *Dir* Stephen C Soong *Founded* 1971.
Aims Established to raise the standard of translation by assisting in the training of Chinese and other languages and by encouraging those engaged in scholarly pursuits to translate important works of Chinese and other languages, in order to cater to the needs of the developing society and to promote cultural exchanges.
Publications *Bulletin of the HKTS* (see Sec 6, Journals).

Hungary

A MAGYAR ÍRÓK SZÖVETSÉGÉNEK MÜFORDITÓI SZAKOSZTÁLYA (Literary Translators' Section of the Union of Hungarian Writers)
Bajza utca 18, H-1062 Budapest VI *Contact* György Radó, Petöfi Sándor utca 9, H-1052 Budapest.
Member of FIT.

India

INDIAN SCIENTIFIC TRANSLATORS ASSOCIATION (ISTA)
c/o INSDOC, Hillside Rd, New Delhi 12 *Founded* 1962, with charter membership of 60.
Membership Over 200, including several life members and a number of Indian national institutions, scientific and academic bodies as institutional members, e.g., Jawaharlal Nehru University, Osmania University, several Defense Research laboratories, Indian Agricultural Research Institute, Birla Institute of Technology, Tea Research Association, Central Hindi Directorate, Central Institute of Hindi, Central Institute of English and Foreign Languages, Kerala Bhasha Institute. Membership is open to all persons and institutions subscribing to the association's aims, especially to those who benefit directly or indirectly from the promotion of scientific and technical translation. ISTA provides professional translators a platform for mutual intercourse and for resolving translation and professional problems.
Aims (1) to promote facilities for scientific and technical translation in India; (2) to improve the status and service conditions of translators; (3) to promote training facilities for scientific and technical translation and to take such measures as would lead to the mainte-

nance of a high standard; (4) to convene conferences or conduct seminars on scientific and technical translation; (5) to cooperate with national and international organizations with similar objectives; (6) to bring out publications which will tend to the realization of the aims of the group.
Activities/Programs Symposiums: 1973, "Language Barrier in Technology Transfer," unanimously recommending the establishment of a National Institute of Scientific and Technical Translation to be established by the government for meeting the enormous translation needs of Indian science, technology, and education, and to undertake an integrated program of (1) conducting surveys to fix priority-based translation needs of the country; (2) dissemination of foreign science information through an express service; (3) selective translation of foreign journals on a regular basis; (4) translation of high-quality foreign-language textbooks, research monographs, etc, into English and into Indian languages; (5) translation of research papers on the request of Indian scientists; (6) training of competent translators; (7) research in translation technique, lexicography, terminology, etc; (8) compilation of bilingual and multilingual dictionaries and other translation tools; (9) maintenance of a translation and terminology bank in cooperation with the translation units functioning in various organizations; (10) maintenance of contacts with international translation agencies.

1976, "Role of Scientific and Technical Translation in the Development of India," recommending the following activities: (1) to conduct All-India Qualifying Examinations for scientific and technical translators, essential and effective for quality control of translators; (2) to organize the teaching of languages—Hungarian, Nordic, East European, etc—for which little or no facilities exist in India; (3) to undertake research projects in terminology and lexicology in foreign as well as Indian languages (Sanskrit and Pali), an area that has remained practically unexplored.
Publications *JISTA,* Journal of the Indian Scientific Translators Association (see Sec 6, Journals).

Indonesia

HIMPUNAM PENTERJEMAH INDONESIA (Association of Indonesian Translators)
Jalan Cikini Raya 73 (TIM), Jakarta.
Member of FIT.

International

ASSOCIATION INTERNATIONALE DES INTERPRÈTES DE CONFÉRENCE (AIIC) (International Association of Conference Interpreters)
14 rue de l'Ancien-Port, CH-1201 Geneva, Switzerland *Tel* 31 33 23 *Telex* LAIIC *Exec Secy* M Gucassoff-Gingrich *Founded* 1953, registered according to French law.
Membership 1450 members in five continents (53 countries) in 1977; 200 are per-

manently employed by international organizations, the rest are free-lance; admission is subject to strict procedures guaranteeing the professional performance of its members.

Aims Through the Commission for Admission and Language Classification, AIIC (1) assesses and guarantees the levels of linguistic competence of its members; (2) ensures the maintenance of high ethical standards throughout the profession (these include absolute observance of professional secrecy); (3) establishes rules governing conditions of work which are binding upon its members everywhere; (4) enters into and periodically revises agreements with the UN family, EEC, and the Intergovernmental Coordinated Organizations; (5) seeks to establish technical standards in regard to conference facilities; (6) establishes criteria designed to improve the standards of training in interpreters' schools and accords recognition to diplomas of schools meeting the required standards.

Publications *Code of Professional Conduct; Efficient Planning of Conference Interpretation; Statuts* (French only); *Reglement Interieur* (French only); *AIIC Yearbook and Corrigendum* (English & French); *AIIC Bulletin* (multilingual); *AIIC Minimum Rates* (English & French); *Minimum per Diem Rates* (English & French); *Letter of Appointment* (English & French); *Ecoles d'Interprètes dont le Diplome est Reconnu par l'AIIC* (French only); *Kongresssentren—Ein Fiasco?* by Dr W Jumpelt (German & French), *AIIC, What It Is, What It Does* (English, French, Spanish & Portuguese), *Inter-Standard ISO 2603 Booths for Simultaneous Interpretation*—equipment (English, French & German); *Charte de l'Interprète Permanent* (Fr.), *Checklist for Rating Permanent Booths and Simultaneous Equipment* (English & French), *Checklist of AIIC Practice in the Non-agreement Sector* (English).

See Sec 5 for Code of Professional Conduct & Efficient Planning of Conference Interpretation.

ASSOCIATION INTERNATIONALE DES TRADUCTEURS DE CONFÉRENCE (AITC) (International Association of Conference Translators)

Palais Wilson, Case postale 31, CH-1211 Geneva 14, Switzerland *Tel* (022) 32 92 93 *Telex* ASTRAD-GENEVE *Pres* Margaret Levick.

Membership 320 in 1977. Membership is open to all free-lance and permanent translators, and members are classified according to their mother tongue. Within the meaning of the association's constitution (1) the term "free-lance translator" refers to any translator working in connection with an international conference or for an international organization essentially on a temporary basis, under a contract of employment which does not provide for affiliation to the employer's pension fund or under a contract relating to the performance of particular tasks (e.g., work done at home); (2) the term "permanent translator" refers to any translator working for an international organization and contributing to the pension fund for that organization.

Aims The Association represents the profession of conference translator and its purposes are (1) to study the problems arising from the exercise of the profession; (2) to defend the moral and material interests of those who practice it, and to maintain high professional standards. Within the scope of this definition, the Association lays down a set of rules constituting the ethical code of the profession.

See also Sec 5 for AITC Professional Code.

FÉDÉRATION INTERNATIONALE DES TRADUCTEURS (FIT) (International Federation of Translators)

5 Square Thiers, F-75116 Paris, France *Founded* 1953 at the I World Congress, Univ of Sorbonne, Paris.

Pres Pierre-François Caillé, 185 ave Victor Hugo, F-75116 Paris, France *Vice Pres* Anna Lilova, rue Sveta Gora 17, Sofia, Bulgaria; Ewald Osers, 33 Reades Lane, Sonning Common, Reading RGA 9LL, UK; Hans Schwarz, Olbrichstrasse 53, D-6000 Frankfurt/Main, West Germany *Secy Gen* René Haeseryn, Heivelstraat 269, B-9110 Sing-Amandsberg, Belgium *Treas* Jacques Goetschalckx, 30 rue Belle-Vue, Lorentzweiler, Luxembourg.

Members of Council Henry Fischbach, US; Malou Höjer, Sweden; Josef Kot, Czechoslovakia; Zdenko Lesić, Yugoslavia; Vilguelm Levik, USSR; Hans-Jürgen Pfisterer, West Germany; György Radó, Hungary; Ernst B Steffan, Switzerland; Zygmunt Stoberski, Poland.

Membership 34 translators associations in 29 countries: Argentina, Australia, Austria, Belgium, Brazil, Bulgaria, Canada, Czechoslovakia, Finland, France, Guatemala, Hungary, Indonesia, Italy, Japan, the Netherlands, Norway, Poland, Rumania, South Korea, Spain, Sweden, Switzerland, UK, Uruguay, USA, USSR, West Germany, Yugoslavia.

Aims Founded under the auspices of UNESCO in order to group professional translators throughout the world, to make them and the general public aware of the importance of their profession, and to render the profession a factor in the establishment of friendly relations between peoples of all nations.

Activities/Programs Congresses: 1953, Paris, France; 1956, Rome, Italy; 1959, Bad Godesberg, West Germany; 1963, Dubrovnik, Yugoslavia; 1966, Lahti, Finland; 1970, Stuttgart, West Germany; 1974, Nice, France; 1977, Montreal, Canada; 1980, to be held in Warsaw, Poland.

Committees & Chairpersons Literary Translators, Elena Nikolova, Str San Stefano 8, Sofia, Bulgaria; Technical & Scientific Translators, Henry Fischbach, PO Box 8, Hastings-on-Hudson, NY 10706 USA *Tel* 914-478-3558, 212-687-4183; Special Committee for the Enforcement of the 1976 FIT Recommendation, Bogdan Novković, Djure Jakšića 11, YU-11000 Belgrade, Yugoslavia; Managerial & Editorial, *Babel*, Pierre-François Caillé, 185 ave Victor Hugo, F-75116 Paris, France; Developing Countries, Pierre-François Caillé; International Translation Bibliography, René Haeseryn, Heiveldstraat 269, B-9110 Sint-Amandsberg, Belgium; FIT Translation Prize, Harriet Nordbäck-Linder, Gyllenstiernsgatan 8, S-115-26 Stockholm, Sweden; Statutes & Regulations, Hans-Jürgen Pfisterer, Rohrbacher Str 138, D6900 Heidelberg, West Germany; Terminology & Documentation, Jacques Goetschalckx, 30 rue Belle-Vue, Lorentzweiler, Luxembourg; Problems of Translating Legal Documents, Sándor Karcsay, Árpád fejedelem útja 38, H-1023 Budapest II, Hungary; Training & Qualification of Translators, Derry Cook Radmore, 7 Oaklands Grove, Cowplain, Portsmouth PO8 8PR, UK; History & Theory of Translation, György Radó, Petofi Sándor utca 9, H-1052 Budapest V, Hungary; Organization of the IX Congress (1980, Warsaw, Poland), Zygmunt Stoberski, Aleja Niepodłeglosci 67 m 69, PL-02-626 Warsaw, Poland; Copyright, Patricia Crampton, Rookery Farm House, Calne, Wiltshire SN11 OLH, UK.

Publications *Babel,* an international journal of translation (see Sec 6, Journals).

Israel

ISRAEL ASSOCIATION OF TRANSLATORS & EDITORS (IATE)

PO Box 541, Herzlia *Chpn* Amos Carmel *Secy Gen* Uriel Ofek *Treas* Abraham Kadima *Exec Comm* Ami Shamir, Arieh Hashavia, Zohar Shavit *Founded* 1979.

Membership 112 professional Israeli translators, organized to protect the welfare, interests, and rights of Israeli translators, and editors. Owing to the continuous state of inflation, the IATE's main activities are concentrated on monetary problems and reasonable remuneration for assignments. The association is recognized by the Histadruth (Israeli Federation of Labor) as a trade union.

Italy

ASSOCIAZIONE ITALIANA TRADUTTORI E INTERPRETI (AITI) (Italian Association of Translators and Interpreters)

Via Macedonia 72, I-00179 Rome.
Publications *Il Traduttore.*
Member of FIT.

Japan

JAPAN SOCIETY OF TRANSLATORS (JST)

The Shiroyama Mansion, Room 203, 1-33-1, Nakanoku, Tokyo.
Member of FIT.

THE NATIONAL TRANSLATION INSTITUTE OF SCIENCE AND TECHNOLOGY (NATIST)

3-5-11, Kita Aoyama, Minato-ku, Tokyo.

Aims Founded in 1965 and officially organized in 1967 under the sponsorship of the National Council of Science and Technology to introduce quality control of translations from and into Japanese. Since relatively few foreigners read Japanese fluently enough to translate from it, most translations in the recent past were of necessity made by Japanese, translating from their own language into other languages (mostly English) not their own. According to R Yeomans, a Canadian translator and theoretician, who visited Japan in 1973 to become acquainted with the country's professional translation programs and reported on his visit in *Babel* (19, no 4, 1974), although the number of certified translators was given as 4000 at the end of 1972, the only detailed figures available were for 1970.

Activities/Programs The Institute differs from all other associations in other countries in that its functions include language teaching, translator training, language proficiency examinations, information exchange with government agencies and private enterprise, and certification of translators. Language and translation training is conducted through seminars, correspondence courses, and on-the-job training in industry. Examinations are given twice a year in five foreign languages (English, French, German, Russian, Spanish), and tests are given in a number of subject fields: agriculture, chemistry, engineering (civil, electrical/electronic, systems) fisheries, metallurgy, mining, nuclear industry, patents, pharmaceutical science, physics (applied), international licensing, and export publicity.
Member of FIT.

TRANSLATION SERVICE CENTER (TSC)

c/o The Asia Foundation, 31 Kowa Bldg #8, 19-1 Shirokanedai 3-chome, Minato-ku, Tokyo 108 *Tel* (03) 441-8291 *Cable* ASIAF TOKYO *Dir* James L Stewart *Sr Man Ed* Kano Tsutomu *Sr Amer Ed/Translator* to be appointed *Founded* May 15, 1978.
Steering Committee Maeda Yoshinori, chairperson; Amagi Isao, Thomas Blakemore, Thomas Hague, Ichimura Shin'ichi, Kubota Kinuko, Oyamada Takashi, Saito Makoto, Seki Yoshihiko, Shimanouchi Toshiro.
Japanese Selection Committee Saeki Shoichi, Fukushima Shintaro, Homma Nagayo, Hosoya Chihiro, Iwao Sumiko, Mochida Takeshi, Suzuki Shigenobu, Takeyama Yasuo, Yano Toru.
American Advisory Committee Robert A Scalapino, chairperson; Norman Cousins, Frank Gibney, Walter Hoadley, Everett Kleinjans, Philip E Lilienthal, David MacEachron.
Aims Established by The Asia Foundation in San Francisco and Toyota, with the financial support of the Japan Foundation and the Japan-United States Friendship Commission, the Center's basic aims are (1) to serve Americans and other readers of English by putting into English the best of Japanese writing today—what Japanese are saying to each other in their own language and country; (2) to provide more effective intercultural communication by establishing and maintaining a standard of excellence in the translation of Japanese into English; (3) to serve American publishers by solving difficult technical problems and high costs inherent in identifying, translating, and editing suitable Japanese materials; (4) to serve Japanese writers, scholars, and thinkers by stimulating direct communication and exchange of views with their professional counterparts abroad; (5) to serve as a focal point of facilitation and coordination for Americans and Japanese interested in cross-cultural communication through translation.
Activities/Programs The Chapter's activities have been planned as a way to help balance the exchange of ideas between Japan and other countries. At present, partly because written Japanese presents special difficulties in comprehension and translation, very little temporary Japanese thinking and writing reaches the Western reader. In contrast, thousands of books and articles are translated each year from English into Japanese. The relative pau-

city of Japanese work that is disseminated to other countries has been described by Japanese and Westerners alike as deplorable, embarrassing, even inexcusable. There is wide agreement that one of the best methods of broadening the American and European readership of recent Japanese writing is through the publication of selected Japanese works in a cross section of high-quality American and other English-language publications, ranging from the scholarly to the popular, from academic journals and university monographs to the opinion-editorial (OpEd) pages of American newspapers.
The Center is also prepared to use out-of-house resources in translating, editing, proofreading; but regardless of where the initial translation has been made, the Center's Japanese editor will assume the final responsibility for the accuracy and fidelity of all translations while the American editor will be responsible for the quality of the English in the text.
While all articles selected for translation will be written by Japanese authors, subject matter will not be limited to descriptions of things Japanese. Priority is to be given to business- and economics-related material, to articles on Southeast Asia, China, and the United States and those discussing common problems of industrialized societies and the world today. Material is to be selected from leading general circulation Japanese magazines, specialized academic and professional journals, and from portions or chapters of current books in print.
Publications *TSC Newsletter* (see Sec 6, Journals).

Korea, South (Republic of Korea)

ASIAN WRITERS' TRANSLATION BUREAU

Korean Center of International PEN, Seoul *Founded* 1970.
Membership 16 PEN centers in the Asian and Pacific region: Australia, Ceylon, Taiwan, Hong Kong, India, Indonesia, Iran, Israel, Japan, Korea, Lebanon, New Zealand, Philippines, Thailand, Turkey, Vietnam.
Aims To effect lively international exchange of literature through translation and publication of the selected works of literature and other related cultural works originating from the nations of Asia, thereby promoting better mutual understanding, cooperation, and lasting friendship. To fulfill its aims the Translation Bureau is scheduled to carry out the following literary and other related cultural activities: 1) translating and publishing meritorious works of literature originating from each of the member nations of the Translation Bureau; (2) conducting relevant literary interchange programs among the member nations; (3) staging other necessary and effective programs to promote better understanding and friendship among the men of letters in the region.

SOCIETY OF TRANSLATORS OF KOREA

Univ of Kyung-Hee, Seoul *Contact* Prof Gonie Bang.
Member of FIT.

The Netherlands

FOUNDATION FOR THE PROMOTION OF TRANSLATION OF DUTCH LITERARY WORKS

Singel 450, NL-Amsterdam *Tel* (020) 23 10 56 *Founded* 1954.
Aims The Foundation for Translations, as it is called for short, is subsidized by the Dutch Ministry of Culture, Recreation, and Social Works, and by the Belgian Ministry of National Education and Culture, since the literary works whose translation it seeks to promote are written in the Dutch language. Dutch is spoken by about 18,000,000 people, about 13,000,000 of which live in Holland and about 5,000,000 in the northern half of Belgium, or Flanders. The Foundation's work is conducted by a committee of eight members, representatives of: The Society of Dutch Authors, The Dutch Literary Society, Dutch Center of International PEN, Royal Dutch Publishing Association, Society of Flemish Authors, Royal Flemish Academy of Language and Literature, Flanders Center of International PEN, and the Society for the Promotion of Flemish Literature.
Activities/Programs Dutch literature is presented abroad in numerous ways. The Foundation publishes two journals, and conducts a regular correspondence with foreign publishers and literary bodies, documenting the background of specific books and authors, and submitting either a part-translation in French, German, or English of the work in question or the complete translation in manuscript or bound volume. Regular visits are paid to cultural centers throughout the United States and Europe, to make presentations to publishers, official agencies, literary agents, and editors of literary journals. Of equal importance in this sphere are the annual book fairs, such as the annual Frankfurt event, where the Foundation has its own booth and members of its staff are in constant contact with the world of international publishing.
The translations the Foundation promotes are the work of free-lance translators who, after they pass rigorous screening by linguistic experts, are called upon on a regular basis. They are of necessity a small group, since few translators are able to make superior literary translations from Dutch into other languages. In addition, one translator is invited to visit the Foundation each year to refresh his/her knowledge of the Dutch language and literature.
The Foundation further acts as an intermediary agent between Dutch publishers and those abroad on all matters concerning Dutch literature. It acts as an information center, compiles data, issues biographies and bibliographies. Members of the staff attend conferences and international congresses.
Since translations from a relatively unfamiliar language like Dutch might, in principle, face poor sales abroad, one of the major tasks of the Foundation is allocating financial support to aid the publication of translations. Such support has often tipped the scale in favor of publication.
Publications *Writing in Holland and Flanders,* quarterly bulletin, which concentrates on Dutch and Flemish authors and contains extracts from their work, articles on newly-published books and reprints; *Netherlands Books,* a

quarterly distributed to Dutch communities abroad, foreign universities with courses or chairs in the Dutch language and literature, and foreign libraries.

INTERNATIONAL TRANSLATIONS CENTER (ITC)

101 Doelenstraat, NL-2611 NS Delft, *Tel* (015) 14 22 42; 14 22 43 *Telex* 316 ITC NL *Dir* D van Bergeijk *Founded* 1961.

Aims Established as the European Translations Center under the auspices of the European Productivity Agency of the Organization for European Economic Cooperation, the predecessor of the Organization for Economic Cooperation & Development (OECD), and renamed International Translations Center in 1976, "to encourage, improve, and facilitate the use of literature published in less accessible languages and of interest in science and industry, and also to promote international cooperation in this field."

Activities The ITC is the most comprehensive of the several networks of translations agencies, holding centers, and international clearinghouses developed in Europe, the US, and Latin America. Although a foundation under Dutch law, ITC is directed and guided by an international Board of Management, composed of representatives of national translations centers from Belgium, Denmark, France, West Germany, Greece, the Netherlands, Norway, Spain, Sweden, and Switzerland. Any national or international scientific institutions, universities, research centers, and translating bureaus can join the network, contribute material to the Center by notifying it of translations prepared by them or for them.

The ITC's main objectives are: (1) to act as a referral center in relation to the national centers; (2) to maintain and develop an information network for announcement of translations; (3) to facilitate access to such translations; (4) to provide, on request, information on the existence of translations; (5) to cooperate with institutions engaged in similar activities and to serve as a coordinating center of an international network for improved utilization of translations. The Center does not prepare translations itself, nor does it order translations.

Since its founding, ITC has compiled a catalog of over 500,000 translations, mainly from East European and Asiatic scientific and technical literature. Its own collection of translations comprises about 140,000 items. This data is stored in a data base, which will be offered for EURONET, the European On-Line Information Network.

Publications *World Transindex; Translation News* (see Sec 6, Journals) *Journals in Translation.*

THE LOW COUNTRIES TRANSLATION STUDIES GROUP

Translation Studies Program, General Literary Studies, Univ of Amsterdam, Spuistraat 210, NL-1012 VT Amsterdam *Tel* (020) 525-3873 *Contact* James S Holmes.

Aims A loosely knit circle of scholars in the Netherlands and Belgium working in the field of translation studies and research, whose nucleus consists of James S Holmes (University of Amsterdam), José Lambert (University of

Leuven), André Lefevere (University of Antwerp), and Raymond Van den Broeck (Vlaamse Hogeschool, Antwerp). The group meets informally from time to time to discuss relevant problems and maintains close touch with translation scholars elsewhere, particularly in Slovakia (Anton Popovič) and Israel (Itamar Even-Zohar and Gideon Toury).

Activities/Programs Organized the colloquium on "Literature and Translation" held in Belgium in 1976, its proceedings published under the title of *Literature and Translation: New Perspectives in Literary Studies* (Leuven, Belgium: Acco, 1978); and "Translation Theory and Intercultural Relations" held in Tel Aviv, Israel, in 1978, its proceedings forthcoming. A third colloquium is to be held in Antwerp in 1980.

NEDERLANDS GENOOTSCHAP VAN VERTALERS (NGV) (Netherlands Society of Translators)

Prinsessestraat 2, NL-2012 LR Haarlam *Pres* G J M Fritschy *Vice-Pres* J C Roos *Secy* Elisabeth van der Zee, van Wassenaerlaan 4, NL-1215 PB Hilversum *Founded* 1956, with an initial membership of a few dozen.

Membership Over 600

Aims (1) to promote the interests of translators and interpreters; (2) to encourage a better understanding of the work of translators; (3) to enhance the quality of their work. The objectives are laid down in the Statutes, amended in 1977, which also stipulate conditions for membership, number and duties of the honorary board, finances, and annual meeting. The NGV consists of three sections: technical-scientific, literary, and court interpreters.

Activities/Programs At the request of the Netherlands Ministry of Culture and in accordance with the FIT 1976 Recommendation, the NGV has submitted to the Ministry a series of proposals, relating to the legal protection of translators and translations and the means to improve the status of translators in the Netherlands. Apart from the annual meeting, the NGV have a conference each year, while special meetings and excursions open to the membership are organized throughout the year by the individual sections.

Publications *Newsletter* (six times a year); *Van Taal tot Taal* (quarterly); an annual alphabetical list of members with addresses, working languages, and subject fields. To mark its 20th anniversary, the association published *Vertalen Vertolkt* in a limited edition.

Member of FIT.

WERKGROEP VERTALERS (The Translators Working Group)

Vereniging van Letterkundigen/Vakbond voor schrijvers (Dutch Soc of Authors), Vossuisstraat 24, NL-1071 AE Amsterdam *Tel* (020) 79-7644 *Secy* Cora Polet *Founded* 1958.

Aims Brings together some 150 professional literary translators, among them most of the established translators in the Netherlands. In the past the Group has conducted successful campaigns for higher minimum rates, for a standard publishing contract for literary translations, and for stipends and other subsidies for literary translators. In conjunction with the Literary Section of the Netherlands Society of

Translators (see Nederlands Genootschap van Vertalers), the Group organizes meetings each year on a variety of themes (group translation, translation criticism, translation of specific literary genres). Each spring an annual Translation Day takes place, when translators meet in language sub-groups to discuss their translations.

Norway

NORSK OVERSETTERFORENING (Norwegian Association of Translators)

Radhusgt 7, Oslo 1.
Member of FIT.

Poland

ZWIĄZEK LITERATÓW POLSKICH—KOMISJA TŁUMACZY (Translators Commission of the Union of Polish Writers)

ul Krakowskie Przedmieście 87/89, PL-00-079 Warsaw *Contact* Zygmunt Stoberski, Aleja Niepodległosei 67/m 69, PL-02-626 Warsaw.
Member of FIT.

Rumania

UNIUNEA SCRIITORILOR DIN REPUBLICA SOCIALISTĂ ROMÂNIA (Translators Section, Union of Writers of the Rumanian Socialist Republic)

Şoseaua Kiseleff 10, Bucharest.
Member of FIT.

Spain

ASOCIACIÓN PROFESIONAL ESPAÑOLA DE TRADUCTORES Y INTÉRPRETES (APETI) (Spanish Professional Association of Translators and Interpreters)

Biblioteca Nacional, Paseo de Calvo Sotelo 20, E-Madrid 1.
Publications *Boletín Informativo de APETI.*
Member of FIT.

Sweden

SVENSKA FIT-KOMMITTÉN (Swedish Committee of FIT)

Rosengatan 5, S-111-40 Stockholm *Contact* Harriet Nordbäck-Linder, Gyllenstiernsgatan 8, S-115-26 Stockholm.
Member of FIT.

Switzerland

ASSOCIATION SUISSE DES TRADUCTEURS ET INTERPRÈTES (ASTI) (Swiss Association of Translators and Interpreters)

Case postale 2726, CH-3001 Berne, *Pres* Eric E Thilo, ave de Gambach, CH-1700 Fribourg *Secy* Constantin Rosset, Erlenweg 2, CH-3700 Spiez.

Aims A nonprofit association, founded in accordance with the Swiss Civil Code, to defend the moral, social, economic, and legal interests of its members and to promote contacts between them and similar organizations in other countries. ASTI is strictly neutral in all matters that are not connected with the professional activity of its members, particularly in matters of politics and religion. Members are bound to observe the strictest professional integrity in their dealings with their clients, employers, or partners, and rigorous fraternal loyalty in their relations with one another. They are pledged to professional secrecy.
Member of FIT.

Union of Soviet Socialist Republics

SOVIET PO KHUDOZHESTVENNOMU PEREVODU SOYUZA PISATELEI SSSR (Council on Literary Translation of the Union of Writers of the USSR)
Ul Vorovskogo 52, Moscow *Contact* Feliks Kuznyetsov.
Member of FIT.

United Kingdom

FEDERATION OF TRANSLATION COMPANIES OF GREAT BRITAIN
44 Fulham Rd, London SW3 6HQ *Tel* (01) 589 8872 *Secy* J H Gale.
Membership Seven companies.
Aims A professional body of leading translation companies in Great Britain, undertaking maintenance of honorable business practices, to observe high standards of work, to refrain from misleading advertising, to provide clients with reliable translation services on most subjects and in most languages.

THE TRANSLATORS ASSOCIATION
84 Drayton Gardens, London SW10 9SD *Secy* George D Astley *Affil* The Society of Authors.
Member of FIT.
See also Sec 5 for *Specimen Contract.*

THE TRANSLATORS' GUILD
Lloyds Bank Chambers, 24A Highbury Grove, London N5 2EA *Tel* (01) 407 4755 *Affil* The Institute of Linguists *Founded* 1955.
Membership The Guild Committee recommends to membership of the Guild those Fellows and Members of the Institute who can satisfy the Council that their work as translators—from one or more languages into their language of habitual use (usually the mother tongue)—is of a uniformly high standard as regards the use of technical terminology, accuracy, readability of translations, and presentation. Members are admitted in only those languages and subjects in which they have satisfied the Committee of a proper degree of competence, suitability for membership being based on success in the Translator's Diploma examination as well as on testimonials covering quality of work and personal character. They must also be able to provide evidence of three years' experience as translators.

The names and particulars of members of the Guild appear in *Index of Members of the Translators' Guild* which is kept up-to-date by periodic new editions and by means of supplements issued quarterly to holders of the *Index.*

The Secretary and staff, replying to inquiries for translators, put forward the names of members of the Guild only. In order to avoid discrimination in putting forward names, a punched card system is in use, which enables the operator to give the inquirer names and full particulars on individual cards, of all members possessing the qualifications required for the assignment, which are then mailed.

The Guild holds meetings at which matters of importance to the profession are discussed and decided. Some sessions of these meetings are open to the public, as well as to matriculated students, affiliates, and associates of the Institute who are undergoing courses of training as translators recognized by the Council of the Institute.

Aims To encourage cooperation between members of the Institute who are regularly engaged in translating and to present the range of services they offer to the public-at-large. It comprises those Fellows and Members of the Institute who work as technical, scientific, commercial, or literary translators.

Publications *Membership of the Institute of Linguists; The Translator's Diploma and Membership of The Translators' Guild.*

Member of FIT.
See also Sec 5 for *The Translators' Guild: You and Your Translator,* and Sec 6, Journals for *The Incorporated Linguist.*

United States of America

AMERICAN ASSOCIATION OF LANGUAGE SPECIALISTS, *see* The American Association of Language Specialists (TAALS)

AMERICAN LITERARY TRANSLATORS ASSOCIATION
Box 688, Mail Sta 1102, The Univ of Texas at Dallas, Richardson, TX 75080 *Pres* A Leslie Willson, PO Box 7939, Austin, TX 78712 *Vice Pres & Pres Elect* Miller Williams, Univ of Arkansas, Fayetteville, AR 72701 *Founded* 1978.
Membership About 300.
Aims To promote the quality of literary translations in the English-speaking world and to expand the market for such translations published in English, to bring literary translators together at annual meetings to exchange ideas on all aspects of literary translation, to focus on translation as an art that enriches the study of the Humanities, to incorporate a variety of functions: (1) a clearinghouse for translators, translations in progress, and suggestions for possible new translations; (2) a special library collection of book translations, published in English, of contemporary arts and humanities and journals publishing translations; (3) a research service to coordinate information on questions of copyright, costs of translation in the US and abroad, federal and private foundations which support translations, institutions involved in the teaching and practice of translation; (4) a professional referral service for the

Dallas-Fort Worth area to assist business and industry with technical translations (in preparation is a directory of translators living in the metroplex area); (5) a program of workshops at the University of Texas at Dallas in the theory and practice of translation, writing, exploration into aspects of the translation process and intensive language/culture courses.
Publications *Translation Review* (see Sec 6, Journals).

AMERICAN SOCIETY OF INTERPRETERS (ASI)
1010 Vermont Ave NW, Suite 917, Washington, DC 20005 *Tel* 202-783-3871 *Pres* H F Broch de Rothermann *Vice Pres* Marguerite Borchardt, 345 E 54 St #5H, New York, NY 10022, 212-355-0135 *Founded* 1965.
Membership 40 conference interpreters based in three countries (USA, Canada, Panama) and working in ten languages: Arabic, Dutch, English, French, German, Italian, Japanese, Portuguese, Russian, and Spanish. All members are conference interpreters, both simultaneous and consecutive.
Aims A nonprofit, tax exempt professional and educational organization with two basic purposes: (1) to foster a higher code of ethics among interpreters in the Western Hemisphere; (2) to improve working conditions and practices and to recommend professional standards. Its members are pledged to uphold specific principles in the interest of their own profession and the general public. ASI is made up exclusively of professional interpreters who must meet the performance standards set forth by the Society.
Publications *Membership List; Interpretation Services Handbook.*
See also Sec 5 for *ASI Code of Professional Standards & Guidelines.*

AMERICAN TRANSLATORS ASSOCIATION (ATA)
Box 129, Croton-on-Hudson, NY 10520 *Tel* 914-271-3260 *Staff Admin* Rosemary Malia *Pres* Josephine Thornton, Mellon Bank NA, Mellon Sq, Pittsburgh, PA 15230, 412-232-5751 *Pres Elect* Thomas Bauman *Secy* Ben Teague *Treas* Royal L Tinsley, Jr *Founded* 1959.
Membership Over 1300 members in almost every state of the nation and a score of foreign countries, including not only those actively engaged in the profession of translating (salaried translators, agency-owner translators, freelance translators, editors), but also students, teachers, and others who are working toward a direct and active role in the translating profession, and some 50 institutional and corporate members. Annual dues range from $20 (student members) to $250 (sustaining members). Active membership is open to any citizen or resident of the US or Canada who is professionally engaged in translating, interpreting, or closely related work.
Aims "To promote and advocate the recognition of translation as a profession; to formulate and maintain standards of professional ethics, practices, and competence; to improve the standard and quality of translation; to establish a system of mutual assistance, including a reference library; to publish periodicals, bulletins, notices, glossaries, dictionaries, reports,

and any other publication that may advance translation and the interests of the profession; to promote social and professional relations among its members; to organize and support lectures, courses, and the training of translators; to provide a medium for collaboration with persons in allied professions; to conduct any and all other activities to effect and further the above-named objectives and promote the general welfare of the Association."

Activities/Programs During the first two decades since its first board elections in 1960, the ATA has established several regional chapters and has developed numerous services and programs for its members: (1) *Professional Services Directory,* listing 407 of its members who request inclusion and indicating their accreditation by test; (2) an Accreditation Program (see Sec 5), establishing minimum standards for nationwide certification through tests; (3) Translator Training Guidelines (see Sec 5), a model curriculum for training translators at the university level, including a bibliography of source material useful to the translator and the teacher of translation; (4) Code of Professional Ethics (see Sec 5), professional rights and responsibilities, and a Committee on Ethics and Practices, whose services are available to members to mediate professional disputes and maintain a high standard of ethical practice; (5) Alexander Gode Medal (see Sec 3, USA).

Publications *ATA Chronicle* (see Sec 6, Journals).

Member of FIT.

ASOCIACION PROFESIONAL DE TRA-DUCTORES (APT) (Professional Association of Translators)
PO Box 1146, Hato Rey, Puerto Rico 00919.

ASSOCIATION OF PROFESSIONAL TRANSLATORS (APT)
c/o Josephine Thornton, Mellon Bank NA, International Dept, 2432 Mellon Square, Pittsburgh, PA 15230 *Tel* 412-232-5751 *Founded* 1974

Membership About 75.

Aims (1) to establish translating as a profession and to strive for professional and economical advancement; (2) to propagate the use of foreign languages to benefit better communication and understanding between peoples and nations; (3) to engage in activities of an educational nature such as serving as a consulting agency for academic institutions or actively participating in the process of designing and implementing of better translator traning programs; (4) to promote, formulate, and recommend standards of accreditation and certification; (5) to seek new members in the professional fields; and (6) to provide an active and reliable source for sponsorship, assistance, and cooperation.

Activities/Programs (1) Certification: in conjunction with Carnegie-Mellon University, the APT offers a Certification Program, with examinations held twice a year by appointment; (2) Translator Training: in conjunction with Carnegie-Mellon University, professional in-house translators of APT have provided Technical Translation Workshops in French, German, Russian, and Spanish since 1975; APT also offers an internship program to stu-

dents who have completed two Technical Translation Workshop courses at Carnegie-Mellon University—internships are presently offered at Mellon Bank NA and Koppers Company; (3) Translator Placement: employment opportunities are notified to members either by phone or through the *Newsletter.*

Publications *APT Directory of Translators* (forthcoming); *Newsletter* (six times per year), edited by Sarah B Mishelevich, 6346 Caton St, Pittsburgh, PA 15217.

ATLANTA ASSOCIATION OF INTER-PRETERS AND TRANSLATORS (AAIT)
PO Box 52554, Atlanta, GA 30355 *Tel* 404-261-2322 *Pres* Denise H Crist *Secy* Gisela Nuckolls

Membership Open not only to professional translators and interpeters, but also to persons or groups (schools, colleges, libraries, companies, etc.) who support the goals of the association.

Aims To encourage liaison with various governmental agencies and diplomatic relations with similar groups in the international field, and to observe the established Code of Ethics which states: a professional translator or interpreter must know the limits of his/her competence and undertake only those tasks which are within his/her competence, evidence of which are (1) a diploma from a recognized school for the training of translators or interpreters; (2) accreditation by the ATA; (3) accreditation by the US Dept of State or Dept of Defense.

CENTER FOR INTER-AMERICAN RELATIONS
680 Park Ave, New York, NY 10021 *Tel* 212-249-8950 *Staff* Ronald Christ, Rosario Santos, Greg Kolovakos *Founded* 1966.

Aims A private, nonprofit, membership organization with the general purpose of increasing understanding among the peoples of the Western Hemisphere, and more particularly of developing a greater degree of awareness and knowledge of the hemisphere within the US.

Activities/Programs The Literature Department has both a translation program (see Sec. 4, USA, Brooklyn College Translation Workshop) and a three-time-yearly magazine of Latin American literature in translation.

Publications *REVIEW.*

See also Sec 1, 1974 for *PEN American Center (Latin American Translation Conference).*

CENTER FOR THE BOOK
Library of Congress, Washington, DC 20540 USA *Exec Dir* John Y Cole *Founded* October 13, 1977, by an Act of Congress, PL 95-129.

Aims To stimulate appreciation of the essential role of the book and printed word in American society. Drawing on the resources of the Library of Congress, the Center works closely with other organizations (1) to explore important issues in the book and educational communities; (2) to encourage reading; (3) to encourage research about books and about reading.

The Center's goal is to serve as a useful catalyst by bringing together authors, publishers, librarians, booksellers, educators, scholars, and readers to discuss common concerns and to work toward the solution of common problems. The Center's interests include the educa-

tional and cultural role of the book; the history of books and printing; the future of the book, especially as it relates to new technologies and other media; the international flow of books and the contribution of the book and the printed word to international understanding; authorship and writing, the publishing, design, and production of books; the distribution, access, and use of books and printed materials; reading; literacy; and the role of the institutions and professions of the book world.

Activities/Programs The international flow of books and ideas is a major concern of the Center. A symposium on "Japanese Literature in Translation", cosponsored with the Library's Asian Division, was held on May 17–18, 1979, with discussions focusing on linguistic aspects of translation, translating modern fiction and poetry, translating from the literature of the social sciences, translating into the medium of film, and the publishing of translations into English of Japanese writing.

CHINESE-ENGLISH TRANSLATION AS-SISTANCE GROUP (CETA)
9811 Connecticut Ave, Kensington, MD 20795 *Tel* 301-946-7007 *Exec Secy* J Mathias *Founded* 1971.

Membership A group of individuals from government and academic institutions working together as volunteers to develop tools for Chinese-English translation.

Aims To utilize newly developed techniques in computer printing of Chinese characters to produce a "living" dictionary containing modern terms as an expandable computer-based file that can be updated as new terms and new uses are identified. Through the cooperative efforts of all its participants, the group is able to maintain a dictionary that reflects changes and the growth of linguistic knowledge by constant correction and expansion.

Activities/Programs (1) a computer-based Chinese-English general dictionary of 106,000 terms in current use, now being revised and expanded; (2) companion dictionaries of 10,000 colloquial expressions and 525,000 scientific and technical terms; (3) a computer-stored reference file of about 11,600 Chinese characters and the associated Pinyin romanizations and tones, radical numbers, and total stroke numbers, which includes some 4000 alternate pronunciations and is capable of printing or of displaying Chinese characters, Japanese Kana, Korean symbols, and the Roman, Greek, and Cyrillic alphabets.

Also (1) a bibliography of Chinese dictionaries in all languages; (2) development of the dictionary file for use in on-line computer retrieval systems; (3) application of computer technology to research in Chinese language characteristics; (4) coordination of research information among linguists in the academic and government communities; (5) assessment of current systems of Chinese-English machine translation.

CETA also serves as a means of facilitating communication and for exchange of information with the objective of promoting cooperative efforts and avoiding needless duplication. The principal methods are a periodically issued bulletin and continuous communication by mail.

Publications *CETA Bulletin.*

COLORADO TRANSLATORS ASSOCIATION
1643 Krameria St, Denver, CO 80220 *Contact* Sidonie H Safonov.

COLUMBIA UNIVERSITY TRANSLATION CENTER
School of the Arts, Math 307A, Columbia Univ, New York, NY 10027 *Tel* 212-280-2305 *Dirs* Frank MacShane, Robert Payne, William Jay Smith, Willard R Trask *Man Ed* Dallas C Galvin *Founded* 1972, with a grant from the National Endowment for the Arts.

Aims To serve as a central organization to advance the art of literary translation in the US and to represent the needs of the literary translator. Through a variety of programs, the Center seeks to bring the literary sensibility to the practice of translation, to increase the number and improve the quality of works currently being published in the US, and to encourage the translation into English of difficult and little-known languages, particularly those of Asia and Africa. The Center invites eminent poets, professional writers, and translators from the US and abroad to form its national and international governing boards. Using their expertise as a continuing guide to help achieve its goals, the Center has designed a number of programs of artistic and financial assistance. Direct monetary support is awarded to assist nonprofit presses to bring out works that otherwise might not be published. Generally, these are anthologies, and four have been brought out to date. The Center also maintains a directory of literary translators which is available to editors, writers, publishers, and television news centers that may need translators for special projects or full-time jobs. A subsidiary function is to stimulate international cultural exchange. In 1977, the Center sponsored a visit of four Hungarian poets and the editor of *The New Hungarian Quarterly* in celebration of the publication of *Modern Hungarian Poetry,* a subventionary book of the Center. As part of the Center's Writer Exchange Program, the poets gave readings in Hungarian and English at the Library of Congress and at universities across the country. A new program to bring writers and poets from Latin America was begun in 1978.

Publications *Translation* (see Sec 6, Journals).

See also Sec 3, USA, for *Awards and Fellowships.*

CONCORDIAT
Translation & Interpretation Dept, Monterey Inst of Foreign Studies, PO Box 1978, Monterey, CA 93940 *Pres* Lydia H Vollmer *Vice Pres & Recording Secy* Sally Dungan *Treas* Alain Thayer *Corresponding Secy* Ann Breiter *Founded* 1976.

Aims An independent professional organization of the students and alumni of the Department of Translation and Interpretation at the Monterey Institute of Foreign Studies (see Sec 4, USA), modeled along the lines of the Association d'Interprètes et de Traducteurs of the Geneva Ecole d'Interprètes, and the first organization of this kind in the US, formed to inform its members of innovations and new directions in the Institute's training program, to keep its members abreast of general developments within the profession, and to encourage professionalism, high ethical standards, and solidarity among the members.

Publications *The Concordiat* (see Sec 6, Journals).

DELAWARE VALLEY TRANSLATORS ASSOCIATION (DVTA)
617 E Chelten Ave, Philadelphia, PA 19144 *Contact* Theodore E Morrow.

GUILD OF PROFESSIONAL TRANSLATORS (disbanded in 1978)
5914 Pulaski Ave, Philadelphia, PA 19144 *Dir* Charles Parsons.

Aims Founded in 1973 as an international union of practical translators sharing English as a working language, with members in 14 countries, to establish and maintain high standards of professionalism in the practice of translation.

Publications *Translation Referral Directory* (1974); *Professional Translator* (bimonthly); various specialized bilingual reference materials.

INTER-AMERICAN ASSOCIATION OF TRANSLATORS (AIT) (Asociación Interamericana de Traductores)
1324 Jonquil St NW, Washington, DC 20012 *Pres* François Latortue *Founded* 1976.

Aims Organized for the following professional, cultural, and scientific purposes: (1) to provide a professional forum for the translators of the Americas; (2) to further the knowledge and appreciation of translation as a science and an art and to enhance the status of the translator; (3) to uphold, promote, and protect the moral and professional interests of translators and to advocate and advance the recognition of translation as a profession; (4) to foster the dissemination of high professional standards and a code of professional ethics among translators; (5) to cooperate with institutions and organizations interested in obtaining translating services and to help them meet their needs, with due regard to equitable pay rates and fair working conditions.

Publications *Escolopendra* (see Sec 6, Journals).

METROPLEX CHAPTER OF ATA
PO Box 34380, Dallas, TX 75234 *Contact* Mike Stacy.

MID-AMERICA CHAPTER OF ATA (MICATA)
8301 E 166 St, Belton, MO 64012 *Contact* Doris Ganser.

NALANDA FOUNDATION TRANSLATION COMMITTEE
1345 Spruce St, Boulder, CO 80302 *Tel* 303-444-0211 *Cable* NALANDA *Exec Dir* Larry Mermelstein *Dir* Vajracarya the Venerable Chögyam Traungpa (Rinpoche) *Dir of Studies* (Loppön) Lodrö Dorje, *Lecturer* Lama Ugyen Shenpen *Translators* David Cox, Dana Dudley, Christine Keyser, Robin Kornman, Jud Levinson, Reginald Ray, John Rockwell, C Ives Waldo III, Scott Wellenbach, Gerry Wiener *Founded* 1973.

Aims A division of Nalanda Foundation, a nonprofit educational corporation, whose major division is Naropa Institute, an institution of higher learning offering BA and MA degrees, and currently holding candidacy status for accreditation. The Committee's purpose is to collect, preserve, and translate the vast body of literature of Tibetan Buddhism, with the principle focus being Tibetan language materials, with a secondary and growing emphasis on Sanskrit Buddhist literature.

See also Sec 4, USA for *Naropa Institute.*

NATIONAL TRANSLATION CENTER
Library of Congress, Washington, DC 20540 *Tel* 202-426-5000 *Telex* 710-822-0185 *Libn of Congress* Daniel J Boorstin.

Aims Establishment proposed and recommended by the 1976 Librarian's Task Force on Goals, Organization, and Planning. Principal goals: (1) to undertake a survey of outstanding books in the humanities published in foreign languages that should be translated (or retranslated) into English; (2) to assemble an up-to-date record of such books currently under translation or already commissioned for translation by American, Canadian, or British publishers; (3) to compile and distribute a roster of translators who have already published acceptable translations, in an effort to improve the low estate of the translating art in the US; (4) to form a permanent national commission on translation, each of whose members would be delegated to select a subcommittee of senior scholars, native and foreign, specializing in the relevant language and culture (the subcommittee would be responsible for advising scholars in choosing appropriate works and translators); (5) to seek out those relatively few publishers in English-speaking lands who already bring out a significant number of translations, with intent to aid them in finding subsidies for translations from governments, foundations, cultural associations, and private philanthropy; the Center should also aid such publishers in appropriate ways to increase the sale of translations; (6) to publish a newsletter and later a quarterly journal that would inform the educated public of the work of the translation center and plans for future publications. The journal should also provide space for publication of articles on the theory of translation by English-speaking and foreign authors.

NATIONAL TRANSLATION CENTER (disbanded in 1971)
The Univ of Texas, 2621 Speedway, Austin, TX 78705.

Membership Established on January 1, 1965, by the Ford Foundation, with a grant of $150,000 annually for five years. It was governed by a National Advisory Board of 13, and among the many scholars, writers, poets, editors, and translators who served on the Board during the Center's six-year existence were: Hannah Arendt, William Arrowsmith, W H Auden, Joseph Barnes, Saul Bellow, Heinrich Blücher, Keith Botsford, Clarence Brown, Peter Davison, Dudley Fitts, Robert Fitzgerald, Gerald J Gross, John Houseman, Donald Keene, Paul Henry Lang, Philip Lilienthal, Robert Lowell, Jackson Mathews, Vincent McHugh, Sidney Monas, Roger Shattuck, Charles Singleton, Fred D Wieck, and Helen Wolff.

Aims To support the quality, availability, and financial reward of literary translation into English of texts having cultural and artistic significance, including works in the humanities and arts, in the social and natural sciences, or any other domain of genuine contemporary relevance.

Activities/Programs A fellowship program, established in 1966, was designed to be an effective help to translators. The fellowships were available to applicants for a wide variety of purposes and were renewable.

The Center's best-articulated program was a fund, used in three ways:

(1) Grants were made from a Revolving Fund to commission individual translators. With these grants, the Center expected to set an example of the highest possible standards of translation; to make available important but previously neglected foreign works; to sponsor new translations to replace existing unsatisfactory ones; and to encourage professional translators to improve their techniques as well as to bring into the craft of translation writers and poets who had not previously been attracted to it (see Sec 3, USA). Commissions in 1965 and 1966 ranged from $1000 to $5000 and averaged under $3000. These were made on the basis of an agreement between the applicant and the Center, and were repayable to the Fund itself, from fees and royalties paid to the translator, within the five years following publication of the commissioned translation, at the rate of 50% of all royalties paid, up to 50% of the Center's commission. The balance of any royalties were to be retained by the translator. Up to one-half of the amount of commission was payable to the translator on signature of the contract, and the balance on completion of the project. Applicants were expected, if their projects were not in the public domain, to inquire from the original publisher whether English-language translation rights were available. Commissions were not to be given until the applicant was legally free to exercise these rights. In exceptional circumstances the Center was prepared to cooperate with the applicant in obtaining such rights, by stating its interest in the project, but any sums paid for such rights were to be paid at the expense of the applicant. The Center considered applications at any stage in a project, and was willing to support a project from its inception, when a partial translation already existed and assistance was required to complete it, or when a translation was already completed and needed, to achieve its definitive form, checking or criticism, whether stylistic or linguistic.

(2) The Center set aside from its Revolving Fund a specific fund to support a pilot project in the preparation of carefully edited, faithful, bilingual prose translations of the major works of post-classical literature, along the lines of the Loeb Classical Texts.

(3) A special fund was set aside to provide nonrepayable grants of up to $500 to cooperate with magazine editors and others wishing to improve the standards of translation by making available to translators grants for the translation of works of less than book length, to tender flexible assistance to such projects as would not be eligible under the commissioning program, but would, nevertheless, advance the Center's aims, and to assist in specific surveys

of translation needs (to commission careful, objective reviews of published translations and to study specific problems in translation, as well as its history and theory).

The Center was especially interested in maintaining a log of translations published, projected, or in progress, and in acting, when possible, as a clearinghouse for information on translation and translators, in order to help in avoiding costly duplications of effort—informing translators, editors, and publishers of works needing translation, assisting editors and publishers seeking translations or translators, and occasionally evaluating translations through its own consultants.

The Center was interested in all aspects of translation, in its study as well as its practice, in sponsoring, coordinating, or furthering in any way it could imaginative studies of translation in all fields, including theater, film, music, etc, whether by individuals, groups, or institutions.

In 1968, the Center added a new program, to bring to the Center a limited number of translators to reside in Austin and work with the staff and other available specialists on specific projects. The purpose of the program was to train beginning translators and assist more experienced ones by providing them with transportation, a modest stipend and a cost-of-living allowance.

The Center sponsored two translation prizes, the first National Book Award in Translation and the Cesare Pavese Prize for a translation from the Italian.

Publications *Delos* (see Sec 6, Journals).

NATIONAL TRANSLATIONS CENTER
The John Crerar Library, 35 W 33 St, Chicago, IL 60616 *Tel* 312-225-2526 *Telex* 910-221-5131 *Chief* Ildiko D Nowak *Founded* 1946.

Aims Established and funded by Special Libraries Association; (1) to serve as an international depository and information source for unpublished English translations of the world's scientific and technical materials available from any known source in the English-speaking countries; (2) to make translations available, regardless of the source from which they can be obtained, and to avoid unnecessary duplication of translating efforts. The Center receives copies and/or notifications of unpublished translations, maintains a locator file of over 500,000 items, and provides copies of or information about translations on a nonprofit, service fee basis. The Center provides services such as customized and on-demand (own database only) manual searching, document delivery, with subject coverage of all fields of theoretical and applied sciences. Inquiries may be made by letter, telephone, or telex.

Activities/Programs In 1976 a grant of $15,230 from the National Endowment for the Humanities enabled the Center to undertake a study to determine the amount of translating from other languages into English now being carried on, where such translating is being done, availability of the translations, the need in various humanistic disciplines for such an information clearinghouse, and the cooperation likely to be forthcoming for the establishment and operation of a center.

Publications *Translations Register-Index* (see Sec 6, Journals).

NEW ENGLAND TRANSLATORS ASSOCIATION (NETA)
35 Catherine Dr, Peabody, MA 01960 *Contact* Alice Berglund.
Membership Chapter of ATA.

NORTHERN CALIFORNIA TRANSLATORS ASSOCIATION (NCTA)
15 Pearl St, San Francisco, CA 94103 *Contact* Thomas R Bauman.
Membership Chapter of ATA.

NORTHERN OHIO TRANSLATORS ASSOCIATION (NOTA)
243 Stanmary Dr, Berea, OH 44017 *Contact* Lee Wright.

PEN AMERICAN CENTER TRANSLATION COMMITTEE
47 Fifth Ave, New York, NY 10003 *Tel* 212-255-1977 *Chmn* Robert Miller *Contact* Christine Friedlander *Founded* 1959.
Membership Reza Baraheni, Emile Capouya, Ronald Christ, B J Chute, Frances Frenaye, Serge Gavronsky, Mirra Ginsburg, Peter Glassgold, Talat Sait Halman, Karen Kennerly, Peter Kussi, Rika Ellen Lesser, Jean R Longland, Barbara S Miller, Richard Plant, Theodore Purdy, Gregory Rabassa, Michael Roloff, Raymond Rosenthal, John Shepley, Grace Schulman, Marian Skedgell, Beatrice Stillman, Sophie Wilkins, Helen Wolff.
Aims To work for the recognition, appreciation, and benefit of translators. As an international organization, PEN has been particularly conscious in recognizing the important role of this enduring art.
Publications *The World of Translation* (New York: PEN American Center, 1971); Proceedings of the "Conference on Literary Translation," held in New York in 1970; papers by 39 translators, writers, poets, editors, and publishers representing 13 countries.
See also Sec 3 for *Calouste Gulbenkian Foundation Prize, Goethe House-PEN Translation Prize, PEN Translation Prize* and Sec 5 for *Manifesto on Translation, The Bill of Rights.*

REGISTRY OF INTERPRETERS FOR THE DEAF (RID), *See* National Interpreter Training Consortium (Sec 4, USA)

SOCIETY OF FEDERAL LINGUISTS (SFL)
PO Box 7765, Washington, DC 20044 *Pres* Everette E Larson, Hispanic Division, Library of Congress *Founded* 1930.
Membership Federal employees who use one or more foreign languages in their work. The Society welcomes as members all employees of the US Government who are translators or interpreters, as well as other categories of Federal employees who are required to use foreign languages in their work—foreign language abstractors, research analysts, editors, catalogers. Supervisors of such employees are also eligible for membership. Persons in nongovernment language employment are admitted as "Associate" members.
Aims To promote the professional status and competence of its member-linguists, to seek to establish professional standards and training programs, to furnish its members information

on language tools and techniques, and to advise them on job opportunities in foreign-language fields. The Society holds frequent meetings which provide professional and social contacts, and which serve as a forum for Government and private authorities on translation, communication, and other relevant topics.

In the past, the Society has presented to the US Civil Service Commission information and demands which resulted in significant improvement in job standards and classifications for Federal translators and interpreters. Since then, the Society has continued to maintain interest in this subject and has presented its views to the Commission from time to time.

Publications *The Federal Linguist* (see Sec 6, Journals).

SOUTHERN CALIFORNIA CHAPTER OF ATA

Medical Library, LAC/USC Medical Center, 1200 N State St, Los Angeles, CA 90033 *Contact* Gillian Olechno.

THE AMERICAN ASSOCIATION OF LANGUAGE SPECIALISTS (TAALS)

1000 Connecticut Ave NW, Washington, DC 20036 *Tel* 202-298-6500 *Exec Secy* Idette Johnson Swetye *Pres* Lisa Valyiova, 225 E 57 St, New York, NY 10022, 212-751-4668 *Founded* 1957.

Membership 215 interpreters and translators based in 12 countries of the Western Hemisphere—Argentina, Brazil, Canada, Chile, Colombia, Guatemala, Mexico, Panama, Peru, the US, Uruguay, Venezuela—and in Europe and Japan. Over 40 of them are permanently employed by international organizations, governmental agencies, and universities; the others work on a free-lance basis.

Aims A professional association in the Americas that represents language specialists working at the international level, either in conferences or in permanent organizations, and determines their qualifications and standards. The association vouches for the language competence of its individual members through a rating system. The TAALS standards, both of professional ethics and working conditions, are binding on its members everywhere. All qualified conference-level language specialists are eligible for membership. Applications are accepted through October 1 of each year, and new members are admitted by a two-thirds majority at the annual General Assembly.

Publications *Yearbook 1979.*

See also Sec 5 for *TAALS Professional Code for Language Specialists.*

TRANSLATORS' ASSOCIATION OF CENTRAL TEXAS (TRACT)

3214 Beverly Rd, Austin, TX 78703 *Contact* Mike Conner.

THE WORD GUILD, INC

119 Mount Auburn St, Harvard Sq, Cambridge, MA 02138 *Tel* 617-492-4656 *Pres* Zelda Dlugo Fischer.

Aims A national free-lance collaboration specializing in literary, scholarly & scientific translations of all major languages of Europe as well as Japanese and Arabic. Copy editing of translated texts & reading for publishers.

Publications *The Word Guild Magazine* (see Sec 6, Journals).

Member of ATA.

Uruguay

COLEGIO DE TRADUCTORES PÚBLICOS DEL URUGUAY (Society of Certified Translators of Uruguay)

25 de Mayo 395, Piso 3 Ap 5, Montevideo.

Member of FIT.

Yugoslavia

SAVEZ DRUŠTAVA I UDRUŽENJA KNJI-ŽEVNIH PREVODILACA JUGOSLA-VIJE (Union of Societies of Literary Translators of Yugoslavia)

Francuska 7, YU-11000 Belgrade.

Member of FIT.

SAVEZ DRUŠTAVA ZNANSTVENIH I TEHNICKIH PREVODILACA JUG-OSLAVIJE (Federation of Associations of Scientific and Technical Translators of Yugoslavia)

Klaiceva 42/1, YU-4100 Zagreb

Member of FIT.

3
Awards/Fellowships/Grants/Prizes

There is general agreement among translators that the very existence of translation prizes and grants and the competition for excellence of performance that these may engender does a great deal to publicize the profession itself and to raise the standards of literary translation as well as the status of the individual literary translator.

Ewald Osers of The Translators' Association of London, one of the recipients of the Nathhorst-FIT International Prize in 1977, has stated that in a literary activity which offers so little financial reward as translation, "the existence of prizes is important. They hold out the hope of a very occasional small windfall for a translator who normally, by any standard of comparison, is underpaid and who quite often, like the translator of poetry, gets no payment at all for his/her labor of love. Translation prizes also draw attention to literary translation and provide much-needed publicity for this still undervalued activity."

It is probably not unfair to state that two of the milestones in the history of translation in the United States, where the profession has been particularly neglected and disdained, have been the establishment of the annual PEN Translation Prize in 1963 and the first National Book Award in Translation in 1967.

The awards are arranged by country, with a special designation, International, for those administered by international associations or organizations. Although most of the information has been gathered from responses to a questionnaire, some of the data has been compiled from secondary sources.

Brazil

ODORICO MENDES TRANSLATION PRIZES
Brazilian Academy, Ave Presidente Wilson 203, 20,000 Rio de Janeiro.

Awarded annually for a distinguished translation of foreign literature into the Portuguese language.

Canada

CANADA COUNCIL TRANSLATION PRIZES
Canada Council, Box 1047, 151 Sparks St, Ottawa, ON K1P 5V8.

Awarded to two distinguished translations of any year, one in French, one in English, since 1974. The original cash prize of $2,500 was increased to $5,000 in 1976.

1974 Alan Brown & Jean Paré.
1975 Sheila Fischman & Michelle Tisseyre.
1976 John Glassco & Jean Simard.

France

MARTHE FIUMI-LEROUX TRANSLATION PRIZE
Société des Poètes français (Soc of French Poets), 38 rue du Faubourg-St-Jacques, F-75014 Paris.

Known also as the "Gran Premio Franco-Italien" and established by friends of the Italian poet Lionello Fiumi in memory of his wife, the annual award is presented alternately to a French writer translating and commenting on contemporary Italian poetry, and to an Italian writer translating and commenting on French poetry. Past recipients have included:

1957 Eugène Bestaux.
1958 Guglielmo Lo Curzio.

1959 André Pezard.
1960 Carlo Pellegrini.
1969 Roger Clérici.

JULES JANIN PRIZE
French Academy, Inst of France, 23 quai de Conti, F-75006 Paris.

Monetary prizes awarded annually for translation of a Latin or Greek work published within the past three years.

LANGLOIS PRIZE
French Academy, Inst of France, 23 quai de Conti, F-75006 Paris.

Monetary prize awarded annually for a translation of verse or prose from a foreign language.

PORTUGUESE—FRENCH TRANSLATION PRIZE
Association pour le Développement des Études Portugaises et Brésiliennes (ADEPB) (Association for the Development of Portuguese and Brazilian Studies), 117 rue de Rennes, F-75006, Paris.

Established in 1978 in collaboration with the Calouste Gulbenkian Foundation of Portugal, the prize of 5000 French francs has thus far only been announced for 1978 and is to be presented in 1979 for a translation into French of a contemporary Portuguese work.

PRIX DU MEILLEUR LIVRE ÉTRANGER
20 rue Oudinot, F-Paris VII *Secy* J Wittorski.

Although not awarded for the translation, the award, established in 1948, depends to a great degree on the relative excellence of translation and is awarded annually for what is regarded by a jury as the best foreign book published in a French version by a French publisher.

1950 *Monsieur le Président* (Bellenand) translated by George Pillement, Francisca

Garcias, & Yves Malartic from the Spanish of Angel Asturias.
1951 *Barrabas* (Stock) translated by Marguerite Gay & Gerd Mautort from the Swedish of Pär Lagerkvist.
1953 *Le fous du roi* (Stock) translated by Pierre Singer from the English of Robert Penn Warren.
1954 *Alexis Zorba* (Plon) translated by Yvonne Gauthier from the Greek of Nikos Kazantzakis.
1955 *Rentrez chez vous Bögner* (Seuil) translated by André Starcky from the German of Heinrich Böll.
1956 *Le Partage des eaux* (Gallimard) translated by L. F. Durand from the Spanish of Alejo Carpentier.
1957 *Dans les forêts* (Gallimard) translated by Sylvie Luneau from the Russian of Melnikov Pechersky.
1958 *L'Homme sans qualité* (Seuil) translated by Philippe Jaccottet from the German of Robert Musil.
1959 *Justine et Balthazar* (Buchet Chastel) translated by R Giroux from the English of Lawrence Durrell.
1960 *Les 40 ans de Mrs Eliot* (Stock) translated by Claude Elsen from the English of Angus Wilson.
1961 *Pays de neige* (Albin Michel) translated by Armel Guerne from the Japanese of Yasunari Kawabata.
1962 *Le Tambour* (Seuil) translated by Jean Amsler from the German of Günter Grass.
1963 *Les enfants de Sanchez* (Gallimard) translated by Céline Zins from the English of Oscar Lewis.
1964 *Le magicien de Lublin* (Stock) translated by Gisèle Bernier from the English translation of Isaac Bashevis Singer's original Yiddish; *La Gnose* (Seuil) translated by Jeanne Henri Marrou from the English of R M Grant.
1965 *Le Centaure* (Seuil) translated by L Casseau from the English of John Updike; *Autobiographie* (Gallimard) translated by Marie

Canavaggia from the English of John Cowper Powys.

1966 *Niembsch ou l'immobilité* (Seuil) translated by B Lortholary from the German of Peter Hartling; *Marcel Proust* (Mercure de France) translated by Georges Cattaui from the English of D Painter.

1967 *La femme des sables* (Stock) translated by Georges Bonneau from the Japanese of Abe Kobo.

1968 *Le Premier cercle* (Laffont) translated by H G Kybarthi; *Le Pavillon des cancéreux* (Julliard) translated by Alfreda & Michel Aucouturier, Lucile & Georges Nivat, & J P Semon from the Russian of Aleksandr Solzhenitsyn.

1969 *Cent ans de solitude* (Seuil) translated by Claude & Carmen Durand from the Spanish of G García Márquez.

1970 *Trois tristes tigres* (Gallimard) translated by Albert Bensoussan from the Cuban Spanish of C Cabrera Infante.

1971 *Cités a la dérive* (Seuil) translated by Catherine Lerouvre & Chrysa Prokopaki from the Greek of Stratis Tsirkas; *Le choc du futur* (Denoel) translated by Sylvie Laroche & Solange Metzger from the English of Alvin Toffler.

1972 *Le Seigneur des anneaux* (Christian Bourgois) translated by Francis Ledoux from the English of J R R Tolkien; *Agression violence* (Calmann Lévy) translated by Rémi Laureillard & Hélène Bellour from the German of Frédéric Hecker.

1973 *Les oranges de sang* (Lettres Nouvelles/Denoel) translated by Alain Delahaye; *Cassandra* (Lettres Nouvelles/Denoel) translated by Jacqueline Bernard; *Le Cannibale* translated by René Daillie, *Le Gluau* translated by Aanda Golem, all from the English of John Hakes; *Enterre mon coeur* (Stock) translated by Gisèle Bernier from the English of Dee Brown.

1974 *Les Boutiques de eanelle* (Lettres Nouvelles/Denoel) translated by Thérèse Douchy, Georges Sidre, & Georges Lisowski; *Le Sanatorium au croque mort* translated by Thérèse Douchy, Allan Kosko, Georges Sidre, & Suzanne Arlet, both from the Polish of Bruno Schulz; *Une voix dans le choeur* (Seuil) translated by Alfréda & Michel Aucouturier from the Russian of Abraham Tertz (André Siniavskii).

1975 *Todo modo* (Lettres Nouvelles/Denoel) translated by René Daillie from the Italian of Leonardo Sciascia; *La Mort dans la vie de Freud* (Gallimard) translated by Brigitte Bost from the English of Max Schur.

1976 *L'ange des Ténèbres* (Seuil) translated by Maurice Manly from the Spanish of Ernesto Sabato; *Poésies choisies* (Gallimard) translated by Jean Lambert from the English of W H Auden

1977 *Le Cinquième Evangile* (Fayard) translated by Henri Louette from the Italian of Mario Pomilio; *La Chair, la mort et le diable* (Denoel) translated by Constance Thompson-Pasquali from the Italian of Mario Praz.

1978 *L'herbe qui ne meurt pas* (Gallimard) & *Terre de fer ciel de cuivre* (Gallimard) translated by Munevver Andac from the Turkish of Yachar Kemal; *Adieu prairies heureuses* (Stock) translated by Diane de Margerie & Xavier Jaujard from the English of Kathleen Raine.

Germany, West (Federal Republic)

GERMAN ACADEMY OF LANGUAGE & POETRY PRIZE

German Academy of Language & Poetry, Alexandraweg 23, D-61 Darmstadt.

Monetary prize of 6000 German marks awarded annually for a single translation or a life's work.

GERMAN ACADEMY TRANSLATION PRIZE

German Academy for Language and Poetry, Alexanderweg 23, Glückert-Haus, D-6100 Darmstadt.

Awarded in the sum of 6000 marks for a single work, or a body of work.

INTER NACIONES e V

Referat I/3, Kennedyalle 91-103, D-5300 Bonn-Bad Godesberg.

An organization funded in part by the government and in part by cultural institutions and established to subsidize translations of books by German authors into "international" languages—English, French, Spanish, Russian—with other languages (such as Italian or Portuguese) considered in specific instances. Assistance is provided for translations in science, belles lettres, children's literature, nonfiction (art, popular science, topography and travel), and specialized works (adult education, vocational studies, etc).

Conditions The precondition for a subsidy is the existence of a contract between a German and a foreign publisher, or evidence that negotiations over rights are being concluded, and the foreign publisher's demonstration that the book concerned can only be published at a reasonable retail price if the translation costs are subsidized. Applications for assistance can be made only by the German publisher, based in the Federal Republic or in West Berlin, who holds the rights to the book. If the book is selected for assistance, an agreement between the German publisher and Inter Naciones is concluded. Inquiries from foreign publishers must be directed to the holder of publishing rights in West Germany, who is required to submit an application accompanied by the following information: (1) a declaration by the foreign publisher stating that publication can only go ahead if the subsidy applied for is granted; (2) the name and qualifications of the translator under consideration; (3) the identity of the person who will evaluate the translation; (4) size of printing planned; (5) probable retail price; (6) probable publishing date; (7) subsidy applied for to cover the costs of translation and evaluation; (8) probable main sales area.

Hungary

MEMORIAL MEDAL OF THE HUNGARIAN PEN CLUB

Hungarian PEN Club, Vörösmarty ter 1, Budapest 5.

Awarded annually to reward outstanding translations of Hungarian literature into for-eign languages. Since 1948, when the prize was established, 42 medals have been presented to writers and translators of various nations. The Memorial Medal carries no monetary award.

In 1979 Anne-Marie de Backer was the recipient for her translations and services in making Hungarian literature better known in the French-speaking world.

International

IBBY HONOR LISTS

The Children's Book Council, 67 Irving Pl, New York, NY 10003 USA *Dir* John Donovan.

The International Board on Books for Young People (IBBY), with headquarters in Zurich, Switzerland, is an international, cross-disciplinary organization interested in promoting greater understanding among the children of the world through children's books. It has national sections in approximately 40 countries with the purpose of encouraging a greater exchange, by way of translations among countries, of the best of children's literature published worldwide. In 1978, IBBY announced that it will include translators of children's books on its Honor List for the first time. IBBY Honor Lists are prepared every two years and include books that each of the national sections considers worthy of worldwide attention and international publication.

First US translator honored: Sheila La Farge, for her cumulative work, with her translation of *The Glassblower's Children* by Maria Gripe ((Delacorte/Seymour).

C B NATHHORST PRIZE

International Federation of Translators, 5 Square Thiers, F-75116 Paris, France *Committee for the Translation Prize* Harriet Nordbäck-Linder (Sweden), pres; Pierre-François Caillé (France), I J Citroen (The Netherlands), Henry Fischbach (USA), R. Haeseryn (Belgium), G Radó (Hungary), R Sato (Japan).

Established in 1974 by a grant of 10,000 kroner from the Swedish Nathhorst Foundation "to honor the role of translation in enriching world literature, disseminating scientific knowledge, and bring the peoples of the world and their aspirations closer together." The dual prize is intended to be awarded every three years as grants become available, one grant for a literary translation, another for a scientific one.

Conditions Candidates for the prize are submitted by the member societies of FIT, with each society requested to submit the names of two candidates. Candidates from the US are sponsored by ATA.

1970 Ervino Pocar (Italy), literary; Alexander Gode (US), scientific-technical. Judges: Pierre-François Caillé (France), J Citroen (The Netherlands), R Sato (Japan), Henry Fischbach (US), Zlatko Gorjan (Yugoslavia), Harriet Nordbäck-Linder (Sweden), Bronisław Zieliński (Poland).

1974 Kenji Takahashi (Japan), literary; Ingvar Gulberg (Sweden), scientific-technical.

1977 Zoltán Csuka (Hungary), Ewald Osers (UK).

Israel

TSCHERNIHOVSKI TRANSLATION PRIZE

Hebrew Assn of Writers, PO Box 7111, Tel Aviv.

Monetary prize of 4000 Israeli pounds awarded biennially to two translators for outstanding translations into Hebrew.

Japan

JAPAN TRANSLATION CULTURAL PRIZE

Japan Soc of Translators, Shiba Mansion #208, 5-11-6, Toranomon, Minato-ku.

Awarded annually to encourage translation from and into the Japanese language, and consisting of a trophy and a cash award of 10,000–20,000 Japanese yen.

1974 Shukushi Kakurai, Yasuharu Ito, Katsuya Baba, and Tomokazu Oguri, for *Parzifal* by Wolfram von Eschenbach; Takero Oiji for *The Vision of Williams;* Yasuo Deguchi, for *Keats' Poetical Works;* Toshio Kuroda and Hidehiko Kashiwagi, for *Histoire de la Philosophie Islamique.*

1976 Iwao Kinoshita, for a translation into German of *Kojiki* (Records of Ancient Manners); Edward G Seidensticker, for *The Tale of Genji.*

1977 Isao Mikami, for *Selected Dramas of Shakespeare;* Hiroko Usui, Kazuko Komada, et al, for *Selected Writings of Florence Nightingale;* Edwin McClellan, for *A Dark Night's Passing* from the Japanese of Naoya Shiga.

JAPAN TRANSLATION PRIZE FOR PUBLISHERS

Japan Soc of Translators, Shiba Mansion #208, 5-11-6, Toranomon, Minato-ku.

Awarded annually to a Japanese publisher of a translation into Japanese of a foreign literary work.

1976 For their contributions to the translation of foreign literature into Japanese: Ikubundo, Kokushu Kankokai, Field Enterprises, Lenkyusha, Eichosha, Kodansha International, and TBS- Britannica.

1977 Hyoronsha, for *Les géants de la littérature mondiale* (25 vols); Gyosei for *Märchen der Weltliterature* (12 vols); Kanakando Shuppansha, for *Shinkyugaku* (Acupuncture and Moxibustion), and Kodansha International, for *War Criminal* by Saburo Shiroyama.

The Netherlands

MARTINUS NIJHOFF TRANSLATION PRIZE

Prince Bernhard Fund, Leidsegracht 3, NL-Amsterdam.

Established in 1953 to commemorate the poet Martinus Nijhoff, the prize of 5000 Dutch florins (originally 2,000 florins) is awarded annually on January 26, the date of the poet's death, "for a translation of a literary work into or from Dutch—alternately, if possible." Past recipients have included:

1954 Aleida G Schot, for works of 19th-century Russian writers; Bertus van Lier, for Sophocles' *Antigone.*

1955 James S Holmes, for Dutch poetry.

1956 H W J M Keuls, for Dante's *La Vita Nuova.*

1957 Dolf Verspoor, for Dutch poetry into French.

1958 Max Schuchart, for *Lord of the Rings* by Tolkien. Bert Voeten, for dramatic works, mainly English.

1959 Francisco Carrasquer, for Dutch poetry into Spanish: *Antologia de poetas holandeses contemporaneos.*

1960 Gerda van Woudenberg, for contemporary Dutch poetry. Evert Straat, for his body of work, especially Shakespeare's *Love's Labour Lost, Euripides & Heracles,* and *Iphigenia in Aulis.*

1961 Roy Edwards, for M Nijhoff's *Pen op papier* and other Dutch prose into English.

1962 Johannes Piron, for modern Dutch prose into German; Charles B Timmer, for 19th-century Russian writings into Dutch.

1963 Giacomo Prampolini, for Dutch and Frisian literature into Italian; C N Lijsen, for French prose into Dutch.

1964 Ludwig Kunz, for contemporary Dutch prose into German; Ernest van Altena, for Villon's poetry into Dutch.

1965 J Hemelrijk, Sr, for the comedies of Plautus into Dutch; James Brockaway, for Dutch writing into English.

1966 Alexander Brotherton, for contemporary Dutch prose into English; Gerrit Kouwenaar, for foreign contemporary drama into Dutch.

1967 Ida G M Gerhardt, for Vergil's *Georgics* and other Latin literature into Dutch; Felipe M Lorda Alaiz, for Dutch drama and prose into Spanish.

1968 Olga Krijtová, for Dutch writing into Czech; Marco Fondse, for Russian writing into Dutch.

1969 John Vandenbergh, for James Joyce's *Ulysses* and British and American writing into Dutch.

1970 Else Hoog, for British and American writing into Dutch; L Roelandt, for Multatuli's *Max Havelaar* and other Dutch fiction into French.

1971 E Kummer, for Céline's *Voyage au bout de la nuit* into Dutch.

1972 H B Jassin, for Multatuli's *Max Havelaar* and other Dutch writing into Indonesian.

1973 Adrienne Dixon, for Harry Mulisch's *Het Stenen Bruidsbed* and other Dutch writing into English; C A G van den Broek, for Garcia Márquez' *Cien años de soledad* and other Spanish writing into Dutch.

1974 Barber van de Pol, for Julio Cortázar's *Rayuela* and other Latin-American writing into Dutch.

1975 H R Radian, for Dutch writing into Rumanian.

1977 Júlia Májeková, for Dutch writing into Slovak.

1978 Ingrid Wikén Bonde, for Dutch writing into Swedish; Karel van het Reve, for Russian writing into Dutch; Robert Lemm, for Latin-American writing into Dutch.

Norway

BASTIAN PRIZE

Norwegian Assn of Translators, Fr Nansens Pl 6, Oslo

Monetary prize and a statuette for an outstanding translation published during the preceding year.

THE NORSEMEN'S FEDERATION TRANSLATION GRANT

Nordmanns-Forbundet, Raadhusgt 23b, Oslo 1.

An annual grant of 15,000 Norwegian kroner (approximately $2700) given to a foreign publisher as a contribution toward translation of a Norwegian work, preferably one of modern fiction. The grant is made directly to the publisher, although actual payment is not made until after the translation has been published.

Conditions Applications should be submitted no later than March 1 of each year.

NORWEGIAN TRANSLATION PRIZE

Norwegian Cultural Council, Rosenkrantzgate 11, Oslo 1.

Monetary prize of 15,000 Norwegian kroner, awarded annually for translations of foreign literature.

Poland

POLISH AUTHORS' PRIZES

Polish Authors' Agency, Hipoteczna 2, Warsaw.

Two annual prizes of 15,000 Polish zlotys each, awarded for distinguished translations of Polish literature into foreign languages.

POLISH PEN CLUB PRIZES

Palace of Culture & Science, Warsaw.

Initiated in 1928 and awarded irregularly, the prizes of 15,000 Polish zlotys are awarded for distinguished translations of Polish literature into foreign languages and for translations of foreign literature into Polish.

Translations of Polish works into foreign languages:

Paul Cazin, for *Pan Tadeusz* by Adam Mickiewicz (into French); Jan Tomcsanyi, for *The Peasants* by W Reymont (into Hungarian); George Rapall Noyes, for *Pan Tadeusz* by Adam Mickiewicz (into English).

1948 Frantisek Halas, for works of Adam Mickiewicz and Juliusz Slowacki (into Czech).

1957 Julije Benesic, for diverse works (into Croatian).

1960 Istvan Meszaros, for diverse works (into Hungarian); Jean Bourilly, for works of Juliusz Slowacki (into French).

Translations of foreign literature into Polish:

1928 Aniela Zagorska, for *Victory* by Joseph Conrad, and for her other translations.

1932 Tadeusz Boy-Zelenski, for French literature.

1935 Jozef Wittlin, for the *Odyssey.*

1937 Edward Boye, for Cervantes' *Don Quixote.*

1938 Gabriel Karski, for translations of French literature.

1939 Maria Godlewska, for works of John Galsworthy, Aldous Huxley, and Katherine Mansfield (from English).

1948 Leopold Staff, for his body of work, especially Leonardo da Vinci, Michelangelo, and Goethe's *Reinecke Fuchs*.

1949 Stefan Srebrny, for the Greek Classics, especially Aeschylus' *Oresteia*.

1950 Adam Wazyk, for *Eugene Onegin* by Pushkin, and the works of Rimbaud, Apollinaire, and Vladimir Mayakovski.

1951 Waclaw Rogowicz, for French literature.

1952 Ludwik Hieronim Morstin, for the works of Calderon and Lope de Vega.

1954 Kazimierza Illakowiczowna, for Tolstoy, Schiller, and Hungarian writers.

1956 Julian Rogozinski, for his translations from French.

1959 Zofia Jakimecka, for translations from the Italian; Roman Koloniecki, for his body of work.

1960 Bronislaw Zielinski, for his body of work.

1961 Wladyslaw Broniewski, for her translations from the Russian.

Portugal

PORTUGAL TRANSLATION PRIZE
Portugal State Secretariat for Information & Tourism, Palazio Foz, Lisbon 2.

A monetary prize of 30,000 Portuguese escudos, awarded biennially for a distinguished translation of a literary, scientific, or cultural work written by a Portuguese author.

PRÉMIO PORTUGAL—PORTUGAL PRIZE FOR POETIC TRANSLATION
Portugal State Secretariat for Information & Tourism, Palazio Foz, Lisbon 2.

The prize, consisting of a trip to Portugal, is given by the International Poetry Association (Associazione Internazionale di Poesia), based in Rome, with the cooperation of the State Secretariat of Information & Tourism of Portugal.

1973 Jean R Longland, Curator of the Library, The Hispanic Society of America, for her translations of medieval and modern Portuguese poetry.

Rhodesia

RHODESIAN PEN CLUB TRANSLATION PRIZE
PEN International, Rhodesia Ctr, PO Box 1900, Salisbury.

Annual monetary prize of 50 Rhodesian dollars for a translation into English of a novel written in Shona/Ndebele languages.

South Africa

NEDERLANDSE BANK TRANSLATION PRIZE
South African Academy of Science & Arts, PO Box 538, Pretoria 0001.

An annual prize of 150 rand for a translation of belles lettres from any language other than Modern Dutch into Afrikaans.

United Kingdom

ALICE HUNT BARTLETT PRIZE
The Poetry Soc, 21 Earls Ct Sq, London SW5.

An annual prize of £200 given to the poet the Society most wishes to honor. In the case of poems translated into English, the prize is divided equally between the original poet and the translator.

Conditions Applications should be submitted no later than December 31 of each year.

JOHN FLORIO TRANSLATION PRIZE
The Translators Assn, The Soc of Authors, 84 Drayton Gardens, London SW10 9SD. *Tel* (01) 373-6642 *Sec* George D Astley

Established in 1963 under the auspices of The Italian Institute and The British Italian Societ, the prize—originally £200 and increased to £500 in 1976—is awarded annually for an outstanding translation from the Italian commissioned in the UK and published by a British publisher. Only translations of Italian 20th-century works of poetry, fiction, criticism, history or belles lettres, biographical studies, and travel books are considered. The sum to be awarded each year is decided by the Translation Committee.

Conditions (1) the translation must have been published in the year of the award; (2) books must be submitted by the publisher, and there is no limit to the number of translations submitted by any one publisher; (3) three copies of the work, which may be proof copies, and three copies of the original must be submitted and addressed to The John Florio Prize, c/o of the above address; (4) the closing date for each year is March 1 of the year following publication, but it is helpful if entries are sent in well before that date.

Judges A panel of three judges is appointed by the Committee. Its decision is final and without appeal. If, in the opinion of the judges, there are two candidates of equal eligibility, the prize may be divided between them; also, if no entry reaches the required standard, the prize may be withheld.

1963 Donata Origo, for *The Deserter* by Giuseppe Dessi; Eric Mosbacher, for *Hekura* by Fosco Maraini.

1964 Angus Davidson, for *More Roman Tales* by Alberto Moravia; E R Vincent, for *A Diary of One of Garibaldi's Thousand* by G C Abbas; H S Vere-Hodge, for *The Odes of Dante*.

1965 W C Darwell, for *Dongo, The Last Act* by P Luigi Bellini delle Stelle & Urbano Lazzaro (MacDonald).

1966 Stuart Woolf, for *The Truce* by Primo Levi (Bodley Head); Jane Grigson & Father Kenelm Foster, for *The Column of Infamy* prefaced by *Of Crimes and Punishments* by Allesandro Manzoni & Cesare Beccaria.

1967 Isabel Quigly, for *The Transfer* by Silvano Ceccherini (Eyre & Spottiswoode).

1968 Muriel Grindrod, for *The Popes in the Twentieth Century* by Carlo Falconi (Weidenfeld & Nicolson); Raleigh Trevelyan, for *The Outlaws* by Luigi Meneghello (Michael Joseph).

1969 Sacha Rabinovitch, for *Francis Bacon: From Magic to Science* by Paolo Rossi (Routledge & Kegan Paul); William Weaver, for *A Violent Life* by Pier Pasolini (Cape).

1970 Angus Davidson, for *On Neoclassicism* by Mario Praz (Thames & Hudson).

1971 William Weaver, for *The Heron* by Giorgio Bassani (Weidenfeld & Nicolson) and *Time and the Hunter* by Italo Calvino (Cape).

1972 Patrick Creagh, for *Selected Poems of Giuseppe Ungaretti* (Penguin).

1973 Bernard Wall, for *Wrestling with Christ* by Luigi Santucci (Collins).

1974 Stephen M Hellman, for *Letters from Inside the Italian Communist Party* by Maria Antonietta Macciocchi (New Left Books).

1975 Cormac O'Cuilleanain, for *Cagliostro* by Roberto Gervaso (Gollancz).

1976 Frances Frenaye, for *The Forests of Norbio* by Giuseppe Dessi.

1977 Ruth Feldman & Brian Swann, for *Shema, Collected Poems of Primo Levi* (Menard Pr).

SCHLEGEL-TIECK TRANSLATION PRIZE
The Translators Assn, The Soc of Authors, 84 Drayton Gardens, London SW10 9SD *Sec* George D Astley.

Established through funds provided by the German Federal Republic, the prize of £1600 (originally £500) is awarded annually for a distinguished translation published in the UK by a British publisher. Entries must be translations of German 20th-century works of literary merit and of general interest. The translator may be of any nationality, provided the work is under a British imprint. The award is presented in the spring of each year at the London Embassy of the German Federal Republic.

1965 Michael Bullock for *The Thirtieth Year* by Ingeborg Bachmann (Deutsch) and *Report on Bruno* by Joseph Breitbach (Jonathan Cape).

1966 Ralph Manheim, for *Dog Years* by Günter Grass (Harcourt).

1967 James Strachey, for *Works of Sigmund Freud* (Norton).

1968 Henry Collins, for *History of the International* by J Braunthal (Praeger).

1969 Leila Vennewitz, for *The End of the Mission* by Heinrich Böll (Weidenfeld).

1970 Eric Mosbacher, for *Society Without the Father* by Alexander Mitscherlich (Tavistock).

1971 Ewald Osers, for *The Scorched Earth* by Paul Carell (Harrap).

1972 Richard Barry, for *The Brutal Takeover* by Kurt von Schuschnigg (Weidenfeld); Anthony Palastanga, for *The Gift Horse* by Hildegard Neff (Deutsch).

1973 Geoffrey Strachan, for *Love and Hate* by Irenaus Eibi Ei-besfeldt (Methuen).

1974 Geoffrey Skelton, for *Frieda Lawrence* by Robert Lucas (Secker).

1975 John Bowden, for *Judaism and Hellenism* by Martin Hengel (SCM Pr).

1976 Marian Jackson, for *War of Illusions* by Fritz Fischer (Chatto & Windus).

1977 Charles Kessler, for *Wallenstein—His Life Narrated* by Golo Mann (André Deutsch); Ralph Manheim, for *The Resistible Rise of Arturo Ui* by Bertolt Brecht (Eyre Methuen).

1978 Michael Hamburger, for *German Poetry 1910–1975* (Carcanet New Pr).

SCOTT-MONCRIEFF TRANSLATION PRIZE

The Translators Assn, The Soc of Authors, 84 Drayton Gardens, London SW10 9SD *Tel* (01) 373 6642 *Sec* George D Astley.

Established in 1964 under the auspices of The Society of Authors, the prize is awarded annually for an outstanding translation published in the UK and the Irish Republic by a British or Irish publisher. Only translations of French 20th-century works of poetry, fiction, criticism, history or belles lettres, biographical studies, and travel books are considered. The sum to be awarded each year is decided by the Standing Committee. In 1977 the award was £1000.

Conditions (1) the translation must have been published in the year of the award; (2) books must be submitted by the publisher, and there is no limit to the number of translations submitted by any one publisher; (3) three copies of the work, which may be proof copies, and three copies of the original must be submitted; (4) the closing date for each year is December 31, but it is helpful if entries are sent in well before that date.

Judges A panel of three judges is appointed each year by the Standing Committee; its decision is final and without appeal. If, in the opinion of the judges, there are two candidates of equal eligibility, the prize may be divided between them; also, if no entry reaches the required standard, the prize may be withheld.

1965 Edward Hyams, for *Joan of Arc* by Regine Pernoud (Macdonald).

1966 Barbara Bray, for *From Tristram to Yorick* by Henri Fluchère (Oxford U Pr); Peter Wiles, for *A Young Trout* by Roger Vailland (Collins).

1967 John & Doreen Weightman, for *Jean-Jacques Rousseau* by Jean Guehenno (Routledge & Kegan Paul).

1968 Jean Stewart, for *French North Africa* by Jacques Berque (Faber & Faber).

1969 Terence Kilmartin, for *Antimemoirs* by André Malraux (Hamish Hamilton) and *The Girls* by Henry de Montherlant (Weidenfeld & Nicolson).

1970 W G Corp, for *The Spaniard* by Bernard Clavel (Harrap); Richard Barry, for *The Suez Expedition 1956* by André Beaufre (Faber & Faber); Elaine P Halperin, for *The Other Side of the Mountain* by Michel Bernanos (Gollancz).

1971 Maria Jolas, for *Between Life & Death* by Nathalie Sarraute (Calder & Boyars); Jean Stewart, for *Maltaverne* by François Mauriac (Eyre & Spottiswoode) and *The Taking of the Bastille* by Jacques Godechot (Faber & Faber).

1972 Paul Stevenson, for *Germany in Our Time* by Alfred Grosser (Pall Mall Pr); Joanna Kilmartin, for *Sunlight on Cold Water* by Françoise Sagan (Weidenfeld & Nicolson); Elizabeth Walter, for *A Scent of Lilies* (Collins).

1973 Barbara Bray, for *The Erl King* by Michel Tournier (Collins).

1974 John & Doreen Weightman, for *Tristes Tropiques* and *From Honey to Ashes* by Claude Lévi-Strauss (Jonathan Cape).

1975 Brian Pearce, for *Leninism Under Lenin* by Marcel Liebman (Jonathan Cape); Douglas

Parmée, for *The Second World War* by Henri Michel (Deutsch).

1976 Peter Wait, for *French Society 1789–1970* by George Dupeux (Methuen).

1977 Janet Lloyd, for *The Gardens of Adonis* (Harvester Pr); David Hapgood, for *The Totalitarian Temptation* (Secker & Warburg).

1978 John & Doreen Weightman, for *The Origin of Table Manners* by Claude Lévi-Strauss (Cape); Richard Mayne, for *Memoirs* by Jean Monnet (Collins).

United States of America

MILDRED L BATCHELDER AWARD

Children's Services Div, American Library Assn, 50 E Huron St, Chicago, IL 60611 *Tel* 312-944-6780 *Exec Sec* Mary Jane Anderson.

Although not awarded for the translation itself, the award infers relative excellence of translation, and is presented to an American publisher for an outstanding children's book originally published in a foreign language in a foreign country, translated into English, and subsequently published in the United States during the calendar year preceding the appointment of the Mildred L Batchelder Award Committee. Selection is made by the membership of the Children's Services Division from a slate of three to five books nominated by a five-member committee appointed annually by the CSD president. The award, established in 1966, is announced annually on April 2, and a citation is presented at the Membership Meeting of the CSD during the American Library Association's Annual Conference.

1968 Alfred A Knopf, Inc, for *The Little Man* by Erich Kästner, translated by James Kirkup.

1969 Charles S Scribner's Sons for *Don't Take Teddy* by Mrs Friis-Baastad, translated by Elisa Holt Somme McKinnon.

1970 Holt, Rinehart & Winston, Inc, for *Wildcat Under Glass* by Alki Zei, translated by Edward Fenton.

1971 Pantheon Books for *In the Land of Ur* by Hans Baumann, translated by Stella Humphries.

1972 Holt, Rinehart & Winston, Inc for *Friedrich* by Hans Peter Richter, translated by Edite Kroll.

1973 William Morrow & Co for *Pulgg* by S R Van Iterson, translated by Alexander & Alison Gode.

1974 E P Dutton & Company, Inc for *Petros' War* by Alki Zei, translated by Edward Fenton.

1975 Crown Publishers, Inc for *An Old Tale Carved Out of Stone* by A Linevski, translated by Maria Polushkin.

1976 Henry Z Walck, Inc for *The Cat and Mouse Who Shared a House*, retold by Ruth Hürlimann, translated by Anthea Bell.

1977 Atheneum Publishers for *The Leopard* by Cecil Bødker, translated by Gunnar Poulsen.

1978 Harcourt Brace Jovanovich for *Rabbit Island* by Jorg Steiner, translated by Ann Conrad Lammers.

COLUMBIA UNIVERSITY TRANSLATION CENTER

School of the Arts, 307A Mathematics, New York, NY 10027. *Tel* 212-280-2305.

Established in 1973 (fellowships) and 1975 (awards), sponsored annually to encourage excellence in individual works and the development of new translators.

Fellowships Stipends of $10,000 awarded for one year only to American writers who wish to perfect their knowledge of one of the lesser known languages in order to do literary translations from that language. Candidates who show complete proficiency in the language are disqualified, as well as those who have no knowledge, or only a rudimentary knowledge of the language they propose to study. Prospective candidates should send samples (ten or more pages) of their writing—original fiction or poetry and/or translations—together with a self-addressed stamped envelope. Recipients of fellowships may plan their studies as they wish, here or abroad. Stipends are normally paid in quarterly installments. Closing date for applications is January 15.

Conditions for Fellowships In evaluating applications from candidates for fellowships, the committee will consider the following: candidates should (1) be American writers of proven excellence; (2) give reasonable assurance that he/she will work seriously in the field of translation after completion of the fellowship program; (3) choose to study one of the more difficult languages, such as Chinese, Japanese, Persian, Tibetan, Nepalese, Tamil, Bengali, Thai, Burmese, and the African languages; (4) give proof of linguistic aptitude necessary to carry out the proposed language study; (5) choose their place of study and give proof of availability of adequate educational facilities—candidates are not restricted to Columbia University; (6) indicate that a substantial body of literature is available in the language of his/her choosing—and that the works are not available in English translation in the US.

Conditions for Awards Generally of $500, made to American translators who have completed a substantial part of a book-length translation and who have received a serious indication of interest from a publisher (generally expressed by an option letter or by a contract). The award is paid directly to the translator and is not an advance against royalties. Candidates should send the Center samples of their work, together with a self-addressed envelope. Closing date for applications is February 15.

Recipients of fellowships:

1973 Lane Dunlop (Japanese); Karen Kennerly (Japanese).

1974 John Balaban (Vietnamese); Ruta Pempe (Bengali).

1975 Donald A Phillipi (Ainu, Japanese dialect); Terese Svoboda (Puka-Puka and Nuer).

1976 Bruce Carpenter (Japanese); Jan Feidel (Swahili); Mark Rudman (Ukrainian).

1977 Anthony Kerrigan (Rumanian); Paul Auster (Old French); Marco Carynnyk (Byelorussian).

1978 Phyllis Birnbaum (Japanese): *Literary Works by Japanese Women*. Howard Norman (Creole); *Complete Stories and Poems of Paulé Bartón*. Honorable mention, Inara Cedrins: *Anthology of Contemporary Latvian Poetry*.

Recipients of awards:

1975 Ameen Alwan for *The Poetry of Jaime Sabines* (Red Hill Pr); Kofi Awonoor for *Guardians of the Sacred Word: Ewe Poetry* (Nok); Paul Bowles for *The Oblivion Seekers*

and Other Writings by Isabelle Eberhardt (City Lights); May & Hallberg Hallmunddsson for *An Anthology of Icelandic Literature* (Frederick Ungar); Anselm Hollo for *Poems* by Paavo Haavikko (Gnomon Pr); Edmund Keeley for *Selected Poems of Angelos Sikelianos* (Princeton Univ Pr); Stanley Kunitz for *Orchard Lamps* by Ivan Drach (Sheep Meadow Pr); Miklos Vajda, ed for *Modern Hungarian Poetry* (Columbia Univ Pr).

1976 John Balaban for *Vietnamese Folk Poetry* (Unicorn). Steven Berg for *O I'm a Human Being* (Eskimo and Tlingit Poems) (BOA Editions). Elizabeth Bishop & Emanuel Brasil for *Anthology of Modern Brazilian Poetry,* Vol II (Wesleyan Univ Pr). Stefan Congrat-Butlar for *Materials for a History of Translation* (R R Bowker). John Glad for *Poems* by Nikolai Klyuev (Ardis Pr). Diana Der Hovanessian for *Armenian Poetry in Translation* (Columbia Univ Pr). Walter & Anne Knupfer for *The Poetry of America's Immigrants* (in progress). Rika Lesser for *Holding Out: Selections from the Poetry of Rilke* (Abbatoir). Philip Levine & Ernesto Trejo for *The Poetry of Jaime Sabines* (Twin Peaks Pr). Al Poulin, Jr for *Duino Elegies and Sonnets to Orpheus* by Rilke (Houghton-Mifflin). Roy J Rosengrant for *No Day Without a Line* by Yuri Olesha (Ardis Pr). Ewa Zak for *Modern Polish Fiction: An Anthology* (Latitudes Pr). Bill Zavatsky & Ron Padget for *The Poems of A.O. Barnabooth* by Valery Larbaud (Mushinsha).

1977 Eliot Weinberger for *Burn the Boats* by Homero Aridjis (BOA Editions). Mark Strand for *The Poems of Carlos Drummond de Andrade* (Atheneum). Harold Wright for *Poems of Tanikawa Shuntaro* (Leete Islands Pr). Thomas Harper for *In Praise of Shadows* by Jun'ichiro Tanizaki (Leete Islands Pr). John Bierhorst for *Cantares Mexicanos,* Aztec-Nahuatl poetry.

1978 Peter Nosco for *Some Final Words of Advice,* short stories by Ihara Saikaku. David Dell for *Kamayani* by Jai Shankar Prasad (epic verse poem). George Martin for *Fiabe italiane,* vols 1 & 2 by Italo Calvino (Italian folktales). Peter Viereck for poetry of Georg Heym and Stefan George. Frances Barraclough for *Deep Rivers* by José María Arguedas. Jascha Kessler for *The Magician's Garden,* short stories, by Géza Csátu. Jonathan Galassi for *Selected Essays of Eugenio Montale.* Guy Daniels for *Thirty Fables of Ivan Andreyevich Krylov.* John Matthias for *Anthology of Contemporary Swedish Poetry.* Yuri V Karageorge for *Poems of Five Bulgarian Women Poets.* Judith Moffet for *Poetry of Hjalmar Gullberg.* Norman MacAfee for *Poems and an Essay* by Pier Paolo Pasolini. Jan Pallister for *Esanzo: Poems of Antoine-Roger Bolamba.* Chana Bloch for *A Dress of Fire: Selected Poetry of Dahlia Ravikovitch.* Frank Nisetich for *Victory Odes* by Pindar. Meg Bogin for *Selected Poetry of Salvador Espriu.* Victor Power for *Apple on the Treetop,* a novel, by Richard Power. J H Schmitt for *The Devil's Church and Other Stories* by Machado de Assis. Rosmarie Waldrop for *Livre de Questions* by Edmond Jabes. David Unger & Lewis Hyde for *All Alone in the World,* poems, by Vicente Aleixandre.

DENVER QUARTERLY TRANSLATION AWARD
Denver Quarterly, Univ of Denver, Univ Pk, Denver, CO 80208.

Established in 1976 under the editorship of Gerald W Chapman and funded by generous readers of the journal as an annual award of $500 for the most important publishable translation(s) into English of an essay-length work of literary or esthetic theory or criticism.

Conditions The work must be published or accepted for publication in the *Denver Quarterly* during the year of the award. Although the editors offer to be of practical assistance, the translator must assume responsibility for securing permissions, which must be in writing. A copy or photocopy of the foreign-language text must accompany the translation at the time of submission.

There was no award in 1976 and the prize money was held over for the following year. The 1977 award was shared by Reginald Gibbons for "Antonio Machado on Poetry and Literature," *DQ*, XII no 1, Spring, 1977, and Walter Kaufmann for "On Music and Words" by Friedrich Nietzsche, *DQ*, XIII no 1, Spring, 1978.

THE ALEXANDER GODE MEDAL
American Translators Assn, PO Box 129, Croton-on-Hudson, NY 10520 *Tel* 914-271-3260.

Established in 1964 in recognition of the services rendered to the ATA by its first president, Alexander Gode. The original resolution, adopted unanimously by the Association's Board of Directors, reads: "To commemorate his leadership, and to ensure that his example shall for many years to come inspire others wherever translation is practiced, there is hereby established *The Alexander Gode Medal* for distinguished service to the cause of translation, to be awarded annually by the Board of Directors of the Association, without limitation on the nature of the service rendered to the general cause, or the nationality of the recipient."

Conditions Recommendations for the award are made by the ATA Committee on Honors and Awards and submitted to the Board for approval. The award can be made to an individual or an organization, and is not limited to members of the Association. Submissions of suggestions, accompanied by a brief supporting statement, can be made by members of the ATA.

Past recipients have been Alexander Gode, Kurt Gingold, Richard & Clara Winston, The National Translation Center of The University of Texas, Pierre-François Caillé, Henry Fischbach, Carl V Bertsche, Lewis Bertrand, Lewis Galantière, Jean-Paul Vinay, Eliot F Beach, Frederick Ungar, Royal L Tinsley, Jr.

GOETHE HOUSE–PEN TRANSLATION PRIZE
Translation Committee, PEN American Ctr, 47 Fifth Ave, New York, NY 10003 *Tel* 212-255-1977.

Established in 1974 from funds provided by Goethe House, New York City, the annual prize of $500 is awarded for a distinguished book-length translation of a German literary work.

Conditions The work must be published in the US by an established publishing house in the preceding year; technical, scientific, and reference works are not eligible. Selection of books to be judged and final awards are made by a panel of judges. The deadline for submission of books is December 31. Submissions

should be made to the Chairman, Translation Committee. The prize is presented at the annual meeting of the executive board and general membership, held in May at the association's new headquarters in the Salmagundi Club.

1974 Sophie Wilkins, for *The Lime Works* by Thomas Bernhard (Knopf). Judges: Anne Fremantle, George Reavey, Richard Plant.

1975 Peter Sander, for *Ice Age* by Tankred Dorst (a play). Judges: Hortense Calisher, Timothy Foote, Thomas Lask.

1976 Ralph Manheim, for *A Sorrow Beyond Dreams* by Peter Handke (Farrar, Straus & Giroux). Judges: Emile Capouya, Ronald Christ, Elizabeth Hardwick.

1977 Douglas Parmee, for *An Exemplary Life* by Siegfried Lenz (Urizen Books). Judges: Richard Goldstone, Richard Howard, Kate Medina, Richard Plant.

1978 Joachim Neugroschel, for cumulative contributions to the translation of German literature, including *Panorama of the 19th Century* by Dolf Sternberger (Urizen Books) and *The Wonderful Years* by Reiner Kunze (Braziller). Judges: Richard Plant, Michael Roloff, Sophie Wilkins.

1979 Leila Vennewitz, for *And Never Said a Word* by Heinrich Böll (McGraw-Hill).

THE GOLD MEDAL OF THE TRANSLATION CENTER
Translation Center, Columbia Univ, 307A Mathematics, New York, NY 10027 *Tel* 212-280-2305.

Established in 1978 and awarded annually "for a lifetime of excellence" in the field of literary translation.

1978 Willard Ropes Trask.

CALOUSTE GULBENKIAN FOUNDATION TRANSLATION PRIZE
Translation Committee, PEN American Ctr, 47 Fifth Ave, New York, NY 10003 *Tel* 212-255-1977.

Established in 1978, the biennial award of $500 is to be awarded for the first time in 1979 and every alternate year thereafter, for a distinguished translation from the Portuguese.

1979 Helen R Lane, for *The Three Marias* from the Portuguese of Maria Isabel Barreno, Maria-Luisa Horta, and Maria Velho da Costa (Doubleday/Calder & Boyers).

INTERNATIONAL POETRY REVIEW TRANSLATION PRIZE
Competition Chairperson, PO Box 3161, Princeton, NJ 08540 *Founded* 1979.

For a group of translations from one poet (not to exceed 200 lines), first prize: $150; second prize: $75. Winning entries to be printed in the spring 1980 issue of *International Poetry Review,* which will have first publication rights to winning entries, after which rights will revert to the author.

Conditions All translations submitted must be unpublished and not currently involved in other competitions. Judging will be by William Meredith, consultant in poetry at the Library of Congress. Submissions should be accompanied by a short biographical statement and the original language poetry (with source and date, if published). Manuscripts should be postmarked no later than October 15, 1979, and be sent with self-addressed stamped envelope.

ISLANDS AND CONTINENTS TRANSLATION AWARD

PO Box 25, Setauket, NY 11733 *Dir* Jonathan Cohen.

Established in 1977, the award of $1000 is made annually for an outstanding book of poetry translated from another language and published in the US in the current year and is regarded as "poets-translators rewarding their fellow translators for work that merits special praise." Those books published simultaneously in the US and abroad and sold in US bookstores are also eligible.

Conditions Submission by either translator or publisher of three copies of the book with a stamped, self-addressed envelope; if the poetry has been published in English only, submissions should be accompanied by one copy of at least 25 percent of the original text. The deadline for applications is December 31. The announcement of the award is the following May 15.

1977 Hardie St Martin, for *Roots and Wings: Poetry from Spain 1900-1975* (Harper & Row). Judges: Robert Bly, Jonathan Cohen, David Unger.

1978 Lucien Stryk & Takashi Ikemoto, for *The Penguin Book of Zen Poetry* (Swallow Press, 1977). Judges: Robert Bly, Charles Guenther, David Unger. Honorable Mention: John and Bogdana Carpenter, for *Selected Poems of Zbigniew Herbert* (Oxford Univ, 1977).

JAPANESE LITERARY TRANSLATION "FRIENDSHIP FUND" PRIZE

Japan United States Friendship Commission, 1875 Connecticut Ave NW, #709, Washington, DC 20009 *Tel* 202-673-5295. *Chpn* John W Hall *Vice Chpn* James A Linen *Exec Dir* Francis B Tenny.

Established in 1978, the annual award of $1000 will be presented for the first time in 1979 to the translator whose previously unpublished or newly published first translation of a Japanese literary work is judged best by a jury of editors, writers, and established translators. The prize will be administered in cooperation with the Japan Society, Inc, of New York City. Its purpose is to encourage new American translators in the craft of literary translation from the Japanese, and thereby to increase the amount of good Japanese literature available in print for the English-reading public. Translators with book-length works published before January 1, 1978 will not be considered new translators, and will not be eligible for consideration for the award. First translations published after that date, or unpublished manuscripts of new translators may be considered. In the event the prize is awarded to an unpublished manuscript, the sponsors will attempt to assist as necessary in finding a publisher.

Conditions (1) Any work of Japanese literature of any period, known and published in Japanese, of book-length fiction, literary essays and memoirs, drama, or poetry in English translation is eligible. Shorter works, such as a single short story or a selection of only a few poems, will not be eligible. Translations of nonfiction including Japanese scholarship and history will not be considered; (2) The candidate must be an American translator, with no book-length translation published or widely sold in the US before January 1, 1978; (3) in the case of an unpublished manuscript, a trans-

lation in process may be considered provided that the translation is more than half completed.

The jury will judge on the following criteria (in descending order of importance): (1) literary merit of the English; (2) accuracy with which the translation reflects the spirit of the Japanese original; (3) literary merit of the Japanese original, as generally recognized in Japan.

Books and unpublished manuscripts submitted for the prize should be sent to Peter Grilli, Japan Society, Inc, 333 E 47 St, New York, NY 10017, 212-832-1155, before January 31. In the event that no translation is considered of sufficient merit, no prize will be awarded.

THE HAROLD MORTON LANDON TRANSLATION AWARD

The Academy of American Poets, 1078 Madison Ave, New York, NY 10028 *Tel* 212-988-6783.

Established in 1976 and funded by Mrs Harold Morton Landon in memory of her husband, the $1000 prize is awarded biennially to living citizens of the US for published translations of poetry from any language into English. Book-length poems, collections of poems, or verse dramas translated into verse, are considered.

Conditions The deadline for applications is January 1 of even-numbered years. Announcement is Spring of even-numbered years.

1976 Robert Fitzgerald, for Homer's *The Iliad* (Doubleday). Judge: Richard Wilbur.

1978 Galway Kinnell, for *The Poems of François Villon* (Houghton Mifflin), and Howard Norman, for *The Wishing Bone Cycle* (Stonehill Publishing Co).

LOCKERT LIBRARY OF POETRY IN TRANSLATION

Princeton Univ Pr, Princeton, NJ 08540 *Ed* Mrs Arthur Sherwood *Asst Ed* Robert E Brown *Edit Adv* John Frederick Nims.

Established in 1975 and funded by a bequest from Charles Lacy Lockert (1888–1974), scholar and translator of Corneille, Racine, and Dante, the series is expressly intended to publish in worthy translations significant poetry that is in itself poetic, rather than literal.

Conditions Manuscripts of poetry in translation are accepted for review during February and August of each year. Final selections are made in April and October. There is no requirement on the number of pages. Manuscripts are judged with several criteria in mind: the ability of the poetry to stand on its merits simply as poetry in English; fidelity to the tone and spirit of the original, rather than literal accuracy; and the importance of the translated poet to the literature of his/her time and country. Applicants are requested to send manuscripts to the above address and to include a copy of the poems in their original languages as well as any introductory material such as scholarly preface or foreword, and notes, if they are available.

The Library includes translations of both classic and modern works from many languages and cultures, with the original poems printed facing the translation. About two volumes are added to the Library each year. Although those who receive contracts are, in a sense, "winners" of a "competition," the Li-

brary does not consider its series as a contest with an award.

1967 Edmund Keeley & Philip Sherrard, for *George Seferis: Collected Poems (1924–1955)*.

1972 Brian Swann & Ruth Feldman, for *Collected Poems of Lucio Piccolo*.

1975 Edmund Keeley & Philip Sherrard for *Complete Poems of C P Cavafy*, ed by George Savidis.

1975 Alexander Taylor, for *Benny Andersen: Selected Poems*.

1975 Ruth Feldman & Brian Swann, for *Selected Poetry of Andrea Zanzotto*.

1976 Mary Ann Caws & Jonathan Griffin, for *The Poetry of René Char*.

1976 Michael Impey & Brian Swann, for *Selected Poems of Tudor Arghezi*.

1976 Robert Maguire & Magnus Krynski, for *"The Survivor" and Other Poems* by Tadeusz Rozewicz.

1977 Donald D Walsh, for *"Harsh World" and Other Poems* by Angél González.

1979 Ann Winters, for *Salamander: Selected Poems of Robert Marteau*.

1979 Edmund Keeley, for *Ritsos in Parentheses* by Yannis Ritsos.

1979 Patrick Diehl, for Dante's *Rime*.

1980 Edmund Keeley & Philip Sherrard, for *Angelos Sikelianos: Selected Poems*.

NATIONAL ENDOWMENT FOR THE HUMANITIES

Translation Program, Mail Stop 350, Div of Research Grants, 806 15 St NW, Washington, DC 20506 *Tel* 202-724-1672.

The Translations Program provides support for annotated, scholarly translations that contribute to an understanding of the history and intellectual achievements of other cultures and serve as tools for further disciplinary or comparative research.

Conditions Translations from any language, on any topic relevant to the humanities are eligible. The Endowment has a particular interest in applications dealing with non-Western cultures, where the need for translations into English seems to be the greatest. Projects may involve a single scholar or represent a cooperative effort of groups of scholars. Similarly, application may be made to translate a single text or a group or series of related texts. All translations must be accompanied by a critical introduction and explanatory annotation which will locate the work within historical and intellectual contexts.

The program reimburses applicants for whatever time is needed to complete, or significantly advance, the translation of a given text or group of texts. Applicants may request support for up to three years, and need not be affiliated to be eligible to apply.

Projects are evaluated by special panels in accordance with three principal criteria: (1) significance of the work to one or more fields in the humanities; (2) the quality of the translations sample of the specific work for which a grant is sought; (3) the quality of the annotation.

July 1 is the annual deadline; if a grant is approved, funding may be expected to begin on, or after, April 1 of the following year. All prospective applicants should write well in advance of the deadline for detailed guidelines and application materials to the address given above.

Projects funded during 1977:

A Bodrogligeti, Univ of California at Los Angeles. *Islam Among the Turks of Central Asia,* source materials in Karakhanid, Khorazmian, and Chatagay, AD 1000–1800.

W Brinner, Univ of California. *Arabic Tales of the Prophets,* 11th-century Koranic tales from the Old and New Testaments.

P Cachia, Columbia Univ. *Popular Narrative Ballads of Modern Egypt.*

G Cardona, Univ of Pennsylvania. Nāgésa's *Vaiyākaranasiddhāntaparamalaghumañjūsā* (*The Jewel Box of Accepted Views of Grammarians*), major Indian philosophies of language, and grammarians', logicians', poeticians', and ritualists' approach to language, 4th century BC to 18th century AD.

R Dankoff, Univ of Colorado. *Kutadgu Bilig* (The Wisdom of Royal Glory), earliest 11th-century work in Islamic Turkish culture.

D Darst, Florida State Univ. *Reprobación de superstitiones y hechicerías* by Pedro Ciruelo and *Tratado de supersticieas y hechicerías* by Martín de Castanega, treatises on witchcraft and demonology in 16th-century Spain.

T DeBary, Columbia Univ. *Sources of Neo-Confucianism,* major documents of the Chinese philosophical and historical traditions, 11–13th-centuries.

P Debreczeny, Univ of N Carolina. A critical edition and translation of Pushkin's prose fiction, including a history of Pugachev.

M Dols, California State Univ. Ibn Ridwan's *Risālat fī daf'madārr al-abdān bi-ard Misr* (On the Prevention of Bodily Ills in Egypt), 11th-century account of health conditions in Egypt and Muslim understanding of health and causation of illness.

E Dunn Dols, Highgate Rd Social Science Research Station. A I Klibanov's *History of Religious Sectarianism in Russia, 1860s–1917.*

J Eliash, Oberlin College. *al-Kāfi fī 'Ilm ad-Dīn* by Kulayni, a corpus of the sayings of Imams on theology, jurisprudence, and political theory.

V Estes. *Ambrosiastri qui dicitur Commentaruis in Epistulas Paulinas* (Ambrosiaster's Commentaries on the Epistles of St Paul), 4th-century.

M Fearey. *Nevā'ī's Ferhād ü Shirin,* a narrative poem in Old Uzbek (Turkic) establishing that language as a proper vehicle for great literature.

R Goldman & B van Nooten, Univ of California-Berkeley. *The Valmīki Rāmāyana,* an epic Sanskrit poem of 2500 verses.

K Grossberg. *Medieval Japanese Law,* source information about Japan's political system, 14–16th centuries.

J Hangin, Indiana Univ. *Mongolian Folklore Project,* with notes on comparative Altaic folklore.

E Honig & A Trueblood, Brown Univ. Lope de Vega's *La Dorotea,* a lyric drama in prose dialogue with formal choruses and inserted poetry.

F Householder, Indiana Univ. *Syntax of Apollonius Dyscolus,* 2nd century AD with concordance-glossary.

G Jones, Univ of Maryland. *Reports from the Georgia Salzburgers, 1738–41,* lives of Austrian Pietist exiles.

E Keeley, Princeton Univ. A bilingual edition of the poems of Angelos Sikelianos.

D Knechtges, Univ of Washington. *The Wen xuan,* major anthology of Chinese literature, 3rd–6th century AD.

H Lane, Northeastern Univ. *Etienne Bonnot, Abbé de Condillac: Major Philosophical Works, 1746–80.*

A Martinez, SUNY at New Paltz. *A History of the Reign of Gazan Xan.* Rasīdu d-Dīn's 13th-century accounts of civil and military reforms in late medieval Iran.

B Metcalf, Univ of Pennsylvania. *The Bihishtī Zēwar* (The Jewelry of Heaven) by Thanvī, 19th-century Urdu text of guidance to Indian Muslim women on education, religious law, piety, and social responsibilities.

N Morey. *El Orinoco Ilustrado y Defendido, 1745,* by B J Gumilla, an account of the inhabitants, especially now extinct Indian groups, flora and fauna and languages of Colombian and Venezuelan interior lowlands.

A Pace, Univ of Washington. Luigi Castiglioni's *Travels in North America, 1785–87,* observations on Colonial America by a Milanese patrician and botanist.

M Page. *Stories from the Iranian National Legend,* recorded in Shiraz from professional storytellers.

V Rao, Univ of Wisconsin. *The Basavapurāna,* a 13th-century Telugu poem.

D Robinson & A Bigelow, Ohio State Univ. *Riddles of the Russian People,* the first edition (1875) of Savodnikov's collection of 2500 riddles.

H Rolfson, College of St Teresa. Jan van Ruusbroec's *Die Gheestelike Brulocht* (The Spiritual Espousals), a work by the 14th-century Flemish mystic.

D Rosenberg, Duke Univ. Götz von Berlichingen's *Memoirs in Self Defense, 1561,* one of the last records of the dying knightly class.

A Shalkop. *Stephan Ushin's Journal,* a record of life in Alaska by a Russian who remained after the sale of that territory to the US.

P Shashko, Univ of Wisconsin. *Istoriia Slavenobolgarskia* (A Slavo-Bulgarian History), by Paisii of Hilendar, written at the Mt Athos monastery in 1762.

J Shih, George Washington Univ. *Yüan Drama: Plays of Kuan Han-ch'ing, 1260–1368,* on the classical forebear of all Chinese theater.

P Smith, Univ of Lowell. *Hermeneutic Studies on Plato* by H G Gadamer, an examination from the phenomenological viewpoint of modern German philosophy.

S Spectorsky, Queens College of CUNY. *Family Law in Early Islam,* responses to questions of ritual, legal, and dogmatic interest by Ahmad Ibn Haubal (d 855).

T Svoboda. *Nuer Songs from the Sudan,* from an oral tradition now disappearing among the peoples of Sudan.

A Tezla, Univ of Minnesota. *The Hazardous Quest: Hungarian Immigrants in the United States, ca. 1895–1914.*

R Thompson, Harvard Univ. Elishe's *History of Vardan and the Armenian War,* of the Armenian uprising in 450 AD against Iranian overlords.

M Tymoczko. *Aided ConCulainn* (The Death of CuChulainn), the old Irish text, the only pre-Norman version of the epic.

S & M Vasconcellos. *A Century of Gold in Brazil, 1700–99,* sources relating to the discovery and exploration of the metal.

J van Buitenen, Univ of Chicago. *The Ma-habharata* (The Great India), the Sanskrit epic of 100,000 couplets that influenced Southeast Asian civilization from 500 BC to date.

A Veilleux, Cistercian Publications. *Pachomian Sources,* relating to St Pachomius, AD 287–347.

B von Oppen, St John's College. *Letters of Helmuth James von Moltke,* a source on opposition and death under the Nazi regime.

J Wakin, Columbia Univ. *Rawdat al-Nāzir wa-Jannat al-Munāzir* (On the Theory and Methodology of Islamic Jurisprudence) by Ibn Qudama, on comparative jurisprudence within Sunni Islam.

C C Wang. *Lu-shih ch'un-ch'iu* (The Book of Lü Pu-wei), the first "authored" book in Chinese literature (3rd century BC).

Y T Wang, Univ of Pittsburgh. *Record of the Buddhist Monasteries in Lo-yang,* a 6th-century record of the splendor and devastation of this northern Chinese capital.

R Winkes, Brown Univ. *Riegl, the Character of Late Roman Art,* a survey of Roman Imperial Art up to the age of Charlemagne.

A Yu, Univ of Chicago. *The Hsi-yu chi* (Journey to the West), a sixteenth-century Chinese epic narrative of a Buddhist pilgrimage.

S Zenkovsky. *Nikonian Codex,* the late medieval Russian Chronicle of Russian history from the 9th century to 1558, including parts of the "Alexandro-Nevsky Chronicle."

Projects funded during 1978:

W Arndt, Dartmouth College. Pushkin's *Poltava* (1828), a complete verse translation of Pushkin's dramatic poem on the climactic battle in the Ukraine (1709) between Tsar Peter I and Charles XII of Sweden which first settled the modern balance of power in Eastern Europe.

A Bonner. *Selected Works of Ramon Lull (1232–1316).* Seven works of the Catalan philosopher, mystic, and poet, centered on his system of universal thought, the *Ars generalis.*

J Chaves. *Chinese Poetry of the Late Ming Period (1573–1644).* The selection will stress the poetry and poets of the "Kungan School."

T Cleary, Amer Inst of Buddhist Studies. *Hsiu Hua Yen Ao Chih Wang Chin Huan Yuan Kuan* (Fa Tsang's *The Inner Meaning of the Hua Yen*), one of the final works of the great Buddhist patriarch.

R Cushman, Rice Univ. *The Royal Chronicles of Ayutthaya,* a set of documentary source materials for the principal Thai Kingdom and cultural centers in Southeast Asia between 1350 and 1767.

B Dmytryshyn, Oregon Historical Soc. *To Siberia and Russian America: Three Centuries of Russian Eastward Expansion, 1584–1867,* source materials documenting Imperial Russia's expansion into Siberia and the N American littoral.

M Domandi. *Giovanni Cavalcanti's Florentine Histories,* foreign and domestic policies at the beginning of the Medicean ascendancy in the 15th century.

P Gerson. *Pilgrim's Guide to Santiago de Compostela,* one of the earliest travel books in the Western Middle Ages (13th century).

J Haboush. *Hanjungnok (A Journal Written in Leisure),* viewed as one of the major classics of Korean prose literature.

A Hofstadter. Heidegger's *Die Grundprobleme der Phänomenologie (The Basic Problems of Phenomenology)*, containing the text of lectures given in Marburg in 1927.

J Hopkins, Univ of Minnesota. Nicolas de Cusa's *De Docta Ignorantia (On Learned Ignorance)*, presenting a synthesis of his cosmology, ontology, and theology.

W Johnson, Univ of Kansas. *The T'ang Code: Specific Articles, Vol II*, the Chinese Criminal Code, first promulgated in AD 653 and the single most important collection of laws in the history of East Asia.

M Kantor, Northwestern Univ. *First Slavic Lives (Bohemian, Russian, and Serbian Saints)*, semi-secular biographies of princes who were canonized and elevated to the dignity of patron saints.

P Kuepferle. *The Tattva-Prādipikā* (The Illumination of Reality), a 12th-century philosophic text.

D Ludden. *The Manimēkalai*, 6th century, the only Buddhist work written in Tamil.

P Mackay, Univ of Washington. *The Travel Journal of Evliya Celebi, Book 8: Travels in Mainland Greece*, the 17th-century travel book illuminating the history of the Ottoman Empire and Imperial policies.

W Malandra, Univ of Minnesota. *The Yasts* (Hymns of Praise), translations from the Avesta, hymns dedicated to various gods of the ancient Iranian and Zoroastrian pantheon.

C Palisca, Yale Univ. *Music Theory Translation Series*, translation of texts by Aristides Quintilianos, Boethius, Zarlino, Galilei, Koch, and Kirnberger.

J Pessagno. *The Thought of al-Māturīdī—The Kitāb al Tawhīd (Book of the Absolute Unity of God)*, the major speculative work of an acknowledged leader of Islamic speculative theology.

D Rawson, Iowa State Univ. *Gruzenberg Memoirs Translation Project*. The writer, a Jew, recounts conditions of life in his time, 19th-century Russia, for Jews and other minorities.

D Rosenthal. *Tirant lo Blanc*. Martorell, its author, has been described as "the first of that lineage of God-supplanters who try to create in their novels an 'all-encompassing reality' ".

Wm Jay Smith, Hollins College. Jules Laforgue's *Les Moralités légendaires* (1887), and *Berlin, la Cour et La Ville*, (1886), *(Moral Tales and Berlin, the City and the Court)*, works by the poet who deeply influenced 20th-century English and French poetry.

K Stowasser, Univ of Maryland. *The Story of Medieval Egypt: al Maqrīzī's Topographical History*, a 15th-century chronicle discussing legal, dogmatic and sectarian topics regarding the Muslims, Coptic Christians, and Jews.

A F Thurman, Amer Inst of Buddhist Studies. *The Mahāyānasūtralamkāra of Asanga* (Asanga's Ornament of the Mahāyāna Scriptures), a Sanskrit compendium in verse of ethical, spiritual, and philosophical teachings.

W Urban, Monmouth College. *The Chronicle of Balthasar Russow*, a Western account of the great Baltic war between the Teutonic Knights and Ivan the Terrible.

W Wyatt, Hellenic Cultural Soc of SE New England.

A Karkavitsas' *O Zitiānos* (The Beggar) (1896), the first in a proposed series of 19th-century Greek works.

Projects funded during 1979:

E B Ashton, with support from the Swiss Govt Foundation, Pro-Helvetia. Karl Jaspers'

Von der Wahreit (On Truth), embodying Jaspers' contributions to epistemology and the study of man.

Michael Aung-Thwin. *Inscriptions of Pagan: 11th to 14th Centuries, AD, Burma*. Collections of donative records made to the Buddhist church.

Clinton Bailey. *Bedouin Poetry from Sinai and the Negev*. The collection is grouped into didactic poems, women's poems, ballads of romance and of history.

Thomas Barker, SUNY at Albany. *The Heresy Trial of Galileo, In Letters of the Piccolomini Family: A New Perspective*. This hitherto unknown correspondence establishes Galileo's trial to have been a result of political maneuvering rather than religious opposition.

Judith Becker, Univ of Michigan. *Source Readings in Javanese Gamelan Music*. Translations of monographs and articles written by practicing musicians and scholars about traditional Gamelan music.

Eric M Beekman, Univ of Massachusetts, with support from The Foundation for the Promotion of the Translation of Dutch Literary Works. *Library of the Indies*. A literary history, nine novels, and a volume of critical essays, covering the era of Dutch Colonialism (17th to 20th centuries).

John Bierhorst. *The Codex Cantares Mexicanos*, the primary source for Aztec poetry.

Lydia Black, Providence College. *Journals of Yakov Netsvetov, Alaska, 1828–1861*. Accounts picturing life in Alaska's interior among the Eskimoan and Athabascan populations.

Edward W Bodnar, Georgetown Univ. *The Letters of Ciriaco d'Ancona 1443–1447*, records of the Greek and Roman antiquities, particularly inscriptions, extant in the Eastern Mediterranean.

John Boening, Univ of Toledo. *Rainer Maria Rilke's Art Criticism*. Rilke's writing on art, to be organized into (1) his book on the young painters at Worpswede; (2) his monograph and lecture on Rodin; (3) the succession of essays and reviews he wrote for various periodicals.

Daniel Breazeale, Univ of Kentucky. *Fichte: Early Philosophical Writings*, popular lectures, his commentaries and his letters.

Robert D Bruce. *The Book of Chan K'in*, a collection of formal Lacandon narratives appears to be a version of the Mayan narrative of Genesis.

Clark Butler & Christine Seiler, Indiana Univ & Purdue Univ at Fort Wayne. *Hegel's Correspondence*, including letters to and from Goethe, Schiller, Holderlin, Schelling, Fichte, Schlegel, and others.

William E Butler, Amer Soc of International Law. *Russian International Legal History;* V E Grabar's *Materials on the History of the Literature of International Law in Russia, 1647–1917*.

Robert Caponigri, Univ of Notre Dame. *Berenson and Croce in their Correspondence*. Newly discovered, it will act as a base for a comparative study of Berenson's and Croce's theory and practice of art criticism.

David Carrithers, Univ of Tennessee. *Pensées of Montesquieu*. His notebooks, first printed in their original chronological order in 1953.

Ottavio Casale, Kent State Univ. *A Leopardi Reader*, juxtaposing, in chronological order, poems with prose texts relevant to their inception and intent.

John Colarusso, Inst for the Study of Human Issues. *The Nart Sagas*, the most significant oral literary production of the Circassians.

Robert E Conrad. *An Annotated Documentary History of Brazilian Slavery*, documents, gathered by the author over the past 12 years.

Jerrold Cooper, Johns Hopkins Univ. *Sumerian and Akkadian Royal Inscriptions*, translations of all ancient Mesopotamian (Sumerian and Akkadian) royal inscriptions through the end of the old Babylonian period, ca 1600 BC.

Norman Di Giovanni. Stendhal's *"Italian Chronicles,"* fictional and semi-fictional narratives that illustrate the author's interest in the manners and customs of Italy in the 15–17th centuries.

Anne Feldhaus, Fordham Univ. *The Biography of Govindaprabhu*, the 14th-century Marathi text illuminating the Sect's protest against conventions of politeness and sanity as well as the rules of ritual and morality.

Gene Garthwaite, Dartmouth College. *Khans and Shahs: A Documentary Analysis of the Bakhtiyari in Iran*, documents pertaining to the Bakhtiyari tribal confederation, Iran's largest and most powerful nomadic group for the past 200 years.

Herbert Gilliland. *The Life of Captain Alonso de Contreras*, the memoirs of a 17th-century Spanish soldier who traveled throughout the Mediterranean and campaigned in the Caribbean against Sir Walter Raleigh.

Beatrice Gottlieb. *Febvre's "Problème de L'incroyance"* (Belief and Unbelief in the 16th Century).

William Harkins, Columbia Univ. *Anthology of Czech Prose*, illustrating the development of Czech literature and national culture from their beginnings in the Middle Ages up to 1900.

Wilma L Heston. Jamālzādah's *'Sar u Tah-i Yak Karbās'* (The Book of Isfahan), the autobiography of this liberal intellectual, forms an unusual social documentary on traditional non-Western life in early 20th-century Iran.

Michael Holquist, Univ of Texas at Austin. Bakhtin's *Problems in Literature and Aesthetics*, a collection of essays, published in Moscow in 1975, by the Russian critic and philosopher of language.

Alfred L Ivry, Brandeis Univ. *Averroes' Middle Commentary of Aristotle's De Anima*, his interpretation of the treatise of the intellect which became a point of departure for much of later medieval philosophy and culture.

Thorkild Jacobsen. *A Sumerian Sourcebook*, a compendium containing all the major works of Sumerian literature, our primary source for knowledge of the Sumerian civilization.

Michael Jenkins, Angelo State Univ. *Russia Under Peter the Great*, a portrait, not a photograph, a history seen through the eyes of the Enlightenment and with Voltaire in the narrative.

Philip Kolb & Ralph Manheim. *Selected Proust Letters*, chosen from the first three volumes of the authoritative edition being prepared for the Librairie Plon in Paris.

Richard Lariviere. *A Critical Edition of the Hindu Legal Text, "Nāradasmrti,"* a text prescribing modes of conduct (dharma), both legal and religious, for various strata of society.

David C Lindberg, Univ of Madison at Wisconsin. Roger Bacon's *"Philosophy of Light,"* a classic medieval statement of a philosophical tradition in which light was regarded as the key to many hidden realities of the visible and invisible worlds.

Roger D Masters, Dartmouth College. *Collected Writings of Jean-Jacques Rousseau*, seventeen translated texts with annotations of all of Rousseau's works.

Alex Orenstein, Queens College Research Foundation of CUNY. Kotarbinski's *"Lectures on the History of Logic,"* divided into three parts: the history of logic from Aristotle to Frege, the contemporary period, and the history of inductive logic.

Richard Pierce, Alaska Historical Soc. *Russian-American Company Records, 1802, 1817-1867*, 15 percent of the 80,000 documents handed over by the Russians at the Alaska Purchase (1867) here made available for the first time.

Marian Rothstein. *Traditional French Popular Fiction*, tales, revised and reprinted continually from their medieval origins to the 19th century and widely distributed through bookshops and peddlars in markets, remaining best sellers for hundreds of years.

A I Sabra, Harvard Univ. *The Optics of Alhazen*, in which the author developed a new theory of vision considerably beyond the limit reached in the writings of Euclid, Ptolemy, Aristotle, and Galen.

Richard Sherburne, Seattle Univ. *Buddhist Monastic Reform in Central Asia*, the writings of the Abbot Atīśa, illuminating the second period of Buddhism in Tibet—the period that saw the expansion of Indian Buddhism into the territory of its northern neighbor.

Arthur Stabler, Washington State Univ. *An Annotated Edition of André Thevet "On North America."* The French historian-geographer-explorer (1502-1592) made original contributions on the ethnography of a number of North American Indian tribes and on early geographical knowledge.

Eleanor Stump. Boethius' *"In Ciceronis Topica"* (Commentary on Cicero's Topics), contributing a detailed presentation of a philosophically sophisticated method of discovery, the fundamental tool of a dialectic.

Dennis Tedlock, Boston Univ. *The "Popul Vuh" of the Quiché Maya*, an edition combining a critical text in which all emendations are separated from what the manuscript actually says, and a close translation informed both by linguistic considerations and Quiché ethnography.

Charles Timberlake, Univ of Missouri. *The Memoirs of Ivan Petrunkevich*, which provide an inside perspective on the daily functioning of local and provincial government institutions in the 19th century.

Henry Toledano, Hofstra Univ. *Islamic Legal Practice: The Chapter on Procedure and Evidence from Sijilmāsi's "al-ᶜAmal el-Mutlag."* In Muslim Morocco, the attempts to bridge the differences between practical commercial considerations of everyday life and the inflexible Islamic law determined by ethical and religious considerations produced a unique interpretative literature.

E Daymond Turner, Univ of N Carolina, with support from the Comite Conjunto Hispano-Norteamericano para Asuntos Educativos y Culturales, Spain. *Gonzalo Fernandez de Oviedo y Valdes' Historia General y Natural de las Indias* (General and Natural History of the Indies), describing what the soldier Ovieto (1478-1557), Spanish commander of Santa Domingo and official chronicler of the Indies, had observed on his many travels in the New World.

NATIONAL TRANSLATION CENTER (disbanded in 1971)
The Univ of Texas at Austin, 2621 Speedway, Austin, TX 78705.

Between 1965 and 1968 the following grants were made from the Center's Revolving Fund by the National Advisory Board (see Sec 2, USA):

Commissions for 1965 Stanley Kunitz and Max Hayward for *Selected Poetry of Anna Akhmatova*. Barry Eisenberg for *Luna de miel, luna de hiel* and *Los trabajos de Urbano y Simona* by Ramon Perez de Ayala. W S Merwin for *Selected Works of Chamfort*. Lynne Lawner for *Selections from Lettere dal carcere* by Antonio Gramsci. Michael Scammell for *Nikolai Negorev* by Ivan Kushchevsky. Peter Salus for *The Complete Works of Georg Christoph Lichtenberg*. Robin Magowan for *Ecuador* by Henry Michaux. David Luke for *Selected Novellas of Adalbert Stifter*. Walter Clemons, Jr for *Con gli occhi chiusi* by Federigo Tozzi. Christopher Middleton for *Selected Letters of Friedrich Nietzsche*. D S Carne-Ross for *I Canti* by Giacomo Leopardi.

Commissions for 1966 Ulli Beier for *An Anthology of Yoruba Literature*. T Carmi for *An Anthology of Hebrew Verse from Its Origins to the Present*. Douglas M Garman for the first version of the *Education Sentimentale* by Gustave Flaubert. J G Garrard for *The Literaturnye Vospominaniya of Annenkov*. Myron Gubitz for *Leute von Seldwyla* by Gottfried Keller. Daniel Huws for *Selected Poetry of Ingeborg Bachmann*. Leonard J Kent and Elizabeth Knight for *Selected Work of E T A Hoffmann*. Elaine Kerrigan for *Selected Don Juan Literature of Spain*. Carolyn Kizer for *Selected Poems of Tu Fu*. W S Kuniczak for Henryk Sienkiewicz's *Trilogy*, including *Ogniem i Mieczem*, *Potop*, and *Pan Wolodyjowski*. Peter Kussi for *Selected Stories by Jaroslav Hasek*. Christopher Logue for Books 17, 18, and 20 of the *Iliad*. Jonathan Mayne for *The Art Criticism of Diderot*, including the *Essai sur la Peinture*. Norman R Shapiro for *French Medieval Love Guides*. Robert C Stephenson for *Los Sueños* by Don Francisco de Quevedo. Willard Trask for *Medieval Portuguese-Galician Lyrics* and *Orlando Innamorato* by Boiardo. David Wevill for *Selected Poetry of Ferencz Juhasz*. Irving Howe and Eliezer Greenberg for *An Anthology of Yiddish Poetry*.

Commissions for 1967 J E Anderson for selected writings of Alain. Stephen Berg for *Tajtkos Eg* by Miklós Radnóti. Joel Carmichael and Lynn Solotaroff for selected letters of Leo Tolstoy. William B Edgerton for selected short stories of Nikolai Leskov. Mirra Ginsburg for collected essays of Yevgeny Zamyatin. Pierce Chandler Hazelton for *Orm og Tyr* by Martin A Hansen. Louis Iribarne for *Insatiability* by Stanislaw Witkiewicz. Christopher Middleton for *Jakob von Gunten* by Robert Walser. James P Scanlan for *History of Young Russia* by Michael Gershenzon. Robert C Stephenson for *Los Sueños of Quevedo*. Paul Beekman Taylor for Old Icelandic "traditional" poetry: *Edda* and the heroic poems from the *Fornaldasögur*.

Charles Tomlinson for selected poems of Giuseppe Ungaretti.

Fellowships for 1967 John Bacon for *Differential und Integral* by Paul Lorenzen. Joseph P Clancy for *Y Gododdin* and a selection from the *Cynfeirdd* and *Gogynfeirdd*. Rolf Fjelde for Ibsen's *Brand*. Edwin Honig for script of *Devotion to the Cross* by Calderón. John M Hummell for Rousseau's *Les Rêveries du promeneur solitaire*. Lenore Mayhew and Wm McNaughton for 120 "Tzu Yeh Poems" in *Yüeh-fu Shih-chi*. Agnes Moncy for *Fortunata y Jacinta* by Perez Galdós.

Fellowships for 1968 Michael Alexander for *Beowulf* into modern English. Marcia Allentuck for selected works of J J Winckelmann and K P Moritz. Leo Black for *Harmonielehre* by Arnold Schoenberg. Ben Johnson for Federigo Tozzi's *Il Podere* and *Tre Croci*. Catherine Leach for *The Memoirs of Jan Chryzostrom Pasek*. Shi Shun Liu for *Eight Great Masters of Chinese Prose*. David Patterson for *Tosephta*. Seymour Palestin for *Lettere di condannati a morte della resistenza italiana*. Adrienne Rich for 20th-century Dutch poetry.

PACIFIC NORTHWEST TRANSLATION AWARD
Mr Cogito Press/Mr Cogito Magazine, Box 627, Pacific Univ, Forest Grove, OR 97116 *Eds* John M Gogol, Robert A Davies.

Established in 1978, the award consists of $100 plus publication of a chapbook by the press for the best poem or group of poems in translation submitted to *Mr Cogito Magazine*.

1978 Frank Kujawinski, for the poems of Stanisław Barańczak (Poland); honorable mention to Magnus J Kryński and Robert A Maguire, for the poems of Anna Świrczyńska.

PEN TRANSLATION PRIZE
Translation Committee, PEN American Ctr, 47 Fifth Ave, New York, NY 10003 *Tel* 212-255-1977.

Established in 1963 through the courtesy of Harry Scherman from funds provided by the Book-of-the-Month Club, the annual prize of $1000 is awarded for a distinguished book-length translation of a foreign literary work from any language into English.

Conditions The work must be published in the US by an established publishing house in the preceding year; technical, scientific, and reference works are not eligible. Selection of books to be judged and final award are made by a panel of three judges. The deadline for submission of books is December 31. Submissions should be made to the Chairman, Translation Committee. The prize is presented at the annual meeting of the executive board and general membership, held in May at the association's new headquarters in the Salmagundi Club.

1963 Archibald Colquhoun, for *The Viceroys* by Federico de Roberto (Harcourt, Brace). Judges: Lewis Galantière, Virgilia Petersen, Ralph Thompson.

1964 Ralph Manheim, for *The Tin Drum* by Günter Grass (Pantheon). Judges: Faubion Bowers, Frances Frenaye, Willard R Trask.

1965 Joseph Barnes, for *The Story of a Life* by Konstantin Paustovsky (Pantheon). Judges: B J Chute, Robert Payne, James Putnam.

1966 Geoffrey Skelton & Adrian Mitchell,

for *The Persecution and Assassination of Jean-Paul Marat, As Performed by the Inmates of the Asylum at Charenton, Under the Direction of the Marquis de Sade,* a play by Peter Weiss (Atheneum). Judges: Patricia Blake, Hans Koningsberger, Donald Keene.

1967 Harriet de Onis, for *Sagarana* by J. Guimarães Rosa (Knopf). Judges: Mildred Ames, Olga Carlisle, Saul Maloff.

1968 Vladimir Markov & Merrill Sparks, for *Modern Russian Poetry* (Bobbs-Merrill). Judges: W H Auden, Justin O'Brien, Ernest J Simmons.

1969 W S Merwin, for *Selected Translations: 1948-1968* (Atheneum). Judges: Frances Keene, Frank MacShane, Ivan Morris.

1970 Sidney Alexander, for *The History of Italy* (Macmillan). Judges: Frances Frenaye, Robert Payne, Muriel Rukeyser.

1971 Max Hayward, for *Hope Against Hope* by Nadezhda Mandelstam (Atheneum). Judges: Anna Balakian, Elizabeth Hardwick, Elizabeth Janeway.

1972 Richard & Clara Winston, for *Letters of Thomas Mann* (Knopf). Judges: Helen Wolff, Richard Howard, Sophie Wilkins.

1973 J P McCulloch, for *The Poems of Sextus Propertius* (Univ of California Pr). Judges: Willard R Trask, Emile Capouya, Guy Daniels.

1974 Hardie St Martin & Leonard Mades, for *The Obscene Bird of Night* by José Donoso (Knopf). Judges: Anne Fremantle, George Reavey, Richard Plant.

1975 Helen R Lane, for *Count Julian* by Juan Goytisolo (Viking/Richard Seaver). Judges: Hortense Calisher, Timothy Foote, Thomas Lask.

1976 Richard Howard, for *A Short History of Decay* by E M Cioran (Viking/Richard Seaver). Judges: Emile Capouya, Ronald Christ, Elizabeth Hardwick.

1977 Gregory Rabassa, for *Autumn of the Patriarch* by Gabriel García Márquez (Harper & Row). Judges: Richard Goldstone, Richard Howard, Kate Medina, Richard Plant.

1978 Adrienne Foulke, for *One Way or Another* by Leonardo Sciascia (Harper & Row). Judges: Ronald Christ, Peter Kussi, Ray Rosenthal.

1979 Charles Wright, for *The Storm and Other Poems* by Eugenio Montale (Oberlin College Field Translation Series). Judges: Serge Gavronsky, John Shepley, William Weaver.

Yugoslavia

YUGOSLAV PEN CLUB AWARD
Yugoslav PEN Club, 18 Maxim Gorky St. YU-91000 Skopje.

An unspecified monetary prize awarded for the translation of a literary work from and into languages spoken in Yugoslavia.

4

Training & Access
to the Profession

There is a limited but ever-increasing demand for competent translators and interpreters *from* all languages *into* all languages by private industry, international commerce, and governmental and intergovernmental agencies. The increased international exchange in all fields of activity, based on an understanding of foreign cultures, customs, and languages keeps this demand alive and accentuates the necessity of enabling peoples of diverse social and political systems to communicate effectively. It was partially in response to this demand for well-trained linguists and partially from a realization of the advantages of acquiring a thorough background in linguistic competence that academic institutions first established professional translator and interpreter training programs.

Western European countries, like Belgium, France, Germany, and the Netherlands, the centers and domiciles of almost all of Western Europe's cooperative cultural, commercial, industrial, and diplomatic activity, have a relatively well developed post-World War II tradition and maintain and support high-quality training programs on both the undergraduate and graduate levels. In the Western hemisphere, Canada, with its complex problems of bilingualism, understandably has an equally well established tradition and conducts training programs on a scale unknown and undreamed of, for the moment, in the United States.

According to a report presented at the 8th World Congress of the International Federation of Translators in Montreal in 1977 by Royal L. Tinsley, Jr., a professor of German at the University of Arizona, an extensive writer on foreign-language teaching and translation, and a former president of the American Translators Association, "prior to 1971 there were only two schools in the entire U.S. with academic programs designed to train translators and interpreters—Georgetown University in Washington, DC, and the Monterey Institute of Foreign Studies in California. There are now some five or six institutions with complete training programs at the graduate level and numerous colleges and universities throughout the country that offer training in the form of one or more courses."

Institutions with four- or five-year degree programs offer broad curricula of courses that include all the basic and advanced aspects of the discipline, e.g., theory and practice, history of translation, lexicology and terminology, documentation, computer aids to translation, linguistics and translation, and in most cases require a commented translation from a foreign language into one's mother tongue.

Most of the information in this section was gathered through questionnaires mailed to all known training centers throughout the world and was provided by the directors (or their representatives) of the individual translation and/or interpretation training programs. In some cases, where questionnaires were not returned, information was verified by the use of secondary printed sources.

Australia

THE AUSTRALIAN NATIONAL UNIVERSITY
Translation Program, The Humanities Research Ctr, The Australian National Univ, PO Box 4, Canberra ATC 2600 *Tel* 49511 *Dir* Ian Donaldson.

Belgium

ÉCOLE D'INTERPRÈTES INTERNATIONAUX
Université de l'État a Mons (State Univ of Mons), ave du Champs de Mars, B-7000 Mons *Tel* (065) 315171 *Dir* Lucien Cosson *Staff* 39.
    Certificate/Degree License in Translation, License in Interpretation.
    Languages Dutch, English, German, Italian, Spanish. Optional: Danish, Greek, Portuguese.

HOGER INSTITUUT VOOR VERTALERS EN TOLKEN
Anvers.

    Program Government institute offering four-year course of studies leading to the degree of Licensed Translator and Licensed Interpreter.

HOGER RIJKSINSTITUUT VOOR VERTALERS EN TOLKEN
Brussels *Dir* Gustave Cammaert.
    Program Government institute offering a four-year course of studies.
    Certificate/Degree Licensed Translator, Licensed Interpreter.

L'INSTITUT D'ENSEIGNEMENT SUPÉRIEUR LUCIEN COOREMANS
Brussels.
    Program Government institute offering a four-year course of studies.
    Certificate/Degree Licensed Translator, Licensed Interpreter.

L'INSTITUT LIBRE MARIE HAPS
Université catholique de Louvain (Catholic Univ of Louvain), Brussels.
    Program Offers four-year course leading to the degree of Licensed Translator, Licensed Interpreter.

L'INSTITUT SUPÉRIEUR DE L'ÉTAT DE TRADUCTEURS ET D'INTERPRÈTES
Rue Joseph Hazard 34, B-1180 Brussels *Dir* Jean Nieulandt *Deputy Dir* Jean Leclercq *Staff* 69 *Founded* 1958 (to train translators and interpreters at university level).
    Program Government institute offering a four-year course of studies. About 730 students.
    Certificate/Degree Licensed Translator, Licensed Interpreter.
    Publication *Equivalences* (see Sec 6, Journals).

Canada

CARLETON UNIVERSITY
Russian and Linguistics Translation Program, Ottawa, ON K1S 5B6 *Acting Chpn* B W Jones.
    Program The development of students who have attained special translating skills in the Russian language, and in the analysis and usage of language, by combining specific language training in Russian and in linguistic analysis with practical training in translation.

The program is designed to satisfy a range of different professional and academic interests, with one of the major areas of concentration language and linguistics with the option of translation training.

Curriculum (1) Tutorial in Linguistics: directed readings in the theory of translation; (2) Honors Essay: an annotated translation of a substantial piece of text, with oral defense before a panel consisting of a member of the Russian Department, a member of the Linguistics Department, and a professional translator from the Association of Translators and Interpreters of Ontario or the Department of the Secretary of State; (3) Russian Translation: a course of contrastive grammar and stylistics of Russian, English, and French, theory of translation, and extensive exercises in text translation from and into Russian.

LAURENTIAN UNIVERSITY
School of Translators and Interpreters, Lake Ramsey Rd, Sudbury, ON P3E 2C6 *Tel* 705-675-1151 *Dir* A F M Arbuckle *Staff* T Asongwed, S Capaldo, C Ratkoff-Rojnoff, C Romney, P Jindt, A Manning, L Nordstrom-Thirion, R Henry *Founded* 1968.

Program In Canada, the Federal and Provincial Government Services require a great number of translators in various languages, especially in French and English. Canadian industry and commerce also require the services of personnel familiar with foreign conditions, who are able to speak the languages concerned, as well as to carry out high-level translation.

The degree which is conferred after four years of study makes use of linguistic methods and provides an insight into the nature of language, as well as an introduction to its problems and the problems of terminology in general. The program's distinguishing feature, as compared to programs of other translator schools in Canada, is that it is the only one which is bilingual; its purpose is to train not only Francophone, but also Anglophone students, to translate into their mother tongue.

Certificate/Degree BS in Language.

Languages French into English.

Curriculum The four-year program includes a thorough study of translation theory; translation workshops; French, English, and a third language; documentation and terminology; scientific vocabulary, actual translation of administrative, commercial, legal, scientific, and technical texts. An Interpretation Workshop is a special elective in the techniques and practice of consecutive and simultaneous interpretation, with sight translation used as a vehicle for voice training and enhancement of the student's general knowledge.

Member ATA.

LAVAL UNIVERSITY
School of Translation, University City, PQ G1K 7P4 *Tel* 418-656-2131.

Certificate/Degree BA in Translation.

McGILL UNIVERSITY
School of Translation, Montreal, PQ, H3C 3G1.

Certificate/Degree Offers a Diploma in Translation for a three-year evening course in a major and a minor language for final examination scores of 80 percent in the major and 70

percent in the minor language; and a Certificate of Proficiency for 70 percent and 60 percent, respectively.

THE SAULT COLLEGE OF APPLIED ARTS & TECHNOLOGY
Translator-Traducteur, East Algoma Campus, 180 Mississauga Ave, Elliot Lake, ON *Tel* 705-848-2285.

Program Two-year course of studies leading to a Diploma in Translation.

Curriculum Theories of translation, structure and style of source and target languages; literature of source and target languages; translation workshops; French for Anglophones; English for Francophones; written communications; oral communications; expository English prose; expository French prose.

UNIVERSITY OF BRITISH COLUMBIA
German Dept, Vancouver, BC V6T 1W5 *Tel* 604-228-5151 *Dir* L Miller *Staff* 3.

Program Offers an initial training in the translation of difficult literary and technical materials. Normal duration of the course is one academic year.

Certificate/Degree Diploma in Translation.

Languages German into English.

Requirements Applicants must have a BA and have above average competence in German and English. Graduation requires a reading knowledge of French. Training or experience in a scientific or technical field, eg, biology, economics, chemistry, forestry, computer science, etc, is an advantage. A parallel diploma program is offered in French.

UNIVERSITY OF BRITISH COLUMBIA
Linguistics, Vancouver BC V6T 1W5 *Tel* 604-228-4256 *Staff* Bernard Saint-Jacques.

Program Linguistic Theories of Translation: the presentation and evaluation of various linguistic and sociolinguistic theories of translation. Students are exposed to a wide selection of theories by authors of diverse linguistic backgrounds. Part of the student's workload consists of preparing, presenting, and evaluating orally a theory written in his/her language of expertise. Sociolinguistics: this course examines stylistic variations, sociolinguistic rules, language and social change, the function of language varieties, and deals with problems of bilingualism. It is conducted as a seminar.

Certificate/Degree Diploma in Translation offered by the French and German departments.

UNIVERSITY OF MONCTON
Dept of Translation and Languages, Faculty of the Arts, Moncton, NB E1A 3E9 *Tel* 506-858-4214 *Dir* Roland Viger *Staff* Christel Gallant, Frédéric Grognier, Daniel Deveau.

Certificate/Degree BA in Translation.

Languages English into French.

Curriculum Introduction to translation and its elements; Anglicisms and Canadianisms; stylistic comparison of French and English; editing translations; documentation and terminology; commercial, economic, literary, legislative and administrative translation; lexicology and terminology; introduction to and seminars in simultaneous interpretation. Reading of current writings in translation theory, terminology, and contrastive linguistics required.

UNIVERSITY OF MONTREAL
Translation Sec, Dept of Linguistics and Philology, CP 6128 Succursale A, Montreal, PQ H3C 3J7 *Tel* 514-343-6220 *Dir* André Clas *Staff* 15 full-time, 20 part-time.

Certificate/Degree BA in Translation, MA in Translation, MA in Terminology.

Languages French and English.

UNIVERSITY OF OTTAWA
School of Translators and Interpreters, ON K1N 6N5 *Dir* Brian Harris.

Program Although the School was only established in 1971, the university had been offering translation courses since 1936, the first Canadian university to do so. The present program offers an MA in Applied Linguistics (Translation), and consists of research-oriented seminars followed obligatorily by some form of dissertation. It is not intended as a basic training program for professional translators, but to increase awareness of the processes that underlie efficient translation and to stimulate much needed research. The full slate of MA seminars has been designed to encourage the following specializations: technical translation, "creative" (dynamic) translation, terminology and documentation, automation of translation, linguistic research on translation, conference interpreting.

Languages The working languages of the program are English and French, and all students need a good knowledge of both. All seminars are bilingual, ie, they may be conducted in either of the working languages. However, the school recognizes the importance of other languages, and hence students' research may be conducted in a third language.

It is to be noted that the accepted international standard for translators is that they should be able to translate from two languages into their own mother tongue. Several important international organizations such as the United Nations make this requirement, as do a number of European translation schools. In view of the needs of the Canadian market, this program does not insist on a third language.

Curriculum Courses and seminars include the following: history of translation, translation theory, computer aids to translation, esthetics of translation, lexicology and terminology, linguistics and translation, interpretation, automation research, terminology and documentation, technical translation. Supplementary requirements may take any one of the following forms according to the student's experience and interests (for all options there is an oral defense before a jury): (1) a commented translation of not less than 5000 words; (2) a commented bilingual or multilingual terminology file, containing at least 100 terms in each language; (3) a minimum of three commented interpretations (simultaneous or consecutive), each lasting not less than 20 minutes; (4) a thesis reporting the student's original research on an historical or contemporary aspect of translation. The school has its own reading room which holds about 1000 volumes. It also houses a computer terminal linked to the Computer Center of the University, which can provide the software necessary for small-scale terminology banks and experiments in machine translation.

Research Projects An investigation of "natural translation" (NT) was established in 1977 at the University with the aid of a grant from the Canada Council for the purpose of collecting data on "the natural foundation of professional and artistic translation, the translating done in everyday circumstances by people who have had no special training for it." The research team consists of Brian Harris (project dir), Bianca Sherwood, Francis Smyth, and Lilian Nygren, most of whose recent work has consisted of a search and analysis of translation data gathered in earlier research on bilingualism. This earlier research includes J Ronjat's 1913 university thesis on the development of language observed in a bilingual child; Werner F Leopold's study of a bilingual child conducted in the 1930s; a number of other linguistic case studies of bilingual children; Harris' paper "The Importance of Natural Translation."

Publications "Working Papers in Translatology," edited by Brian Harris. No. 1: *To Pammachius: On the Best Method of Translation* (St Jerome, Letter 57), 1976. No. 2: *The Importance of Natural Translation,* 1977. Also forthcoming: "Componential Analysis and Translation Theory" by P Newmark; "Batteaux et Nida" by L Vincent.

Czechoslovakia

CHARLES UNIVERSITY
Translation and Interpretation Sec, Faculty of Social Sciences, Ovocny TRH 4, Prague *Tel* 228 441.

Program Courses in the role of translation in the development of Czech culture, theory of translation, and problems of translating literary and nonliterary texts.

Finland

TURUN KIELI-INSTITUUTTI (Turku Language Institute)
Aurakatu 11, Turku *Tel* 17 418 *Dir* Liisa Peltomaa *Founded* 1966.

Faculty Approximately one half of the faculty are native speakers of the foreign language they teach. The staff is further supplemented by specialists in the various subject fields.

Program A three-year course for the training of translators and interpreters in English, Finnish, French, German, with optional courses given in Swedish, the second official language of Finland. The Institute functions under the control of the Department of Science and Higher Education of the Finnish Ministry of Education, and is owned by a private foundation, but receives state support. Future plans foresee the integration of the Institute in the University of Turku as an independent department.

Certificate/Degree Diploma Translator, with advanced training in commerce and technology, law and administration, and medicine.

Curriculum Acceptance performance in the following examinations: (1) translation from Finnish into a student's basic target language (mother tongue) and vice-versa, including a text of a general nature and one in the student's field of specialization; (2) translation

from the student's second active language into Finnish; (3) conversation in both foreign languages; (4) optional tests in simultaneous and consecutive interpretation.

France

UNIVERSITY OF SORBONNE
École Supérieure d'Interprètes et de Traducteurs (L'ESIT), Centre Universitaire Dauphine, Université de la Sorbonne Nouvelle, Place du Marechal de Lattre de Tassigny, F-75116 Paris *Tel* 505 14 10 poste 42-06 *Dir* M Gravier *Founded* 1957.

Faculty D Moskowitz (Translation); D Seleskovitch (Interpretation).

Curriculum Courses of study in translation, interpretation, and research.

Certificate/Degree Translator Diploma, Conference Interpreter Diploma.

Germany, West (Federal Republic)

EUROPÄISCHES ÜBERSETZUNGS KOLLEGIUM (European Translators' College)
Postfach 26, D-4172 Straelen/Niederrehin 1 *Founded* 1978 under the patronage of Samuel Beckett, Heinrich Böll, Max Frisch, Robert Minder, and the late Mario Wandruszka.

Program Planned for many years, the College has been designed to offer German and foreign translators an opportunity to gather for the purpose of exchanging working methods and the results of their research. Housing facilities (apartments), workrooms, and an extensive library of basic sources of material on translation will enable translators-scholars to work in an atmosphere created specifically for the profession and its related fields. Future plans embrace close cooperation with translators' associations and academic translator training centers, and a data-processing unit for the registration and storage of terminology, nomenclature, and diverse versions of translations of the same material and will enable a wide dissemination of exemplary translations/interpretations of specific concepts.

FACHHOCHSCHULE DES LANDES, NORDRHEIN-WESTFALEN
Fachhochschule Köln-Fachbereich Sprachen, Fachhoschule des Landes Nordrhein-Westfalen, Aachener Strasse 217, D-5000 Cologne.

JOHANNES GUTENBERG-UNIVERSITÄT MAINZ
Fachbereich Angewandte Sprachwissenschaft (Dept of Applied Linguistics), An der Hochschule, D-6728 Germersheim *Tel* (07274) 1091 *Dean of Faculty* Horst W Drescher.

Certificate/Degree Translator's Diploma, Interpreter's Diploma.

Languages Guided translation/interpretation training available in Arabic, Danish, Dutch, English, French, Italian, Polish, Portuguese, Russian, Spanish, German for foreign students. Program includes visiting translators/interpreters from European Community countries and from the West German Foreign Office, Bonn.

RUPRECHT-KARL-UNIVERSITÄT, HEIDELBERG
Institut für Übersetzen und Dolmetschen (Inst of Translation and Interpretation), Landfriedstrasse 12, D-6900 Heidelberg 1.

Faculty About 60 members of the Institute, the Institute of Applied Linguistics, and the Institute of German and Foreign-language Philology; also visiting professional free-lance translators and interpreters.

Program Studiengang für Diplomübersetzer und Diplomdolmetscher (Course of Studies for Translator's Diploma and Interpreter's Diploma)

Languages Czech, Dutch, English, French, Italian, Polish, Portuguese, Russian, Spanish, Swedish.

SPRACHEN- UND DOLMETSCHER-INSTITUT, MÜNCHEN
Language and Interpreter Inst, Staatlich anerkannte Fachakademie für Fremdsprachenberufe, Amalienstrasse 73, D-800 Munich *Founded* 1952.

UNIVERSITÄT DES SAARLANDES
Angewandte Sptachwissenschaft sowie Übersetzen und Dolmetschen, Im Stadtwald, Bau 4, D-6600 Saarbrücken.

Languages English, French, Italian, Russian, Spanish.

Israel

HEBREW UNIVERSITY
Translation Program, Ctr for Applied Linguistics, Hebrew Univ, Jerusalem *Dirs* Chaim Rabin, Shoshana Blum-Kulka.

TEL AVIV UNIVERSITY
Chair of Translation Theory, Tel Aviv University, Ramat-Aviv, Tel Aviv *Tel* 416111 *Chpn* Itamar Even-Zohar *Faculty* Gideon Toury.

Program Courses in the theory of translation (with emphasis on literary translation), methodology of translation studies (including translation analysis), and history of translation. These courses are included in the curriculum of the university's Department of Poetics and Comparative Literature, but are open to students of all departments (linguistics, Hebrew language and literature, English language and literature, French language and literature, Arabic language and literature, etc). A project on the "History of Translation into Hebrew" is now in progress.

Symposia March 1978, "Translation Theory and Intercultural Relations" including discussions of (1) orientation in translation theory; (2) text analysis and translation; (3) literary translation and system interference; (4) translational manifestations and translatability; (5) translational norms and literary systems.

Publications *Translation Theory and Intercultural Relations:* proceedings of a symposium (see Sec 6, Books); an analytical inventory list of translations into Hebrew 1928–1948; a bibliography of Scandinavian literature in Hebrew translation (forthcoming).

Mexico

EL COLEGIO DE MÉXICO
Programa para la formación de traductores (Translator Training Program), Camino al Ajusco 20, Mexico 20 DF *Dir* Monique Lagros Chapuis *Founded* 1974

Program A two-year course and a research program for the solution of problems originating from the translation of nomenclature. Since 1976, the Program has been working toward implementation of a Plurilingual Terminological Word Bank, to include Spanish as a working language and to be conducted in collaboration with the Bureau of Terminology of the European Communities Commission in Luxembourg and with the Breau of Translations of the State Secretariat in Ottawa. The Program's Seminar on Terminology has published in Mexico and Luxembourg the following terminological glossaries in Spanish: *Glossaire de Statistique* (Doc 1412/75 CCE Luxembourg), *Glossaire Multilingue de l'Informatique* (Doc 3403/69 CCE Luxembourg), *Glossaire de Base "Crèdit et investissements,"* (Doc 3617/69, CCE Luxembourg), *La Clè des Mots* (CILF, no 3, 1972), *Résumé terminologique de l'Informatique,"* (École de traduction de l'Université de Montréal).

INSTITUTO ALLENDE
El Taller Xochiquetzal, Univ of Guanajuato, San Mieguel de Allende, GTO, Guanajuato *Membership* Stella Quan, Mary Gambee, Patricia Goedicke, Deborah Kent, Collete Pratt, Antonio Beckwith, Bonnie Carroll *Founded* 1977.

Program El Taller Xochiquetzal is comprised of San Miguel residents who, with the participation of occasional visitors from Ireland, Argentina, and Chile, have been working on Spanish-English and English-Spanish translations of Latin American literature. In 1978, the first Latin American Women Writers' Conference, consisting of lectures, readings, discussions, interviews, and a translation workshop, was held.

INSTITUTO DE INTÉRPRETES Y TRA-DUCTORES (IIT) (Institute of Interpreters and Translators)
Rio Rhin 40, Mexico 5, DF *Tel* 5 66 77 22 *Dir* Jacobo Chencinsky.

UNIVERSIDAD DE LAS AMÉRICAS
Translation/Interpretation Program, Universidad de las Américas, Apartado 100, Santa Catarina Mártir, Puebla *Dir* Tanya Gordon.

Certificate/Degree MA in Intercultural Communication; Postgraduate Certificate in Translation/Interpretation.

Member ATA.

The Netherlands

UNIVERSITY OF AMSTERDAM
Instituut Voor Vertaalkunde (IVV) (Institute for Translator Training), Oude Turfmarkt 145-147, NL-1012 GC Amsterdam *Tel* (020) 525-2449, 2450 *Chpn Exec Comm* F J Cremer *Founded* 1964.

In the Netherlands the training of translators and teaching and research in translation studies at the university level are concentrated in two institutes affiliated with the University of Amsterdam, the Institute, and the Department of General Literary Studies (see next entry).

Program The Institute concentrates its activities primarily on the training of technical and literary translators. Students are admitted only after having passed a matriculation examination. The course of study extends over four years and leads to a diploma of Translator. Emphasis in the curriculum is primarily on intensive practice in translation from and into a mother tongue (language A), usually Dutch, into and from either English, French, or German (language B), as well as translation into the mother tongue from a third language (language C), which may be English, French, German, Italian, Spanish, or Russian. Other subjects included in the curriculum are general linguistics, translation studies, A-language competence, B- and C-language grammar and competence, and B- and C-culture background knowledge. Final requirements for the diploma include three extensive translations, B into A, A into B, C into A, and a research paper. The teaching and administrative staff of the Institute are appointed by the University of Amsterdam, which also provides all financial support.

Research projects Research at the Institute is directed to general and language-pair-restricted translation theory and to differential linguistics and stylistics. A main project is a series of bibliographies, to be completed by 1980, of theoretical statements on translation dating from earlier times, ranging from Antiquity to a cut-off date of 1945, and if not world-wide in scope, at least covering the entire Western cultural area, including Hebrew and Arabic as well as the Slavic languages.

UNIVERSITY OF AMSTERDAM
Translation Studies Program, General Literary Studies, Spuistraat 210, NL-1012 VT Amsterdam, *Tel* (020) 525-3873, 3865 *Chpn* James S Holmes *Founded* 1967.

Program Leads to the degree of doctorandus, an official degree indicating the all-but-dissertation level. Admission to the program is open to all students with the degree of "candidate" (equivalent to an American Bachelor's degree) in a language. The program is *not* directed toward training practical translators, but on enabling students to gain scholarly insight into the problem surrounding the phenomena of translating and translations.

Requisites for degree Includes participation in introductory courses and seminars, individual study, and guided research leading to a thesis or two extensive papers. Areas covered in the examination are: (1) introduction to general literary studies; (2) fundamentals of translation studies; (3) the theory and methodology of translation studies; (4) translation theory and its history; (5) descriptive translation studies and the history of translation; (6) applied translation studies, including translation criticism and translation didactics. The program can normally be completed within two and a half years after the candidate's degree.

Plans are now pending approval of the Dutch Ministry of Education for the consolidation of both the Translation Studies Program and Institute for Translation in a new department of Vakgroep Vertaalwetenschap (Translation Studies), placing emphasis on both translator training and teaching and research in translation studies.

Projects *Approaches to Translation Studies,* a series of books devoted largely or exclusively to the general field of translation studies, translation history, translation theory and its history, translation analysis and evaluation—ranging over schools and scholarly disciplines in an endeavor to include a very broad spectrum of research.

Publications *A Basic Bibliography of Books on Translation Studies: 1956–1976,* James S Holmes, ed, 1978. A survey of the most significant and influential writings on translating and translations issued in book form during the past two decades with emphasis placed on those in English, French, and German. Only the most important titles from the extensive Eastern European scholarly literature are included.

Switzerland

UNIVERSITY OF GENEVA
École de Traduction et d'Interprétation (School of Translation and Interpretation), 3 Place de l'Université, CH-1211 Geneva 4 *Tel* (022) 25 63 50 *Dir* R E Williams.

Program To train translators and interpreters in seven languages: Arabic, English, French, German, Italian, Russian, and Spanish.

Certificate/Degree Diploma in Translation & Interpretation.

Publications *Französisch-Deutsches Taschenwörterbuch* by J Agad & R P Schwarz, 1970. *Le vocabulaire barometre dans le langage économique* by J Delattre & G de Vernisy (English into French, 1967). *Manuel de l'interprete* by Jean Herbert, 1965 (also editions in Dutch, English, German, and Spanish). *La prise de notes en interprétation consècutive,* by Jean-François Rozan, 1970.

United Kingdom

BRADFORD COLLEGE
School of Combined Studies, Div of Language Studies, Great Horton Rd, Bradford, West Yorkshire *Tel* 34844 *Dir* J S Hoyle.

Program Diploma Course for Translators and Foreign Correspondents.

Languages French, German, Italian, Spanish, with English required as mother tongue.

EALING COLLEGE OF HIGHER EDUCATION
Applied Language Studies, School of Language Studies, St Mary's Rd, Ealing, London W5 5RF *Tel* (01) 579 4111 *Dir* J D Winslow.

Faculty Drawn from the school's 46 teachers engaged in foreign language instruction.

Program Four-year course leading to a BA in Applied Language Studies.

Languages English, French, German, Russian, Spanish.

POLYTECHNIC OF CENTRAL LONDON

School of Languages, 9-18 Euston Center, Drummond St, London NW1 3ET *Tel* (01) 388 2551 *Dir* Peter Newmark.

Program Course of studies leading to a BA in Modern Languages or a Diploma in Technical and Specialized Translation.

Languages Arabic, Dutch, French, German, Italian, Polish, Portuguese, Russian.

UNIVERSITY OF BRADFORD

Modern Languages Ctr, Wardley House, Bradford, Yorkshire *Tel* 33466 *Dir* R B Tilford.

Faculty Approximately 15 members of the Center and several interpreters and translators from the staffs of national and international governmental agencies and industry and commerce.

Program A four-year course in modern languages leading to a BA and graduate courses leading to a Postgraduate Diploma in Interpreting and Translating.

Languages French, German, Russian, Spanish, with English required as a mother tongue.

UNIVERSITY OF SALFORD

Modern Languages, Salford M5 4WT *Tel* (061) 736 5843 *Dir* Martin B Harris.

Program Four-year course in modern languages leading to a BA in Modern Languages.

Languages French, German, Italian, Russian, Spanish.

UNIVERSITY OF SURREY

Linguistic and International Studies, Stag Hill, Guildford, Surrey GU2 5XH *Tel* (0483) 71281 *Dir* B P Pockney.

Program BS in Linguistic & International Studies, embracing courses in translation and computer aids to translation.

Languages French, German, Russian, Swedish.

United States of America

BALL STATE UNIVERSITY

Spanish/English Translation Course, Foreign Languages, Muncie, IN 47306 *Tel* 317-285-1226 *Dir* Rita Gardiul.

Languages Guided translation practice available in Spanish.

Curriculum Basic courses offered include such subjects as structure and style of both English and Spanish, expository prose writing, problems involved in translating diverse literary forms.

Member ATA.

BARNARD COLLEGE

Translation Studies, 606 W 120 St, New York, NY 10027 *Tel* 212-280-2052 *Dirs* Serge Gavronsky, Barbara Stoler Miller.

Program "Translation: Access to Cultural Communication" is a pilot project supported by the National Endowment for the Humanities and designed to explore the multiple processes of translation. It was conceived to allow undergraduate students to develop through a rigorous practice in textual analysis as well as in related semiotic fields, a refined understanding of the linguistic, literary, and philosophic traditions of other cultures, and the way in which these cultures have been transmitted and assimilated into our own.

Curriculum A Translation Seminar and a body of courses focus on the complex ways in which humanistic activity involves the translation of ideas, emotions, and forms across barriers of time, space, and language. The basic courses offered do not constitute a major, but are designed to permit students to broaden their knowledge of humanistic traditions while complementing and enriching the specialization inherent in a major program: (1) Oriental Encounters: The American Experience; (2) The Antilles: A Bicultural Introduction; (3) French and English as Literary Languages; (4) The Science of Linguistics and the Art of Translation; (5) Translation Seminar: The Theory and Practice of Translation; (6) Translations, Transformations, and Distortions.

BRANDEIS UNIVERSITY

Literary Studies 204, Joint Grad Program in Literary Studies, Shiffman Hall, Waltham, MA 02154 *Dir* Harry Zohn.

Faculty Members of the departments of Romance/Comparative Literature and of Germanic & Slavic Languages. Past visiting translators have included Richard Winston, Robert Szulkin, Peter Sander, Martin Robbins.

Languages Guided translation offered in Danish, French, German, Hebrew, Italian, Russian, Spanish, Yiddish.

BRIGHAM YOUNG UNIVERSITY

Computer-assisted Translation, Translation Sciences Inst, 130 B-34, Provo, UT 84602 *Tel* 801-374-1211 *Dir* Eldon G Lytle.

Program Formerly part of the program of the Language and Intercultural Research Center, TSI is now a separate research organization developing computer aids to human translators for reviewing, editing, and sometimes setting type for translators. The goal is to achieve an operational computer-assisted translation system by 1979. Some progress is also being made in synthesizing natural-sounding voice by computer.

Certificate/Degree German Certificate in Computer-assisted Translation.

Languages Guided translation practice available in Chinese, French, German, Portuguese, Spanish.

Member ATA.

BRIGHAM YOUNG UNIVERSITY

Language and Intercultural Research Ctr, 240 B-34, Provo, UT 84602 *Tel* 801-374-1211 *Dir* V Lynn Tyler *Founded* 1970.

Program The Language and Intercultural Research Center (LIRC) functions as a specialized research organization within the College of Humanities. It exists to serve the academic community, The Church of Jesus Christ of Latter-day Saints (Mormon), governmental and educational institutions, private enterprises, and the general public. It operates with two major ongoing goals: (1) research, development, service, and training for enhancing communication throughout the world; (2) sharing with others, on a reciprocal basis, resources to further language and intercultural research.

Major Research Interests & Services (1) Language Description/Classification: under a recently organized New World Languages Program, grammars and dictionaries are to be prepared in several Mayan languages. Other research to be conducted includes further lexical and comparative studies of Indian languages of North, Central, and South America. Limited geolinguistic research has been prepared for specific groups.

(2) Language Acquisition/Instruction: although there is no easy way to learn a foreign language, there are certainly variables that can make one way easier than others. Research seeks to identify these variables and determine the best ways to combine and manipulate them. The effectiveness of the computer for improving language skills and applying remedial teaching techniques to English reading and writing services, English as a second language, French, and Italian is being researched by several professors. The study of one foreign language and its effect on subsequent foreign-language learning has also been analyzed. Experimental and innovative language-learning classes are encouraged at Study Abroad Centers in Madrid, Paris, Vienna, and Mexico City, as well as on campus.

(3) Language Evaluation: now nearing completion is a Foreign Language Achievement Test Series (FLATS), examinations in 25 languages to measure two fundamental areas of language competence on first-year and intermediate levels—basic knowledge (grammar, phonology, vocabulary, and culture), use of knowledge (speaking, listening and reading comprehension, writing, and interacting). The Center administers available tests to students from any college or university. These institutions receive test results and determine the grades and amount of credit for each student. Tests in the following languages are available: Afrikaans, Cakchiquel, Cantonese, Danish, Dutch, English as a second language, Farsi (Persian), Finnish, German, Hebrew (modern), Indonesian, Italian, Japanese, Korean, Mandarin, Navajo, Norwegian, Portuguese, Samoan, Serbo-Croatian, Spanish, Swedish, Tahitian, Thai, Tongan, Vietnamese.

(4) Language Translation: Certificate programs for the training of translators in German and Spanish have recently been established.

(5) Intercultural Communication Resources: *Intercultural Communicator Resources,* published by LIRC, is one of the most comprehensive bibliographies on intercultural communication and is proving a valuable aid to researchers.

(6) Intercultural Communicative Indicators: basic research has been conducted for the development of lexicons which will organize, categorize, and make practical use of numerous concepts and findings relevant to such communication. Language will be the base, but nonverbal communication, thought patterns, and many other elements will be included in what is now being called the art and science of Languetics.

(7) Communication Learning Aids: the publication *Intercultural Communicating* presents an introduction to some of the basics of intercultural communication by reviewing cultural differences and similarities between the US culture and that of other countries, giving cautions to help prevent miscommunication and suggestions for understanding ideas across cultures.

(8) Culturgrams: these are four-page summaries prepared to help church authorities, missionaries, students, and other travelers gain an initial understanding of the people whose countries they are visiting. They touch briefly on customs and courtesies (greeting, visiting, eating, gestures, personal appearance), people (attitudes, population, language, religion, holidays), life-style (family, dating and marriage customs, income and possessions, work schedules, diet, recreation), and nation (history and government, economy, education, transportation and communication, land and climate). They also include a short phrase list with English spelling, foreign spelling, and pronunciation. Culturgrams have been prepared for 61 cultural areas and a special one on Berlin.

Publications A series of English language textbooks for several languages; publications by individual members of the College of Humanities; Communication Learning Aids; Languages and Linguistics Symposia; Translation Seminar; Symposia on Intercultural Communications and Language Concerns; Conference on Language of the Mormons; individual articles.

Member ATA.

BRIGHAM YOUNG UNIVERSITY

Translator Certification, Spanish & Portuguese, 164 FOB, Provo, UT 84602 *Dir* Marian McMaster.

Certificate/Degree Translator Certificate in Spanish.

Member ATA.

BROOKLYN COLLEGE, CITY UNIVERSITY OF NEW YORK

Summer Translation Workshop, Comparative Literature/Modern Languages & Literatures, Bedford Ave & Ave H, Brooklyn, NY 11210 *Coordinators* Gerald Storzer (212-780-5451,5452), Gregory Kolovakos (212-249-8950).

Program The workshop, sponsored in cooperation with The Center for Inter-American Relations in New York City and held at The Graduate Center of CUNY, 33 W 42 St, NY, features guest lectures by writers, translators, critics, editors. Included among those who have lectured in the past are Octavio Armand, Meg Bogin, Ronald Christ, JoAnne Engelbert, Edith Grossman, Elizabeth Lowe, Julio Marzán, Gregory Rabassa, Alastair Reid, Grace Schulman, and Alex Szogyi.

Languages French and Spanish.

Requirements All interested students at both the graduate and undergraduate levels are requested to submit samples of their translations, or—if they have not previously translated—samples of creative writing.

Curriculum A lecture by a guest speaker, followed by sessions of theory, practical exercises, and student editing. Text used is "The Translation Workshop Booklet of Selected Texts."

BROWN UNIVERSITY

Introduction to Literary Translation, Comparative Literature, Brown Univ, Providence, RI 02912 *Tel* 401-863-2818.

Program Two courses are offered: (1) Comparative Literature 171, conducted by Alan S Trueblood, treating literary translation as a lit-

erary phenomenon in relation to the creative process, the critical process, literary tradition, literary history; materials from the particular languages represented by the students enrolled are the subject of close scrutiny; (2) Comparative Literature 272, conducted by Edwin Honig, covering the structure and style of English and of a foreign language, history and theories of translation, and problems involved in the translation of particular genres.

CALIFORNIA STATE UNIVERSITY, Center on Deafness, *see* National Interpreter Training Consortium (NITC)

CARNEGIE-MELLON UNIVERSITY

Translation and English Language Ctr, Baker Hall 232D, Schenley Park, Pittsburgh, PA 15213 *Tel* 412-621-2600 *Dir* Concetta Carestia Greenfield.

Faculty James Antos, M Hammour, Faud H Megally, David Pahnos, Afroditi Panaghis, Hellmut Rennert, Howard Selekman, Antoinette Tuma, James Wehner, Michael Zimecki.

Program A $14,500 grant made in 1976 by the Pittsburgh Foundation to further development of the Translation Center made possible "an innovative program in translation that will open new career opportunities for students and benefit the business and industrial community." The funds were earmarked for a major cooperative effort between the Center and the Association of Professional Translators (see Sec 2, USA) in (1) development of a certification system to insure that candidates have attained satisfactory proficiency levels for the profession; (2) establishment of internships or traineeships with local industry and business to give students practical experience in preparing for careers; (3) identification of experienced translators from the association's membership to serve as part-time instructors in such areas of expertise as foreign business correspondence or banking; (4) developing a translation referral service as a clearinghouse for requests from business and industry, thus offering students a chance to do supervised translations for pay.

The Center was founded with programs in three general areas: translation theory, scientific/technical translation, and literary translation. More than 70 students enrolled. Generally, engineering and science students selected the scientific/technical workshops to develop adjunct linguistic skills useful in professional careers. Many companies that conducted job interviews were keenly interested in hiring professionals with bilingual backgrounds. Humanities and creative writing students elected the literary translation workshops.

The CMU translation programs provide opportunities for developing practical skills that are highly marketable, as well as broad liberal educational goals—among them, understanding of cultural diversities and enlightened awareness of linguistic complexities. The programs also tie in with a professional minor in technical translation in French, German, and Spanish, which is especially recommended for students in professional fields such as science, engineering, and technical writing, where foreign language proficiency can constitute an important auxiliary skill.

The two-year program in technical translation is designed for international students who have completed their secondary school

studies and who desire training in technical translation and/or interpretation from English into their native language and vice-versa. The program leads to Certification in Translation; units earned are also applicable in full or in part toward a BS degree in Technical Writing and Translation. The Translation Center's outstanding facilities and activities in Technical Terminology (Computerized Technical Terminology Bank, technical translation workshops and services, etc) make it possible to use new techniques and innovative instructional materials to prepare foreign students for admission to American universities.

TARGET Multilingual Terminology Bank is a joint effort of the Center and the Computer Science Department with a stated purpose of collecting foreign language technical terminology in order to meet the increased demand for up-to-date professional documentation of current terminology in all fields of international business. The dictionary includes terms in English, French, German, Spanish, and Arabic and is programmed to permit the addition of other languages as demand directs and resources permit.

The system consists of two major components; a large data base of technical terms constantly being increased and refined, and an interactive retrieval network which provides an up-to-date access to the data base, structured to allow it to be expanded and refined continuously—both by lexicographers assigned the task and by translators in the midst of their translation activity.

The project promises to facilitate and speed up the translation process through a system of interaction between translator and machine and is gaining support from both translators and industry. Completed translations are often used as a source of terms to be entered into the data base.

The Center has been performing translations for local firms for over three years. During that time it has assembled a group of qualified translators whose fluency in languages is matched by their competence in the technology of the material being translated. All are either professionals or graduate students under the supervision of the Center's faculty.

Translation of technical documents from and into any foreign language is offered by the Center, and every possible effort is made to honor the specific deadline of the client. In all cases an agreement is signed with the client specifying fees and length of time required to complete the translation. All documents submitted to the Center remain confidential both in the original and in the target language.

COLUMBIA UNIVERSITY

Linguistics, 401 Philosophy Hall, Columbia Univ, New York, NY 10027 *Tel* 212-280-3925 *Dir* Joseph L Malone.

Program Linguistics S4212D: Linguistics and the Translation of Poetic Language, (to be offered during the 1979 summer session) presents linguistics as a tool in the translation of poetry and other text genres whose structure depends crucially on phonetic and phonological patterns. Particular attention is paid to quite recent developments in linguistics (eg, by Paul Kiparsky) relevant to the analysis of rhyme, meter, parallelism and other sound-based configurations. Materials include monolingual and bilingual texts (poems, proverbs, songs, etc) in a variety of languages, some chosen by the instructor and others by the students. Parts of the syllabus offered by Linguistics is cross-listed with the Humanities Translation Studies program of Barnard College (see above).

DICKINSON COLLEGE
Translation Seminar, Spanish & Italian, Carlisle, PA 17013 *Tel* 717-243-5121 *Dir* Earl E Fitz.

Program A seminar, restricted to seniors majoring in French, German, Portuguese, or Spanish, which is both theoretical and practical in nature.

GALLAUDET COLLEGE, Sign Language
Programs, *see* National Interpreter Training Consortium (NITC)

GEORGETOWN UNIVERSITY
Div of Interpretation and Translation, School of Languages and Linguistics, 485 & 487 Nevils Bldg, 1221 36 St NW, Washington, DC 20057 *Tel* 202-625-4571, 4572 *Mailing address* 37 & O Sts NW, Washington, DC 20057.

Faculty Margareta Bowen and David Bowen, full-time. Part-time lecturers and consultants are drawn from international and governmental agencies in Washington, or they are free-lance translators/interpreters. Usually, they belong to one of several professional associations, for example TAALS, AIIC, ATA (see Sec 2).

Programs The division offers two distinct Certificate programs, one in translation and one in interpretation. Since both provide professional training they are outside the normal degree structure, not leading to a degree but rather to a Certificate of Proficiency.

Requirements Applicants must have completed secondary education in the US or their home country and must also pass the entrance examination, administered only on campus. Although students are not required to hold a degree in order to qualify, most students do hold at least a Bachelor's Degree or its equivalent. Successful candidates usually have spent some time abroad; often they have held jobs in business or government organizations or have engaged in studies other than languages only. General background is particularly important, as well as ease of expression in the active language.

The Division does not provide language teaching programs. Candidates must already know their languages before entering in order to concentrate on the techniques required for this type of profession and on specialized vocabularies.

Certificates of Proficiency in Translation This program provides general training in written translation and grants a certificate in a specific language combination to students who have successfully completed at least two translation courses in the given language combination.

Certificate of Proficiency as a Conference Interpreter The objective of this program is to train conference interpreters (see Sec 7, Conference Interpreters). Interpreters are rated according to the following language combinations: A—principal *active* language *into* which

one interprets (normally one's native language), B—other *active* language(s) *into* which one interprets with near-native fluency, C—passive language(s) *from* which one interprets regardless of difficulties of terminology or idiom. Active languages included in this program are at present: English, French, Spanish, and German. Passive Italian and Portuguese are accepted provided there is sufficient enrollment. Applicants must normally know three of the acceptable languages. Only in exceptional cases will admission with two languages, both active, be considered—such candidates must be truly bilingual.

Languages The main courses offered are: French into English and English into French, Spanish into English and English into Spanish. Usually courses embracing other combinations of languages, English, German, Italian, Portuguese, and Russian are offered.

Interpretation curriculum The interpretation program consists of courses in (1) simultaneous interpretation; (2) consecutive interpretation; (3) public speaking; (4) terminology workshop; (5) parliamentary procedure; (6) interpretation as a profession.

Publications The Division publishes and distributes an eight-page bulletin containing a detailed description of all aspects of its complex program of studies: undergraduate students minoring in translation; typical cases of translation minors; entrance examinations; prerequisite courses offering students a background in English, history, philosophy, economics, political science (government); certificate examinations.

INDIANA UNIVERSITY
Linguistics, Lindley Hall 401, Bloomington, IN 47405 *Tel* 812-337-6457 *Chpn* Fred W Householder.

Faculty Charles S Bird, Daniel A Dinnsen, John A Goldsmith, F Roger Higgins, Carleton T Hodge, Robert F Port, Linda Schwartz, Thomas A Sebeok, Albert Valdman.

Program Guided translation is available in French, a large number of African languages, Sanskrit.

KEARNEY STATE COLLEGE
Translation/Interpretation, Foreign Languages, Kearney, NE 68847 *Tel* 308-236-4249 *Dir* Betty Becker Theye.

Faculty Jerald L Fox, Richard Detsch, Aristedes Sosa, J Thomas, Antonio Paez.

Certificate/Degree BA with minor/major in translation and/or certificate. Guided translation in French, German, Spanish.

Curriculum Subjects covered include the structure of English and French, translation workshops, literary translation and interpretation, student translations of texts, others.

Member ATA.

MARYGROVE COLLEGE
Foreign Language Translation, Foreign Languages, Detroit, MI 48221 *Tel* 313-862-8000 *Dir* Edelgard DuBruck *Faculty* Sara Heikoff Woehrlen.

Program Technological, scientific, and technical translation.

Certificate/Degree AA in Translation; BA in Foreign Language Translation; Master of

Education with Cognate in Foreign Language Translation.

Languages English, French, German, Spanish.

MEMPHIS STATE UNIVERSITY
Foreign Languages, Memphis, TN 38152 *Dir* Franklin O Brantley.

Faculty French: Raymonde Niel, Reginald Dalle, Sharon Harwood, Basil Ratiu, Harold Watson; German: Leo Connolly, Richard O'Connell, Robert Smythe; Russian: Tamara Miller; Spanish: Franklin Brantley, William Brewer, Mary Jane Fenwick, José Freire, Felipe Lapuente, Nicholas Rokas.

Program Offers language and translation courses in French, German, Russian, Spanish.

Member ATA.

MONTCLAIR STATE COLLEGE
Translating/Interpreting, Spanish & Italian, Upper Montclair, NJ 07043 *Tel* 201-893-4285 *Dir* Norman Fulton.

Faculty JoAnne Engelbert, Ana Rambaldo, John Zahner, Norman Fulton.

Certificate/Degree Certificate in Translating/Interpreting; track of BA in Spanish.

Member ATA.

MONTEREY INSTITUTE OF FOREIGN STUDIES
Translation & Interpretation, 425 Van Buren St, Monterey, CA 93940 *Tel* 408-649-3113 *Dir* Wilhelm-Karl Weber.

Faculty Barbara Moser, Brenda Rendon, Sylvie Lambert, Laurence Batisse, Tamara Kantor, Holly Mikkelson. Visiting translators include Theodor Fagan, John Upton.

Program To meet the need for expert translators and interpreters in increased international exchanges in science, politics, management and culture, the Institute offers an MA in Intercultural Communication with an emphasis on either Management Studies or International Studies. These degree programs are open to all graduate students who have sufficient language proficiency in their chosen working language combinations.

Certificate/Degree The MA in Intercultural Communication is awarded only in conjunction with a postgraduate Certificate which stipulates either *Translation* (English and one foreign language), or *Interpretation* (English and two foreign languages). The MA with an Emphasis on Management Studies gives the student exposure to translation and interpretation skills in addition to more extensive work in the fields of Economics and International Business Management. Students work in English and one other language, which must be a strong B. The MA with an Emphasis on International Studies gives the student a background in translation and interpretation skills in addition to more extensive work in International Studies.

Languages Since the Institute does not provide language training programs, students entering the program must already have superior linguistic competence and as near-native fluency in their languages as possible. The Department of Translation and Interpretation offers programs in the following languages: English, French, German, Russian, and Spanish. Languages are classified according to proficiency as: *Language A* (principal or mother tongue), *Language B* (second, or "major" language), *Language C* (third, or "minor" language).

Language A, according to accepted professional definitions, is a principal or mother language in which the student has complete mastery of vocabulary, grammatical structure, and ease of oral and written expression. *Language B* differs from *Language A* in that the student has a less comprehensive vocabulary, possibly a slight accent, and not as complete a mastery of the complexity of the grammatical structures. The student must, however, be able to express in *Language B* all nuances and messages. *Language C* is one in which the student has complete passive understanding. It does not imply accentless mastery of oral expression; however, the student must be able to express adequately any message in *Language C*. All students must have English as either their A or B language. They must also give acceptable proof of superior linguistic competence in the English language and one or two of the other languages for which the department offers programs of study. Students entering these programs must have a BA or an equivalent degree from an accredited institution.

Curriculum The basic courses required of all students include: Consecutive Interpretation; Conference Reporting Techniques; Sight Translation; Simultaneous Interpretation; Basic Translation Exercises; Translation into English; Translation Theory.

Member ATA.

NAROPA INSTITUTE
1111 Pearl St, Boulder, CO 80302 *Tel* 303-444-0202 *Cable* NALANDA.

Program A major division of Nalanda Foundation, an institution of higher learning offering BA and MA degrees, and currently holding candidacy status for accreditation. Offers a language program in Sanskrit and Tibetan, with emphasis in its series of courses and workshops on the development of translation skills. The program is taught and administered by the Nalanda Foundation Translation Committee (see Sec 2, USA) and includes extensive training in Asian philosophies and cultures.

NATIONAL INTERPRETER TRAINING CONSORTIUM (NITC)
c/o Deafness Research & Training Center, New York University, 80 Washington Sq E, New York, NY 10003 *Tel* 212-598-2305.

Program Established in 1974, sponsored in part by a grant from the Rehabilitation Services Administration, Dept of Health, Education, and Welfare, Washington, DC, and to end March 31, 1980, by which it is foreseen that each state will have an institution for the training of sign language interpreters. Six institutions in the US have joined to conduct programs for training interpreters throughout the country: Center on Deafness, California State Univ, Northridge, CA 91324, 215-885-2611; Sign Language Programs, Gallaudet College, Kendall Green, Washington, DC 20002, 202-447-0837; Deafness Research & Training Ctr, New York Univ, 80 Washington Sq E, New York, NY 10003, 212-598-2305; Program for Deaf Students, St Paul Technical-Vocational

Inst, 235 Marshall Ave, St Paul, MN 55102, 612-227-9121; The Rehabilitation Ctr, College of Education, Univ of Arizona, Tucson, AZ 85721, 602-884-3601; Dept of Special Education & Rehabilitation, Univ of Tennessee, Knoxville, TN 37916, 615-974-2321.

The six members of NITC conduct the following programs for training interpreters: (1) upgrading: improving the skills of people who have been interpreting but are not yet certified; (2) beginning: training people who know sign language to become interpreters; (3) trainers: preparing teachers to train interpreters in their home states; (4) consumers: teaching deaf people how to best use interpreting services; (5) low-verbal: training interpreters to work with deaf people with minimal language skills.

For information for sources of additional information on specific careers, and lists of training programs, contact: American Speech & Hearing Assn, 10801 Rockville Pike, Rockville, MD 20852; Bureau of Education of the Handicapped, US Office of Education, Washington, DC 20202; Conference of American Instructors of the Deaf, 5034 Wisconsin Ave NW, Washington, DC 20016; Professional Rehabilitation Workers with the Adult Deaf, 814 Thayer Ave, Silver Spring, MD 20910; Registry of Interpreters for the Deaf (RID), PO Box 1339, Washington, DC 20013. See also the publication, *Careers in Deafness* (Washington, DC: Gallaudet College Public Service Programs, 1977).

NEW YORK UNIVERSITY
School of Continuing Education, Foreign Language Program, 3 Washington Sq N, New York, NY 10003 *Tel* 212-598-2296 *Dir* Gerard R Wolfe.

Faculty Spanish: William Puga; French: Ernest van Haagen.

Program Seminars in Spanish and French with a certificate of proficiency awarded for successful completion.

NEW YORK UNIVERSITY, Deafness Research & Training Center, *see* National Interpreter Training Consortium (NITC)

NOTRE DAME COLLEGE
Foreign Language Professional Translating Program, Modern Languages, 4545 College Rd, S Euclid, Cleveland, OH 44121 *Tel* 216-381-1680 *Dir* Sister M Cesarie, SND.

Faculty Ingrid Bahler, Clara Thurner, Sister M Chaminade, SND. Visiting translators include Leland Wright, Maria Neiden, Ciba Vaughn, Josephine Leach.

Program Courses preparing students for Certification in Translation include a workshop in general translation (practice in translating letters, booklets, brochures, and articles for magazines and newspapers); a workshop in business correspondence (translation of documents, papers, and letters used in international trade); a seminar in selected topics, based on the student's major (translation of scientific, technical, medical, mathematical and legal papers).

Languages French into English, German into English, Spanish into English.

Member ATA.

OAKLAND UNIVERSITY
Translation Certificate Program, Modern Languages & Literatures, Rochester, MI 48063 *Tel* 313-377-2060 *Dir* R A Mazzara.

Faculty R Gerulaitis, C Linsalata, C Urla.

Languages Guided translation training available in French, German, Russian, Spanish.

OHIO UNIVERSITY
Translation Program, Modern Languages/English/Comparative Literature, Ellis Hall, Athens, OH 45701 *Tel* 614-594-5096.

Program A part of graduate programs in Modern Languages and in English, with a faculty consisting of all departments, including a faculty of creative writing.

Languages French, German, Spanish.

THE POETRY CENTER OF THE 92ND ST YM-YWHA
Translation Workshop, 1395 Lexington Ave, New York, NY 10028 *Tel* 212-427-6000 *Dir* Richard Howard.

Program The workshop, consisting of eight weekly two-hour sessions, places emphasis on principles (applicable to any translation into English from any language) rather than on the production of publishable manuscripts. However, practical matters are not out of reach and attention is paid to such concerns as period style, verse, and discrepancies between commercial and literary prose. Exercises, as well as readings from works of master translators, are assigned, and guest translators invited to address the students.

QUEENS COLLEGE, CITY UNIVERSITY OF NEW YORK
German & Scandinavian Studies, 65-30 Kissena Blvd, Flushing, NY 11367 *Tel* 212-520-7173 *Dir* Edward G Fichtner.

Program Stresses translation from German into English.

Certificate/Degree BA in German, with concentration in Translating & Interpreting.

Curriculum Students are required to complete the following courses, in addition to courses in other departments: (1) Principles and Problems of Translating; (2) Translating in the natural sciences: medicine and the biological sciences; physics, chemistry, and the environmental sciences; mathematics and computer science; astronomy and astrophysics; (3) Translating in the arts and humanities: music and the visual arts; imaginative literature and literary criticism; linguistics and communications arts and sciences; (4) Translating in the social sciences: sociology and anthropology; economics and international banking and finance; political science and international law; history and philosophy; (5) Interpreting: simultaneous and consecutive translation and interpretation, interpreting in international travel; (6) independent translating project.

RICE UNIVERSITY
Translation Inst, Spanish/Portuguese/Classics, 6100 S Main, Houston, TX 77001 *Tel* 713-527-4863 *Dir* H N Urrutibéheity.

Faculty Joan R Boorman, James A Castañeda, Graciela Daichman, Lane Kauffmann.

Program The courses offered cover the usual theoretical and practical aspects of translating,

and cultural contact, international relations, and international organizations.

Certificate/Degree Professional certification in translation and interpretation.

ROSE-HULMAN INSTITUTE OF TECHNOLOGY

Technical Translation Program, 5500 Wabash Ave, Terre Haute, IN 47803 *Tel* 812-877-1511 *Dir* Peter F H Priest.

Program Requires completion of science or engineering courses, and is designed to provide not only pre-professional translator training, but also to encourage that rational dexterity and semantic sensitivity which will enhance any student's professional prospects. It is regarded as the only undergraduate foreign language program in the US devoted exclusively to technical translation.

Curriculum For students who enter with no previous knowledge of Russian or German, the first year courses are similar to most standard elementary courses, with the exception that the teaching approach emphasizes grammar and translation. Students begin to read graded material dealing with science or engineering. Second year courses study in particular depth those aspects of grammar that are characteristic of scholarly scientific and technical writing. The third year courses differ radically from traditional foreign language courses, which emphasize literature and literary criticism. Students concentrate on learning the stylistics of technical writing, the high frequency scientific vocabulary, and reading and discussing significant works related to the history and philosophy of science and engineering, such as "Prerequisites for Scientific and Technological Progress," "The Role of Mathematics in Modern Science," "What Einstein Got From Dostoyevsky," Max Planck's "Religion and Science," or Einstein's "My Worldview." Students also begin to learn the art and techniques of translation with small individual projects. Each Russian student, for example, translates, edits, and tape-records his translation of a Soviet-made filmstrip (or slide set) that is actually used for teaching science or engineering in the USSR. German students translate timely articles from *Die Zeit* or a strictly engineering newspaper like *VDI Nachrichten*. Students at the fourth-year level work independently in their own subject area on a major Russian to English or German to English translation project of approximately 100 pages. Translations are not approved until they meet professional standards.

ST MARY-OF-THE-WOODS COLLEGE

Translation Training Program, French & Spanish, St Mary-of-the-Woods, IN 47876 *Tel* 812-535-4141 *Dir* Camille Garnier.

Faculty French: Gary Godfrey; Spanish: Sister Beth Kelso, Felix Illaraz.

Certificate/Degree The college offers a translation major (undergraduate) and aims at having its students accredited by the ATA.

Languages French and Spanish into English; English into Spanish.

ST PAUL TECHNICAL-VOCATIONAL
INSTITUTE, *see* National Interpreter Training Consortium (NITC)

SAN FRANCISCO STATE UNIVERSITY

Translator Training Program, German Studies, San Francisco, CA 94132 *Dir* Edith Fried.

Program Offers German into English and English into German curriculum, which includes a translator internship program at Wells Fargo Bank in San Francisco, to be conducted under the direction of the head of the bank's Translation Section, Thomas Bauman.

STANFORD UNIVERSITY

Program in Translation & Interpretation, German Studies, Stanford, CA 94305 *Tel* 415-497-1068 *Dir* Walter F W Lohnes *Assoc Dir* Ulrike Lieder.

Program The program leads to Certificates in General Translation at the BA level, and in Advanced Translation or Interpretation at the MA level. It can be combined with degree programs in any subject area, including German. It is primarily designed to provide students with a valuable ancillary skill which will enhance their professional prospects in any field. By combining certificate and degree, the greatest amount of flexibility is assured. A solid linguistic foundation in German combined with the ability to translate documents from a number of fields provides a valuable asset for the student and can open up career possibilities in international relations, international law or business, diplomacy, journalism, editing and publishing, communications, other fields. Students in the natural sciences should find these skills to be useful tools in the preparation for their careers. The program can also serve those who want an exceptionally strong background in German Studies. Each student participates in at least one Stanford Overseas Program and in the final year must produce an original translation of a literary or documentary work.

Curriculum Students normally enter the program in their junior year. In addition to fulfilling the requirements of their major subject, they must complete the following courses:

Translation of Texts in the Social Sciences: this series concentrates on (1) the translation of current nonliterary materials, selected from German newspapers, periodicals, government publications, and from the fields of business, political science, medicine, anthropology, law, and economics; (2) occasional sessions devoted to the interpretation of bilingual conversations and negotiations (*Verhandlungsdolmetschen*); (3) general aspects of the theory of translation, as well as lexicography.

Translation Workshops: in these, each student is expected to produce independently an original translation from his/her major field of interest.

Internship for Translators: an internship in the translation department of a major bank.

Advanced Translation: this series leads to the Certificate in Advanced Translation, and includes practice translations of difficult texts and critical comparisons of accepted translations with the originals.

Interpretation: this sequence introduces the student to the two principal techniques in interpretation, simultaneous and consecutive, with discussions of various aspects of the activity—ethics, parliamentary procedure, conference and escort interpreting, writing of reports and précis.

Literary translation: whenever student interest warrants, a special literary translation workshop is offered, in which students have the opportunity to translate literary works, or philosophical or critical writings. Translations of this nature may later be developed into a thesis. In recent years, the need to translate philosophical and critical writings has increased and has led to the establishment of several journals.

Member ATA.

STATE UNIVERSITY OF NEW YORK (SUNY), BINGHAMTON

Translation Training Program, Comparative Literature, Binghamton, NY 13901 *Tel* 607-798-3582, 6763 *Dir* Marilyn Gaddis Rose.

Faculty French: Marilyn Gaddis Rose; German: Roger Norton; Spanish: Julio Rodriguez-Luis; Hebrew: Marcia Doron; Classical Greek & Latin: Zoja Pavlovskis; Italian, Russian: Frank F Seeley. Visiting translator: André Lefevere (Dutch, French, theory).

Program The program is an outgrowth of the Translation Workshop, established in January, 1971. In 1973, it received funding from the US Office of Education, allowing it to expand its staff and curricular base. It offers an interdisciplinary graduate curriculum in the theory and practice of translation. Workshop courses enable students to work with published translators on projects of professional scope; these courses are open to all graduate students in the Schools of Arts and Sciences, Advanced Technology, Management, and General Studies, and are posited upon fluency in a source language (usually foreign), effective expression in a target language (usually English), and knowledge of the subject(s) to be translated. In addition, students specializing in translation are advised on appropriate individual course sequences depending upon their interests: literary, commercial, legal, technical, scientific, scholarly translation. Program courses may be taken in preparation for accreditation examinations, such as those given by the American Translators Association (see Sec 2, USA), or may be applied toward an advanced degree. A Translation Referral Service, directed by the program for the larger Binghamton community and industrial area, provides students an opportunity to do supervised translation for remuneration.

Certificate/Degree A graduate Certificate in Translation Program is available. It may be taken either in conjunction with a graduate degree or as a separate graduate track. Since 1970–1971, graduate students in Comparative Literature have had the option of minoring in translation and doing an edited translation in lieu of an MA thesis or PhD dissertation.

Languages Guided translation practice is available in most modern and classical languages, both Western and non-Western; Aramaic, Armenian, Chinese, Czech, Danish, Dutch, French, German, Greek (Classical & Modern), Hebrew, Hindi, Indonesian, Italian, Latin, Malay, Polish, Portuguese, Rumanian, Russian, Scandinavian, Spanish. The curriculum complements especially well the area studies certificate program: Judaic, Latin American, Medieval and Early Renaissance, Russian and Eastern European, and Southwest Asian and North African.

Curriculum Suitable both for those who wish

to develop translation skills while pursuing an advanced degree, and for those who wish to add translation skills to their present educational background.

Symposia 1976, "Translations in the Humanities: Forum on Translation Problems and Practice"; "Translation as Data: Theory for Translation"; "Poe, Baudelaire, and His Rival Translators"; "Translation as Expression: Blossoms from *Sunflower Splendor*"; "Translation and the Oral Tradition."

Publications *Translation in the Humanities* edited by Marilyn Gaddis Rose (SUNY at Binghamton, 1977).

Member ATA.

UNIVERSITY OF ARIZONA, The Rehabilitation Center, *see* National Interpreter Training Consortium (NITC)

UNIVERSITY OF ARKANSAS
Program in Translation, Comparative Literature, CC 224 Univ of Arkansas, Fayetteville, AR 72701 *Tel* 501-575-4301 *Dir* Miller Williams.

Faculty Members of the Faculty of English and of Foreign Languages. Two visiting translators are invited each year to direct workshops and hold individual conferences with each of the degree students. Recent visitors have been Margaret Sayers Peden, John Ciardi, John Nims, Lucien Stryk, and Rainer Schulte.

Program The program was begun in 1973 as a workshop and enlarged to a degree program in 1975. Candidates are required to hold a bachelor's degree and to demonstrate—upon entering the program—a satisfactory knowledge of two foreign languages. If the degree is not in the literature of English or a foreign language, period and genre courses may be required as background work not counting toward the degree.

Languages Guided translation practice is available in Chinese, French, German, Italian, Russian, Spanish.

Curriculum The following courses are required: Workshops in Translation, in Fiction Writing, and in Poetry Writing, Form and Theory of Poetry and of Fiction, in which structure and style of the source language, structure of English, history and theories of translation, problems involved in translating particular literary forms are covered.

UNIVERSITY OF CALIFORNIA, SANTA BARBARA
Translation-Interpretation Program, French & Spanish Dept, Santa Barbara, CA 93106 *Tel* 805-961-3112, 2131 *Dir* Alexandre Rainof.

Program The program combines the efforts of more than one department of the university. The Departments of French and Italian and of Spanish and Portuguese collaborate to offer a series of specialized post-graduate courses in interpretation and translation to and from English, French, and Spanish. The courses are, in their orientation and content, designed to provide the student with a wide technical background for public service and similar activities. The German Department has a similar program.

Certificate/Degree Certificate in Translation and Interpretation in French; Certificate in Translation and Interpretation in Spanish.

Requirements Candidates must meet the general requirements for admission to graduate study as well as the following special requirements: (1) an undergraduate major in either French or Spanish; (2) one of the following: an academic year at a university in a French-speaking or Spanish-speaking country; extensive work experience using Spanish or French; bilingual facility (written or oral) in English and either Spanish or French.

Curriculum The program offers two series of specialized courses in translation and interpretation, French and Spanish into English and English into Spanish and French—introduction to translation, introduction to interpretation, advanced translation, conference interpretation. These courses may be combined with electives from related departments: biological sciences, chemistry, economics, environmental studies, political science, psychology, sociology.

Member ATA.

UNIVERSITY OF CALIFORNIA, SANTA BARBARA
Translation-Interpretation Program, Germanic Languages, Univ of California, Santa Barbara, CA 93106 *Tel* 805-961-2131 *Dir* Roselinde Konrad.

Program Similar to that offered by the French and Spanish departments (see above) and the courses offered constitute a one-year program leading to a certificate. The emphasis is on written translation with some interpreting included in the curriculum.

Certificate/Degree Certificate in Translation and Interpretation in German and English.

Requirements Besides the general requirements for admission to graduate study, candidates must have an academic year's study as a regular student at a recognized university in a country in which German is the national language (including German-speaking Switzerland), or equivalent.

Curriculum The program requires the satisfactory completion of the following courses: reading of German texts, oral comprehension, introduction to consecutive interpretation, translation of general and technical German texts into English (reversed where German is the target language), writing and translation of business materials, summarizing of specialized German texts in English (or English texts in German), translation of specialized texts from German into English (or vice versa).

Member ATA.

UNIVERSITY OF CALIFORNIA, SANTA CRUZ
Summer Translation Inst, Santa Cruz, CA 95064 *Tel* 408-429-0111 *Coord:* Paul Mann.

Faculty Gabriel Berns, professor of Spanish Literature at USCS; Anya Kroth, instructor of Russian, USCS; Paul Mann, doctoral candidate and lecturer, USCS; Peter Whigham, translator of Provençal and Italian literature. Guest faculty includes Richard Howard, Hardie St Martin, Sidney Monas, Stephen Kessler, Rita Rait-Kovaleva (USSR).

Program An intensive four-week program designed to introduce students to the art of translating foreign literature into English, and to allow advanced students an opportunity to sharpen their skills. The Institute is open to

students in language and literature, as well as to teachers, writers, and persons interested in careers as professional literary translators. It is divided into four sections: French, Spanish, Russian, and Greek and Latin. Readings, films, lectures, and discussions on topics ranging from translation theory to ways of publishing literary translations supplement the workshops. Students receive ten quarter units of upper division credit in literature upon successful completion of work.

THE UNIVERSITY OF IOWA
International Writing Program, School of Letters, Iowa City, IA 52242 *Dir* Paul Engle.

Program Brings established and published writers of high reputation from around the world to live at the university, write their own books, meet with other writers, and give talks on the literary scene of their countries. Most of the invited writers have never before met the other invited writers from the countries represented in the program. An important part of their stay at the university is translation. Some turn American texts into their own languages, others help prepare anthologies of writing from their own literature. The program pays gifted young Americans from the "Writers Workshop" to work with other members, making translations in contemporary, idiomatic American speech, even though the Americans may not know the original language. This process is referred to as "co-translation" and several books have resulted from it.

Publications *Iowa Translation Series.*

THE UNIVERSITY OF IOWA
MFA Program in Translation, Comparative Literature, 425 English-Philosophy Bldg, Iowa City, IA 52242 *Tel* 319-353-3341 *Chpn* Daniel Weissbort.

Program Translation has long been associated with the university. In 1962, a Translation Workshop, which became a model for such workshops elsewhere, was established and first taught by Edmund Keeley and Mark Strand. Since 1967, the International Writing Program (IWP), founded by Paul and Hualing Engle, has brought distinguished foreign writers to the campus each year. Publishing of poetry in translation, both anthologies and collections of individual poets, is sponsored by the IWP, and writing students also interested in translation have the opportunity to work on these projects as well as with individual visiting writers.

The MFA program permits a balanced course of study, taking into account the need to develop literary skills in English and to acquire an understanding of the cultural background of the foreign literature. Course work is structured to the needs and interests of individual students. The importance of an awareness of the tradition of translation itself, its role in literary culture, as well as of the historical development of translation theory is recognized.

Requirements The student, who will normally have had three years of its equivalent of college-level work in a foreign language must submit a short statement explaining his/her interest in and understanding of "translation," and examples of his/her written work in English—this may include original or translated poetry or prose (not criticism), though ideally examples of both original writing and translation should be submitted.

Curriculum An example of a course of study designed for a person interested primarily in translation from Chinese and Japanese would include central courses: Translation Workshop, Foreign Literature (not in translation), History and Theory of Translation, Seminars (Writers Workshops); basic courses include: Asian Society through Literature, Ethnology of Japan, Ethnology of China, Buddhist and Hindu Iconography, Art of China, Art of Japan, Religion of Japan, History of Pre-modern China, Modern China, Pre-modern Japan to 1867, Modern Japan, Recent Revolutionary Developments in East Asia, Structure of Japanese, Religion in China.

In addition to course work and an examination in practical criticism, the student must complete a thesis, which represents the culmination of his/her work. This will be a literary translation of a collection of poems or short stories, a novel or a drama, with an introduction placing the work in its literary context, both national and international. The thesis must be judged of a sufficiently high standard to merit serious consideration for publication.

In the Translation Workshop, concentration is initially on the identification of typical problem areas of translation. Group exercises provide a focus for a review of general methodological questions, as well as the range of possible solutions of specific problems. During the Fall semester visiting writers in the International Writing Program take part in Workshop activities.

UNIVERSITY OF MISSOURI
Romance Languages, 27 Arts & Science, Columbia, MO 65201 *Dir* Margaret Sayers Peden.

Program MA in Spanish with an Area of Study in the Techniques of Translating Literary Material, approved by the department in 1977. Since the Fall semester, 1978, a candidate for the MA in Spanish may elect to include in his/her program an area of study in translating.

Requirements Candidates must meet requirements for general master's degree and complete 36 hours of course work on the grad-

uate level, distributed as follows: (1) Spanish and Spanish American literatures, 21 hours divided between the two fields; (2) History of the Spanish language, 3 hours; (3) workshop in literary translations, 6 hours; (4) creative writing as offered by the department of English, writing of fiction, writing of poetry, advanced writing of fiction, advanced writing of poetry.

UNIVERSITY OF PUERTO RICO
Grad Program in Translation, PO Box 22613, UPR Sta, Rio Piedras 00931 PR *Tel* 809-764-000 *Dir* Angel Jorge Casares.

Faculty Marshall Morris, Carmen Diaz Zayas, Sara Irizarry, Carlos H Soto

Program An MA program in English into Spanish, Spanish into English, and French into Spanish.

UNIVERSITY OF TENNESSEE, Special Education & Rehabilitation, *see* National Interpreter Training Consortium (NITC)

UNIVERSITY OF TEXAS AT ARLINGTON
Scientific & Technical Translation, Soviet & East European Center, 226 Hammond Hall, Arlington, TX 76019 *Tel* 817-273-3161 *Dir* Charles T McDowell.

Faculty Rimma Palangian, Jack Palangian, Jim Wilmeth, John Stuart. Guest translators are Yuri Smigunov, Y Kostarchuk, Pete Collins.

Program The Center emphasizes translation workshops and seminars, linguistics and translation, computer aids to scientific & technical translation, and the translator's resources.

Certificate/Degree Scientific & Technical Translation Certificate in Russian into English.

UNIVERSITY OF TEXAS AT AUSTIN
Germanic Languages, PO Box 7939 TX 78712 *Tel* 512-471-4123 *Staff* A Leslie Willson.

Program One of visiting German-language authors and translators whereby one is in residence each semester, and is devoted exclusively to literary translation and the history and theories of translation.

UNIVERSITY OF WISCONSIN
East Asian Languages & Literatures, 1208 Van Hise Hall, Madison, WI 53706 *Tel* 608-262-9876.

Faculty Joseph S M Lau, Arthur Chen.

Curriculum Although the department offers no independent program in translation, it offers a course, Problems in Translation, which emphasizes the practice rather than the theory of translation. It is conducted in the manner of a workshop in which the instructor and students work together to discuss the various problems arising from the actual practice of translation. In view of the different backgrounds of the students, the workshop is divided into two streams, Chinese into English, English into Chinese. Efforts are devoted to discussing works in existing translations and to weekly assignments of a short piece of writing in the original as well as its translated version(s).

UPSALA COLLEGE
Translators Training Program in German, East Orange, NJ 07019 *Tel* 201-266-7209 *Dir* Ellen von Nardroff.

Certificate/Degree BA major in German Translation. Requisite in program is internship with Ad-Ex Translations International, New York.

WEST CHESTER STATE COLLEGE
The Art of Translation, Foreign Languages, West Chester, PA 19380 *Tel* 215-436-2383 *Dir* Alfred D Roberts.

Program Techniques of translating literary, journalistic, technical, and scientific texts.

Curriculum Practice in the skills of formal translating from the foreign language into English and vice versa; analysis of the problems encountered by the translator and what to do about them; a study of the literature on translation, particularly a review of current books and periodicals in the field; a survey of international activities of translators, professional translators' organizations, and schools for translators; an assessment of job opportunities for translators.

5
Guidelines: Codes of Practices/Model Contracts/Copyright/Legislation

Guidelines for translators and interpreters are a relatively recent phenomenon, necessitated by the growth of the profession during the past 25 years and the increasing complexity of dealing with clients and employers (frequently across international borders) of dissimilar natures: governmental and intergovernmental agencies, national and international organizations, national associations and institutes, and private enterprise. Like guidelines for other professions, crafts, and trades, they consist in the main of codes of standards or principles for determining courses of action and policies, usually established by professional associations founded with these objectives in mind: to protect members, to promote their welfare, and to stabilize their relations with the community.

Although every national or regional translators' and interpreters' association in all countries is known to have its own statutes and codes, it was the UNESCO-sponsored International Federation of Translators (FIT) that first set down a series of recommended principles for "the protection of translators and of translations," a lengthy document intended as a model for its member societies, existing under a variety of economic and political systems. The instrument takes into account (1) the general legal position of translators; (2) measures to insure the application in practice of protection afforded translators under international conventions and in national laws relating to copyright; (3) the social and fiscal situations of both free-lance and salaried translators; (4) special training and working conditions, including writing programs, seminars, workshops, terminology banks, standardization and development of international scientific and technical terminology; (5) the manner in which the principles and norms set forth in the instrument may be adopted by developing countries.

To the best of one's knowledge, the documents reproduced in this section have been compiled and published collectively for the first time. Prior to their appearance here, most of them have been known primarily to members of the individual associations or within the borders of one country.

Introductory paragraphs preceding several of the documents reproduced here have been set in italics to indicate that the comments are made by the Editor and are not a part of the original document.

American Association of Language Specialists, see The American Association of Language Specialists (TAALS)

American Institute of Physics

Required Translation Agreement

The new copyright law that went into effect on January 1, 1978 contains a provision which changes the traditional copyright status of commissioned works such as translations.

Prior to 1978, a commissioned translation was considered a "work made for hire," and as such, copyright could properly be claimed by the publisher. Under the new law, copyright to "a work made for hire" still vests with the publisher initially; however, a commissioned translation may now be defined as a "work made for hire" *only* if there is an express written agreement signed by the translator stating that this is so. Accordingly, under the new law, if the American Institute of Physics and its member societies are to claim copyright to the English translations of articles in their translation journals as they have in the past, translators must state in writing that their translations are "works made for hire."

Since it is essential to the publishing and marketing activities of AIP and its member societies that copyright be held by AIP or the respective AIP member society, we must require that you agree in writing that any translation you prepare at the request of AIP, an AIP member society, or anyone producing or publishing journals or other works on their behalf, is a "work made for hire."

This letter may serve as the required agreement if you will sign the enclosed copy in the place provided below and return it to us, thereby indicating that unless and until you otherwise advise us in writing, all translations you prepare for publication in AIP or AIP member society journals are to be considered "works made for hire." We have enclosed a stamped self-addressed envelope for your convenience in returning the signed agreement.

Susan Gordon
Translations Office

AGREED:——— Date:———

Member Societies of AIP: American Physical Society, Optical Society of America, Acoustical Society of America, Society of Rheology, American Association of Physics Teachers, American Crystallographic Association, American Astronomical Society, American Association of Physicists in Medicine, American Vacuum Society.

American Society of Interpreters

Code of Professional Standards

I. Purpose and Scope

a. This Code sets forth the rules of professional practice for members of this Society.

b. The provisions of this Code shall be binding upon all members. Members are pledged to support the society in implementing them.

II. Professional Standards

a. Members are pledged to secrecy regarding information obtained in their professional capacity.

American Society of Interpreters (cont.)

b. Members are pledged to refuse any financial profit or personal advantage that may be derived from third parties through revelation of information obtained in their professional capacity.

Members are pledged to submit their professional differences to arbitration by the Society, without prejudice to subsequent legal action.

III. Standards for Short-Term Appointments

Members are pledged to rendering the best possible service, and to undertake all possible steps to that end. When in an organizing or supervisory capacity, members shall also consider the cost effectiveness of their recommendations and actions. They shall also determine whether the use of the relay system may tend to improve services or reduce costs without prejudice to quality.

a. Members are pledged to abide by the terms and conditions accepted by them in connection with an assignment, without prejudice to subsequent, possible evaluation of these arrangements by the Society.

b. Members may request release from a professional commitment in exceptional circumstances only, and provided that: (1) they give a valid reason; (2) they give sufficient advance notice; and (3) they provide a replacement acceptable to the person responsible for staffing arrangements, at no additional cost.

c. Members shall not work on a gratis basis, except in welfare cases or in national or international emergencies.

d. Members are pledged not to accept fees and staffing arrangements which are inferior to those recommended by the Society.

e. Fees shall be paid on a daily basis for each day of the assignment. For the sake of simplicity, fees shall be quoted in US dollars, and shall be payable in that currency, or its convertible equivalent, and shall be free of all encumbrances.

f. Members shall not accept sub-standard travel arrangements. They will always require the shortest and most convenient mode of travel available.

g. Members are pledged to the elimination of illegal and unethical practices in the interpreting profession.

IV. Professional Guidelines

The following terms and conditions are presently (November 1, 1978) secured by contract conference interpreters in good professional standing in the United States:

1. Daily compensation: $190.00.
2. Minimum number of interpreters per language booth at the above rate: 2 interpreters.
3. Minimum paid study time for technical conferences: 2 days.
4. Per diem allowance, when applicable (for each day or fraction of day away from residence): $50.00 per day.
5. Minimum per diem for traveling when applicable: 1 day each way.
6. Fees and allowances are payable for each calendar day or part thereof.
7. Appointments are payable on a through basis including intervening days and/or weekends, whether worked or not.
8. Traveling costs between interpreter's residence and site of conference, and return, are paid by the conference organizers.
9. Cancellation of appointments are subject to: (a) 100% compensation with less than 30 days notice, (b) 50% compensation with less than 60 days notice, but more than 30 days.

American Translators Association (ATA)

Accreditation

In 1963 the ATA (see Sec 2, USA), one of whose aims is the improvement of the standards and quality of translation, established a committee on accreditation, charged to create and carry out a program by which the Association would accredit translators. The program, worked out over a period of years and first put into practice with exams in 1972, has several objectives: (1) if translating is to gain recognition as a profession, someone must define and measure the skills it requires; accreditation is a start toward defining what minimal skills ATA believes translators should have; it also provides one means of evaluation; (2) accreditation offers translator and client a way to measure the translator's competence and commitment; an accredited translator gives objective proof of having enough basic skills and training to function as a professional in this field; (3) ATA has long intended to create a special class of members, of proven merit as translators, who have shown their willingness to take part in professional activities; when the time comes to set up standards for admission to this class, experience gained in the accreditation program will be useful as a guide to means of evaluation.

As of 1978, close to half of all ATA members had taken the exams and nearly 300 translators had received their certificates. Members seem to regard accreditation as a desirable and useful service, and translation users are recognizing the benefits that the program holds for them too.

Active or associate members of ATA may take an accreditation exam in any language pair offered: French, German, Portuguese, Russian, or Spanish into English; English into German and Spanish. Exams are taken with the aid of dictionaries and other reference tools. They consist of five passages, of which the examinee is requested to choose three and translate them in writing within three hours. The accreditation program is not a teaching medium. The completed translations become the exclusive property of the Committee, which does not discuss general or specific problems of the translations with anyone.

For detailed information concerning schedules of tests, conditions, grading, and ground rules, translators are requested to write to Accreditation Committee, American Translators Association, PO Box 129, Croton-on-Hudson, NY 10520.

Code of Ethical Practices and Professional Rights

It shall be the duty of every translator:

1. To translate with the greatest fidelity and accuracy he can command, endeavoring always to give his readers and audiences the impression they would have if they could read or hear the original.

2. To maintain professional discretion and in particular to respect the rights of his client or employer by divulging nothing he may have learned in his professional capacity that is harmful to their interests; and to derive no personal profit or advantage from any confidential information he may have acquired in his professional capacity.

3. To accept no assignment for which he knows himself to be less than well qualified in either language or understanding of the subject, except with the prior knowledge of his client or employer; and to refuse any assignment which he believes he cannot properly complete within the time allowed.

4. To share professional knowledge with his colleagues on a reciprocal basis.

5. To refrain from any action likely to discredit the profession, and in particular to abstain from engaging in unfair competition.

6. To seek or accept no work on terms that are humiliating to him or to the profession.

7. To refuse any assignment that he believes to be intended for illegal or dishonest purposes, or against the public interest.

8. To be loyal to his colleagues and to his profession and to agree to settle professional differences by arbitration, whenever possible.

Every translator shall have the right:

1. To receive the same consideration and the same status as are generally accorded the members of other professions, including prompt payment for his services.

2. To charge such professional fees as are commensurate with his experience, degree of specialized knowledge and quality of work, taking into account such guidelines as may be laid down by his professional society.

3. To demand working conditions that will enable him to perform his services with efficiency and dignity.

4. To refuse to quote a fee on a competition basis or without having seen the work to be translated.

5. To seek, by legislation or other means, the same social and fiscal benefits and tax classifications granted to members of other professions.

6. To enjoy in the case of translations intended for publication or performance, equitable publicity of this kind traditionally granted authors of technical, literary, and dramatic works, including mention of his name on the title page and jacket of the published translation, or in the theater program, and in the advertising of his translation by the publisher or producer.

7. To share, in the case of commercially published or produced works, in the fortunes of his translation, and in particular to receive a proportional share of the royalties as well as an advance payment.

8. To assist, in the case of translations intended for publication or performance, that no substantial changes be made without his consent or, alternatively, that his name be removed as translator or adapter, without prejudice to the agreed payment.

Profile of a Competent Professional Translator

The following characteristics are not necessarily exhaustive nor given in any order of priority, but illustrate what many translators themselves believe should be considered by companies or individuals seeking services:

1. Gives evidence of thorough knowledge of both source and target languages, as well as more-than-average familiarity with the particular subject matter.

2. Has adequate skill and experience as a translator, as evidenced by work samples, letters of reference/recommendation, published translations, and—in some cases—by a certificate of accreditation issued by the ATA.

3. As a corollary to the preceding two items, proof of competence as a translator is of utmost importance, since mere knowledge of a second language does not in itself indicate significant ability in translating into or from that language.

4. Refrains from seemingly broad or exaggerated promotional claims about professional capabilities and does not accept assignments beyond such capabilities.

5. Provides full information on the nature and scope of services offered.

6. Brings unsolved problems to the client's attention.

7. Respects reasonable deadlines.

8. Maintains the confidentiality of all information contained in translation assignments.

9. Quotes fees for an assignment only after prior examination of the material to be translated. If not feasible or practical, quotes an estimated fee based on preliminary information received, subject to confirmation after detailed examination of the material.

10. Charges professional fees commensurate with prevailing rates and in accordance with economic-financial requirements, professional capabilities and/or specialized knowledge.

11. Has access to and makes use of current reference tools, equivalent to those found in an up-to-date professional library. Also has the requisite equipment (e.g., typewriter, dictation machine, etc.) to provide for a complete service.

12. Holds membership and actively participates in local and national professional associations.

Profile of a Competent Translator and of an Effective Translator Training Program

This document embraces and reflects numerous and diverse answers to many frequently asked questions on the levels of competence the translator is expected to reach; e.g., how does one get to be a translator? and how much science does one need to know to be a scientific translator? The profile was piloted by V. Lynn Tyler, associate director of the Language and Intercultural Research Center, Brigham Young University, Provo, Utah, and contains contributions by many established practicing translator-members of the ATA. Since the profile is still in an interim or draft stage, translators and all persons and institutions associated with any aspect of translation are requested to respond to the questions and collective answers and to submit contributions based on their own experience and knowledge.

I. What standards should professional translators be expected to meet?

A. A highly developed sense of intellectual integrity, responsibility, and ethical conduct, which in practical terms means:

1. Not accepting assignments beyond one's language and/or subject competence. A translator should be able to meet minimum standards imposed by his client, who initially judges his competence. The level of competence will also be influenced by the amount of research time the translator is willing to devote.

2. Continuing the ongoing process of self-education and improvement. The translator should be familiar with current developments both in linguistic usage and scientific/technical advances. He should polish his competence in English reading and writing skills and increase his vocabulary.

3. Bringing unsolved problems to the client's attention (eschewing guesswork). The client himself may need to be educated about what can be expected of the translator and the translation.

4. Keeping confidential unpublished information the translator is commissioned to translate.

5. Respecting deadlines mutually agreed to.

6. Helping to upgrade the performance of the profession as a whole by improving the quality of the work, increasing consciousness of existing standards, and evaluating performance and training programs.

7. Sharing knowledge and resources with one's colleagues.

8. Refraining from unseemly or exaggerated promotional claims. The best "promotion" is word of mouth.

9. Abstaining from unsolicited criticism of translations by others.

B. Language and subject-matter requirements:

1. Sound knowledge of source language, equivalent to at least four years of intensive and ten years of sporadic study.

2. Above-average writing ability in the target language, equivalent to that of (self- or otherwise) educated native speakers.

3. Reasonable familiarity with the subject matter, equivalent to that which can be acquired by at least one year (preferably two) of formal education or job experience in the particular field.

4. Access to and assiduous consultation of recent reference books, equivalent to those found in fairly up-to-date professional libraries.

5. Contact with more experienced fellow translators or more knowledgeable linguists and scientists, and the willingness to consult with them (on a reciprocal basis).

6. Translators should also adhere to accepted standard terminology when such exists, to high standards of legibility, and to standard abbreviations, transliteration systems, etc.

7. Familiarity with other standard procedures such as: the use of standard invoicing or billing procedures, familiarity with how to give and receive proper credit (always put the translator's name on the translation, even though someone else may remove it later), copyrighting of translations, especially articles and books.

II. What training is required to be able to attain such standards?

A. Training of student translators:

1. Preliminary courses providing a fairly extensive knowledge of and ability to reason in the subject matter of the translation.

2. Survey-type courses would acquaint the student translator with standard references and sources.

3. Sound reading knowledge and grasp of the language from which one is translating.

4. Training to develop the ability to express oneself in lucid, straightforward English.

5. The potential translator should be taught to identify a number of languages which he will not work with and be familiar with two forms of the language, if two exist.

6. A major outside foreign languages allows the translator to learn the terminology and logic of another discipline.

7. Intensive, direct training in translation theory and practice.

8. Sessions of cultural immersion in foreign study programs useful.

9. Student translators should be given guidance in job-hunting and in developing speed in translation.

10. Standards of training should be reflected by ATA accreditation exams.

B. Continued training of professionals:

1. Periodic participation in advanced "post-graduate" workshops, seminars, correspondence courses, etc., notably in specialized subject-matter areas.

2. The ATA or other professional body should set and govern minimum standards for professional translators, though the consumer or client still may have the last word in setting and evaluating the standards he requests.

III. What/who are clientele/markets for translators?

1. The U.S. Government and its myriad agencies.

2. U.S. and foreign "multinational" corporations and their subsidiaries.

3. U.S. and foreign importers and exporters.

4. Commercial and nonprofit research institutions.

5. Pharmaceutical, chemical, machinery, etc. manufacturers not covered by any of the above categories.

6. Engineering and construction firms with foreign connections.

American Translators Association (ATA) (cont.)

7. Patent attorneys.
8. The publishing industry.
9. Municipal governments in "bilingual" U.S. cities.
10. Graduate schools of U.S. universities.
11. The United Nations and its affiliated agencies.
12. Foreign diplomatic, commercial, scientific, and other representatives in the U.S.

IV. What specific fields of translation have special requisites?

A. Literary requires:

1. Above average knowledge of the source language.
2. Highly developed writing ability in the target language.
3. Comprehensive background in the culture (specifically the literature), history and social customs of other countries (notably that of the source language).

Rewards: intellectual satisfaction, public exposure, reasonable deadlines, byline credit.

Drawbacks: limited economic opportunities ("feast or famine") because of limited market and general lower rates than other fields of translation; lack of retirement benefits (except perhaps in a salaried position).

B. Scientific/technical requires:

1. Moderately extensive scientific/technical knowledge (theoretical and/or practical).
2. Familiarity with specific terminology (and, in the absence thereof, to "know what you don't know").
3. A reasonably up-to-date scientific/technical library.
4. Access to reproduction facilities (for graphs and figures).
5. In most cases, impeccable typing ability and good layout sense (or an associate typist who has these attributes).

Rewards: fairly steady income, with generally higher rates than in the field of literary translation, a broad market, the opportunity to expand one's subject-matter knowledge.

Drawbacks: often "impossible deadlines, the necessity of being a Jack/Jane of all subjects," fairly high cost of reference books, lack of retirement benefits (unless working in a salaried position).

C. Commercial requires:

Most of the same qualifications as scientific/technical translation, but perhaps to a lesser degree.

V. Desiderata for literary translators.

1. Learn at the start, once and for all, the mechanics of manuscript preparation. Present clear, clean, correctly punctuated manuscripts that leave as little work as possible for the editor.
2. Cultivate style. Read widely and observe how stylistic effects are achieved. If possible take courses in stylistics. Consider and study differences among the styles of language as well as among writers.
3. Try to keep up with linguistic and literary developments in the source and target languages.
4. Cultivate respect for the author. Try to ascertain his intentions. Identify with him, empathize with him; if you dislike his ideas, try to see how he arrived at them.
5. Feel free to save an author from his mistakes, but don't make the mistake of indulging your own prejudices.
6. Learn to recognize what is novel and unique in the author, what is standard usage in the source language. Try to reproduce these effects.
7. Whenever you have time, read at least some of your translation aloud. Often the ear detects false notes better than the eye. Cultivate your ear: for dialogue, for prose rhythms, for logic.
8. In translating dialect, don't try to render the text into any specific dialect. Create something artificial that sounds to every dialect speaker like someone else's dialect.
9. Remember that everything is untranslatable and nothing is; there is always some solution, almost always a pretty good solution.
10. Laborare et orare!

Profile of a Professional Quality Translation

The following criteria have been suggested by translators for us in the evaluation of translated materials:

1. The presentation style and format should be in accordance with the nature and purpose of the translation and with the client's specification (e.g., neatness, accuracy, reproducibility, etc.).

2. The non-technical translation should be written in the phrases which might have occurred naturally and spontaneously to an educated native of the target language, had he wanted to express the same ideas and the same shades of meaning. Hence, the non-linguist reader should not be aware that he is in fact reading a translation.

3. The technical translation, which requires clarity and accuracy in every respect, should not contain any phrase or statement that seems wrong, incongruous, unnatural or implausible to any reader who is knowledgeable in the subject matter. Highly specialized or preferred terminology, when supplied by the client to the translator, should be incorporated. Failing this, the translation must be judged on its merits—is the meaning conveyed accurately? Can equipment be operated and/or adjusted properly with the aid of the translated text?

4. For all translations, but particularly true for advertising and promotional materials, the principal criterion should be the undistorted communication of exact meanings while taking into account the culture and psychology of the intended audience. To this end, a translation frequently involves rewriting the original text in an attempt to reproduce in the target language the closest natural equivalent of the source-language message. Above all, it must be remembered that translation of all kinds is a creative, intellectual process and not a mere mechanical transfer of words.

5. No evaluation of translated materials is complete until the translator has been informed whether the translation meets the above criteria and the client's specifications. In today's world of rapid technological and linguistic change, the best way for a translator to keep abreast of current terminology usage is the feedback provided by those who read and evaluate the translation.

Proposed Guidelines for a College-level Translator Training Program

The following set of guidelines was prepared between 1970 and 1972 by the Translator Training Committee of the ATA in response to requests by colleges and universities contemplating the initiation of academic programs designed to prepare students for a career in translation.

At the time, the Committee felt obligated to point out to such institutions that they had a solemn responsibility to make it clear to their students that while successful completion of such a program will provide the student with certain skills, it cannot provide any assurance that these skills will find a ready market, nor can any academic program or degree provide such assurance.

The Committee felt a further obligation to call attention to the fact that there were at the time no reliable statistics available to give even an approximate picture of the current and future needs in the field of translation. In view of this situation, and the fact that there is an apparent current decrease in governmental and free-lance translation work in the Washington–New York area, institutions were advised to proceed with caution in the development of translator training programs. The Committee was optimistic concerning future translation needs and felt that there were indications that these needs will increase, but in view of the apparent situation and the lack of reliable statistics this note of caution seemed advisable at the time.

The guidelines were designed with that student in mind who is majoring in a foreign language and who wants a minor in translation, particularly in the field of scientific-technical translation. In the opinion of the Committee, a student who completed a program covering the suggested areas of knowledge and skill would have a minimum basic competence as a translator, from one foreign language into English in a non-literary field, roughly equivalent to the competence of the academically trained but inexperienced student in any other field. He should be qualified to enter an institution which specializes in graduate-level training for translators and interpreters, or to begin his on-the-job training in a governmental agency, in an industrial translation department, or as a free-lance translator. He will obviously *not* be a highly competent professional translator, no more than the graduating engineering student is a highly competent professional engineer.

In view of the lack of information concerning future job opportunities in translation, some institutions may be well advised to offer students in fields other than foreign languages the core program consisting of the Translation Workshops, which should provide them with enough acquaintance with translation to enhance their value as scientists, business administrators, engineers, etc., or provide them with an excellent research tool in a foreign language. The prerequisite for either program is two years of college-level study in the language, or an equivalent background.

It is obvious that the Translation Workshops should be taught by persons with experience in professional translation, and experienced translators are usually available in a community for part-time teaching. In the event such instructors are not available, the ATA is contemplating a workshop during the summer of 1973 to train instructors for these courses.

It is important to keep in mind the professional translator who earns the bread for his children by practicing his professional skills. Students of translation must translate, and real translation for a client is more effective in developing skills than is meaningless practice translation after the student has developed some competence. But in every community there are opportunities for emergency, charity, and courtesy translation work which do not deprive professional translators of their right to earn a living. It is incumbent on the instructors of translation programs to determine the nature of requests for translation services and, if the request is for translation of an obviously professional nature, to refer such requests to professional translators in the community, or at least to require payment at professional rates for such services. Translator training programs should not be allowed to become sources of "cheap" translation for the community nor for the campus. Such a development can only be detrimental to the students themselves when they, in turn, seek to practice as professional translators.

It is the hope of the American Translators Association that instructors will set an example of professionalism for their students by becoming members of ATA, and by encouraging their students to become student members and their institutions to become institutional members of ATA. Only through the active support of the entire profession can the ATA be effective in improving the quality of translation and the image and conditions of the translator.

The following guidelines are based on certain assumptions, namely:

1. The student has had the equivalent of 2 years of college-level study in a foreign language, i.e., students will normally enter the program in their junior year.

2. Translation workshops will be taught by competent, experienced translators and will not serve as "free" translation bureaus.

3. The culture of the source language will be taught as an integral part of the translation workshops as well as of all courses in the source language and its literature.

4. One year of study in the source language country will be emphatically recommended to all students who can possibly achieve it. This will be particularly appropriate for institutions with Junior Year Abroad programs.

5. The program is described in semesters. Institutions on the quarter system, or any other than the 2-semester system, will adjust it to their schedule.

6. The Translation Workshops should be equivalent to at least 3-semester-hour courses for a total of 15 semester hours. Each institution is expected to fit the suggested courses or areas of study into its own schedule.

7. Structural studies must be adapted to the nature of each language, since the terminology used in these guidelines is more appropriate for German than for some other languages.

First Semester

1. Structure of the source language: Study of the structure of the source language with special emphasis on root words, prefixes, and suffixes (or some equivalent translation aid appropriate to the given language) to facilitate understanding of words without recourse to a dictionary. There should be an introduction to the stylistics of the language. Upon completion of the course the student must analyze the structure of different types of sentences, and he must generate correctly different types of sentences in the source language.

2. Study of the literature of the source language: Extensive reading of all types of literature in the source language—not more than 25% belles lettres, 75% scientific-technical, business-commercial, journalistic, etc. Upon completion of the course the student must read texts comparable to those studied, without recourse to a dictionary, and with good comprehension. Mistakes are to be expected, but the student should understand the main ideas of the text. The objective is to increase reading speed and comprehension, and to wean the student from the use of a dictionary in his reading.

3. Translation Workshop I: The first 1/3 of the workshop should introduce the student to the history and theories of translation and tools of the trade. The second 1/3 should consist of reading existing translations in various fields and comparing them with the original texts, and with each other when two or more translations of the same text are available. The reading should be done outside the class and class time should be devoted to discussion and questions. The final 1/3 should provide the student with an opportunity to try his hand at translating short texts in various fields; class time should be devoted to discussion and criticism of the translations by the entire class.

Upon completion of the course the student must translate a scientific, technical, journalistic, or commercial/business text of the type covered in the course material. With the aid of an appropriate dictionary he must translate at least 200 words (or the equivalent in ideographic languages) within 50 minutes into reasonably smooth, idiomatic English with a vocabulary appropriate to the subject matter, and with no distortion of meaning. Words which do not appear in his dictionary may be rendered by non-technical words, or by paraphrase, so long as the meaning would be clear to a specialist in the subject field.

4. Structure of English: Study of the structure and some of the historical development of English, and of Latin and Greek roots used in international scientific and technical literature.

5. Elective course work in the anticipated field of translation (science, law, medicine, business, etc.), or in general conceptual fields (philosophy, anthropology, psychology, sociology, etc.), or in fields related to translation (comparative linguistics, philosophy of science, etc.). Students with a strong background in the foreign language or in a field of specialization should be urged to begin study of a second foreign language.

Second Semester

1. Structure and style of the source language: Continued study of structure with increasing emphasis on style appropriate to different purposes; writing different kinds of letters; continued study of word formation and vocabulary building.

Upon completion of the course the student must analyze sentences in the source language, the structure of which presents difficulties in the translation of them into English. He must write a specified type of letter (job application, recommendation, inquiry, etc.) in the source language.

2. Studies in the literature of the source language: Extensive reading of all types of literature in the source languages. At least 70% should be in the scientific-technical, business-commercial, and journalistic fields. Upon completion of the course the student must read any of the course material, and any similar material, without the aid of a dictionary and with good comprehension.

3. Translation Workshop II: Translation outside of class of scientific-technical, business-commercial, journalistic, and some literary texts, with class periods devoted to discussion and criticism of the translations by the entire class.

Upon completion of the course the student must translate a text comparable to those he has been working with. With the aid of an appropriate dictionary he must translate at least 250 words within 50 minutes into smooth, idiomatic English with a vocabulary appropriate to the subject matter.

4. Writing English Expository Prose: Extensive writing of expository prose in English to improve style and correct usage of English.

5. Elective course work in the anticipated field of translation, or in general conceptual fields, or in fields related to translation, or in a second source language.

Third Semester

1. Structure and style of the source language: Continued practice in stylistics, structure, word formation, and vocabulary building; practice in writing précis of various types of articles in the source language. Upon completion of the course the student must make a word-by-word analysis of the structure of a paragraph (or a list of words with the same stem but different meanings may be analyzed); he must read an article in the source language and write an accurate précis of it in the same language.

2. Studies in the literature of the source language: Extensive reading in all types of literature in the source language—25% in the special field of translation, 25% belles lettres, 50% general.

3. Translation Workshop III: Group translation projects—each student should select an article in his field of specialization for the entire

American Translators Association (ATA) (cont.)

class to translate. Each contributor will serve as consultant on technical terminology for his contribution. Selections should obviously be untranslated material and should be of value to the student making the selection. Practice solely as practice should be avoided.

4. Elective course work in a research field or in area studies of the source language area, or in a second source language.

Fourth Semester

1. Structure and style of the source language: Study of the most intricate structures and of advanced stylistics. Upon completion of the course the student must be able to analyze very complicated structures; he must write an abstract in the source language of an article in the same language which deals with a subject in his field of specialization.

2. Study of the literature of the source language: Extensive reading of all types of literature in the source language—50% general, 50% in the field of specialization.

3. Translation Workshop IV: Senior thesis—the student will translate a text of 50–100 pages, depending upon the subject matter. This should be a complete article and it should be something which will represent, in the opinion of the student's major advisor, a pertinent and worthwhile contribution to the available literature in that field. The student must also write an abstract in the source language for the article he has translated. Because of the nature of this course it should carry twice as much credit as the other Translation Workshops.

4. Elective course work in a research field, or in area studies, or in a second source language.

Computer Aids for the Human Translator

The following report was presented at the VIII World Congress of FIT, Montreal, 1977, by Erhardt Lippman, a research staff member at IBM, where he is engaged in computational linguistics and text-processing studies. He is also the chairman of the Committee on Computer-Aided Translation of the American Translators Association.

1. Current Translation Practice

Despite extensive efforts over the past 25 years to automate all or part of the process of language translation, the vast majority of translations prepared today for government, industry, and the rest of the private sector are still being produced by human translators employing conventional methods that do not involve the use of computers. The translation production process typically includes the following sequence of steps:

1. preparation of a draft translation by the translator (usually handwritten, less frequently dictated or typed);
2. typing of the draft (unless that was the original mode of transcription in step 1);
3. review and revision of the translation;
4. typing of a clean copy of the revised translation, with provisions for insertion of figures and tables;
5. proofreading, correction, and print preparation;
6. production of the final printed document.

Not only are the individual steps time-consuming in themselves, but substantial delays tend to occur between the completion of one step and the initiation of the next, resulting in lengthy overall production times.

Still more serious for certain classes of translation users are the long delays inherent in the present process between the time when an original document appears and the time when it is available in translated form. Such delays can have an extremely adverse impact both (1) on the workings of government entities and businesses required by law to produce all documents in two or more languages and (2) on the competitive position of international companies producing products requiring extensive sales and service literature. A variety of attempts to automate the translation process have been carried out to overcome the delays and disadvantages in manual translation production. Historically, there have been two fundamentally different approaches towards the use of computers in attempting to automate all or part of the trans-

lation process: machine translation (MT) and automatic translation aids.

2. Machine Translation (MT)

Machine translation research was actively pursued in university and industrial laboratories in the late 1950s and 1960s with liberal government support, primarily in the U.S. The goal was the development of computer programs which could produce high-quality translations at high speed and low cost, with a minimum of human intervention. Accordingly, MT systems were designed in such a way as to place the computer at the center of the translation process, autonomously carrying out all steps in the generation of a typed translation draft, from lexical analysis of the input text to generation of the output language sentences. The bilingual human was relegated to the role of posteditor, i.e., a person responsible for fixing up inadequacies in the output of the translation program. Because of the emphasis of MT on the extraordinarily difficult task of developing systems to replace the human translator during the draft translation phase (step 1) MT research has largely ignored the problems of automating subsequent steps in the translation production process (steps 2 to 6).

Although the major research efforts in MT contributed to greatly increased scientific understanding of the nature of human languages and to the development of computer-based techniques for natural language processing, none of the practical goals of MT with respect to quality, speed, or cost has ever been realized. This negative assessment of practical capabilities represents the cumulative result of several independent evaluations of MT system performance beginning with the ALPAC Report in 1966 (Automatic Language Processing Advisory Committee, National Academy of Sciences, National Research Council, Washington, DC, 1966) and ending with a seminar on machine translation sponsored by the U.S. Foreign Broadcast Information Service in 1976 ("FBIS Seminar on Machine Translation," *American Journal of Comparative Linguistics,* Microfiche 46, 1976). The key findings of the ALPAC report regarding system performance were the following:

1. the raw machine output was of such low quality as to be of very limited value without extensive human postediting;
2. postediting was as time-consuming as conventional human translation and resulted in a somewhat inferior product;
3. because of the added input keyboarding and machine processing steps, postedited MT was both more costly and slower than conventional translation.

3. Automatic Translation Aids

In contrast to the widespread and highly publicized activity in MT in the 1950s and 1960s, work on automatic translation aids proceeded on a very modest scale in centers in Europe, remaining largely unknown in North America until 1966, when it received favorable mention in the ALPAC Report. The automatic translation aid approach differs from that of MT, since its central aim is not to replace the human translator during the original translation process, but rather to increase his productivity by providing him with computer aids in carrying out some of the more routine but time-consuming parts of his job, such as searching for the translations of technical terms in specialized dictionaries. In the most highly developed of these (that of the German Bundeswehr's translation center in Mannheim) the translator would begin his work by scanning the text to be translated, underlining individual words and phrases whose technical translations he was not sure of. The underlined terms would then be entered in a computer in the order of their occurrence and automatically looked up during a subsequent batch computer run in a large English–German technical dictionary stored in machine-readable form. The printed output of the run, a glossary giving the German translation(s) of each of the underlined terms in the order of their occurrence in the text (a so-called text-related glossary), was then given to the translator for use in the preparation of his translation.

The German Bundeswehr's pilot operation at Mannheim was evaluated in 1965 in a series of controlled experiments. The principal result was that translators working with the aid of text-related glossaries required on average only 60% as much time to prepare their draft translations as they did when working unaided. In addition, it was observed at the review and revision stage that, when text-related glossaries were used, the frequency of terminology errors was reduced by an average of 40%—a significant increase in quality. The fact that quality was improved, rather than degraded as in the case of MT, appears to support the soundness of an approach where the translator retains full control of the translation process, especially of those aspects requiring a high degree of human intelligence.

4. Computer-Assisted Translation and Text Processing

Computer-assisted translation and text processing significantly extends the earlier European work on automatic translation aids in two important respects: first, it takes full advantage of the flexibility of a man/machine interactive environment with TV-like display terminals and typewriters connected to a computer to provide the translator with a wide variety of lexical processing choices including single-term lookup and lexical browsing, where the display images may be printed if hard copy is desired. Second, it provides a full complement of text-processing aids for interactive editing, layout, and text manipulation (permitting, e.g., the ready inclusion within a text of tables and previously translated "boiler-plate" information—a U.S. term meaning material repeated without change from one report, contract, or magazine issue to the next). Not only are these facilities of greater usefulness in the initial draft translation phase, but they also provide the key to a major streamlining of the remaining steps required for getting the translation into print-ready form; that is, they can readily be employed by both the technical editor at step 3 and the proofreader and layout person at step 5 to expedite their work, while completely eliminating the necessity of the two typing phases (steps 2 and 4).

Such system aids are designed to make it maximally simple for inexperienced computer users such as translators, terminologists, lexicographers, editors, and typists. The goal of these aids is to streamline the entire translation production process from the reception of a source text to the printing of the finished version of the translation, thereby significantly increasing the productivity of the translator. In this connection, the user can perform the following tasks interactively with the computer:

1. enter and/or edit a text, e.g., a translation or a dictionary;
2. look up dictionary entries and browse through dictionaries and other reference files;
3. update dictionaries or other text files;
4. print text or dictionaries in formatted or unformatted layout on terminals or high-speed printers;
5. obtain statistical information on translations and/or (machine-readable) source language texts;
6. delete, merge, and duplicate text files or text portions;
7. permit other users to share texts and dictionaries on-line to the computer;
8. obtain instructions on how to use the system.

Advantages and benefits include:

a. increased productivity through accelerated dictionary and terminology lookup, rapid and convenient revision of successive translation drafts, and high-speed layout and printing of translations;
b. reduction or elimination of the uninteresting work that is normally associated with the creation of a technical translation;
c. easily activated automatic insertion of previously translated text portions and boiler-plate information;
d. reduced handling and consumption of paper through emphasis on the use of visual displays rather than printed output during all but the final processing step.

To summarize: While the difficulties of machine translation remain unsolved, the computer is a tool that can greatly assist the human translator.

Inter-American Development Bank

General Translation Agreement

The Inter-American Development Bank (hereinafter designated "the Bank" and——— (hereafter designated "the translator"), residing at ———— hereby agree as follows:

1. *Term of Agreement.* The translator undertakes to translate personally into *(language)* ———— such material as he may specifically accept for that purpose from the Translation Section of the Bank between the date of this Agreement and December 31, 1978.

2. *Preparation and delivery of translations.*

a. The translation(s) made under this Agreement shall, on or before the date(s) specified on the respective Translation Order, be delivered to the Translation Section of the Bank or transmitted to the aforesaid Section by registered mail in sufficient time to arrive at that destination on or before the date(s) specified.

b. The translation(s) shall be typewritten, double-spaced, in original and one copy, on unlined letter-size paper (8-1/2″ × 11″) on one side only. The original is to be prepared on bond paper; the copy may be prepared on light-weight manifold paper. The pages shall be numbered consecutively, and the finished work shall be relatively free of erasures and corrections.

3. *Compensation.* Upon timely receipt of complete, accurate and well-written translation(s), the Bank shall compensate the translator at the rate of:

a. $40.00 per thousand words in the original text if the number of words translated is not more than 3,000 per day, i.e., if the number of words in the original text, divided by the number of calendar days elapsed between the date of the translation order and the delivery date specified in such order, is not more than 3,000 words; or

b. $45.00 per thousand words in the original text if the number of words translated is more than 3,000 per day computed as per *a.* above.

4. *Benefits excluded.* It is understood that the translator is an independent translator and, as such, shall not be entitled to any of the benefits established specifically for employees of the Bank.

5. *Taxes.* The translator shall be responsible for the payment of all taxes, as may be incurred as the result of the payment of compensation provided for herein. The translator acknowledges and understands that the Bank does not deduct or withhold any taxes from any sum of money paid for services to be performed hereunder and that the Bank shall incur no obligation for the payment of taxes.

6. *Property rights.* All translations made under this Agreement shall become the sole property of the Bank, which may publish them in whole or in part, adapt them freely, and issue or reissue them in any country, with or without mention of the name of the translator, who, on his part, relinquishes to the Bank any rights concerning copyright that may be granted by the national legislation of any country, or by international conventions.

7. *Confidentiality.* The translator is aware that in discharging his obligations pursuant to this contract he may have access to privileged and confidential information of the Bank, a public international organization. The translator agrees that under no circumstances shall he disclose to any person or organization, in any manner or form, now or after the expiration of this contract, such information or any part thereof.

8. *Termination.* This Agreement shall remain in force until December 31, 1978, unless terminated by the Bank at an earlier date. The Bank shall have the right to terminate the Agreement by giving the translator fifteen (15) days notice at his last known place of residence.

| The Translator | For the Inter-American Development Bank |

International Association of Conference Interpreters (AIIC)

Code of Professional Conduct (extracts)

Art. 2. (a) Members of the Association shall be subject to strict professional secrecy. This applies to all persons and all information gathered in the course of non-public meetings attended in a professional capacity.

(b) No member shall derive personal profit or advantage from any confidential information acquired while acting in a professional capacity.

Art. 3. Members of the Association shall refrain from accepting conference engagements they do not feel qualified to undertake. Acceptance shall be regarded as guaranteeing a high professional standard of interpreting.

Art. 6. Members of the Association shall refuse, for themselves as

International Association of Conference Interpreters (AIIC) (cont.)

well as for interpreters recruited on their recommendation working conditions not in accordance with those laid down by the Association.

Art. 8. (a) Members of the Association shall only accept a conference engagement when they are aware of the exact conditions of this engagement and have made sure that their identity and conditions of payment are known to the conference organizer. Thus, they cannot accept any engagement which does not imply clearly established contractual relations between themselves and the conference organizer. Members shall use the Letter of Appointment of the Association or take it as a basis for their non-governmental conferences.

(b) When members are engaged as interpreters, they perform no other task.

Art. 11. (d) Members of the Association engaged to work on the same team of interpreters shall accept a conference engagement only if all the free-lance members are engaged at the same rate of remuneration, subject to the case of beginners covered by a special arrangement between AIIC and some organizations.

Efficient Planning of Conference Interpretation

The following suggestions, issued in October 1973, are addressed to organizers of conferences who have decided to use consecutive or simultaneous interpretation and wish for some guidance on how to tackle the practical problems that are involved in handling the interpretation service efficiently. They cover choice of type of interpretation; recruitment of interpreters; working arrangements; facilities; and fees.

The hints given here are the fruits of many years' experience in conference interpreting and the organization of efficient interpreting teams acquired by members of the AIIC. Additional information can be obtained from Secretariat, AIIC, 14 rue de l'Ancien Port, CH-1201 Geneva, Switzerland.

Choice of Type of Interpretation

Consecutive interpretation, where the interpreter takes notes in the Conference Room and translates these when the speaker has finished his statement, is suitable when two, or at most three languages are used. Consecutive interpretation is obviously longer than simultaneous, but for drafting committees, press conferences, and other special meetings offers greater flexibility.

Simultaneous interpretation is the method of choice for all large meetings, with the interpreters working in sound-insulated booths, talking into microphones and heard by delegates in their earphones. For further information on simultaneous, see "working conditions" below.

Under very special conditions, or with small groups, it is permissible to use out-of-booth simultaneous interpretation. The interpreter has a headset, sits in the room and whispers into a microphone for participants using headsets to listen. At meetings where there may be only two delegates of one given language, *whispered* interpretation, where the interpreter sits between the two delegates and gives the interpretation sotto voce for them only, is permissible, and may prove less expensive than including this language in the official list.

In any case, the choice of the foregoing types of interpretation should *always* be decided in conjunction with a consultant interpreter, who has the experience to advise which is most suitable and efficient.

Recruitment of Interpreters

Never engage amateurs. Conference interpreting is a special job requiring proper qualification like any other professional activity. A command of languages is a prerequisite, not of itself a qualification. Make sure your interpreters have this qualification, preferably by membership in AIIC which is a guarantee of professional ability. AIIC publishes a *Yearbook* listing all members by country and town, with their language combinations.

The choice and number of interpreters, and hence their fees depend on a number of factors which include the languages to be used, the type of conference, the amount of preparatory work, the length and frequency of sittings, and the number of concurrent sittings.

Organizers should also be aware that the interpreters required can of-

ten not all be recruited on the spot, especially where several languages are involved. Provision must therefore be made for the payment of travel expenses and a subsistence allowance to those interpreters recruited away from the conference venue.

If the subject of the meeting is highly specialized, in addition to a possible increase in fees and size of team, it may be necessary to arrange expert briefings for the interpreters prior to the conference. Such briefing sessions are considered in the period of engagement.

Book interpreters well in advance, especially when the conference cannot be held outside the peak periods of May, June, September, and October. Recruitment in the quieter periods makes for better team planning.

The ideal procedure is to enlist the assistance of an experienced professional interpreter, to take over all arrangements with regard to interpretation. He will be responsible for selecting the interpreters and forming a team to cater for both the language combination and the workload. He will take charge of the team's working arrangements before and during the conference and serve as a permanent link between his colleagues and the organizing committee. He is answerable to his colleagues for their working conditions, and should be consulted at every stage of the organization of the conference. He will see that each interpreter is engaged by a letter of appointment signed by the conference organizer, who thus knows the name, address, qualifications, and fees of interpreters engaged for a given period and job, while the interpreter in signing guarantees his ability to render efficient services.

"Organizer" here means the actual sponsoring of the conference; interpreters do not accept letters of appointment signed by commercial intermediaries who may be handling the material organization of the conference.

Working Arrangements

Your consultant interpreter will help you here, once you give him the information about your conference: subject, languages, number of halls, draft program and time schedule of sessions, building where the conference will be held and whether this has built-in facilities in halls you will use with simultaneous interpretation.

For *consecutive* interpretation, interpreters will sit as close as possible to the Chairman, have a full view of participants and be able to hear them clearly. They should receive a full set of documents and be provided with facilities for taking notes. If the hall is to be darkened for slide projection, small table lamps should be provided for the interpreters. If you are not using the services of a consultant interpreter, always ask your team what arrangements they need to perform their job.

For *simultaneous* interpretation, remember it is in your best interest to get the help of a consultant interpreter to handle your service in the most effective manner. There should be cooperation between your consultant interpreter, the sound engineer, and the conference secretary. Ask interpreters whether in their experience the installation you plan to use is satisfactory.

Facilities for Simultaneous Interpretation

Permanent installations. Literature is available on the architectural problems at the design stage of conference halls or buildings, so that the simultaneous interpretation system can be installed as part of the facilities as a whole and not just added later. The Secretariat of AIIC can supply literature on the subject.

Movable installations. When halls with good permanent facilities cannot be hired, movable equipment can be used for conferences organized on a periodical basis in different countries or as a one-time event. It can be hired from firms specialized in this sector, or in some cases as a semipermanent feature included in hotel or institutional conference facilities. When working with movable equipment, consult a conference sound engineer to make sure that the room is acoustically satisfactory and booths have proper sound installation.

Minimum dimensions for movable booths. Height 230 cm (90 in), depth 240 cm (94 in), width 250 cm (98 in), window over full width. The interpreters' voices must be inaudible in the adjacent booth as well as outside. This means a combination of sound insulation and ventilation.

Ventilation. Each booth must be provided with a fresh-air inlet and an exhaust fan, both of which should be silenced. The resulting carbon dioxide concentration in the booth when in use should not be more than 0.10. Sustained mental effort is hampered at higher concentrations, sometimes even found in poorly ventilated conference rooms.

Position. In full view of chairman, speakers, and screens or blackboards. No delegates should be permitted to stand or pass in front of booths, and interpreters should be able to leave booths and hall without walking in front of delegates.

Doors should be easy to open. Side panels should have glass windows for visual communication with the next booth. Shelving for documents on side wall, and two coat hooks, if possible.

Seating should be roomy and comfortable. Two chairs per booth.

Desk. Working depth minimum 50 cm (20 in), 72 cm (28 in) from floor. Covered with elastic or foam material for protection against impact noise.

Equipment in booths. For each interpreter separate headset, selector, and volume control of incoming channels (including other booths), switch for microphone and pressbutton temporary cut-out. Tell-tale should light up when microphone is on the air. Pushbutton to signal chairman or speaker. It is also useful to have a special switchover arrangement in the booth to alternate the outgoing channels for small-team situations where each interpreter may need to work in both directions without changing microphones. Reading lamps should be provided, of a make which does not encumber the table.

Equipment for delegates. For each delegate headset, channel selector and volume control. There are many types, radio or wired. The consultant interpreter and the sound engineer will advise on what is most suitable for your particular conference. The choice and location of microphones depends much on the type of meeting; always consult both the team leader, sound engineer, and conference secretary when deciding microphone layout, which is of decisive importance to the success of the meeting. Not more than one microphone must be switched at a time as dual transmission interferes with reception in the interpreters' booths. Switching may be done by the sound technician from a central panel. In large conference rooms some electrical or manual arrangement is necessary to enable him to identify the person about to speak. Alternatively, the microphones may be fitted with individual switches operated by the speaker himself. All microphones should have an "on" light.

Miscellaneous

Documents. The success of your meeting depends on its preparation, and this includes interpretation. Each interpreter should receive all available documents well beforehand. If papers are to be read from text it is mandatory for interpreters to receive copies in extenso in the original language, plus translations if these have been made. If no documents are to be used, minutes of former meetings and other publications on the subject will enable the interpreters to gain the necessary background.

Interpreters' room. This is where interpreters can read, keep documents, and receive messages. It should be within easy reach of booths.

Contacts with conference organizers. One person from the Secretariat should, in the case of big meetings, be appointed to handle contacts with interpreters.

Extra-conference events. Interpreters' duties do not include sightseeing trips, private parties, and the like. They do include visits to technical plants, hospital laboratories, or other places directly connected with the conference topics. Consult the interpreters or their team leader before making final arrangements.

Translations. Written translation is a job for translators and not covered in appointment of interpreters. Your consultant interpreter can probably help you find translators. You may also get help from the AIIC, International Association of Conference Translators [see Sec 2, International] Case postale 31, CH-1211 Geneva 14, Switzerland.

Speed of delivery for written papers. Should not be more than ten lines a minute or one page of double-spaced typescript in 2-1/2 minutes. Lecturers should be informed of their total time and reading speed well in advance.

Fees

Fees are based on a daily rate for each day or part of a day covered by the appointment. They are free of tax or commission and must be transferable to the country in which the interpreter is domiciled.

AIIC rates are subject to periodic cost-of-living adjustment (applicable January 1 or July 1); minimum daily rates under an agreement with major international organizations in Europe are available from the AIIC Secretariat.

International Association of Conference Translators (AITC)

Practical Guide for Users of Conference Language Service (extracts)

As all organizers of international meetings know, language plays an important role in such meetings and is a key problem. The use of professional interpreters to enable participants at international meetings to communicate orally is standard practice, and a guide to help users in the proper employment of interpreter services has been published by the International Association of Conference Interpreters (AIIC). The use of other language staff, namely, revisers, translators, précis-writers, and editors, in connection with most international meetings is also standard practice. This guide is designed to assist employers in the proper utilization of their services.

Work of this type, which involves the "manipulation" of languages, requires great concentration, and is particularly exacting during a conference, when all staff are subjected to a considerably higher degree of nervous tension than during calmer periods. The conference organizer must bear this in mind and calculate as accurately as possible the number of staff required in each category, on the basis of the output which can reasonably be expected without adverse effect on the quality of the work produced.

Translation

A translation service consists of translators and revisers, together with secretarial and, if possible, documentation services.

Translators

Translators are linguists who have devoted many years of their life to mastering the technique of faithfully rendering in their mother tongue texts drafted in other languages. They must therefore have the necessary cultural background and open-mindedness to enable them to adapt to all the fields—economic, legal, scientific, technical, etc.—in which they are required to work. In this connection, it will be noted that in order to include only high-quality translators in its annual register of active members, AITC examines only the candidacies of translators who have at least 500 days' practical experience with international organizations.

Like their colleagues the interpreters, translators form an integral part of any multilingual international meeting: while the interpreter is expected to give instantaneous oral interpretation, the translator works from written texts of which he is expected to provide a considered, strictly accurate and thoroughly documented translation in a clear, precise style. In short, the text which leaves his hand should constitute a document or basis for discussion quite as valid as that drafted in the original language. In the case of treaties, conventions, protocols, or resolutions, etc., formally binding upon two or more countries, his translations in the official languages of the conference have the same binding value as the original text, and all versions should be regarded as equally authentic. In other words, the translator must make no mistakes, however small, since such mistakes may have serious consequences.

Translation is therefore a job which requires the utmost application and cannot be done in haste. Consequently, it is desirable that conference services should be so organized that the translators have all the time they need for the proper fulfillment of their task.

One reason why a translator makes a point of translating only into his mother tongue is the need for the strictest accuracy in his written work, for experience has shown that nobody can ever acquire the same mastery of a foreign language as he has of his mother tongue. Conference organizers therefore have to provide one or more translators for each of the languages used at the conference, the precise number being determined by the expected volume of work and the time allowed for doing it.

Revisers

The reviser is usually a linguist who has spent most of his life in translation work and who, through his extensive knowledge of that work, his linguistic experience, his sure judgment and style, has acquired sufficient authority to advise his fellow translators and revise their work. He makes sure that the translation of documents is of a very

International Association of Conference Translators (AITC) (cont.)

high quality. His main function is to read through the translated documents and correct errors of style or substance, settle points relating to the interpretation of sentences or words and, if a text is too long to be dealt with by a single translator within the fixed deadline, ensure consistency of style and terminology throughout the translated document.

Because of his authority and experience, the reviser is often called upon to act as head of a team. As such, he arranges the work of the translators, distributes the texts to them on the basis of their competence, speed, and the deadlines to be met, etc.

A reviser is expected to revise each day the work of three or four translators, depending upon the difficulty of the translations and the quality of the translators. Lastly, the reviser may, if necessary, be asked to translate particularly important and urgent texts himself and to advise authors of documents on points of terminology, style, presentation, etc.

Précis-writing

In the ordinary context, "précis" means a concise summary of the content of a book, article, or document, i.e., of something that is written. In the context of international meetings, it means a concise summary, prepared in writing, of the views and arguments advanced orally by delegates during a meeting. Great skill is obviously required in preparing such a summary. For instance, identification by the précis-writer of the salient points of an argument has to be instantaneous. Verbal accuracy is more important in writing than in speaking. The speaker can be seen by his audience, and his expression and tone of voice give color to what he says; in fact, it may be through his expression and tone of voice that he makes his real meaning clear. The writer, on the other hand, has only the printed word to offer, and if the words he uses are imprecise, they may be open to a number of interpretations, particularly when they implicitly convey an opinion. It should be emphasized that the written précis of a meeting is very often the only lasting record of its proceedings, and, in all cases, constitutes an authoritative reference document.

Précis-writing is a task for professionals. To do his job properly, the précis-writer for international meetings should be a linguist, following the discussions in the languages used by the speakers and resorting to the interpreter's version only when a speaker uses a language in which the précis-writer is not proficient. He must also have an excellent command of his mother tongue so as to express concisely and clearly what each speaker has said. Finally, he must have sound judgment, since it is he who decides in the first instance what points are important for the record and what points may be omitted.

Functions of the précis-writer. The précis-writer is responsible for preparing, from notes he has taken during a meeting, a summary (précis) in his mother tongue of the proceedings of that meeting. He is not responsible for preparing a verbatim record, i.e., an account in extenso of all that has been said during a meeting. A verbatim record does not serve the same purposes as a summary record, being a transcript, made by typists, of notes taken by shorthand stenographers, and is much more difficult to read than a summary record, which not only summarizes the statements but also arranges them in the form of a coherent text which focuses attention on the decisions. A verbatim record is also more costly, and as a result is very seldom called for except in large international organizations, which occasionally supplement summary records by having transcriptions made in extenso of debates in which the speeches are generally of a political nature.

Functions of the reviser. The reviser must have an overall grasp of the scope and purposes of the conference, its background and the relevant documentation, and of conference procedure and terminology in general. He must dovetail and unify sections written by different précis-writers so as to produce a continuous, balanced, and consistent record, and must also ensure its factual correctness (names of delegates, accuracy of references to previous resolutions, etc.).

Where the précis-writer has worked from a delegate's written statement, the reviser must check to see that the précis-writer has given an adequate reflection of it. The reviser should himself have done précis-writing at an earlier stage in his career, and thus have a proper appreciation of the problems involved and the ability to solve them.

Depending on the volume of work, the reviser may have to engage in

revising translations of resolutions, etc. He will in any case ensure that partial texts of resolutions in the making, as reflected in the discussions, and the texts of the resolutions as finally adopted, are in proper relation to each other.

Editing

In the terminology used in international organizations the word editor ("editeur") has the meaning it carries in English. Thus an editor is someone whose work it is to prepare for printing texts drafted either by their authors or by translators. He is needed for large conferences.

The editor's functions. There are several possibilities at large conferences.

1. If he is editing translations or summary records, which have already been revised in the language services, his task is largely confined to preparing the texts materially. He prepares a cover-page for the (printed or mimeographed) volume in which the edited summary records of the session, for example, are to appear. He makes out a list of contents and a list of the symbols and abbreviations used in the records and drafts any explanatory notes that may be required.

2. In the case of verbatim records, which have not passed through the language services, the editor may and is indeed required to alter the text of oral statements. This he does as tactfully as he can; yet the speakers are the first to be grateful to him for having tidied up their language, if not their ideas.

3. Where he is dealing with original texts (for example papers read at scientific conferences) for publication, he must be in a position to get personally in touch with the authors and suggest to them any improvements he thinks should be made in the presentation of the text itself, the tables or the illustrations; he must check with them that the tables have titles, that all the illustrations have captions, and that all the blocks are satisfactory.

When the final text is ready the editor prepares the manuscript for printing. He is also responsible for correcting the proofs.

Practical Guides

International Congress Science Series, published by the Union of International Associations, 1 rue aux Laines, B-1000 Brussels, Belgium are guides designed to help users in the proper employment of language services, both interpreting and translating:

International Congress Organization: Theory and Practice. Ideas and advice from leading specialists; a series of practical suggestions, classified by subject; a typical agreement between the international secretariat and the host country, detailing their respective responsibilities and duties; classified bibliographical data. Available only in French.

Congress Organizers' Manual, by Lucien R. Duchesne, Administrative Director of International Chamber of Commerce. A detailed compendium of all the organizational operations involved in running an international congress; tables, time-charts, model cards, and instructions, together with a large wall-chart (30 in. × 50 in.) for use in arranging a congress. Bibliography and subject index. Available in English and French.

Proceedings of the 3rd Congress of International Congress Organizers and Technicians, Rome 1962: Audio-Visual Equipment, Associated Exhibitions, Public Relations. Appendices: the text of the 1962 Customs Convention, draft code for indicating languages by the use of colors, nomenclature applicable to statutory bodies and to international meetings. Available in English and French.

Practical Guide for Users of Conference Interpreting Services, prepared by the International Association of Conference Interpreters (AIIC), and designed to aid employers in the proper utilization of interpretation services. Available in French, English, and Spanish.

Professional Code

Article 1. The provisions of the present Code are binding on all the members of the Association.

Article 2. A translator must in all circumstances act in an international spirit. He must not engage in any form of activity incompatible with his duties or likely to be detrimental to the dignity of his profession. (Under the Constitution, the term "free-lance translator" applies to all revisers, translators, précis-writers, and editors working in connection with international conferences or for international organizations under temporary contracts of employment or contracts relating to the performance of particular pieces of work, e.g., translation carried out at home).

Article 3. The translator must observe professional secrecy. He may at no time communicate to anybody information which he has obtained in the course of his duties and which has not been made public. He is not relieved of this obligation on the expiration of his contract.

Article 4. A translator may not accept an appointment or work which is outside his competence.

Article 5. Translators must maintain friendly relations amongst themselves and observe their duties of moral support and solidarity. They shall refrain from all forms of unfair competition.

Article 6. Any dispute between members of the Association on professional questions may be submitted to the Disciplinary Board.

Article 7. Except in cases of emergency translators shall not undertake duties other than those provided for in their contract.

Article 8. Translators shall not consent to work in conditions liable to be detrimental to the quality of their work. In this connection, they must insist on the observance of the Rules of the Annex on the duration of the working week, on the writing of summary records and on travel.

Article 9. Members of the Association must select a professional domicile, which shall be the only place where they may be recruited as local staff. Such domicile may not be changed for a period of less than a year. Any change must be notified without delay to the Executive Secretary.

Article 10. Except in cases of *force majeure,* a translator shall not withdraw from a contract unless he can give notice within the requisite period, supply a valid reason and propose a competent substitute.

Article 11. Members of the Association shall not accept a contract which is not in conformity with the professional rules adopted by the General Assembly and reproduced in the Annex, unless they are allowed to make appropriate reservations.

Article 12. The members of the Association shall refrain from any action detrimental to the Association.

Article 13. The members of the Association who fail to observe the said provisions shall be liable to the disciplinary measures specified in the Constitution.

Annex

Remuneration and Subsistence Allowance

Rule 1. Remuneration shall be on a monthly or daily basis. It must be transferable to the member's country of domicile. A full day's pay shall be due for a fraction of a day. Remuneration is due for all days covered by the period of employment including Sundays and holidays. Every free-lance translator engaged elsewhere than at his professional domicile shall receive a subsistence allowance fixed according to a scale published periodically.

Rule 2. In the case of non-consecutive engagements outside the country of domicile, contracts must provide either for repatriation or for payment of salary and subsistence allowance during intervals.

Length of Working Week

Rule 3. The length of the working week must not exceed 40 hours, spread over 5 or 6 days. If, owing to unforeseen circumstances, a translator is called upon to work longer, he shall receive compensation, in the form either of time off, or of an equivalent number of days of paid leave at the end of the contract. In addition, any work done on a Sunday, a holiday or a non-working day or after 8 P.M. shall entitle the translator to compensation in the form of monetary payment or time off. Normally, the length of the working week should not exceed 35 hours when the translator is asked to remain on duty until midnight (evening shift) and 30 hours if he is required to remain on duty after midnight (night shift).

Writing of Summary Records

Rule 4. The précis-writer must insist on being allowed reasonable time to write the record. The team responsible for the précis of a meeting lasting between two and three hours shall consist of three précis-writers; the taking of notes and the subsequent drafting of the record represent at least a full day's work for each of the précis-writers concerned. (This rule is based on U.N. practice. Naturally, any other method which does not involve more work for the précis-writer is acceptable.)

The period of note-taking shall be reduced when the subject before the meeting is particularly difficult or when the speakers read written statements at speed. The team shall be relieved when a meeting lasts for more than three hours.

Cancellation of Contracts

Compensation. Rule 5. In case of cancellation of contract by an organization, and unless the translator is offered an equivalent engagement, the organization shall pay him/her the following compensation:

a) 50% of the salary for the whole period of the engagement if the contract is cancelled more than 30 days before the start of the engagement;

b) 100% of the salary for the whole period of the engagement if the contract is cancelled within 30 days of the start of the engagement, or for the period of the engagement to run if the contract is cancelled during the engagement.

Notice. Rule 6. A minimum of 3 days' notice shall be given in case of cancellation of contract by either side during the engagement; subsistence allowance is due during that period in addition to the salary due for the whole of the remainder of the contract, in accordance with Rule 5(b).

Travel

Rule 7. As compensation for the time spent in travel before and after his engagement, a translator shall be paid salary and subsistence allowance for two half-days' work. For any further day's travel, he shall be paid full salary and subsistence allowance. These payments are subject to the following conditions:

(a) for this purpose, travel-time is reckoned on the basis of the speediest route from domicile to place of work;

(b) the translator must travel on the day or days immediately preceding or following his engagement;

(c) during that time, the translator must not be in receipt of pay from any other organization.

Rule 8. The employer shall defray the translator's traveling expenses between his domicile and place of employment as follows:

Travel by rail or boat: First class, with sleeper or cabin for night journeys;

Travel by air: Tourist class may be accepted provided the organization allows the translator 30 kg (66 lbs) of free luggage and

one day's rest with salary and per diem for journeys of more than 9 hours and less than 16 hours;

two days' rest with salary and per diem for journeys of more than 16 hours and less than 21 hours;

three days' rest with salary and per diem for journeys of 21 hours or more.

The length of the journey is reckoned from airport to airport. Days' rest may be taken during a stop en route or on arrival.

International Federation of Translators (FIT)

Code of Ethical Practices and Professional Rights

The FIT code, representing a guideline for the adoption of similar codes by translators' societies throughout the world, is identical to that of the American Translators Association, which was instrumental in wording the FIT text.

The Legal and Social Status of the Translator

In 1972 and 1976 the FIT Committee for the Legal and Social Status of the Translator conducted companion surveys among FIT's member associations. The following report of the results of the surveys (extensively extracted here) was submitted by Hans Schwarz of West Germany, chairman of the FIT Committee, vice-president of FIT, and president of the Bundesverband der Dolmetscher und Übersetzer (BDÜ).

Because of the low rate of returns, the sometimes incomplete or incorrect statements, and the heterogeneous nature of the translating profession, one cannot claim that the results of this survey are generally valid or even complete. It was, for example, not possible to include any information . . . (from) countries whose . . . associations did not participate in the survey. The following aspects were given consideration when evaluating the information received:

International Federation of Translators (FIT) (cont.)

legislation regulating professional practice;
legislation concerning protection of the title "Translator";
recommendations on fees and anti-trust law provisions;
work and service contracts for translators;
copyright law;
tariff agreements for salaried translators;
legislation concerning the certification of translators;
tax laws;
social security and old-age pension schemes;
rules of professional conduct and codes of ethics of the associations and professional courts of honor and arbitration.

Legal Status

The results of the survey showed that the legal status of the translator differs considerably from country to country. In most countries, there is either absolutely no, or only unsatisfactory, regulation of the translator's legal status, apart from the international or national copyright laws that apply to translators. Under no circumstances is the legal situation in keeping with the translator's important role as a link and promoter of understanding between nations. Only a few countries have laws regulating admission and the practice of the profession of translator that set forth a job profile, the necessary course of training, and the examinations and qualification criteria that protect the title of "Translator," codify the rights and duties of the profession, and provide for regulation of the practicing translator's conduct by state or professional organs and/or courts of honor and arbitration.

The degree of government control of the translating profession in the individual countries depends primarily on their various constitutions and on the opinion of the legislative or executive body concerning what public need exists for protection against the activities of unqualified or unreliable translators going beyond that offered by general national law. Such protection is in particular need when important public law tasks are to be performed (for example, court interpretation, translation of legal documents, or expert linguistic advice to courts and public authorities).

We can distinguish three stages of legislative measures regulating the profession of translator, the individual stages depending on the scope of the laws.

The first stage . . . consists of protection of the title "Translator" or of connected titles and functional designations, such as "diploma translator, state-examined translator, officially appointed and sworn or authorized translator or linguistic expert." In such cases, the appropriate laws determine the conditions under which the use of these professional designations is legally permissible and/or the conditions under which they can be awarded (for example, after proof of having passed the appropriate state examinations, of having reached the minimum age and of having practiced the profession for a given minimum period, of having fulfilled the obligation to register, etc.). Legal regulation of the right to use the title "Translator" or the other previously mentioned functional designations does not, however, prohibit the practice of translation by those not so qualified. The entitlement to use these professional and functional designations is, usually, however a "seal of quality" granted by the government, thus considerably facilitating practice of the profession and protecting the public against unqualified translators.

The second stage . . . is that which regulates admission to professional practice. As a rule, it will consist of provisions concerning admission to and the right to practice the profession (for example, personal and professional requirements such as minimum age, no criminal record, proof of suitable training and graduation from a university or other academic institution and/or proof of many years of practical translating work, professional rights and duties, courts of honor and arbitration, scales of fees, etc.).

The third stage . . . is that concerning professional self-regulation with statutory powers in the form of a public corporation with compulsory membership, its own professional courts, and a legally binding scale of fees.

The survey revealed the following legal provisions in the individual countries that returned reports:

Argentina. Act of Parliament No. 20305 of 25 April 1973 regulating the official appointment and swearing-in of court translators, including protection of the title "Sworn Court Translator."

Federal Republic of Germany. Some of the member states (*Länder*) of the Federation (FIT) have legal provisions concerning the official appointment and swearing in of linguistic experts, court interpreters and translators and legal protection of the title "Diploma Translator/Diploma Interpreter," "State-Examined Translator/Interpreter."

German Democratic Republic. The GDR introduced statutory regulation of the admission and registration of freelance linguists (interpreters and translators) on 5 April 1974. The qualification criteria for freelance linguists are graduation from a university or other academic institution as linguist (interpreter/translator) or philologist, coupled with proof of several years of successful activity as a linguist. In exceptional cases, linguists who have passed no recognized examination but can prove many years of practice and capability as a linguist can be admitted.

Denmark. In Denmark, Act of Parliament No. 213 of 8 June 1966 regulates the admission of interpreters and translators to professional practice (licensing). The main criteria for admission to the profession are the following: (1) the applicant must be of Danish nationality; (2) the applicant must be resident in Denmark; (3) the applicant must have completed the 25th year of life; (4) the applicant may be under no legal incapacity or guardianship, nor may his estate be in the hands of an official receiver; (5) the applicant must pass a special examination. The Minister of Commerce is responsible for enforcement of this act, his ministry laying down the qualification criteria and appointing the examining boards. The Danish law also regulates certain fields of professional practice and use of the professional designations "Interpreter" and "Translator."

Holland. In Holland, the Act of Parliament of 6 May 1878 as amended on 20 April 1928 regulates the official appointment of sworn court interpreters and translators and their professional practice.

Poland. Poland has no statutory regulations concerning the official appointment of sworn court translators.

Sweden. Sweden has statutory regulations governing professional practice and use of the professional designations.

Copyright Law as Applying to Translators

Translators copyright is protected on the international and supra-regional level by a number of conventions, including the 1952 Universal Copyright Convention and its 1971 revision.

The national copyright laws of the signatory states go a long way toward giving translators the same copyright protection that they enjoy under these international conventions. In spite of a general improvement in the provisions of copyright law, the copyright protection of the translator is still largely dependent on the rights of the author of the original work. The reason for this is that copyright law—with only a few exceptions—gives the translator only the legal status of one who has modified a work and not the legal status of co-originator. One must also remember that present copyright laws generally protect only literary, scientific and artistic works, whereas the majority of translations made and published today enjoy no copyright protection (for example, advertising and information brochures, price lists, operating instructions, etc.).

The legal position of the translator is made even worse by the fact that the author of a work usually also assigns the right to translate the work into a different language to the publisher when he assigns his rights as author. The translator is however always at a disadvantage when dealing with publishing companies, being the economically weaker party. . . . One question connected with copyright law as applying to translators is worthy of mention: that of the remuneration received by translators in some countries as a royalty for the loaning of a copyright-protected translated work by public libraries (the so-called library penny). Such copyright provisions exist in the Federal Republic of Germany and in Sweden.

Social Status of the Translator

Like his legal status, the translator's social status differs from country to country and is equally unsatisfactory in most cases. This is largely due to the fact that intellectual performance is generally undervalued in comparison with manual performance, a widespread trend in our times.

Generally speaking, one can say that the income of salaried translators is far higher than that of freelance translators. A number of countries, including the Federal Republic of Germany, have model agreements regulating the salary scales of translators employed in industry and above all those employed by the government, these agreements being negotiated by the several trade unions. The trade unions, with their large numbers of members, their financial strength (union dues), and their political weight can exert a far greater influence on the legislative and executive bodies and the economy of a country than, for example, the small and relatively poor associations and other bodies representing the interests of the translators. A further factor is that these professional associations are not usually competent to negotiate and conclude rate agreements under labor law.

Except for a few countries, the general economic situation of freelance translators is more than unsatisfactory. Adequate safeguarding of the social status of the translator is possible only in those countries in which there are official scales of fees for translators or in which recommendations on fees are legally permissible.

Recommendations on fees. "Official scales of fees" contain minimum and maximum fees that are legally binding on the translator and his client. Such legally prescribed scales of pay not only protect the individual client and the general public from excessive demands by the individual translator, they also protect the profession against ruinous competition from within. Since one of the aims in laying down the scales of fees is to ensure an appropriate income for the individual translator, such a scale of fees also has an important social regulatory function. This function, however, can be properly carried out only if the scale of fees is constantly adapted to general price developments, particularly in times of rapidly declining purchasing power. As the legal machinery is rather slow-moving, fee scales do not always keep pace with general prices.

The recommendations on fees usually found in those countries in which no official scales are in force and no limitations exist in the form of anti-trust law provisions, are recommendations that are usually made by the professional organizations representing the translators' interests that are published in the form of so-called "catalogues of services." Such catalogues usually contain the units on which invoices are based (e.g., words, lines, or pages in the case of translations), the rates for writing foreign-language advertising copy, for checking other translators' translations, for certifying documents, for typing and other ancillary costs (e.g., stamps, telephone), sales or value-added tax, and specimen work and service contracts. The recommendations made in such catalogues are usually based on surveys of fees in the area of application made by the professional association among their members and, sometimes, non-members.

Although such recommendations on fees have a certain regulatory effect, it is in general found to be relatively slight because of the absence of legal backing. The recommendations are by no means legally binding on the translator and his client. Many members of our profession ignore the recommendations, but the main offenders are the uncounted persons from other walks of life who dabble in translating as a secondary source of income. In the freelance sector in particular, this state of affairs has led to a situation in which the income of the freelance translator in many countries does not even equal the national average of the working population.

An international survey revealed that the following countries have laws or regulations on the fees of translators and/or interpreters:

Argentina. Act of Parliament No. 20305 of April 1973 lays down minimum and maximum fees for sworn court interpreters.

Austria. Act of Parliament of February 19, 1975, regulates the remuneration of witnesses, experts, interpreters, jurors, and lay judges in court proceedings.

Bulgaria. Statutory regulations govern the remuneration of translators, including standard contracts between translators and publishing firms.

Federal Republic of Germany. The Act of Parliament of October 1, 1969, as amended on November 2, 1976, regulates the remuneration of court witnesses and court experts (including interpreters and translators).

German Democratic Republic. The Statutory Regulation of April 5, 1974, regulates the remuneration of freelance interpreters and translators.

Greece. Articles 52 and 53 of Act of Parliament No. 3026 (1954) regulate the remuneration of lawyers for the translation and certification of documents.

Poland. A Polish law regulates the remuneration of literary and technical-scientific translators, sworn court translators, and conference in-

terpreters and provides a standard contract to be executed by the translator and the publishing house in case of book translations.

As far as the publication of recommendations on fees and of specimen work and/or service contracts is concerned, the survey and other investigations conducted by the FIT Committee for the Legal and Social Status of the Translator revealed that most countries have anti-trust regulations that prohibit this (exceptions do exist, e.g., Austria and Switzerland). All member states of the European Economic Community (EEC) prohibit the publication of such recommendations, but there are two partial exceptions. In the Federal Republic of Germany, the Foreign Office regulations on the remuneration of freelance linguists; and in The Netherlands, officially registered and approved general conditions of contract that regulate the legal relationship between clients and members of the Dutch Association of Translators (NGV).

Social Security and Old-Age Pensions

The translator's situation with regard to social security and support in the event of sickness, accident, disability, and old age also differs from country to country. Salaried translators are found to be in a far better position than freelance translators.

Only a few countries have compulsory social insurance for freelancers or voluntary social security schemes for the translating profession. Freelance translators in the other countries are in a particularly difficult position, and far worse off than salaried translators as far as social security and old-age pensions are concerned. As their course of training is usually long, their economic performance is concentrated on a considerably shorter period than the average for the population in general. The time required for education and on-the-job training has become longer, and there is a trend toward even longer training periods in many places despite attempts to introduce reforms. The result is that the working life of the translator, particularly the academically-educated translator, is usually limited to 30-35 years, while about 50 years is normal in many other walks of life.

This has far-reaching consequences, especially in connection with the old-age pensions of freelance translators, as these have less time than others to build up reserves to maintain a certain standard of living after retirement. Because of this situation, and the often ruinous competition and fiscal disadvantages that hinder making provision for old age, many a freelance translator is obliged to work far beyond the normal retirement age in order to survive.

In this context, one outstanding example is worth mentioning, namely a newly introduced Polish law providing for pensions for writers and literary translators (see *Babel*, no. 2, 1976, p. 76, "Translations in Poland" by Zygmunt Stoberski).

Tax Law

In most of the reporting countries, translators are subject to the general tax laws, whereas some countries have special regulations applying to freelance translators (relief from business tax and turnover tax on scientific translators and reduced value-added tax rates).

Codes of Professional Conduct and Ethics; Professional Courts of Honor and Arbitration

A number of FIT member societies have codes of professional conduct and ethics regulating the rights and duties of the profession and courts of honor and arbitration to settle disputes concerning these, e.g., the American Translators Association, Translators Guild of Bulgaria, The Translators Guild (UK), West German Federal Association of Interpreters and Translators. Numerous other member associations have regulated these matters in their statutes. [See other entries in this Section.]

Summary and Conclusions

With the exception of the copyright protection granted to translators which is now reflected by the national legislations of many countries as a result of international agreements, there is little legislation to protect the translator and hence his security from the legal and social standpoints. Copyright protection alone is not enough to secure the legal and social status of the translator, regulating, as it does, only one aspect of the complex problem.

Only adequate national legislation can bring about considerable improvement in the translator's legal and social status. The national pro-

International Federation of Translators (FIT) (cont.)

fessional associations of translators will have to greatly intensify their efforts to obtain legislative action, concentrating primarily on legal regulation of admission to professional practice and improvement of the translator's security. A good basis for such efforts is to be found in the FIT Recommendation of 1977, as this touches upon the main problems of our profession and proposes means of improving the translator's status.

Legal Regulation

The problem of the legal regulation of professional practice is very complex because of the heterogeneous composition of the translating profession (salaried translators, freelance translators, literary translators, scientific-technical translators, conference interpreters and translators, court interpreters, etc.), and because of the differing interests of the groups that comprise the profession as a whole. The only common denominator that can be found is the requirement for personal and professional qualification in order to practice the profession, associated with commensurate remuneration for the services performed. Legal regulation of professional practice and protection of the title "Translator" is a reliable guarantee against continued exploitation of the translator by commercial plunderers of all types. The only way to remedy this situation and create order is to introduce legislative regulation, which should give consideration to the following aspects:

1. Admission criteria: proof of personal qualification and proof of linguistic and professional qualification (criteria such as minimum term of professional training, university or other academic graduation, many years of successful practical activity).

2. Rules for professional practice: the rights and duties of the translator; professional courts of honor and arbitration.

3. Rules on protection of the title "Translator."

4. Regulation of fees for freelance translator services (official scales of fees), including work and service contracts.

5. Legal measures or regulations ensuring the old-age security of freelance translators (inclusion in existing state pension plans or establishment of professional old-age pension plans with compulsory contributions).

This demand for legislative regulation of professional practice is fully in keeping with the Recommendation on the Legal Protection of Translators. It is the logical step toward implementing the UNESCO recommendations intended to secure the quality of translations and the professional training and qualification that are prerequisites to translation services of high quality.

Recommendation on the Legal Protection of Translators and Translations and the Practical Means to Improve the Status of Translators

The original text of this document was prepared over a number of years by member associations of FIT, then examined by an intergovernmental committee of technical experts which applied the finishing touches, and approved unanimously by UNESCO's 145 member states at a general conference held in Nairobi, Kenya, in November 1976. It covers every conceivable issue and contingency that affects or might affect translators and their professional activities. It defines the terms "translation, translator, and user" and the scope of application of these terms.

The General Conference of the United Nations Educational, Scientific and Cultural Organization, meeting in Nairobi from 26 October to 30 November 1976, at its nineteenth session,

Considering that translation promotes understanding between peoples and co-operation among nations by facilitating the dissemination of literary and scientific works, including technical works, across linguistic frontiers and the interchange of ideas,

Noting the extremely important role played by translators and translations in international exchanges in culture, art, and science, particularly in the case of works written or translated in less widely spoken languages,

Recognizing that the protection of translators is indispensable in order to ensure translations of the quality needed for them to fulfill effectively their role in the service of culture and development,

Recalling that, if the principles of this protection are already contained in the Universal Copyright Convention, while the Berne Convention for the Protection of Literary and Artistic Works and a number of national laws of Member States also contain specific provisions concerning such protection, the practical application of these principles and provisions is not always adequate,

Being of the opinion that if, in many countries with respect to copyright, translators and translations enjoy a protection which resembles the protection granted to authors and to literary and scientific works, including technical works, the adoption of measures of an essentially practical nature, assimilating translators to authors and specific to the translating profession, is nevertheless justified to ameliorate the effective application of existing laws,

Having decided, at its eighteenth session, that the protection of translators should be the subject of a recommendation to Member States within the meaning of Article IV, paragraph 4, of the Constitution,

Adopts, this twenty-second day of November 1976, the present Recommendation.

The General Conference recommends that Member States apply the following provisions concerning the protection of translators and translations by taking whatever legislative or other steps may be required, in conformity with the constitutional provisions and institutional practice of each State, to give effect, within their respective territories, to the principles and standards set forth in this Recommendation.

The General Conference recommends that Member States bring this Recommendation to the attention of the authorities, departments or bodies responsible for matters relating to the moral and material interests of translators and to the protection of translations, of the various organizations or associations representing or promoting the interests of translators, and of publishers, managers of theatres, broadcasters and other users and interested parties.

The General Conference recommends that Member States submit to the Organization, at such times and in such forms as shall be determined by the General Conference, reports on the action taken by them to give effect to this Recommendation.

I. Definitions and Scope of Application

1. For purposes of this Recommendation:

(a) the term "translation" denotes the transposition of a literary or scientific work, including technical work, from one language into another language, whether or not the initial work, or the translation, is intended for publication in book, magazine, periodical, or other form, or for performance in the theatre, in a film, on radio or television, or in any other media;

(b) the term "translators" denotes translators of literary or scientific works, including technical works;

(c) the term "users" denotes the persons or legal entities for which a translation is made.

2. This Recommendation applies to all translators regardless of:

(a) the legal status applicable to them as: (i) independent translators; or (ii) salaried translators;

(b) the discipline to which the work translated belongs;

(c) the full-time or part-time nature of their position as translators.

II. General Legal Position of Translators

3. Member States should accord to translators, in respect of their translations, the protection accorded to authors under the provisions of the international copyright conventions to which they are party and/or under their national laws, but without prejudice to the rights of the authors of the original works translated.

III. Measures to Ensure the Application in Practice of Protection Afforded Translators under International Conventions and in National Laws Relating to Copyright

4. It is desirable that a written agreement be concluded between a translator and the user.

5. As a general rule, a contract governing relations between a translator and a user, as well as where appropriate any other legal instrument governing such relations, should:

(a) accord an equitable remuneration to the translator whatever his or her legal status;

(b) at least when the translator is not working as a salaried translator, remunerate him or her in proportion to the proceeds of the sale or use of the translation with payment of an advance, the said advance being retained by the translator whatever the proceeds may be; or by the payment of a sum calculated in conformity with another system of remuneration independent of sales where it is provided for or permitted by national legislation; or by the payment of an equitable lump sum which could be made where payment on a proportional basis proves insufficient or inapplicable; the appropriate method of payment should be chosen taking into account the legal system of the country concerned and where applicable the type of original work translated;

(c) make provision, when appropriate, for a supplementary payment should the use made of the translation go beyond the limitations specified in the contract;

(d) specify that the authorizations granted by the translator are limited to the rights expressly mentioned, this provision applying to possible new editions;

(e) stipulate that in the event that the translator has not obtained any necessary authorization, it is the user who is responsible for obtaining such authorization;

(f) stipulate that the translator guarantees the user uncontested enjoyment of all rights granted and undertakes to refrain from any action likely to compromise the legitimate interests of the user and, when appropriate, to observe the rule of professional secrecy;

(g) stipulate that, subject to the prerogatives of the author of the original work translated, no change shall be made in the text of a translation intended for publication without seeking the prior agreement of the translator;

(h) assure the translator and his translation similar publicity, proportionately to that which authors are generally given, in particular, the name of the author of the translation should appear in a prominent place on all published copies of the translation, on theatre bills, in announcements made in connection with radio or television broadcasts, in the credit titles of films and in any other promotional material;

(i) provide that the user ensure that the translation bear such notices as are necessary to comply with copyright formalities in those countries where it might reasonably be expected to be used;

(j) provide for the resolution of any conflicts which may arise, particularly with respect to the quality of the translation, so far as possible, by means of arbitration or in accordance with procedures laid down by national legislation or by any other appropriate means of dispute settlement which on the one hand is such as to guarantee impartiality and on the other hand is easily accessible and inexpensive;

(k) mention the languages from and into which the translator will translate and without prejudice to the provisions of paragraph 1 (a), further specify expressly the translator's possible use as an interpreter.

6. In order to facilitate the implementation of the measures recommended in paragraphs 4, 5, and 14, Member States should, without prejudice to the translator's freedom to enter into an individual contract, encourage the parties concerned, in particular the professional organizations of translators and other organizations or associations representing them, on the one hand, and the representatives of users, on the other, to adopt model contracts or to conclude collective agreements based on the measures suggested in this Recommendation and making due allowances for all situations likely to arise by reason either of the translator or of the nature of the translation.

7. Member States should also promote measures to ensure effective representation of translators and to encourage the creation and development of professional organizations of translators and other organizations or associations representing them, to define the rules and duties which should govern the exercise of the profession, to defend the moral and material interests of translators and to facilitate linguistic, cultural, scientific and technical exchanges among translators and between translators and the authors of works to be translated. To this end, such organizations or associations might undertake, where national law permits, in particular, the following specific activities:

(a) promote the adoption of standards governing the translating profession; such standards should stipulate in particular that the translator has a duty to provide a translation of high quality from both the linguistic and stylistic points of view and to guarantee that the translation will be a faithful rendering of the original;

(b) study the bases for remuneration acceptable to translators and users;

(c) set up procedures to assist in the settlement of disputes arising in connection with the quality of translations;

(d) advise translators in their negotiations with users and cooperate with other interested parties in establishing model contracts relating to translation;

(e) endeavor to arrange for translators individually or collectively, and in accordance with national laws or any collective agreements which may be applicable on this subject, to benefit with authors from funds received from either private or public sources;

(f) provide for exchanges of information on matters of interest to translators by the publication of information bulletins, the organization of meetings or by other appropriate means;

(g) promote the assimilation of translators, from the point of view of social benefits and taxation, to authors of literary or scientific works, including technical works;

(h) promote the establishment and development of specialized programs for the training of translators;

(i) cooperate with other national, regional, or international bodies working to promote the interests of translators, and with any national or regional copyright information centers set up to assist in the clearance of rights in works protected by copyright, as well as with the UNESCO International Copyright Information Center;

(j) maintain close contacts with users, as well as with their representatives or professional organizations or associations, in order to defend the interests of translators; and negotiate collective agreements with such representatives or organizations or associations where deemed advantageous;

(k) contribute generally to the development of the translating profession.

8. Without prejudice to paragraph 7, membership of professional organizations or associations which represent translators should not, however, be a necessary condition for protection, since the provisions of this Recommendation should apply to all translators, whether or not they are members of such organizations or associations.

IV. Social and Fiscal Situation of Translators

9. Translators working as independent writers, whether or not they are paid by royalties, should benefit in practice from any social insurance schemes relating to retirement, illness, family allowances, etc., and from any taxation arrangements, generally applicable to the authors or literary or scientific works, including technical works.

10. Salaried translators should be treated on the same basis as other salaried professional staff and benefit accordingly from the social schemes provided for them. In this respect, professional statutes, collective agreements, and contracts of employment based thereon should mention expressly the class of translators of scientific and technical texts, so that their status as translators may be recognized, particularly with respect to their professional classification.

V. Training and Working Conditions of Translators

11. Member States should recognize in principle that translation is an independent discipline requiring an education distinct from exclusive language teaching and that this discipline requires special training. Member States should encourage the establishment of writing programs for translators, especially in connection with translators' professional organizations or associations, universities or other educational institutions, and the organization of seminars or workshops. It should also be recognized that it is useful for translators to be able to benefit from continuing education courses.

12. Member States should consider organizing terminology centers which might be encouraged to undertake the following activities:

(a) communicating to translators current information concerning terminology required by them in the general course of their work;

(b) collaborating closely with terminology centers throughout the world with a view to standardizing and developing the internationalization of scientific and technical terminology so as to facilitate the task of translators.

13. In association with professional organizations or associations and other interested parties, Member States should facilitate exchanges of translators between different countries, so as to allow them to improve their knowledge of the language from which they work and of the socio-cultural context in which the works to be translated by them are written.

14. With a view to improving the quality of translations, the following principles and practical measures should be expressly recognized in

International Federation of Translators (FIT) (cont.)

professional statutes mentioned under sub-paragraph 7 (a) and in any other written agreements between the translators and the users;

(a) translators should be given a reasonable period of time to accomplish their work;

(b) any documents and information necessary for the understanding of the text to be translated and the drafting of the translation should, so far as possible, be made available to translators;

(c) as a general rule, a translation should be made from the original work, recourse being had to retranslation only where absolutely necessary;

(d) a translator should, as far as possible, translate into his own mother tongue or into a language of which he or she has a mastery equal to that of his or her mother tongue.

15. The principles and norms set forth in this Recommendation may be adapted by developing countries in any way deemed necessary to help them meet their requirements, and in the light of the special provisions for the benefit of developing countries introduced in the Universal Copyright Convention as revised at Paris on 24 July 1971 and the Paris Act (1971) of the Berne Convention for the Protection of Literary and Artistic Works.

VII. Final Provision

16. Where translators and translations enjoy a level of protection which is, in certain aspects, more favorable than that provided for in this Recommendation, its provision should not be invoked to diminish the protection already acquired.

Resolutions Adopted at the VIII Congress, 1977 (extracts)

Resolution II: a recommendation that (1) national member societies of FIT should bring the UNESCO "Recommendation on the Legal Protection of Translators and Translations . . ." to the attention of their respective national authorities, departments, or bodies responsible for matters relating to the moral and material interests of translators; (2) national member societies of FIT should urge their respective national authorities, departments, or bodies responsible for matters relating to the moral and material interests of translators to give effect to the principles and standards set forth in the UNESCO "Recommendation," in particular by the introduction of laws and implementing regulations to include, inter alia, stipulations and provisions concerning qualification criteria and requirements, rights, and duties of translators as well as the authority granted to professional organizations and bodies of translators to establish model contracts and rates relating to translation and the conclusion of wage tariff agreements; (3) national member societies of FIT submit to the competent FIT Committee for Translator's Legal and Social Status reports on the action taken and the results achieved by them; such national reports to be communicated to all member societies of FIT and to be evaluated by the said Committee and reported to the next World Congress for consideration and further action.

Resolution IV: the literary translators present, (1) realizing the important part played by *Babel*, urge all member societies to support this organ by keeping its board fully and regularly informed about their activities and by encouraging their members to contribute articles, reviews, and notes. . . . ; (2) realizing the practical value of an SOS service, first on a national and subsequently on an international scale, urge all member societies to take active steps towards the organization of such a service, and to keep the chairman of the Commission on Literary Translators informed on progress made along these lines; (3) welcoming the suggestion of the publication of an anthology of European poetry, to be followed by similar works covering Latin America, North America, Africa, and Asia, call on member societies to submit masterpieces of poetry in translation from their own countries to the chairman of the Commission on Literary Translation; (4) call on member societies to encourage the organization of international conferences of literary translators, with FIT participation, between this and the next Congress, to discuss common problems; (5) urge all member societies to work towards the conclusion of bilateral agreements between member societies,

to promote closer contacts exchange of experience, and the exchange of translators for limited periods; (6) welcome the news of the project of a Literary Translation College to be set up in the Federal Republic of Germany and urge all member societies to support this project in every possible way; (7) call on the organizers of future congresses again to provide ample space in the congress programs for progress reports on the current state of translation theory and its relevance to translation practice; (8) realizing the economic difficulties frequently encountered in the publication of translated works, urge all member societies to use their best efforts—both with their own governments and with institutions, foundations, etc.—to obtain subsidies which would enable the publication of deserving works in translation; (9) realizing the inadequacy of the remuneration for certain types of literary translation and bearing in mind the great publicity value of translation prizes, urge all member societies to induce public or private sources of money in their countries to set up more prizes for outstanding translations.

Resolution VI: that (1) in order to fit training programs to the needs of employees and clients, more research be undertaken to clarify the criteria and standards that determine so-called "good" translations in the various fields; (2) all training courses and degrees in translation include a practicum, i.e., a period of practical working experience alongside an experienced translator; (3) if it is possible for them to do so without undue financial burden, translation students spend a year in the country or the cultural milieu of their second language, and some period in the country or milieu of their third language; (4) FIT and UNESCO work together to stimulate the setting-up of international scholarships and exchange programs for translation students, teachers, and professors, and for working translators wishing to improve their professional qualifications.

Resolution VII: (1) considering the common objective in certain regional areas where other languages prevail, with substantially different interests; considering the difficulty in communicating effectively with the Secretary of FIT frequently on the part of the countries in geographically remote areas; and considering what has been accomplished by FIT over the past years and the global tasks it is expected to perform in the immediate future, FIT shall have its Regional Committees for Asian-Oceanic, Latin-American, and African areas under the chairmanship of the FIT Committee for the Developing Countries . . . who will coordinate the efforts of the countries concerned in respective regions and the endeavors of the national societies now in existence or to be organized in the future. . . .

Resolution IX: that FIT urge comparatists to increase the systematic teaching and study of the history, theory, and practice of literary translation—this motion to be transmitted to the International Comparative Literature Association (ICLA), American Comparative Literature Association (ACLA), Canadian Comparative Literature Association (CCLA).

Resolution X: a clause to be inserted in all translation contracts, whether literary or scientific, namely, that no such translation may be published before proofs of the said translation—which has been submitted to and accepted by a publisher—have been read, approved, and signed by the translator.

Further to this, nothing should either be added to or deleted from the translation by others, without the signed agreement of the translator.

Resolution XII: in view of the fact that machines and/or computers are playing and will continue to play an important role in the field of translation, FIT and its affiliates should examine and publish the availability of suitable computer training centers. While present pioneers in the field have become more knowledgeable in direct proportion to the expansion of the system itself, future members of the profession will have to have an advance knowledge of it, if they are to profit from it. Therefore, (1) FIT inquires, where such training centers exist: prerequisites for participation in the program, costs and length of the program, specific skills to be obtained; (2) FIT and its affiliates publish these findings in their respective journals; (3) if no such programs are available for the members of the profession (but only to private institutions and their employees), FIT encourages institution of such programs and keeping its members posted on any program in this field.

Resolution XIII: considering that new possibilities to translate mean raising of the living standards of the translators, the board of FIT and all member societies should draw attention to the new fields of enlarging translating activity. Member societies should urge private, governmental, and other official or semiofficial institutions interested in translation, to exploit all new fields and possibilities to enlarge translation activity.

International Organization for Standardization (ISO)

International Standard ISO 2603-1974 (E): Booths for Simultaneous Interpretation—General Characteristics and Equipment

This standard was initiated as the result of a request from the International Association of Conference Interpreters (AIIC). During the course of its preparation, reference was made to earlier studies made by this Association and to observations made on recent installations.

The design of interpretation booths is governed by three requirements: (1) acoustically separating of different languages spoken simultaneously; (2) providing good two-way communication between the booths and the conference hall; (3) placing the interpreters, whose booths are their work-place, in conditions of comfort that will enable them to continue to exert the intense effort of concentration required of them.

Copies of this Standard, which discusses all aspects of interpretation booths (accessibility, size, windows, acoustics, air conditioning, lighting, working surfaces, seating, control panels, microphones, etc.), are available from ISO, 1 rue de Varembe, CP, CH-1211 Geneva, Switzerland.

Literary Translators' Association of Canada

Model Translation Agreement for Book Publication

This model agreement was prepared in 1977 and distributed to participants of the VIII World Congress of the International Federation of Translators (FIT), held in Montreal, Canada, in May 1977. The document is accompanied by a "Guide to Negotiations," intended to be used as an adjunct to the form of agreement. Both are addressed primarily to Association members, but should prove informative to all translators and publishers in the English-speaking world as well.

Agreement

Between: *(Publisher's name and address)*_____ and: *(Translator's name and address)*_____ it is agreed that:

1. *(Purpose of the agreement)* The PUBLISHER has commissioned the TRANSLATOR to translate a text of _____ words contained in the work entitled _____ written by _____. The translation of said text is hereinafter called the WORK.

2. *(Translator's obligations)* The TRANSLATOR undertakes to furnish a faithful and careful translation conforming to the standards upheld by the Literary Translators' Association. He will submit the text of the WORK before the _____ day of _____, 19_____, barring unforeseen circumstances beyond his control (force majeure).

If the manuscript is not delivered by the above date, the PUBLISHER may demand its delivery, in writing, allowing six months' grace, after which period, if delivery has still not been made, the PUBLISHER may terminate this agreement in writing delivered to the TRANSLATOR, who shall then return the sum paid to him under Clause 5.

3. *(Force majeure)* If the TRANSLATOR is obliged to leave his work incomplete for reasons beyond his control, he will so advise the PUBLISHER. The latter shall pay him an amount proportionate to that part of the WORK delivered.

4. *(Fixed payment)* The PUBLISHER undertakes to pay the TRANSLATOR the sum of _____ dollars, calculated in the following manner: _____.

5. *(Manner of payment)* The PUBLISHER undertakes to pay the TRANSLATOR the sum of _____ dollars at the time of signing the present agreement, which amount shall be not less than one third of the sum prescribed in Clause 4.

6. The remainder of the sum prescribed in Clause 4 will be paid in the following manner: _____.

7. *(Unilateral breaking of agreement by publisher)* The TRANSLATOR shall be entitled to an amount proportionate to that part of the WORK completed in the event that this agreement is breached by the PUBLISHER. Said amount shall in no circumstances be inferior to the amount mentioned in Clause 5.

8. *(Translator's responsibility)* The TRANSLATOR will not be held responsible for loss or consequential damages resulting from the exploitation of the WORK, but is responsible for any errors or omissions in translation.

9. *(Copyright)* The copyright to the WORK shall be registered in the TRANSLATOR's name.

10. *(Royalties)* Besides the sum provided for in Clause 4, the PUBLISHER shall pay the TRANSLATOR a royalty equivalent to _____ percent of the price indicated in his catalogue on each book sold in excess of _____ copies. He shall provide the TRANSLATOR with twice-yearly statements of monies received or receivable relating in any way to the WORK.

11. *(Resale rights)* If the PUBLISHER sells the WORK to another publisher, or licenses another publisher to publish the WORK, the PUBLISHER shall undertake to pay or to cause such other publisher to pay to the TRANSLATOR the royalty provided for in Clause 10.

12. *(Subsidiary rights)* The TRANSLATOR shall retain subsidiary rights accruing from the exploitation of the work.

13. *(Non-publication or failure to reprint)* If the PUBLISHER does not publish the WORK within _____ months of its acceptance by him or if, the WORK being out of print, the PUBLISHER does not republish it within one year of notice from the TRANSLATOR of his intent to invoke this clause, the TRANSLATOR shall regain full disposition of the rights to his WORK.

14. *(Correction of manuscript by the translator)* The TRANSLATOR shall have the right to make corrections to his entire text before it is sent to the typesetter, especially where the manuscript has been submitted in sections.

15. *(Corrections made by the publisher)* The TRANSLATOR shall see and approve any editorial changes made by the PUBLISHER in his text before said text is sent to the typesetter. No deduction from the sum mentioned in Clause 4 shall be made as a result of any such corrections. The TRANSLATOR shall likewise approve the title of the WORK in writing.

16. *(Correction of printed text)* The TRANSLATOR shall have the right to see all printer's proofs of the text and to make such corrections as he deems necessary or desirable. He shall, however, reimburse the PUBLISHER for any typesetting costs for which he is responsible in excess of ten percent of the initial cost of typesetting. The PUBLISHER must provide the TRANSLATOR with pertinent written evidence of such excess cost.

17. *(Return of manuscript and proofs)* The PUBLISHER shall return to the TRANSLATOR the manuscript of the WORK and all printer's proofs corrected by the TRANSLATOR.

18. *(Changes required by the author and publisher)* Any changes in the text to be translated, after the translation has started, shall be counted as additional text at the agreed rate, provided such changes are not made necessary by an error or omission on the TRANSLATOR's part.

19. *(Supplementary material requested by the publisher)* Supplementary material required by the PUBLISHER (Introduction or Preface written by the TRANSLATOR, compiling of an index or bibliography, etc.) shall be remunerated separately.

20. *(Translator's name)* The TRANSLATOR's name or pseudonym shall appear on the cover, title page, and jacket of the WORK, and in all advertisements, press releases, and review slips pertaining to the WORK.

21. *(Free copies)* The TRANSLATOR shall receive _____ complimentary copies of his WORK, and shall have the right to buy additional copies at the normal author's discount.

22. *(Cooperation from the publisher)* For any questions pertaining to the text, the TRANSLATOR should consult _____. The PUBLISHER will assist the TRANSLATOR to communicate with the author if necessary.

23. The present agreement replaces and rescinds any previous agreements pertaining to the WORK.

Made this _____ day of _____, 19____.

PUBLISHER _____ TRANSLATOR _____

Guide to Negotiations

Translation for Book Publication

We use the word "agreement" in preference to "contract" since "agreement" is less restrictive than "contract" and any omission noted after signing may be corrected by supplementary agreement. It will be apparent that not all clauses of the agreement are applicable in every case. It will also be apparent that some translators will be able to obtain better terms than others.

Literary Translators' Association of Canada (cont.)

Word Count   The Association recommends that the word count of the source language text be included in the agreement.

Fee Calculation   In Canadian practice, this word count is normally the basis of fee calculation. The rate per word is left to the individual translator, with the observation that the maximum rate for Canada Council grants to publishers for aid to translation is 5¢ per word. A minimum of 6¢ is therefore not unreasonable. For long-term agreements a cost of living adjustment provisions may be desirable.

Force majeure   An unforeseeable and unavoidable event which prevents fulfillment of an obligation. Examples: strike, illness, death, earthquake, blizzard, flood, war, insurrection, etc.

Notification of Grant   The Canada Council agrees that the translator should be advised of the amount of its grant to the publisher for his translation. He has a right to this notification and should insist that he receive it. The Association considers that the notification should include the word-count basis of the grant.

Modalities of payment   The practice is very diverse. A suggestion is a third in advance, a third on delivery of the manuscript, a third within 30 days of acceptance of the manuscript. Some publishers prefer 1/2 in advance, 1/2 on acceptance. Whatever the formula, the Association suggests insistence on an advance and payment to be completed within 30 days of acceptance.

Delivery of the manuscript in installments, with proportionate installment payments, may be considered appropriate; e.g., delivery in thirds of the total, the first covered by an advance of a third, and the balance to be paid for in two more payments of a third, each due within a stated time after delivery of the remaining installments of the manuscript.

Royalty basis fee   Where the basis of the fee is royalties, there should be an adequate non-refundable advance. Optimism can be poorly rewarded.

Downward adjustments   There should be no withholding of any portion of the fee for "editorial expenses," meaning copy editing or minor revisions. Where a translation proves to be inadequate and a second translator must be engaged to revise it, it is reasonable for a portion of the fee to be applied to the cost incurred. The Canada Council makes these two points clear where its grants are concerned. The Literary Translators' Association is prepared to arrange independent evaluation in case of disagreement over the quality of the work.

Additional payments   The Association considers the following to be appropriate additions to the basic agreement for the translator of recognized competence:

Royalty   In consideration of the translator's contribution to the success of a book which is exceptionally well received by the public, the translator should receive, in addition to the basic fee, a royalty of 2-1/2 % of the retail price of the book on sales beyond 5000 copies (the Guild of Professional Translators in the U.S. recommends 3% on sales after 3000 copies); for the translation of a work in the public domain (50 years after the death of the author), the standard author's royalty (usually 10 to 15%). He should receive regular sales reports.

Subsidiary rights   The translator should have the right to compensation for the use of his work for subsidiary purposes, i.e., reprints (including school and deluxe editions, book club and paperback editions), serial rights, anthology, excerpts and abridgments (except for review and promotion), and also use in other media (radio, television, theater, etc.) and commercial use (not book promotion) depending on circumstances. In some countries a distinction is made between subsidiary rights (reprints, etc.) and derived rights (other media, etc.).

Non-publication   In our opinion the waiting period before recovery of rights should be 12 to 18 months.

Translator's responsibility   Both the publisher and the translator should have read the text to be translated before signing an agreement. Clause 8 asserts the translator's responsibility for his own errors and omissions but assures that he cannot be held responsible for consequential damages in case, for instance, of libel arising from the content or tone of a book.

The purpose and scope of the book should be clearly agreed upon, in particular the language register to be used (level and quality of language); the registers for a popularization and for a learned treatise in the same field, for instance, will be very different; the precise readership for whom the text is intended may not be self-evident.

The translator should not agree to translate a text which he is in-capable of translating. Nor should he agree to translate a poor text; if he does, he risks being blamed for the shortcomings of the original text. If a translator is willing to accommodate a publisher who insists on having a poor text translated, and agrees to edit or adapt as well as translate, his authority to do so should be firmly established in the understanding of the author, his additional responsibility clearly stated in the agreement, and his fee adjusted appropriately.

The translator must have control over his text. Editorial changes must have his consent.

The translator may wish to substitute "last galley proofs" for "all proofs," but should realize that this will reduce the extent of his control. He may need to remind his editor which proofs he should see. Copy editing is not his responsibility but he should exercise great vigilance in proof correction to assure that his work is presented to the best advantage.

The manuscript and corrected printer's proof may in the future have a certain market value.

Length of translation   There seems to be a widespread conviction that English translations are shorter than French original texts and the corollary. This is a myth and should be laid to rest. A translated text in either direction tends if anything to be longer than the original, though it may be shorter depending on the subject and style of the author. For practical purposes the two should be expected to be approximately the same.

Supplementary material   Introductions, etc., provided by the translator should be considered as separate from the translation and paid for additionally. *Indexes* can be exceedingly complicated and time consuming. Translators would best involve themselves only with their translation, not even their alphabetical rearrangement. Regarding *bibliographical material*, translators should realize that the bibliographical style of the author may require adaptation in order to conform to that laid down by the publisher. If new bibliographical material is considered appropriate, the translator may accept total or partial responsibility for it but should not be obliged to do so.

Recognition   The translator's name should appear on the cover, jacket, and title page of the published translation, in blurbs and all publicity and promotional material, on review slips sent out with books for review. When the translated work is reproduced in whole or in part, the translator's name and full title of the book should appear whenever the author's name appears. If a translation has undergone major revision by a second translator, the Association considers it appropriate, as is the practice in many countries, for the translator's name not to appear on the cover, jacket, or title page but on some other page, or else for the revisor's name to appear as co-translator. The revisor should insist on some such arrangement.

Copyright   The Association is of the opinion that copyright to the translation should be in the translator's name. Under present Canadian copyright law, the translator has no rights over his translation in the absence of stipulation in his agreement with the publisher. The Association has already submitted a recommendation in anticipation of the law's revision, and will make further representations at the appropriate time.

A translator, in obtaining copyright to his work, should ascertain what that copyright consists of. The author, in his original contract, often retains no continuing interest in anticipation of translation, and the publisher may sell the translation rights outright to a second. If the author does retain a continuing interest, the terms may restrict freedom of movement in the use of the translation for subsidiary purposes, or in its transfer to another publisher in case of nonpublication or failure to reprint.

Copyright may be registered, prior to publication, for a fee of $10, with the Copyright and Industrial Design Branch, Bureau of Intellectual Property, Department of Consumer and Corporate Affairs, Place du Portage, Hull, Québec. Such registration is not necessary, however, *if* the copyright symbol © appears beside the translator's name in the book. But if it does not, he does not have copyright. Whether or not registration has been made, if copyright is included in his agreement and the symbol does not appear in the book beside his name, he should consult a lawyer.

Free copies   Some publishers, but by no means all, seem to consider that a translator should be grateful to receive even a single copy of his published translation. Some translators already receive ten copies, and the Association considers six to ten to be a reasonable expectation, with purchase terms in any event equal to the author's.

Author cooperation   This does not seem to be a widespread problem, but when it arises it is serious. A translator urgently needs the cooperation of the author, no matter how impeccable his text may be. Some authors do not realize that the difference between the source and target languages often necessitate clarification of the thought behind the text; on the other hand, some, having an inflated idea of their own understanding of the target language, attempt to impose undue literality on the translator. Publishers should impress on authors the importance of their cooperation with and availability to the translator, but discourage intervention to an extent which undermines the exercise of the translator's judgment.

Additional remarks   Certain of the clauses in the agreement cover matters of fundamental policy to which the Association attaches great importance.

Identification of the translator's name with his work is not only a right due the translator but a right due the public; it is acknowledgment of responsibility on the translator's part. The quality of the translation can make or break the author's work in another language, and the translator's name therefore follows closely behind the author's in importance.

The translator's right of control over his text (Clauses 14 to 17) is also fundamental, presuming adequate quality. While the conscientious translator will be grateful for suggestions leading to minor improvements, he is the best judge of the author's intentions. Editorial interference without the translator's consent is altogether unacceptable. It is likewise unthinkable that the book title not be subject to the translator's approval. (Clause 15)

The Association is aware that on occasion there is disagreement on the acceptability of a translation, and envisages the establishment of a procedure for adjudication of such cases, and possibly other disputes, under conditions acceptable to publishers.

The proposal of royalties for translators (Clauses 10 to 12) is the one most likely to encounter hostility on the part of certain publishers. The Association points out that under the terms proposed (2-1/2 on sales over 5000 copies) the royalties accruing to the translator will be nil except in exceedingly rare cases. Even then, the sums involved are modest to say the least: sales of 5,100 copies of a $5 book, $12.50; sales of 5,500, $62.50; sales of 6,000, $125. The provisions proposed envisage only the outside chance of best-seller sales, in which case the success will certainly be largely attributable to the skill of the translator.

In the agreement, Clauses 1 to 8 inclusive and Clauses 14, 15, 16, 18 and 19 should be considered non-negotiable. Clauses 17, 20 and 21 should not decently be refused. Clauses 9 to 15 inclusive are highly desirable but perhaps unobtainable at the moment from certain publishers.

New York State Supreme Court

January 9, 1975 Decision Granting a Translator Exemption of Payment of the Unincorporated Business Tax

In 1972 the New York State Tax Commission ruled that Arthur Tannenbaum, an established practicing translator and interpreter, was required to pay an Unincorporated Business Tax for the years 1966 and 1967. The Commission's determination was based on its contention that the petitioner was not engaged in the practice of a profession, and that the State requires a license in order to engage in a profession.

On January 9, 1975, the Appellate Division of the New York State Supreme Court reversed the Commission's ruling, affirming that "petitioner was engaged in the practice of a profession and was thus entitled to exemption from assessment of unincorporated business taxes." Although other translators are known to have filed unsuccessful briefs contesting the Tax Commission's rulings, none of them are known to have sought a court ruling to test the Commission's rulings.

Inasmuch as the landmark decision may have far-reaching consequences for all translators and interpreters in the United States who meet established professional standards, and, in the words of Arthur Tannebaum, "brings the translator and interpreter a step closer to recognition as a profession," the full text of the decision by Hon. J. Clarence Herlihy, Presiding Justice, State of New York Supreme Court, Appellate Division, Third Judicial Department, is reproduced here.

Petitioner was a translator and interpreter during the years of 1966 and 1967. He attended the Geneva University Interpreter's School in Geneva, Switzerland, from 1946 to 1950, receiving a diploma as a translator-interpreter of German, French, and English after extensive language studies and 48 courses in translation and interpretation, plus numerous courses in law, international law, and history. In 1957 he received a Bachelor of Arts degree from the College of the City of New York. He is a member of the American Translators Association. Petitioner's services were rendered to government agencies, law firms, and corporations, and his income derived from translating and interpreting from one language to another with respect to testimony in court, court documents, technical texts, and scientific dissertations. The State Tax Commission has determined that petitioner's activities as a translator and interpreter did not constitute the practice of a profession within the purview of subdivision (c) of section 703 of the Tax Law.

The sole issue presented is whether petitioner was engaged in the practice of a profession exempt from the unincorporated business tax. This is a question of law. (*Matter of Voorhees* v. *Bates*, 308 N.Y. 184, 188.)

Traditionally, and by Commission regulation, the definition of a profession includes "any occupation or vocation in which a professed knowledge of some department of science or learning, gained by a prolonged course of specialized instruction and study, is used by its practical application to the affairs of others, either advising, guiding or teaching them, and in serving their interest or welfare in the practice of an art or science founded on it." (*Matter of Geiffert* v. *Mealey*, 293 N.Y. 583, 585; 20 NYCRR 203.11) We have recently listed factors which should also be taken into consideration in determining whether certain activities constitute the practice of a profession. (*Matter of Rosenbloom* v. *State Tax Comm.*, 44 A D 2nd 69.) Even more recently, this court has concluded that, in addition, the services performed must involve something more than the type generally performed by those in the broader categories of a trade, business, or occupation. (*Matter of Koner* v. *Procaccino*, _____ A D 2nd _____ October 31, 1974.)

We conclude that petitioner's vocation as a translator and interpreter fulfills the requirements of a profession. The record establishes that during the years under review he was devoted in his work to public service in a traditionally professional sense. His service of spontaneous and accurate translation and interpretation of a foreign language was vital, not only in courts of record, but in international forums. His is a science of learning, the knowledge of which can be acquired only after a prolonged course of specialized study, instruction, and experience. The record reveals that petitioner's diploma from the University of Geneva is tantamount to a degree in translating and interpreting now being conferred at such university and at American colleges and universities. Although licensing of a translator and interpreter is not presently required, this is only one factor which should be given consideration (*Matter of Rosenbloom* v. *State Tax Comm.*, supra). The requirement by the State of a license in order to engage in a profession is not necessarily a satisfactory standard by which to classify the nature of an occupation. (*Matter of Teague* v. *Graves*, 261 App. Div. 652, 655, affd. 287 N.Y. 549.) That petitioner clearly was qualified and legally authorized to practice a profession is well demonstrated by the record. Nor do we find it fatal that petitioner wrote no books or articles in the field of interpreting and translating and did not engage in the teaching of these subjects, a factor upon which respondent apparently placed great emphasis in reaching its determination. Petitioner's knowledge and skill were applied to the affairs of others in serving their interests by bridging the gaps caused by language barriers in highly technical and scientific matters.

In our opinion, under all the circumstances, respondent's determination is without legal basis and contrary to law, and should be annulled. Petitioner was engaged in the practice of a profession and thus entitled to exemption from assessment of unincorporated business taxes for the years in question.

This determination should be annulled, and the matter remitted for further proceedings not inconsistent herewith, with costs.

PEN American Center

Bill of Rights (by Ivan Morris & Robert Payne, 1968)

Since translation of works of literature by the very nature of the task is the creation of a new work, the translator must be regarded as sovereign. The translator's chief obligation is to create the work in a new lan-

PEN American Center (cont.)

guage with the appropriate music and the utmost response to the silences of the original. The unit of translation is the entire work: and the imagination of the translation is concerned above all with this unity.

The privileges of the translator therefore include the right to be regarded as the maker of a new work, and he should be recompensed accordingly. His name shall be given a proper prominence, and he shall possess continuing rights over his work during its life. The honor of translation demands that translators of literary works shall in future be regarded as artists rather than as skilled craftsmen.

Manifesto on Translation

The following document was drawn up by the American PEN Translation Committee (see Sec 2, USA), whose then chairman, Robert Payne, has been one of this country's most fervent fighters for "the translator's rights"—and, in fairness to the investing publisher, "the translator's obligations to the publisher." Dated September 1969, the Manifesto was first made public and distributed at the 36th International PEN Congress in Menton, France, and was later published in The World of Translation *(NY: PEN American Center, 1971), a report on the proceedings of the Conference on Literary Translation, New York City, 1970.*

A Call for Action. The time has come for translators to come out into the open and to agree on a common course of action. For too long they have been the lost children in the enchanted forest of literature. Their names are usually forgotten, they are grotesquely underpaid, and their services, however, skilfully rendered, are regarded with the slightly patronizing and pitying respect formerly reserved for junior housemaids.

Our culture, and indeed all cultures, are thoroughly rooted in translation, and the translator is the unacknowledged vehicle by which civilizations are brought about. We could have no Bible without Tyndale, no Proust without Scott-Moncrieff, no *Tale of Genji* without Arthur Waley. Most of what we know of the past has come to us through translation, and much of our future will inevitably depend on translation. We are the heirs of all the cultures of the past only because the translators have made these cultures available, and without the translator, the lost child, we are all lost.

Too often the translator is brushed aside as though he were some mechanical contrivance adept at converting one language into another. Since he is often poor, it is assumed that he came to his poverty honorably; and his name, if it appears at all, is usually printed in small type, in accordance with his reputation for humility. Reviewers rarely notice his existence. Publishers in their advertisements rarely pay any attention to him. Since the reviewer is the public's sole guide to the quality of the translation, and since only the publisher can give prominence to the translator's name, he remains largely anonymous and the quality of his work is unknown. As a consequence, the translator finds himself far too often in a shadowy no man's land, where he is scarcely distinguishable from the shadows.

Who knows the names of translators? Who cares? Yet the names deserve to be known, and it is necessary that we should care about them. It is absurd that they should be relegated to their own private no man's land, with no court of appeal and without recourse to the usual benefices reserved for authors. They are the proletarians of literature with nothing to lose but their chains.

The duties of translators are well known. Since the time of the first translators, they have always argued that their task was to make a faithful rendering of the works they are translating. They know that it is not enough to convey the substance of these originals accurately; they must employ all their gifts of imagination and resourcefulness to make versions which mirror the original rhythms, assonances, structure and style. A sentence in Japanese, for example, has to be examined patiently, broken up into its separate parts and then refashioned before it can be expressed in English; and what is true of Japanese is equally true of all oriental languages, and to a lesser extent of all modern European languages. Translation is therefore reconstruction and re-creation, a creative act of immense difficulty and complexity. A translator may spend hours unraveling and recreating a single paragraph. He must somehow suggest the rhythm and structure of the original, and write in a style that conveys the style of the original. He must have a deep and far-reaching knowledge of two languages. The original author is luckier: he needs to know only one language.

Ideally, the best writers should be asked to make translations, and

every good writer should at one time or another assume the burden of translation. Rilke translated Paul Valéry, Baudelaire translated Edgar Allan Poe, Dostoyevsky translated Balzac: but such happy conjunctions are very rare. In our own time great works of literature have been translated too often by writers with an insufficient command of the resources of the English language, but on the whole the level of translation has been higher than we had any right to expect under prevailing conditions. Obviously there are reasons why good writers often refuse to embark on translation. The rewards are small, the work arduous, the time can be spent more profitably. Nevertheless, the standard of translations improves every year, and every year there are more and more dedicated translators.

The duties of a translator are well known, but his rights have never been satisfactorily formulated. The American PEN Translation Committee believes that the time has come to re-examine the situation. A Bill of Rights for translators is long overdue, and it is proposed to call a Conference on Literary Translation to discuss these rights in the spring of 1970 [see Sec 3].

The Rights of Translators. Among the subjects to be discussed are the following:

(a) The translator has the right to continuing royalties as long as his translation is in print. He is inseparable from the translation. Under no conditions whatsoever should he accept an outright fee for his work. Even if the royalty is very small, amounting to as little as 2%, such an arrangement is eminently necessary in order to guarantee his *continuing rights.* (This royalty should not be deducted from the author's royalties.) Without these, he becomes merely a pawn in the game, sacrificed as soon as he has fulfilled his elementary duty in the eyes of the publisher. A translator does not deserve to be treated as a pawn.

(b) A model contract suitable to publishers, authors, and translators in preparation.

(c) The name of the translator should *always* appear on the title page and in the promotional matter issued by the publisher. It is not possible to insist on any relative size for the name of the translator on the title page, but in general it should be two-thirds the size of the name of the original author. The translator's name should also appear on the jacket.

(d) In general, the translator should retain the same proportional scale of royalties for his own work as does the author of the original work.

(e) Advances to translators based on fixed fees per thousand words, i.e., $20 per thousand words in current American practice, are clearly unworkable in cases of highly wrought imaginative fiction, and some new basis for computation is needed. It would be absurd to pay a translator of Thomas Mann or Paul Valéry at the same rate as a translator of any "sexpot" novel, but translators are in fact being paid according to the number of words and not according to the inherent difficulties of the task.

(f) Translators are continually faced with the need for special dictionaries, and it is suggested that in addition to an advance and royalties a translator should receive an honorarium to cover the cost of dictionaries.

(g) Translations made in England have been published in the United States only after large-scale revisions have been made, without any mention of the names of the translators responsible for the revisions. This is inherently dishonest, for the reader has no way of knowing who is ultimately responsible for the translation.

Translators' Conference. While the prime purpose of the Translators' Conference to be held in New York in the spring of 1970 will be to draw up a model contract and a Bill of Rights for Translators, there are other urgent matters to be discussed. Among them are the following:

Professorships of Translation. Although translations have been made since the beginning of recorded history and many of the best minds have been engaged in this appallingly difficult task, no chair of translation has ever been established. There have been "colleges" of translation instituted for the purpose of translating the Bible, but the art and craft of translation have never been taught as a major subject in a university.

This is a shocking state of affairs, which should be remedied as soon as possible. Such professorships should properly be established in all the major universities. Only in this way shall we have the possibility of constant professional study of the theory and practice of translation as distinguished from philology and linguistics. Exchange professorships with foreign countries are also urgently needed. The establishment of professorships will have the effect of producing an improvement in the quality of translations. Ultimately, it is a question of giving dignity to an art which has hitherto received only a grudging respect.

Exchange Fellowships. In addition to professorships there is need of exchange fellowships, because the art of translation is best pursued with constant meetings with translators from abroad. It is not so much a question of asking the foreign translators to take up positions in universities, but it is very necessary that they come to America and meet translators. This could be done under the auspices of PEN. It is especially desirable that translators from the African and Asian nations should be invited for a minimum period of two or three months. Ideally, of course, they would be attached to the universities, but this may not always be possible.

Prizes. The PEN Translation Committee hopes to establish a number of regional prizes for translation. At the very least there should be prizes for the best translations from the literatures of Asia, Latin America, France, Germany, Italy, Spain, and Scandinavia. We would also like to see an annual prize for the best translation from Russian, making no distinction whether the work comes from the Soviet Union or from emigré writers. We would like to see prizes for the best translation from the Japanese and the languages of India-Pakistan. These prizes, if well publicized, would encourage publishers to produce more translations.

Publishers. There are already a number of publishers and editors on the PEN Translation Committee, and it is hoped to add more. The Committee should keep in very close touch with them.

Translations from Russian. As long as the Soviet Union and other totalitarian regimes insist on censoring their writers and sending them to prison camps, their literature will be subject to intolerable strains. In these countries, the best writers write "for the drawer" against the day when, by a miracle, they will be allowed to write freely. Censorship was light under the Czars; under the Soviets it is all-pervasive, and not a word can be printed without the imprimatur of a government functionary. And this is true of all totalitarian regimes, and may become increasingly true throughout the world.

Like writers everywhere, Russian writers want to be read, they want to be known, they want their emotions to be shared and their ideas to be understood. They will go to almost any lengths to see that their books are read abroad if they cannot be read in Russia. Translators who receive their manuscripts then find themselves attempting to resolve intensely difficult moral problems, for they know that the publication of their translations will inevitably place the author in jeopardy and they will bear a moral responsibility for his fate. There are no simple solutions. We cannot say: "Let us publish, and be damned. We know that the author wanted his works to appear in translation and his intention outweighs all other considerations." Many imponderables have to be weighed, for no one has the right to sentence a man to a prison camp, which may also be a sentence of death.

The PEN Translation Committee believes that there is need to re-examine the situation and to establish certain guidelines in consultation with as many experts as possible. This is also a question to be discussed at the forthcoming Conference, at which time it is hoped to invite a representative of the Soviet and other governments and any writers who have been heavily censored.

Untranslated Works. Translation has always been a rather haphazard affair depending on considerations which do not necessarily have anything to do with the real value of the work translated. The Arabs translated Greek works on philosophy, astronomy, and medicine because they needed them and thus saved them for posterity; they did not translate the plays of Aeschylus and Sophocles or the lyric poets, and we are therefore all the poorer. Some works translated by the Arabs are known to be lost. Chance has played its part, and even today translations often come about by chance.

Index of Translations. We need an Index of Translations, similar to the annual *Books in Print,* and we also need an Index of Works to Be Translated. This should properly be in the care of a university with a department of translation. A comparatively long list of works that need to be translated can be easily compiled, together with another list of works which have been translated inadequately. We have no adequate translations of Ariosto or Tasso. *The Dream of the Red Chamber,* acknowledged to be the greatest of the Chinese novels, has never been translated in full. There are no comprehensive anthologies of Indian or Japanese poetry. Strangely, there is no body of translations from the Vietnamese. As far as we know, neither the American Government nor any American university has made any conspicuous attempt to make Vietnamese culture known, and it is only with the greatest difficulty that one can find an occasional translation of a Vietnamese poem.

We have nothing from the Nepalese language, and precious little from the Arabic languages. If there is an outstanding novelist in Indonesia, we have not heard of him. Tibetan poetry is still unknown territory, and we are almost totally ignorant of the African languages. There is clearly a need for a comprehensive program to fill up the gaps, and we might very well begin with a serious study of the literature of the emerging African nations.

The question of inadequate translations is quite easily resolved when the books are out of copyright. What happens when the books are still in copyright? Edmund Wilson's strictures on the translation of *Doctor Zhivago* have not been satisfactorily answered, and there would seem to be a prima facie case for a new translation which would convey the poetry and rhythm of the original more adequately. Similarly, André Malraux's *Antimémoires* deserved a translator with a keener sense of the music of the original. In both cases, we are presented with modern classics in an English dress which fails to convey their extraordinary beauty. Under present circumstances nothing can be done and we shall have to wait until the works go out of copyright before a new translator can improve on them. This is not a very serious matter where minor works are concerned; it is a very serious matter indeed when it is a question of masterpieces.

Wherever we look, we find work for translators to do. There are urgent needs reflecting the contemporary situation, and we need a crash program for translations from modern Chinese and Vietnamese and from the African languages. But we are also living at a time when it has become necessary to re-examine our past and bring to light the important forgotten works of the past. We might begin by examining the 500 volumes of Migne's *Patrologia* to discover what the Christian fathers were saying. It is not suggested that those immense volumes should be translated in full, but at least we should be permitted to have some idea of the treasures contained in them. What about Bruno's *De Immenso?* The more one contemplates our lack of translations, the more urgent appears the necessity of bringing into existence a publishing house supported by Foundations, which will be devoted solely to translations.

A Journal for Translators. We believe that each country should have a translator's journal which will present translations, reviews of translations, and a continuing commentary on the problems of translation. It should not be in the hands of a small academic élite, but represent the broad interests of translators all over the country. Many of the problems confronting translators would be solved by the existence of such a journal, which would provide them with a voice after an eternity of silence.

Although the journal would consist chiefly of translations and critical commentaries, it would also serve to promote the interests of translators and offer them a forum and a debating ground. They would learn what works are being translated and what works need to be translated. Through the journal serious efforts can be made to raise the standard of translation. Above all, the journal would serve as the translators' vehicle of communication with the outside world, which has rarely listened to them, because they have rarely been heard.

Translators are faced with a choice. Either they can continue to do nothing to improve their lot or they can join together to ensure that at long last they will receive their due. The choice is between apathy and active engagement in a struggle for recognition, between silence and the living voice. The world of translation is still largely undiscovered and unexplored, and the time has come to set the projects in order and to learn what can and what cannot be done.

The Rights of the Translator

During the late 1960s, the Translation Committee of American PEN (see Sec 2, USA) held a series of meetings on questions arising from translation. Feeling that a new attitude toward translators was long overdue, the Committee drew up a list of urgent recommendations for the attention of translators and publishers and issued the following statement:

"Since the translator is the re-creator of a work, which is only as good as his final rendering, we believe that he should be given continuing rights in the income arising from his work. We believe it is to the advantage of the publisher to extend to him these benefits. In this way publishers will attract more qualified translators and writers of proved literary ability, and at the same time improve the level of contemporary translations."

The Rights of the Translator was published in 1977 and disseminated to both the translating and publishing communities.

The translator is an essential link between various historical periods and diverse cultures. Without him, our world would be parochial and impoverished. His function of recreating a literary work in his own tongue makes him a collaborator of the author in contributing to civ-

PEN American Center (cont.)

ilization. Nevertheless, the tranlator's role is little appreciated, and he himself is generally underpaid. PEN feels that the basic facts about the translator's cultural role ought to be publicized, and his position in the literary world redefined, so that the rewards of the profession are brought into just proportion with the talent and energy it demands.

Reviewers should recognize that a translated work is not a product of spontaneous generation, but the result of arduous and dedicated effort, which deserves informed criticism and appreciation.

Publishers should recognize that the translator is in a real sense the co-author of the work in the language of the translation. He should therefore enjoy certain rights as a matter of course.

This is *not* a model contract. It is intended to provide guidelines only, as all contracts of this kind are subject to negotiation. The figures suggested should be regarded as the minimum, as many translators have been able to negotiate higher fees.

1. The professional translator should receive a regular contract, similar to an author's contract, stipulating the terms of the agreement between him/her and the publisher.

2. The translator's name should appear on the title page of the work, on the jacket, and in all publicity releases and advertisements.

3. Copyright in the translation, whenever legally possible, should be in the translator's name. In any case, the translator's name should appear on the copyright page.

4. The translator of literary prose (fiction, criticism, biography, etc.) should receive a rate *not less than* $30.00 per thousand English words. As the general price level and book prices in particular advance, this minimum should be raised proportionately. Translations of difficult languages and of difficult manuscripts should command a higher fee.

5. In addition, the translator should have a continuing share in all income derived from his/her translation of the work. To begin with, that share should be expressed in a royalty on sales of the work. The suggested royalty should be a minimum of 2% of the list price of the original published edition. For a translation of a work in the public domain, the translator should receive a royalty of not less than 5% of the list price.

6. The translator should have a continuing share in all subsidiary earnings deriving from the use of the translation—including first and second serial rights, book-club sales, sales of the translated version to foreign publishers, paperback and clothbound reprints, anthologies, dramatizations and recordings in all media, etc., as are stipulated in the publisher's contract with the author of the book. The translator should also enjoy a continuing share of revenue deriving from the sales of translations made from his/her translation.

7. The translator should receive 10 free copies of the work he/she has translated, and shall have the right to buy additional copies at the standard author's discount of 40%.

8. If a translated work goes out of print, the right of full ownership in the translation should revert to the translator, who may then attempt to place it elsewhere with another publisher, subject to agreement with the author or other holder of the copyright to the original.

9. The translator's contract should specify a time limit within which the work must be published. A suggested limit is 18 months to 2 years after delivery to the publisher and acceptance by the publisher of the completed translation. If the work is not published within a reasonable period, the translator should request that the rights revert to him/her, and all moneys already paid to the translator by the publisher should be non-returnable.

10. It is assumed that the publisher will furnish the translator with the copy-edited manuscript and/or galleys for the translator's approval.

11. Since the translator is the author of his/her text, its integrity should be respected and no changes in it should be made without the translator's consent.

Registry of Interpreters for the Deaf

Code of Ethics

Preamble

Recognizing the unique position of an interpreter in the life of a deaf person, the Registry of Interpreters for the Deaf sets forth the following principles of ethical behavior which will protect both the deaf person and the interpreter in a profession that exists to serve those with a communication handicap.

In the pursuit of this profession in a democratic society it is recognized that through the medium of interpreters, deaf persons can be granted equality with hearing persons in the matter of their right of communication.

It is further recognized that the basic system for self-regulation governing the professional conduct of the interpreter is the same as that governing the ethical conduct of any business or profession with the addition of stronger emphasis on the high ethical characteristics of the interpreter's role in helping an often time misunderstood group of people.

The standards of ethical practice set forth below encourage the highest standards of conduct and outline basic principles for the guidance of the interpreter.

Code of Ethics

1. The interpreter shall be a person of high moral character, honest, conscientious, trustworthy and of emotional maturity. We shall guard confidential information and not betray confidences which have been entrusted to him.

2. The interpreter shall maintain an impartial attitude during the course of his interpreting avoiding interjecting his own views unless he is asked to do so by a party involved.

3. The interpreter shall interpret faithfully and to the best of his ability, always conveying the thought, intent and spirit of the speaker. We shall remember the limits of his particular function and not go beyond his responsibility.

4. The interpreter shall adopt a conservative manner of dress upholding the dignity of the profession and not drawing undue attention to himself.

5. The interpreter shall recognize his own level of proficiency and use discretion in accepting assignments, seeking for the assistance of other interpreters when necessary.

6. The interpreter shall use discretion in the matter of accepting compensation for services and be willing to provide services in situations where funds are not available. Arrangements should be made on a professional basis for adequate remuneration in court cases comparable to that provided for interpreters of foreign languages.

7. The interpreter shall never encourage deaf persons to seek legal or other decisions in their favor merely because the interpreter is sympathetic to the handicap of deafness.

8. In the case of legal interpreting, the interpreter shall inform the court when the level of literacy of the deaf person involved is such that literal interpretation is not possible and the interpreter is having to grossly paraphrase and restate both what is said to the deaf person and what he is saying to the court.

9. The interpreter shall attempt to recognize the various types of assistance needed by the deaf and do his best to meet the particular need. Those who do not understand the language of signs may require assistance through written communication. Those who understand manual communication may be assisted by means of translating (rendering the original presentation verbatim), or interpreting (paraphrasing, defining, explaining, or making known the will of the speaker without regard to the original language used.)

10. Recognizing his need for professional improvement, the interpreter will join with professional colleagues for the purpose of sharing new knowledge and developments, to seek to understand the implications of deafness and the deaf person's particular needs, broaden his education and knowledge of life, and develop both his expressive and his receptive skills in interpreting and translating.

11. The interpreter shall seek to uphold the dignity and purity of the language signs. We shall also maintain a readiness to learn and to accept new signs, if these are necessary to understanding.

12. The interpreter shall take the responsibility of educating the public regarding the deaf whenever possible recognizing that many misunderstandings arise because of general lack of public knowledge in the area of deafness and communication with the deaf.

National Certification of Interpreters

Certification is only open to members of the national Registry of Interpreters for the Deaf.

I. Certificates

Comprehensive Skills Certificate: The interpreter possessing this certificate has met at least the minimum requirements for expressive translating and interpreting. The interpreter possesses skills to handle reverse translating and interpreting situations represented by the various communication levels of the deaf.

Expressive Translating Certificate: The interpreter possessing this certificate has met at least the minimum requirements for expressive translating, which is used in situations that call for exact wording. Minimal reverse translating skills are required.

Expressive Interpreting Certificate: The interpreter possessing this certificate has met at least the minimum requirements for expressive interpreting. Minimal reverse interpreting skills are required.

Reverse Skills Certificate: The interpreter possessing this certificate has met at least the minimum requirements to do reverse translating and interpreting only. This may be done orally, manually, or be in writing as dictated by ability or necessity. (Hearing-impaired persons may also qualify for this certification.)

Special Certificates: A local chapter may award a special certificate in a particular methodology to an interpreter who may be eminently qualified to work in his local community but who, because of his limited acquaintance with the field, may not be able to pass the evaluation for a national certificate. The RID Certification Board will establish guidelines for these special evaluations.

Specialized Area Competency: The RID Certification Board will develop within the year certification in specialized areas of interpreting such as: legal, religious, etc. This certification will be built upon the Comprehensive Skills Certificate. The Specialized Area Competency cannot be awarded unless the interpreter holds a Comprehensive Skills Certificate.

Note: An interpreter need not hold all certificates. The Comprehensive Skills Certificate is the embodiment of all the three other certificates. The other certifications imply a specific skill. An interpreter may want to work up to the Comprehensive Skills Certificate by taking one or both expressive evaluations first.

II. Self-Screening Questionnaire

This questionnaire is designed to help you decide if you are ready for an evaluation. An affirmative response to 10 of the 12 questions indicates possible readiness for an evaluation.

1. Have you read *Interpreting for Deaf People* and are you familiar with the Code of Ethics and its implications?

2. Does your skill go beyond just an ability to expressively sign and fingerspell directly to a deaf person?

3. Have you had minimal satisfactory experience interpreting to the extent that you are familiar with many of the problems involved?

4. Generally, do deaf people consider your skill in interpreting to be adequate at least in some situations?

5. Has anyone previously explained to you that there are four different certificate possibilities, each involving a different area or level of skill?

6. If response to question five is yes, do you know which certificate might best reflect your own skill and knowledge in interpreting?

7. Can you understand a deaf person who signs and fingerspells to you slowly, but without speech?

8. Have you ever had any association with deaf people in their homes, at their clubs, or at parties?

9. Do you feel that you have a fair enough understanding of deafness and deaf people to respond to questions from general members of the community?

10. Do you think that you have an adequate enough English vocabulary to feel comfortable interpreting in such situations as a courtroom or a hospital?

11. Have you had enough experiences with deaf people that you can discern and adapt to the different levels of language proficiency?

12. Are you the kind of individual who can adapt reasonably well to varied situations and to people with diverse attitudes and personalities?

Code of Ethics with Guidelines

Interpreting shall refer to interpreting or transliterating from sign to speech or from speech to sign. Interpreters:

1. Shall keep all interpreted and assignment related information strictly confidential.

a. Interpreters must not reveal information about any interpreting assignment, including the fact that an assignment is being done. Even the most seemingly innocuous information could be damaging in the wrong hands. To avoid this possibility, and the responsibility which goes with it, interpreters must not say anything about any interpreting job.

b. If a problem arises with the deaf person or hearing consumer and the interpreter feels a need to discuss it with some outside party, she/he should first discuss it with the deaf person, and, if no agreement is reached, the two of them should decide who can advise them.

c. When training other interpreters by the method of sharing actual experiences, interpreters should not reveal any of the following information: name, sex, age, etc., of the deaf or hearing person(s); day of the week, time of day or time of year the situation took place; the location, including the city, state, or agency; other people involved; unnecessary specifics about the situation. It only takes a minimum amount of information to identify the parties involved.

2. Shall render a faithful interpretation, always conveying the content and spirit of the speaker, using linguistic systems and communication modes most readily understood by the persons for whom they are interpreting.

a. Interpreters are not editors and must interpret everything which is said in exactly the same way it was intended. This is especially difficult when the interpreter disagrees with what is being said or feels uncomfortable when profanity is used. Interpreters should remember that they are not at all responsible for what is said, only for conveying information accurately. If the interpreter's own feelings interfere with rendering a faithful interpretation, she/he should withdraw from the situation.

b. While interpreting into sign, the interpreter must communicate in the manner most easily understood by the deaf person(s), be it ASL (American Sign Language), manually coded English, fingerspelling, mouthing, gestures, drawing or writing, etc. It is important for the interpreter and deaf person to spend some time adjusting to each other's way of communicating prior to the actual interpreting situation. When interpreting into speech, the interpreter should speak the language spoken by the hearing person, be it English, Spanish, French, etc.

3. Shall not counsel, advise, or interject personal opinions. Just as interpreters may not omit anything which is said (see no. 2), they may not add anything to the situation even when they are asked to do so by other parties involved. An interpreter is only present in a given situation because two or more people have difficulty communicating, and thus the interpreter's only function is that of facilitator of communication. She/he may not become personally involved because in so doing she/he will take on some responsibility for the outcome, which does not rightly belong to the interpreter.

4. Shall use discretion in accepting assignments with regard to skills, setting, and the persons requesting the service.

a. An interpreter should only accept assignments for which she/he feels ready. However, when an interpreter shortage exists and the only available interpreter does not possess sufficient skill for a particular assignment, this situation should be explained to the deaf and hearing consumers of the interpreting service. If they agree that a lesser-skilled interpreter is better than no interpreter or that they cannot wait until a better-skilled interpreter becomes available, then the lesser-skilled interpreter will have to use his or her best judgment about accepting or turning down the assignment. All interpreters can benefit from additional training in areas in which they lack skill.

b. Certain situations may prove uncomfortable for some interpreters. For example, a male interpreter may feel uncomfortable interpreting for a deaf female patient in the doctor's office. Some interpreters will be uncomfortable in situations where controversial issues are discussed or in religious settings where what is being taught differs from the interpreter's beliefs. An interpreter should not interpret in settings which she/he knows will negatively affect being able to render a faithful interpretation.

c. Interpreters should refrain from interpreting in situations where family members or close personal or professional relationships may affect impartiality. Even the most adept interpreters cannot be expected to mask inner feelings when interpreting for others who may affect their lives in some way. Under these circumstances, especially in legal settings, the ability to prove oneself unbiased when challenged is greatly lessened. In emergency situations it is realized that the interpreter may have to interpret for family members, friends, or close business associates. However, all parties should be informed that the interpreter may not become personally involved in the proceedings.

5. Shall deal with the matter of compensation for services in a professional and judicious manner.

a. Interpreters are trained to work in a professional manner and are considered professionals. Therefore, they should be knowledgeable about fees which are appropriate to that profession.

Registry of Interpreters for the Deaf (cont.)

b. Since a sliding scale of hourly and daily rates has been set up for interpreters in many areas, all interpreters should have an idea of their own level of skill and the expected pay within their category. This can be determined by consideration of several factors, such as: level of certification, length of experience, nature of the assignment, and the total cost of living index ($7.50 an hour may seem high in one geographical area but low in another).

c. There are times when interpreters provide services without charge. This should be done with care and in such a way as to preserve the self-respect of the consumers. In other words, consumers should not feel they are recipients of charity. Care should be taken when interpreting without charge that other interpreters will be protected. In other words, a free-lance interpreter may depend on this work for a living and cannot make it without charging while other persons have full-time work and can interpret as a favor without feeling it is a loss of income.

6. Through the national organization and state chapters, shall seek to uphold the integrity of the profession by encouraging the use of qualified interpreters in order to achieve the highest standards.

Interpreters working as officers and committee members in the national RID and local RID chapters should press for high standards among interpreters. For example, encouraging agencies to hire only certified interpreters and the setting up of a mechanism to achieve compliance with the Code of Ethics are two of the many things which can be done.

An interpreter shall present and conduct herself/himself in a manner appropriate to the interpreting situation.

7. Shall continue to develop her/his interpreting skills and keep abreast of developments in the field. In professional meetings, by joining with professional colleagues for the purpose of sharing information, and by reading current literature in the field.

The American Association of Language Specialists (TAALS)

Professional Code for Language Specialists

I. Aim and Scope

Article 1

(a) This Code sets forth rules of professional conduct by members of the Association.

(b) The purpose of the Code is to ensure professional standards and thereby to encourage the broadest use of language specialists by all who need such services.

(c) Candidates for admission take it upon themselves to observe the Professional Code in its entirety and likewise all other rules and regulations of TAALS.

(d) Members who infringe the Code or otherwise engage in conduct manifestly injurious to the professional reputation of language specialists may be subject to expulsion from the Association or other penalties the procedures for which are outlined in the Bylaws.

II. Code of Ethics

Article 2

(a) Members of the Association shall be subject to strict professional secrecy. This applies to all information gained while acting in a professional capacity.

(b) No member shall derive personal profit or advantage from any confidential information acquired while acting in a professional capacity.

Article 3

(a) Members of the Association shall refrain from accepting engagements they do not feel qualified to undertake. Acceptance shall be regarded as guaranteeing a high professional standard.

(b) The moral guarantee given by TAALS members under paragraph (a) above also covers the quality of the services rendered by nonmembers who have been engaged on the recommendation of TAALS members.

Article 4

(a) Members shall refuse any employment or position which might prejudice the dignity of the profession or conflict with the observance of professional secrecy.

(b) Members shall refrain from any activities which could bring discredit on the profession, including all forms of personal publicity.

Article 5

(a) Members of the Association pledge their unfailing support to their colleagues and to the profession as a whole.

(b) Any difficulty of a professional nature arising between two or more members may be referred to the Council for arbitration.

III. Working Conditions—General

Article 6

Members of the Association shall refuse to work under conditions not in accordance with those laid down by the Association (see Appendix).

IV. Conference Engagements

Article 7

(a) Members of the Association shall accept a conference engagement only when they are aware of the exact conditions of this engagement and have made sure that their identity and conditions of payment are known to the conference (the word is understood to mean the original organizer; any intermediates are specificially excluded): when applicable, the Letter of Appointment shall be used in the form drawn up by the Association.

(b) All contracts and payments shall be direct from the conference to the language specialist.

(c) In the case of organizations without a permanent language services structure, services shall be organized by, and language specialists recruited upon the recommendation of, a recognized professional language specialist.

(d) Members shall perform no other conference duties than those for which they are contracted.

Article 8

(a) Each member shall declare one professional domicile. No member may have more than one professional domicile at the same time.

(b) A change in domicile may be affected upon prior written notification to the Executive Secretary. No member shall be permitted to change professional domicile more often than once every six (6) months.

Article 9

Members of the Association may request to be released from a conference engagement only if they are able to: (a) Give sufficient notice; (b) Show good cause; and (c) Propose a substitute acceptable to the conference organizer.

Article 10

(a) A scale of suggested minimum fees is kept by the Association.

(b) The fees are based on a daily rate. A full day's fee shall be payable for each day or fraction thereof covered by the conference engagement.

(c) Fees are quoted in U.S. dollars or their equivalent. The fees shall be transferable to the language specialist's country of domicile.

(d) Members of the Association engaged to work in the same capacity on the same team shall be paid at the same rate.

Article 11

(a) Fees shall be due for the entire period covered by the conference engagement, including Sundays and other nonworking days.

(b) Fees shall be payable in full without deduction of any commission.

Article 12

Members of the Association may give their services free of charge, provided they pay their own travel and subsistence expenses. (The Council may occasionally waive this provision.)

Article 13

Allowances and Fees for Travel Days

(a) Conference engagements away from the place of domicile shall entitle members of the Association payment of a subsistence allowance (per diem) for each day of absence from the place of domicile and, in addition, a fee for each day required to be spent in travel.

(b) The amounts referred to in (a) above shall be due in full each day or fraction thereof. Members may, however, agree to payment of two-thirds of the subsistence allowance in the form of full board and lodging.

Article 14
Travel
The Mode of travel from domicile to conference, or between consecutive engagements, depends on the practice then current and customary. Members may contact the Association to ascertain the current practice for any given arrangements, and the Association may from time to time publish such practices. In no case, however, may members travel in a mode inferior to that contracted for by the sponsoring organization without the Association's prior consent. (This provision is to be read in conjunction with Article 4 of the Appendix to the Code.)

Appendix to the Professional Code for Language Specialists

Article 1
Duration of Appointments
All contracts shall specify the exact duration of the appointment and contain a cancellation clause providing for the reimbursement of all substantiated expenses and for the payment of: the total remuneration due if the contact or part thereof is canceled or the meeting is terminated sooner than its final date.
Exception: Organizations which are members of the United Nations family. The cancellation clause in effect for these organizations will be as follows:
(a) 50 percent of the total remuneration due if the contract or part thereof is canceled more than 30 days before its effective date;
(b) The total remuneration due if the contract or part thereof is canceled less than 30 days before its effective date or terminated sooner than its final date.
The above paragraphs shall not be operative if the language specialist is offered equivalent employment for the period in question either by the organization canceling the contract or by a third party, or if the reasons for the termination are of a disciplinary character.

Article 2
Subsistence Allowance (per diem): The rate of subsistence allowance (per diem) shall be no less than that specified by the United Nations scale of per diem for staffs in grades P-3 to P-5.

Article 3
Loss-of-Earning Allowance: Whenever applicable, the allowance payable for the first day spent traveling on the outward and return journey shall be half the suggested minimum fee and all additional travel days shall be payable at the full suggested minimum fee.

Article 4
Air Travel: The language specialist may accept economy-class travel accommodations provided his contract includes days of rest at standard fees and, where applicable, per diem, depending on travel time from downtown air terminal to downtown air terminal. Payments in respect of rest days shall be additional to payments in respect of travel days (see Article 3 above).

Travel Time	No. Rest Days Due
9 to 16 hours	One
16 to 21 hours	Two
21 hours or more	Three

Moreover, the contract shall provide for 10 kilos (22 lbs.) excess baggage allowance in excess of the economy class allowance.

Working Conditions for Interpreters

1. General: In the interest of ensuring professional standards, members of the Association shall:
(a) Satisfy themselves that they can see and hear properly;
(b) Warn that simultaneous interpretation without booth may reduce the quality of interpreting below minimum standards;
(c) Endeavor to ensure that interpreting teams are made up in such a way as to avoid regular use of relays.
2. Coordinating interpreters:
(a) It is the responsibility of the coordinating interpreter to ascertain working conditions and fees in effect in the region where the conference is to be held and to see to it that contracts fully meet those conditions: it

is likewise the responsibility of language specialists to respect such working conditions and fees.
(b) If coordinating interpreters cannot be present throughout the conferences they organize, to serve as a link between the conference officials and interpreters, another interpreter shall be appointed as team leader and shall receive all necessary information as well as compensation for such additional responsibility.
3. Number of interpreters:
(a) Interpreters shall not work alone with no possibility of relief. (In exceptional circumstances, and in the mode of consecutive interpretation, an interpreter may work alone; in such cases he shall be paid double the suggested minimum fee.)
(b) A minimum of two interpreters per language is required, except for bilingual conferences, in which case a team of three interpreters is acceptable in certain circumstances.
(c) Exceptionally and for short bilingual meetings not exceeding one half-day or one evening, a team of two bilingual interpreters is acceptable.
4. Scale of suggested fees in the Americas: A list of the suggested minimum daily fees applicable to intergovernmental, governmental, and nongovernmental organizations in the Americas shall be published on January 1 of each year and whenever a fee has been changed.
5. Whispered interpretation: Whispered interpretation is considered to be from one or two languages into another language, for a maximum of two delegates with or without consecutive interpretation from the latter language: three interpreters at the fees laid down in the list mentioned in paragraph 4 above.
6. Briefing:
(a) A briefing period of two full days on full pay during which half a day may be a working period shall be provided in the case of all technical and scientific conferences.
(b) The above briefing period may be replaced by an equivalent period of study at home on full pay if the necessary documents are made available for that purpose.
7. Recording: Interpretation is provided solely for the benefit of the audience. No recording, for whatever purpose, including by members of the audience, may be made without prior consent of the interpreters concerned, who may claim appropriate compensation for such use.
8. Other fees: In the case of conferences held outside the Americas, the suggested minimum fees shall be those of the International Association of Conference Interpreters (AIIC).

Working Conditions for Translators

A. General
1. In the interest of ensuring professional standards, members of the Association shall endeavor to see that the following conditions prevail in all working situations:
2. *Facilities and Working Area:* The facilities and physical working area provided for translators shall be adequate to permit the production of translations of proper quality. Either dictation equipment or a typewriter in good condition (electric if the translator so prefers) shall be provided for each translator on duty. If translations are to be dictated, an experienced conference typist with proper knowledge of the target language shall also be available. The working area shall be adequately illuminated and ventilated, and reasonable quiet and privacy shall be ensured. Translators shall not be required to share their working area with any distracting activities.
3. *Time Allowed for Work:* Translators shall be allowed sufficient time to complete their work, having regard to the nature and length of the text.
4. *Condition of Text to be Translated:* The material to be translated shall be typewritten or typeset and legible in all respects. A short handwritten text may be accepted in special circumstances, but only if the translator has first satisfied himself that he can read it with no difficulty or possiblity of misunderstanding.
5. *Reference Material:* Translators shall have ready access to the dictionaries they need and, whenever possible, to documents and information (including marked-up copies) required for proper understanding of the text to be translated and production of a good translation.

B. Conferences
6. Members of the Association shall ensure that, in addition to the foregoing general conditions, the following specific conditions with respect to conferences are observed:

The American Association of Language Specialists (TAALS) (cont.)

7. *Hours of Work:* The normal working day shall be eight hours. Shift work shall be agreed upon in advance.

8. *Composition of Translation Teams:* When a conference engages two or more translators to work simultaneously into the same target language, at least one of them shall be accorded the title and duties of "Reviewer" or "Reviser" and paid at an agreed higher rate. A conference may also engage a team composed exclusively of experienced reviewers/revisers.

9. *Working Languages:* A translator shall not be required to work into languages other than those in which he has an A classification.

10. *Documentation:* In addition to the reference material mentioned in paragraph 5 above, background documentation for the conference (special glossaries, reports of previous meetings, documents under consideration, etc.) shall be made available for ready reference.

C. Scales of Suggested Fees

11. A scale of suggested minimum daily fees for conference engagements in the Americas shall be published on January 1 of each year and whenever a fee has been changed.

12. The Association shall also publish each year and whenever necessary a scale of suggested minimum fees for non-conference free-lance translation work, which is usually remunerated on a word-count basis.

13. For both conference and non-conference translation work performed outside the Americas, the suggested minimum fees shall be those of the Association, or those of the local professional association of translators, whichever are higher.

D. Copyright

14. It is understood that translators are entitled to the same protection in respect of their translations as is accorded to authors under international copyright conventions. The translator may, however, voluntarily waive these rights.

15. Where the authors(s) of a report, document, or article are names, the translator(s) of that publication should be accorded equal mention.

The Translators Association (London)

Specimen Contract

The following document, dated January 1975, covers the essential points necessary for the protection of the translator's interests and avoidance of disputes with publishers as the work proceeds, and is accompanied by:

"All the clauses incorporated have been found acceptable to one publisher or another and written into contracts which have been studied. Translators will find a resistance from some publishers to certain clauses, particularly those concerning retention of copyright (see note on Clause 3), royalties, and an interest in serial rights. However, there is no reason why, if they are acceptable to some well-established publishers, they should not become general practice in due course and it is therefore up to the translator to negotiate the best possible terms, bearing in mind the value of a continuing interest in his work.

"The nature and scope of translation is immensely varied and the individual may well find it necessary to insert special clauses not contained in the specimen contract to meet his/her own and the publisher's requirements."

MEMORANDUM OF AGREEMENT made this *(date)* between *(Publisher's name and address)* hereinafter called the PUBLISHERS of the one part and *(Translator's name and address)* hereinafter called the TRANSLATOR of the other part whereby it is mutually agreed as follows:

1. The Translator shall provide the Publishers with a faithful translation into English of the complete and unabridged work entitled *(foreign title)* hereinafter called the Work.

2. The Translator undertakes to deliver to the Publishers _____ copies of his Translation of the Work by *(date)* in the absence of delays due to circumstances beyond his control.
No alteration shall be made in the Translation without seeking the consent of the Translator. If this consent is refused, the Publishers may nevertheless make such changes they think fit, in which event the

Translator may withdraw his name from the Translation, without, however, relinquishing any of his rights under this agreement.

3. In consideration of the payments hereinafter mentioned in this Agreement the Translator grants the Publishers an exclusive license to print, publish, and sell his translation throughout the world in volume and serial form in limited territory as agreed: UK and Commonwealth, or North America (USA and Canada), or World English rights.

NOTE: Under the Copyright Act 1956, copyright, in the absence of any agreement to the contrary vests automatically in the Translator. The wording of this clause is designed to ensure that the Translator does not assign his copyright to the Publishers and at the proof stage the Translator should check that the Copyright notice (© John Smith 1975) is in his/her name. Territories specified in the clause can be deleted as required. Negotiations as to advance payment on signature will depend on the standing of the Translator. Established Translators may expect the terms outlined in this clause. Others may have to accept an advance of one third of the provisionally agreed total.

4. The Publishers shall pay the Translator the sum of _____ per thousand words of the English translation: an estimated one half to be paid on signature of this Agreement and the balance within four weeks of the delivery of the Translation.

NOTE: Under no circumstances should the Translator agree to payment of the balance being dependent on publication alone as it will be seen that this could be delayed indefinitely.

Publishers may well wish to replace the term "delivery" by "acceptance" or "approval." Where competent Translators and responsible Publishers are concerned such a change may not be important but in exceptional cases it can lead to difficulties. Delivery in a state ready for press appears to be a satisfactory way of obviating any suggestion of acceptance or approval.

If Translators are not aware of the current rates for the language from which they translate, advice can always be obtained from The Translators Association.

5. On all copies of the Publishers' original edition of the Translation after the first _____ copies the Publishers shall pay the Translator a royalty of _____ percent of the published price rising by _____ percent for every additional _____ copies.

NOTE: Many (perhaps most) Publishers still refuse to pay the Translator any royalties (in which case Clauses 5, 6, and 7 will not be required). However, a growing number are beginning to do so. The Translator should point out that it is the policy of the Association to press for this and that he/she is merely asking for a small percentage of the earnings of the book at a point when the Publishers have covered their costs and are making a profit.

6. In respect of any English edition published by a reprint house or reprint club under license from the Publishers, the Publishers shall pay to the Translator _____ percent of the actual amount to which he/she is entitled.

The Publishers shall pay the Translator 10% of their share of the net receipts from the sale of the serial rights.

In the event of a sale by the Publishers of the paperback rights, the Publishers shall pay the Translator a royalty of _____ percent, rising _____ percent for every additional _____ thousand copies.

7. The Publishers shall make up the royalty accounts under Clauses 4 and 5 hereof twice yearly on dates to be agreed and shall settle any sums within three months of the agreed dates.

8. All rights in the Translation not specifically mentioned in this Agreement shall remain the exclusive property of the Translator.

9. The Publishers undertake that the Translator's name shall appear on the title page and jacket of every edition of the Translation and in all publicity material (catalogues, advertisements, etc.) concerning it.

10. The Translator shall be entitled to receive _____ presentation copies of every new edition of the Translation. He/she is further entitled to purchase additional copies for his own use at a discount of one third from the published price.

11. The cost of Translation alterations made by the Translator in the proofs and correction of alterations made by the Publishers, unauthorized by the Translator (other than correction of printer's errors) above 10% of the original cost of typesetting shall be paid by the Translator. The Translator undertakes to read, check, and correct proofs of the work and to return them to the Publishers within _____ days of their receipt.

NOTE: In agreeing to a specified number of days, the Translator should bear in mind the length and nature of the work.

12. The Translator guarantees to the Publishers that he will not in-

troduce into the said Translation any matter of an objectionable or libelous character which was not present in the original work. In reliance on such a guarantee the Publishers undertake to hold the Translator harmless from all suits and all manner of claims and proceedings or expenses which may be taken against or incurred by them on the grounds that the said Translation contains anything objectionable or libelous.

NOTE: Has been agreed (1974) by the Publishers' Association (London) and must be inserted in all contracts.

Members undertaking the translation of out-of-copyright work may wish to know the usual termination clause recommended in The Society of Authors' *Notes on Publishing Contracts*, which is as follows:

"If the publishers fail to fulfill or comply with any of the provisions of this agreement within one month after written notification from the author of such failure or if they go into liquidation or if after all editions of the work published under their own imprint are out of print or off the market they have not within six months of a written request from the author issued a new edition or impression of at least 1,500 copies then and in any of these events this agreement shall automatically determine and all rights revert to the author without prejudice to any claim which the author may have for monies due and/or damages and/or otherwise.

"Some forms of contract provide that if the publishers fail to reprint a new edition after due notice from the author, the contract shall terminate only if the author refunds any unearned balance of the advance and buys back blocks, stereoplates, etc., at a proportion of their original cost. This is unreasonable."

13. If the Publishers go out of business, whether voluntarily or otherwise, the Translator shall recover the full disposal of his Translation.
IN WITNESS whereof we have hereunto set our hands.

For and on behalf of PUBLISHER

Translator   Director

N.B.: In case of dispute between the Translator and the Publishers, the Translator is strongly advised to seek the guidance of the Association.

The Translators' Guild (United Kingdom)

You and Your Translator

Your translator is a professional collaborator, and to do his/her job properly he/she needs the same degree of cooperation you give your accountant or lawyer. Nominate an executive, if possible one who knows a foreign language (even if it is not the one involved in the translation work), whom your translator can consult about any problems that arise.

Your work may involve manuscripts for publication abroad as brochures, sales and prestige literature, etc., or foreign texts wanted purely for internal intelligence. Translations for publication, which besides being accurate—as all translation must be—will need special attention to terminology and style and will cost more than those wanted solely for information because they take the translator substantially longer to deal with properly. When commissioning work for publication, study the details of the translator's background and experience, and ask for samples of previous work done for publication.

The original supplied to the translator should, for both the translator's and the client's sake, be edited to make sure it is correct. Photocopies should be clear—a translator may justifiably charge extra for working from a blurred photocopy or badly handwritten text which is hard to read.

Priority treatment, which may involve working at high speed or outside normal working hours to meet an urgent deadline, or allowing a particular assignment to "jump the queue" of work already accepted (which usually means working overtime to meet these other commitments) is subject to a surcharge negotiable between translator and client, with a minimum of 33 ⅓%.

The word count is based on the original text to help the client get a rough idea of the cost and time involved (an average output, of high quality work, is about 2000 words a day for publication and perhaps 50% higher for information work). This applies to fairly continuous text; discontinuous text (lists of components or isolated words on engineering drawings) will probably involve a surcharge or be charged on the basis of time spent. (See below for *Fees 1975*).

Enough time and enough information are two main factors in insuring satisfactory results. Besides the actual translating and stylistic polishing, time is needed for terminology research. Plan your translation needs well in advance—work done in a hurry costs more and may well be inferior; and top-quality translators are seldom available at a moment's notice. Give your translator all the information you can—literature on your own or competitor's products, glossaries of technical terms, earlier translations of similar texts, and so on. The translator *must* have any illustrations accompanying the text; as these were provided to help the reader of the original text, they are all the more essential for the translator.

Knowledge of the subject by the translator is important, as no one can properly translate what he/she does not fully understand. Make sure that your translator does have a sound basic grasp of the specialist field concerned; this is absolutely imperative when the translation is intended for publication.

Above all, never ask a translator to translate *from* his/her own language. However well a translator knows another language, his/her command of it will never equal that of his own—and the results can easily be ludicrous and damage your own reputation. A very few people, through special circumstances of upbringing, may be competent to work into two languages; *no* translator with a sense of professional responsibility will offer to work into three or more languages.

Fees 1975

In April 1975 the Guild conducted a survey with a view to establishing the going rate for translations in the United Kingdom. Results showed these rates to cover a range from £12–£15 per 1000 words for a straightforward text to £15–£25 for texts of a relatively specialized nature, and £25 upwards (sometimes considerably upwards) for highly specialized texts. There was significant variation as to source language, except for Chinese and Japanese, which occupy the upper end of the scale. The rate charged for translations from English into a foreign language seem to be 30–40% higher. The figures refer to United Kingdom clients; rates paid abroad are often considerably higher.

This information is intended to serve as a guide to the practitioner or client unwilling to look further into the complexities of the present system of charging for translations. At the urgent request of both translators and clients, the Guild Committee has (in addition to conducting a limited survey of full-time translators) earnestly reconsidered the whole subject of charging for translations, which is at present in a state of flux.

It appears that recent United Kingdom monopoly legislation prohibits the prescription or publication of minimum charges. The Guild, therefore, can only release information on the going rate—even though, in an inflationary situation, the practical value of such figures or rate brackets must be problematical. Guild members will probably find it practical and acceptable to clients to raise their fees annually by the amount of the rise in the cost-of-living index. Since the publication of the last "Scale of Fees" in the January 1976 issue of *The Incorporated Linguist* [see Sec 6, Journals], to date this increase has been 19%.

Two other developments have complicated this picture: (1) the growing preference for charging on the basis of the target language, the language of the end product, and (2) the widespread practice of calculating charges (usually based on the target language) on a line count rather than a word count.

The supporters of the target language system base their attitude on the facts that (1) book publishers, the editors or journals commissioning translations, and certain other clients, have always used this system, and (2) their own expenses, such as typing fees, fees to consultants, and indeed even stationery and postage costs are related to the length of the finished article. The supporters of the source language system are mostly translation agencies anxious to be able to give an instant quotation to their clients.

The case for a line count, and hence for a quotation based on lineage, is chiefly one of convenience—and since a 55-stroke standard line (as now used in many countries) accommodates an average of 10 English words, conversion is easy enough. Moreover, a line count, as compared with a word count, will show far less variation between source and target languages since the breaking up of long compound words into several shorter ones, or the use of prepositional constructions instead of inflection, will automatically tend to iron out the differences. The line-count practice is now universal in Germany and Switzerland, and gaining ground elsewhere, even among translation agencies in the United Kingdom.

The Translator's Guild (United Kingdom) (cont.)

There is, finally, another method of charging—no doubt the most professional—the quotation "for the job." This is already practiced by several translators and willingly accepted by their clients; it is particularly suitable for non-standard jobs (work involving editing, précis-writing, research, diagrams, etc., or translations of greatly varying degrees of complexity).

The Guild Committee has spent a great deal of time discussing the rival claims of the different methods; it has come to the conclusion that it would be impossible in the present situation to impose any particular practice on all translators or users of translators. The Committee leans very strongly towards the "quotation for the job"; where this is not appropriate, it favors a line charge. On the issue of source language versus target language, it was found that the majority of the Committee preferred a target language count.

A Translator on Your Staff

An increasing number of medium-sized firms are recruiting their first staff translator or translators; for most of them this will be their first encounter with the professional linguist. While they may have long experience of employing design engineers or research scientists, and know what these workers need to be able to give their best, they often have very little idea of the sort of working conditions a translator has a right to expect.

I. Office Accommodation

Ideally, a translator needs an office to himself; at most, two translators can work efficiently in the same room. Translating is a task demanding concentration and lack of distractions, and the modern "open-plan" office is totally unsuitable.

The translator will spend the major part of his working day reading from texts which may often be in small print or in the form of a rather blurred photocopy: he/she therefore needs the best possible lighting conditions, as much natural daylight as possible, good glarefree general room lighting, and a desk lamp fitted with an effective shade.

Similar physical aids to fatigue-free working are a desk offering ample scope for arranging dictionaries and reference books (the type with pull-out shelves to right and left is specially suitable); the size of desk normally supplied for a typist is definitely not large enough, although one or two of the drawers could be well fitted with the angled racks for typing paper which are common in typists' desks. Ample shelf space for reference books is essential, with filing cabinets for storing reference literature and copies of translations.

The translator may often have to discuss a text with specialist visitors to his office, and there should be enough room and chairs for them to be able to work uncramped and in comfort.

II. Reference Material

A full-time free-lance translator will normally expect to spend something between £100–150 a year on dictionaries, handbooks, journals, technical encyclopedias, and similar reference books, and a firm employing a staff translator must expect to invest at least a similar sum to enable the translator to keep abreast of his/her subject. Some of the reference material can, of course, be available to the translator on short-term loan from the company's own technical library (to which the translator should have easy access). But there will be a sizeable nucleus of reference literature—especially dictionaries in regular use—which a translator will need to have constantly at hand for his/her exclusive use.

Problems connected with the company's particular technology will frequently crop up in a translator's work, and he/she should have unimpeded access at all times to engineers, research scientists and the like for help in solving these. During the first few weeks in the job, the translator should be introduced to the heads of various departments in the firm likely to help him/her in this way; this problem-solving can usually be done by telephone, and the translator should have his/her own extension, listed in the firm's house directory. The translator is a specialist in his/her own right, and a climate of professional collaboration with other specialists in the firm should be fostered from the outset.

III. Workload and Working Methods

When dealing with the major European languages and translating texts required for internal intelligence, an average daily output of good quality translation will be about 2000–3000 words. Texts intended for publication, as sales or prestige literature, will take substantially longer, and 1500–2000 words a day would be a reasonable average. While a higher output will be occasionally possible to meet an urgent deadline, these are the averages on which the translator's output should be based when drawing up work schedules.

It should be remembered, when forecasting deadlines for work, that the staff translator commonly suffers from interruptions (translating odd items of corresponding, spending an hour or a whole day interpreting for a party of foreign visitors to the firm) which will eat into his/her working day, and the translator's work may also include extra duties such as editing and proofreading.

Working methods can vary from one company to another, and from one translator to another, and a certain amount of flexibility and experiment may be needed to find the best arrangement. Some translators prefer to type their own drafts of translations (a translator should not be expected to produce final, clean typescript, and it would be uneconomical to have him/her spend time doing so), while others work best by dictating to a tape-recorder or shorthand-typist and then revising the transcript for final typing. Some users may be satisfied with a taped translation alone, saving the time and expense of typing. Another way of saving time and effort is the "read through," with user and translator quickly scanning the text together and selecting significant passages for full translation.

The office of The Institute of Linguists and The Translators' Guild offers guidance on matters connected with translation staff, or suggests outside sources of expert advice.

Ad Hoc Interpretation

Ad hoc interpreters are persons completely fluent in at least 2 languages and their task is to ensure perfect communication between persons who do not understand each other's languages. Ad hoc interpretation is used: (1) for discussions between two persons, usually businessmen or technical experts, and informal talks in small groups consisting of up to five persons; (2) for on-site visits, e.g., to factories; (3) for exhibitions and trade fairs; (4) for court proceedings; (5) for reception desk inquiries at congresses and conferences; (6) for shopping and sight-seeing expeditions.

For interpretation under headings 1–5 above, it is important that the interpreter should be properly briefed beforehand. Whenever possible he should be provided with the relevant documents and as much background information as possible so that he/she can cooperate effectively in the process of two-way communication.

There is a clear distinction between ad hoc interpreting and conference interpretation. In the former case, interpreters usually work without taking notes and translate sentence by sentence, occasionally two or three sentences at a time. International conference interpretation (consecutive, simultaneous, and whispering) is used for speeches and discussions at meetings—probably with a chairman and a set agenda—normally consisting of more than five participants, usually sitting in a hall or round a table.

The fees for conference interpreting are laid down by the International Association of Conference Interpreters (AIIC) in Geneva, and the latest information on these fees may be obtained directly from the association's secretariat, 14 rue de l'Ancien-Port, CH-1201 Geneva, Switzerland (022) 31-33-23.

Translator's Terms of Business

Translation rights. The Translator will assume that the client owns translation rights to the original text, or will be using the translation only for purposes of study, etc., in which the question of infringement of rights does not arise. In all cases, the client undertakes to keep the translator harmless from any claim for infringement of translation rights.

Fees and quotations. In the absence of any specific agreement on the rate to be charged, this shall be fixed by the translator. Any rate quoted or discussed before sight of the text is liable to amendment when the text is received. Subject to this statement, questions shall be binding on either side for up to two months. All other special expenses incurred in the course of translation shall also be charged separately.

Copyright. In the absence of a specific written agreement to the contrary, copyright in the text of the translation remains the property of the translator. In the case of texts intended for publication, it is understood that the translator gives the client license to publish in return for the agreed fee and when this has been paid. When copyright is assigned in full, this is likewise effective only on completion of payment. When the translator retains the copyright, the printed text shall, unless he/she agrees in writing to the contrary, carry the words: © (English, etc.) text (Translator's name) 19_____.

Delivery and payment. Any delivery date agreed on between translator and client shall be binding on the translator only if he/she has had sight of the full text to be translated; and is superseded if additions or substantial amendments are made by the client subsequently. If the time allowed for completing the work is such that means of delivery other than normal first class mail are necessary, the cost of these shall be chargeable to the client. Payment shall be effected within a month of the delivery of the translation and the rendering of an invoice. Overdue amounts shall be subject to an interest of 2.5% per 4-week period. Any complaint about the translator shall be made by the client, either to the translator or to the TG Disputes Committee, within a month of the delivery of the translation.

Cancellation. Work once commissioned and then cancelled shall incur a cancellation charge of 10% of the total fee as a minimum, to compensate for the time booked but not used. If work has been started (either research or actual translation) the client shall be liable for the cost of the portion completed plus 10% of the total fee. The work completed shall be available to the client.

Safekeeping of client's documents. The translator is responsible for the safekeeping and confidentiality of the client's documents, etc., only while these are actually in his/her keeping, and not while in transit to or from the client. The translator will, if requested, insure documents in transit, at the client's expense.

Libel. The translator guarantees to the client that he/she will not introduce into the translation any matter of an objectionable or libelous character which was not present in the original work. In reliance on such a guarantee the client undertakes to hold the translator harmless from all suits and all manner of claims and court proceedings or expenses which may be taken against or incurred by him/her on the grounds that the translation contains anything objectionable or libelous.

UNESCO

International Copyright Information Center

The following extracts, pertaining to a "Draft model contract for the purpose of the translation of a work," have been culled from the Final Report of a meeting of officials of regional or national copyright information centers and specialists in the field of copyright or publishing, held at UNESCO House, Paris, June 30 to July 4, 1975.

The draft contract, an integral part of the program undertaken by UNESCO in the field of translation, concerns relations between publishers and translators in developing countries, and "is intended to safeguard the rights of a professional category, the protection of which is entirely ensured in the large majority of countries by the international multilateral conventions and by national laws, but is not always applied in practice."

30. Almost all the participants intervened in the discussion which took place on this subject. The basic observations concern the following:

(i) the need to avoid including percentages in the text, even in an illustrative manner, as had been the case in the other draft model contracts submitted to the meeting. The role of a model contract is to furnish a framework, which, subsequently, the users are to complete in the way they seem most adequate;

(ii) the advisability of waiting until the General Conference of UNESCO adopts a recommendation on the protection of translators before preparing, in the light of the content of this recommendation, the draft text which will be submitted for comments to governments of Member States of UNESCO and interested professional organizations;

(iii) the danger that a model contract setting forth an adequate protection of the interests of translators would discourage publishers from using it, especially in developing countries;

(iv) the usefulness of submitting to users of the model contract, as alternatives, two methods of remuneration for the translator: a lump sum and a percentage on the sale price of copies of the published translation, instead of proposing only this second method.

31. Some experts having expressed the fear that the protection the draft affords the translator be acquired at the expense of the rights of authors, other participants, as well as the observer of the FIT and the Secretariat, recalled that under the international conventions and national laws the translator is assimilated to an author without the protection accorded him/her diminishing in any way the copyright in the original work, which, moreover, has been expressly recognized by the General Conference of UNESCO.

Recommendations

The meeting recommended that the main objectives of the International Copyright Information Center should be, among others, to listing in the developing countries:

(9) (i) the requirements in the field of translation, from and into what languages and in which disciplines;

(ii) existing possibilities for making translations from and into what languages and in what disciplines;

(10) to undertake a study on the implications for developing countries which may arise from the transfer of translation rights, depending on whether the latter is based on a linguistic zone, a country, or a specific geographical region, or any combination of the above;

(11) undertake the preparation of a draft model contract applicable to translators in developing countries, mainly in the light of the recommendation that the General Conference of UNESCO may adopt on the protection of translators and after having received the suggestions of the interested circles.

US Congress

Bilingual Courts Act

In 1977, Democratic Senator Dennis DeConcini, Chairman of the Judicial Improvements Subcommittee, introduced legislation sponsored by senators Allen of Alabama, Bayh of Indiana, and Kennedy of Massachusetts, designed to guarantee the services of a competent interpreter in Federal Court proceedings to every citizen who is not fluent in English. In his speech introducing the bill, Senator DeConcini stated that "our citizens of Spanish, Puerto Rican, Chinese, native American and other heritages who do not adequately understand English as well as our deaf citizens who must communicate by sign language are in effect denied real justice under the law without this guarantee....

"The fifth amendment, providing that 'no person . . . shall be deprived of life, liberty or property without due process of law,' supports my belief that the Bilingual Courts Act should apply to both criminal and civil proceedings. Surely any legal proceeding that allows a party to an action to be deprived of life, liberty or property without first insuring that he fully understands what is happening at the trial lacks in basic and fundamental fairness and thus violates the due process clause.

"The proposals contained in this legislation are certainly not novel. Article 2(a) of the Canadian Bill of Rights, adopted in 1960, guarantees every person the right to the assistance of an interpreter in any proceeding in which he is involved if he does not understand or speak the language in which the case is being heard. In addition, the Constitution of the State of New Mexico explicitly provides that in all criminal proceedings the defendant is entitled 'to have the charge and testimony interpreted to him in a language that he understands.'

"Fundamental fairness, the integrity of the fact-finding process, the potency of our adversary system of justice and the Constitution demand the enactment of the Bilingual Courts Act."

(Excerpts from Senator DeConcini's address and the text of the bill were taken from the April 20, 1977 issue of the Congressional Record, *pages S 6041–6042.)*

S. 1315

Be it enacted by the Senate and House of Representatives of the United States of America in Congress assembled, that this Act may be cited as "Bilingual Courts Act."

Conduct of Bilingual Proceedings

Sec. 2. (a) Chapter 119 of title 28, United States Code, is amended by adding at the end thereof the following new section:

1827. Bilingual proceedings

"(a) (1) In any criminal action, whenever the judge determines, on his own motion or the motion of a party to the proceedings, that (A) the defendant does not speak and understand the English language with a fa-

US Congress (cont.)

cility sufficient for him to comprehend either the proceedings or the testimony, or (B) in the course of such proceedings, testimony may be presented by any person who does not so speak and understand the English language, the court, in all further proceedings in that action, including arraignment, hearings, and trial, shall order an oral simultaneous translation of the proceedings, or an oral simultaneous translation of that testimony, to be furnished by an interpreter in accordance with the provisions or subsection (b) of this section.

"(2) In any civil action, whenever the judge determines on his own motion or on the motion of a party to the proceedings, that (A) a party does not speak and understand the English language with a facility sufficient for him to comprehend either the proceedings or the testimony, or (B) in the course of such proceedings, testimony may be presented by any person who does not so speak and understand the English language, in all further proceedings in that action, including hearings and trial, the court shall order an oral translation of the proceedings to be made by an interpreter in accordance with the provisions of subsection (b) of this section. The judge shall also determine, in the interests of justice, whether the translation shall be simultaneous, consecutive, or summary in nature, except that if a party requests a simultaneous translation, the court shall give the request special consideration.

"(3) In any criminal or civil action, the judge, on his own motion or on the motion of a party to the proceedings, may order all or part of the non-English testimony and the translation thereof to be electronically recorded for use in verification of the official transcript of the proceedings.

"(4) The defendant in any criminal action, or a party in any civil action, who is entitled to a translation required under this section, may waive the translation in whole or in part. The waiver must be expressly made by the defendant or party upon the record and approved by his attorney and by the judge. An interpreter shall be used to explain the nature and effect of the waiver to the non-English speaking defendant or party.

"(5) The term 'judge' as used in this section shall include a United States magistrate and a referee in bankruptcy.

"(b) (1) The district court in each judicial district shall maintain on file in the office of the clerk of the court a list of all persons in that district who have been certified as interpreters by the Director of the Administrative Office of the United States Courts under section 604 (a) (12) of this title.

"(2) In any action where the services of an interpreter are required to be utilized under this section, the court shall obtain the services of a certified interpreter from within the judicial district, except that, where there are no certified interpreters in the judicial district, the court, with the assistance of the Administrative Officer of the United States Courts, shall determine the availability of and utilize the services of certified interpreters from nearby districts. Where no certified interpreter is available from a nearby district, the court shall obtain the services of an otherwise competent interpreter."

(b) the Analysis of chapter 119, of title 28, United States Code, is amended by adding at the end thereof the following new item: "1827. Bilingual proceedings."

Facilities and Personnel for Bilingual Proceedings
Sec. 3. Section 604(a) of title 28, United States Code, is amended—
(1) by redesignating paragraph (12) as paragraph (13); and
(2) by inserting immediately below paragraph (11) the following new paragraph:
"(12) Under section 1827 of this title, (A) prescribe, determine, and certify the qualifications of persons who may serve as certified interpreters in bilingual proceedings, and in so doing shall consider the education, training, and experience of those persons; (B) maintain an updated master list of all interpreters certified by him, and report annually on the frequency of requests for, and the use and effectiveness of interpreters in bilingual proceedings pursuant to the provisions of this Act; (C) provide, or make readily available to each district court, appropriate equipment and facilities for the translation of non-English languages; (D) prescribe, from time to time, a schedule of reasonable fees for services rendered by such interpreters and, in those districts where the Director considers it advisable based on the need for interpreters, authorize the employment by the court of certified full-time or part-time interpreters; and (E) pay out of moneys appropriated to the judiciary for the conduct of bilingual proceedings the amount of interpreter's fees of costs of recording, unless the court, in its discretion, directs that all or part of those fees or costs incurred in a civil proceeding in which an interpreter is utilized pursuant to section 1827 (a) (2) of this title be apportioned between the parties or allowed as costs in the action."

Appropriations
Sec. 4. There are hereby authorized to be appropriated to the Federal judiciary such sums as may be necessary to carry out the amendments made by this Act.

Effective Date
Sec. 5. The amendment made by this Act shall take effect on the date which is six months after the date of enactment of this Act.

Federal Translation Coordinating Council Act of 1978

This legislation was introduced in the House of Representatives, Washington, DC, on June 15, 1978, by Congressman John Breckinridge of Kentucky. It is reproduced from the Congressional Record, *Proceedings and Debates of the 95th Congress, Second Session, Vol. 124, No. 92, and was preceded by the following statement:*

"It has come to my attention that the translation community within the Federal Government suffers from a number of problems due to a lack of coordination between various Government departments and agencies involved in translation work. Among these problems is a lack of standard meanings for many foreign terms, discrepancies in grade assignments and contract funding among translators employed in the Federal Government, duplication of work, and inadequate training of personnel. This lack of coordination has also resulted in a complete lack of comprehensive information on the number and location of translators employed in either the private or Government sector, or even a complete listing of all commercial firms engaged in translation work."

A BILL

to establish a Federal Translation Coordinating Council to improve the quality of foreign language translations available for use by the Federal Government.
Be it enacted by the Senate and House of Representatives of the United States of America in Congress assembled:

Short Title
Section 1. This Act may be cited as the "Federal Translation Coordinating Council Act of 1978."

Findings
Section 2. The Congress hereby finds that
(1) the number of translators employed by the Federal Government and the proficiency of such translators have been declining in the last several years;
(2) the community of translators in the United States suffers from a duplication of effort, and lacks the coordination of effort and the sufficient continuity of training necessary to ensure that translations of high quality, including consistency in terminology and standardization of such translations, are available in the United States;
(3) there is insufficient information available to the Congress and to the public regarding the translation capabilities of the Federal Government;
(4) great discrepancies exist with respect to grade assignments and contract funding among the various translators who are employed by the Federal Government;
(5) there are virtually no comprehensive statistics regarding the number of translators, the types of translation, and the costs of translation activities in the United States;
(6) foreign language enrollments in institutions of higher education in the United States dropped 30 percent between 1968 and 1974 and appear to be continuing to decline;
(7) in 1975, only 24 percent of the secondary school students in the United States were studying any foreign language and even fewer are doing so now;
(8) only 17 percent of the students in the United States who receive instruction in a foreign language are able to speak, read, or write such language with proficiency; and
(9) the International Education Act of 1969, which provides for grants for international studies and research has never been funded.

Establishment of Council

Section 3. There is hereby established as an independent organization in the executive branch of the Federal Translation Coordinating Council.

Functions of Council

Section 4. (a) Before the date determined under section 11 to be the date on which the Council ceases to exist, the Council shall—

(1) make such recommendations as may be necessary to coordinate all Federal programs, activities, and endeavors involving translation;

(2) determine, evaluate, and, where possible, improve the quality and quantity of translation available to interested persons;

(3) conduct a survey of the community of translators in order to determine the number and capabilities of translators whose services may be available to the Federal Government;

(4) determine which institutions of higher education in the United States provide training in skills for translation;

(5) determine the needs of the Federal Government for translation services;

(6) determine which foreign countries maintain translation systems and evaluate such systems for purposes of comparison and improvement of the quality of translation in the United States; and

(7) after consultation with persons in the community of translators and other persons interested in translation, determine such principles, standards, and procedures for translation as the Council may deem appropriate.

(b) (1) In order to perform the functions established in subsection (a), the Council shall utilize pertinent available information, studies, reports, statistics, and other data gathered or compiled by any department, agency, or instrumentality of the Federal Government, or by any other public or private source.

(2) Upon request of the Council, the head of any Federal department, agency, or instrumentality shall furnish to the Council such information as may be necessary for carrying out the functions of the Council and as may be available to such department, agency, or instrumentality.

Membership

Section 5. (a) The Council shall be composed of 10 members as follows:

(1) a delegate of the Secretary of State;

(2) a delegate of the Secretary of Defense;

(3) two representatives appointed by the President from among officers and employees of the Federal Government who are involved in intelligence activities for the Federal Government and who exercise significant decision making authority relating to translation and related fields;

(4) two representatives appointed by the President from among officers and employees of the Federal Government (one of whom shall be from the National Science Foundation) who exercise significant decision making authority relating to translation and related fields in any Federal department or agency which requires translation services; and

(5) four representatives appointed by the President who are experts in translation including persons from institutions of higher education and private organizations actively involved in translation.

(b) The Chairman of the Council shall be designated by the President from among those members serving on the Council pursuant to subsection (a).

(c) (1) Members of the Council who are full-time officers or employees of the United States shall receive no additional pay on account of their service on the Council.

(2) Members of the Council, other than those referred to in paragraph (1), shall receive $120 for each day (including travel time) during which they are actually engaged in the performance of the duties of the Council.

(3) While away from their homes on regular places of business in the performance of services for the Council, members of the Council shall be allowed travel expenses, including a per diem allowance in lieu of subsistence, in the same manner as employees of the Federal Government are allowed such expenses under subchapter I of chapter 57 title 5, United States Code.

Staff

Section 6. (a) The Council may appoint such staff as it considers desirable without regard to the provisions of title 5, United States Code, governing appointments in the competitive service. The Council may pay such staff without regard to the provisions of chapter 51 and subchapter III of chapter 53 of such title, relating to classification and General Schedule pay rates, except that no individual so appointed may receive pay in excess of the annual rate of basic pay in effect for grade GS-18 of the General Schedule under section 5332 of such title.

(b) Upon request of the Council, the head of any Federal department or agency may detail to the temporary duty with the Council on a reimbursement basis such personnel within his administrative jurisdiction as the Council may need or believe to be useful for carrying out its functions under section 4(a). Any such detail shall be without loss of seniority, pay, or other employment status.

Reporting and Implementation

Section 7. (a) The Council shall transmit to the President, the Congress, and the Secretary of State a report which shall include

(1) recommendations with respect to the coordination of overall policy and development of objectives and priorities for all Federal translation activities, including any suggestion for Executive action or modification of any Federal program relating to translation;

(2) any recommendation for legislation with respect to the implementation of the principles, standards, and procedures for translation determined by the Council pursuant to paragraph (7) of section 4(a); and

(3) a compilation of all data and information described in paragraphs (3) through (6) of section 4(a).

(b) The Secretary of State shall coordinate and implement as is practicable, any recommendation included in the report transmitted to him pursuant to subsection (a).

Public Inspection

Section 8. To the extent permitted by law, all appropriate records and papers of the Council shall be made available for public inspection during regular office hours.

Rules and Regulations

Section 9. The Council shall have the authority to prescribe such rules and regulations as it may consider necessary to carry out the provisions of this Act.

Termination

Section 10. The Council shall cease to exist one calendar year after the date on which the President appoints the last of all of the members to be appointed by him to the Council pursuant to paragraph (3) through (5) of section 5.

Congressman Breckinridge concluded his introduction of the above bill with the following evaluation:

"In establishing the Council, I do not wish to imply that all Government translation work is bad; most of it is good and a great deal of it is excellent. But serious problems do exist in the translation community and they require our attention. This bill is not intended to be a final version, but is introduced with the hope that it will begin the process whereby we may begin to seek out solutions to the many problems that exist in this vital area."

US Copyright Act of 1976—Public Law 94-553

Sections Pertaining to Translations

The new copyright law, which became effective in January 1, 1978, and superseded the old copyright law, US Copyright Act of 1909, contains a number of references to translations of foreign works and their copyrightability: definitions of a "derivative work" and a "work made for hire," exclusive rights in copyrighted works (the preparation of derivative works based on copyrighted work), and ownership of copyright of "works made for hire." These excerpts are here reproduced verbatim. They are followed by explanatory excerpts from Copyright Handbook *(Bowker, 1978) by Donald F. Johnston, a book which is, according to the preface, "intended primarily for use by publishers, librarians, educators, and authors, who regularly, or from time to time, have need for direct access to information about the new law."*

Definitions—From Sec. 101

A "derivative work" is a work based upon one or more preexisting works, such as a translation, musical arrangement, dramatization, fic-

US Copyright Act of 1976—Public Law 94–553 (cont.)

tionalization, motion picture version, sound recording, art reproduction, abridgment, condensation, or any other form in which a work may be recast, transformed, or adapted. A work consisting of editorial revisions, annotations, elaborations, or other modifications, which, as a whole, represent an original work of authorship, is a "derivative work."

A "work made for hire" is (1) a work prepared by an employee within the scope of his or her employment; or (2) a work specially ordered or commissioned for use as a contribution to a collective work, as a part of a motion picture or other audiovisual work, as a translation, as a supplementary work, as a compilation, as an instructional text, as a test, as answer material for a test, or as an atlas, if the parties expressly agree in a written instrument signed by them that the work shall be considered a work made for hire. . . .

Exclusive rights in copyrighted works—From Sec. 106

. . . the owner of copyright under this title has the exclusive rights to do and to authorize any of the following: . . . (2) to prepare derivative works based upon the copyrighted work; . . .

Ownership of copyright—From Sec. 201

(b) Works Made for Hire.—In the case of a work made for hire, the employer or other person for whom the work was prepared is considered the author for purposes of this title, and, unless the parties have expressly agreed otherwise in a written instrument signed by them, owns all of the rights comprised in the copyright.

Notice of copyright: Visually perceptible copies—From Sec. 401

(a) General Requirement.—Whenever a work protected under this title is published in the United States or elsewhere by authority of the copyright owner, a notice of copyright as provided by this section shall be placed on all publicly distributed copies from which the work can be visually perceived, either directly or with the aid of a machine or device.

(b) Form of Notice.—The notice appearing on the copies shall consist of the following three elements:

(1) the symbol © (the letter C in a circle), or the word "Copyright", or the abbreviation "Copr."; and

(2) the year of first publication of the work; in the case of compilations or derivative works incorporating previously published material, the year date of first publication of the compilation or derivative work is sufficient. . . .; and

(3) the name of the owner of copyright in the work, or an abbreviation by which the name can be recognized, or a generally known alternative designation of the owner.

On pages 48–49 of *Copyright Handbook*, Johnston comments:

"Works Made for Hire. In the case of works made for hire, the employer or the one who commissioned the work is considered to be the author [201(b)]. A work-made-for-hire category has been part of U.S. copyright law for a long time. Congress wanted to retain the concept in the new law, but decided to limit specifically the types of works that can fall within it. The new law provides for two categories.

"*Works by Employees.* A work prepared by an employee within the scope of his or her employment is a work made for hire [101 'work made for hire']. The employer owns all of the rights of copyright in the work unless the employer and employee have agreed otherwise in a written instrument signed by them [201(b)].

"Often, the employer–employee relationship is clear as is the 'scope of employment' issue. Sometimes, however, there is room at least for argument. The employer, for example, could consider preserving a record of the facts, establishing the employment and its scope. The employer should also consider, in some cases, drawing up a formal agreement that reflects the work-made-for-hire status of the work. (Note 4: a discussion of when a person is considered an 'employee' for work made for hire purposes, see Angel and Tannenbaum, 'Works Made for Hire Under S. 22,' *New York Law School Law Review* 22 (1976): 209; 221–225.)

"Theoretically, an employer's work made for hire can be any type of work since the employer–employee relationship can cover just about anything. Two of the most frequent types of 'employer' works made for hire are periodicals (as collective works) and periodical contributions prepared by employees of the publication. . . .

"*Specially Ordered or Commissioned Works.* The new law's second category of a work made for hire relates to works that are specially ordered or commissioned [101 'work made for hire']. There are two requirements for this category. First, the parties must expressly agree in a written instrument signed by them that the work shall be considered a work made for hire. Second, the work must be specially ordered or commissioned for use as one or more of the following: 1. translation; . . ."

6
Journals/Books
Journals/Bulletins/Newsletters

With the exception of *Delos,* a short-lived publication that translators still refer to as the most distinguished journal of its kind every published, and *Babel,* the official journal of the International Federation of Translators, which serves an international audience with material on the protection of translators, news of member societies of FIT, multilingual lexicography and terminology, most publications devoted to translational matters are issued by individual associations to serve intra-organizational purposes. The two leading American publications, the *ATA Chronicle* and the slightly older *Federal Linguist,* published by the American Translators Association and The Society of Federal Linguists, respectively, are intended to inform members of matters of interest to the practicing professional translator. The most recent addition to the growing number of publications is *Translation Review,* the official journal of the American Literary Translators Association (ALTA) which is devoted exclusively to humanistic and literary translation.

A number of professional journals of a purely linguistic nature, published either by linguistic societies or trade publishers serving the linguistic community, regularly devote sections of each issue to problems related to both linguistics and translation. Of these the most prestigious are the Canadian journal, *Meta* (formerly *Translators Journal*), published by a combine of Canadian associations and councils; the German journals *Fremdsprachen, Lebende sprachen, Der Sprachmittler;* the Dutch *Levende talen;* and *The Incorporated Linguist,* published by the Institute of Linguists in the United Kingdom.

ABRATES
Associação Brasileira de Tradutores (Brazilian Assn of Translators), Rua Almirante Barroso 97, 3 andar, Rio de Janeiro, Brazil *Tel* 221-4486. *Founded* 1976.
Official bulletin of the Brazilian association.

AIIC BULLETIN
Association Internationale des Interprètes de Conférence, 14 rue de l'Ancien-Port, CH-1201 Geneva, Switzerland.
Official newsletter of the International Association of Conference Interpreters.

ATA CHRONICLE
American Translators Assn, Box 129, Croton-on-Hudson, NY 10520 USA *Tel* 914-271-3260. *Ed* Isabel A Leonard, PO Box 55, Hingham, MA 02043 USA *Tel* 617-749-1540.
The official journal of the American Translators Association, the largest translators' society in the United States, published ten times a year, distributed free to its membership. Non-member subscription: $25 per year. In 1976 the journal greatly expanded its format and coverage and now contains Association news, dictionary reviews, news of FIT and other translators' societies, miniglossaries, informative articles on every aspect of the profession, "Members in the News" column, periodic "profiles" of individual ATA members, "Problem Corner," letters to the editor, and classified advertising.

L'ACTUALITÉ TERMINOLOGIQUE
Centre de Terminologie, Ministry of Supply and Services, Publications Div, Ottawa, ON K1A OS9, Canada *Founded* 1968.
Monthly bulletin of the Canadian Direction générale de la terminologie et de la documentation, Ministry of Supply and Services.

L'ANTENNE (The Antenna)
Translators' Soc of Quebec, 1010 rue Sainte-Catherine W #841, Montreal, PQ H3B 3R5, Canada *Tel* 514-866-9101 *Founded* 1970.
A news bulletin published seven or eight times a year.

BABEL: International Journal of Translation
Published by the Hungarian Academy of Sciences (Akadémiai Kiadó), distributed by Kultura, H-1389 Budapest, PO Box 149, Hungary, *Managerial and Edtl Committee* Pierre-François Caillé, 185, ave Victor Hugo, F-75116 Paris, France *Ed* György Radó, Petofi Sándor utca 9, H-1052 Budapest, Hungary. *Founded* 1955.
Published quarterly by the International Federation of Translators (FIT) with the support of UNESCO, the official organ of the Federation has been the leading such journal of an international nature since its founding. It is addressed to translators, interpreters, philologists, literary historians, linguists, librarians, publishers, editors, copyright agencies, universities, and to the general public that wishes to be informed of FIT's activities to further mutual understanding by promoting translation.
Individual issues contain articles, bibliographies, and lexicographical information and reviews pertaining to the following: the practice and theory of translation and interpretation, professional aspects of the profession (ethics, material conditions, client relations), translation programs, translator-training programs, activities of Member Societies, legal problems (copyright).

LA BANQUE DE MOTS
Conseil International de la Langue Français (International Council of the French Language), 105 Ter rue de Lille, F-75007 Paris, France.

BULLETIN DE L'ASTI
Swiss Translators and Interpreters Assn, 11 ave de Gambach, CH-1700 Fribourg, Switzerland.
Published bimonthly for members of the Association and deals mainly with internal organizational matters.

BULLETIN DE LA TRADUCTION
Le Bureau de Terminologie, Commission des Communautes Européennes (Commission of the European Communities), Division IX/C/1, 1 ave de Cortenbergh, B-1040 Brussels, Belgium *Tel* 35 00 40 *Telex* COMEURBRU 21 877.

BULLETIN D'INFORMATION
Chambre Belge des Traducteurs, Interpretes et Philologues, De Haynlaan 110, B-1090 Brussels, Belgium. *Ed* G Becklandt, Koning Leopold II laan 37, B-9000 Ghent, Belgium *Tel* (091) 22 53 56.
Official bulletin of the Belgian association.

BULLETIN D'INFORMATION DE L'ASSOCIATION DES TRADUCTEURS LITTÉRAIRES DE FRANCE
80 blvd Pasteur, F-75015 Paris, France *Founded* 1973.
Quarterly bulletin of the Association published for its membership.

BULLETIN OF THE HKTS
The Hong Kong Translation Society, PO Box 335, Kowloon Central Post Office, Kowloon, Hong Kong *Tel* 5-468161 *Ed* C C Liu.
Official informative newsletter of the Society (published once every two months, usually in Chinese), devoted to disseminating news of the profession and the activities of the society as well as printing speeches made at the Society's meetings and bibliographical items of interest.

LA CLÉ DES MOTS

Conseil International de la Langue Française (International Council of the French Language), 105 Ter rue de Lille, F-75007 Paris, France.

THE CONCORDIAT

Monterey Inst of Foreign Studies, PO Box 1978, Monterey, CA 93940 USA *Founded* 1976.

Quarterly journal of Concordiat (see Sec 2, USA), an independent organization of the students and alumni of the Department of Translation & Interpretation, intended to serve as a link between students and alumni working professionally in translation and interpretation.

DELOS, a journal on & of translation
(defunct)

Delos was published by the National Translation Center at the University of Texas at Austin under the editorship of D S Carne-Ross and with an editorial board which included William Arrowsmith, W H Auden, Keith Botsford, Roger Shattuck, George Steiner, and David Wevill. The first of 12 scheduled issues appeared in April 1968 and continued until issue 6 in 1971 when the journal ceased publication. While centrally concerned with translation and literature in translation, the magazine was also a general review of interest to a broad public (as well as to specialists). It was designed to make translation and its problems known as widely as possible and to attract to the craft of translation and to serious consideration of its problems, those who had not participated before or given translation serious consideration. Regular features included translations of fiction, plays, poetry; essays and critical studies on translation in the broadest sense of the term; reviews of translations, a clearinghouse for translations known to be in progress and titles for which publishers were seeking translators; notes on contributors; listings of grants made from the Center's Revolving Fund by the National Advisory Board (see Sec 2, USA).

EQUIVALENCES

Association pour la Promotion de l'Étude des Langues Modernes (Assn for the Promotion of the Study of Modern Languages), Institut Supérieur de l'État de Traducteurs et d'Interpretes, rue J Hazard 34, B-Brussels, Belgium. *Ed* J M van der Meerschen *Founded* 1970.

Triquarterly with text mainly in French; occasionally in Dutch, English, German, Italian, & Spanish.

ESCOLOPENDRA

Inter-American Assn of Translators (AIT), 1324 Jonquil St NW, Washington, DC 20012 USA.

Official bulletin of the association of professional translators of the Americas, with a special interest in those translators and interpreters who are associated with US governmental agencies, the OAS, and international agencies and organizations.

THE FEDERAL LINGUIST

Soc of Federal Linguists, PO Box 7765, Washington, DC 20044 USA *Founded* 1967.

Edtl Bd Elemer Bako, Irene V Bald, Elsie P Brown, Sandra Deem, Wanda Feeley, Murray L Howder, Thomas L Jones, Thomas Lagergreen, Everette E Larson (Man Ed), Rita Llaverias, Louvan Nolting, Leopoldina Nowak

Dependent on the availability of resources, the journal has been issued irregularly, but appears approximately twice a year in a double issue. The reports, surveys, and analytical essays resulting from the Society's current program are presented regularly.

FREMDSPRACHEN: Zeitschrift für Dolmetscher, Übersetzer und Sprachkundige

Karl-Marx Universität, Hauptabteilung Öffentlichkeitsarbeit, Abteilung Wissenschaftliche Publikationen, DDR-701, Leipzig, German Democratic Republic *Distributor* Buchexport, Zeitungsvertriebsamt, Exportabteilung, Strasse der Pariser Kommune 3/4, 1004 Berlin, East Germany.

Contains texts in English, French, German, Russian, and Spanish, deals with the latest developments in these languages, and contains specialized vocabularies. Annual subscription: 20 East German marks, with postal expenses to be added for non-socialist countries. Specimen copies available from the university.

IN OTHER WORDS

Wycliffe Bible Translators, Inc, 19891 Beach Blvd, Huntington Beach, CA 92648 USA *Ed* Carey Moore.

Devoted to Bible translation; supersedes *Translation*.

THE INCORPORATED LINGUIST

The Inst of Linguists, 24a Highbury Grove, London N5, UK *Ed* D Cook-Radmore *Founded* 1962.

Official journal of The Institute of Linguists and its subsidiary, The Translators' Guild.

INFORMATIO

Association of Translators and Interpreters of Ontario, 202-260 Dalhousie St, Ottawa, ON K1N 7E4, Canada *Founded* 1971.

INTERPRETE

Longo Editore, Via Rocca ai Fossi 6, CP 431, I-48100 Ravenna, Italy *Ed* Alfio Longo.

Published irregularly with texts in English or Italian.

INTERPRÈTE

Assn d'Interpretes et de Traducteurs, Case Strand 388, CH-Geneva, Switzerland *Ed* Violette Collins *Founded* 1946.

Official quarterly journal of the Swiss Association of Interpreters and Translators.

JEITA JIHO

Japanese-English Interpreters & Translators Assn, PO Box 19546, Washington, DC 20036 USA *Founded* 1975.

A bulletin of the Association featuring articles and news items on Japanese-English translation.

JISTA

Indian Scientific Translators Assn, c/o INSDOC, Hillside Rd, New Delhi 12, India *Founded* 1964.

Quarterly journal of the ISTA (see Sec 2, India).

THE JOURNALS OF PIERRE MENARD

Peter Hoy, 97 Hollywell St, Oxford, UK.

A private journal featuring book reviews, monographic articles, essays on the theory and practice of translation into and from most European languages, each issue devoted to one translation.

LANGUES ET TERMINOLOGIES

Conseil International de la Langue Français (International Council of the French Language), 105 Ter rue de Lille, F-75007 Paris, France.

A fortnightly informational journal containing announcements of conferences, congresses, and new books and publications on language and terminology.

LEBENDE SPRACHEN: Zeitschrift für fremde Sprachen in Wissenschaft und Praxis

Verlag Langenscheidt KG, Crellestrasse 29, 1000 Berlin 62, West Germany *Founded* 1956.

Quarterly journal devoted to foreign languages in science, with texts in English, French, German, Italian, Spanish, and each issue containing articles on language and translation. Circ 4000. DM 35 annually.

LEVENDE TALEN

Vereniging van Leraren in Levende Talen (Assn of Teachers in Modern Languages), Wolters-Noordhoff B V, Box 58, Oude Boteringestraat 52, Groningen, The Netherlands. *Ed* P J Slagter *Founded* 1912.

Published six times a year with texts in Dutch, English, French, German, Italian, Russian, Spanish.

META

School of Translation, Univ of Montreal, C P 6128, Succursale A, Montreal, PQ H3C 3J7, Canada *Founded* 1956.

Ed André Clas *Edtl Bd* Bruce Barkman, Daniel Slote, Jean-Paul Vinay, Roger Boivineau, Paul A Horguelin, Jean Hesse, Marcel Marquis, Irene V Spilka, François Geuthier, Pierre Marchand *Contrib Eds* P F Caillé (Paris), Jean Delisle (Ottawa), Henry Fischbach (New York), Christel Gallan (Moncton), Roger Goffin (Brussels), M Govaert (Anvers), L Hirschberg (Brussels), B Hunter Smeaton (Calgary), R W Jumpelt (Bad Godesberg), A Lane (Munich), H J Pfisterer (Heidelberg), T A Pilley (London), Jacqualine C Romney (Sudbury).

A quarterly journal published in cooperation with the Society of Translators of Quebec, Association of Translators and Interpreters of Ontario, and the Council of Translators and Interpreters of Canada. Contains essays on all aspects of translation and interpretation, book reviews, and bibliographies of writings on translation and related fields. Although the material, usually in French and occasionally in English, tends to be of interest to Canadian translators, much of it pertains to universal translation themes. Formerly titled *Journal des Traducteurs* (Translators Journal).

MITTEILUNGSBLATT
Österreichischer Übersetzer- und Dolmetscher-Verband "Universitas" (Austrian Soc of Translators and Interpreters "Universitas"), Institut für Dolmetscherausbildung an der Universität Wien, Dr Karl Lueger-Ring 1, A-1010 Vienna, Austria *Tel* 42 76 11, 336 *Secy* Liese Katschinka.

Official bulletin of the Austrian translators and interpreters association.

MITTEILUNGSBLATT DES SCHWEIZE-RISCHER ÜBERSETZER- UND DOL-METSCHER-VERBANDES
Assn Suisse de Traducteurs et Interprètes, Case postal 2726, CH-3001 Berne, Switzerland.

Official bulletin of the Swiss Association of Translators and Interpreters.

MITTEILUNGSBLATT FÜR DOLMET-SCHER UND ÜBERSETZER
Bundesverband der Dolmetscher und Übersetzer (BDÜ) (Federal Union of Interpreters and Translators). Wolfgangstrasse 148, D-6000 Frankfurt 1, West Germany. *Ed* Hans Schwarz *Founded* 1955.

Bimonthly official bulletin of the German association. Circ 3500.

NÉOLOGIE EN MARCHE
Office de la Langue Français (Office of the French Language), Govt of Quebec, Canada.

NEWS TRANSLATION
The East-West Ctr, East-West Communication Inst, 177 East-West Rd, Honolulu, Hawaii 96822 USA *Cable* EASWESCEN.

PRACTICAL PAPERS FOR THE BIBLE TRANSLATOR
United Bible Societies, Europe Regional Ctr, rue du Trone 160, B-1050 Brussels, Belgium *Ed* Rev E McG Fry.

Contains New Testament abstracts; supersedes in part *Bible Translator*.

PROFESSIONAL TRANSLATOR (defunct)
Edited by Charles Parsons, this was the official bimonthly journal of the Guild of Professional Translators which was established to serve the interests of practical translators who shared English as a working language. Both ceased to exist in 1978.

RETX (Russian-English Translators Exchange)
Translation Research Inst, 5914 Pulaski Ave, Philadelphia, PA 19144 USA *Ed* Charles Parsons.

An informal newsletter by and for practicing translators of Russian. Features include new and difficult terms, comparison translations, dictionary reviews, employment notices. 10 issues per year. Subscription: $10 per year, individual; $20 per year, corporate.

RENDITIONS: A Chinese-English Translation Magazine
Comparative Literature and Translation Ctr, Inst for Chinese Studies, The Chinese Univ of Hong Kong, Shatin, NT, Hong Kong *Tel* 12-612211 *Ed* George Kao *Exec Ed* Stephen C Soong *Founded* 1973.

An English language journal published biannually, devoted primarily to translations of Chinese writings past and present and covering broadly the humanities, both contemporary and classical. Issues contain the original Chinese text of a part of the contents, and its contributors are from many countries and range from students to scholars of international reputation. Both the magazine and its publications, Renditions Books, are widely used by students of Chinese language and literature the world over.

SIGN LANGUAGE STUDIES
Linstok Pr, 9306 Mintwood St, Silver Spring, MD 20901.

SPRACHE UND DATENVERARBEI-TUNG
Max Niemeyer Verlag, Postfach 2140, D-7400 Tübingen, West Germany.

A new periodical, established ca 1976, which regularly devotes attention to machine translation.

DER SPRACHMITTLER: Informationshefte des Sprachendienstes der Bundeswehr
Bundesministerium der Verteidigung, Postfach 161, D-5300, Bonn, Germany *Founded* 1960.

Official organ of the VÜ, the German association of translation agencies. Features information on fees, rates, intra- and inter-associational politics, reviews of new dictionaries.

T A INFORMATIONS
Assn pour le Developpement de la Traduction Automatique et de la Linguistique Appliquée (Assn for the Development of Machine Translation and Applied Linguistics), Editions Klincksieck, 11 rue de Lille, F-75007 Paris, France *Founded* 1965.

Published formerly as *Traduction Automatique* (Machine Translation), the semiannual journal is devoted to the application of machine translation to language and contains book reviews, abstracts of articles, charts, illustrations.

TSC NEWSLETTER
Translation Service Ctr, c/o The Asia Foundation, 31 Kowa Bldg #8, 19-1 Shirokanedai 3-chome, Minato-ku, Tokyo 108, Japan *Tel* 03-441-8291 *Cable* ASIAF TOKYO. *Dir* James L Stewart *Man Ed* Kano Tsutomu *Sr American Ed/Translator* to be appointed.

Founded in 1978 with the first issue dated January 1979, the newsletter is intended to inform its recipients of the activities of the Translation Service Center (see Sec 2, Japan).

TECHNICAL PAPERS FOR THE BIBLE TRANSLATOR
United Bible Soc, 56 Craigton Rd, Aberdeen AB1 7UN, UK. *Ed* Paul Ellingworth *Founded* 1950.

Contains New Testament abstracts, book reviews. In 1972 superseded in part *Bible Translator*. Semiannual.

TECHNICAL TRANSLATION BULLETIN
Aslib, 3 Belgrave Sq, London SW1X 8PL, UK *Founded* 1955.

TERMINOLOGICAL INFORMATION
Directorate for Translation & Terminology Services, European Parliament, PO Box 1601, Luxembourg, Belgium.

TETRADI PEREVODCHIKA (The Translator's Copybooks)
International Relations Publishing House, Moscow, USSR *Ed* L S Barkhudarov *Founded* 1964.

Published annually in a single issue averaging 100–120 pages, the Soviet journal contains articles under four classifications: translation theory, literary translation, oral interpretation, translation exercises and practice.

TRADUIRE
Société Française des Traducteurs, 1 rue de Courcelles, 75008 Paris, France *Ed* Florence Herbulot *Founded* 1955.

Official journal of the Society, published in tabloid format, and containing book reviews and bibliographies.

TRANSLATION
Translation Ctr, School of the Arts, Math 307A, Columbia Univ, New York, NY 10027 USA *Tel* 212-280-0235 *Founded* 1973. *Edtl Bd* Frank MacShane, Robert Payne, William Jay Smith.

Published twice yearly, contains exceptional translations of poems, short stories, excerpts from novels, articles on translation theory and problems, and reports of symposiums and conferences held by the Center. Incorporates the *Newsletter*, containing notes on conferences, suggestions of work in need of translation, and articles on events of interest to translators and the literary community.

TRANSLATION NEWS
International Translations Ctr, 101 Doelenstraat, NL-2611 NS Delft, The Netherlands *Ed* D van Bergeijk *Founded* 1978.

A newsletter, published irregularly, reporting about the activities of the Center and other items of interest in the field of documentation of translations and related fields. Issued free of charge to subscribers of *World Transindex* and on request.

TRANSLATION REVIEW
American Literary Translators Assn (ALTA), Box 688, Mail Sta 1102, The Univ of Texas at Dallas, Richardson, TX 75080 USA *Eds* Rainer Schulte, James P White *Founded* 1978.

A quarterly publication of the first association of literary and humanistic translators in the United States, designed to cover a wide spectrum of activities: book reviews (significant creative and critical books in the contemporary arts and humanities, new translations of older works, books and essays which are about the translation process, special translation issues of journals and magazines); feature essays (about publishers of translations, translators, original authors, special aspects of the translation process); listings (journals publishing translations, dictionaries and reference materials, books on the theory and practice of translation, translations in progress, translation programs in the United States, national and international translation conferences, translation awards and scholarships).

TRANSLATIONS REGISTER-INDEX
National Translations Ctr, The John Crerar Library, 35 W 33 St, Chicago, IL 60616 USA *Dir* Ildiko D Nowak.

A monthly translations accession bulletin listing translations reported by agencies or free-lancers. A Directory of Sources included in each issue lists participating translators and agencies. Copies of the translations are not deposited at the Center; clients requesting reported translations are referred to the agency or translator. Translations contributed to the Center by industrial organizations, government agencies, academic institutions, and research organizations become part of the Center's collection. As of 1977, the Center listed over 750,000 translations from about 40 languages.

TRANSLATØREN
Translatørforeningen (Assn of Danish Sworn Translators), Bornholmsgade 1, DK-1266 Copenhagen K, Denmark *Ed* Jesper Lundbye *Founded* 1939.

Official bulletin of the Association of Danish Sworn Translators, issued five times a year. Text in Danish, Norwegian, Swedish, and occasionally in English, French & German. Circ 900.

TRANSST
Translation Studies Program, General Literary Studies, Univ of Amsterdam, Spuistraat 210, NL-1012 VT Amsterdam, the Netherlands *Tel* (020) 525-3873 *Man Ed* Dirk Bloemraad *Edit Group* F F de Haan, James S Holmes, R H van Lindonk, Raymond Van den Broeck.

Irregular mimeographed international newsletter reporting on research in progress, books recent and forthcoming, recently published articles, available reprints of papers, and news of interest to translation scholars. Published by the Translation Studies Program and the Institute for Translator Training, both of the University of Amsterdam (see Sec 4, the Netherlands). Clearinghouse for the Scientific Committee on Translation of the International Association of Applied Linguistics (IALA) and the Translation Studies Committee of the International Association for Comparative Literature (AILC). Supported by a subsidy from the University of Leuven. Available free to all bona fide translation scholars.

DER ÜBERSETZER
Verband deutschsprachiger Übersetzer literarischer und wissenschaftlicher Werke e V (VDÜ) *Ed* Eva Bornemann, A-4612 Scharten, Vitta 7, Austria.

Published more or less monthly, the bulletin appears in four pages and is devoted predominantly to literary translations.

VAN TAAL TOT TAAL
Gerrit van der Veenstraat 29/III, NL-1077 DN Amsterdam, the Netherlands *Tel* (020) 71-4106 *Editl Bd* Christine Oberman, F F de Haan, F J A Mostern *Founded* 1978.

Quarterly review of the Nederlands Genootschap van Vertalers (see Sec 2, the Netherlands), mostly in Dutch with occasional texts in other languages. Annual subscription: 20 Dutch florins.

THE WORD GUILD MAGAZINE
The Word Guild, Inc, 119 Mt Auburn St, Harvard Sq, Cambridge, MA 02138 USA *Tel* 617-492-4656 *Founded* 1977.

Features regular articles on various aspects of translation by Harry Zohn of Brandeis University.

WORLD TRANSINDEX
International Translation Ctr (ITC), 101 Doelenstraat, NL-2611 NS Delft, The Netherlands *Tel* (015) 142242; 142243 *Telex* 31673 ITC NL *Ed* D van Bergeijk *Founded* 1978.

Published jointly with the Directorate General for Scientific and Technical Information Management of the Commission of the European Communities (see Sec 8, Belgium), and the Scientific and Technical Documentation Center of the Centre National de la Recherche Scientifique in Paris, the monthly publication is a merger of three former publications: *Translation Bulletin*, *Bulletin des Traductions*, and *World Index of Scientific Translations and List of Translations Notified to the International Translations Center*.

World Transindex announces yearly about 32,000 translations from Asiatic and Eastern European languages into Western languages, and some translations from Western languages into French and Spanish, and includes a Source Index and an Author Index, both cumulated annually. The data, produced by means of the PASCAL system, stores all information in a central data base which permits the production of print-outs and will, in the future, be available for on-line access and in a microfiche edition.

Books

The first extensive English-language bibliography of material pertaining to translation appeared in 1964 in *Toward a Science of Translation* by Eugene A Nida, the noted linguist and biblical scholar, and listed a selection of nearly 2000 diverse source materials dealing not only with the discipline itself, but with what the author regarded as related fields: linguistic structure, psychology (as related to semantics and perception of symbols), anthropology, information theory, machine translation, theology (special problems of Bible translation, the author's area of authority), and stylistics and literary criticism. It was followed in 1970 by an even more extensive international bibliography covering the years 1962–71, the most comprehensive thus far undertaken, *The Science of Translation: An Analytical Bibliography* in two volumes and a supplement, by three distinguished European specialists, K-R Bausch, Josef Klegraf, and Wolfram Wilss. A third volume is now in preparation.

A truly comprehensive encyclopedic bibliography, planned as volume two of the overall project *Materials for a History of Translation* will cover all writings in all languages, including everything that has ever appeared in all journals and periodicals, and will embrace and be classified under such headings as: awards, fellowships, grants, prizes; bibliographies; associations and centers; children's literature; dictionaries, glossaries, thesauri, terminological data banks; directories, indexes, and services; dissertations and theses, drama; film dubbing; legislation and guidelines; interpretation; linguistics and semantics; machine translation and computer-aids to translation; the translators' market place; music; poetry; proceedings of congresses, conferences, symposiums, and seminars; publishers and publishing; theology, religion and scripture; theory and practice of translation; sign language interpretation and translation; and transliteration.

The books listed below, either in print or available in university and some public libraries, comprise a very basic international selection of American, British, Canadian, Western European, and Soviet material intended for the student preparing to enter the profession, and include all contemporary studies containing important bibliographies or bibliographic footnotes. In view of the recent establishment of diplomatic and cultural relations with the People's Republic of China, the consequent renewal of interest in the Chinese-speaking world at large, and the increased need in the West of highly trained language specialists in this area, a selection of the most important recent Far East writings on both Chinese-English and English-Chinese translation and its extraordinary interpretative and linguistic problems is included. These works have been culled mostly from extensive contemporary bibliographies provided by the Institute of Chinese Studies of The Chinese University of Hong Kong and by the Hong Kong Translation Society (see Sec 2, Hong Kong).

ACTES DU COLLOQUE INTERNATIONAL DE LINGUISTIQUE ET DE TRADUCTION, MONTRÉAL, 30 SEPTEMBRE–3 OCTOBRE 1970
André Clas, ed. Montréal: Presses de l'Université de Montréal, 1971.

ADAM'S DREAM: A CASEBOOK ON TRANSLATION
Ben Belitt. New York: Grove Press, 1978, 186 pp.

AFTER BABEL: Aspects of Language and Translation
George Steiner. New York: Oxford Univ Press, 1975, 507 pp.

Although much space is devoted to the history and theory of translation as it is commonly understood, translation is but a part of the complicated discussion based on the author's contention that "the problem of the nature of translation appears to be central to that of language itself. . . ." This book has applied poetics, literary criticism, and the history of cultural forms to aspects of natural language. Its focus throughout has been on the act of translation. Select bibliography of 198 entries from 1813 to 1973.

AKTUAL'NYE PROBLEMY TEORII KHUDOZHESTVENNOGO PEREVODA (Topical Problems of the Theory of Artistic Translation)
Z Kul'manova, ed. Moscow: Union of Writers of the USSR, 1967, 2 vols.

Proceedings of the All-Soviet symposium, Feb–Mar 1966.

AN APPROACH TO TECHNICAL TRANSLATION: AN INTRODUCTORY GUIDE FOR SCIENTIFIC READERS
CA Finch. London & New York: Pergamon (Library of Industrial and Commerical Education and Training), 1969, 70 pp.

APPROACHES TO TRANSLATION STUDIES
Assen/Amsterdam: Van Gorcum.

Devoted largely or exclusively to the general field of translation studies with emphasis on translation theory and its methods and history, examples of translation analysis and evaluation, works of methodological significance, applied translation problems.

THE ART AND PROFESSION OF TRANSLATION: Proceedings of the Asia Foundation Conference on Chinese-English Translation
T C Lai, ed. Hong Kong: The Hong Kong Translation Society, 1977.

THE ART OF TRANSLATION
Theodore Horace Savory. London: Jonathan Cape, 1957; Chester Spring, PA: Dufour Editions, 1961, 159 pp.; enlarged edition. Boston: The Writer, 1968, 191 pp., paperback 1969.

Frequently referred to as "the best book on the subject in English," it contains nine essays on the work, art, and principles of translation, on the translation of the classics and poetry, translating the Bible, and educational and scientific translation.

ASPECTS OF TRANSLATIONS
Andrew Donald Booth et al. Preface by A H Smith. London: Secker & Warburg (Communication Research Ctr, Univ College, Studies in Communication, N 2), 1958, 145 pp.

Bibliographical footnotes.

THE ASTONISHMENT OF WORDS: An Experiment in the Comparison of Languages
Victor Proetz. Foreword by Alastair Reid. Afterword by Charles Nagel. Austin: University of Texas Press, 1971, 187 pp.

Includes selected passages from English literature, with parallel French and German translations.

ATT VARA TOLK, TEKNIK, UTBILDNING, ARBETSMÖJLIGHETER
Harriet Nordbäck Linder. Stockholm: Natur och Kultur, 1972.

AUGUST WILHELM SCHLEGEL AS A TRANSLATOR OF SHAKESPEARE
Margaret E Atkinson. Oxford: Basil Blackwell, 1958, 67 pp.

AUTOMATIC LANGUAGE TRANSLATION: Lexical and Technical Aspects, With Particular Reference to Russian
Anthony G Oettinger. Foreword by Joshua Whatmough. Cambridge, MA: Harvard University Press (Harvard Monographs in Applied Science, No 8), 1960.

AUTOMATIC TRANSLATION
Dimitrii Yu Panov. Translated from the Russian by R Kisch. Edited by A J Mitchell. London, New York: Pergamon, 1960, 73 pp.

AUTOMATISCHE SPRACHÜBERSETZUNG
Stefan Nündel et al. Berlin: Akademie-Verlag, 1969, 1972, 1976. 3 Bde.

AUTOMATISCHE ÜBERSETZUNG. Untersuchung am Beispiel der Sprachen Englisch und Deutsch
Klaus Brockhaus. Braunschweig: Vieweg (Schriften zur Linguistik, Bd 2), 1971.

LES BELLES INFIDÈLES
Georges Mounin. Paris: Cahiers du Sud, 1955, 159 pp.

BIBLIOGRAPHIE DE LA TRADUCTION AUTOMATIQUE (Bibliography of Mechanical Translation)
E & K Delavenay. The Hague: Mouton (Janua linguarum, Series A, No 11), 1960; New York: Humanities Press, 1967.

BIBLIOGRAPHY OF ENGLISH TRANSLATIONS FROM MEDIEVAL SOURCES, 1944-1968
Mary A Ferguson. Columbia Univ Press, 1974.

A BIBLIOGRAPHY OF WRITINGS ON THE PRINCIPLES AND METHODS OF TRANSLATION WITH SELECTED TITLES OF TRANSLATED WORKS AND RELATED WRITINGS
Hong Kong: The Extramural Studies Dept, The Chinese Univ of Hong Kong.
Contains ca. 200 entries, divided into English and Chinese writings.

CHILDREN'S BOOKS IN TRANSLATION
Göte Klinberg, Mary Ørvig, and Stuart Amor, eds. Stockholm: Almquist & Wiksell International for The Swedish Institute for Children's Books, 1978, 172 pp.
Proceedings of the Third Symposium of the International Research Society for Children's Literature, held at Södertälje, Sweden, in 1976. 17 essays based on lectures given by attending representatives of 15 countries.

CHIN-TAI FAN-YI SHIH-HUA (Modern English-Chinese Translation: A Critical Survey)
Han Ti-hou. Hong Kong: Swindon, 1969.
Originally an MA thesis for the Chinese Dept of The Univ of Hong Kong. Describes the intellectual background in China between 1898 and 1919 against which translation work was carried on, and assesses the work of three prominent Chinese translators, Yen Fu, Lin Shu, and Fu Tung Hua.

CHUNG-KUO WEN-HSUEH YING-YI HSÜ-T'AN (Notes on Some English Translations of Chinese Literature)
Sha Feng. Hong Kong: Ta-kuang, 1976.

CHUNG-SHIH YING-YI HSU-T'AN (Notes on Some English Translations of Chinese Poetry)
Sha Feng. Hong Kong: Ta-kuang, 1964.

CONFERENCE INTERPRETING
Patricia E Longley. London: Pitman, 1968.

THE CRAFT AND CONTEXT OF TRANSLATION: A Critical Symposium
William Arrowsmith & Roger Shattuck, eds. Austin, TX: Univ of Texas Press for Humanities Research Center, 1961, 206 pp.; Garden City, NY: Anchor Books, 1964, 374 pp.
Essays by Peter Arnott, W Arrowsmith, Smith Palmer Bovie, D S Carne-Ross, Robert W Corrigan, Richard Howard, Denver Lindley, Sidney Monas, Jean Paris, Kenneth Rexroth, George D Schade, R Shattuck, Frederick Will, Werner Winter, Theodore Ziolkowski. Ten of the essays were originally delivered at a Symposium on Translation held at The Univ of Texas in November, 1959.

DEUTSCHE ÜBERSETZUNGSTHEORIE IM 18. JAHRHUNDERT (1734-1746)
Anneliese Senger. Bonn: Bouvier (Abhandlungen zur Kunst-, Musik- und Literarturwissenschaft, Bd 97), 1971.

DEUX LANGUES, SIX IDIOMES
I de Buisseret. Ottawa: Carleton-Green, 1975.

DICTIONARIES OF FOREIGN LANGUAGES
Robert Lewis Collison. New York: Hafner, 1955, 210 pp.
A bibliographical guide to the general and technical dictionaries of the chief foreign languages, with historical and explanatory notes and references.

DICTIONARY FOR THE ANALYSIS OF LITERARY TRANSLATION
Anton Popovič. Edmonton, Alberta: Dept of Comparative Literature, University of Alberta, 1976. 2nd edition. Nitra, Czechoslovakia: Dept of Literary Communication, Pedagogical Faculty Nitra.

DOLMETSCHDIALOGE ENGLISCH UND DEUTSCH. Ein Übungsbuch für das Gesprächsdolmetschen
Wolf Friederich. Munich: Max Hueber, 1960, 1965.

DRYDEN AND THE ART OF TRANSLATION
William Frost. New Haven: Yale Univ Press, 1955, 100 pp.
Includes bibliographical footnotes.

EARLY THEORIES OF TRANSLATION
Flora Ross Amos. New York: Octagon, 1973, 184 pp.
Original edition issued in series: Columbia University Studies in English and Comparative Literature.

ELIZABETHAN TRANSLATIONS FROM THE ITALIAN
Mary A Scott. Boston & New York: Houghton Mifflin, 1916.

THE ENGLISH BIBLE: A History of Translations from the Earliest English Versions to the New English Bible
F F Bruce. London: Lutterworth, 1961, 1970.

ENGLISH BIBLICAL TRANSLATION
Astley Cooper Partridge. London: Deutsch (The Language Library), 1973.

ENGLISH TRANSLATION THEORY: 1650-1800. Approaches to Translation Studies 2
T R Steiner. Assen/Amsterdam: Van Gorcum, 1975, 159 pp.
Part I, The Theory, focuses on the substance of English translation theory: precursors to Dryden, English and French translation theory in the 17th century. Part II, The Documents, brings together for the first time the major writings about translation published in England between 1650 and 1800, texts by Sir John Dehman, Abraham Cowley, John Dryden, the Earl of Roscommon, Laurence Echard, Sir Edward Sherburne, Alexander Pope, William Guthrie, Thomas Gordon, Philip Francis, Thomas Francklin, Samuel Johnson, George Colman, Christopher Smart, the *Gentleman's Magazine* (anonymous), and William Cowper.

ENGLISH TRANSLATORS AND TRANSLATIONS
J M Cohen. London: Longmans, Greene (Writers and Their Work, No 142), 1962.

ESSAY ON THE PRINCIPLES OF TRANSLATION
Alexander Fraser Tytler. London: J M Dent/New York: E P Dutton, 1907. New York: Garland, 1970, 416 pp.
"Facsimile . . . made from a copy in the Harvard University Library." On original title page: The second edition, corrected, and considerably enlarged. London: printed for T Cadell, W Davies, W Creech, Edinburgh, 1797.

ESSAYS IN TRANSLATION FROM FRENCH
R L Graeme Ritchie & Claudine L Simons. Cambridge: Univ Press, 1952, 405 pp.

FACTORS IN A THEORY OF POETIC TRANSLATING. Approaches to Translation Studies 5
Robert de Beaugrande. Assen/Amsterdam: Van Gorcum, 1978, 186 pp.
Using as its starting point Rilke's *Duineser Elegien* (Duino Elegies) and the problem of translating them into English, this study traces those processes as a set of consistent, multiphase language strategies that encompass operations as contextualization, structuring, rearrangement, objectivation, and revision.

FAITHFUL ECHO
Robert Brainerd Ekvall. Foreword by Arthur H Dean. New York: Twayne, 1960, 125 pp.
Autobiographical.

FAN-I CH'ANG-SHIH CHIEN-TAN (Common Sense about English Translation)
Lo Sau. Hong Kong: Ta-kuang, 1976.

Examples from journalistic material with emphasis on current American idiom and slang and their treatment.

FAN-I CHIH I-SHU (The Art of Translation)
Chang Ch'i-ch'un. Hong Kong: Chih-wen, 1973, 269 pp.

A classic work on the problems of English-Chinese and Chinese-English translation, with illustrations of the various techniques employed in solving problems, and the different attitudes of individual translators.

FAN-I LUN-TSA (Selected Essays on Translation)
Huang Chia-teh. Shanghai: West Wind Monthly, 1940, 305 pp.

A rich collection of essays on translation by prominent men of letters: general principles of translation, translation of names, translation of poetry, history of translation. Regarded as an important work on translation theory during the years after the May 4th Movement.

FAN-YI TI CHI-CH'IAO (The Technique of Translation)
Chien Gochuen. Taipei: Kai-ming, 1972.

A theoretical and practical manual for Chinese to English translation and vice versa.

FAN-YI YEN-CHIU (A Study of Translation)
Sau Kuo. Taipei: Ta-ti, 1962.

Various problems of translating English into Chinese: grammar, rhetoric, punctuation, prosody. Contains a list of the Key to Translation and Chinese and English indexes.

FEASIBILITY STUDY ON FULLY AUTOMATIC HIGH QUALITY TRANSLATION
Winfred P Lehmann & Rolf Stachowitz. Austin, Texas: Linguistics Research Center, University of Texas at Austin (Report No RA DC-TR-71-295), 1971.

THE FIRST ENGLISH TRANSLATIONS OF THE CLASSICS
C H Conley. New Haven: Yale Univ Press, 1927; Kennikat Press, NY: Port Washington, 1967, 158 pp.

THE FORKED TONGUE: A Study of the Translation Process
Burton Raffel. The Hague: Mouton (De proprietatibus litterarum, Series maior, No 14), 1971, 181 pp.

DAS FREMDE KUNSTWERK, ASPEKTE DER LITERARISCHEN ÜBERSETZUNG
Ralph-Rainer Wuthenow. Göttingen: Vandenhoeck & Ruprecht (Palaestra, Bd 252), 1969.

FUG UND UNFUG DES ÜBERSETZENS. Sachlichpolemische Betrachtungen zu einem literarischen Nebengeleise
Walter Widmer. Cologne: Kiepenheuer & Witsch, 1959.

LES GRANDS TRADUCTEURS FRANÇAIS
Edmond Cary. Geneva: Librairie de L'Université, Georg & Cie, 1963, 135 pp.

GRUNDFRAGEN DER ÜBERSETZURIGS-WISSENSCHAFT. Materialien einer wissenschaftlichen Konferenz des Dolmetscher-Institutes der Karl-Marx-Universität Leipzig. Oktober 1965
Albrecht Neubert, ed. Leipzig: Verlag Enzyklopädie (Beuhefte zur Zeitschrift Fremdsprachen, Bd 2), 1968.

HANDBOOK OF MACHINE-AIDED TRANSLATION
Herbert E Bruderer. New York: American Elsevier, 1977.

HAN-I "HA-MU-LEI-T'E" YEN CHIU (A Critical Study of the Chinese Translation of "Hamlet")
Chau Sui-cheong Simon. Hong Kong: The Univ of Hong Kong, 1976.

Chapter 1, a brief history of Shakespearean translation in China; chapter 2, the criteria and principles adopted, as well as the limitations of translations of Shakespeare; chapter 3–4, comparison of the work of individual translators and exploration of the difficulties involved; chapter 5, examination of each version against its background and an assessment of its merits.

HISTORICAL TRANSLATION THEORY: A Basic Bibliography
James S Holmes. Amsterdam: Translation Studies Program, Department of General Literary Studies, University of Amsterdam (Amsterdam Publications and Prepublications in Translation Studies), 1977.

HSI-YÜ HAN-I-LING YEN-CHIU (A Study of the English Translation of Chinese Idioms)
Chang P'ei-chi. Peking: Commercial Press, 1958; reprint, 1964.

Explains the nature of Chinese idioms and the methods of translating them into English. With an index of ca. 1000 idioms discussed in the text.

HUO-YUNG YUNG-WEN FAN-YI FA (Practical English Translation)
Su Chao-lung. Hong Kong: Yi-mei, 1971.

IN ANOTHER LANGUAGE: A Record of the Thirty-Year Relationship between Thomas Mann and His English Translator, Helen Tracy Lowe-Porter
John C Thirwall. New York: Knopf, 1966.

INTERLINGUISTICA. Sprachvergleich und Übersetzung. Festschrift zum 60. Geburtstag von Mario Wandruszka
Karl-Richard Bausch & Hans-Martin Gauger, eds. Tubingen: Niemeyer, 1971.

INTERLINGUISTIK: Umrisse einer neuen Sprachwissenschaft
Mario Wandruszka. Munich: R Piper, 1971.

INTERNATIONAL BIBLIOGRAPHY OF DICTIONARIES, 5th edition
Edtl direction: Helga Lengenfelder. Munich: Verlag Dokumentation; New York & London: R R Bowker, 1972, 511 pp.

Approximately 5000 titles divided and subdivided into groups and nearly 120 subgroups. Index of authors and editors and a directory of publishers.

INTERNATIONAL JOURNAL OF AMERICAN LINGUISTICS
Translation Issue (20, No. 4). Bloomington, IN: Waverly Press for Indiana University, 1954; reprint, New York: Kraus, 1965.

INTERNATIONALE BIBLIOGRAPHIE DER ÜBERSETZUNG (International Bibliography of Translation, vol 1)
Henry Van Hoof. Munich: Verlag Dokumentation, 1973, 591 pp. (Handbook of International Documentation and Information, Vol II, in English and German.)

THE INTERPRETERS OF FOREIGN LANGUAGES AMONG THE ANCIENTS
H S Gehman. Lancaster, PA: Intelligencer Printing, 1914, 67 pp. Bibliography.

A study based on Greek and Latin sources, and originally a PhD thesis, Univ of Pennsylvania.

INTERPRETING FOR INTERNATIONAL CONFERENCES: Problems of Language and Communication
Danica Seleskovitch. Washington, DC: Pen & Booth, 1978, 154 pp.

Translated and adapted from the French, *L'interprète dans les conférences internationales—problemes de langage et de communications* (Paris: Minard, Lettres Modernes, 1968).

INTRODUCCIÓN A LA TRADUCTOLOGÍA
Gerardo Vásquez-Ayora. Washington, DC: Georgetown Univ Press, 1977.

AN INTRODUCTION TO MACHINE TRANSLATION
Emile Delavenay. New York: Praeger, 1960, 144 pp. English version by the author and Katharine M Delavenay.

INTRODUCTION TO SEMANTICS AND TRANSLATION
Katharine G L Barnwell. Bucks, UK: Summer Institute of Linguistics, 1974.

ISKUSSTVO PEREVODA (The Art of Translation)
Kornei Chukovskii. Moscow-Leningrad: Academia, 1936, 222 pp.

A discussion of typical blunders in translation into Russian.

KHUDOZHESTVENNYI PEREVOD: Bzaimodeistviye i Vzaimoobogashcheniye Literatur (Artistic translation: Interaction and Mutual Enrichment of Literatures)
Union of Writers of the USSR. Yerevan: State Univ of Yerevan, 534 pp.

Collection of essays edited by V Kh Ganiev. Includes bibliographical references.

KHUDOZHESTVENNYI PEREVOD I LITERATURNYE VZAIMOSVIAZI (Artistic Translation and Literary Intercommunication)
Givi Gachechiladze. Moscow: Sovetskii pisatel', 1972, 262 pp.
Bibliographical references.

DIE KUNST DER ÜBERSETZUNG
Clemens Podewils, ed. München: Oldenbourg (Bayerische Akademie der schönen Künste, Jahrbuch *Gestalt und Gedanke*, Nr 8), 1963.

DIE KUNST DES ÜBERSETZENS
Paul Cauer. Berlin: Weidmann, 1896.

KUO-CHI FAN-I SHOU-TS'E (International Translation Handbook)
Hu Tzu-tan, ed. Taipei: T'ien-jen, 1974, 551 pp.
A bilingual collection of examples of public and private documents, announcements, correspondence, advertisements, etc., providing a handy reference guide to official writing for non-native English speakers. Contains a bilingual glossary of place names and names of institutes.

LANGAGE ET TRADUCTION
P Daviault. Ottawa: Secrétariat d'Etat, 1972.

LANGUAGE & INFORMATION: Selected Essays on Their Theory & Application
Yehoshua Bar-Hillel. Reading, MA: Addison-Wesley, 1964.

LANGUAGE AND MACHINES; Computers in Translation and Linguistics; a Report
National Research Council (Automatic Language Processing Advisory Committee). Washington: National Academy of Sciences, 1966, 124 pp.
Includes bibliographical references.

LANGUAGE SERVICES IN INDUSTRY
Ian F Finlay. Foreword by Sir Frank Roberts. London: Lockwood, 1973, 155 pp.
Includes bibliographies.

LANGUAGE STRUCTURE AND TRANSLATION: Essays
Eugene A Nida. Stanford, CA: Stanford University Press, 1975.

LANGUAGE TODAY: A Survey of Current Thought
Mario Pei. New York: Funk & Wagnalls, 1967, 150 pp. Chapter 3, "Problems of Semantics," dicusses the language of diplomacy, the changing meaning of words, the language of propaganda, language by age group, the problems of cultural misunderstanding.

LATIN TRANSLATION, PRINCIPLE TO PRACTICE
George Hamilton Cowan. London: Macmillan; NY: St Martin's, 1964, 184 pp.

LINGUISTIC ANALYSIS & PROGRAMMING FOR MECHANICAL TRANSLATION
Silvio Ceccato, ed. New York: Gordon & Breach, 1961.

LINGUISTIC AND ENGINEERING STUDIES IN THE AUTOMATIC TRANSLATION OF SCIENTIFIC RUSSIAN INTO ENGLISH
2 vols. Erwin Reifler, ed. Technical report prepared by the Dept of Eastern and Slavic Languages and Literatures and Dept of Electrical Engineering, University of Washington. Seattle: Univ of Washington Press, 1960, 492 pp.

LITERARY TRANSLATION: The Theory and the Practice
Jiri Levy. Translated from the Czech by Suzanne Flatauer, Assen, Amsterdam: Van Gorcum, 1977.
Approaches to Translation Studies 4. When the late Jiri Levy, who taught at the University of Brno and was the pioneer of translation studies in Czechoslovakia, first published his *Umeni Preklady* (The Art of Translation) in 1963, it was hailed as a landmark in literary translation studies by those who could read the Czech text. The English version includes revisions and expansions made by the author before his death.

LITERATURE AND TRANSLATION: New Perspectives in Literary Studies
James S Holmes, Jose Lambert, Raymond Van den Broeck, eds. Leuven, Belgium: Acco, 1978.
Extensive bibliography.

LA MACHINE À TRADUIRE. Histoire des Problèmes Linguistiques
Georges Mounin. The Hague: Mouton (Etudes sur le Traitement automatique du Langage, No 2; Janua linguarum, Series minor, No 32), 1964.

MACHINE TRANSLATION
A Donald Booth, ed. Amsterdam: North Holland, 1967.

MACHINE TRANSLATION AND APPLIED LINGUISTICS
Viktor Yu Rozencvejg. Wiesbaden: Athenaion (Soviet Papers in Formal Linguistics, Bde 16, 17), 1974. 2 Bde.

MACHINE TRANSLATION OF LANGUAGES
William N Locke & A Donald Booth, eds. Cambridge, MA: Massachusetts Institute of Technology, 1955, 1957, 1965; reprint, Westport, CT: Greenwood, 1976.

MAN-T'AN FAN-YI CHI HSIEH-TSO (Remarks on Translation and Composition)
Tseng Yüeh-nung. Taipei: Student's English Digest Association, 1971.
Comments on the principles of translation with several sample student translations followed by the author's comments and improved versions.

MANUEL DE L'INTERPRÈTE. Comment on devient interprète de conférences
Jean Herbert. Geneva: Georg, 1952, 1966. Also Dutch (1968), English (1952, 1968), and German (1952) translations.

MECHANICAL RESOLUTION OF LINGUISTIC PROBLEMS
Andrew Donald Booth, L Brandwood & J P Cleave. New York: Academic Press, 1958, 306 pp.
Includes bibliographies.

MEMOIRS OF AN INTERPRETER
A H Birse. London, 1967.

METHODEN DER PHILOLOGIE. Methodenprobleme der Übersetzung
Manfred Thiel, ed. Munich & Vienna: Oldenbourg (Enzyklopädie der geisteswissenschaftlichen Arbeitsmethoden, 5. Liferung), 1975.

MIRROR ON MIRROR: Translation, Imitation, Parody
Reuben Arthur Brower. Cambridge, MA: Harvard Univ Press, 1974, 183 pp.
In the author's words, the book consists of discussions of (1) the shape and problem of translation; (2) two books which challenge the full energy and intent of the translators—Homer and the Bible; (3) allusive-translations, inserted parenthetically into the texture of a work otherwise original; (4) levels of diction in translation; (5) imitations; (6) special problems of rendering rough texture and high polish; (7) original authors (Joyce), who took special interest in the translation of their own works; (8) the limits of the possible and conceivable definition of the desirable in translation.

NABOKOV TRANSLATED: A Comparison of Nabokov's Russian & English Prose
Jane Grayson. London: Oxford University Press (Oxford Modern Languages and Literatures Monographs, No 24), 1977.

THE NAME AND NATURE OF TRANSLATION STUDIES
James S Holmes. Amsterdam: Translation Studies Section, Department of General Literary Studies, University of Amsterdam (Amsterdam Publications and Pre-publications in Translation Studies), 1975.

THE NATURE OF TRANSLATION: Essays on the Theory and Practice of Literary Translation
James S Holmes, ed. Frans de Haan & Anton Popovič, assoc. eds. Bratislava: Publishing House of the Slovak Academy of Science (Approaches to Translation Studies, No 1); The Hague: Mouton, 1970, 232 pp.
Papers presented at an "International Conference on Translation as an Art" held in 1968 in Bratislava, Czechoslovakia, planned by the Translators' Section of the Slovak Writers Union.

NORMOT ŠEL TIRGUM VE-HA-TIRGUM HA-SIFRUTI LE-IVRIT BA-ŠANIM 1930–1945 (Translational Norms and Literary Translation into Hebrew, 1930–1945)
Tel Aviv University. Tel Aviv: The Porter Institute for Poetics and Semiotics, 1977, 296 pp.
　　Based on a 1976 Ph.D. dissertation and published in the *Literature, Meaning, Culture Series,* #6.

NOTES ON BIBLE TRANSLATION. With Drills
John Beekman, ed. Santa Ana, CA: Summer Institute of Linguistics, 1965, 1967, 1970. 3 vols.

O KHUDOZHESTVENNOM PEREVODE (On Artistic Translation)
A V Fedorov. Leningrad: Khudozhestennaya literatura, 1941, 257 pp.
　　A discussion of belletristic literature by a leading Soviet Russian specialist in translation theory and technique.

O SZTUCE TŁUMACZENIA
Michał Rusinek, ed. Wrocław: Ossolineum, 1955.

OLD TESTAMENT TRANSLATION PROBLEMS
A R Hulst. Leiden: Brill (Helps for Translators, Vol. 1), 1960.

ON ENGLISH TRANSLATION
Ronald Arbuthnott Knox. Oxford: Clarendon Press, 1957, 26 pp.

ON MACHINE TRANSLATION
Paul L Garvin. The Hague: Mouton (Janua linguarum, Series minor, No 128), 1972.

ON ROMANTICISM AND THE ART OF TRANSLATION: Studies in Honor of Edwin Hermann Zeydel
Gottfried F Merkel, ed. Princeton, NJ: Princeton University Press, 1956.

ON TRANSLATING POETRY
C Day-Lewis. Abington-on-Thames: Abbey Press (Jackson Knight Memorial Lecture, 2), 1970.

ON TRANSLATION
Hilaire Belloc. Oxford: Univ Press, 1931, 44 pp. Also in *Selected Essays; Bookman* 74: 32–39, 179–185.

ON TRANSLATION
Reuben A Brower, ed. Cambridge: Harvard Univ Pr, 1959, 297 pp; Oxford Univ Press/Galaxy, 1966, 296 pp.
　　A collection of essays in the "Harvard Studies in Comparative Literature." I. Translators on Translation: a series of practical reports "on the process of translation by a number of distinguished present-day translators—Achilles Fang, Dudley Fitts, John Hollander, Rolfe Humphries. Roman Jakobson, Douglas Knight, Richmond Lattimore, Jackson Mathews, B Q Morgan, Edwin & Willa Muir, Vladimir Nabokov, Eugene A Nida, Justin O'Brien,

Anthony G Oettinger, Renato Poggiolo, Willard V Quine. "Although difference is of the essence in this group, one concern is common to all of them: the necessity of trying to approximate the form of the original. . . . One conclusion emerges from their common preoccupation: that the translator is a 'creator, that like the original author he is ordering and expressing experience in dramatic and rhythmic speech." II. Approaches to the Problem. III. A Critical Bibliography of Works on Translation by Bayard Quincy Morgan. This is an attempt to present a wide selection of sources which will serve the needs of the student of the subject.

OSNOVY OBSHCHEGO I MASHINNOGO PEREVODA (Fundamentals of General and Machine Translation)
I Revzin & V Yu Rozencvejg. Moscow: Izd-vo Vyshshaya shkola, 1964. French translation: *Introduction à la théorie de la traduction.* Brussels: Ecole Supérieur de Traducteurs et d'Interprètes (Mémoire G Chantrain), 1968.

OSNOVY OBSHCHEI TEORII PEREVODA (Principles of a General Theory of Translation)
A V Fedorov. Moscow: 1968, 3rd revised & enlarged edition. Dutch translation: *Fundamentele begrippen der algemene vertaaltheorie.* Antwerpe: Katholieke Vlaamse Hogeschool 1973.

PEREVOD I SMYSLOVAYA STRUKTURA (Translation and Sense Structure)
L A Chernyakhovskaya. Moscow: International Relations, 1976.

POETIKA UMELECKÉHO PREKLADU. Proces a Text
Anton Popovič. Bratislava: Tatran, 1971. 2nd edition: *Téoria umeleckého prekladu. Aspekty textu a literárnej metakomunikácie.* Bratislava: Tatran (Ed OKNO, zv 14), 1975.

POEZIYA I PEREVOD (Poetry and Translation)
Efim G Etkind. Leningrad: Sovetskii pisatel', 1963, 428 pp.
　　Bibliographical footnotes.

POSLEDOVATEL'NYI PEREVOD. Teoriya i metody obucheniya
R K Min'yar-Beloruchev. Moscow: Military Publishing House of the Ministry of Defense, USSR, 1969.

POSOBIYE PO PEREVODU RUSSKOI KHUDOZHESTVENNOI PROZY NA ANGLIISKII YAZYK (Handbook of Translation of Literary Prose into English)
M M Morozov. Moscow: Izd-vo literatury na innostrannykh yazykakh, 1956, 145 pp.

PREKLAD A VÝRAZ
Anton Popovič. Bratislava: Vydavatel'stvo Slovenskej akadémie vied, 1968.

PŘEKLAD LITERÁRNIHO DÍLA. Sbornik současných zahraničnich studii
Josef Čermák, et al. Prague: Odeon (Český preklad, svaz 12), 1970.

PREMIÈRE RENCONTRE INTERNATIONALE DES TRADUCTEURS LITTÉRAIRES À VARSOVIE
Michał Rusinek, ed. Warsaw: Centre Polonais PEN, 1959 (PEN Bulletin du Centre Polonais).

PRINCIPLES AND PROBLEMS OF BIBLICAL TRANSLATION: Some Reformation Controversies and Their Background
W Schwarz. Cambridge: Cambridge University Press, 1955.

PRINTSIPY KHUDOZHESTVENNOGO PEREVODA (Principles of Artistic Translation)
F Batyushkov, K Chukovski & K Gumilev. Petrograd: 1919.
　　First Russian attempt toward a systematic discussion of translation problems.

LA PRISE DE NOTES EN INTERPRÉTACONSÉCUTIVE
Jean-François Rozan. Geneva: Georg, 1956, 1970, 1973.

DAS PROBLEM DER ÜBERSETZUNG
Hans Joachim Störig, ed. Stuttgart: Goverts; Darmstadt: Wissenschaftliche Buchgesellschaft (Wege der Foschung, Bd 8), 1963, 1969.

PROBLEMAS DE LA TRADUCCIÓN
Puerto Rico: Univ of Puerto Rico Press for Graduate Program in Translation, Faculty of Humanities, 1978.

DE PROBLEMATIEK VAN DE LITERAIRE VERTALING
Raymond van den Broeck. Leuven (Dissertation, Catholic University of Leuven), 1970. 3 vols.

PROBLEME UND THEORIEN DES ÜBERSETZENS IN DEUTSCHLAND VOM 18. bis zum 20. Jahrhundert
Winfried Sdun. Munich: Max Hueber (Sprachen der Welt), 1967.

PROBLÈMES DE LA TRADUCTION AUTOMATIQUE
Georges Gougenheim, ed. Paris: Klincksieck (Association pour la Traduction automatique et la Linguistique appliquée, Documents, No 2), 1968.

PROBLÈMES LITTÉRAIRES DE LA TRADUCTION. Textes des conférences presentées au cours d'un séminaire organisé pendant l'année académique 1973–74
Leiden: Brill (Travaux de la Faculté de Philosophie et Lettres de l'Université Catholique de Louvain, 15), 1975.

LES PROBLEMES THEORIQUES DE LA TRADUCTION (Theoretical Problems of Translation)
Georges Mounin. Preface by Dominique Aury. Paris: Gallimard, 1963, 296 pp.
　　Includes bibliography.

PROBLEMS OF TRANSLATION: A Handbook for Chinese Translators of English
Francis Price Jones. Hong Kong: Chinese Christian Literature Council, 1969.
A theoretical discussion of various aspects of translation: transliteration, punctuation, translation as a literary form, translation of poetry, sentence construction.

PROTEUS, HIS LIES, HIS TRUTH: Discussions of Literary Translation
Robert Martin Adams. New York: Norton, 1973, 192 pp.
Bibliography.

PRZEKŁAD ARTYSTYCZNY. O sztuce tłumaczenia, księga druga
Seweryn Pollak, ed. Wrocław: Ossolineum, 1975.

QUALITY IN TRANSLATION: Proceedings of the Congress of International Federation of Translators (FIT), Bad Godesberg, 1959
Edmond Cary & R W Jumpelt. Oxford: Pergamon, 1963.

RÉPERTOIRE BIBLIOGRAPHIQUE DE LA TRADUCTION
L Albert & J Delisle. Ottawa: Bibliotheque Morisset (Université d'Ottawa), 1975.

RUSSKIYE PISATELI O PEREVODE 18–20 VV. (Russian Writers on Translation of the 18th–20th Centuries)
A V Fedorov and Yu D Levin, eds. Leningrad: Sovetskii pisatel', 1960, 696 pp.

THE SCIENCE OF TRANSLATION: An Analytical Bibliography
Karl Richard Bausch, Josef Klegraf, & Wolfram Wilss. Tubingen, W Germany: Tübinger Beiträge zur Linguistik, 1970.
Vol I: 1962–1969. Supplement 1962–69. Vol 2: 1970–71. A third volume is in preparation.

SCIENTIFIC AND TECHNICAL TRAINING AND RELATED ASPECTS OF THE LANGUAGE PROBLEM
J E Holmstrom, ed. Paris: UNESCO (Documentation and Terminology of Science), 1958.

SCIENTIFIC AND TECHNICAL TRANSLATING AND OTHER ASPECTS OF THE LANGUAGE PROBLEM
NY: UNESCO, 1957, 282 pp.

SCIENTIFIC AND TECHNICAL TRANSLATION
Isadore Pinchuck. London: André Deutsch; Boulder, CO: Westview Press, 1977, 269 pp.
A thorough examination of the theory and practice of translating scientific and technical material, with examples confined to German into English. Bibliography.

LE SECOND VRAI AMI DU TRADUCTEUR ANGLAIS-FRANÇAIS ET FRANÇAIS-ANGLAIS
Félix François Billot. Paris: Gliven, 1956.

SIMULTANEOUS INTERPRETING: A PRACTICE BOOK
Paul V Hendrickx. London: Longmans, 1971.

SKETCHES FROM A LIBRARY WINDOW
Basil Anderton. Cambridge: Heffer, 1920; Freeport, NY: Books for Libraries, 1968.
See pp. 38–70 for "Lure of translation."

SLOVO O PEREVODE (A Word About Translation)
Vilen N Komissarov. Moscow: International Relations, 1973, 215 pp.
Bibliography.

SOME REMARKS ON TRANSLATION AND TRANSLATORS
John Swinnerton Phillimore. Oxford: Univ Press, 1919, 22 pp. The English Association, Pamphlet #22.

SOUS L'INVOCATION DE SAINT JÉROME
Valéry Larbaud. Paris: Gallimard, 1946. 341 pp.

SPECIFICATION FOR THE PRESENTATION OF TRANSLATIONS
London: British Standards Institution (British Standard 4755: 1971), 1971.

SPEZIALPROBLEME DER WISSENSCHAFTLICHEN UND TECHNISCHEN ÜBERSETZUNG
Harry Spitzbardt, ed. Halle/Saale: Niemeyer (Linguistische Studien), 1972.

SPRACHEN: Vergleichbar und Ünvergleichbar
Mario Wandruszka. Munich: Piper, 1969.

SPRACHWISSENSCHAFT UND ÜBERSETZEN. Symposium an der Universität Heidelberg, 1969
P Hartmann & H Vernay, eds. Munich: Max Hueber (Commentaciones Societatis Linguisticae Europarae, Vol. 3), 1970.

STUDIEN ZUR THEORIE DES ÜBERSETZENS IM ZEITLATER DER DEUTSCHEN AUFKLÄRUNG 1730-1770
Thomas Huber. Meisenheim an Glan: Hain (Deutsche Studien, Bd 7), 1968.

STUDIEN ZUR ÜBERSETZUNGSWISSENSCHAFT
Leipzig: Verlag Enzyklopädie (Beihefte zur Zeitschrift *Fremdsprachen*, Bd 3/4), 1971.

STUDIES IN CHINESE THOUGHT
Arthur F Wright, ed. Chicago: Univ Press, 1962.
Contains the well-known essay by I A Richards, "Towards a theory of translating."

STUDIES IN ELIZABETHAN TRANSLATION
Julia Gracia Ebel. New York, 1964, 113 pp. typescript. Thesis, Columbia Univ.
Includes bibliography.

A STUDY OF SIMULTANEOUS INTERPRETATION
Henri Charles Barik. Ann Arbor, MI: University Microfilms (Dissertation, University of North Carolina, 1969), 1970.

STYLISTIQUE COMPARÉE DU FRANÇAIS ET DE L'ANGLAIS. Méthode de traduction
Jean-Paul Vinay & J. Darbelnet. Paris: Didier (Bibliothèque de stylistique comparée, No 1), 1958, 1966.

SYNTAX ORIENTED TRANSLATOR
Peter Z Ingerman. New York: Academic Press, 1966.

SZTUKA PRZEKŁADU W POGLĄDACH LITERACKICH POLSKIEGO OŚWIECENIA
Jadwiga Zitarska. Wrocław: Ossolineum (Studia z okresu Oświecenia, tom 10), 1969.

TECHNICAL TRANSLATOR'S MANUAL
J B Sykes, ed. New York: Chickrell Library, 1971, 173 pp.

TECHNIK DES ÜBERSETZENS ENGLISCH UND DEUTSCH. Eine Systematische Anleitung für das Ubersetzen ins Englische und ins Deutsche für Unterricht und Selbststudium
Wolf Friederich. Munich: Max Hueber, 1969.

TECHNISCHE TEXTE RICHTIG ÜBERSETZEN. Ein Ratgeber für die Praxis
Gottfried Feidel. Düseeldorf & Wien: Econ Verlag, 1970.

TEKHNIKA PEREVODA NAUCHNOI LITERATURV S ANGLIISKOGO YAZYKA NA RUSSKII (Technique of translating scientific literature from English into Russian)
M Morozov. Moscow, 1934.

TEN YEARS OF TRANSLATION: Proceedings of the Congress of the International Federation of Translators (FIT), Dubrovnik, 1963
I J Citroen, ed. Oxford: Pergamon, 1967.

TEORIYA I KRITIKA PEREVODA (Theory and criticism of translation)
B A Larin, ed. Leningrad: Univ of Leningrad Press, 1962, 166 pp.
Bibliographical footnotes.

TEORIYA PEREVODA I PEREVODCHESKAYA PRAKTIKA. Ocherki lingvisticheskoi teorii perevoda
Ya I Recker. Moscow: International Relations, 1974.

DIE THEORIE DE LITERARISCHEN ÜBERSETZUNG. Romanisch-deutscher Sprachbereich
Rolf Kloepfer. Munich: Fink (Freiburger Schriften zur romanischen Philologie, Bd 12), 1967.

THÉORIE ET PRATIQUE DE L'INTERPRETATION, AVEC APPLICATION PARTICULIÈRE A L'ANGLAIS ET AU FRANÇAIS
Henri Van Hoof. Munich: Max Hueber, 1962, 190 pp.
Contains list of professional associations of interpreters. Bibliography.

THEORIE UND PRAXIS DES ÜBERSETZENS UND DOLMETZENS. Referate und Diskussionsbeiträge des internationalen Koloquiums am Fachbereich Angewandte Sprachwissenschaft der Johannes Gutenberg-Universität Mainz in Germersheim (1975)
Horst W Drescher & Signe Scheffzek, eds. Bern: Herbert Lang, Frankfurt/Main: Peter Lang (FAS), 1976.

THE THEORY AND PRACTICE OF TRANSLATION
Eugene A Nida & Charles R Taber. Leiden: E J Brill, 1969
Includes an extensive bibliography.

TIEN-NAO FAN-I (Machine Translation)
Loh Hsiu-chang. Hong Kong: The Machine Translation Research Group, The Chinese University of Hong Kong, 1975.
Short introduction to the principles and procedures as well as the history and future of machine translation, with an appendix including samples of machine translations.

TOWARD A SCIENCE OF TRANSLATING
Eugene A Nida. Leiden: E J Brill; New York: Heinman, 1965, 331 pp.
Contains special reference to principles and procedures involved in Bible translating.

LA TRADUCCIÓN LITERARIA Y SUS PROBLEMAS
Olaf Blixen. Montevideo: Instituto de Filología, Universidad de la República, 1954, 72 pp.

TRADUCCIÓN: literatura y literalidad
Octavio Paz. Cuadernos marginales, 18. Barcelona, Tusquets Editor, 1971, 78 pp.

LA TRADUCTION
Jean-René Ladmiral, ed. Paris: Didier, 1972. (*Langages*, No 28).

LA TRADUCTION DANS LE MONDE MODERNE
Edmond Cary. Geneva: Librairie de l'Université, 1956, 196 pp. At head of title: École d'interprètes, Université de Geneve.

LA TRADUCTION EN JEU
Paris: Seghers; Laffont (Cahiers du Collectif Change, No 19), 1974.

TRADUCTION. Mélanges offerts en mémoire de G Panneton
Jean P Vinay. Montreal: Institut de Traduction, 1952.

LA TRADUCTION SCIENTIFIQUE ET TECHNIQUE
Jean Maillot. Paris: Editions Eyrolles, 1969, 1970.

TRADUCTIONS ET TRADUCTEURS
Georges Mounin. Italian translation: *Teoria e storia della traduzione*. Torino: Einaudi (Piccola Biblioteca Einaudi, No 61), 1965. German translation: *Die Übersetzung. Geschichte, Theorie, Anwendung*. München: Nymphenburger Verlag, 1967. (French text not published).

LA TRADUZIONE
Trieste: LINT, 1973, 420 pp. Proceedings of a meeting held at the Università degli studi in Trieste, April, 1972.
In French or Italian; includes bibliographies.

TRANSCRIPTION AND TRANSLITERATION: An Annotated Bibliography on Conversion of Scripts
Hanan Wellisch. Silver Spring, MD: Institute of Modern Languages, 1975, 133 pp.

TRANSLATING
I F Finlay. London: English U P, 1971.

TRANSLATING: A Profession
Paul A Horguelin, ed. Proceedings of the 8th World Congress of FIT, Montreal, 1977. Ottawa: Canadian Translators & Interpreters Council, 1978, 576 pp.
English, French. Preface by Pierre-François Caillé. Foreword by the editor.

TRANSLATING LITERATURE: The German Tradition from Luther to Rosenzweig
André Lefevere. Assen, Amsterdam: Van Gorcum, 1978, 128 pp.
Approaches to translation studies. Part I, Establishing the Tradition: texts by Martin Luther, J G Schottel, J Ch Gootsched, J J Bodmer, J J Breitinger, G E Lessing, J G Herder, J W Goethe, Wilhelm von Humboldt, A W Schlegel, Friedrich Schlegel, Novalis, and Friedrich Schleiermacher. Part II, Internal Criticism of the Tradition: texts by Jacob Grimm, Friedrich Nietzsche, Karl Vossler, Arthur Schopenhauer, Walter Benjamin, Ulrich von Wilamowitz-Moellendorf, Rudolf Borchardt, and Franz Rosenzweig.

TRANSLATING POETRY: Seven Strategies and a Blueprint
Approaches to Translation Studies 3. André Lefevere. Assen/Amsterdam: Van Gorcum, 1975, 127 pp.
The study is based on a comparison of Catullus' 64th poem, an Alexandrian short epic on the love and marriage of Peleus and Thetis, with English translations of it published between 1870 and 1970: phonemic, literal, metrical, prose, rhymed, blank-verse.

TRANSLATION: Applications and Research
Richard W Brislin, ed. New York: Gardner Pr, distributed by Halsted Pr, 1976, 312 pp.
A collection of 11 essays by specialists in linguistics, psychology, sociology, literature, and education that "have the common element of increasing our understanding of the range of skills a translator must have and the range of places in which the skills of a translator can be used."

TRANSLATION, AN ELIZABETHAN ART
F O Matthiessen. New York: Octagon Books, 1965, 232 pp. First issued in 1939 by Harvard Univ Press. Bibliographical footnotes. On Hoby's Courtier (1561), North's Plutarch (1579), Florio's Montaigne (1603), and Philemon Holland, the translator general.

TRANSLATION AND TRANSLATORS: A Round Table Discussion in Rome, November, 1961
Ladislas Gara et al. London: International PEN, ca. 1963.

TRANSLATION AND TRANSLATIONS, THEORY AND PRACTICE
J P Postgate. London: Bell, 1922, 206 pp.

TRANSLATION FROM FRENCH
R L Graeme Ritchie & James M Moore. Cambridge: Univ Press, 1918, 1931, 258 pp.

TRANSLATION FROM THE CHINESE
Arthur Waley. New York: Knopf, 1941. 1st edition, 1919.

TRANSLATION IN THE HUMANITIES
Marilyn Gaddis Rose, ed. Binghamton, NY: State Univ of New York at Binghamton, 1977, 82.
Proceedings of a forum sponsored by the Department of Comparative Literature, November, 1976.

TRANSLATION OF SCIENTIFIC RUSSIAN
Vladimir A Pertzoff. New York: Exposition, 1964, 147 pp.

TRANSLATION THEORY AND INTERCULTURAL RELATIONS
Proceedings of a symposium held in Tel Aviv University, March, 1978 (forthcoming).

TRANSLATIONS FROM EUROPEAN LITERATURE PUBLISHED IN 108 AMERICAN LITTLE MAGAZINES, 1909-1959
George Marvin Tatum. Chapel Hill, NC: 1960, 397 pp. Micro-opaque. Lexington, KY: Univ of Kentucky Press, 1962, 5 cards.

TRANSLATORS AND TRANSLATING: Selected Essays from the American Translators Association Summer Workshops, 1974
T Ellen Crandell, ed. State University of New York at Binghamton, Department of Comparative Literature, 1974.

TRES CONFERENCIAS SOBRE LA TRADUCCIÓN (Three Lectures on Translation)
Río Piedras, Puerto Rico: Escuela Profesional de Traductores, Universidad de Puerto Rico, 1971, 94 pp.
Essays on various aspects of translation by three scholars-translators, Jorge Enjuto, Mi-

chael Reck, and George Delacre, including a study of two different Spanish versions of the preamble and first article of the Constitution of the United States, demonstrating a variety of dubious divergences and cases of ambiguity.

TROIS STYLISTES, TRADUCTEURS DE POUCHKINE: Mérimée, Tourguenev, Flaubert. Essai de traduction comparée
André Meynieux. Paris: Librairie de cinq continents (Cahiers d'Etudes littéraires, No 2; Etudes critiques, No 1), 1962.

UNESCO: Literature Translations Program.
Paris: 1966, 45 pp.

ÜBERSETZEN. Vorträge und Beiträge vom Internationalen Kongress literarischer Übersetzer in Hamburg, 1965
Rof Italiaander, ed. Frankfurt/Main: Athanäum, 1965, 192 pp.
German, English, or French.

ÜBERSETZEN II: Sprache und Computer
Stuttgart: Kohlhammer, 1967. (Sprache im technischen Zeitalter, Nr 23.)

ÜBERSETZER UND DOLMETSCHER. Theoretische Gundlagen, Ausbildung, Berufspraxis
Volker Kapp, ed. Heidelberg: Quelle & Meyer (Uni-Taschenbücher, Nr 325), 1974.

DIE ÜBERSETZUNG DER BIBEL IN AFRIKANISCHE SPRACHEN
Ernst Dammann. Munich: Fink (Abhandlungen der Marburger gelehrten Gesellschaft, 1972, Nr 3), 1972.

DIE ÜBERSETZUNG NATURWISSENSCHAFTLICHER UND TECHNISCHER LITERATUR. Sprachliche Massstäbe und Methoden zur Bestimmung ihrer Wesenszüge und Probleme
Rudolf Walter Jumpelt. Berlin-Schöneberg: Langenscheidt Bibliothek für Wissenschaft und Praxis, Bd 1), 1961.

ÜBERSETZUNGSPROBLEME IN DEN DEUTSCHEN ÜBERSETZUNGEN VON DREI ANGLO-AMERIKANISCHEN KURZGESCHICHTEN: Aldous Huxley's "Green Tunnels," Ernest Hemingway's "The Killers" and "A Clean, Well-Lighted Place"
Jans-Joachim Kann. Munich: Max Hueber (Mainzer amerikanische Beiträge, Bd 10), 1968.

ÜBERSETZUNGSPROBLEME IN FRUHEN MITTELALTER
Philipp von Heck. Tübingen: J C B Mohr (P Siebeck), 1931, 303 pp.

ÜBERSETZUNGSWISSENSCHAFT
Wolfram Wilss, ed. Heidelberg: Julius Gross (IRAL Sonderband GAL '74/1; Kongressbericht der 6. Jahrestagung der Gesellschaft für Angewandte Linguistik GAL E V Bd 1), 1974.

VERTALEN VERTOLKT. Verhalen over vertalen
Gerard Fritschy et al. Amsterdam: Nederlands Genootschap van Vertalers, 1976.

THE VIRTUES OF TRADUCEMENT: Sketch of a Theory of Translation
Paolo Valesio. The Hague: Mouton, 1976. *Semiotica,* 18, No 1).

VOPROSY ISTORII I TEORII KHUDOZHESTVENNOGO PEREVODA (Issues of the history and theory of artistic translation)
Pavel I Kopanev. Minsk: Izd-vo BGU, 1972, 295 pp. Bibliography.

VOPROSY KHUDOZHESTVENNOGO PEREVODA: sbornik statei (Problems of artistic translation: collection of articles)
Vi M Rossel, ed. Moscow: Sovetskii pisatel': 1955.
Proceedings of a symposium dealing with realistic traditions of Russian translators, the place of translations in a national literature, and the attitude to the national peculiarities of the original.

VOPROSY TEORII KHUDOZHESTVENNOGO PEREVODA
Givi Gachechiladze. Tiflis: Izd-vo literatura da Chelovneba, 1964.

VOPROSY TEORII KHUDOZHESTVENNOGO PEREVODA
T A Rushkaya, ed. Moscow: Sovetskii pisatel', 1971.

VORAUSSETZUNGEN FÜR MASCHINELLE ÜBERSETZUNG. Probleme, Lösungen, Aussichten
Rolf Stachowitz. Frankfurt/Main: Athenäum (Athenäum-Skripten Linguistik), 1973.

LE VRAI AMI DU TRADUCTEUR ANGLAIS-FRANÇAIS ET FRANÇAIS-ANGLAIS
Félix François Billot. Paris: Les Presses universitaires de France, 1930, 266 pp.

VVEDENIYE V TEORIYU PEREVODA (Introduction to a theory of translation)
A V Fedorov. Moscow: Idz-vo literatury na inostarnnykh yazykakh (Biblioteka fifiologa), 1953, 1958. French translation: *Introduction à la théorie de la traduction.* Brussels: École Supérieure de Traducteurs et d'Interprètes (Mémoire R Deresteau & A Sergeant), 1968.

VVSOKOYE ISKUSSTVO: O PrintziPakh Khudozhestvennogo Perevoda (The Lofty Art: On the Principles of Artistic Translation)
Kornei Chukovskii. Moscow, Goslitizdat, 1941, 256 pp.; Iskusstvo, 1964, 313 pp.; 2nd revised edition, 1969.
Bibliography and footnotes.

WESTERN LITERATURE AND TRANSLATION WORK IN COMMUNIST CHINA
Wolfgang Bauer. Frankfurt/Main: Metzner, 1964.
A study conducted in Hong Kong in 1962 under the auspices of the Modern Chinese History project of the Far Eastern Institute of the University of Washington. Gives a detailed account of translation work as well as principles and problems of translation in China, 1949–1962. Contains useful tables and diagrams.

WHY RE-CREATE? A CONVERSATION ABOUT TRANSLATIONS
Burton Raffel & Vincent J Cleary. San Francisco: Chandler & Sharp, 1973, 34 pp.

THE WORLD OF TRANSLATION
PEN American Center. New York: 1971, xvi, 400 pp.
A self-publication, edited by B J Chute and designed and typeset by S Congrat-Butlar. Proceedings of the Conference on Literary Translation, held in New York in 1970. Papers by 39 translators, writers, poets, editors, and publishers from 13 countries, discussing the problems of translation and of translators, and inquiring into the Bill of Rights for Translators (see Sec 5, PEN American Center). Publication made possible by contributions from Harcourt, Brace, Jovanovich and Victor Weybright, and by a grant from the National Endowment for the Humanities.

WSTĘP DO TEORII TŁUMACZENIA
Olgierd Wojtasiewicz. Wrocław: Ossolineum, 1957.

YAZYK I PEREVOD. Voprosy obshchei i chastnoi teorii perevoda (Questions of a General and Personal Theory of Translation)
L S Barkhudarov. Moscow: International Relations, 1975.

YI-HSUEH KAI-LUN (Principles of Translation)
Chang Chen-yü. Taipei: Jen-jen, 1966.
A systematic work on the history of translation in China and of translation from Chinese to English and vice versa, quoting widely from existing translations of Chinese and English works.

YI-LIN HSU-YÜ (Notes on Translation)
Sha Feng. Hong Kong: Ta-kuang, 1973.
Comments on the Chinese translation of English journalistic writings on current affairs.

YING-WEN CHUNG-YI FA (How to Translate from English to Chinese)
Lee Mu-hua. Taipei: Hua-mei, 1970, 489 pp.
Chapters 1–4, principles of translation; chapter 5, different versions of nine short stories and passages from the classics; chapter 6, English-Chinese translations by well-known translators.

YING-WEN FAN-I SHOU-TS'E (A Handbook of English Translation)
Helen Ng. Hong Kong: Wan-li, 1966.

YING-WEN FAN-YI FANG-FA HO SHIH-LI (Methods and Examples of English-Chinese Translation)
Liu T'ien-min. Hong Kong: Won-yit, 1964.
Principles and methods of translation, with Chinese translations of three short stories with the author's comments.

YING-WEN FAN-YI TSO-WEN TSO-WEN TIEN-FAN (A Guide to English Translation and Composition)
Yin Jang-ch'e. Hong Kong: World, 1974.

YING YI CHUNG: YING-HAN FAN-YI KAI-LUN (Principle of Translation: English to Chinese)
Phillip Sun & Serena Fung. Hong Kong: Department of Extramural Studies, The Chinese Univ of Hong Kong, 1975.
Practical aspects of translation from English to Chinese with explanations of how the different parts of speech may be treated and also the use of footnotes.

YING-YÜ FAN-I CHIANG-TSO (Lectures on Translation)
Mincio Fon. Hong Kong: San-yu, 1972.
Various aspects of English-Chinese translation practice, with an appendix containing 38 examples of model translations taken from the translation papers of the Hong Kong Secondary Examination, 1952–1964.

YING-YÜ HSIEN CHING (Pitfalls for Chinese Students Learning English)
Jen Ch'ung. Hong Kong: Ta-kuang, 1977.

YI-YÜ MAN-T'AN (Remakers on Translation)
Hsü Yao. Hong Kong: San-yu, 1972.

Short articles on the practical aspects of literary and journalistic translation.

YOUR FUTURE IN TRANSLATING AND INTERPRETING
J F Hendry. New York: Richards Rosen Press, 1969, 128 pp.

ZIELSPRACHE: Theorie und Technik des Übersetzens
Fritz Güttinger. Zurich: Manesse, 1953, 234 pp.
Includes bibliography.

7

Register of Translators & Interpreters

Although the terms translation and interpretation, or translator and interpreter, are often used interchangeably by the general public (they share a common goal: the transfer of message between two different languages), professionally and practically speaking, the two concepts and designations comprise distinct activities, practices, and professions, and require distinctly different education, preparation, and professional training. And although translation is generally regarded in daily parlance as the overall designation for the process of rendering in one language words, statements, utterances, thoughts expressed in an entirely different language, translation basically refers to *written* rather than *oral* communication. Interpretation, on the other hand, while also translation, is *oral* conversion and communication.

Because translators and interpreters tend and choose to classify themselves and to organize within their own distinct activities and with distinct labels, the profession as a whole has here been divided into the following characteristic and predominant categories: (1) agencies; (2) industrial, scientific & technical translators; (3) humanistic/literary translators; (4) conference translators; (5) conference interpreters.

All information is based on data provided by the individual translators and/or interpreters in response to special questionnaires designed to elicit all relevant data identifying the professional's competence in languages and subject fields.

Collectively, the translators and interpreters listed in the Register represent active and/or passive proficiency in the following 73 languages and/or their variants:

Afrikaans	Faroese	Latin	Scottish-Gaelic
Anglo-Saxon	Finnish	Latin (Medieval)	Serbo-Croatian
Arabic	French	Latvian	Slovak
Armenian	French (Old)	Lithuanian	Slovenian
Bengali	Georgian	Macedonian	Spanish
Bulgarian	German	Malay	Spanish (Galician)
Burmese	Greek	Marathi	Swedish
Byelorussian	Greek (Classical)	Norwegian	Tamil
Castilian	Hebrew	Nuer (African)	Telugu
Catalan	Hindi	Persian (Farsi)	Thai
Chinese	Hungarian	Pinyin	Tibetan
Choctaw	Indonesian	Polish	Turkish
Croatian	Irish	Portuguese	Ukrainian
Czech	Irish (Old)	Portuguese (Brazilian)	Urdu
Danish	Italian	Provençal	Vietnamese
Dutch	Japanese	Provençal (Old)	Yiddish
Dutch/Flemish	Kannada	Rumanian	
English	Korean	Russian	
Estonian	Laotian	Sanskirt	

In the alphabetical listings that follow in each subsection, the pertinent categories of data and information are designated by the following abbreviations:

TL target language(s), *into* which a translation is made

SL source language(s), *from* which a translation is made

UDC Universal Decimal Classification, the genre or subject field representing the translator's area of competence and/or preference

Affil affiliation in a professional translational capacity with an academic institution, governmental agency, or national or international organization, association, or institution

Accred accreditation, followed by the association, society, or academic institution from which formal and officially recognized accreditation has been obtained

Memb membership in a recognized professional translators' or interpreters' association, society, or center

Awards awards/fellowships/grants/prizes (see also Sec 3) received in recognition of, or for the purpose of conducting, purely translational activity

Two categories of translators and interpreters have not been included in this register: (1) court interpreters, who serve primarily within the US federal, state, and municipal court systems and who are at the present identified exclusively with local associations, such as California Court Interpreters Association (CCIA), are in the process of organizing nationally. Substantive information on the ultimate structure, objectives, and codes of conduct and ethics were not available at press time; however, individual court interpreters are registered within the subsectional categories; (2) sign language interpreters and translators, who serve a unique purpose in providing the deaf with interpretations of messages through the use of artificial sign languages designed and developed to transcodify the language of the community, are discussed in detail in Registry of Interpreters for the Deaf (see Sec 2, USA) and in National Interpreter Training Consortium (see Sec 4, USA).

Directly following each category division (except for Agencies) is an index which classifies the target and source languages of each translator/interpreter listed. To identify regional accessibility of each translator/interpreter, the standard two-letter state abbreviations have been used for those based in the United States, and an abbreviated form for other countries has been used as follows:

Ang—Angola	Gr—Greece	PR—Puerto Rico
Arg—Argentina	Guat—Guatemala	Rum—Rumania
Austral—Australia	Indo—Indonesia	Sen—Senegal
Aust—Austria	Ire—Ireland	S Afr—South Africa
Bel—Belgium	Isr—Israel	S Arab—Saudi Arabia
Bul—Bulgaria	It—Italy	Sp—Spain
Cam—Cameroon	Lux—Luxembourg	Sw—Sweden
Can—Canada	Mex—Mexico	Switz—Switzerland
Col—Colombia	Mor—Morocco	Thai—Thailand
Czech—Czechoslovakia	Neth—The Netherlands	Tur—Turkey
Den—Denmark	N Cal—New Caledonia	UK—United Kingdom
Ecua—Ecuador	N Hebr—New Hebrides	Urug—Uruguay
Eth—Ethiopia	Nor—Norway	Ven—Venezuela
Fr—France	Pan—Panama	VI—Virgin Islands
Ger—Germany, W	Port—Portugal	

Acronyms used in all subsections of the Register to identify national and international associations, societies, centers, institutions, and organizations, and governmental and inter-governmental agencies, are identified as follows:

AAIT—Atlanta Association of Interpreters & Translators (USA)

ABRATES—Associação Brasileira de Tradutores (Brazilian Association of Translators) (Brazil)

ACIT—Association of Conference Interpreters of Turkey (Turkiye Konferans Tercümanlari Derneği) (Turkey)

AIIC—Association Internationale des Interprètes de Conférence (International Association of Conference Interpreters) (Switzerland)

AIT—Asociación Internacional de Traductores (Inter-American Association of Translators) (USA)

AITC—Association Internationale des Traducteurs de Conférence (International Association of Conference Translators) (Switzerland)

AITI--Associazione Italiana Treduttori e Interpreti (Italian Association of Translators & Interpreters) (Italy)

ALTA—American Literary Translators Association (USA)

APETI—Asociación Profesional Española de Tradutores e Intérpretes (Spanish Professional Association of Translators & Interpreters) (Spain)

APT—Association of Professional Translators (USA)

ASI—American Society of Interpreters (USA)

ASTI—Association Suisse des Traducteurs et Interprètes (Swiss Association of Translators & Interpreters) (Switzerland)

ATA—American Translators Association (USA)

ATAQ—Association des Traducteurs Anglophones du Québec (Association of Anglophone Translators of Quebec) (Canada)

ATIE—Associação dos Tradutores et Interpretes do Estado do Rio de Janeiro (Association of Translators & Interpreters of the State of Rio de Janeiro) (Brazil)

ATIO—Association of Translators & Interpreters of Ontario (Canada)

ATLF—Association of Literary Translators of France (France)

ATPI—Association of Public Translators & Interpreters of Brazil (Brazil)

BDÜ—Bundesverband der Dolmetscher und Übersetzer e. V. (Federal Association of Interpreters & Translators) (West Germany)

CBTIP—Chambre Belge des Traducteurs, Interprètes et Philologues (Belgian Chamber of Translators, Interpreters, & Philologists) (Belgium)

CCIA—California Court Interpreters Association (USA)

CITA—Court Interpreters & Translators Association (USA)

CIUTI—Conférence Internationale Permanents des Directeurs des Instituts Universitaires de Traducteurs et Interprètes (International Permanent Conference of Directors of University Institutes of Translators & Interpreters) (France)

CPDT—Centre de Préparation Documentarie á la Traduction (France)

CTA—Colorado Translators Association (USA)

DOE—Department of Energy (USA)

DVTA—Delaware Valley Translators Association (USA)

EEC—European Economic Community (headquarters, Belgium)

EIT—École d'interprètes et traducteurs de la Chambre de Commerce de Paris (School of Interpreters & Translators of the Chamber of Commerce of Paris) (France)

ESIT—École Supérieur d'Interprétation et Traduction (School of Interpretation & Translation, University of Paris) (France)

FAT—Föreningen Auktoriserade Translatorer (Association of Authorized Translators) (Sweden)

GAIT—Guatemalan Association of Interpreters & Translators (Guatemala)

IAEA—International Atomic Energy Agency (headquarters, Austria)
ICITO/GATT—Interim Commission for the International Trade Organization/General Agreement on Tariffs & Trade (Switzerland)
ILO—International Labor Office (Switzerland)
INTELSAT—International Telecommunications Satellite Consortium (USA)
ISETI—Institut Supérieur de l'Etat de Traducteurs et Interprètes (State Higher Institute of Translators & Interpreters) (Belgium)
ISTA—Indian Scientific Translators Association (India)
JEITA—Japanese-English Interpreters & Translators Association (USA)
JPRS—US Joint Publications Research Service (USA)
LDF—Landesverband der Dolmetscher und Fremdsprachenlehrer (National Association of Interpreters & Foreign Language Teachers) (West Germany)
MICATA—Mid-West Chapter of ATA (USA)
NATIST—National Translation Institute of Science & Technology of Japan (Japan)
NATO—North Atlantic Organization Treaty (headquarters, Belgium)
NCCI—Northern California Court Interpreters (USA)
NCTA—Northern California Translators Association (USA)
NEH—National Endowment for the Humanities (USA)
NETA—New England Translators Association (USA)
NGV—Nederlands Genootschap van Vertalers (Netherlands Association of Translators) (The Netherlands)
NOTA—Northern Ohio Translators Association (USA)
NTA—Nevada Translators Association (USA)
OARS—Organization of Asian Research Scholars (USA)
OAS—Organization of American States (USA)
PAHO—Pan American Health Organization (USA)
SFL—Society of Federal Linguists (USA)
SFT—Société Française des Traducteurs (French Society of Translators) (France)
STIC—Société des Traducteurs et Interprètes du Canada (Society of Translators & Interpreters of Canada) (Canada)
STQ—Society of Translators of Quebec (Canada)
TA—The Translators Association of the Society of Authors (UK)
TAALS—The American Association of Language Specialists (USA)
TG—The Translators' Guild of the Institute of Linguists (UK)
TRACT—Translators' Association of Central Texas (USA)
Universitas—Österreichischer Übersetzer und Dolmetscherverband (Austrian Translators & Interpreters Association) (Austria)
VDÜ—Verband deutschsprachiger Übersetzer literarischer und wissenschaftlicher Werke (Association of German-speaking Translators of Literary & Scientific Works) (West Germany)
VS—Verband deutscher Schriftsteller (Association of German Writers) (West Germany)

Agencies

Translation agencies, also known as bureaus or services, are commercial enterprises or firms capable of undertaking a variety of extensive translation and/or interpretation assignments in numerous subject fields by employing permanent or free-lance services of many translators of diverse backgrounds, education, training, experience, and expertise in specialized subject fields.

Because most agencies translate from and into most or all major world languages in most or all subject fields, no Classified-by-Language Index follows this section. However, particular specializations have been highlighted in each entry, especially when these have been emphasized by the agencies.

AAA LANGUAGE SERVICES, INC 22255 Greenfield Rd #118, Southfield, MI 48075 USA *Tel* 313-569-5699, 5681, 5599 *Dirs* Gabriel N Issa, Michele R Nemchek, Sylvia Santos *Staff* 9 *Founded* 1965.

TL & SL any world language, specialists in Arabic. **UDC** commerce, industry, science, technology.

Memb ATA.

AAA LINGUISTIC SERVICE 58 S Waverly St, Brighton, MA 02135 USA *Tel* 617-782-7888 *Dir* Walter Grant *Staff* 4 *Founded* 1974.

TL & SL all languages. **UDC** no restrictions, with specialization in the sciences and technologies.

Memb The Word Guild.

ACADEMIC CONSULTING ASSOCIATES PO Box 911, East Falmouth, MA 02536 USA *Tel* none, assignments via mail *Dir* Vera Verhovskoy *Staff* 3 *Founded* 1975.

TL English. **SL** French, German, Greek, Italian, Latin, Latvian, Russian, Scandinavian, Slavic. **UDC** education, ethics/morals, government, history, linguistics/philology, literature (criticism, drama, folklore, history, prose), religion/scripture, theology.

AD-EX TRANSLATIONS INTERNATIONAL, INC 630 Fifth Ave, New York, NY 10020 USA *Tel* 212-581-2380 *Dir* Bernard Bierman *Staff* 3 *Founded* 1963.

TL & SL all major languages. **UDC** an industrial translation service handling foreign-language documentation involving all subject fields and subdivisions of such fields.

AD-EX TRANSLATIONS INTERNATIONAL/USA 3220 Alpine Rd, Portola Valley, CA 94025 USA *Tel* 415-854-6732 *Dirs* R Addis, J B Fitzgerald, R Abilock *Staff* 10 plus contract translators, editors, typists *Founded* 1959.

TL & SL all major languages. **UDC** all major scientific, technical, and industrial fields. **Memb** ATA.

AGNEW TECH-TRAN INC PO Box 789, Woodland Hills, CA 91365 USA *Tel* 213-340-5147 *Dir* Irene Agnew *Staff* 40 *Founded* 1964.

TL & SL all languages. **UDC** all phases of technical translation, including marketing, graphics, and typesetting.

AJAX TRANSLATORS ASSOCIATES INC 1720 Lawrence Ave E, Scarborough, ON M1R 2YJ, Canada *Tel* 416-755-6668, 2977 *Dirs* Armand Claereboudt, Claudette Claereboudt *Staff* 6 translators, 3 typists, 1 proofreader *Founded* 1964.

TL & SL English & French. **UDC** all subject fields, with specialization in cinema, fashion, fire protection products, footwear, games & toys, hospital (administration, products), medical products, model building, porcelain and china, safety products.

ALL LANGUAGES SERVICE 67 Yonge St #1105, Toronto, ON, Canada *Tel* 416-361-0303 *Dir* Maurice Penzo *Staff* 4 plus 200 free-lance translators and interpreters *Founded* 1971.

TL & SL over 70 major languages. **UDC** all subject fields.

AMERIND PUBLISHING CO (P) LTD N-56 Connaught Circus, New Delhi 110001, India *Tel* 4-4957, 4-3584 *Dir* Gulab Primlani *Staff* 3 *Founded* 1969.

TL English, Hindi. **SL** German, Japanese, Russian. **UDC** areonautics, agriculture, biology, biomedicine, botany, economics, engineering (civil, electrical, hydraulic), fisheries, genetics, history, metallurgy, mineralogy, oceanography, philosophy, sciences. **Memb** ISTA.

ANSEL TRANCOLIT TRANSLATIONS PO Box 2157, Teaneck, NJ 07666 USA *Tel* 201-836-1949 *Dir* Selig O Wassner *Staff* 1 *Founded* 1968.

TL Hebrew, Italian, Portuguese, Swedish. **SL** French, German, Polish, Russian, Spanish. **UDC** archeology, biology, business, documentation, ecology, economics, electronics, fisheries, maritime law, oceanography, philosophy.

ARABIC-ENGLISH TRANSLATION SERVICES, INC 343 E 30 St, New York, NY 10016 USA *Tel* 212-685-7472 *Dirs* Frank Foz, Omneya Tewfik, Mona Sadek *Founded* 1967.

TL & SL Arabic & English. **UDC** areonautics, agriculture, architecture, automotive, aviation, bacteriology, banking/finance, biochemistry, biology, building/construction, chemistry, commerce, communications, computers, ecology, economics, electronics, engineering (chemical, sanitary), fuel technology, information science, law (international), machine tools, medicine, microbiology, military science. **Memb** ATA.

ARMSTRONG TECHNICAL TRANSLATIONS PO Box 27204, San Francisco, CA 94127 USA *Tel* 415-564-3550 *Dir* John Armstrong.

TL English. **SL** all major languages. **UDC** all subject fields.

ARTECO TECHNICAL SERVICES LIMITED 159 Bay St #804, Toronto, ON M5J 1J7, Canada *Tel* 416-364-3684 *Dir* Jean-Jacques Bass *Staff* 5 *Founded* 1967 (incorporated 1972).

TL & SL all Western languages, but mainly English, French, Italian, Spanish. **UDC** all subject fields.

Accred The Canadian Manufacturers' Assn.

BENEMANN TRANSLATION CENTER 760 Market St #1048, San Francisco, CA 94102 USA *Tel* 415-982-7658 *Dir* Federico C Benemann.

TL & SL all languages. **UDC** all subject fields.

Memb ATA.

BESSETTE, CREVIER, PARENT, TANGUAY & ASSOCIATES 110 Cremazie Blvd #1001, Montreal, PQ H2P 1B9, Canada *Tel* 514-382-6930 *Dirs* Pierre Tanguay, Michel Tanguay, Marie-Thérèse De Coorde *Staff* 3 *Founded* 1961.

TL English, French. **SL** Italian, Polish, Portuguese, Spanish. **UDC** agriculture, architecture, astronomy, automotive, aviation, biochemistry, biology, botany, building/construction, business, chemistry, communications, crystallography, ecology, education, electronics, engineering (all areas), forestry, fuel technology, geodesy, geography, geophysics, industry, linguistics/philology, machine tools, meteorology, microbiology, mineralogy, paper/pulp, physics/mechanics, plastics/polymers, political economy/science, public administration, railroad technology, sciences (natural), shipping, surveying, telecommunications, transportation, welding.

BI LANGUAGE SERVICES 403 Executive Center Blvd, El Paso, TX 79902 USA *Tel* 915-544-8300 *Dir* Josefina A Salas-Porras *Staff* 3 *Founded* 1970.

TL & SL English, French, German, Italian, Spanish. **UDC** agriculture, automotive, banking/finance, business, food/nutrition, insurance, interpreting, law, machine tools, petroleum technology, solar energy, textiles.

BLOUIN TRANSLATIONS REGD 1568 Carling Ave #4, Ottawa, ON K1Z 7M5, Canada *Tel* 613-728-9088 *Dirs* Leonard Bernard Hilaire, Leonard Georges Blouin *Staff* 2 plus 7 contract translators *Founded* 1966.

TL & SL English & French. **UDC** agriculture, architecture, building/construction, business, electronics, engineering (electrical, mechanical), forestry, government, human resources, industry, insurance, law, military science, paper/pulp, patents/trademarks, printing, public administration, sports, statistics, transportation, veterinary medicine, welding.

BONZON, SIMEON PO Box 1277, Manila, Philippines *Tel* 79-14-83 *Dirs* K P Villanueva, Noemi S Cruz *Founded* 1973.

TL & SL English, Philipino (major dialects), Spanish. **UDC** aesthetics, communications, documentation, education, electronics, engineering (electrical), government information

science, library science, meteorology, paper/pulp, philosophy, printing, telecommunications.

BRUNSWICK TRANSLATORS PO Box 369, East Brunswick, NJ 08816 USA *Tel* 201-257-0251 *Dir* Stanley Epstein *Founded* 1956.

TL English. **SL** Dutch/Flemish, French, German, Italian, Polish, Portuguese, Rumanian, Russian, Scandinavian, Spanish, Ukrainian. **UDC** all subject fields.

BUREAU OF PUBLICATIONS 721 Capitol Mall, Sacramento, CA 95814 USA *Tel* 916-445-7608 *Dir* Liliana Loofbourow *Staff* 2 *Founded* 1963.

TL & SL English & Spanish. **UDC** education, government, legislation.

Memb ATA.

CAL INTERNATIONAL TRANSLATION SERVICE 71 Ontario St. Toronto, ON M5A 2V1, Canada *Tel* 416-862-8262 *Dir* Pierre M Jolin *Staff* 8 plus 60 free-lance translators *Founded* 1963.

TL English, French, and all listed source langaues on a weekly basis. **SL** Arabic, Cantonese, Danish, Dutch, English, Finnish, French, German, Greek, Italian, Japanese, Mandarin, Portuguese, Russian, Serbo-Croatian, Spanish, Swedish. **UDC** all subject fields; also word processing services and rental of simultaneous multi-channel interpretation equipment.

CALDERON LANGUAGE TRANSLATIONS 1358 E 61 St, Tulsa, OK 74136 USA *Tel* 918-743-3692 *Dir* Juan Calderon *Staff* 2 *Founded* 1973.

TL English, French, Spanish. **SL** French, German, Italian, Portuguese, Spanish. **UDC** archeology, art, banking/finance, business, commerce, education, engineering (electrical, hydraulic, industrial, mechanical, municipal, sanitary), petroleum technology, religion/scripture, shipping, taxation, technology, theology, transportation.

Accred National Translator Certification Service.

CARL DEMRICK ASSOCIATES, INC 30 S Broadway, Yonkers, NY 10701 USA *Tel* 914-963-7006 *Dirs* Linda Hellmann, Irving Elman *Staff* 3 *Founded* 1936.

TL English, French, German, Italian, Spanish. **SL** Danish, Dutch, French, German, Italian, Norwegian, Portuguese, Spanish, Swedish. **UDC** all subject fields.

Memb ATA.

CENTRAL TRANSLATIONS 14 College St, Belfast BT1 6BT, Northern Ireland *Tel* (0232) 646122 *Dir* H A Meek *Founded* 1922.

TL English. **SL** Dutch, French, German, Greek, Italian, Portuguese, Russian, Spanish. **UDC** archeology, architecture, art, building/construction, iron/steel industry, literature (history, prose), painting, sculpture/plastic arts.

Affil Royal Inst of British Architects, London.

CHOW, BANNIE P L 567 24 Ave #203, San Francisco, CA 94121 USA *Tel* 415-387-8879; 433-7164.

TL & SL Chinese (3 dialects: Cantonese, Mandarin, Shanghainese) & English. **UDC** government, history, law (criminal, civil), social services, sociology.

English Somerset Maugham: "The Moon & Sixpence" (pending).

Accred Monterey Inst of Foreign Studies (Translator's Certificate). **Memb** Concordiat.

DUKE TRANSLATION SERVICE 2022 Campus Dr. Duke Univ, Durham, NC 27706 USA *Tel* 919-684-2623 *Dir* H J Ypma *Staff* 4 *Founded* 1973.

TL & SL all languages. **UDC** all subject fields.

DURSTON & ASSOCIATES 65 E Scott, Chicago, IL 60610 USA *Tel* 312-787-2978 *Dir* Donna Durston *Founded* 1970.

TL & SL French & Spanish. **UDC** advertising copy, law, manuals (convention, operational, training).

DUSSAULT TRANSLATION LIMITED 100 Adelaide St W, Toronto, ON M5H 1S3, Canada *Tel* 416-366-5405 *Dir* Jacques Dussault *Staff* 28, including 15 professional translators *Founded* 1950.

TL & SL French & English. **UDC** all subject fields.

E L B LANGUAGES GROUP LTD 61 Carey St, London WC2A 2JG, UK *Tel* 01-242-9276 *Telex* 24224 *Dirs* A C W Crane, D E Lee, T P·E Beglan, Laurence Viney *Staff* a large panel of translators working in the UK and 25 other countries.

TL & SL all major languages, including those of the Far and Middle East (Arabic, Chinese, Farsi, Japanese) and Eastern Europe, some 60 in all.

EDITORIAL EXCELSIOR CORPORATION Two N First St, San Jose, CA 95113 USA *Tel* 408-293-3734 *Dir* Héctor Pereyra-Suárez *Staff* 4.

TL French, Portuguese, Spanish. **SL** English,· French, Portuguese, Spanish. **UDC** agriculture, archeology, art, automotive, business, commerce, copyright, education, engineering (civil), forestry, law, literature (children's), mining, political science, psychology, religion/scripture, sciences (medical), zoology.

EFFECTIVE LEARNING, INC 7 N MacQuesten Pkwy, PO Box 2212, Mt Vernon, NY 10550 USA *Tel* 914-664-7944 *Dir* William Brandon *Founded* 1969.

TL & SL Bulgarian, Finnish, French, German, Hebrew, Italian, Portuguese, Spanish. **UDC** anthropology, automotive building/construction, commerce, communications, education, government, graphics, human resources, industry, journalism, literature, logic, metaphysics, paper/pulp, philosophy, political science, printing, psychology, publishing, recreation/games, religion/scripture, sciences, technology.

ESPERANTO LANGUAGE SERVICE CO 452 Aldine #501, Chicago, IL 60657 USA *Tel* 312-549-0982 *Dir* R Kent Jones *Staff* 1 *Founded* 1969.

TL & SL English & Esperanto. **UDC** engineering (civil, hydraulic, sanitary).

Accred National Translator Certification Service.

EURAMERICA TRANSLATIONS INC 50 E 42 St, New York, NY 10016 USA *Tel* 212-490-1382 *Dir* Yuri Radzievsky *Staff* 10 full-time and 15 part-time translators; 75 consultants *Founded* 1975.

TL & SL 35 major world languages. **UDC** all subject fields.

EUROLARTS, INC 5407 41 St NW, Washington, DC 20015 USA *Tel* 202-686-6766 *Dir* Ismael S Dieguez *Staff* 4 *Founded* 1969.

TL & SL English, French, Italian, Portuguese, Spanish. **UDC** all scientific subject fields.

FLAMBARD (EUROPEAN) LIMITED—TRANSLATIONS Milburn House, Newcastle-on-Tyne NE1 1NW, UK *Tel* Newcastle (0632) 621798, International (44 632) 612798 *Dir* C T Percival.

TL & SL European languages. **UDC** all subject fields.

FOREIGN RESOURCES ASSOCIATES 603 W 13 St #104, Austin, TX 78701 USA *Tel* 512-478-9014 *Dir* Duncan Anderson *Founded* 1973.

TL English. **SL** French, German, Japanese, Russian. **UDC** engineering, sciences.

GFE TRANSLATION CO 6807 Winter Lane, Annandale, VA 22003 USA *Tel* 703-354-0491 *Dir* H Julich *Staff* 6 *Founded* 1971.

TL English, French, German. **SL** all European languages and Japanese. **UDC** aeronautics, automotive, chemistry, communications, computers, electronics, engineering, information science, iron/steel industry, medicine, metallurgy, military science, optics, photography, physics/mechanics, plastics/polymers, railroad technology, sciences, telecommunications, textiles.

GALAXY SYSTEMS, INC 1523 17 St NW, Washington, DC 20036 USA *Tel* 202-667-7400 *Dir* Tadahiko Nakamura *Staff* 2 *Founded* 1973.

TL & SL English & Japanese. **UDC** astronomy, automotive, banking/finance, biochemistry, biology, building/construction, business, chemistry, commerce, communications, ecology, economics, engineering (chemical, civil), fuel technology, government, industry, information science, interpreting, journalism, legislation, literature, microbiology, navigation, patents/trademarks, petroleum technology, philosophy, photography, plastics/polymers, political economy/science, public administration,· sports, standards, statistics, transportation.

Accred US Dept of State Certification.

GERMAN AMERICAN COMMERCIAL & LEGAL INTERPRETER & TRANSLATION SERVICE 46 W 69 St, New York, NY 10023

USA·*Tel* 212-877-1434 *Dir* Olaf R Brauer *Staff* 3 *Founded* 1962.

TL & SL English & German. **UDC** all subject fields.

HEBREW TRANSLATION SERVICE 22 Cornelia St, New York, NY 10014 USA *Tec* 212-989-1742 *Dir* Israel R Eiss *Founded* 1968.

TL & SL English, Hebrew, Yiddish. **UCD** all subjects fields.

Memb ATA.

HOLT FRENCH TRANSLATING BUREAU LTD 11 Yorkville Ave #304, Toronto, ON M4W 1L2, Canada *Tel* 416-924-9379 *Dir* Charles Metz *Staff* 6.

TL & SL English & French. **UDC** business, food/nutrition, medicine, pharmacology, technology.

HOUSE OF TRANSLATION/LES TRADUCTIONS SAUTEMENT 205 Gilmour St, Ottawa, ON K2P ON9, Canada *Tel* 613-233-2200 *Dir* Elsie Saumure *Staff* 3 *Founded* 1963.

TL & SL English & French. **UDC** agriculture, archeology, business, commerce, communications, dairy farming, economics, education, ethics/morals, history, labor relations, municipal affairs, political economy/science, poultry farming, psychiatry, psychology, religion/scripture, social sciences, sociology, statistics, telecommunications, theology.

Memb ATIO.

ITA INTERNATIONAL, INC 4010 Washington, Kansas City, MO 64111 USA *Tel* 816-561-3955 *Dir* John M Kirk *Staff* 30 *Founded* 1958.

TL & SL Arabic, Bulgarian, Chinese, Czech, Danish, Finnish, Flemish, French, German, Greek, Hindi, Hungarian, Icelandic, Indonesian, Italian, Japanese, Korean, Latin, Lettish, Norwegian, Persian (Farsi), Polish, Portuguese, Rumanian, Russian, Serbo-Croatian, Spanish, Swedish, Tagalog, Thai, Turkish, Vietnamese. **UDC** all subject fields.

INLINGUA SCHOOLS OF LANGUAGES 500 N Michigan Ave #530, Chicago, IL 60611 USA *Tel* 312-644-0700 *Dir* William A Reilly *Founded* 1968.

TL & SL all languages. **UDC** all subject fields.

THE INSTITUTE LANFRANCO 350 S Figueroa St #177, Los Angeles, CA 90071 USA *Tel* 213-687-9651 and 2107 Van Ness Ave, San Francisco, CA 94109 USA *Tel* 415-776-7888 *Dirs* Eugene Davie, GianFranco Vignutelli, Don Disler *Staff* 35 *Founded* 1971.

TL & SL all major languages. **UDC** all subject fields.

Memb ATA.

INTERNATIONAL LANGUAGE & TRANSLATION SERVICES Wilburn Plaza, 2221 W Lindsey, #200D, Norman, OK 73069 USA *Tel* 405-360-4822 *Dir* Richard G Price *Founded* 1977.

TL & SL all major languages. **UDC** law, sciences.

INTERNATIONAL LANGUAGE SERV-ICES 3005 E Skelly Dr #180, Tulsa, OK 74105 USA *Tel* 918-299-3469. *Dir* B W Mufti.

TL & SL Arabic, Chinese, Dutch, French, German, Italian, Japanese, Serbo-Croatian, Russian, Spanish. **UDC** all subject fields.

INTERNATIONAL RESOURCE CONSUL-TANTS 1023 Hilgard Ave, Los Angeles, CA 90034 USA *Tel* 213-477-4587 *Dir* Inez Asher *Staff* 1 *Founded* 1975–76.

TL & SL all major languages. **UDC** all subject fields.

INTERNATIONAL TECHNOLOGY TRANSFER ASSOCIATES, INC 200 W 57 St #800, New York, NY 10019 USA *Tel* 212-765-5924 *Dirs* Leon Mindlin, Mary Jane Wilkie *Staff* 5 *Founded* 1976.

TL & SL all major languages. **UDC** advertising (industrial), engineering, technology.

Memb ATA.

JACOBSON TECHNOLOGY LTD PO Box 24009, Tel Aviv, Israel 61240 *Tel* 972-3-471565 *Dirs* Thelma Jacobson, Jonathan Segal *Founded* 1973.

TL & SL English & Hebrew. **UDC** computers, electronics, engineering (aerospace, electrical), information science, maintenance and operation, missiles/rocketry, sciences (applied), telecommunications.

Memb Inst of Electrical and Electronics Engineers (USA), Israel Engineers' Assn, Israel Soc for Technical Communication, Israel Soc of Periodical Editors.

JAPANESE LANGUAGE WORKSHOP 16 California St, San Francisco, CA 94111 USA *Tel* 415-956-8325 *Dir* Motome A Harriman *Founded* 1974.

TL & SL English & Japanese. **UDC** all subject fields.

THE LANGUAGE CENTER, INC 71 Valley St, South Orange, NJ 07079 USA *Tel* 201-762-4455 *Dirs* Michael S Zane, Eleanor P Stetson *Staff* 12 and 91 free-lance specialists *Founded* 1961.

TL & SL all major languages. **UDC** all industrial, medical, scientific, and technical fields, legal and patent work.

Memb ATA, Conference Translator's Assn of Amer.

THE LANGUAGE GUILD INSTITUTE, INC 75 E 55 St, New York, NY 10022 USA *Tel* 212-421-4555, 4556 *Dir* Marina Fedorovskaya *Staff* 2 *Founded* 1942.

TL & SL Arabic, Burmese, Chinese, Czech, Danish, Dutch, English, Finnish, French, German, Greek, Hebrew, Hindi, Hungarian, Icelandic, Indonesian, Italian, Japanese, Korean, Malayan, Norwegian, Persian, Polish, Pushto, Russian, Spanish, Swedish, Thai, Turkish, Ukrainian, Urdu, Vietnamese. **UDC** all subject fields with exception of astrology, brewing, choreography, dairy farming, engraving, metaphysics, occultism, poultry farming, stockbreeding, witchcraft.

THE LANGUAGE LAB 501 Madison Ave, New York, NY 10022 USA *Tel* 212-838-6631 *Dir* Elena Paz *Staff* 10 *Founded* 1971.

TL & SL all modern languages. **UDC** all subject fields.

THE LANGUAGE SERVICE, INC PO Box 8, Hastings-on-Hudson, NY 10706 USA *Tel* 212-687-4183; 914-478-3558. *Dirs* Henry Fischbach, Stefi Fischbach, Monica Fischbach, Peter Fischbach *Staff* 7 *Founded* 1950.

TL & SL Arabic, Chinese, English, Farsi, Hebrew, Hindi, Japanese, and all European languages. **UDC** bacteriology, biochemistry, biology, biomedicine, chemistry, dentistry, entomology, epidemiology, food/nutrition, genetics, medicine, microbiology, optometry, paramedicine, parasitology, pharmacology, psychiatry, public health, sciences (life, medical), veterinary medicine, zoology.

Accred ATA. **Memb** ATA, Amer Chemical Society, Amer Med Writers Assn (AMWA), Conference Translator's Assn of Amer.

LATIN AMERICAN ASSOCIATION PO Box 13154 Sta K, Atlanta, GA 30324 USA *Tel* 404-231-0940 *Dirs* Frank X Nuñez, Gladys Nuñez, Dee Dougherty *Staff* 7 *Founded* 1976.

TL English, Spanish. **SL** English, Portuguese, Spanish. **UDC** anthropology, art, business, ceramics, chemistry, communications, education, ethics/morals, genealogy, genetics, geography, history, journalism, literature (folklore), navigation, painting, psychology, religion/scripture, social sciences, statistics, taxation, theology, transportation.

Memb Freelance Translators Assn.

LINDNER TRANSLATIONS, INC 29 Broadway, New York, NY 10006 USA *Tel* 212-269-4660; 799-6049 *Staff* 1 *Dir* Valerie E Lindner.

TL & SL all languages. **UDC** archeology, automotive, banking/finance, biochemistry, building, business, chemistry, commerce, communications, computers, copyright, electronics, engineering, law, medicine, metallurgy, microbiology, patents/trademarks, physics, plastics, sciences, telecommunications.

Memb ATA, Conference Translator's Assn of Amer.

LINGUISTIC SYSTEMS, INC 116 Bishop Richard Allen Dr, Cambridge, MA 02139 USA *Tel* 617-864-3900 *Dirs* John J Moss, Martin Roberts *Staff* 21 *Founded* 1967.

TL & SL all major languages. **UDC** all subject fields.

MARKETMAN-TRANSLATIONS 13A ave du Pesage, B-1050 Brussels, Belgium *Tel* (02) 648 03 17 *Dir* George Vourliotis.

TL & SL Dutch, English, French, German, Greek, Italian, Spanish. **UDC** all subject fields.

MEDIA FACTORY, INC 1 Union Square W, New York, NY 10003 USA *Tel* 212-243-1008 *Dir* Ronald Globus *Founded* 1974.

TL & SL all languages. **UDC** all subject fields.

Memb ATA.

MEDICAL-PHARMACEUTICAL TRANS-LATION SERVICES, INC 343 E 30 St, New York, NY 10016 USA *Tel* 212-685-7472 *Founded* 1959.

TL & SL all major languages. **UDC** bacteriology, biochemistry, biology, biomedicine, entomology, epidemiology, food/nutrition, genetics, microbiology, psychiatry, psychology, sciences (medical), veterinary medicine.

Memb ATA.

MIDDLE EAST INFORMATION AGENCY PO Box 1588, New York, NY 10017 USA *Tel* 212-243-1975 *Dir* Ray Lord *Founded* 1968.

TL English. **SL** French, Persian (Farsi, Iranian), Russian, Turkish. **UDC** economics, law (international, maritime, property), legislation, political economy, psychiatry, psychology, sociology, statistics, surveying.

MONTREAL TRANSLATION CENTRE 1345 Redpath Crescent, Montreal, PQ H3G 1A1, Canada *Tel* 514-282-1223 *Dirs* Guy Coté, L P Nolet, M Coté *Staff* 4 *Founded* 1974.

TL & SL English, French, Italian, Latin, Portuguese, Rumanian, Spanish. **UDC** administration, advertising & public relations, banking/finance, data processing, humanities, industrial processes, industrial relations, law, sciences (health, physical).

NELLES TRANSLATIONS 53 W Jackson Blvd, Chicago, IL 60604 USA *Tel* 312-922-7774 *Dir* Peter Nelles *Staff* 2 *Founded* 1959.

TL English, French, German, Spanish. **SL** Chinese, Dutch, French, German, Italian, Japanese, Portuguese, Russian, Spanish, Swedish. **UDC** aesthetics, bacteriology, chemistry, electronics, engineering (chemical), fuel technology, geophysics, iron/steel industry, linguistics/philology, metallurgy, mineralogy, mining, optics, painting, patents/trademarks, petroleum technology, pharmacology, plastics/polymers, recreation/games, textiles, theater, welding, zoology.

Memb ATA.

NEW YORK LANGUAGE INSTITUTE 2395 Palisade Ave, Riverdale, NY 10463 USA *Tel* 212-796-9685 *Dir* David L Meth *Staff* 2 *Founded* 1975.

TL & SL English & Japanese. **UDC** general interpreting and translating, calling upon experts in specialized fields when outside expertise is needed.

POLISH TRANSLATING SERVICE 1050 N State St, Chicago, IL 60610 USA *Tel* 312-787-4440 *Dirs* Stan & Roman Lobodzinski *Staff* 3 *Founded* 1957.

TL English. **SL** Polish, Russian.

POLYGLOT TRANSLATIONS 230 Prince Edward Rd #1B, Kowloon, Hong Kong *Tel* 3-372994 *Dir* Husein Rofé.

TL English. **SL** Arabic, Chinese, Dutch, French, German, Indonesian, Italian, Malaysian, Persian, Portuguese, Spanish, Swedish, Turkish. **UDC** anthropology, archeology, astrology, banking/finance, economics, education, ethnography, insurance, linguistics/philology, occultism, philately, photography, psychology, religion/scripture, shipping, sociology, transportation.

Affil Asian Development Bank, Manila (chief translator, 1970–75). **Memb** AITC.

POLYGLOTS, INC 802 Chester Ave, Yeadon, PA 19050 USA *Tel* 215-626-5000 *Dir* Elizabeth M Bolen *Founded* 1973.
TL & SL all languages. **UDC** all subject fields.

PROFESSIONAL TRANSLATING SERV-ICES Roberts Building, 28 W Flagler St #540, Miami, FL 33130 USA *Tel* 305-371-7887 *Dir* Luis a de la Vega *Staff* 12 *Founded* 1973.
TL & SL Arabic, Chinese (4 dialects), Czech, Danish, Dutch, English, Finnish, French, German, Greek, Haitian Creole, Hebrew, Hungarian, Italian, Japanese, Norwegian, Polish, Portuguese, Russian, Spanish, Swedish, Thai, Turkish, Ukrainian, Vietnamese, Yiddish. **UDC** all subject fields.
Memb ATA.

PROFESSIONAL TRANSLATORS 2924 28 Ave NE, Portland, OR 97212 USA *Tel* 503-281-4493 *Dir* Sam Markson *Staff* 5 *Founded* 1971.
TL & SL French, German, Japanese, Polish, Russian, Spanish, Swedish. **UDC** brewing, business, commerce, computers, data processing, engineering (chemistry), forest products, forestry, industry, law, mathematics, paper/pulp, political science.
Memb ATA.

RAINBOW SYSTEMS, INC 2727 Duke St, Box 5, Alexandria, VA 22314 USA *Tel* 703-751-1592; 301-949-4219 *Dir* M S Soloviev, George Rabchevsky *Founded* 1970.
TL & SL over 30 languages. **UDC** all subject fields.

ROSETTA STONE ASSOCIATES, INC 142 Main St, Nashua, NH 03060 USA *Tel* 603-882-1760 *Dir* John F Furey *Staff* 3 *Founded* 1972.
TL & SL all major languages. **UDC** all subject fields.

ROUTLEDGE ASSOCIATES 25 Woodhayes Rd, London SW19 4RF, UK *Tel* (01) 947 5614 *Dir* R A Routledge *Founded* 1972.
TL & SL Arabic, Afrikaans, Bulgarian, Czech, Danish, Dutch, Flemish, French (modern & medieval), German, Greek (modern & classical), Hebrew, Hungarian, Italian. Latin (classical & medieval), Norwegian, Polish, Portuguese, Rumanian, Russian, Serbo-Croatian, Spanish, Swedish, Yiddish. **UDC** anthropology, archeology, architecture, art/art history, arts/crafts, bacteriology, banking/finance, biomedicine, commerce, communications, copyright, documentation, economics, education, genealogy, government, graphics, heraldry, history, jurisprudence, law (international, maritime, property), legislation, library science, linguistics/philology, literature, medicine, microbiology, military science, music, painting, patents/trademarks, petroleum, pharmacology, philosophy, political economy/science, psychiatry, psychology, religion, sciences (medical), sociology.
Accred all staff translators must have accreditation through the TG or an accredited institution of translator training.

SCIENCE INFORMATION ASSOCIATES c/o Charles M Stern, 241 W 97 St, New York,

NY 10025 USA *Tel* 212-864-4453 *Dirs* Charles M Stern, E L Juliet *Founded* 1963.
TL English, Spanish. **SL** Danish, Dutch, French, German, Italian, Rumanian, Spanish, Swedish, others. **UDC** banking/finance, business, chemistry, communications, engineering (civil, industrial, municipal), history, iron/steel industry, literature (prose), paper/pulp, patents/trademarks, printing, sciences (medical), statistics.

SCIENTIFIC INFORMATION CONSUL-TANTS LTD 661 Finchley Rd, London NW 2 2HN, UK *Tel* 01-794-2217 *Dir* E G Gros *Staff* 5.
TL English. **SL** Czech, French, German, Hungarian, Russian.

SCIENTIFIC TRANSLATIONS INTER-NATIONAL LTD (STI) POB 1154 Jerusalem, Israel *Tel* (02) 812601, 812671, 812731 *Telex* 25445 (INTRA IL) *Dirs* Stefan S Sella, Jerome Sella *Staff* 64 employees in Israel, 11 outside Israel in USA-Europe marketing network *Founded* 1973.
TL Arabic, English, Farsi, French, German, Hebrew, Italian, Polish, Portuguese, Rumanian, Russian, Spanish. **SL** English, French, German, Hebrew, Italian, Polish, Rumanian, Russian, Spanish. **UDC** all subject fields.

SPANISH INTERNATIONAL PO Box 763, Hollywood, CA 90028 USA *Tel* 213-786-1601 *Dir* Gerardo J Tosco. *Founded* 1977.
TL & SL English & Spanish. **UDC** all subject fields except governmental projects.

SPANISH INTERPRETING AND TRANS-LATING SERVICE 2 N Riverside Plaza #1333, Chicago, IL 60606 USA *Tel* 312-782-8115 *Dirs* Frida Freudman, Ernest Freudman *Staff* 5 *Founded* 1967.
TL & SL English & Spanish. **UDC** business, computers, data processing, engineering, information science, insurance, interpreting, law, literature.
Memb ATA.

THE SPANISH LANGUAGE CENTER OF NEW YORK 51 E 42 St, New York, NY 10017 USA *Tel* 212-687-0535, 0536 *Dir* Ralph A Alvarez *Founded* 1939.
TL & SL English, French, German, Italian, Japanese, Russian, Spanish. **UDC** all subject fields.

SPICA TRANSLATIONS INC Tower A, Place Vanier, 333 Rider Rd, Ottawa, ON K1L 8B9, Canada *Tel* 613-741-5315 *Dirs* G Holtzwarth, P Leizour, S Fourcand, D Holtzwarth *Staff* 12 translators, 3 revisers *Founded* 1976.
TL English, French. **SL** Dutch, English, French, German, Italian, Spanish. **UDC** aeronautics, athletics, automotive, aviation, banking/finance, building/construction, business, commerce, communications, data processing, ecology, economics, electronics, engineering (aerospace, civil, electrical, mechanical, sanitary), forestry, geodesy, government, industry, journalism, machine tools, meteorology, mineralogy, mining, navigation, photography, plastics/polymers, poultry farming, public administration, shipbuilding, sports, technology, telecommunications, transportation.

Accred Government of Canada (Secy of State, Min of National Defense, Min of Transport, Dept of the Environment, Dept of Industry and Commerce, Dept of Mines, Energy, and Resources).

SUNLONE, INC 1603 S Highland Ave, Arlington Hts, IL 60005 USA *Tel* 312-439-4312 *Dir* Nora Liu *Staff* 4 *Founded* 1965 (incorporated 1973).
TL Chinese, English, French, German, Hungarian, Japanese, Spanish, and through freelance translators all languages in which technical material is published **SL** Chinese, Dutch, French, German, Hungarian, Italian, Portuguese, Spanish. **UDC** biochemistry, biology, ceramics, chemistry, food/nutrition, iron/steel industry, medicine, metallurgy, paper/pulp, patents, petroleum technology, physics, sciences (applied, medical, natural), and especially toxicology.
Memb ATA.

TECHMEDIA-MARKOV ASSOCIATES 501 Fifth Ave, New York, NY 10017 USA *Tel* 212-687-7955 *Dir* George Markov *Founded* 1977.
TL & SL English, Russian, and major European languages. **UDC** all subject fields.

TECHNICAL SERVICES 32 Broadway, New York, NY 10004 USA *Tel* 212-425-5540 *Dir* Alice L Picard *Founded* 1974.
TL Spanish, Portuguese. **SL** French. **UDC** archeology, aviation, chemistry, law, literature (prose), meteorology.

TRANSAFRICA Transafrica Via Trieste 34, I-Brescia, 25100 Italy *Tel* 030-55080 *Dir* Giancarlo Parapini *Staff* 2 *Founded* 1951.
TL French, Italian. **SL** Arabic, Dutch, English, German, Luganda, Portuguese, Spanish, Swahili. **UDC** general translation.

TRANSEMANTICS, INC 1901 Pennsylvania Ave NW #407, Washington, DC 20006 USA *Tel* 202-659-9640 *Dirs* Marcel X Rocca, Alfred V Roberts *Staff* 12 *Founded* 1970.
TL & SL most modern languages. **UDC** most subject fields with specialization in accountancy, advertising, aerospace & aviation, agriculture, banking/finance, energy, engineering, international trade, law, law enforcement, management, medicine, public health, sciences (physical, social), telecommunications.
Memb ATA.

TRANS-INTER-SCIENTIA (TIS) PO Box 16, Tonbridge, Kent TN11 8DY, UK *Tel* (0892) 870 641 *Dir* A McMath.
TL & SL English, French, German. **UDC** all subject fields, with specialization in the sciences.
Affil Aslib.

THE TRANSLATION CENTER, INC 2 Vernon St, Medford, MA 02155 USA *Tel* 617-395-0900 *Dir* Claude W Nash *Staff* 3 plus an associated staff of free-lance translators in the US and over 200 native specialists overseas *Founded* 1969.
TL & SL all modern languages. **UDC** all fields of commerce, law, science, technology.
Memb ATA.

TRANSLATORS' POOL LTD 1 Rachel St, Tel Aviv, Israel *Tel* 03-238532, 230574, 241780 *Cable* TRAPOOL TELAVIV *Dirs* Alisa & Yohanan Goldman *Staff* 3 plus about 100 freelance translators *Founded* 1960.

TL & SL Arabic, Hebrew, Persian, and most European languages. UDC all subject fields.

TRANSTEK ASSOCIATES, INC 143 Main St, Reading, MA 01867 USA *Tel* 617-944-1947 *Dir* M Emelianoff *Staff* executive, editing, and production personnel, with over 2,000 freelance translators available *Founded* 1962.

TL & SL all languages. UDC all subject fields.

G J WIEDEMANN TRANSLATING SERVICE 86 Albert St, Cambridge, ON N1R 3N5, Canada *Tel* 519-621-6534.

TL & SL German & English. UDC automotive, banking/finance, commerce, communications, documentation, economics, government, iron/steel industry, machine tools, philately, public administration.

Memb ATA.

YAMA TRANS 24228 Hawthorne Blvd, Torrance, CA 90505 USA *Tel* 213-378-8700 *Dir* Eiichi Yamamoto *Staff* 1 *Founded* 1975.

TL & SL English & Japanese. UDC astronomy, astrophysics, business, computers, data processing, documentation, electronics, engineering, physics, political economy/science, sciences (applied, earth, information, library, natural).

Industrial, Scientific & Technical Translators

Translators who work with material of a purely factual or pragmatic nature (rather than literary, esthetic, poetic, or belletristic) are listed alphabetically in this section. Each entry contains the basic identifying professional designations: target language(s), source language(s); specialized subject fields of the translator's competence and/or preference; affiliation with an academic institution, international organization, private enterprise, or government agency; recognized accreditation from an association or translator-training program; and membership in a recognized professional association. These facts are, in some instances, accompanied by a selected bibliography of published translations arranged by source language, original author's name, English title, publisher's name, and year of publication.

It should be noted that in many instances these translators may also work with humanistic or literary material, but because the major portion of their professional activity appears to be in the purely administrative, commercial, legal, industrial, scientific, or technical areas, they have been listed in this section.

ABILEAH, MIRIAM M PO Box 1203, Sta A, Toronto, ON M5W 1G6, Canada.

TL English. SL French, German. UDC bacteriology, biochemistry, biology, biomedicine, botany, chemistry, ecology, epidemiology, fisheries, food/nutrition, forestry, medicine, microbiology, pharmacology, physiology, sciences (applied, life), veterinary medicine, zoology.

German K Beyermann: *Chemistry: An Introduction for Medical Students* (George Thieme, 1975). M Tausk: *Pharmacology of Hormones* (George Thieme, 1975). Translations mostly not for publication, but for the internal use of researchers and scientists.

Memb Amer Med Writers Assn.

ABILOCK, ROBERT Ad-Ex Translations International/USA, 3220 Alpine Rd, Portola Valley, CA 94025 USA *Tel* 415-854-6732.

TL English. SL French, German. UDC computers, electronics, iron/steel industry, metallurgy, physics, telecommunications, technology.

Memb ATA.

ADAM, E W 231 E 89 St Apt 2F, New York, NY 10028 USA *Tel* 212-348-6800.

TL English, German, Portuguese. SL French, German, Portuguese, Spanish. UDC banking/finance, business, commerce, education, electronics, engineering (electrical, industrial, mechanical), insurance, law (international), legislation, literature (drama, prose), painting, patents/trademarks.

ADAMS, JOYCE Epidemiology, Univ of California, Davis, CA 95616 USA *Tel* 916-752-1378.

TL English. SL German, Russian. UDC archeology, art history, cinematography, epidemiology, food/nutrition, history, medicine, parasitology, religion, veterinary medicine.

ADAMSON, URSULA B 1332 Barcelona Dr, Akron, OH 44313 USA *Tel* 216-867-0175.

TL German. SL English. UDC engineering (civil, mechanical, nuclear), genealogy, iron/steel industry, material testing, metallurgy, standards, technology, welding.

Memb ATA.

ADAO, DEOLINDA M 7334 Schmidt Lane, El Cerrito, CA 94530 USA.

TL English, French, Portuguese, Spanish. SL Portuguese, Spanish. UDC banking/finance, business, commerce, economics, law (international, maritime, property), taxation.

Memb ATA, NCTA (treas & staff adm).

AGRANOV, ISRAEL 5005 Richenbacher Ave, Alexandria, VA 22304 USA *Tel* 703-370-1497.

TL & SL English & Russian. UDC bacteriology, banking/finance, biochemistry, biomedicine, business, chemistry, commerce, documentation, education, engineering (industrial), interpreting, law (property), linguistics, sciences (applied, medical, natural).

Author of *English-Russian Patent Dictionary* (TSNIIPI, 1973). *Glossary of English-Russian Patent Terms,* Issue 2 (Translation Bureau of the All-Union Inst of Scientific and Technical Information, 1971).

AISWORTH, CARLOS A 50-18 68 St, Woodside, NY 11377 USA *Tel* 212-651-9494.

TL & SL English & Spanish. UDC agriculture, automotive, business, chemistry, commerce, communications, computers, data processing, electronics, engineering (aerospace, electrical, industrial, mechanical), industry, insurance, iron/steel industry, machine tools, medicine, pharmacology, photography, physics, telecommunications.

Memb ATA.

AKKERMAN, FEDDE H 52784 Sporn Dr, South Bend, IN 46635 USA *Tel* 219-272-6933.

TL English. SL Dutch, French, German. UDC chemistry, general science, literature (prose).

Memb ATA.

ALBIZU, EDDY MARIA 1462 Lombardy Blvd, Bay Shore, NY 11706 USA *Tel* 516-666-9107.

TL & SL English & Spanish. UDC business, engineering (electrical, civil), instrumentation & controls.

Memb ATA.

ALEX, KURT 6517 N Nordica, Chicago, IL 60631 USA *Tel* 312-631-0663.

TL & SL English & German. UDC automotive, building/construction, chemistry, engi-

neering (chemical, electrical, hydraulic, mechanical), fuel technology, industry, iron/steel industry, machine tools, metallurgy, optics, petroleum technology, physics, plastics/polymers, sciences (applied, natural), standards, technology, transportation, welding.
Memb ATA.

ALVAREZ, ELENA A 5500 Friendship Blvd #N1004, Chevy Chase, MD 20015 USA *Tel* 301-656-7277.
TL Spanish. **SL** English, French. **UDC** banking/finance, economics.
Affil World Bank (senior translator/reviser). **Memb** ATA.

ANACKER, NICOLE MARIE 61 Singingwood Lane, Orinda, CA 94563 USA *Tel* 415-254-5646.
TL English. **SL** French. **UDC** agriculture, banking/finance, building/construction, business, commerce, communications, computers, data processing, documentation, economics, electronics, engineering (civil, electrical, hydraulic, industrial, mechanical), medicine, mining, sciences (medical), sociology, surveying, telecommunications, transportation, veterinary medicine.
Affil International Engineering Co. **Memb** ATA, NCTA.

ANDRIESSE, ELLA Palestrinalaan 4, NL-1217 CE Hilversum, Netherlands *Tel* (035) 43014 c/o Rotem, 222 E 51 St #3C, New York, NY 10022 USA.
TL Dutch. **SL** English, French, German. **UDC** international law.

ARANGO, LUIS EDUARDO 3333 Lauriston Pl, Fairfax, VA 22030 USA *Tel* 703-698-8758.
TL English. **SL** Spanish. **UDC** aeronautics, aviation, communications (satellite).
Affil INTELSAT (senior translator).

ARMSTRONG, JOHN W PO Box 27204, San Francisco, CA 94127 USA *Tel* 415-564-3550.
TL English. **SL** Danish, French, German, Italian, Norwegian, Russian, Spanish, Swedish. **UDC** electronics, engineering (electrical, nuclear), telecommunications.
Affil Armstrong Technical Translations. **Memb** ATA.

BALABAN, JOHN 306 S Gill St, State College, PA 16802 USA *Tel* 814-865-6381.
TL English. **SL** Vietnamese. **UDC** both oral and literary poetry of Vietnam.
Vietnamese *Vietnamese Folk Poetry* (a collection of oral folk poems without single composers, taped in Vietnam in 1971–72), (Unicorn, 1974). Also the works of Rumanian poets, Lucian Blaga, Stephan Doinas, B. Fundolanu, Aurel Rau, and V. Voiculescu (in *Translation*, Columbia Univ, 5, 1978).
Affil Pennsylvania St Univ. **Awards** 1974 Columbia-PEN Translation Fellowship; 1977 Columbia Univ Translation Grant.

BALIG, H 112 rue du Pinson, B-1170 Brussels, Belgium *Tel* (02) 660 67 35.
TL German. **SL** English. **UDC** electronics, engineering (electrical).
Memb CBTIP, TG.

BALK, LYDIA R 23 Windsor Rd, Clifton, NJ 07012 USA *Tel* 201-773-4084.
TL English. **SL** French, German. **UDC** chemistry, commerce, engineering (electrical), sciences (applied, medical).
Memb ATA.

BANDA, FRANCISCO C 3724 Ingomar St NW, Washington, DC 20015 USA *Tel* 202-362-3627.
TL English. **SL** Spanish. **UDC** agriculture, botany, biomedicine, commerce, fisheries, government, law, shipping, transportation.

BARB, WOLFGANG GERSON Spring Wood, Hedgerley Lane, Gerrards Cross, Bucks SL9 7NS, UK *Tel* (2813) 86962, 87712.
TL English. **SL** French, German. **UDC** biochemistry, chemistry, cosmetics, patents/trademarks/licenses, pharmacology, plastics/polymers, synthetic textiles.
Memb TG.

BARRACLOUGH, FRANCES HORNING 1341 Slaterville Rd, Ithaca, NY 14850 USA *Tel* 1-607-273-5038.
TL & SL English & Spanish. **UDC** agricultural economics, anthropology, archeology, economics, history, land tenure, literature (drama, folklore, poetry, prose, songs), music, political science, psychology, sociology.
Spanish José María Arguedas: *Deep Rivers* (Univ of Texas, 1978). Solon Barraclough: *Agrarian Structure in Latin America* (Lexington Books, 1973).
Affil Ithaca College. **Memb** ALTA. **Awards** Columbia Univ Translation Center Grant.

BAUMGART, ARTHUR E 39 Tula Pl, NW, Ft Walton Beach, FL 32548 USA *Tel* 904-243-4122.
TL English. **SL** German, Polish, Spanish. **UDC** aeronautics, business, commerce, electronics, engineering (electrical), telecommunications.
Memb ATA.

BECK, CHARLENE J 149 Rivercrest Dr, Coraopolis, PA 15108 USA *Tel* 412-264-4176.
TL English. **SL** French, Spanish. **UDC** building/construction, engineering (civil, electrical, hydraulic), mining, surveying.
Accred ATA. **Memb** APT, ATA.

BEERBAUM, MIRA S 345 Taft, Sebastopol, CA 95472 USA *Tel* 707-823-2516.
TL English. **SL** Russian. **UDC** aeronautics, biochemistry, biomedicine, epidemiology, fisheries, food/nutrition, genetics, iron/steel industry, machine tools, medicine, microbiology, mining, oceanography, petroleum, sciences (applied, earth, life, natural, social), standards.
Accred Monterey Inst of Foreign Studies (Certificate). **Memb** ATA.

BELLAGAMBA, MARIA CAROLINA PO Box 2129, Panama 9A, Panama *Tel* 267227; 640437.
TL English, Spanish. **SL** French, Italian, Portuguese, Spanish. **UDC** anthropology, art, communications, data processing, economics, information, taxation (legislation & treaties).

Spanish Macon & Merino Manon: *Financing Urban & Rural Development through Betterment Levies: The Latin American Experience* (Praeger, 1977).
Affil Inter-American Center of Tax Administrators. **Memb** AIIC, TAALS.

BELLEGARDE, SERGE 238 Southampton Dr, Silver Spring, MD 20903 USA *Tel* 202-381-8616, 8703.
TL French. **SL** English, Portuguese, Spanish. **UDC** administration, government, political science.
Affil OAS. **Memb** AIT.

BERGER, S EDMUND 298 Grayton Rd, Tonawanda, NY 14150 USA *Tel* 716-832-7316.
TL English. **SL** French, German, Italian, Serbo-Croatian. **UDC** biochemistry, engineering (chemical), food/nutrition, medicine, metallurgy, petroleum, plastics, sciences (earth, life, medical), textiles.
Memb ATA.

BERGLUND, ALICE M 35 Catherine Dr, Peabody, MA 01960 USA *Tel* 617-535-2140.
TL English. **SL** French, German, Russian. **UDC** biochemistry, chemistry, engineering (chemical), metallurgy, patents, pharmacology.
Affil International Translation Co.

BERGMANN, VERA 182 Garth Rd, Scarsdale, NY 10583 USA
TL English, German, **SL** French. **UDC** brewing.
Affil Schwarz Services International (consultants to the brewing industry). **Memb** ATA.

BERNAYS, HELLA FREUD 1864 Riverside Dr, Columbus, OH 43212 USA *Tel* 614-488-4407.
TL English. **SL** German. **UDC** psychiatry, psychology.
German H Argelander: *Initial Interview in Psychotherapy* (Behavioral Pub, 1976). Charlotte Buhler: *Psychology for Contemporary Living* (Hawthorn, 1968). Albert Haller: *The Vitamin Hunters* (Chilton, 1962). Also the works of A A Brill, Paul Federn, Sigmund Freud, F Fromm-Reichmann, Carl C Jung, Ludwig Marcuse, A A Meerloo, Hans Sachs.

BERRIZ, HILARIO A 1150 NW 11 St, Miami, FL 33136 USA *Tel* 305-547-1952; 548-3319.
TL Spanish. **SL** English. **UDC** banking/finance, commerce, data processing, economics, insurance, law, public administration.
Affil State of FL. **Memb** ATA.

BERRY, VIRGINIA EVA 285 Madison Ave, New York, NY 10017 USA *Tel* 212-689-8810.
TL English. **SL** French, Italian, Spanish. **UDC** commerce, economics, insurance, law, machine tools, mining, patents, public administration, shipping, textiles.
Accred Univ of Geneva. **Memb** ATA.

BERSON, ALAN CHARLES 74 Ridgmount Gardens, London WC1E 7AX UK *Tel* (01) 6361990.
TL English. **SL** French, Russian, Spanish. **UDC** art, banking/finance, biology, business,

economics, government, law, legislation, medicine, political economy, sociology.

Spanish Alfonso E Pérez Sánchez: *The Famous Italian Drawings of the Madrid Collections* (Phaidon, 1977).

Memb ATA, TA, TG, Inst of Linguists.

BERTSCHE, ALISON PO Box 129, Croton-on-Hudson, NY 10520 USA *Tel* 914-271-3260.
TL English. **SL** German. **UDC** sciences (information, medical).
Affil Interlingua Translations. **Memb** ATA.

BERTSCHE, WILLIAM I 11 Broadway, New York, NY 10004 USA *Tel* 212-344-2930.
TL English. **SL** Dutch, French, German, Italian, Portuguese, Scandinavian, Spanish. **UDC** chemistry, commerce, economics, engineering, insurance, law, medicine, patents, sciences, taxation.
Memb ATA (past pres).

BIANCO, CELSO 140 West End Ave, New York, NY 10023 USA *Tel* 212-595-2573.
TL English. **SL** Portuguese (Brazilian). **UDC** sciences (medical).
Memb ATA.

BICK, WALTER 38 Airyhall Ave, Aberdeen AB1 7QX UK.
TL English. **SL** German. **UDC** agriculture, biochemistry, chemistry, farming, horticulture, peat production & utilization.
Memb TG.

BIDERMAN, ARTHUR 425 Riverside Dr #4D, New York, NY 10025 USA *Tel* 212-662-4643.
TL English. **SL** Russian. **UDC** electronics, engineering (civil), mathematics (applied), physics.
Memb ATA.

BIGGS, R R 49 Pine Walk, Carshalton Beeches, Surrey SM5 4HA, UK *Tel* (01) 643 1620.
TL English. **SL** French. **UDC** architecture, art, automotive, building/construction, chemistry, engineering (chemical, civil), mining, petroleum, printing, sciences (earth), surveying, viniculture.
Memb TG.

BINSFELD, GUILLAUME Blvd Sylvain Dupuis 223/Bte 13, B-1070 Brussels, Belgium *Tel* (02) 215 48 93; 522 57 08.
TL French, German. **SL** English. **UDC** automotive, brewing, commerce, construction of glass annealing lehrs, data processing, economics, engineering (chemical, electrical, mechanical), plastics, printing, sports, technology.
Memb CBTIP.

BIRDWOOD, GEORGE F B Westmeon, Langley Hill, Kings Langley, Herts, UK *Tel* (09277) 63996.
TL English. **SL** German. **UDC** sciences (medical, natural).
Affil Ciba-Geigy Scientific Publications. **Memb** TG **Awards** 1969 Youhotsky Prize for technical translation.

BLAU, MARCELLE R 1335 Meadow Lane, Yellow Springs, OH 45387 USA *Tel* 513-767-7611.
TL English. **SL** Russian. **UDC** sciences (medical).

BOER-HOFF, LOUISE ELENA Linnaeusparkweg 71, NL-Amsterdam, Netherlands *Tel* (020) 935287.
TL English. **SL** Dutch. **UDC** psychology.
Memb Dutch Soc of Translators.

BOGAERT, DIRK Lichtaartseweg 199, B-2410 Herentals, Belgium *Tel* (014) 21 33 88.
TL Dutch. **SL** English. **UDC** business, commerce, navigation, philately, shipping, transportation.
Memb CBTIP.

BOLTON, PHYLLIS L 18 Windermere Rd, Upper Montclair, NJ 07042 USA *Tel* 201-744-1672.
TL English. **SL** French, German, Russian. **UDC** chemistry, geology, petroleum, plastics, pulp/paper.
Russian M O Korshun et al: *Methods in Microanalysis: Simultaneous Rapid Combustion* (Gordon & Breach, 1964).
Memb ATA.

BOMSE, MARGUERITE D 8301 Ridge Blvd, Brooklyn, NY 11209 USA *Tel* 212-680-0041.
TL English. **SL** French, German. **UDC** art, banking/finance, business.
Memb ATA.

BONNEKAMP, SONJA M 47 Firs Close, London N10 3HR, UK *Tel* 883 9917.
TL & SL Dutch & English. **UDC** agriculture, commerce, dairy farming, ecology, education, fisheries, food/nutrition, history, industry, literature, occultism, painting, poultry farming, public health, sciences (medical), shipping, stockbreeding, theater, witchcraft.
English R Prawder Jhabvala: *To Whom She Will* (De Toorts, 1958). **German** Nobel Prize Laureates: *Nobel Lectures (Medicine, Chemistry, Physics)* (Elsevier, 1964).
Memb TG, Dutch Soc of Translators.

BONNING, H K 24 Upper Belgrave Rd, Clifton, Bristol BS8 2XL UK *Tel* (0272) 35736 *Telex* 449530 (BOING G).
TL English. **SL** French, German, Italian, Spanish. **UDC** agriculture, finance, hydrology, law (commercial), taxation.
German D Bronger: *Forms of Spatial Integration* (Verlag Ferdinand Schöningh, 1978). Hans-Joachim Wenzel: *Rural Population* (Lenz-Verlag, 1974).
Memb TG.

BORCHARDT, MARGUERITE 345 E 54 St #5H, New York, NY 10022 USA *Tel* 212-355-0135.
TL & SL English & French. **UDC** agriculture, art, banking/finance, commerce, economics, engraving, history, insurance, medicine, painting, public administration.
German Heinrich Brunner: *Cuban Sugar Policy from 1963 to 1970* (Univ of Pittsburgh, 1977).
Accred US Dept of State. **Memb** ASI.

BOSTWICK, GARY L c/o Manatt, Phelps, Rothenberg & Tunney, 1888 Century Pk E, Los Angeles, CA 90067 USA *Tel* 213-556-1500.
TL English. **SL** German, Spanish. **UDC** automotive, economics, engineering (mechanical) government, law, technology.
Memb ATA.

BOURGOIN, EDWARD G PO Box 28365, Washington, DC 20005 *Tel* 301-589-1714.
TL English. **SL** French, Portuguese, Spanish. **UDC** banking/finance, communications, economics, government, law (international), legislation, military science, political economy, statistics, taxation.
French Abdulhamid Brahimi: "Economic Prospects of the Arab World" (pending). **Spanish** Edmundo Solorzano Diaz: "The Perfect Planet" (pending). Mario Rietti: "Money and Banking in Latin America" (pending).
Affil World Bank. **Memb** ATA, TAALS.

BOURS, JOHN F 44 Prospect Park W, Brooklyn, NY 11215 USA *Tel* 212-768-4378.
TL English. **SL** Spanish. **UDC** banking/finance, commerce, government, history, iron/steel industry, philately.
Memb ATA.

BRACE, G Institut Français du Pétrole, boîte postale 311, F-92506 Rueil-Malmaison, France *Tel* (01) 749 02 14.
TL English. **SL** French. **UDC** automotive, chemistry, engineering (chemical), geology, geophysics, petroleum, plastics, sciences (earth).
French Alphonse Schilling: *Automobile Engine Lubrication* (Scientific Publications, 1972). Also co-author of *Technical Dictionary of Terms Used in the Petroleum Industry* (Editions Technip, 1979).

BRADLEY, FRED 19 Bagley Wood Rd, Kennington, Oxford OX1 5LY UK *Tel* (0865) 735 430.
TL English. **SL** German. **UDC** arts/crafts, astronomy, biography, education, history, industry, optics, railroad, sciences (natural), technology.
German Fleck: *The Origin and Development of a Scientific Fact* (Chicago Univ, 1977). Scheerer: *The Leica and the Leica System* (Fountain, 1964). Kisselbach: *The Leicaflex Book* (Heering, 1969). Scheerer-Macovec: *The Leica and the Leicaflex* (Fountain, 1969). Kisselbach-Windisch: *Manual of Modern Photography* (Heering, 1970). Also numerous photography manuals and books on woodcarving, metal craft, fungi, skiing.
Memb TA.

BRAMTOT, JUAN ADOLFO 5529 Woodenhawk Circle, Columbia, MD 21044 USA *Tel* 301-997-1845.
TL Spanish. **SL** English. **UDC** all fields of commerce, science, technology.
English H V Kaltenborn: *Europe Now: A First-Hand Report* (Aspas-Madrid, 1946). Kenneth E Boulding: *Economic Analysis* (Revista de Occidente, 1947). John Rhode: *Men Die at Cyprus Lodge* (Aspas-Madrid, 1945).
Memb ATA.

BROADBENT, KIERAN PATRICK PO Box 8500, Ottawa, K1G 3H9, Canada *Tel* 613-996-2321.

TL English. SL Chinese, German. UDC agriculture, commerce, dairy farming, ecology, entomology, food/nutrition, forestry, geography, government, information science, library science, political economy/science, poultry farming, sociology, stockbreeding, viniculture.

Author of *Chinese-English Dictionary of China's Rural Economy* (Farnham Royal, 1978). *A Terminological Study of Agricultural Economics and Rural Social Economy in China* (Oxford Univ, 1975).

Accred Civil Service. **Affil** International Development Research Center. **Memb** TG.

BRODOVIKOFF, L Duinparklaan 76, B-8458 Oostduinkerke, Belgium *Tel* (058) 51 19 75.

TL & SL English, French, Russian. UDC chemistry, computers, cybernetics, engineering (chemical, civil, electrical, hydraulic, industrial, mechanical, municipal, sanitary), industry, information science, iron/steel industry, machine tools, metallurgy, mineralogy, mining, patents/trademarks, plastics, sciences (applied), statistics, technology, welding.

English Charlotte Brönte: *Jane Eyre* (La Boétie & Marabout, 1949). Elisabeth Gaitskell: *Life of Charlotte Brönte* (La Boétie, 1950). **Russian** Dostoyevsky: *Crime and Punishment* (La Boétie, 1948).

Memb CBTIP.

BRONSTEIN-VINAVER, BLANCHE 4 rue des Eaux, F-75016 Paris, France *Tel* 288 68 07.

TL French, Polish, Russian. SL English, German, Polish, Russian. UDC chemistry, economics, medicine, metallurgy.

English K W Kapp: *Social Costs of Business Enterprise* (Flammarion, 1976). Also the collected works of I Sachs. **German** E Baumler: *A Century of Chemistry* (Econ-Verlag, 1963); *In Search of the Magic Bullet* (Quatre Vents, 1973).

Memb ATLF.

BROWN, GORDON KEITH 360 Olentangy St, Columbus, OH 43202 USA *Tel* 614-267-4490.

TL English. SL Dutch, French, German, Russian. UDC chemistry, iron/steel industry, metallurgy, welding.

Affil Hoosier Translation Service.

BRUCH, KARL Fischbacher Weg 1, D-6232 Bad Soden, West Germany *Tel* (06196) 2 66 68.

TL German. SL English. UDC anthropology, archeology, art, bacteriology, epidemiology, medicine.

English Sahle Sellassie: *Shinega's Village* (Erdmann, 1972).

Memb TG. **Awards** 1973 Charles Frerk Memorial Prize.

BURDICK, DAVID L 1806A Withington Rd, China Lake, CA 93555 USA *Tel* 714-446-6876.

TL English. SL Russian. UDC astrophysics, mathematics, optics, physics.

Russian N G Basov, ed: *Electronic Characteristics and Electron-Phonon Interaction in Superconducting Metals and Alloys* (Consultants Bureau, 1977); *Microwave Studies of Exciton Condensation in Germanium* (Consultants Bureau, 1978). V N Tsytovich: *Theory of Turbulent Plasma* (Consultants Bureau, 1977).

Affil Naval Weapons Center. **Memb** ATA.

BURLEIGH, W ALFRED 11606 Ashley Dr, Randolph Hills, Rockville, MD 20852 USA *Tel* 301-770-7285.

TL Spanish. SL English. UDC all scientific and technical fields.

Affil OAS. **Memb** AIT.

BUTCHER, CLIFTON H Steward Towers 705, 200 Ft Meade Rd, Laurel, MD 20810 USA *Tel* 301-725-7172.

TL English. SL French, German. UDC electronics, government, linguistics, telecommunications.

Accred Memb ATA.

BUTTERFIELD, VALERIE 23 Edward Rd, Hampton Hill (Middlesex) TW12 1LH, UK *Tel* (01) 979 3886.

TL English. SL German. UDC engineering (control), textiles.

Accred/Memb TG.

BUTTERWORTH, BASIL 13 Garden Close, Hayling Island, Hampshire PO11 9AD, UK *Tel* (07016) 5487.

TL English. SL Dutch, French, German, Italian, Spanish. UDC building/construction, ceramics (bricks, tiles).

German K-W Stock & A Meiners: *Silesia Confiserie Manual No. 2* (Silesia-Essenzenfabrik, 1973). Also numerous technical papers for research organizations, especially the Centre Scientifique et Technique du Bâtiment, Paris.

Accred/Memb TA.

CADMUS, SPENCER V, JR 771 27 St, San Francisco, CA 94131 USA *Tel* 415-826-9140.

TL English. SL Russian. UDC banking/finance, commerce, ecology, economics, education, government, history, human resources, labor relations, linguistics/philology, literature (criticism, folklore, history, prose), political economy/science, public administration, sciences (social), social services, sociology, statistics, taxation, transportation.

Russian N K Mikhailovskii: *A Cruel Talent* (Ardis, 1978).

Affil JPRS (contract translator).

CAPALDO, STEPHEN J 461 Arnley, Sudbury, ON P3C 1J1, Canada *Tel* 705-675-3096.

TL English. SL French, Russian. UDC economics, political economy/science, social sciences.

Memb ATIO, Concordiat.

CARDOZO, MANOEL DA SILVEIRA 1004 Sigsbee Pl NE, Washington, DC 20017 USA *Tel* 202-832-5392.

TL English. SL Castilian, French, Italian, Portuguese. UDC dairy farming, food/nutrition, genealogy, government, photography.

Affil The Catholic Univ of America (Oliveira Lima Library).

CARMELL, PAMELA LEE 704 W 44 St #1E, Kansas City, MO 64111 USA *Tel* 816-753-6245.

TL English. SL Spanish. UDC banking/finance, commerce, communications, meat processing, refrigeration.

Memb ALTA, ATA, MICATA.

CAROZZI, ALBERT VICTOR Geology, Univ of Illinois, NHB 254, Urbana, IL 61801 USA *Tel* 217-333-3008.

TL English. SL French, German. UDC geology, mineralogy, petrography, sciences (earth), sedimentology.

French Louis Agassiz: *Studies on Glaciers* (Hafner/Macmillan, 1967). Lucien Cayeux: *Carbonate Rocks (Limestones and Dolomites)* (Hafner/Macmillan, 1970). Benoit De Maillet Telliamed: *On the Diminution of the Sea* (Univ of Illinois, 1968). **German** Abraham G Werner: *On the External Characters of Minerals* (Univ of Illinois, 1962). Also the works of J B Lamarck, E Raspe.

CARRASCO, ALVITO 5912 Cantwell Dr, Cleveland, OH 44124 USA *Tel* 216-461-8559.

TL English. SL Portuguese. UDC sciences (medical).

Accred/Memb ATA.

CHÁIREZ, JESÚS LÓPEZ Rio Elba 436, Col del Valle, Monterrey, Nuevo Léon Mexico *Tel* (83) 56 31 19.

TL Spanish. SL English. UDC hydrology, water well drilling technology.

Memb ATA.

CHECKETTS, RICHARD JOHN Summit Translations, Cleeve Hill, Cheltenham, Glos 9L52 3QD UK *Tel* (0242) 67 4913.

TL English. SL French, Spanish. UDC data processing, education, fuel technology, insurance.

Accred/Memb TG.

CHENAIL, JACQUES 1-319 rue Frank, Ottawa, ON K2P OX7, Canada *Tel* 613-232-9182.

TL French. SL English. UDC aeronautics, aviation, government, navigation, photography.

English Henry B Mayo: *Ottawa-Carleton Review* (Govt of Ontario, 1977).

CHEVALLIER, MAURICE GEORGES 8 Marquis Close, Wembley (MDDX), UK *Tel* (01) 902 6745.

TL English. SL French. UDC commerce, glass & glassware.

Memb TG.

CHIAPPERINI, FELICE F 165 W 66 St, New York, NY 10023 USA *Tel* 212-787-9129.

TL English. SL French. UDC astrology, astronomy, ethnography, geography, meteorology, philosophy, theology, viniculture.

Memb ATA.

CHISMAN, ANNA McG 725 S Fairfax St, Alexandria, VA 22314 USA *Tel* 703-548-3316.

TL English. SL French, Spanish. UDC busi-

ness, finance, law (international), telecommunications.
Affil OAS. **Memb** AIT, TAALS.

CLAFF, CHESTER E, JR PO Box 2038 (Monteilo), Brockton, MA 02403 USA *Tel* 617-583-2354.
TL English. **SL** French, German. **UDC** business, chemistry, engineering (chemical), plastics, sciences (natural).
German Diether Arndt: "Manganese Compounds as Oxidizing Agents in Organic Chemistry" (pending).
Memb ATA.

CLINQUART 8 rue Médoquerie, St Benoit F-86000 Poitiers, France.
TL French. **SL** English. **UDC** agriculture, anthropology, botany, ecology, ethnography, forestry, navigation, sciences (natural), sociology.
English Richard Adams: *Watership Down* (Flammarion, 1976). James Dickey: *Deliverance* (Flammarion, 1971). Bronislaw Malinowski: *Coral Gardens* (Maspero, 1974). C W Mills: *The Sociological Imagination* (Maspero, 1967). Also the works of George McDonald Fraser, William Bradford Huie, Bertrand Russell.
Affil Univ of Poitiers. **Memb** ATLF, SFT.

COHEN, JOEL E 1230 York Ave, Box 20, New York, NY 10021 USA *Tel* 212-360-1942.
TL English. **SL** French. **UDC** computers, ecology, epidemiology, genetics, parasitology, psychology, sciences (medical).
French Abraham Moles: *Information Theory and Aesthetic Perception* (Univ of Illinois, 1966).

COLES, DOROTHY T 424 E 84 St, New York, NY 10028 USA *Tel* 212-288-0600.
TL English. **SL** French, German, Spanish. **UDC** banking/finance, business, communications, law (international), political economy/science, telecommunications.
Affil UN (Conference Services). **Memb** ATA.

COLLAZO, JAVIER L 68 Manitou Circle, Westfield, NJ 07090 USA *Tel* 201-233-5761; 232-8557.
TL Spanish. **SL** English. **UDC** most scientific and technical fields especially aeronautics, computers, telecommunications.
Memb ATA.

CONNER, R MICHAEL 3214 Beverly Rd, Austin, TX 78703 USA *Tel* 512-452-3033.
TL English. **SL** Russian. **UDC** sciences (earth, geology).
Memb ATA, TRACT.

CONRAD, ISAAC JOHN 9 Wentworth Close, Finchley, London N3 1YP, UK *Tel* (01) 346 5732.
TL English. **SL** French, German, Italian, Spanish. **UDC** agriculture, automotive, food/nutrition, horticulture, industry, iron/steel industry, political economy/science, shipping, transportation.

French A Tanagras: *Psychophysical Elements in Parapsychological Traditions* (Parapsychological Foundation, 1967).
Memb TA, TG.

CORBYN, D R 16 Strathnaver Pl, Hodge Lea, Milton Keynes (Bucks) MK12 6JD, UK *Tel* (0908) 314 585.
TL English. **SL** French, German. **UDC** most areas of aeronautics, communications, engineering (mechanical), sciences (natural).
German Walter Weyer: *Know and Like the South of France* (Albion Scott, 1975). Verena von Jevin: *Know and Like Sicily* (Albion Scott, forthcoming). Georg Mergl: *Know and Like the Greek Mainland* (Albion Scott, forthcoming). Franck Weimert: *Know and Like the Greek Islands* (Albion Scott, forthcoming).
Memb TA.

CORCORAN, NOEL 62 Ringley Rd, Whitefield, Manchester M25 7LN, UK *Tel* (061) 766 2903.
TL English. **SL** French, German. **UDC** astronomy, chemistry, electronics, engineering (electrical), geophysics, information science, optics, sciences (natural), technology.
French Jack Manenc: *Structural Thermodynamics of Alloys* (Reidel/Dordrecht, 1973). B Trémillon: *Chemistry in Non-Aqueous Solutions* (Reidel/Dordrecht, 1974). H Poitou: *Group Dynamics* (Academic, forthcoming).
Memb TG.

CORIAT, ALAIN POB 104, Caracas, Venezuela *Tel* (01) 310811.
TL French, Spanish. **SL** English. **UDC** commerce, copyright, economics, law, legislation, patents/trademarks.
Memb ATA.

COSSU, FRANCO PO Box 1268, South Pasadena, CA 91030 USA *Tel* 213-799-1012.
TL English. **SL** Italian. **UDC** most areas of banking, jurisprudence, law, legislation, patents/trademarks, taxation, political science/economy.
Memb ATA.

COTTA, HORTENSIA ZALDIVAR Orinoco #404 Ote, Col de Valle, Garza Gracía, Nuevo Léon, Mexico *Tel* 56 47 02.
TL English. **SL** Spanish. **UDC** banking/finance, business, education, law.
Memb ATA.

COUTIL, JEANNE M 440 Moran Rd, Grosse Pointe Farms, MI 48236 USA *Tel* 313-882-3013.
TL & SL English & French. **UDC** art, automotive, commerce, economics (foreign trade), industry, literature (history, prose), painting, social services.
Accred Marygrove College. **Memb** ATA.

CRADDOCK, JOHN THOMAS Ray Park Ave, Maidenhead, Berkshire, UK *Tel* (0628) 24931.
TL English. **SL** Danish, French, German, Norwegian, Spanish, Swedish. **UDC** agriculture, business, construction, economics, engi-

neering (mechanical), paper/pulp, political economy.
Memb Aslib (Technical Translation Group), TG.

CRAFTON, PHYLLIS 45 Mountwood Rd, Swampscott, MA 01907 USA *Tel* 617-595-5614.
TL English. **SL** French. **UDC** aeronautics, banking/finance, communications, copyright, law, military science, missiles/rocketry.
Memb ATA.

CREUTZ, ROBERT T 373 K St, Boston, MA 02127 USA *Tel* 617-269-4532.
TL English. **SL** Danish, Norwegian, Russian. **UDC** communications, computers, cybernetics, data processing, electronics, engineering (electrical), information science, optics, physics/mechanics, sciences (applied).

CROWLEY, CHRISTINE A 23 Division St #3, Pittsburgh, PA 15205 USA *Tel* 412-921-7716.
TL English. **SL** French, German. **UDC** urethane chemistry (German only).
Memb APT, TA.

CROZY, ALAN 4 Mallory Ave, Caversham Park, Reading, UK *Tel* (0734) 477922.
TL English. **SL** French, German, Italian, Russian, Spanish. **UDC** agriculture, bacteriology, biochemistry, biology, biomedicine, dairy farming, entomology, fisheries, food/nutrition, medicine, microbiology, paper/pulp, pharmacology, political economy/science, poultry farming, psychiatry, public health, shipbuilding, veterinary medicine.
Russian Larionov: *Cancer Chemotherapy* (Pergamon); *Nitrogen Fixation* (McMillan). Sharov: *Basic Arthropan Stock* (Pergamon, 1966).
Accred/Memb TG.

CRUMMEY, JOYCE ADAMS Epidemiology, Univ of California, Davis, CA 95616 USA *Tel* 916-752-1378.
TL English. **SL** German, Russian. **UDC** arts, biography, geography, history, literature (prose), philology, psychiatry, psychology, religion, sciences (applied, natural), veterinary and human medicine.
German Carl Hentze: "Gods and Drinking Serpents" (*History of Religions*, 4 No. 2). Also the works of Herbert Fischer, Horst Gies, Hans Mommsen, and Eberhard Jäckel in collections.

CRUZ, AMAURY 1216 Algeria, Coral Gables, FL 33134 USA *Tel* 305-446-2842.
TL & SL English & Spanish. **UDC** automotive, communications, government, law, public administration, scuba diving, social services.
Memb ATA.

CUELLAR, BERTHA V DE Canelo 604, Col Valle de Sta Engracia, Garza García, Nuevo Léon, Mexico. *Tel* (83) 78 28 14.
TL Spanish. **SL** English. **UDC** banking/finance, commerce, communications, human resources, iron/steel industry, music, social services, statistics, transportation.
Memb ATA.

CUNNINGHAM, DALE S Uniworld Languages, Translation Drawer, Haddonfield, NJ 08033 USA *Tel* 609-795-2251.

TL English. SL German. UDC agriculture, bacteriology, biochemistry, biology, biomedicine, botany, brewing, chemistry, computers, crystallography, epidemiology, information science, insurance, linguistics, literature (children's), medicine, patents, pharmacology, plastics, sciences (applied, life, medical, natural), veterinary medicine.

German Gerhard Gollwitzer: *The Joy of Drawing* (Sterling, (1961); *Abstract Art* (Sterling, 1961). Dieter Krauter: *Experimenting with the Microscope* (Sterling, 1963). Harald Doering: *A Bee Is Born* (Sterling, 1962). Also the works of Rudolf Dittrich, Bruno Knobel, Walter Sperling, Susanne Strose, and scores of 19th and 20th century German and French scientists.

Memb ATA, SFL.

CUNNINGHAM, MARIANNE 324 Grace St, Pittsburgh, PA 15236 USA *Tel* 412-653-1971.

TL German. SL English. UDC automotive, business, engineering (mechanical), law (international, property), legislation.

Accred Carnegie-Mellon Univ. **Affil** Contraves Goerz Corp.

Memb ATA.

DALY, MARILYN M 21 Cherry Tree Rd, Loudonville, NY 12211 USA *Tel* 518-465-0796.

TL English. SL French. UDC athletics, computers, international affairs, medicine.

Memb ATA, Concordiat.

DAMBERGS, NIKOLAJS 6315 Jubilee Rd, Halifax, NS B3H 2G6, Canada *Tel* 902-422-4572.

TL English. SL French, Latvian, Russian. UDC biochemistry, biology, chemistry, fisheries, food/nutrition, oceanography.

Affil The Translation Bureau, Secy of State, Canada. **Memb** ATA.

DAVIES, RITA F 28 Candlewood Dr, Andover, MA 01810 USA *Tel* 617-475-8836.

TL English. SL Serbo-Croatian. UDC accounting, arts, banking/finance, chemistry, commerce, documentation, economics, history, medicine, mining, pharmacology.

Memb ATA.

DAVISON, LUCILE S 50 Tomlinson Rd, Woodbury, CT 06798 USA *Tel* 203-263-4207.

TL English. SL French, German, Japanese, Russian. UDC biochemistry, chemistry, engineering (chemical), petroleum technology, plastics.

Memb ATA.

DEARS, PATRICIA HELENE 6333 Walnut St #1A, Pittsburgh, PA 15206 USA *Tel* 412-665-1111.

TL English. SL Portuguese, Spanish. UDC banking/finance, commerce, economics, iron/steel industry.

Accred Carnegie-Mellon Univ. **Memb** APT.

DELHEY, LISELOTTE SCHWARZEN-BERG Southern Peru Copper Corp, Casilla 165, Villa Cuajone 213, Tacna, Peru.

TL Spanish, German. SL English. UDC business, law, medicine, petroleum, refining.

Memb ATA, CCIA.

DELISLE, JEAN 27 rue des Cedres, Limbour, PQ J8V 1C8, Canada *Tel* 819-827-2452.

TL French. SL English. UDC commerce, photography, public administration, telecommunications, transportation.

Author of numerous articles on translation and interpretation in *Meta*.

Affil Univ of Ottawa. **Memb** STQ.

DELL, KATHRYN M 32 Overlook Rd, Ardsley, NY 10502 USA *Tel* 914-693-1698.

TL English. SL French, Spanish. UDC all medical sciences.

Memb ATA.

DE PALMENAER, ROGER 2 ave Marius Renard, Bte 10, B-1070 Brussels, Belgium *Tel* (02) 522 17 65; 537 13 08.

TL French, Dutch/Flemish. SL English. UDC brewing, chemistry, engineering (chemical, marine), food/nutrition, genetics, law (maritime, property), navigation, petroleum, plastics/polymers, sciences (medical), viniculture.

Memb CBTIP.

DEPORTE, PAUL V 4000 Denfeld Ave, Kensington, MD 20795 USA *Tel* 301-946-3194.

TL English. SL French, Russian, Spanish. UDC bacteriology, biochemistry, biomedicine, parasitology, public health.

Affil National Inst of Health. **Memb** ATA, SFL.

DERRICK, FRANCIS WILLIAM 3 rue Antoine de Saint-Exupéry, F-94800 Villejuif, France *Tel* 678-64-59.

TL English. SL French. UDC aeronautics, aviation, navigation.

DE VERE, ROSEMARY 1449 19 Ave, San Francisco, CA 94122 USA *Tel* 415-566-5597.

TL English. SL French. UDC arts, economics, medicine, political science, sciences (earth).

French Albert Leprince: "Therapeutic Colors and Metals" (pending).

Memb NCTA, Concordiat.

DEVINNEY, MARGARET KLOPFLE 100 Union Ave, Delanco, NJ 08075 USA *Tel* 609-764-1250.

TL English. SL Dutch, French, German. UDC aeronautics, astronomy, astrophysics, biomedicine, computers, electronics, human resources, optics.

Memb ATA, DVTA.

DE VRIES, JAN Tragel 4, B-1780 Hekelgem, Belgium *Tel* (053) 66 99 22.

TL English. SL Dutch, French. UDC history, jurisprudence, navigation, social services.

Memb CBTIP.

DICKENSON, U R 7 Church Close, Ranton, Stafford ST18 9JE, UK *Tel* Seighford (078575) 617.

TL & SL English & German. UDC automotive, computers, data processing, engineering (electrical, mechanical), iron/steel industry, machine tools, metallurgy, welding.

Memb BDÜ, TG.

DIEGUEZ, ISMAEL S 5407 41 St NW, Washington, DC 20015 USA *Tel* 202-362-3280.

TL Spanish. SL English, French, Italian, Portuguese. UDC aeronautics, astronautics, aviation, communications, electronics, mechanics, missiles, navigation, photography, viniculture.

Memb TAALS.

DIERCKX, MARC J Antwerpsesteenweg 48/2, B-2140 Westmalle, Belgium *Tel* (031) 12 35 89.

TL & SL Dutch & English. UDC commerce, economics, engineering (mechanical), law (international, maritime, property), legislation, patents/trademarks, shipping.

Memb CBTIP.

DIGGS, NANCY 1160 Lytle Lane, Dayton, OH 45409 USA *Tel* 513-299-0211.

TL English. SL French, German, Spanish. UDC business, commerce.

Memb ATA.

DILSON, JESSE 201 E 30 St, New York, NY 10016 USA *Tel* 212-685-3121.

TL English. SL French, German, Russian. UDC almost all areas of science and technology, with specialties in computers, cybernetics, electronics, mathematics, and physics.

French Marcel Baudot et al: *Encyclopedia of the War 1939–45* (Facts on File, Inc, forthcoming).

Memb The Word Guild.

DI VIRGILIO, LISE 3000 Gouin Blvd E, Montreal, PQ H3M 1B6, Canada *Tel* 514-334-8178.

TL French. SL English. UDC banking/finance, brewing, commerce, communications, economics, government, literature (science fiction), paper/pulp, printing, publishing.

English Thom Sullivan: *Adventures in Darkness* (Editions Sélect, 1978). Thelma G. Thurstone: *The Red Book* (Science Research Associates, 1970); *The Blue Book* (Science Research Associates, 1977).

Affil Schoo¹ of Translation, Univ of Montreal. **Memb** ATA, STQ.

DOBES, RONALD KEITH 868 Lighthouse Ave #0, Pacific Grove, CA 93950 USA *Tel* 408-372-1708.

TL English. SL German. UDC astronomy, aviation, banking/finance, biochemistry, chemistry, computers, economics, fuel, medicine, microbiology, military science, missiles/rocketry, political economy/science, sciences (medical).

German Theodor Veiter: "Ethnic Conflict and Rights for Ethnic Groups" (pending).

Affil Monterey Inst of Foreign Studies. **Memb** Concordiat.

DOCAL, SONIA J 2947 Tilden St NW, Washington, DC 20008 USA *Tel* 202-362-2459.
   TL & SL English & Spanish. **UDC** agriculture, banking/finance, business, communications, dairy farming, documentation, education, human resources, public administration, public health, telecommunications, transportation.
   Affil Agency for International Development. **Memb** ASI.

DOLBERG, ALEXANDER 63 Drayton Gardens, London SW10, UK *Tel* (01) 373-9690.
   TL English. **SL** Russian. **UDC** literature (criticism, history, science fiction), most scientific and technical fields.
   Russian A. Solzhenitsyn: *Cancer Ward* (Bodley Head, 1968); *The Love Girl and the Innocent* (Bodley Head, 1970). I Daniel: *Prison Poems* (Calder & Boyars, 1972).
   Memb TG.

DOTZAUER, HERBERT H 21025 Lassen St #224, Chatsworth, CA 91311 USA *Tel* 213-998-1524.
   TL English. **SL** French, German, Italian, Spanish. **UDC** accounting, banking/finance, economics, missiles/rocketry, political economy.
   Memb ATA.

DRUCK, KITTY L 13 Penlaw Rd, Lawrenceville, NJ 08648 USA *Tel* 609-896-9494.
   TL English. **SL** Czech, French, German, Russian, Spanish. **UDC** biochemistry, biology, biomedicine, chemistry, ecology, engineering (chemical), medicine, microbiology, pharmacology, sciences (life, medical, natural).
   Memb ATA.

DRUMMOND, HELGA 12 Thornbury Wood, Chandler's Ford, Eastleigh, Hampshire SO5 1DQ UK *Tel* (04215) 3800.
   TL English. **SL** German. **UDC** food/nutrition, literature (history), public health, social services.
   German Bertold Spuler: *History of the Mongols* (Routledge & Kegan Paul, 1972).
   Memb TG.

DUBE, BERNARD PO Box 805, Saint-Basile-le-Grand, PQ JOL 1SO, Canada *Tel* 514-653-5318.
   TL French. **SL** English. **UDC** automotive, commerce, communications, engineering (electrical, industrial, mechanical), government, human resources, machine tools, public administration, statistics, welding.
   Memb ATA, STQ.

DU BOIS, ARDEN E M 584 Parkwood Lane, Naples, FL 33940 USA *Tel* 813-261-3789.
   TL English. **SL** French, Portuguese, Spanish. **UDC** agriculture, automotive, biomedicine, botany, epidemiology, fisheries, forestry, geography, public health.
   Memb AIT, SFL.

DUNGAN, SALLY MURRAY 1020B Tenth St, Santa Monica, CA 90403 USA *Tel* 213-394-6585.
   TL English. **SL** French, Spanish. **UDC** banking/finance, building, commerce, computers, data processing, law, political economy/science, telecommunications.

DWIN, ALFRED W PO Box 3013, West End, NJ 07740 USA *Tel* 201-870-1567.
   TL English. **SL** Spanish. **UDC** banking/finance, commerce, mining, textiles.
   Spanish Moises Saenz: *The Peruvian Indian* (Strategic Index of the Americas, 1943). Simon Bolivar: *Selected Writings* (Banco de Venezuela, 1951).
   Memb ATA.

ECK, HANNELORE Z 3046 Mount Olivet Rd, Kalamazoo, MI 49004 USA *Tel* 616-345-2635.
   TL English. **SL** French, German. **UDC** bacteriology, biochemistry, biomedicine, chemistry, economics, medicine, patents/trademarks, public health, sciences (medical).
   Affil Upjohn International. **Memb** ATA.

EGBERT, SUSAN M 203 Randall St, San Francisco, CA 94131 USA *Tel* 415-641-9135.
   TL English. **SL** French. **UDC** business, finance, government, military science, mining, oceanography, psychology, sciences, sports, technology.
   Accred Monterey Inst of Foreign Studies. **Memb** ATA.

EHRLICH, LOTTE 16980 Marquez Ave, Pacific Palisades, CA 90272 USA *Tel* 213-454-8718.
   TL English. **SL** Czech, French, German. **UDC** bacteriology, ceramics, food/nutrition, law, literature (prose), public health.
   German Bircher-Benner: *Arthritis Nutrition and Rheumatism Plan* (Nash, 1972).
   Memb ATA (Southern California chapter).

EHRMANN, ROLF-HELMUTH 1446 Garden St, Park Ridge, IL 60068 USA *Tel* 312-825-0408.
   TL English. **SL** German. **UDC** most areas of science and technology with emphasis on medical sciences and legal agreements, contracts, patents.
   Memb ATA, VDÜ.

EICHLER, GREGORY PAUL 227A Collingwood, San Francisco, CA 94114 USA *Tel* 415-863-0828.
   TL English. **SL** Dutch, German, Portuguese, Spanish. **UDC** banking/finance, commerce, documentation, insurance, law (international, property), legislation, political economy, public administration, taxation, telecommunications.
   Memb NCTA.

EISINGER, ELAINE 226 W 72 St, New York, NY 10023 USA *Tel* 212-787-4087; 867-9360.
   TL & SL English & French. **UDC** legal documents.
   Memb ATA.

ELIASSAF, JEHUDAH 9 Asher St, Haifa, Israel *Tel* (04) 22 46 86.
   TL English. **SL** German, Russian. **UDC** chemistry.
   Russian S R Rafikov et al: *Determination of Molecular Weights and Polydispersity of High Polymers* (Israel Program for Scientific Translations, 1964). P M Ogibolov et al: *Structural Polymers Testing Methods* (Israel Program for Scientific Translations, 1974).

ELLISON, JOAN AUDREY 74 Doneraile St, Fulham, London SW6 6EP, UK *Tel* (01) 731-5988.
   TL English. **SL** Norwegian, Swedish. **UDC** culinary arts, food/nutrition.
   Swedish Karin Fredrikson: *The Great Scandinavian Cookbook* (Allen & Unwin, 1966). Lennart Thölén: *The Best of Scandinavian Cooking* (Paul Hamlyn). Karin Fredrikson: *The New Scandinavian Cookbook* (Allen & Unwin, 1979).
   Memb TA.

ENGLE, ERNA 80-20 Broadway, Elmhurst, NY 11373 USA *Tel* 212-899-1173.
   TL English. **SL** French, German, Portuguese, Russian, Spanish. **UDC** biochemistry, genetics, medicine, sciences (medical).

ESCOBAR, F JAVIER, JR 2710 Reagan, Dallas, TX 75219 USA *Tel* 214-522-7691.
   TL English, Italian, Spanish. **SL** French, Italian, Spanish. **UDC** athletics, banking/finance, business, documentation, economics, government, law, photography.
   Accred/Memb ATA (Metroplex chapter, pres).

ETORE 8 Allée Berlioz, F-94800 Villejuif, France *Tel* (16-1) 677 11 82.
   TL French. **SL** English. **UDC** biology, ethology, literature (prose), psychiatry, psychology, sociology, zoology.
   English R. Evans: *Konrad Lorenz: The Man and His Ideas* (Flammarion, 1977).

EVANS, GORDON G 51 South Rd, Bedford, MA 01730 USA *Tel* 617-275-8854.
   TL English. **SL** French, German, Russian. **UDC** biochemistry, chemistry, spectroscopy.
   Affil Tufts Univ. **Memb** ATA.

EVANS, WILLY VUYSJE 219 Strathmore Dr, Syracuse, NY 13207 USA *Tel* 315-475-7949.
   TL English. **SL** Afrikaans, Dutch, Flemish. **UDC** history, literature (criticism, folklore, history, prose), political economy/science.
   Memb ATA.

EVERETT, BRENDA HUFF PO Box 13, Williamstown, MA 01267 USA *Tel* 413-637-3116; 799-7569.
   TL English. **SL** French, Italian, Spanish. **UDC** anthropology, archeology, food/nutrition, literature (prose).
   Italian Renzo de Felice: *Interpretations of Fascism* (Harvard Univ, 1977).
   Accred Conference Interpreters Inst, Paris.

EVIA, ELSA Q DE GARZA 5 de Mayo Ote, 111 San Pedro, Garza García, Nuevo Léon, Mexico *Tel* (83) 56 91 85.
TL English. SL Spanish. UDC education, ethics, government, human resources, literature (prose), public health, social sciences.
Memb ATA.

FAIN, CHERYL ANN Monterey Inst of Foreign Studies, PO Box 1978, Monterey, CA 93940 USA *Tel* 408-373-6941.
TL English. SL German. UDC art, business, ecology, economics, education, government, history, literature (drama, history, prose), music, political economy/science, recreation, social services, theater, tourism.
German Ulrich Dibelius: "Perspectives on Mozart" (pending).
Memb ATA, Concordiat.

FAINBERG, ALEXANDER 34 Greville Hall, Greville Pl, London NW6 5JS, UK *Tel* (01) 328 2882.
TL & SL English & German. UDC advertising, banking/finance, commerce, economics, insurance, law, publicity.
Memb TG.

FAIRFIELD, FRANÇOISE 6627 Yale #711, Westland, MI 48185 USA *Tel* 313-326-5179.
TL & SL English & French. UDC advertising, engineering (mechanical), iron/steel industry, metallurgy.
Memb ATA.

FARBER, CAROL A 6001 140 Ave #D361, Redmond, WA 98052 USA *Tel* 206-885-7439.
TL & SL English & Spanish. UDC aeronautics, aviation, banking/finance, commerce, economics, education, engineering (aerospace, electrical), fisheries, law (international), machine tools, medicine, mining, sociology, transportation.
Affil Bellevue Community College (part-time) Memb ATA.

FELDMANN, ALBERT A PO Box 5568, Univ Sta, Seattle, WA 98105 USA *Tel* 206-325-7790.
TL & SL English & German. UDC aeronautics, art, astrophysics, automotive, aviation, ceramics, communications, electronics, engineering (aerospace, electrical, hydraulic, mechanical), engraving, fuel, machine tools, metallurgy, meteorology, military science, missiles/rocketry, oceanography, optics, physics, plastics, sciences (applied, natural), technology, telecommunications.
Accred/Memb ATA.

FENTON, LU 435 W 57 St, New York NY 10019 USA *Tel* 212-586-6814.
TL English. SL German. UDC travel and historical background, application techniques of consumer products based on natural and synthetic raw materials.
German Hans Blum: *Africa* (Abrams, 1976). Karl Brugger: *The Chronicle of Akakor* (Delacorte, 1976). Ernst Haas: *In Germany* (Viking, 1977). J Stephan Jellinek: *Formulation and Function of Cosmetics* (John Wiley, 1970). Also in-house technical reports on the application of industrial raw materials in various industries

for chemical companies, and inter-company reports of pharmaceutical companies on animal and clinical tests of new preparations.

FERREIRA, MARIO D PO Box 4, Middlesex, NJ 08846 USA *Tel* 201-469-1473.
TL English. SL French, German, Italian, Portuguese, Spanish. UDC automotive, banking/finance, communications, electronics, iron/steel industry, international law, machine tools, metallurgy, patents/trademarks, photography, telecommunications.
Memb ATA.

FERSHEE, SUSAN 5724 McGee, Kansas City, MO 64113 USA *Tel* 816-333-0386; 842-1230.
TL & SL English & German. UDC commerce, documentation, military science, shipping, social science, social services.
Accred/Memb ATA, MICATA.

FFORDE, KATHLYN Watery Lane Cottage, Dilwyn, Hereford HR4 8JJ UK *Tel* Pembridge (05447) 283.
TL English. SL French, German. UDC agriculture, bacteriology, biochemistry, dairy farming, food/nutrition, food science and technology, literature (prose), microbiology, sciences (life).
Memb TG.

FICKAU, BARBARA 3510 S 12 St #201, Sheboygan, WI 53081 USA *Tel* 414-457-0226.
TL German. SL English. UDC automotive, aviation, government, transportation.
Memb ATA.

FIELDS, HARRY ALFRED 23 Field View, Derby Rd, Caversham, Reading-Berkshire RG4 OHB, UK *Tel* (0734) 476 711.
TL English. SL French, Italian. UDC aeronautics, automotive, aviation, banking/finance, biochemistry, building, commerce, communications, computers, cybernetics, data processing, economics, electronics, engineering (all areas), industry, insurance, machine tools, metallurgy, military science, missiles, petroleum, shipbuilding, shipping, telecommunications, welding.
French Jean-Jacques Servan-Schreiber: *The Radical Alternative* (MacDonald, 1970); *Egyptian Art* (Octopus, 1971).
Memb TA.

FINCH, G KIRK, II 11603 Chantilly Lane, Mitchellville, MD 20716 USA *Tel* 301-464-1654.
TL English. SL Russian. UDC automotive, aviation, business, communications, computers, government, information science, medicine, military science, public administration, technology.
Memb ATA.

FISCHER, HANS W Nieder-Ramstaedter Str 27, D-6100 Darmstadt, West Germany *Tel* (0 61 51) 496 60.
TL English. SL German. UDC business, electronics, engineering (electrical, mechanical), jurisprudence.
Memb ATA, VDÜ.

FISCHLIN, JÜRG EDGAR Rainweg 2, C H-8704 Herrliberg, Switzerland *Tel* (01) 915 36 39.
TL German. SL English, French. UDC automotive, business, commerce, copyright, data processing, economics, engineering (industrial, mechanical), engraving/prints, government, graphics, information theory, literature (prose), machine tools, paper/pulp, printing.
English Gerald Clark: *The Impatient Giant—Red China Today* (Daphnis, 1968).
Memb TG.

FISHER, PHILLIP L The Dow Chemical Company, 2020 ARC, Midland, MI 48640 USA *Tel* 517-636-1599.
TL English. SL French, German. UDC biochemistry, chemistry, engineering (chemical), plastics/polymers, textiles.
Memb ATA.

FITZGERALD, BETTY J 202 Overlook Dr, McMurray, PA 15317 USA
TL English. SL German. UDC automotive, aviation, economics, food/nutrition, law (property), literature (criticism, history, prose), philosophy, photography, political economy/science.
German Reinhard Kammer: *Zen and Confucius in the Art of Swordsmanship* (Routledge & Kegan Paul, 1977).
Memb ATA.

FLEMING, RICHARD Auberrow House, Wellington, Herefordshire HR4 8AJ, UK *Tel* 043-271-558.
TL English. SL Swedish. UDC agriculture, anthropology, archeology, botany, brewing, building, dairy farming, ecology, education, engineering (civil), fisheries, food/nutrition, forestry, fuel, horticulture, literature (folklore), poultry farming, psychiatry, psychology, shipbuilding, stockbreeding, veterinary medicine, viniculture, witchcraft, zoology.
Swedish Sevelius, Pettersson & Olsson: *Keeping Your Horse Healthy* (David & Charles, 1973).
Memb TA.

FLINN, PATRICIA A 3544 Shadeland Ave, Pittsburgh, PA 15212 USA 412-761-6414.
TL English. SL French, German. UDC coal mining, law.
Memb APT, ATA.

FOCKENS, ROBERT PAUL Caixa Postal D-20, 60000 Fortaleza, Ceará, Brazil.
TL & SL English & Portuguese. UDC brewing, food/nutrition, microbiology, sciences (life, medical), soccer, solar energy.
Memb ATA.

FOGARTY, CHRISTOPHER MARTIN 30 E Elm St, Chicago, IL 60611 USA *Tel* 312-664-7651.
TL English. SL Spanish. UDC contractual documents and technical specifications for hydro-electric projects, engineering (civil, hydraulic).
Memb ATA.

FONTANA, ADELE 14A Porter Rd, Medford, MA 02155 USA *Tel* 617-395-2671.
TL English. SL French. UDC business, data processing, linguistics/philology.
Memb ATA, NETA.

FORSTER, MARCEL P 7 place de la Fechere, B-5860 Chastre, Belgium *Tel* (10) 65 73 16.
TL English. SL French. UDC engineering (civil, electrical, hydraulic, industrial, mechanical), geophysics, industry, iron/steel industry, machine tools, metallurgy, mining, photography, railroads, welding.
Memb CBTIP.

FOZ, FRANK 343 E 30 St, New York, NY 10016 USA *Tel* 212-685-7472.
TL Arabic, Catalan, French, Italian, Portuguese, Spanish. SL English. UDC sciences (medical, paramedical, pharmaceutical).
Memb ATA.

FRANÇOIS, ROBERT R 1112 Beryl #15, Redondo Beach CA 90277 USA *Tel* 213-372-9937.
TL & SL English & French. UDC aeronautics, automotive, aviation, building, computers, economics, electronics, engineering (aerospace, civil, electrical, hydraulic, industrial, marine, mechanical), law (international, maritime), machine tools, mining, petroleum (off-shore drilling), telecommunications.
Memb ATA, SFT.

FRASER, DOUGLAS ATHOL 22 Gresley Rd, London N19 3JZ, UK *Tel* (01) 272 5664.
TL English. SL French, German, Italian, Japanese, Russian. UDC biology, chemistry, ecology, medicine.
Memb TG.

FRENTZ, LEROY BRAND, III 1119 Bucknell Dr, Davis, CA 95616 USA *Tel* 916-758-6989.
TL English. SL Russian. UDC agriculture, military affairs, sciences (earth), sociopolitical writings.
Russian *Great Soviet Encyclopedia* (Macmillan, 1973–79). Valentin Turchin: *The Phenomenon of Science* (Columbia Univ, 1977).
Memb ATA.

FREY, HENRY ARTHUR Goldhaldenstrasse 20a, CH-8702 Zollikon/ZH, Switzerland.
TL English. SL French, German. UDC architecture, art, banking/finance, geography, history, insurance, law.
German Elissa Aalto & Karl Fleig: *Alvar Aalto: Projects and Final Buildings* Vol. III (Architektur Artemis, 1978). Roland Rainer: *Livable Environments* (Architektur Artemis, 1972). Leopold Reidemeister et al: *Foundation Emil G Bührle Collection* (Artemis, 1973). Emil Schulthess: *The Amazon* (Collins & Sons, 1962). Also the works of Emil Egli, Alfred Roth, Carlo Testa.

GARCIA-DONOSO, PILAR Avenida Colón 2278, PO Box 237, Quito, Ecuador *Tel* 232-049; 450-809.
TL Spanish. SL English. UDC agriculture, anthropology, banking/finance, building/construction, business, commerce, communications, computers, data processing, documenta-

tion, economics, education, engineering (civil, industrial), ethnography, food/nutrition, fuel, government, history, human resources, industry, information science, jurisprudence/law, linguistics, petroleum, photography, political economy/science, psychology, public administration, sciences (life), social sciences, sociology, statistics, technology, telecommunications, transportation.
Memb AIT, SFT.

GARDNER, FRED HUGO 35 Pattison Rd, GB-London NW2 2HL, UK *Tel* (01) 794-8976.
TL English. SL French, German. UDC business, commerce, geology, history, jurisprudence, law (international), music, patents, theater.
German Karl May: *Captain Cayman* (Neville Spearman, 1970); *Canada Bill* (Neville Spearman, 1970).
Memb TA.

GAUDY, CARLOS A 5038 Hazeltine Ave #201, Sherman Oaks, CA 91423. *Tel* 213-995-3232.
TL English. SL Spanish. UDC biochemistry, chemistry, engineering, government, industry, law/legislation, metallurgy, photography, sciences.
Accred Los Angeles Superior Court. **Memb** ATA, CCIA.

GAWN, PETER 1045 Alenmede Crescent, Ottawa ON K2B 8H2, Canada *Tel* 613-820-8138.
TL English. SL French.
Affil Canadian Government Translation Bureau (dir). **Memb** ATIO.

GELD, ISIDORE 8854 Heraldry St, San Diego, CA 92123 USA *Tel* 714-278-5509.
TL English. SL Russian. UDC chemistry, corrosion, engineering (chemical) industry, iron/steel industry, metallurgy.
Russian I Geld: *Theory of Corrosion and Protection of Metals* (Macmillan, 1966).
Memb ATA.

GENIS, MARIGOLD Apartado 2568, San Jose, Costa Rica *Tel* 41 15 30.
TL English. SL Spanish. UDC agriculture, education, information science, rural development.
Memb AIT.

GERAN, PETER 425 Hanna, Birmingham, MI 48009 USA *Tel* 313-642-8507.
TL English. SL Hungarian, Rumanian. UDC architecture, banking/finance, business, commerce, economics, education, engineering (electrical), ethics, geography, government, history, insurance, law, linguistics/philology, petroleum, philosophy, political economy/science, public administration, social sciences, sociology, transportation.
Memb ATA.

GERGAY, PETER A 9763 Bluestem Path, Salinas, CA 93907 USA *Tel* 408-633-3992.
TL English. SL Hungarian. UDC business, chemistry, medicine, political economy/science, sciences (applied), sociology.
Memb ATA.

GILBOY, PETER THOMAS Sostres 25, Viv 18, E-Barcelona 24, Spain *Tel* (34-3) 214 48 69.
TL & SL English & Spanish. UDC building/construction, patents/trademarks, textiles.
Memb TG.

GILLMEIER, INGRID E 1415 S 88 St, West Allis, WI 53214 USA *Tel* 414-475-2371.
TL English. SL German. UDC business, chemistry, electronics, engineering (electrical, hydraulic, mechanical, power plant—fossil and nuclear), machine tools, metallurgy.
Accred/Memb ATA.

GIROD, CHRISTIANE 109 E 39 St, New York, NY 10016 USA *Tel* 212-751-5544; 201-652-2134.
TL French. SL English. UDC banking/finance, building/construction, business, engineering (civil, chemical), shipping.
Memb ATA.

GISBEY, ALBERT EDWARD Zugspitzweg 32, Postfach 1550, D-8192 Geretsried 1, West Germany *Tel* (0 81 71) 6 04 60.
TL English. SL French, German, Russian. UDC biochemistry, chemistry, medicine, pharmacology, veterinary medicine.
Memb TG.

GIST, GLADYS SALAZAR 19732 NW Fifth Pl, Miami, FL 33169 USA *Tel* 305-651-2070; 446-7608.
TL & SL English & Spanish. UDC agriculture, business, education, linguistics, literature, psychology.
English Peggy Fisher: *JCI World* (Jaycees International); *Citizen, Our Concern* (Jaycees International, 1974).
Accred/Memb ATA.

GLATZ, EVA M 645 Water St, New York, NY 10002 USA *Tel* 212-964-0423.
TL English. SL German. UDC banking/finance, business, commerce, history, insurance, law, psychiatry, religion/scripture.

GOLDBLATT, HAROLD 10900 Bucknell Dr, Silver Spring, MD 20902 USA *Tel* 301-946-2048.
TL English. SL French. UDC sociology.
French Maurice Halbwachs: *The Causes of Suicide* (Routledge & Kegan Paul/Free Press, 1978).
Affil Dept of Housing.

GOLDMAN, YOHANAN E 1 Rachel St, Tel Aviv, Israel *Tel* (03) 238 532; 230 574.
TL English. SL French, German, Hebrew, Hungarian, Italian, Rumanian. UDC aeronautics, athletics, aviation, banking/finance, building, commerce, communications, computers, data processing, ecology, economics, education, electronics, engineering (all areas), government, history, industry, insurance, law (all areas), machine tools, medicine, metallurgy, music, photography, political economy/science, printing, psychiatry, psychology, public administration, social services, sports, theater.
Hebrew Ephraim Kishon: *Look Back, Mrs Lot* (Atheneum/Andre Deutsch/Penguin, 1961); *Noah's Ark, Tourist Class* (Atheneum/

Andre Deutsch/Penguin, 1963); *Wise Guy, Solomon* (Atheneum/Andre Deutsch/Penguin, 1968). *Blow Softly in Jericho* (Atheneum/Andre Deutsch/Penguin, 1972). Also the works of Joseph Lapid, Aharon Megged, Yerahmiel Weingarten.
Affil Translators Pool (Israel).

GOLDNER, LOREN R 1332 Riverside Dr #54, New York, NY 10033 USA *Tel* 212-781-9351.
TL English. **SL** French, German. **UDC** banking/finance, business, economics, history, philosophy, political economy, sociology.
German Friedrich Katz: *The Secret War in Mexico: Germany, the Great Powers, and the Mexican Revolution* (Univ of Chicago, 1979).

GÓMEZ, MARY FRANCES LEYVA 1737 N Arrowhead Ave, San Bernardino, CA 92405 *Tel* 714-882-0042.
TL & SL English & Spanish. **UDC** agriculture, banking/finance, business, commerce, documentation, economics, education, government, insurance, law, legislation, library science, public health sciences (medical), taxation.
Memb ATA, CCIA.

GONZÁLEZ, SARITA GALLARDO Blvd R Arellano, D10, Bayamón, PR 00617 USA *Tel* 809-783-1105.
TL English. **SL** Spanish. **UDC** banking/finance, law.
Memb ATA.

GORHAM, DON CYRIL 7214 16 Ave, Takoma Park, MD 20012 USA *Tel* 301-434-0797.
TL English. **SL** Japanese. **UDC** art, automotive, banking/finance, building, business, commerce, communications, documentation, economics, education, ethics, fisheries, government, history, industry, information science, jurisprudence, law (international), legislation, patents/trademarks, philosophy, political economy/science, printing, religion, social services, sociology, taxation, transportation.
Memb ATA, SFL.

GORDON, ALICIA A 4457 Rosewood, Los Angeles, CA 90004 USA *Tel* 213-663-4718.
TL English. **SL** French, Spanish. **UDC** athletics, automotive, commerce, communications, education, electronics, engineering, pharmacology, political science.
Accred Chamber of Commerce of Spain.
Memb ATA.

GORSKI, JADWIGA 3867 Glenwood Rd, Cleveland Heights, OH 44121 USA *Tel* 216-382-7550.
TL Polish. **SL** English. **UDC** geography, government, law (international), political science, public health, social services, telecommunications, transportation.
Memb ATA, NOTA, Acad of Political Science. **Awards** 1960 City of Cleveland Mayor's Award of Distinction, for translation of driver's manual for foreign language driving classes.

GOSDEN, A 14 ave du Cerf, B-1330 Rixensart, Belgium *Tel* (02) 653 10 72.

TL English. **SL** Dutch, French, German, Italian. **UDC** accountancy, banking/finance, engineering (chemical, civil), metallurgy, petroleum, technology.
Memb CBTIP, TG.

GOULD, DENNIS E 85 Thanington Rd, Canterbury, UK *Tel* (0227) 68 796.
TL English. **SL** Swedish. **UDC** communications, education, food/nutrition, geography, logic, meteorology, sports, transportation.
Memb TG.

GRAF, VLADIMIR 1812 Atkinson Pl, Pittsburgh, PA 15235 USA *Tel* 412-371-6532.
TL English, French, German. **SL** Russian. **UDC** engineering (electrical, industrial, mechanical), industry, machine tools, metallurgy.
Memb ATA.

GRIETTI, MARIO RFD #2, Burlington, CT 06013 USA *Tel* 203-673-0389.
TL English. **SL** Italian. **UDC** archeology, art, automotive, banking/finance, botany, building, ecology, engineering (electrical, industrial, mechanical), fuel, geography, government, history, industry, insurance, iron/steel industry, machine tools, metallurgy, military science, philately, railroad technology, shipping, sports, technology, transportation.
Memb ATA.

GRIFFITH, RICHARD 142 South St, Red Bank, NJ 07701 USA *Tel* 201-741-1570.
TL English. **SL** Dutch, French, German, Spanish. **UDC** bacteriology, biochemistry, biomedicine, chemistry, engineering (industrial), food/nutrition, medicine, microbiology, paper/pulp, patents/trademarks, petroleum, pharmacology, plastics, sciences (applied, medical), textiles, veterinary medicine.
Memb ATA.

GRIMES, WILLIAM J PO Box 55, Hingham, MA 02043 USA *Tel* 617-749-0772.
TL English. **SL** French, German, Russian. **UDC** automotive, biology, biomedicine, electronics, medicine, meteorology, patents/trademarks, railroad technology, transportation, zoology.
Memb ATA, NETA (pres), TG.

GUBACK, DENISE IMPENS 608 W Michigan Ave, Urbana, IL 61801 USA *Tel* 217-328-1104.
TL English. **SL** Dutch, French, German, Spanish. **UDC** business, commerce, communications, ecology, food/nutrition, industry, law, paper/pulp.
Affil Univ of Illinois. **Memb** ATA.

GUISE, MARILIA ALVAREZ DE SOUZA Rua Conselheiro Lafaiete 703 #4, Rio de Janeiro, Brazil *Tel* 287-1502.
TL Portuguese, Spanish. **SL** English. **UDC** agriculture, communications, education, human resources, literature (all areas), social sciences, veterinary medicine.
Affil Inter-American Inst of Agricultural Sciences of the OAS. **Memb** AIT, ATPI.

GWIRTSMAN, JOSEPH J Exxon Research & Engineering Co, PO Box 121, Linden, NJ 07036 USA *Tel* 201-379-3947; 474-3884.
TL English. **SL** French, German, Polish, Russian. **UDC** chemistry, engineering (chemical), fuel, patents/trademarks, petroleum technology, plastics/polymers, sciences (applied).
Memb ATA.

HAAS, GERDA 55 Bardwell St, Lewiston, ME 04240 USA *Tel* 207-784-8708.
TL English. **SL** German. **UDC** library science, medicine, psychiatry, psychology.
German the works of Max Frisch, Peter Handke, Tilmann Moser, Erwin Schrödinger, Karl Vierordt.
Affil Bates College Library. **Memb** ATA, NETA.

HABBERTON, ANDREW PO Box 3435, San Rafael, CA 94902 USA *Tel* 415-472-1916.
TL English. **SL** French, German, Italian, Portuguese, Spanish. **UDC** agriculture, chemistry, engineering (petroleum), geology, law (patent), legislation, shipbuilding.
Memb ATA.

HAHN, MARIE 808 N Market St, Frederick, MD 21701 USA *Tel* 301-662-1598.
TL English. **SL** German. **UDC** bacteriology, biology, genealogy, history, library science, medicine, microbiology, music, public health, theology.
German Samuel Urlsperger: *First Continuation of the Detailed Report on the Salzburg Emigrants Who Have Settled in America* (Univ of Georgia, 1972).
Affil Hood College.

HAIGH, BASIL 28 Roman Hill, Barton, Cambridge CB3 7AX, UK *Tel* (022) 026 2391.
TL English. **SL** Russian. **UDC** anatomy, bacteriology, biochemistry, biomedicine, epidemiology, genetics, microbiology, neurosciences, pathology, pharmacology, physiology, psychiatry, psychology, public health, sciences (medical), toxicology.
Russian A R Luria: *Higher Cortical Functions in Man* (Basic Books, 1966); *Human Brain and Psychological Processes* (Harper & Row, 1966); *The Working Brain* (Penguin, 1973). Zdrodovskii & Golinevich: *The Rickettsial Diseases* (Pergamon/Oxford, 1960).
Memb TG.

HAJDU, MARGARET BLAKEY 1061 Inlet Dr, Marco Island, FL 33937 USA *Tel* 813-394-7410.
TL English. **SL** French, German, Hungarian. **UDC** bacteriology, biochemistry, biology, chemistry, crystallography, ecology, epidemiology, genetics, parasitology, pharmacology, public health, sciences (biomedical).
Hungarian Tibor Doby: *Discoverers of Blood Circulation* (Abelard-Schuman, 1963).
Memb ATA.

HALL, MARIE J 314 Rancocas Ave, Delanco, NJ 08075 USA *Tel* 609-461-1999.
TL English. **SL** Polish, Russian. **UDC** agriculture, biology, botany, business, ecology, education, geography, food, law (military), lit-

erature (children's), medicine, oceanography, political science, psychology, religion, sciences (applied, earth, life, medical, natural), theater, zoology.

Polish W. Zaweyski: "Maria Dominika" (pending). **Russian** A N Leont'ev: *Activity, Consciousness, and Personality* (Prentice-Hall, 1978). *Soviet Military Law* (Dept of Commerce, 1967).

HALLEUX, NICOLE rue du Bois de Feluy 24-7180, B-7180 Marche-les-Ecaussines, Belgium *Tel* (067) 44 33 84.

TL French. **SL** English. **UDC** art, banking/finance, business, commerce, economics, insurance, law, legislation, literature (criticism, prose, science fiction), painting, political economy/science, public administration, public health.

Memb CBTIP.

HAMILTON, GLENDA CHAPELLE 6298 Warner Dr, Los Angeles, CA 90048 USA *Tel* 213-931-5851.

TL English. **SL** French. **UDC** aeronautics, aviation, ecology, engineering (aerospace, industrial), public administration, technology, urban planning.

Memb ATA.

HAMMOND, EDGAR 33 Blakemere Rd, Welwyn Garden City, Herts AL8 7PQ, UK *Tel* (070 73) 206 52.

TL English. **SL** French, German. **UDC** chemistry, optics, painting and paints, paper/pulp, plastics, particle technology.

German Bernd Koglin et al: *Selected Translated Papers of the Institut für Mechanische Verfahrenstechnik* (Karlsruhe Univ, 1972).

Memb TG.

HAMMOND, ROBIN EWART 12 Field Way, Cambridge CB1 4RW, UK *Tel* (0223) 49761.

TL English. **SL** French, Russian. **UDC** law (civil), metallurgy (extractive, ferrous, nonferrous, physical, processing, etc), especially concurrence of metal ores and petroleum and gas, and prospecting for these.

Russian Glembotskii et al: *Flotation* (Primary Sources, 1963). V M Plyatskii: *Extrusion Casting* (Primary Sources, 1965). E M Savitskii: *Alloys of Palladium* (Primary Sources, 1966). P M Starkov: *The Problem of Acute Hypothermia* (Pergamon, 1960).

Accred Civil Service Interpreter's Certificate. **Memb** TG.

HANFF, KONSTANTY Z 112-50 78 Ave #5A, Forest Hills NY 11375 USA *Tel* 212-793-9115; 362-3650.

TL English. **SL** German, Polish, Russian. **UDC** anthropology, architecture, art, bacteriology, banking/finance, biochemistry, biomedicine, building/construction, business, ceramics, chemistry, commerce, epidemiology, food/nutrition, law, linguistics/philology, logic, machine tools, microbiology, military science, political economy/science, sciences (medical), standards, technology.

Memb ATA.

HANNA, GEORGE M 75 Comstock Ave, Staten Island, NY 10314 USA *Tel* 212-698-0250.

TL English. **SL** Arabic. **UDC** automotive, business, education, political science, public administration.

Affil New York Univ. **Memb** ATA.

HANNEMANN, ERNST 2536 W Warnimont Ave. Milwaukee, WI 53221 USA *Tel* 414-281-5525.

TL & SL English & German. **UDC** communications, electronics, engineering (electrical, industrial, mechanical), machine tools, metallurgy, standards, telecommunications.

Memb ATA.

HARDIN, RON Villa Clara, Motsa Illit, Judean Hills, Israel *Tel* (02) 539 705.

TL English. **SL** Dutch, French, German, Russian. **UDC** aerospace, astronomy, astrophysics, botany, ecology, electronics, geophysics, horticulture, linguistics, mathematics, meteorology, oceanography, physics, seismology, systems analysis, viniculture.

Russian A Kh Khrgian: *Meterology—A Historical Survey* (Israel Program for Scientific Translations, IPST, 1970). B V Kukarkin: *Pulsating Stars* (IPST, 1975). I M Soskin, ed: *Handbook of Hydrological Studies in Oceans and Seas,* (IPST, 1977). S V Vonsovskii: *Magnetism* (IPST/John Wiley, 1974). Also the works of numerous Soviet scientists in the above subject fields.

Affil Keter Publishing.

HARDY, CLAUDIA 1106 Lake Grove SE, Grand Rapids, MI 49506 USA *Tel* 616-676-6339; 949-9483.

TL French. **SL** English. **UDC** beauty products, commerce, sales training materials.

Memb ATA.

HARRIS, DAVID Weichselstrasse 37, D-1000 Berlin 44, West Germany.

TL English. **SL** German. **UDC** aesthetics, anthropology, building/construction, economics, education, ethics, government, information science, literature (drama, prose), medicine, military science, philosophy, political economy/science, psychology, public administration, sociology, theater.

HASNAIN, QAMAR PO Box 2132, Jeddah, Saudi Arabia *Tel* Jeddah 35220.

TL English. **SL** Arabic, Persian, Urdu. **UDC** Arab-Muslim-Middle East affairs, commerce, economics, education, ethics, geography, government, history, human resources, industry, information sciences, law, legislation, linguistics/philology, military science, political economy/science, public administration, religion, sociology, theology.

Arabic Noman Mahir Kanaani: *Limelight on the North of Iraq* (Dal al-Jumhuriya, 1965). Noori al-Rawi: *Iraq in Pictures* (Dar al-Jumhuriya, 1966). *North of Iraq* (Dar al-Jumhuriya, 1966). **Persian** "Shia Rituals" (pending).

Memb TA, TG.

HASSELRIIS, HELEN 52 Seasongood Rd, Forest Hills, NY 11375 USA *Tel* 212-268-1540; 867-2370.

TL English. **SL** Dutch, French, German, Italian, Portuguese, Spanish. **UDC** biochemis-

try, botany, chemistry (industrial), dairy farming, engineering (mechanical), horticulture, medicine, patents/trademarks, poultry farming, veterinary medicine.

Memb ATA.

HAUSMAN, M J One Hart St, Providence, RI 02906 USA *Tel* 401-272-9006.

TL English. **SL** French. **UDC** agriculture, economics, poetry.

Affil Brown Univ. **Memb** ALTA.

HAWTHORNE, ROBERT E 48 Marland Rd, Colorado Springs, CO 80906 USA *Tel* 303-633-9679.

TL English. **SL** French, Norwegian, Swedish. **UDC** aeronautics, athletics, aviation, banking/finance, business, commerce, communications, economics, electronics, engineering (electrical, marine), geography, government, industry, iron/steel industry, military science, mining, missiles, navigation, physics/mechanics, shipbuilding, shipping, sports, transportation, welding.

Accred Qualified US Navy Translator & Interpreter in French & Swedish. **Memb** ATA, CTA.

HAYES, JOHN H Clover House, Parrotts Close, Croxley Green, Herts WD3 3JZ, UK *Tel* (092) 37 79728.

TL & SL English & German. **UDC** automotive, engineering (mechanical), machine tools, machine tool electronics.

Affil Hayes Engineering Services. **Memb** TG.

HAYWARD, SALLY 111 Ladbroke Rd, Redhill, Surrey RH1 1JT, UK *Tel* Redhill 65196.

TL English. **SL** Dutch, French, German, Italian, Spanish, **UDC** art, aviation, commerce, economics, education, engineering (industrial), industry, insurance, iron/steel industry, literature (children's history, prose), mining, music, painting, patents, printing, psychiatry, shipping, statistics.

Memb TA, TG.

HEDDY, MARC P 73 W Cedar St, Boston, MA 02114 USA *Tel* 617-523-4613.

TL English. **SL** French, Vietnamese. **UDC** business, computers, data processing, economics, genealogy, law, political economy/science.

Accred Defense Language Inst (Monterey, CA).

HEETER, MARIA CELINA G R 2607 N 16 St, Arlington, VA 22201 *Tel* 703-243-3048.

TL Spanish. **SL** English. **UDC** law, political science, social sciences, telecommunications.

Accred Catholic Univ. **Affil** Amer Assn for the Advancement of Science. **Memb** ATA.

HELLMANN, ULRIC 37 Yarrow Rd, Fairfield, CT 06430 USA *Tel* 203-259-4856.

TL & SL English & German. **UDC** automotive, engineering (electrical, industrial, mechanical), industry, iron/steel industry, machine tools, metallurgy, patents, philately, physics/mechanics, sciences (applied), technology.

HELMICK, JOHN G 2351 Willamette St, Eugene, OR 97405 USA *Tel* 503-342-4554.

TL English. **SL** German, Greek. **UDC** biology, business, chemistry, commerce, ecology, economics, engineering (mechanical, nuclear), geophysics, linguistics, literature (criticism, prose), logic, mathematics, metallurgy, music, petroleum, pharmacology, physics, sciences (all), sociology, technology.
Memb ATA.

HEPNER, GEORGE D, III PO Box 93, Selinsgrove, PA 17870 USA *Tel* 717-743-7439, 1791.
TL English. **SL** French, German, Italian. **UDC** agriculture, botany, ecology, fisheries, linguistics, zoology.
Memb ATA.

HERMAN, FRED W 265 Atlanta Dr, Pittsburgh, PA 15228 USA *Tel* 412-341-7954.
TL English. **SL** French, German. **UDC** engineering (mechanical), metallurgy, literature (drama, poetry).
German *An Introduction to the Language of German Industry* (Carnegie-Mellon Univ, forthcoming).
Affil Carnegie-Mellon Univ. **Memb** APT, ATA.

HERRMANN, HELLMUTH H 82-60 168 St, Jamaica, NY 11432 USA *Tel* 212-380-1440.
TL & SL English & German. **UDC** aeronautics, arts, automotive, aviation, building/construction, commerce, communications, computers, data processing, ecology, electronics, engineering (aerospace, chemical, civil, electrical, hydraulic, industrial, marine, mechanical, municipal, sanitary), geography, history, insurance, iron/steel industry, law, machine tools, medicine, metallurgy, military science, patents/trademarks, plastics, sciences (applied), technology, telecommunications, transportation.
English *Handbook of Modern Budgetary Practices* (A Hamilton Inst, 1978). **German** Johann Willsberger: *Gold* (Degussa, 1976).
Affil Langenscheidt Verlag (Munich). **Memb** VDÜ (former member and co-founder).

HERTZER, WILLIAM 138 Lichty Blvd, Waterloo IA 50701 USA *Tel* 319-234-4994.
TL German. **SL** English. **UDC** engineering (automotive, agricultural), patents/trademarks, standards.
Memb ATA, BDÜ.

HERZER, IVO 9635 Podium Dr, Vienna, VA 22180 USA *Tel* 703-938-4345; 527-4200.
TL English. **SL** French, German, Italian, Russian, Serbo-Croatian. **UDC** business, economics, electronics, military science, political science, telecommunications.
Russian A A Pervozvanskii: *Random Processes in Nonlinear Control Systems* (Academic Press, 1965).
Memb ATA.

HILDEBRANDT, RUDI HENRY 5021 Carol St, Skokie, IL 60077 USA *Tel* 312-677-1664.
TL English. **SL** German, Spanish. **UDC** agriculture, architecture, arts, banking/finance, building/construction, commerce, engineering (civil, industrial, mechanical), forestry, geogra-

phy, history, iron/steel industry, machine tools, military science, sports, welding.
Accred/Memb ATA.

HIRSCHHORN, HOWARD H 1215 Pizarro St, Coral Gables, FL 33134 USA *Tel* 305-445-8349.
TL English. **SL** French, German, Spanish. **UDC** anthropology, biomedicine, ethnography, fisheries, food/nutrition, literature (poetry), medicine, microbiology, parasitology, pharmacology.
Memb CBTIP, VDÜ.

HOCKELBERG, WENDY B 348 S Atlantic Ave, Pittsburgh, PA 15224 USA *Tel* 412-361-1077.
TL English. **SL** French, Portuguese, Spanish. **UDC** banking/finance, commerce, engineering (mechanical), insurance, law.
Accred/Memb APT, ATA.

HORTON, CLAUDE W, SR Rte 1, PO Box 203A, Granger, TX 76530 USA *Tel* 512-859-2814.
TL English. **SL** French, German. **UDC** acoustics, geology, geophysics, mathematics, physics/mechanics.
Affil Univ of Texas (emeritus). **Memb** ALTA.

HOWE, K BENNETT 104 Newhall St, Lynn, MA 01902 USA *Tel* 617-593-5912.
TL English. **SL** German, Russian. **UDC** aerospace, botany (edible & useful wild plants), sciences (earth, life).
Memb ATA, Word Guild.

HOWELL, WARREN M, JR PO Box 876, Purcellville, VA 22132 USA *Tel* 703-338-6412.
TL English. **SL** French, Portuguese, Spanish. **UDC** agriculture, banking/finance, computers, dairy farming, economics, forestry, government, history, horticulture, law (international), farm machinery, petroleum, stockbreeding, taxation.
Portuguese Renato Ribeiro: "*Nationalization of Foreign Property in International Law*" (pending).
Memb AIT.

HUMMEL, JÖRG GOTTLIEB Livry-Gargan-Str 33, D-8080 Fürstenfeldbruck-Buchenau, West Germany *Tel* (08141) 26 158.
TL German, Polish. **SL** English. **UDC** automotive, commerce, documentation, engineering (civil, industrial), history, patents, public administration, railroad technology, standards, transportation.
English Edmund Wilson: Selection of essays from *The Bit Between My Teeth, Shores of Light, Axel's Castle, Classics and Commercials* (PIW, 1974).
Memb BDÜ, VDÜ.

ILSINK, YVONNE Y 1302 Oddstad Blvd, Pacifica, CA 94044 USA *Tel* 415-355-6672.
TL English. **SL** Dutch, Spanish. **UDC** business, commerce, computers, data processing, insurance, law (taxation) literature (children's) taxation.
Memb NCTA.

INTERDONATO-McNEIL, RITA 15819 Millbrooke Lane, Laurel, MD 20810 USA *Tel* 301-953-9432.
TL English. **SL** Italian, Spanish. **UDC** arts, banking/finance, business, economics, food/nutrition, government, law (property), linguistics/philology, taxation.
Memb ATA.

IRVING, ROBERT ALEC SNOW Cavendish Villa, Cavendish Rd, Bath, UK
TL English. **SL** Arabic. **UDC** aeronautics, architecture, astronomy, automotive, aviation, building/construction, chemistry, commerce, communications, documentation, electronics, engineering (aerospace, chemical, civil, electrical, hydraulic, industrial, mechanical), fuel, geography, geophysics, government, iron/steel industry, machine tools, military science, missiles, petroleum, physics/mechanics, plastics, sciences (natural), shipbuilding, shipping, standards, surveying, taxation, technology, telecommunications, textiles, transportation.
Memb TG.

IYER, MURLI M A-13/E, DDA Flats, Munirka, New Delhi 110 067, India
TL English, Hindi. **SL** English, Hindi, Russian. **UDC** art, athletics, chemistry, commerce, communications, documentation, education, engineering (aerospace, chemical, civil, electrical, mechanical), information science, literature (children's, folklore, history, science fiction), sciences (natural, social), sports, standards.
Russian Soviet technological works for the Cement Research Instit of India.
Memb ISTA.

JACOBS, RACHEL 213-02 75 Ave, Bayside, New York, NY 11364 USA *Tel* 212-464-2342.
TL English. **SL** Spanish. **UDC** banking/finance, commerce, economics, education, law (contracts, documents, international, maritime, property).
Memb ATA.

JACOBY, FRANK R 14 Glencrest Ave, Dover, NH 03820 USA *Tel* 603-742-7136.
TL English, German. **SL** Hebrew. **UDC** legal, medical.
Memb ATA.

JAMES, MADELEINE 14 Dorryn Ct, Trewsbury Rd, London SE26 5DR, UK *Tel* 778-3160.
TL & SL English & French. **UDC** art, building, commerce, engineering (civil, mechanical), law (commercial), painting, plastics, railroad technology, transportation.
Memb TG.

JARDINE, DOUGLAS KENNEDY Mariénia, F-64210 Guéthary, France *Tel* (59) 26 51 04.
TL English. **SL** French. **UDC** agriculture, biology, ecology, ethics, food/nutrition, virology.
French Jacques Barbizet: *Human Memory and Its Pathology* (Freeman, 1970). Jean Trémolières: "To Share One's Bread" (pending). Constant Vago & Max Bergoin: *Viruses of Invertebrates* (Academic, 1968). G Blaha: *Methods of Testing for Resistance in Phytoph-*

thora Disease (Longman, 1974). Also numerous articles, mostly for the Centre National de la Recherche Scientifique, France.
Memb TG.

JEBOKJI, KAREN BROWNING 17261 E Cypress St #9, Covina, CA 91722 USA *Tel* 213-339-4846.
TL & SL English & French. **UDC** banking/finance, commerce, communications, copyright, economics, fuel, government, history, horticulture, law, literature (prose), music, political economy/science, religion, sciences (life, medical, social).
Affil Interworld Music Group, Inc. **Memb** Concordiat.

JENKS, ROYTON HUBERT Piper's Moon, Paddock Close, St Mary's Platt, Seven Oaks, Kent TN18 8NN, UK *Tel* Borough Green (0732) 884 442.
TL English. **SL** French. **UDC** building, commerce, communications, computers, data processing, documentation, economics, electronics, engineering (civil, mechanical), metallurgy, political economy, public administration, railroad technology, telecommunications, transportation.
French numerous articles for International Railway Congress Assn, Brussels, and International Union of Railways, Paris.
Memb TG.

JERISON, IRENE 503 W Rustic Rd, Santa Monica, CA 90402 USA *Tel* 213-454-9553.
TL English. **SL** French, German, Polish, Russian. **UDC** biology, biomedicine, communications, ecology, education, government, human resources, literature (children's, criticism, drama, history, lyrics, songs), medicine, paleontology, philosophy, political economy/science, psychiatry, psychology, sciences (applied, earth, life, medical, natural, social), sociology, zoology.
Memb ATA.

JOHANNSEN, H Highlands, Mt Bures, Suffolk, UK *Tel* (0787) 227 208.
TL & SL Danish & English. **UDC** agriculture, commerce, ethics, nutrition, horticulture, medicine, metaphysics, philosophy, poultry farming, psychology, refractories, religion, theology.
Memb TG.

JOHNSTON, IRMGARD D PO Box 628, Wyandotte, MI 48192 USA *Tel* 313-282-3300.
TL & SL English & German. **UDC** automotive, banking/finance, business, ceramics, chemistry, engineering (civil, electrical, mechanical), metallurgy, telecommunications.
Memb ATA.

JOLLY, STEPHEN B 69B Grange Rd, London W5 5BU, UK *Tel* (01) 567-2346.
TL English. **SL** Czech, German, Russian. **UDC** biochemistry, chemistry, engineering (chemical, civil, mechanical, sanitary), geophysics, metallurgy, sciences (earth).
Czech Josef Čapek: *Harum Scarum* (Methuens, 1963). Julius Fučik: *Report from the Gallows* (Fore/Spencer, 1951). Jiri Langer: *Nine Gates* (James Clarke, 1961). Jiří Mucha: *Al-*

phonse Mucha: His Life and Art (Heinemann, 1966). Also the works of E Kulka, V Nezval, A Vostra, A Zweig, numerous others.
Memb TG.

JONES, IAN PETER 7 rue Dante, Luxembourg-Ville, Luxembourg *Tel* 442 540.
TL English. **SL** French, Spanish. **UDC** banking/finance, electronics, engineering (civil, electrical), law, linguistics/philology, missiles/rocketry, music (jazz), technology.

JONES-DAIX, EVELYNE 7 rue Dante, Luxembourg-Ville, Luxembourg *Tel* 442 540.
TL French. **SL** English. **UDC** banking/finance, commerce, computers, data processing, food/nutrition, industry, law, technology.
Accred ISETI.

JORDAN, DEREK 415-A Woodfield Dr, Ottawa, ON, K2G 4B7, Canada *Tel* 613-225-0576.
TL English. **SL** German. **UDC** agriculture, automotive, aviation, biology, ecology, geography, geophysics, medicine, metallurgy, mining, psychiatry, psychology, transportation.
German Gerhard Bosch: *Infantile Autism* (Springer, 1970). R F Schmidt et al: *Fundamentals Neurophysiology* (Springer, 1975). Paul Matussek: *Internment in Concentration Camps and Its Consequences* (Springer, 1975). Wilhelm Reich: *The Bion Experiments on the Origin of Life* (Farrar, Straus, Giroux, 1979). Also the works of W Zeil.
Affil Government of Canada (staff translator). **Memb** TG.

JUNCAL, JULIO ANGEL 3917 Benton St NW, Washington, DC 20007 USA *Tel* 202-333-3297.
TL Spanish. **SL** English. **UDC** art, banking/finance, business, documentation, economics, government, history, law (international), legislation, medicine, political economy/science, psychology, public administration, public health, sciences (social), sociology, taxation.
Memb ATA.

KAGIE, JOHANNES L Terpstraat 12, NL-Berkel/Rodenrijs, Netherlands *Tel* (01891) 4752.
TL & SL Dutch & English. **UDC** anthropology, archeology, automotive, banking, building, commerce, copyright, documentation, economics, engineering (civil, hydraulic, industrial, mechanical), engraving, ethnography, genealogy, geography, government, heraldry, history, industry, information science, iron/steel industry, law (international, maritime, property), legislation, library science, linguistics, machine tools, metallurgy, patents/trademarks, petroleum, plastics, political economy/science, printing, railroad technology, religion, sciences (social), sociology, surveying, taxation, transportation.
Memb ATA.

KAMAL, SHUCKRAN A PO Box 7, Chattanooga, TN 37401 USA *Tel* 615-875-5899.
TL English. **SL** Arabic. **UDC** banking/finance, economics, education, ethics, food/nutrition, fuel, geography, government, history, human resources, literature (children's, criti-

cism, drama, feminist, folklore, history), philology, social services, sociology, theater.
Memb ATA, SFL.

KANDINER, HAROLD J Old Coach Rd, Summit, NJ 07901 USA *Tel* 201-277-0491.
TL English. **SL** German, Russian. **UDC** chemistry, energy, engineering (chemical), fuel, petroleum.
Memb ATA.

KAPULSKI, ISAC H 727 Oakton St, Evanston, IL 60202 USA *Tel* 312-475-3192.
TL English. **SL** Hebrew, Spanish, Portuguese. **UDC** automotive, aviation, building/construction, commerce, documentation, economics, engineering (civil, mechanical), geodesy, public administration, transportation.
Accred Univ of Jerusalem. **Affil** Universal Languages, Inc. **Memb** ATA.

KARGLEDER, CHARLES L Languages, Spring Hill College, Mobile, AL 36608 USA *Tel* 205-460-2152.
TL English. **SL** Spanish. **UDC** aesthetics, agriculture, art, communications, commerce, dairy farming, economics, education, ethics, government, history, metaphysics, philosophy, political science, poultry farming, psychology, religion, social services, sociology, sports, stockbreeding, theater, theology, transportation.
Memb ATA.

KARKALAS, OLGA 1007 W Lindley Ave, Philadelphia, PA 19141 USA *Tel* 215-324-3794.
TL English. **SL** German, Russian, Ukrainian. **UDC** agriculture, anthropology, bacteriology, biochemistry, biology, biomedicine, botany, chemistry, ecology, entomology, epidemiology, fisheries, food/nutrition, forestry, genetics, horticulture, medicine, microbiology, oceanography, paleontology, parasitology, pharmacology, plastics, psychiatry, psychology, public health, sciences (life, medical, natural), statistics, stockbreeding, veterinary science, viniculture, zoology.
Memb ATA, DVTA.

KARRIKER, ROBERT J PO Box 2637, Boulevard Sta, Norman, OK 73070 USA *Tel* 405-329-4119.
TL English. **SL** Bulgarian, Russian. **UDC** building/construction, chemistry, linguistics/philology, railroad technology.
Russian *Flow Detection in Rails* (Dept of Transportation, forthcoming).
Memb ATA.

KATZMARK, JUDITH WEICH 43 Dearborn Pl #59, Goleta, CA 93017 USA *Tel* 805-964-6653.
TL & SL English & Spanish. **UDC** agriculture, arts, astrology, automotive, banking/finance, biomedicine, commerce, documentation, education, food/nutrition, fuel, genealogy, history, law, library science, linguistics/philology, literature, philosophy, political science, religion, transportation.
Memb ATA.

KAUFMAN, HELENE SARA 3360 Cote Ste Catherine Rd #15, Montreal, PQ, Canada *Tel* 514-737-6324.
TL English. SL French. UDC athletics, biomedicine, business, genetics, insurance, sciences (medical).
Memb ATA, ATAQ.

KAWASAKI, HIROKO 245 S Rampart Blvd #301, Los Angeles, CA 90057 USA *Tel* 213-388-8073.
TL & SL English & Japanese. UDC business, chemistry, ecology, history, medicine, patents/trademarks.

KAWECKI, ALICJA T Bell Laboratories, Room 6B-303, 600 Mountain Ave, Murray Hill, NJ 07974 *Tel* 201-582-2255.
TL English. SL French, Italian, Polish, Russian, Ukrainian. UDC astronomy, biology, chemistry, communications, computers, medicine, sciences (life), telecommunications.
Accred Polytechnic of Central London.
Memb ATA, STQ.

KELLNER, HUGO MARIA 3240 Iroquoid Rd, Caledonia, NY 14423 USA *Tel* 716-538-6327.
TL English. SL German. UDC chemistry, engineering (chemical), meteorology, photography, physics, religion, theology.
German Evelyn Waugh: *The Life of Ronald Knox* (Echter, 1965).

KELLY, WILLIAM F PO Box 726, Bothell, WA 98011 USA *Tel* 206-488-3762.
TL English. SL French, Russian. UDC aeronautics, astrophysics, biology, biomedicine, botany, chemistry, copyright, economics, engineering (civil, hydraulic), epidemiology, fisheries, forestry, geodesy, geology, information science, linguistics/philology, medicine, metallurgy, meteorology, microbiology, military science, mineralogy, missiles, oceanography, optics, paper/pulp, patents/trademarks, petroleum, pharmacology, physics/mechanics, plastics, political economy, sciences (earth, life, medical, natural), sociology, textiles.
Memb ATA.

KEMENDO, JOSEPH P 410 E Courtland, San Antonio, TX 78212 USA *Tel* 512-733-8397.
TL English. SL French, Italian, Spanish. UDC business, economics, history, military science.
Memb ATA.

KENT, WALTER, JR 878 Cahill Dr W, Ottawa, ON K1V 9A2, Canada *Tel* 613-521-0045.
TL English. SL Russian. UDC agriculture, bacteriology, biochemistry, biology, biomedicine, chemistry, computers, data processing, ecology, engineering (chemical, civil, hydraulic), entomology, fisheries, food/nutrition, geodesy, geophysics, iron/steel industry, literature (science fiction), machine tools, medicine, metallurgy, microbiology, mineralogy, oceanography, paleontology, patents, pharmacology, plastics, psychiatry, psychology, sciences (applied, earth, life, medical, natural), standards, stockbreeding, technology, telecommunications, transportation, veterinary medicine, welding, zoology.
Russian L B Bernshtein: *The Kislaya Guba Tidal Power Plant* (CISTI, 1977). N Ya Kats: *The Bogs of North America in the Book of Swamps of the World* (CISTI, 1976). State Committee on the Use of Atomic Energy, USSR: *Uranium Hexafluoride Analysis Methods* (CISTI, 1976). A B Vistelius et al: *Statistical Identification of Ideal Granites and Their Transformation Products* (CISTI, 1978). Also hundreds of scientific and technical papers in all fields by numerous authors.
Affil Translation Bureau, Canadian Secy of State Dept. Memb ATA, ATIO.

KEOGH, BRENDAN TEMPLE c/o Sheila Lyons, 205 Raleigh House, Dolphin Sq, London SW1, UK
TL English. SL French, German, Russian, Spanish. UDC archeology, astronomy, astrophysics, banking/finance, business, communications, economics, electronics, genealogy, government, information science, occultism, philosophy, photography, political economy/science, psychology, recreation/games, sciences (applied, medical), sociology, technology.
Memb ATA, TG.

KERR, LUCILLE P Via Achillini 6/10, I-00141 Rome, Italy *Tel* (06) 827 2632.
TL English. SL Italian. UDC medical sciences, microbiology, parasitology, pharmacology.
Memb ATA.

KEY, DAVID BRIAN 1220 N Pierce St #705, Arlington, VA 22209 USA
TL English. SL Spanish. UDC athletics, brewing, economics, history, viniculture.
Spanish Jorge Kattan Zablan: "Birth, Spread, and Development of a Theatrical Character: Don Juan" (PhD diss).
Accred Monterey Inst of Foreign Studies.
Memb NCTA.

KHIN, U 7904 Deepwell Dr, Bethesda, MD 20034 USA *Tel* 301-365-1087.
TL & SL English & Burmese. UDC agriculture, anthropology, art, athletics, building/construction, education, geography, government, jurisprudence, political economy/science, public health, taxation.

KIDD, DAVID L 109 Mill Creek Dr, Arlington, TX 76010 USA *Tel* 817-261-3405.
TL English. SL German. UDC acoustics, aeronautics, applied mathematics, aviation, chemistry, communications, computers, cybernetics, economics, electronics, engineering (mechanical), helicopters, instrumentation, metallurgy, military procurement, missiles, physics/mechanics, plastics, sciences (medical), specifications, standards, technology, vibration.
Affil Bell Helicopter Textron. Memb ATA.

KIM, CHEONG-HWAN 334 Chatham Rd, Columbus, OH 43214 USA.
TL English. SL Japanese, Korean. UDC chemical technology, metallurgy, pollution.

KING, BRENDA NEWMAN 119 Seafoam Ave, Monterey, CA 93940 USA *Tel* 408-372-1843.
TL English. SL French. UDC agriculture, architecture, art, banking/finance, botany, building/construction, chemistry, commerce, ecology, economics, engraving, ethics, fuel, metallurgy, metaphysics, petroleum, philosophy, political economy/science, religion, sciences (natural), solar energy, sports, technology, theater, transportation, zoology.
Accred Monterey Inst of Foreign Studies.
Memb ATA, Concordiat.

KING, GEORGE & MADELEINE 10 bis, route du Pavé des Gardes, F-92310 Sevres, France *Tel* 027 56 37.
TL & SL English & French. UDC aeronautics, agriculture, automotive, aviation, building/construction, computers, communications, engineering, information science, iron/steel industry, metallurgy, meteorology, oceanography, plastics, public works, telecommunications, transportation.

KING, IRENE B 8131 Carrleigh Pkwy, Springfield, VA 22152 USA *Tel* 703-569-9697.
TL English. SL German, Spanish. UDC agriculture, anthropology, archeology, education, government, law (international, maritime), legislation, literature (children's, drama), political science.
Memb Concordiat.

KING, SOPHIE rue du Roetaert 147, B-1180 Brussels, Belgium *Tel* (021) 376 65 01.
TL English. SL French, German. UDC commerce, economics, literature, political economy, yoga.
French A van Lysebeth: *Pranayama* (Allen & Unwin, forthcoming).
Memb TG.

KIRK, KATHLEEN L 3032 Rodman St NW #23, Washington, DC 20008 USA *Tel* 202-244-3737.
TL English. SL French, Spanish. UDC agriculture, art, banking/finance, economics, law, medicine, commerce, education, history, linguistics, psychology, political science, sciences (natural, social), theater.

KITTENBACHER, PAUL E 3402 Burning Tree, Garland, TX 75042 USA *Tel* 214-272-9427.
TL English. SL German, Spanish. UDC broadcasting applications (audio, video), data processing, electronics, engineering (electrical, mechanical), radio transmitters and antenna systems, telecommunications.
Memb ATA (Metroplex chapter).

KNUDSEN, WALTRAUD 31299 White Rd, Willoughby Hills, OH 44092 USA *Tel* 216-944-2390.
TL & SL English & German. UDC agriculture, automotive, business, engineering (electrical), horticulture, music, taxation.
Memb ATA, NOTA.

KOEHLER, HENRY M 5000 S East End Ave, Chicago, IL 60615 USA *Tel* 312-493-7976; 440-2794.

TL English. **SL** German. **UDC** dentistry, sciences (medical).

German Bauer/Gutowski: *Gnathology* (Quintessence, 1977). Schijatschky: *Life-Threatening Emergencies in the Dental Practice* (Quintessence, 1975). Harnisch: *Apicoectomy* (Quintessence, 1975).

KOENIG, HANS J 4833 Fremont Ave S, Minneapolis, MN 55409 USA *Tel* 612-825-4395.

TL English. **SL** German. **UDC** aeronautics, agriculture, athletics, automotive, aviation, banking, building/construction, chemistry, commerce, communications, computers, education, electronics, engineering (most fields), film dubbing, geography, government, industry, insurance, jurisprudence, law, machine tools, medicine, military science, patents, photography, plastics, politics, textiles, transportation.

Memb ATA.

KOENIG, JULES 350 Fifth Ave, New York, NY 10001 USA *Tel* 212-594-8218.

TL English. **SL** Dutch, French, German. **UDC** accounting, banking/finance, business, copyright, economics, government, insurance, law (international), patents/trademarks, taxation.

Affil Interworld Translation Services. **Memb** ATA, SFL.

KÖHLER, WILLI Strubbergstr 19, D-6000 Frankfurt/Main 90, West Germany *Tel* (0611) 786 967.

TL German. **SL** English. **UDC** psychiatry, psychology, sociology.

English Hilde Bruch: *Learning Psychotherapy* (Fischer, 1977). Theodore Lidz: *Origin and Treatment of Schizophrenic Disorders* (Fischer, 1976). Ann Grace Mojtabai: *Mundome* (Fischer, 1978). Charles Brenner: *Psychoanalytic Technique and Psychic Conflict* (Fischer, 1979). Also the works of Alred Adler, Phyllis Greenacre, Arthur Janov, Manuel J Smith.

Memb VS.

KOMOROWICZ, EDITH 752 Kedron Ave, Morton, PA 19070 USA *Tel* 215-543-8197.

TL English. **SL** French, German, Hungarian, Italian, Russian. **UDC** agriculture, biochemistry, chemistry, electronics, medicine, paper/pulp, pharmacology, patents, petroleum, photography, plastics, textiles.

Memb ATA, DVTA.

KONDOR, RUBEN Mameyasdim 21, Jerusalem, Israel *Tel* (02) 528 421.

TL English, German. **SL** Dutch, French, Hungarian, Italian, Russian. **UDC** biochemistry, chemistry, engineering (chemical), food/nutrition, hydraulics, irrigation, metallurgy, microbiology, physics, plastic, statistics, viniculture.

German W Leithe: *The Analysis of Air Pollutants* (Humphrey Science, 1970). **Russian** A F Belyaev et al: *Transition from Deflagration to Detonation In Condensed Phases* (Israel PST, 1975). Ya M Paushkin: *Organic Polymeric Semiconductors* (Wiley & Sons, 1974).

Affil International Irrigation Information Center.

KONSTANTIN, ANATOLE E 10 Live Oak Rd, Norwalk, CT 06851 USA *Tel* 203-847-9754.

TL English. **SL** Polish, Russian, Ukrainian. **UDC** business, engineering (industrial, mechanical).

Russian V Tretyak: *The Hockey I Love* (Lawrence Hill, 1977).

KOWALSKI-NARDONE, ANNE-MARIE Viale Giustiniano Imperatore 76, I-00145 Rome, Italy *Tel* (06) 51 39 753.

TL French, Italian. **SL** English. **UDC** commerce, education, medicine.

Memb AITI, SFT.

KRAWUTSCHKE, PETER W 4204 Waldorf, Kalamazoo, MI 49007 USA *Tel* 616-343-5028.

TL English. **SL** German. **UDC** business, medicine, military science, paper/pulp.

German Frank R Bahr: *Introduction to Scientific Acupuncture* (German Academy for Auricular Medicine, 1978).

Affil Western Michigan Univ. **Memb** ATA.

KUBOTA, HISASHI 910 W Outer Dr, Oak Ridge, TN 37830 USA *Tel* 615-483-5220.

TL English. **SL** Japanese. **UDC** biochemistry, chemistry, fuel, metallurgy, nuclear engineering & science, patents/trademarks, plastics, sciences (applied).

Memb ATA, JEITA.

KUMIN, JUDITH 36 Holworthy St, Cambridge, MA 02138 USA *Tel* 617-661-6733.

TL English. **SL** Dutch, French, German. **UDC** law (international), political economy/science.

Memb ALTA.

LABRADA, EMILIO B Organization of American States, Washington, DC 20006 USA *Tel* 202-381-8611; 703-698-5331.

TL & SL English, Portuguese, Spanish. **UDC** agriculture, automotive, banking/finance, business, commerce, documentation, economics, education, food/nutrition, forestry, geography, government, history, human resources, industry, information science, law, philosophy, photography, political economy/science, public administration, shipping, sports, statistics, taxation, telecommunications, transportation.

Memb AIT, TAALS.

LACHMANN, ALICE D 1305 Gibson Pl, Falls Church, VA 22046 USA *Tel* 703-536-7520.

TL French. **SL** English. **UDC** biology, chemistry, food/nutrition, medicine, pharmacology, psychiatry.

Memb ATA.

LADY, EVERETT L 1658 Liholiho St #202, Honolulu, Hawaii 96822 USA *Tel* 808-536-9932.

TL English. **SL** Russian. **UDC** mathematics, sciences (natural).

Affil Univ of Hawaii. **Memb** ATA.

LAKIS, ELAINE ANN 7310 E Main St, Lima, NY 14485 USA *Tel* 716-582-1671.

TL English. **SL** German. **UDC** banking/finance, business, commerce, computers, data processing, economics, government, history, military science, political science, sports, viniculture.

Memb Concordiat.

LAMBERT, JEAN LOUIS FRANÇOIS 2111 Montreal Rd #153, Ottawa, ON K1J 8M8, Canada *Tel* 613-741-4423.

TL English, French. **SL** French, German, Serbo-Croatian. **UDC** criminology, geography, geology, history, linguistics, locks and keys, oceanography, political science, security plate tectonics, transportation.

Memb ATA.

LANGMAN, IDA K 116 S Raleigh Ave #7B, Atlantic City, NJ 08401 USA *Tel* 609-344-5410.

TL English. **SL** Portuguese, Spanish. **UDC** biology, botany, ecology, horticulture, sciences (natural).

Memb DVTA.

LANNIEL, JEAN MARTIN PO Box 834, Havertown, PA 19083 USA *Tel* 215-449-4480.

TL English. **SL** French. **UDC** aeronautics, agriculture, aviation, bacteriology, biochemistry, biology, biomedicine, botany, chemistry, copyright, electronics, engineering (civil, industrial, mechanical), history, patents/trademarks, theater, veterinary medicine.

Memb ATA.

LAPORTE, MARIE AUGUSTA 6618 Shady Brook #3183, Dallas, TX 75206 USA *Tel* 214-692-7725.

TL & SL English, French, Spanish. **UDC** banking/finance, business, documentation, engineering (electrical, mechanical), machine tools, metallurgy, petroleum.

Memb ATA (Metroplex chapter).

LA ROCHE, MARGARETE M SCHWABE 50 Bartlett Ave, Pittsfield, MA 01201 USA *Tel* 413-499-3804.

TL & SL English & German. **UDC** business, education, law, sciences (social).

Accred/Memb ATA.

LASQUIN, FRANÇOIS 41 rue Taitbout, F-75009 Paris, France *Tel* (1) 583 57 44; 874 30 45.

TL French. **SL** English. **UDC** anthropology, astrophysics, ecology, economics, ethnography, food/nutrition, literature (poetry, prose, science fiction), occultism, pharmacology, political economy/science, psychiatry, psychology, sciences (social), sociology, underground & counterculture (drugs, all areas of slang, rock music).

English William Burroughs, Jr: *Speed* (Olympia, 1971). Jerry Rubin: *Do It* (Seuil, 1970). Philip Jose Farmer: *A Feast Unknown* (Champ Libre, 1973). Terry Andrews: *The Story of Harold* (André Ballaud, 1976). Also the works of Stewart Brand, Noam Chomsky, Eldridge Cleaver, Dylan Thomas, William Jon Watkins, others.

Memb ATLF.

LATORTUE, FRANÇOIS 1324 Jonquil St NW, Washington, DC 20012 USA *Tel* 202-882-6554; 381-8616.
TL French. **SL** English. **UDC** economics, education, law (international), legislation, statistics.
Affil OAS (chief, French section). **Memb** AIT (pres).

LAVOOTT, ROSE 13 Lincoln St #2, Jerusalem, Israel.
TL English. **SL** Czech, Russian. **UDC** biology, botany, theology, zoology.
Czech O Prochazka: *Crusaders in the Holy Land* (private, 1958). **Russian** V L Komarov, ed: *Flora of the USSR,* Vols 7–8, 10–15, 18–19, 21 (IPST, 1969–75). N A Rynin: *Interplanetary Flight and Communication* (IPST, 1970). K Skryabin: *Nematodes,* Vols 3–6 (IPST, 1972–75).

LAWSON, VERONICA 20 Tooks Ct, Cursitor St, London EC4A 1LB, UK *Tel* (01) 242-8710.
TL English. **SL** French, German. **UDC** automotive, engineering (mechanical, nuclear), insurance (marine), law (maritime, property), literature (prose), patents/trademarks, sciences (earth, especially vulcanology), textiles (weaving).
French Haroun Tazieff: *The Making of the Earth* (Saxon House, 1974).
Affil Polytechnic of Central London. **Memb** TA, TG.

LAWTON, DAWN HARI General Delivery, Hiram, OH 44234 USA *Tel* 216-569-7909.
TL Spanish. **SL** English. **UDC** art, arts & crafts, communications, fashion, law (international), textiles.
Memb ATA.

LEAMAN, LOUIS 26 Columbia St, Brookline, MA 02146 USA *Tel* 617-277-2253.
TL English. **SL** French, German, Russian. **UDC** biochemistry, biology, chemistry, engineering (chemical), medicine, patents/trademarks, pharmacology, sciences (applied, medical), veterinary medicine.
Memb ATA, NETA.

LEBOVITZ, CARL H 2917 Richmond Ave, Mattoon, IL 61938 USA *Tel* 217-234-3267.
TL English. **SL** Bulgarian, Russian, Ukrainian. **UDC** most areas of science & technology.
Accred Georgetown Univ.

LEDERMAN, DOV B 5 Rashbam St, Bnei Brak, Israel *Tel* (9723) 78 98 56.
TL English. **SL** Hebrew, Polish, Russian. **UDC** aeronautics, astrophysics, engineering (aerospace, mechanical), meteorology, missiles/rocketry, physics/mechanics.
Russian Ya B Zel'dovich & Yu P Raizer: *Physics of Shock Waves and High-Temperature Hydrodynamic Phenomena* (Academic, 1966). Ye V Stupochenko et al: *Relaxation in Shock Waves* (Springer, 1967). L E Kalikhman: *Elements of Magnetogasdynamics* (Saunders, 1967). V P Shidlovskiy: *Introduction to Dynamics of Rarefied Gases* (American Elsevier, 1967). Also numerous translations in the sciences and technologies, mainly of Heat-Transfer (Soviet Research and Fluid Mechanics).

LE DOCTE, EDGARD Meiddelweg 121, B-3030 Heverlee, Louvain, Belguim *Tel* (016) 22 75 51.
TL English. **SL** Dutch, French. **UDC** art/art history, banking/finance, commerce, economics, genealogy, geography, government, jurisprudence, law (international, maritime, property), legislation, political economy.
Author of *Legal Dictionary in Four Languages—Dutch, English, French, German* (Oyex, 1978).
Accred Univ of Cambridge (Proficiency Certificate). **Memb** CBTIP.

LEFFLER, DONALD R 219 E Wilshire Ave, Fullerton, CA 92632 USA *Tel* 714-525-6674.
TL English. **SL** French, German, Russian, Spanish. **UDC** aeronautics, aviation, biochemistry, biology, biomedicine, chemistry, communications, computers, data processing, electronics, engineering (aerospace, chemical, electrical, hydraulic, industrial, mechanical), machine tools, medicine, metallurgy, military science, mining, missiles/rocketry, patents/trademarks, petroleum, pharmacology, plastics/polymers.
Memb ATA.

LEONARD, ISABEL A PO Box 55, Hingham, MA 02043 USA *Tel* 617-749-1540.
TL English. **SL** Dutch, French, Italian, Portuguese, Spanish. **UDC** engineering (nuclear), metallurgy, patents/trademarks.
French Jean Pouquet: *Earth Sciences in the Age of the Satellite* (Reidel, 1974).
Accred Univ of Bath. **Affil** *ATA Chronicle* (ed). **Memb** ATA.

LEOPOLD, CARON JENNIFER 752 West End Ave #17B, New York, NY 10025 USA *Tel* 212-866-6219.
TL English. **SL** French. **UDC** agriculture, banking/finance, biology, commerce, computers, dairy farming, data processing, ecology, education, engineering (hydraulic), entomology, fisheries, food/nutrition, forestry, geography, history, horticulture, literature (criticism, drama, history, science fiction), mineralogy, mining, oceanography, parasitology, psychology, sciences (all areas), stockbreeding, theater, veterinary medicine, viniculture.
French Richard Armand, Robert Lattes, Jacques Lesourne: *The Management Revolution* (MacDonald, 1972). Jacqueline Beaulieu-Garnier: *Urban Geography* (Longmans, Green, 1967). Philippe Jullian: *La Belle Epoque* (William Morrow, 1978).
Accred Inst Français du Royaume.

LET, NICHOLAS P 1326 W Fargo Ave #509, Chicago, IL 60626 USA *Tel* 312-465-1781.
TL & SL Czech, English, Slovak. **UDC** agriculture, automotive, aviation, biochemistry, biology, biomedicine, chemistry, electronics, engineering (electrical, hydraulic, industrial), iron/steel industry, machine tools, medicine, metallurgy, patents/trademarks, transportation, welding.
Memb ATA.

LETOURNEAUT, RAFAEL 1208 San Miguel Ave, Coral Gables, FL 33134 USA *Tel* 305-442-0314.

TL English. **SL** Spanish. **UDC** communications, education, government, human resources, legislation, literature (drama), public administration, social services, theater, transportation.
Affil Amaury Cruz & Associates.

LEWIS, ELIZABETH M 2465 Glenwood Dr, Boulder, CO 80302 USA *Tel* 303-442-2574.
TL English. **SL** Spanish. **UDC** banking/finance, business, commerce, economics, education, government, history, law, political science, religion, women's studies.
Spanish Elena Urrutia, ed: "Women: Image and Reality" (pending).
Accred Monterey Inst of Foreign Studies. **Memb** ATA, Concordiat.

LI, PAMELA M 3459 Stratford Rd NE, Atlanta, GA 30342 USA *Tel* 404-233-2686.
TL English. **SL** Spanish. **UDC** agriculture, anthropology, archeology, arts/crafts, astrology, athletics, aviation, commerce, communications, copyright, education, ethics, geography, government, graphics, history, horticulture, industry, information science, music, painting, photography, political science/economy, religion, telecommunications, theater, transportation.
Memb AAIT, ATA.

LIEDER, ULRIKE E German Studies, Stanford Univ, Stanford, CA 94305 USA *Tel* 415-497-0417.
TL & SL English & German. **UDC** agriculture, business, ceramics, education, history, iron/steel industry, political science, railroad technology, sociology, sports.
German the works of Edgar Bonjour, Hans-Jürg Hauser, Marlies Näh, Margit Baumann, Hans Kurz (in *Modern Switzerland,* SPOSS, 1978).
Memb ATA, NCCI, NCTA.

LIGHT, LISE R 4607 SE 3rd Court, Des Moines, IA 50315 USA *Tel* 515-285-8917.
TL & SL English & French. **UDC** business, music, photography, psychology, social services.
Accred St Mary-of-the-Woods College (1979). **Memb** ATA.

LINDSEY, DOUGLAS Surgery, Univ of Arizona, Tucson, AZ 85724 USA *Tel* 602-626-7676.
TL English. **SL** German, Yakut. **UDC** medicine.
German abstracts from Dutch, Flemish, French, German, Italian, Portuguese, Russian, Spanish, and Turkish for *Journal of Trauma.*
Memb ATA.

LINKE, EVELYN Basler Str 68, D-8000 Munich 71, West Germany *Tel* (089) 756 161.
TL German. **SL** English. **UDC** biology, biomedicine, genetics, medicine, pharmacology, psychiatry, psychology, sociology.
English Nena & George O'Neill: *Open Marriage* (Scherz, 1972). Robert J Ringer: *Looking Out for Number One* (Moderne, 1978). Leon Uris: *QB VII* (Kindler, 1970). Michael Rogers: *Biohazards* (Hallwag, 1978). Also the works of

Christiaan Barnard, Lance Horner, Golda Meir, Keith Wheeler, numerous others.
Memb VDÜ.

LIU, DAVID YUN-KUO PO Box 59453, Taipei City, Taiwan 100 *Tel* 382-1591; 314-4846.
TL & SL Chinese & English. **UDC** commerce, communications, documentation, economics, government, history, information science, literature (prose), political economy/science, public administration.
English Jacow Trachtenberg: *The Trachtenberg Speed System of Basic Mathematics* (Great China, 1963). Dale Carnegie: *How to Stop Worrying and Start Living* (Lienching, 1978). Charlotte Brontë, retold by A Sweaney: *Jane Eyre* (Hualien, 1965). W Shakespeare, retold: *Lamb's Tales* (Haulien, 1965). Also the works of Daphne du Maurier, Georges Simenon, William Makepeace Thackeray, others.
Memb ATA.

LOEFFLER, ARTHUR GEORGE Casilia Correo 3238, 1000 Correo Central, Buenos Aires, Argentina *Tel* 743-5743.
TL & SL English, German, Spanish. **UDC** agriculture, automotive, banking/finance, chemistry, commerce, communications, computers, cybernetics, dairy farming, data processing, electronics, engineering (all areas), industry, insurance, iron/steel industry, law (all areas), legislation, machine tools, metallurgy, mining, navigation, patents/trademarks, petroleum, plastics, public health, shipbuilding, shipping, technology, telecommunications, welding.
English Robert Gregory: *Business Data Processing and Programming* (Ateneo, 1972). **Author of** an English-German-Spanish *Technical Dictionary for the Automotive Industry*.
Memb TG.

LONDON, JOYCE E Two Glen Cove Rd, Roslyn, NY 11576 USA *Tel* 516-621-4448.
TL & SL English & French. **UDC** biomedicine, chemistry, medicine, microbiology, pharmacology, psychiatry, psychology, sciences (medical).
French A de Cayeux: *Three Billion Years of Life* (Stein & Day, 1969). Jean Dauven: *The Powers of Hypnosis* (Stein & Day, 1969). Michel Gaugeulin: *Cosmic Influences on Human Behavior* (Stein & Day, 1973).
Memb ATA.

LOTTEFIER, PETER J 150 ave de Lévis-Mirepoix, B-1090 Brussels, Belgium *Tel* (02) 427-0696.
TL French. **SL** English. **UDC** law, medicine, microbiology, pharmacology, psychiatry.
Affil Pfizer, Inc (NY) (translation section). **Memb** CBTIP, TG.

LUND, JOHN J 444 China Gulch Rd, Jacksonville, OR 97530 USA *Tel* 503-899-7368.
TL English. **SL** Danish, Dutch, German, Norwegian, Swedish. **UDC** book production, engineering (all areas), library science, mathematics, metallurgy, philosophy.
Danish Svend Dahl: *History of the Book* (Scarecrow, 1958). **Norwegian** Wilhelm Munthe: *American Librarianship from a European Angle* (ALA, 1939).

LYNCH, CHRISTINE ANNE 3129 Rita Ave, Springfield, IL 62703 USA *Tel* 217-753-3601.
TL English. **SL** French. **UDC** agriculture, banking/finance, business, construction machinery (dozers, graders, scrapers, etc), education, engineering (mechanical, industrial), geography, history, literature (all areas), patents/trademarks, theater.
Affil St Mary-of-the-Woods College. **Memb** ATA.

McALLISTER, KEVIN J Geology, Univ of Texas, Austin, TX 78712 USA *Tel* 512-477-0341.
TL English. **SL** French, German, Italian, Russian, Spanish. **UDC** crystallography, ecology, mineralogy, paleontology, sciences (earth, natural).
Memb TRACT.

McCARTHY, MICHAEL HUGH PATRICK 209 Stafford Rd, Caterham, Surrey, UK *Tel* Caterham 47602.
TL English. **SL** French, German, Russian. **UDC** engineering (civil), iron/steel industry, music, patents/trademarks, technology (glass).
Russian Kh S Kushnaryan: "Problems of the History and Theory of Armenian Monodic Music" (pending).
Memb TG.

McCONNAUGHEY, WILLIAM B 1653 Fairmount Blvd, Eugene, OR 97405 USA *Tel* 503-345-0227.
TL English. **SL** Russian. **UDC** biophysics, geophysics, meteorology, oceanography, physics, technology.
Russian V S Sobolev & Yu M Shkavlet: "Contact and Shielded Transducers" (pending). L G Koreneva et al: "Molecular Crystals in Nonlinear Optics" (pending). I N Uspenskii & A A Mel'nikov: "Design of Automobile Suspensions" (pending). P M Kopylov & A N Tachkov: "Television and Holography" (pending).
Accred/Memb ATA.

McGEE, LILIANE I 6 North St, Wilmington, MA 01887 USA *Tel* 617-658-8003.
TL English. **SL** French, Spanish. **UDC** automotive, banking/finance, biochemistry, building, commerce, communications, computers, data processing, electronics, engineering (all areas), fuel, graphics, insurance, iron/steel industry, law (international), legislation, machine tools, metallurgy, paper/pulp, petroleum, public administration, telecommunications, transportation, welding.
Memb ATA.

McGHEE, JOHN EDWARD 2224 W Westport Rd, Peoria, IL 61614 USA *Tel* 309-685-0920.
TL English. **SL** French. **UDC** agriculture, biochemistry, biology, chemistry, ecology, education, engineering (chemical, industrial), food/nutrition, government, music, plastics, sciences (applied).
Author of numerous articles and reports for industrial and scientific societies and research centers.
Memb ATA.

McGLOTHLIN, WILLIAM O 717A Old County Rd, Belmont, CA 94002 USA *Tel* 415-591-2875.
TL English. **SL** Russian. **UDC** aeronautics, aviation, linguistics, medicine.
Russian Vladimir I Gorelov: "Chinese Grammar" (pending).
Accred Stanford Univ. **Memb** ATA.

McINDOO, TIMOTHY QUINN 1640 N Fourth St, Sheboygan, WI 53081 USA *Tel* 414-452-9078.
TL English. **SL** German. **UDC** engineering (mechanical), literature (poetry, prose), photography.
Memb ALTA, ATA, TRACT.

McINTYRE, JOHN Witts Park 8, D-2000 Hamburg 55, West Germany *Tel* (040) 86 74 81.
TL English. **SL** Danish, French, German, Italian. **UDC** aeronautics, aviation, chemistry, engineering (chemical, electrical, mechanical), patents/trademarks, physics/mechanics, plastic, sciences (applied, natural), welding.
Memb TG.

McMATH, A E L E 11 "The Glebe," Penshurst, Tonbridge, Kent TNL 18DR, UK *Tel* (0892) 870 641.
TL French. **SL** English. **UDC** agriculture, chemistry (analytical), biochemistry, biomedicine, consumer goods, food.
English I Smith & J G Feinberg: *Paper and Thin-layer Chromatography and Electrophoresis* (Shandon Scientific Instruments, 1967).
Accred Aslib (specialist translator). **Memb** CBTIP.

McMILLAN, E NORMAN 1161 New Hampshire Ave NW #1009, Washington, DC 20037 USA *Tel* 202-659-2390.
TL English. **SL** Dutch, French, German, Portuguese, Spanish. **UDC** agriculture, banking/finance, economics, fisheries, forestry, industry, law, legislation, mining, petroleum, philately, sciences (earth), stockbreeding, transportation.
French Danica Seleskovitch: *Interpreting for International Conferences,* with Stephanie Daily (Pen & Booth, 1978).
Affil World Bank. **Memb** ATA, TAALS.

McQUISTON, HENRY 159 Clapboard Ridge, Danbury, CT 06810 USA *Tel* 203-792-2483.
TL English. **SL** French, Russian. **UDC** aeronautics, agriculture, architecture, automotive, aviation, biochemistry, biomedicine, chemistry, computers, cybernetics, economics, education, engineering (chemical, civil, electrical, industrial, mechanical), epidemiology, fuel, genetics, geography, industry, iron/steel industry, law (international), legislation, literature (history), medicine, metallurgy, missiles, paper/pulp, patents/trademarks, petroleum, pharmacology, plastics, psychiatry, public health, sciences (all areas), sociology, statistics, technology, transportation.
Russian V V Novozhilov: *Problems of Cost-Benefit Analysis in Optimal Planning* (International Arts & Sciences, 1970). B M Remennikov: *Economic Problems of Higher Education in the USSR* (International Arts &

Sciences, 1969). V N Nikiforov: "Soviet Historians on Problems of China" (pending). Also over 800 journal articles in the technical, social, and life sciences.

MADDY, MALCOLM C 6532 Coppersmith Rd, Sylvania, OH 43560 USA *Tel* 419-882-0787.
TL English. **SL** French, German, Russian. **UDC** computers, data processing, electronics. **Memb** ATA.

MANSTEAD, JENNIFER 33A Belitha Villas, Islington, London N1, UK *Tel* (01) 607 8195.
TL English. **SL** French, Italian, Rumanian. **UDC** art, business, commerce, economics, engineering (civil), government, law, linguistics, literature (children's, criticism, prose), machine tools, medicine, petroleum, political economy, sciences (nuclear), theater.
Memb TG.

MARCINIK, ROGER L 1456A Chanute Pl, Washington, DC 20336 USA *Tel* 202-563-6061.
TL English. **SL** Russian. **UDC** aviation, commerce, communications, computers, cybernetics, data processing, documentation, ecology, economics, education, geography, government, history, information science, law (international), metaphysics, military science, missiles, philosophy, political economy/science, psychology, public administration, sciences (applied), sociology, technology, telecommunications.
Memb ATA.

MARSH, ALAN 28 Templar Way, Rothley, Leicester, UK *Tel* (0533) 374 197.
TL English. **SL** French. **UDC** engineering (electrical, mechanical).
Memb TG.

MARTIN, JOAN 2641 S Enchanted Hills Dr, Tucson, AZ 85713 USA *Tel* 602-624-6517.
TL English. **SL** German, Russian. **UDC** history, linguistics, sciences (general, medical).
Memb ATA.

MARZOLLINI, PAULINE 1130 Brookview #34, Toledo, OH 43615 USA *Tel* 419-385-0122.
TL English. **SL** Spanish. **UDC** banking/finance, commerce, industry, insurance.
Memb ATA.

MAY, JOHN ERIC Morton-Towers-South #864, 1500 Bay Rd, Miami Beach, FL 33139 USA *Tel* 305-672-1062, 1179.
TL English. **SL** French, German, Italian, Portuguese, Spanish. **UDC** art, banking/finance, commerce, documentation, economics, education, geography, government, history, linguistics/philology, political economy/science, psychology, public health, sociology, taxation, theater.
Memb ATA, SFL.

MAYER, E O 8 rue de la Liberté, B-4840 Welkenraedt, Belgium *Tel* (0032) 87 88 2005.
TL & SL English & German. **UDC** business, commerce, communications, economics, engineering (mechanical), shipping, transportation.
Memb CBTIP.

MECKLENBURG, SUE ANN 613 Woodhaven, Richardson, TX 75081 USA *Tel* 214-690-4666; 243-2321.
TL English. **SL** German. **UDC** banking/finance, building, business, documentation, education, law, medicine, public administration.
Memb ATA.

MEGALLI, ISKANDER Y 5203 Dover Pl, Alexandria, VA 22311 USA *Tel* 703-931-6168; 202-676-0238.
TL Arabic, English. **SL** French. **UDC** aeronautics, agriculture, art, automotive, aviation, banking/finance, commerce, dairy farming, economics, education, fisheries, food/nutrition, forestry, geography, government, history, horticulture, iron/steel industry, law (international), legislation, linguistics/philology, literature (children's, criticism, drama, history, prose, science fiction), military science, mining, mineralogy, petroleum, political science, public administration, sciences (medical, natural), social services, statistics, theater, transportation.
Affil World Bank.

MERRICK, HUGH 22 Empire House, London SW7 2RU, UK *Tel* (01) 584 2098.
TL English. **SL** French, German. **UDC** mountaineering, travel.
German Heinrich Harrer: *The White Spider* (Rupert Hart Davis, 1959). Kurt Diemberger: *Summits and Secrets* (Allen & Unwin, 1971). Hermann Buhl: *Narga Parbat Pilgrimage* (Hodder & Stoughton, 1956). Gunther Oskar Dyhrenfurth: *To the Third Pole* (Werner Laurie, 1955).
Memb TA.

MEYER, R G 19 Withenfield Rd, Manchester M23 9BT, UK *Tel* (061) 998 5622.
TL English. **SL** German. **UDC** engineering (mechanical), law, music, plastics/polymers, sciences (applied), technology, textiles.
Memb TG.

MIKKELSON, HOLLY 230 Carmel Ave, Marina, CA 93933 USA *Tel* 408-384-5909.
TL English. **SL** Spanish. **UDC** agriculture, banking/finance, commerce, economics, education, fisheries, government, iron/steel industry, medicine, military science, mining, petroleum, political economy/science, public health, social sciences, sociology.
Spanish Julio Yao; "The Panama Canal: The Cross a Nation Must Bear" (pending).
Affil Monterey Inst of Foreign Studies. **Memb** ATA, NCTA.

MILLER, CHARLES JOHN Box 23019, S-400 73 Gothenburg, 23, Sweden *Tel* (031) 87 59 20; 59 23 82.
TL English. **SL** Swedish. **UDC** business, engineering (industrial), law, shipping, theology.
Memb TG.

MILNE, MARGO 10 Cranfield Ave, San Carlos, CA 94070 USA *Tel* 415-591-8140.
TL English. **SL** French. **UDC** commerce, engineering (civil, hydraulic), literature, medicine, music, railroad technology, sciences (earth), viniculture.
Memb NCTA.

MISH, JOHN L 64 Sagamore Rd, Bronxville, NY 10708 USA *Tel* 914-337-0819.
TL English. **SL** Chinese, Polish. **UDC** biochemistry, biology, biomedicine, chemistry, history, linguistics/philology, microbiology, patents/trademarks, pharmacology.
Chinese S J Aleni: *Creating an Image of Europe for China* (Monumenta Serica, 1964). Also hundreds of scientific articles translated from German, Dutch, Swedish, Norwegian, Danish, Icelandic, French, Italian, Spanish, Portuguese, Catalan, Rumanian, Latin, Russian, Polish, Czech, Slovak, Bulgarian, modern Greek, Finnish, Turkish, Chinese, Japanese, Manchu, Indonesian, Arabic, and Hindi into German, Polish, French, Italian, Spanish, Latin, Welsh, Basque. **Author of** "A Manchu Scroll in The New York Public Library" (*Bulletin of The New York Public Library*, 52 no. 2, 1948). "The Transcription of Oriental Languages in Chemical Literature" (*Chemical Literature*, 1954). "The World as Language," in *The World of Translation* (PEN Amer Center, 1971), numerous others. Supplement of reading and vocabulary to H A Jäschke: *Tibetan Grammar* (Ungar, 1954). Supplement of modern words and new meanings to John Wortabet, Harvey Porter, eds: *English-Arabic and Arabic-English Dictionary* (Ungar, 1954).
Affil The New York Public Library (Oriental div).

MISHELEVICH, BENJAMIN 6346 Caton St, Pittsburgh, PA 15217 USA *Tel* 412-521-3447.
TL Russian. **SL** English. **UDC** agriculture, automotive, chemistry, communications, computers, cybernetics, economics, electronics, engineering (all areas), fuel, government, horticulture, industry, information science, iron/steel industry, machine tools, metallurgy, mineralogy, mining, patents, petroleum, physics, railroad technology, sciences (applied), shipping, standards, technology, transportation.
Affil Carnegie-Mellon Univ (Translation Workshop). **Memb** APT.

MITCHELL, ANNMARIE DORWART 2509 Stuart St #1, Berkeley, CA 94705 USA *Tel* 415-843-5875.
TL English. **SL** Polish. **UDC** aviation, banking/finance, commerce, economics, education, engineering (airport/aircraft), geography, history, industry, library science, linguistics, meteorology, navigation, political economy/science, technology, transportation.
Accred/Memb ATA. **Affil** Univ of California Library.

MITCHELL, IRENE E 1705 Dale Ct, Fort Collins, CO 80521 USA *Tel* 303-493-7527.
TL English. **SL** German. **UDC** cement manufacture, coal mining, commerce, industry, insurance, mining, printing, sugar beet technology, transportation.
Accred/Memb ATA.

MITTAL, SHRI CHAND CRS, JNU, New Delhi-57, India
TL English. **SL** Hindi, Russian. **UDC** computers, sciences (natural), statistics.
Russian *Problems of Physico-Biogeographic Regionalization of Polar Land* (Amerind, 1979–80). *Scientific Elements of Nature Conservation*

(Amerind, 1979–80). Also several booklets on electronic computers, trade treaties, others.
Affil Jawaharlal Nehru Univ. **Memb** ISTA.

MITTELMANN, GERTRUDE 7 Stoney Rd, Grundisburgh, Woodbridge IP13 6RA, Suffolk, UK *Tel* 047335 502.
TL English. **SL** Arabic, German. **UDC** anthropology, archeology, art, arts/crafts, commerce, economics, education, ethics, graphics, history, literature (children's, folklore), printing, public health, social sciences, sculpture, sociology.
Arabic *The Bird of the Golden Feather* (G Bell, 1969). "Stories from Arab Lands" (4 programs for BBC Jackanory, 1978).
Accred/Memb TG.

MONTENEGRO, MARIO A 3000 Spout Run Pkwy, Arlington, VA 22201 USA *Tel* 703-524-5875.
TL Spanish. **SL** English. **UDC** agriculture, banking/finance, commerce, communications, cybernetics, ecology, economics, education, energy, fisheries, history, human resources, law (international), meteorology, military science, mining, oceanography, petroleum, photography, political science, technology, telecommunications, transportation.
Memb ASI.

MONTERO, BLASS A 24 Mott St, Newark, NJ 07105 USA
TL English. **SL** Portuguese, Spanish. **UDC** electronics, journalism.

MONTERO, SERTORIO SANCHEZ Gregorio V Gelatti 2109, Fraccionamiento FL, Monterey, Nuevo Léon, Mexico. *Tel* 58 79 68.
TL & SL English & Spanish. **UDC** electronics, history, human resources, industry, literature (history, prose), machine tools, metallurgy, metaphysics, soccer, sociology, transportation, welding.
Memb ATA.

MOORE, WOODROW Foreign Languages, Old Dominion Univ, Norfolk, VA 23508 USA *Tel* 703-423-5810.
TL & SL English & Spanish. **UDC** anthropology, art, commerce, communications, documentation, economics, education, ethics, food/nutrition, geography, government, history, human resources, industry, iron/steel industry, law (international, maritime, property), legislation, linguistics/philology, literature (all areas), medicine, music, paper/pulp, political economy/science, public health, religion, shipping, sociology, telecommunications.

MORALES, RUDOLPH M 7336 Player Dr, San Diego, CA 92119 USA *Tel* 714-460-1054; 462-6131.
TL & SL English & Spanish. **UDC** banking/finance, commerce, communications, economics, education, engineering (civil), government, history, industry, insurance, jurisprudence, law (international, property), legislation, linguistics/philology, literature (drama, folklore, history, prose), philosophy, political economy/science, religion, sociology, theology.
Memb ATA.

MOREAU, JEAN J M Bruyère-Ste-Anne 7, B-1300 Wavre, Belgium *Tel* (010) 22 38 89.
TL Dutch, French. **SL** English. **UDC** bacteriology, biochemistry, food/nutrition, medicine, microbiology, sciences (medical, natural).
Memb CBTIP.

MOREHOUSE, KEITH H PO Box 1172, Plymouth, MA 02360 USA *Tel* 617-746-7107.
TL English. **SL** German. **UDC** anthropology, art, aviation, biology, ethnography, literature (criticism, drama, history, poetry), microbiology, military science, railroad technology, sciences (life, social), transportation.
Memb ATA, NETA.

MORIN, ROLAND 6160 Monkland, Montreal, PQ Canada *Tel* 514-488-8833.
TL & SL English & French. **UDC** labor relations' law.
English Pierre Berton: *The Smug Minority* (Du Jour, 1967). **French** *Defensive Driving* (McGraw-Hill, 1966).
Memb ATIO.

MURRAY, STEVEN T 4241 Gilbert St, Oakland, CA 94611 USA *Tel* 415-653-7372.
TL English. **SL** Danish, Dutch, German, Norwegian, Swedish. **UDC** chemistry, crystallography, ecology, engineering (industrial), genealogy, geography, geophysics, graphics, history, industry, literature (prose, science fiction), metallurgy, mineralogy, mining, music, paper/pulp, patents/trademarks, philately, physics, printing, publishing, sciences (natural), shipping, viniculture.
Norwegian Jon Bing & Tor Age Bringsvaerd: Included in *The Best from the Rest of the World* (Doubleday/DAW, 1976).
Memb ATA.

MYERS, GERALD D 6 Bet Zayit, 90 815 Israel *Tel* (02) 527 953.
TL English. **SL** Hebrew, Russian. **UDC** engineering (electrical, nuclear).
Russian O V Ol'shevskii, ed: *Long-Distance Power Transmission—Parameters and Transients* (IPST, 1969). S A Sovalov: *Operating Conditions of the 500-kv Lines of the Unified Power System in the European USSR* (IPST, 1970). N N Tikhodeev, ed: *D-C and A-C Power Transmission* (IPST, 1970). D I Broder, K K Popkov, S M Rubanov: *Biological Shielding of Maritime Reactors* (IPST, 1970).

MYRANTS, G Lexique, Ltd, 54 Hillbury Ave, Harrow, Middlesex, UK *Tel* (01) 907 6066.
TL English. **SL** German. **UDC** copyright, law, legislation, patents/trademarks.
German E Berkenfeld: Chapter in *World Patent Litigation* (Bureau of National Affairs, 1967).
Memb TG.

NACLERIO, GUS 2866 E 197 St, Bronx, New York, NY 10461 USA *Tel* 212-822-1989.
TL English. **SL** French, Italian, Spanish. **UDC** architecture, automotive, aviation, building/construction, commerce, communications, computers, data processing, economics, electronics, engineering (electrical, hydraulic, industrial, mechanical), history, industry, information science, insurance, iron/steel industry, law (international, property), legislation, machine tools, meteorology, military science, mineralogy, mining, patents/trademarks, public administration, public health, railroad technology, sports (soccer), technology, telecommunications, transportation.
Memb ATA.

NARDONE, GERMANO Viale Giustiniano Imperatore 76, I-00145 Rome, Italy *Tel* (06) 51 39 753.
TL Italian. **SL** English. **UDC** business, law, medicine, taxation.
Memb AITI, TG.

NASH, CLAUDE W 2 Vernon St, Medford, MA 02155 USA *Tel* 617-395-0900.
TL English. **SL** German. **UDC** most scientific and technical fields.
German Armin Hermann: *The Genesis of Quantum Theory* (MIT, 1971).
Affil The Translation Center (dir). **Memb** ATA.

NEEDLES, ROBERT C Chemagro Agricultural Div, Mobay Chemical Corp, PO Box 4913, Kansas City, MO 64120 USA *Tel* 816-242-2238.
TL English. **SL** German. **UDC** agriculture, agrochemicals, bacteriology, biochemistry, biology, botany, chemistry, data processing, documentation, ecology, engineering (chemical), entomology, microbiology, zoology.
Memb ATA.

NEIDEN, MARIA 2683 West St, James Parkway, Cleveland Heights, OH 44106 USA *Tel* 216-321-0236; 771-4800.
TL English. **SL** French, German, Spanish. **UDC** automotive, aviation, banking/finance, building/construction, commerce, documentation, economics, engineering (electrical, hydraulic, industrial, marine), fuel, industry, iron/steel industry, law (international, property), machine tools, material handling, metallurgy, mining, paper/pulp, patents/trademarks, plastics, railroad technology, shipping, technology, transportation.
Accred ATA. **Memb** ATA, NOTA.

NEKRASSOFF, VLADIMIR N 1218 Meadowlands Dr E #608, Ottawa ON K2E 6K1, Canada *Tel* 613-225-5307.
TL English. **SL** German. **UDC** animal behavior, biochemistry, biology, biomedicine, chemistry, ecology, entomology, genetics, medicine, microbiology, parasitology, psychiatry, veterinary medicine, zoology.
German Harri Juenger: *The Literatures of the Soviet Peoples* (Ungar, 1970). G F Klostermann et al: *Color Atlas of External Manifestations of Disease* (McGraw-Hill, 1964).
Memb ATA, ATIO, VDÜ.

NIEBAUER, JOHN J, JR 305 Tetra Ct, Glen Burnie, MD 21061 USA *Tel* 301-789-2420.
TL English. **SL** German, Russian. **UDC** automotive, cybernetics, economics, military science, psychology, sociology, statistics
Memb ATA.

NIJK, HENRY G 15 Rechov Achimeir, Ramat Gan, Israel *Tel* (03) 799 946.

TL & SL Dutch & English. **UDC** archeology, art, commerce, communications, history, literature (history, prose), political science, psychology, religion, sociology.

English Charles R Boxer: *The Dutch in Brazil, 1624-1654* (Sijthoff, 1977). Edward S Gilfillan, Jr: *Migration to the Stars* (Manteau, 1976). Robert Blake & Jane Mouton: *The New Managerial Grid* (Samson, 1979). Paul Watzlawick: *The Language of Change* (Van Loghum Slaterus, 1978). Also the works of Ann Roth, Rabbi S de Vries.

NOËL, PHILIPPE, 3 rue Rouge, B-1180 Brussels, Belgium *Tel* (02) 375 35 84; 734 62 94.

TL French. **SL** English, Italian. **UDC** aeronautics, agriculture, automotive (road vehicles, equipment, etc), building/construction, engineering (all areas), iron/steel industry, metallurgy, petroleum, railroads, transportation.

Affil Talex SA (head, translation dept). **Memb** CBTIP.

NOWAK, ELIZABETH V 27668 Bennett, Livonia, MI 48152 USA *Tel* 313-549-3850.

TL English. **SL** French, Polish. **UDC** most areas of literature, the sciences and technologies.

Polish Julian Aleksandrowicz; *Perspectives of Ecological Prophylaxis of Leukemia* (Scientific Information Center, Warsaw).

Affil National Instit of Health, National Library of Medicine. **Memb** ATA.

NUÑEZ, BENJAMIN 315 Seventh St NE, Washington, DC 20002 USA *Tel* 202-543-5577.

TL & SL English, Portuguese, Spanish. **UDC** Abro-Braziliana, Afro-Latin America, Indian-Latin America, Latin-America, Portuguese African civilization, technical, scientific, and literary translation.

O'BRYAN, THOMAS R Rte 2, PO Box 205-B2, Nokesville, VA 22123 USA *Tel* 703-754-8933.

TL English. **SL** Indonesian, Malay. **UDC** general and technical subjects.

Indonesian Sarimin Reksodihardjo: *Report on the Lesser Sundas, Indonesia, 1952-1957* (JPRS, 1960). Hasan Muhammad Tiro: *Democracy for Indonesia* (JPRS, 1960). Dipa Nusantara Aidit: *Selected Works,* Vol I (JPRS, 1961). Abdul Haris Nasution: *The Indonesian National Army,* Vol I (JPRS, 1963).

Memb ATA.

ODIAUX, PAULE 16 Everett St, Derry, NH 03038 USA *Tel* 603-434-6631.

TL French. **SL** English. **UDC** accounting, banking/finance, building/construction, commerce, computers, data processing, electronics, geography, industry, law (business), printing, science (natural), technology.

Accred/Memb ATA.

O'GRADY (FREEMAN), LORRAINE 463 West St #A625, New York, NY 10014 USA *Tel* 212-989-2828.

TL English. **SL** French, Spanish. **UDC** aesthetics, anthropology, archeology, architecture, art/art history, banking/finance, choreography, commerce, communications, ecology, economics, education, engineering (civil, mechanical), ethnography, government, graphics, history, jurisprudence, law, literature (all areas), machine tools, metaphysics, music, occultism, painting, philosophy, political economy/science, psychiatry, psychology, public administration, religion, sculpture, sociology, theater, theology.

French Jacques Bergier: *Extra-Terrestrial Visitations from Prehistoric Times to the Present* (Henry Regnery, 1973). **Spanish** José Donoso: *This Sunday* (Knopf, 1967). Also the works of Federico Fellini, Alain Robbe-Grillet, Tristan Tzara, and numerous contributions to *Encyclopaedia Britannica* from Spanish, French, Italian, and Portuguese.

Affil School of Visual Arts. **Memb** ALTA.

OLECHNO, GILLIAN 5862 S Orlando Ave, Los Angeles, CA 90056 USA *Tel* 213-226-7006; 295-3495.

TL English. **SL** French. **UDC** library science, medicine, public health.

Affil Univ of Southern California Med Center. **Memb** ATA (Southern California chapter).

OLECHNO-HUSZCZA, CZESLAW 5862 S Orlando Ave, Los Angeles, CA 90056 USA *Tel* 213-295-3495.

TL English. **SL** Latin, Polish, Russian. **UDC** engineering (electronic), linguistics, literature, medicine.

Polish T Bielecki: *Warsaw Aflame* (Polamerica, 1973). C Banasiewicz: *The Warsaw Ghetto* (Yoseloff, 1968).

Affil Loyola-Marymount Univ. **Memb** ATA.

ORDÁS, RUTH HAGLUND 1520 38 St, Sacramento, CA 95816 USA *Tel* 916-456-5500.

TL English. **SL** Portuguese, Spanish. **UDC** business, food/nutrition, heraldry, history, human resources, law, literature (children's, criticism, drama, folklore, history, prose), medicine, sociology, theater, women's movement.

Memb ATA.

ORDISH, GEORGE 178 London Rd, St Albans, Herts ALL 1PL, UK *Tel* London (76) 57475.

TL English. **SL** French, Portuguese, Spanish. **UDC** agriculture (tropical), crop pest control, Latin American development, pre-Columbian history.

French Alfred Métraux: *The History of the Incas* (Pantheon, 1969). Rémy Chauvin: *The World of Ants* (Gollancz, 1970). R Armand, R Lattès, J Lesourne: *The Management Revolution* (MacDonald, 1972). **Spanish** José María Tey: *Hong Kong to Barcelona in the Junk "Rubia"* (Harrap, 1959). Also the works of R Callois.

Memb TA.

ORDISH, OLIVE 178 London Rd, St Albans, Herts, UK *Tel* St Albans 57475.

TL English. **SL** Dutch, French, German, Italian. **UDC** aesthetics, agriculture, archeology, architecture, art, bacteriology, biology, biomedicine, dairy farming, entomology, genealogy, heraldry, history, literature (all areas), painting, paleontology, poultry farming, sciences (life, natural), stockbreeding, theater, viniculture, zoology.

Dutch B H Slicher van Bath: *The Agrarian History of Western Europe* (Edward Arnold, 1963). W J Hansch, ed: *Drugs; Pollution* (Longman, 1974). **German** Reinhard Bentmann & H Lickes: *European Palaces* (Mondadori/Cassells, 1978). **Italian** Paolo Monelli et al: *La Belle Epoque* (Morrow, 1978). Also numerous technical, scientific, administrative papers for government ministries.

ORENSTEIN, HAROLD STEVEN 3201 Landover St #1504, Alexandria, VA 22305 USA *Tel* 703-548-9821.

TL English. **SL** French, Polish, Russian. **UDC** art history, bacteriology, biochemistry, biology, biomedicine, chemistry, crystallography, education, epidemiology, genetics, linguistics/philology, literature (criticism, drama, prose), medicine, microbiology, military science, music, parasitology, plastics, railroad technology, sciences (life, medical, natural), shipping, theater, transportation, veterinary medicine, zoology.

Affil Library of Congress (Federal Research div).

O'SULLIVAN, ANNA MAE 9709 SW Quail Post Rd, Portland, OR 97219 USA *Tel* 503-244-6241; 297-2287.

TL English. **SL** French. **UDC** commerce, communications, data processing, documentation, education, electronics, industry, library science, literature (children's, poetry, prose, songs), recreation/games, religion, technology, telecommunications.

Affil Portland School of Tutoring and Languages. **Memb** ATA.

PAISLEY, H P 15 Eleven Acre Rise, Loughton, Essex IG10 1AN, UK *Tel* (01) 508-6105.

TL English. **SL** French, German. **UDC** banking/finance, commerce, economics, insurance, law (international, maritime, property), legislation, patents/trademarks, shipping, taxation.

Memb TG.

PARISI, ASSUNTA M Adria/Warren-Teed Laboratories, PO Box 16529, Columbus, OH 43229 USA *Tel* 614-889-1300.

TL English. **SL** French, Italian. **UDC** medicine, patents/trademarks.

Memb ATA.

PATTERSON, LARRY 5501 Luckpenny Pl, Columbia, MD 21045 USA *Tel* 301-730-6713.

TL English. **SL** Russian. **UDC** aviation, business, economics, government, history, law, literature (prose), military science, political science, psychology, public administration, sociology.

Russian the works of V Davidov, Anatoliy Ivashchenko, O A Kunayev, A Mikoyan, numerous others.

Memb ATA.

PATTERSON, LIA MAY 5919 Provost Ave, Montgomery, AL 36116 USA *Tel* 205-284-2639.

TL English. **SL** French, Portuguese, Spanish. **UDC** aeronautics, Air Force, astronautics,

aviation, communications, computers, data processing, engineering (aerospace), geography, geophysics, government, law, missiles/rocketry, railroad technology, telecommunications, transportation.
Memb AIT.

PAUL, DAVID MEL & MARGARETA 4912 W St NW, Washington, DC 20007 USA *Tel* 202-337-2575.
TL English. **SL** Swedish. **UDC** agriculture, biology, literature, microbiology.
Swedish Rolf Edberg; *At the Foot of the Tree* (Univ of Alabama, 1974). Per C Jersild: *The Animal Doctor* (Pantheon, 1975). Karl Erik Lagerlöf, ed: *Contemporary Swedish Prose* (Univ of Minnesota, 1979). Also the works of Per Olof Enquist, Mats Odeen, Arne Sand.
Memb ATA.

PAUWELS, PASCAL Wilgengaarde 10, B-1720 Groot-Bijgaarden, Belgium *Tel* (02) 465 09 67; 218 04 00.
TL Dutch, French. **SL** English, German. **UDC** banking, business, insurance, skin and scuba diving.
Memb CBTIP.

PEARCY, RALPH 1900 S Eads St #412, Arlington, VA 22202 USA *Tel* 703-521-4355.
TL English. **SL** French, German, Italian, Japanese, Spanish. **UDC** biochemistry, biophysics, chemistry, computers, data processing, electronics, literature (science fiction), medicine, metallurgy, microbiology, patents/trademarks, physiology, textiles.
Memb ATA.

PELZ, THEODOR 17 Kidron St, Haifa, Israel *Tel* (00972) 4 252217.
TL English, German. **SL** Dutch, French, German, Hebrew, Italian, Norwegian, Russian, Spanish. **UDC** aeronautics, building/construction, engineering (aerospace, civil, electrical, hydraulic, industrial, marine, mechanical), industry, military science, missiles/rocketry, navigation, physics/mechanics, railroad technology, shipbuilding, shipping, technology, transportation.
Russian Pisarenko, Rudenko, Tret'yachenko, Troshchenko: *High-Temperature Strength of Materials* (IPST, 1969). Bartenev & Zelenev, eds: *Relaxation Phenomena in Polymers* (John Wiley/Keter, 1974). Ogibalov, Malinin, Netrebko, Kishkin: *Structural Polymers—Testing Methods*, Vol I (John Wiley/Keter, 1973). A N Goncharov: *Hydropower Stations—Generating Equipment and Its Installation* (IPST, 1975). Also numerous articles and reports on science and technology.

PEMBERTON, ANNE ELISE 28 Great Brownings, College Rd, London SE21 7HP, UK *Tel* (01) 670 9860.
TL English. **SL** French, Italian, Spanish. **UDC** commerce, insurance.
Accred/Memb TG.

PEÑA, VICKY 100 Hoyt St #3K, Stamford, CT 06905 USA *Tel* 203-327-1026.
TL & SL English & Spanish. **UDC** arts, banking/finance, commerce, communications, education, government, history, human re-sources, literature (prose), political science, religion, sociology, telecommunications, theology.
Memb ATA.

PENNINCKX, WILLY Ringlaan 29, B-1980 Tervuren, Belgium *Tel* (02) 767 76 50.
TL Dutch. **SL** English, French, German, Italian. **UDC** agriculture, banking/finance, commerce, economics, public administration.
Affil Commission of the EEC, Brussels.

PETROV, GEORGE R 915 E St SE, Washington, DC 20003 USA *Tel* 202-547-2909.
TL English. **SL** French, Russian. **UDC** art, biomedicine, commerce, engineering (hydraulic, industrial, mechanical), geography, history, iron/steel industry, literature (prose, science fiction), machine tools, medicine, patents/trademarks, political science, theater.
Russian Konstantin Rudnitsky: *Meyerhold the Director* (Ardis, 1979). Gaito Gasdanov: *An Evening with Claire* (Ardis, forthcoming). Also numerous technical and medical articles, specifications, commercial and legal documents.

PICK, WOLFGANG Nafsikas 16, Corfu-Kanoni, Greece.
TL English, German. **SL** Greek. **UDC** agriculture, archeology, architecture, art, commerce, communications, economics, education, ethnography, history, horticulture, industry, linguistics/philology, literature (all areas), paleontology, philosophy, political economy/science, religion, sculpture, sociology, sports, statistics, theater, theology.

PIERSON, G 16 rue Beaurepaire, F-75010 Paris, France *Tel* (33) 1 208 86 32.
TL French. **SL** Chinese, English, German, Russian. **UDC** agriculture, biochemistry, biology, biomedicine, botany, chemistry, documentation, engineering (chemical), food/nutrition, genetics, horticulture, information science, library science, linguistics/philology, patents/trademarks, photography, plastics, poultry farming, sciences (life, medical, natural).
Affil Centre de Préparation Documentarie à la Traduction (CPDT). **Memb** SFT.

PINTOCOELHO, L C 8600 Lancaster Dr, Bethesda, MD 20014 USA *Tel* 301-986-1866.
TL Portuguese **SL** English, French, Spanish. **UDC** economics, education, meteorology, navigation, oceanography, sailing, science (applied, social).
Affil OAS. **Memb** AIT.

PLATT, JEANETTE 114 N Russel, Mt Prospect, IL 60056 USA
TL English. **SL** Russian. **UDC** industry.
Memb ATA.

PLATZ, ANNA E (Mrs Adolph) 513 Gardiner Rd, Richmond, VA 23229 USA *Tel* 804-285-1010.
TL English. **SL** German, Spanish. **UDC** bacteriology, biochemistry, biomedicine, chemistry, epidemiology, medicine, microbiology, parasitology, pharmaceutics, pharmacology, veterinary medicine.

Accred/Memb ATA. **Affil** Randolph-Macon College.

POCH, WALDEMAR J 19 Cranbury Neck Rd, Cranbury, NJ 08512 USA *Tel* 609-395-1880.
TL English. **SL** Russian. **UDC** communications, electronics, television technology.
Memb ATA.

POLACEK, JIRI Kiriat Bialik-Sabinia, Rechov Hazajit 13, Kiriat Bialik, Israel *Tel* (04) 710 741.
TL & SL English & German. **UDC** agriculture, biochemistry, biology, botany, dairy farming, ecology, forestry, horticulture, machine tools, metallurgy, soil science, viniculture.
Affil Technion (Israel Inst of Technology).

PONTICAS, EFTHYMIAS G 2520 Maryland Ave, Baltimore, MD 21218 USA *Tel* 301-467-4373; 823-1080.
TL & SL English & Greek. **UDC** court interpreting, depositions, immigration services, insurance, marine accidents.

PRADA, ALFREDO 5556 Broadview Rd 3105, Parma, OH 44134 USA *Tel* 216-398-7630.
TL English. **SL** Spanish. **UDC** computers, cybernetics, data processing, engineering (chemical).
Memb ATA, NOTA.

PRIEST, PETER F H Rose-Hulman Inst of Technology, Terre Haute, IN 47803 USA *Tel* 812-877-1511.
TL English. **SL** Russian. **UDC** cybernetics, data processing, documentation, electronics, engineering (electrical, industrial), information science, linguistics, patents/trademarks, photography, physics/mechanics, plastics/polymers, standards.
Accred/Memb ATA.

QUIÑONES, MELVYN O 455 Arlington St, San Francisco, CA 94131 USA *Tel* 415-584-3685.
TL English. **SL** Portuguese, Spanish. **UDC** business, food/nutrition, history, government, law, legislation, literature (prose), machine shop, ships.
Memb ATA.

RACE, CHUMSRI PO Box 2, Rangsit, Thailand *Tel* Bangkok 523-7768.
TL & SL English & Thai. **UDC** aesthetics, agriculture, art, banking/finance, commerce, communications, documentation, ecology, economics, education, fisheries, food/nutrition, forestry, geography, geophysics, government, history, human resources, information science, literature (all areas), petroleum, political economy/science, public administration, sociology.
English John Holt: *Freedom and Beyond* (National Research Council of Thailand, 1977). *Bangkok Transportation Study* (German/Thai Governments, 1976). *Water for the Northeast* (Asian Inst of Technology, 1978).

RAIKHLIN-EISENKRAFT, BIANCA 71 Road of France, Haifa 35706, Israel *Tel* (0⁴) 534 514; 529 205.

TL English. SL French, German, Hebrew, Rumanian, Russian. UDC bacteriology, biochemistry, biology, biomedicine, chemistry, ecology, epidemiology, food/nutrition, medicine, pharmacology, sciences (life, medical), toxicology.

Russian P A Petrishcheva, ed: *Vectors of Diseases of Natural Foci* (IPST, 1965). A A Shlyk: *Metabolism of Chlorophyll in Green Plants* (IPST, 1970). A I Yanushevich: *Acclimatization of Animals in the USSR* (IPST, 1966). Also numerous articles, reports, abstracts.

Affil Israeli Poison Information Center.

RAÏNOF, ALEXANDRE Translation/Interpretation Program, Phelps Hall, Univ of California, Santa Barbara, CA 93106 USA *Tel* 805-961-3111; 213-394-8349.

TL English. SL French, Spanish. UDC aeronautics, aesthetics, agriculture, anthropology, athletics, automotive, banking/finance, building, business, ecology, economics, education, electronics, ethics, history, jurisprudence, law (international, maritime, property), legislation, literature (all areas), petroleum, political science/economy, psychology, solar energy, sports, theater.

Memb ATA, CCIA.

RAJKAY, LESLIE 2447 Pickwick Rd, Baltimore, MD 21207 USA *Tel* 301-448-2961.

TL English. SL French, German, Hungarian. UDC chemistry, engineering (chemical), iron/steel industry, medicine, metallurgy, patents/trademarks, sciences (applied).

Affil Bacon & Thomas (patent engineer). **Memb** ATA.

RAS, MANUEL F 163-07 21 Ave, Whitestone, NY 11357 USA *Tel* 212-352-8493.

TL English. SL Spanish. UDC agriculture, business, chemistry, commerce, communications, dentistry, economics, education, geography, government, history, industry, law, literature, machine tools, navigation, sports, statistics, viniculture.

Memb ASI, CITA.

RASTORFER, REN PO Box 45, New York, NY 10017 USA *Tel* 212-881-2323.

TL English. SL French, German, Spanish. UDC aeronautics, agriculture, astrophysics, automotive, aviation, banking/finance, chemistry, cinematography, commerce, communications, copyright, computers, data processing, economics, electronics, engineering (aerospace, chemical, electrical, mechanical), iron/steel industry, law, machine tools, metallurgy, mining, missiles/rocketry, paper/pulp, patents/trademarks, petroleum, photography, plastics/polymers, sciences (applied), taxation, technology, telecommunications.

Memb ATA.

READING-LECLERCQ, PATRICIA 7130 Chestnut St NW, Washington, DC 20012 USA *Tel* 202-291-3326.

TL English. SL French, Italian. UDC anthropology, dairy products and product standards, ecology (alternate energy sources, nuclear energy, pollution), economics, epidemiology, ethics/morals, ethnography, fisheries, food/nutrition, history, human resources, literature (criticism, folklore, history, poetry, science fiction), marketing, metaphysics, occultism, oenology, petroleum, pharmacology, philology (Romance), philosophy (Marxist), political economy, psychology, public health, sciences (applied), seismology, standards, theology (Roman Catholic), transportation, witchcraft, zoology.

French Jean-Louis Berlandier: *The Indians of Texas in 1830* (Smithsonian Inst/Random House, 1968).

REEDS, JAMES A 200 E 56 St, Kansas City, MO 64113 USA *Tel* 816-361-9221; 276-2261.

TL English. SL German. UDC acoustics, art history, chemistry, electronics, linguistics, metallurgy, phonetics.

Accred ATA. **Affil** General Linguistics Corp, Univ of Missouri. **Memb** ALTA, MICATA.

REES, ELIZABETH S PO Box 54, Pebble Beach, CA 93953 USA *Tel* 408-372-3917.

TL English. SL French. UDC architecture, arts, food, graphics.

Memb ATA.

REHMUS, E EDWARD c/o Haskew, PO Box 835, San Francisco, CA 94101 USA *Tel* 415-387-0896.

TL English. SL French, German, Spanish. UDC anthropology, astrology, bacteriology, biology, commerce, entomology, epidemiology, ethics, ethnography, genealogy, geography, history, linguistics/philology, literature (all areas), medicine, microbiology, occultism, philosophy, religion, theology, witchcraft, zoology.

REIS, DJALMA DOS Estrada do Dendê, 1295-B1 H Apto 203, CEP 21920 Rio de Janeiro, Brazil *Tel* 3-93-4912.

TL Portuguese. SL English. UDC chess, education, history, literature (prose), medicine, petroleum, recreation.

English Gooldman: *Electrocardiography* (Guanabara, 1977).

Memb ATA.

REISENBERGER, RAINER 5 Beer Cart Lane, Canterbury, Kent G1 2NY, UK *Tel* (0227) 53 004.

TL English. SL German. UDC computers, data processing, electronics, engineering (automotive, mechanical), machine tools, motorcycle technology.

Affil Technical Translation & Language Consultancy Service. **Memb** BDÜ, TG .

RIDLEY, CHARLES P 2780 Ross Rd, Palo Alto, CA 94303 USA *Tel* 415-328-7344.

TL English. SL Chinese, French, Japanese. UDC bacteriology, biochemistry, biology, biomedicine, chemistry, ecology, education, entomology, genetics, medicine, microbiology, oceanography, parasitology, pharmacology, political science, zoology.

Chinese C S Chen, ed: *Rural People's Communes in Lien-chiang* (Hoover Inst, 1969).

Memb ATA.

RINGER, WILLIAM CHARLES 1500 W Lake, Fort Collins, CO 80521 USA *Tel* 303-482-6540; 493-0436.

TL English. SL Russian. UDC biochemistry, chemistry, engineering (chemical, hydraulic), geophysics, palynology, paleobotany, plastics/polymers, stratigraphy.

Accred Defense Language Inst. **Affil** Foreign Resources Associates. **Memb** ATA, CTA.

RINGOLD, JEANNETTE K 380 Brandon Way, Menlo Park, CA 94025 USA *Tel* 415-328-2516.

TL English. SL Dutch, French. UDC aesthetics, art, arts/crafts, banking/finance, commerce, education, engineering (sanitary), food/nutrition, history, literature (children's, criticism, drama, history, prose), medicine, painting, psychiatry, psychology, public health, viniculture.

Accred/Memb ATA, NCTA.

RITTERSKAMP, MYRNA S 455 Main St, Oneonta, NY 13820 USA *Tel* 607-432-6304.

TL English. SL German. UDC medicine, patents/trademarks.

Affil Hartwick College. **Memb** ATA.

ROBINSON, EDWIN M 265 ave Defré, Boite 39, B-1180 Brussels, Belgium *Tel* (02) 374 96 15.

TL English. SL Dutch, French, German, Italian. UDC agriculture, business, copyright, economics, government, law (international), military science, music, philosophy, public administration, statistics.

Memb TG.

ROBINSON, HAROLD LANGMEAD Mews Cottage, 28 Reginald Rd. Bexhill-on-Sea, Sussex TN39 3PH, UK.

TL English SL French, German, Italian, Portuguese, Spanish. UDC economics, literature (prose), sociology, taxation.

German Mex Eyth: *The Bridgebuilder* (Sampson, Lowe, 1938). Theodor Plievier: *Stalingrad* (Athaenium, 1948).

Memb TA.

ROCK, EDWARD B 5200 Park Rd, Charlotte, NC 28209 USA *Tel* 704-525-5100.

TL English SL Spanish UDC bank/finance, business, textiles.

Affil Edward B Rock Associates. **Memb** ATA.

RODENAS, MAGDALENA 2401 Calvert St NW, Washington, DC 20008 USA *Tel* 202-483-0207.

TL English, French. SL Spanish. UDC agriculture, art, banking/finance, commerce, ecology, economics, education, engineering (civil), food/nutrition, forestry, history, industry, law, mining, paper/pulp, political economy, public health, remote sensing technology, telecommunications, transportation, urban development.

Affil World Bank. **Memb** APETI.

RODMAN, RICHARD B 65 Locust Ave, Lexington, MA 02173 USA *Tel* 617-861-8149.

TL English. SL German, Russian. UDC astronomy, astrophysics.

Russian Yakov L Al'pert: *Radio Wave Propagation and the Ionosphere,* 2 vols (Plenum, 1974). Iosif S Shklovskii: *Cosmic Radio Waves* (Harvard Univ, 1960); *Stars: Their Birth, Life, and Death* (Freeman, 1978). Boris A Vorontsov-Vel'yaminov: *Extragalactic Astronomy* (Harvard Univ, forthcoming).
Affil Harvard College Observatory (senior translator of Soviet journals, *Soviet Astronomy* and *Soviet Astronomy Letters,* both published by the American Inst of Physics. **Memb** American Astronomical Society, International Astronomical Union.

RODRIGUEZ, PABLO 1619 30 St NW #206, Washington, DC 20007 USA *Tel* 202-965-1694.
TL Spanish. **SL** English, French, Portuguese. **UDC** birth control, statistics, taxation. **Affil** OAS.

ROMEIJN, H Mozartlaan 3, NL-3741 HT Baarn, Netherlands *Tel* (02154) 13749.
TL & SL Dutch & English. **UDC** banking/finance, building/construction, commerce, economics, emigration documents, paper/pulp, police and security, printing, railroad technology, shipping, transportation.
Memb NGV, TG.

ROSE, WALTER 105 Markfield, Courtwood Lane, Croydon, Surrey, UK *Tel* (01) 657 8543.
TL English. **SL** French, German, Italian. **UDC** engineering (civil, mechanical), steel construction.
Memb TG.

ROSENBERG, GERTRAUD 45 Cleary Ct #11, San Francisco, CA 94109 USA *Tel* 415-931-2328.
TL English. **SL** German. **UDC** banking/finance, biology, commerce, data processing, economics, education, government, industry, law, literature (history), medicine, political economy, social services, taxation.
Memb ATA.

RUIZ, VICTOR M PO Box 7524, Oakland, CA 94601 USA *Tel* 415-834-6080.
TL Spanish. **SL** English. **UDC** anthropology, banking/finance, commerce, documentation, economics, education, government, music, psychology, public health, theology, transportation.
English Michael Lorimer: *Lorimer Series for Classical Guitar* (Hansen, 1976).
Accred/Memb ATA, NCTA.

RYBY, IRENE J 104 Merrill Rd, Clifton, NJ 07012 USA *Tel* 201-471-2894.
TL English. **SL** French, German. **UDC** biology, biomedicine, medicine, microbiology, pharmacology, sciences (medical).
Accred/Memb ATA. **Affil** Hoffmann-La Roche, Inc.

SAFONOV, SIDONIE H 1643 Krameria St, Denver, CO 80220 USA *Tel* 303-355-9410; 234-4780.
TL English. **SL** German, Russian. **UDC** aesthetics, commerce, economics, education, electronics, engineering (civil, hydraulic, mechani-

cal), ethics, geography, government, history, linguistics/philology, literature (all areas), logic, meteorology, philosophy, physics, plastics, political economy/science, social sciences, sociology, technology, transportation.
Russian Ts E Mirtskhulava: *Erosion of Canal Beds and Methods for Determining Their Stability* (US Bureau of Reclamation, 1977).
Accred ATA. **Memb** ATA, CTA.

SAKAMOTO, RALPH K 169 Deepdale Pkwy, Albertson, NY 11507 USA *Tel* 516-484-4194.
TL Japanese. **SL** English. **UDC** aeronautics, aviation, archeology, economics, commerce, engineering (aerospace), fisheries, government, law (international), military science, oceanography, philosophy, political science, shipping, theology.
Affil US Dept of State.

SAKLAD, MICHAEL ARTHUR 10 rue du Docteur Roux, F-75015 Paris, France *Tel* (331) 566-7648.
TL English. **SL** French. **UDC** automotive, building/construction, communications, computers, data processing, electronics, engineering (civil, electrical, mechanical, sanitary), iron/steel industry, metallurgy, telecommunications.
French Thierry de Montbrial: *Energy: The Countdown* (Pergamon, 1978). Pierre Rouanet: *Pompidou* (US Govt Commission, restricted). Roger Trinquier: *War, Subversion, Revolution* (US Govt Commission, restricted).
Memb ATA, SFT.

SALMON, LOUIS J 660 Veteran Ave #2, Los Angeles, CA 90024 USA *Tel* 213-479-7293.
TL & SL English & French. **UDC** banking/finance, business, crystallography, economics, engineering (electrical), industry, iron/steel industry, metallurgy, photography, plastics, sciences (applied), technology.
Memb ATA (Southern California chapter).

SAMU, JÁNOS 69 Driggs Ave, Greenpoint, NY 11222 USA *Tel* 212-389-5176.
TL Hungarian. **SL** Danish, English, German, Polish, Russian. **UDC** business, ceramics, construction materials, glass, hotel operations, law, literature (children's), sciences (applied), silicate industry, technology.
English John Powell: *Penology* (Büntetésvégrehajtási Intézet, 1967). Also the works of R. Haukøy, Béla Löcsey, V V Michailova, Y D Stepanov, Kálmán Tóth, László Vissy.
Memb ATA.

SANTALESA, LOUIS A 189-02 35 Ave, Flushing, NY 11358 USA *Tel* 212-445-3722.
TL English. **SL** Italian, Russian, Serbo-Croatian. **UDC** computers, data processing, electronics, engineering (electrical, radar), statistics.
Affil Riverside Research Inst. **Memb** ATA.

SANTOS, M B R 9 Crewdson Rd, London SW9 OLH, UK *Tel* (01) 582-2076.
TL English, Spanish. **SL** Portuguese. **UDC** art, arts/crafts, bacteriology, biochemistry, biology, biomedicine, chemistry, copyright, epidemiology, linguistics/philology, literature (criticism, prose), metallurgy, microbiology,

parasitology, pharmacology, psychiatry, psychology, public health, sciences (medical), theater.
Portuguese R Catz: *Iconoclasm as Literary Technique: A Study of the Satiric Devices* (Prelo, 1978).
Accred/Memb TG.

SASAKI, RYUJI S 193 Riverbrook Ave, Lincroft, NJ 07738 USA *Tel* 201-747-7123.
TL English. **SL** Japanese. **UDC** business, economics, law, patents/trademarks, science & technology (especially chemistry, textiles, biomedicine).
Memb ATA, Word Guild.

SAUSSY, KATHLEEN WHITTEN 1634 Green St #2, Columbia, SC 29201 USA *Tel* 803-771-4855.
TL & SL English & French. **UDC** banking/finance, business, government, literature (prose), social sciences, theater.
Memb ALTA.

SCHECHTER, CHARLES 3124 Draper St, Philadelphia, PA 19136 USA *Tel* 215-332-7366.
TL English. **SL** French, Italian, Portuguese, Spanish. **UDC** banking/finance, business, chemistry, industry, medicine, patents/trademarks, pharmacology.
Memb ATA, DVTA.

SCHNEIDER, RITA PO Box 18180, Jerusalem, Israel *Tel* (02) 52 71 53.
TL English. **SL** Russian. **UDC** geochemistry, geology, geophysics.
Russian A A Beus & S V Grigorian: *Geochemical Exploration Methods for Mineral Deposits* (Applied Publishing, 1977). S V Medvedev, ed: *Seismic Zoning of the USSR* (Keter, 1976). A I Perel'man: *Geochemistry of Elements in the Supergene Zone* (Keter, 1977). A P Vinogradov & G B Udintsev, eds: *Rift Zones of the World Ocean* (Wiley, 1975).

SCHOEN, WILLIE 28545 Bishop Park Dr #114A, Wickliffe, OH 44092 USA *Tel* 216-944-4529.
TL English. **SL** German. **UDC** business, commerce, economics, education, ethics, government, history, insurance, linguistics/philology, literature (folklore, history, prose, songs), metaphysics, occultism, social services, taxation.
Accred/Memb ATA.

SCHULDT, LESLEY M 4827 SE Kelly, Portland, OR 97206 USA *Tel* 503-775-9197.
TL English. **SL** German. **UDC** athletics, computers, data processing, education, government, literature (children's), political science, recreation, sales contracts, sports.
Memb ATA.

SCHULEMANN, DIETRICH F 1211 Sherwood Ave, Richmond, VA 23220 USA *Tel* 804-257-2550.
TL English, German. **SL** Danish, Norwegian, Swedish. **UDC** chemistry, international patents/trademarks, sciences (medical, natural).
Affil A H Robins Co. **Memb** ATA.

SCHULTE, JOSEPHINE H 6623 Callaghan Rd #1703, San Antonio, TX 78229 USA *Tel* 512-696-1909.

TL English. SL German, Spanish. UDC anthropology, archeology, art, commerce, geography, government, history, literature (history), logic, philosophy, political science, shipbuilding, shipping.

Spanish Leopoldo Zea: *Positivism in Mexico* (Univ of Texas, 1974).

SCHUNK, CHRISTIANE 541 Sharp Dr, DeSoto, TX 75115 USA *Tel* 214-223-4342.

TL & SL English, German, Italian. UDC athletics, business, law, oil & gas, political science, sports, travel & tourism.

Accred Translation Inst (Munich). **Memb** ALTA, ATA (Metroplex chapter).

SCHWARTZ, LAURENCE C A 1202 Oakridge Dr, Cleveland Heights, OH 44121 USA *Tel* 216-382-8778.

TL & SL English & German. UDC business (international marketing), engineering (electrical, industrial, marine, mechanical), graphics, industry, iron/steel industry, machine tools, oceanography, photography, printing, recreation, shipbuilding, technology.

Affil Cleveland State Univ, World Trade Education Center. **Memb** ATA, NOTA.

SCHWARZ, RICHARD A Multilingual Services, 808 Townsend Blvd, Towne Point, Dover, DE 19901 USA *Tel* 302-674-2018.

TL English. SL Dutch, French, German. UDC all subject fields.

German Thieme-Becker: *Encyclopedia of Artists* (International Translation, 1978). Hönl, Maue, Westpfahl: *Theory of Diffraction* (US Dept of the Navy, 1978), numerous others. **Memb** ATA.

SCOTT, JOHN SOMERVILLE 74 Park Ave S, London N8 8LS, UK *Tel* (01) 340 3948.

TL English. SL French, German. UDC engineering (civil, sanitary).

Author of *Dictionary of Building* and *Dictionary of Civil Engineering*; co-author, with Newnes Butterworth, of "Dictionary of Public Health Engineering" (pending). **Memb** TG.

SEGURA, VICTOR J 260 Maple Ct #121, Ventura, CA 93003 USA *Tel* 805-647-9345, 6553.

TL English. SL Spanish. UDC agriculture, documentation, law (property), medicine, public health.

Memb ATA (Southern California chapter).

SELON, ANDRÉ Rua Jardim Botânico, 728/apto 1004, Rio de Janeiro, Brazil *Tel* (021) 266 0634.

TL Portuguese. SL English, French. UDC anthropology, banking/finance, commerce, education, ethnography, ethics, food/nutrition, law, literature (Brazilian folklore), navigation, occultism, political economy/science, public administration, social sciences, sociology, sports.

Accred Univ of Sorbonne. **Memb** AIT, ATIE.

SHEEHAN, GEORGE D PO Box 347, Delhi, NY 13753 USA *Tel* 607-746-6122.

TL English. SL French, German, Italian, Portuguese, Spanish. UDC patents/trademarks.

Memb ATA.

SHERRILL, SUSANNE HAMPTON 7124 Harmon Dr, Ventura, CA 93003 USA *Tel* 805-642-2721.

TL English. SL Spanish. UDC astronomy, biology, botany, ecology, food/nutrition, genetics, photography, public health, women's studies.

Memb ATA.

SHEVERS, SANDRA D 6824 Hammerstone Way, Cincinnati, OH 45227 USA *Tel* 513-271-6066.

TL English. SL French, Spanish. UDC chemistry, food/nutrition, paper/pulp, patents/trademarks, pharmacology.

Memb ATA.

SICAUD, PATRICE 55 Wildomar, Mill Valley, CA 94941 USA *Tel* 415-388-1701.

TL French. SL English. UDC aeronautics, banking/finance, commerce, engineering (electrical), fuel, law, literature (science fiction), medicine, political science, sciences (applied).

Memb ATA.

SILVERA, FANNY DEL CARMEN 91 Strawberry Hill Ave #528, Stamford, CT 06920 USA.

TL & SL English & Spanish. UDC engineering (civil), insurance, law, medicine.

Memb ATA.

SILVERMAN, ROBERT H 22 Trowbridge St, Cambridge, MA 02138 USA *Tel* 617-876-4821.

TL English. SL Russian. UDC astrophysics, computers, economics, information science, linguistics, logic, mathematics, physics, transportation.

Russian E V Ovechnikov & M S Fishel'son: *Urban Transportation* (National Science Foundation, 1978, internal use only). A O Slisenko: *Recognizing a Symmetry Predicate by Multihead Turing Machines with Input* (Amer Math Soc, 1976). Various authors: *The Use of Methods from Mathematical Economics and Computer Technology*, collection (National Science Foundation, 1977, internal use only). E G Chistyakova & A K Semenov: *Balance Models of the Urban Economy* (National Science Foundation, 1977, internal use only). Also numerous other scientific and technical works.

Memb ATA.

SIMONNET, ANNE 179 blvd Bineau, F-92200 Neuilly, France *Tel* 747 47 06.

TL French. SL English. UDC anthropology, art, aviation, banking/finance, commerce, education, ethics, food/nutrition, fuel, history, law (international, maritime), linguistics/philology, literature (children's), petroleum, philosophy, political science, recreation, religion, social sciences, sociology, theology.

Accred Univ of California—Santa Barbara. **Memb** ATA.

SIMPKIN, RICHARD E Over Deanshaugh, Elgin, Moray IV30 2JA, UK *Tel* Elgin (0343) 44559.

TL English. SL French, German. UDC automotive, bacteriology, biochemistry, chemistry, ecology, engineering (marine, mechanical), food/nutrition, human resources, literature (prose), machine tools, microbiology, military science, missiles/rocketry, navigation, pharmacology, recreation (sailing), sciences (life), statistics, transportation, welding.

German Berendt: *The Story of Jazz* (Barrie & Jenkins, 1978). von Senger & Etterlin: *Armored Vehicles of the World* (Brassey's, forthcoming). Also the works of Dierich, B Robin, others.

Accred Civil Service Commission Interpretership in French and German. **Memb** BDÜ, TA, TG, SFT.

SINCLAIR, DONALD ALLAN 940 Beaudry St, Ottawa, ON, K1K 3S1, Canada *Tel* 613-746-1224.

TL English. SL Dutch, French, German, Italian, Russian. UDC agriculture, aircraft icing, bird hazards at airports, bacteriology, biochemistry, biology, building, chemistry, ecology, engineering (chemical, civil, electrical, hydraulic, marine, mechanical), geophysics, iron/steel industry, machine tools, medicine, metallurgy, oceanography, patents/trademarks, permafrost studies, physics, sciences (earth, life, medical), shipbuilding, snow and avalanche research, welding.

Accred/Memb ATA (German & Russian). **Memb** STIC.

SLATER, TIMOTHY Postfach 3171, D-8520 Erlangen, West Germany

TL English. SL German. UDC airships, aeronautics, alternative sources of energy, bicycles, data processing, documentation, ecology, engineering (electrical, marine reactor), heraldry, history, information science, literature (science fiction), logic, physics, political economy/science, power plant technology, shipbuilding, shipping, transportation, world affairs.

Memb ATA, BDÜ, TG.

SMITH, BRIAN D 78 Sheringham Ave, Oakwood, London N14 6BG, UK *Tel* (01) 360 3553.

TL English. SL Indonesian. UDC commerce, economics, education, government, history, law, public administration, sociology.

Memb TG.

SMITH, H A 99 North End Rd, London NW11 7TA, UK *Tel* (01) 458 7353.

TL English. SL Dutch, French, German. UDC architecture (military), banking/finance, history, insurance, law (international, patent/trademark, property), taxation.

Dutch E Korb: *Company Strategy* (Saxon House, 1975). **German** Werdinger: *German Company Law* (Oyez, 1975); *Tax Havens* (1975). A Weber: *Investment in Property Abroad* (MacDonald & Evans, 1976). *The Pan Dictionary of Commerce in 5 Languages* (Pan Books, forthcoming).

Memb TG, AITC.

SMITH, MARGARET F Am Weingarten 32, D-6000 Frankfurt/Main 90, West Germany *Tel* (06196) 801-2749.
TL English. **SL** German. **UDC** automotive, computer, data processing, electronics, military science (logistics), technology (automotive).
German D Fischer: *A System for Maintenance Data Collection & Evaluation* (US Dept of the Navy, 1977).
Affil Dept for Technical Documentation. **Memb** ATA, Concordiat.

SMITH, RICHARD E 91-24 88 Rd, Woodhaven, Queens, NY 11421 USA *Tel* 212-750-3244.
TL English. **SL** German, Spanish. **UDC** automotive, aviation, building/construction, communications, computers, data processing, engineering (all areas), government, law, linguistics/philology, machine tools, medicine, navigation, optics, optometry, paper/pulp, photography, physics, plastics, political economy/science, public administration, recreation, sciences (all areas), shipbuilding, shipping, standards, technology, theater, transportation, welding.
Memb ATA.

SMUTS, JOHN 86 Conifer Ave, Poole, Dorset BH14 8RU, UK *Tel* (0202) 743 205.
TL English, German. **SL** Dutch. **UDC** chemistry, engineering (chemical, electrical, marine, mechanical), industry, machine tools, navigation, physics/mechanics, sciences (applied), shipbuilding.
Dutch M Vertregt: *Principles of Astronautics* (Elsevier, 1960).
Memb TG.

SNELL, BARBARA M Sutton's Mill, Cranham, Gloucester, UK *Tel* Painswick (0452) 813373.
TL English. **SL** French, German, Spanish. **UDC** aeronautics, agriculture, arts, aviation, business, commerce, communications, computers, dairy farming, data processing, education, electronics, engineering (electrical, industrial, mechanical), equestrian arts, geography, horse breeding and management, human resources, industry, machine tools, mining, ornithology, photography, plastics, recreation, sports, standards, stockbreeding, telecommunications, transportation.
Accred/Memb TG (ed, newsletter).

SOBCHAK, PATRICIA PO Box 3756, Carmel, CA 93921 USA *Tel* 408-624-1835.
TL English. **SL** Russian. **UDC** agriculture, automotive, business, food/nutrition, forestry, horticulture, music, photography, physics, psychology.
Russian I M Dunskaya: "The Emergence of Quantum Electronics" (pending).
Accred Monterey Inst of Foreign Studies.

SPANGLER, PATRICK S 441 Aster St, Laguna Beach, CA 92651 USA *Tel* 714-494-1342.
TL English. **SL** German, Russian. **UDC** chemistry, computers, engineering (aerospace, chemical, marine, mechanical, nuclear), geophysics, physics, sciences (applied, earth, natural), technology.

SPECTOR, VILMA C 6155 28 St S, St Petersburg, FL 33712 USA *Tel* 813-867-5689.
TL & SL English & Portuguese. **UDC** art, commerce, education, health, industry, literature, music, psychology, public administration, social sciences.
Accred/Memb ATA, NOTA.

STACKHOUSE, KATHLEEN 624 N Euclid St, Pittsburgh, PA 15206 USA *Tel* 412-562-7064.
TL English. **SL** Russian. **UDC** automotive, computers, engineering (mechanical), food, industry, iron/steel industry, machine tools, metallurgy, mining, printing, railroads, transportation.
Memb APT, ATA.

STACY, CHARLES M PO Box 34380, Dallas, TX 75234 USA *Tel* 214-242-8668.
TL English. **SL** French, Portuguese, Russian, Spanish. **UDC** engineering (mechanical), petroleum technology.
Accred/Memb ATA (Portuguese, Spanish). **Affil** Otis Engineering Corp.

STALJANSSENS, LUC 40 ave du Parc, B-1060 Brussels, Belgium *Tel* (02) 537 79 73.
TL French, German. **SL** English, Danish, Dutch, Spanish.
Accred/Memb CBTIP (licensed translator).

STANICH, FRANK S 210 E 47 St #2B, New York, NY 10017 USA *Tel* 212-753-8534.
TL English. **SL** French, German. **UDC** astrology, automotive, business, chemistry, cosmetics, engineering (chemical, mechanical), industry, law, literature (prose), packaging, patents/trademarks, pharmacology, philosophy, photography, sciences (applied, medical, natural, social), textiles.
Memb ATA.

STEENHAGEN, CYNTHIA L 7373 W Florida Ave #18C, Lakewood, CO 80226 USA *Tel* 303-234-4780.
TL English. **SL** French. **UDC** engineering (hydraulic), food/nutrition, psychology, social sciences.
Accred/Memb ATA, CTA.

STERLING, MARILY Normandy Village 24-4, Nanuet, NY 10954 USA *Tel* 914-623-3282.
TL English. **SL** French, German. **UDC** biochemistry, chemistry, education, sciences (medical, natural).
Memb ATA.

STERN, CHARLES M 241 W 97 St (Penthouse K), New York, NY 10025 USA *Tel* 212-864-4453.
TL English. **SL** French, German, Spanish. **UDC** banking/finance, insurance, literature (history), medicine, patents/trademarks, sciences (applied).
French J Fritsch & P Grospierre: *The Manufacture of Biscuits, Cakes, and Wafers* (Pitman & Sons, 1931). **German** Robert Rüdiger Beer: *Unicorn—Myth and Reality* (Litton Educational, 1977). **Spanish** Félix Martí-Ibáñez: *The Crystal Arrow* (Clarkson N Potter, 1964). Au-

gusto Pi Suñer: *Classics of Biology* (Pitman & Sons, 1955).
Memb ATA.

STOCK, JOSEPH W 124 Cimmaron Trail, Enon, OH 45323 USA *Tel* 513-864-7738.
TL English. **SL** German, Russian, Spanish. **UDC** aviation, biomedicine, commerce, communications, copyright, documentation, education, electronics, food/nutrition, government, history, human resources, jurisprudence, law, literature, metallurgy, psychology.
German H F Reimann: *Communications Engineering* (Foreign Technology Div, US Air Force, 1967). Joachim Ulbricht & Werner Makschin: *Fiber Research and Textile Engineering* (Foreign Technology Div, 1971). **Italian** R Galetto & G Inghilleri: *The Relative Orientation of Two Panoramic Photograms* (Foreign Technology Div, 1971). **Russian** Ye M Dudnik & V Kh Oganesyan: *Powder Metallurgy* (Foreign Technology Div, 1968). Also hundreds of scientific and technical works during more than 26 years as chief translator for the US Air Force.
Affil Bureau of Applied Linguistics (dir). **Memb** ATA, SFL.

STOCKS, GEORGE R 89 E King St, Helensburgh, Dunbartonshire, Scotland G84 7RG, UK *Tel* (0436) 4574.
TL English. **SL** French, German, Italian, Spanish. **UDC** agriculture, brewing, commerce, dairy farming, engineering (mechanical), machine tools, psychology, shipbuilding, shipping, taxation.
Memb TG.

STOLL, GERHARD C 206 71 St, Holmes Beach, FL 33510 USA *Tel* 813-778-4917.
TL English. **SL** German. **UDC** automotive, commerce, economics, engineering (mechanical), household appliances, industry, machine tools, plastics, sciences (applied).
Memb ATA.

STRATTA, M CECILE 140 West End Ave, New York, NY 10023 USA *Tel* 212-580-1708.
TL English. **SL** French, Italian, Spanish. **UDC** aeronautics, art, aviation, banking/finance, commerce, communications, copyright, documentation, history, industry, insurance, law (international, maritime, property), legislation, literature (all areas), mining, painting, patents/trademarks, public administration, shipping, taxation, theater, transportation.
Spanish Florencia Varas & José Manuel Vergara: *Coup!* (Stein & Day, 1974). Also numerous arias and liner notes for record albums.

STRICKLER, JULIE ANN Box 314, Center City, MN 55012 USA *Tel* 612-257-5802.
TL English. **SL** German. **UDC** business, economics, linguistics, political economy/science, sociology, viniculture.
Accred Monterey Inst of Foreign Studies. **Memb** ATA, Concordiat.

STRONG, CAROL R 77-16 Austin St, Forest Hills, NY 11375 USA *Tel* 212-520-1802.
TL English. **SL** Spanish. **UDC** anthropology, archeology, business, documentation, eco-

nomics, law (international), literature (children's, folklore, history, lyrics, poetry, science fiction, songs), machine tools, medicine, music, parasitology, pharmacology, philosophy, sciences (medical, natural, social).
Affil Balfour MacLaine International. **Memb** ATA.

STUART, RICHARD ALEXANDER GORDON One Dalhousie Pl, Arbroath, Angus DD11 2BT, UK *Tel* (0241) 74536.
TL English. **SL** French, German, Polish, Russian. **UDC** aeronautics, agriculture, automotive, aviation, commerce, engineering (mechanical), history, iron/steel industry, literature (history), machine tools, military science, textiles.
French Yves Bréferet: *The Cossacks* (Tandem, forthcoming). **Russian** Vera Dolyanski: *Manual of Russian for Adult Beginners* (Rex Collings, 1968).
Memb TG.

STUMPF, MICHAEL LEE 4167 E Alta, Fresno, CA 93702 USA *Tel* 209-255-0156.
TL English. **SL** German **UDC** law, medicine.
Memb ATA (Southern California chapter), CCIA.

SUGANUMA, MASAKO 28-29-205 Hongo 1-Chome Bunkyoku, Tokyo 113, Japan *Tel* (03) 813 9096.
TL English. **SL** Japanese. **UDC** international licensing, export publicity.
Memb TG, NATIST.

SULLIVAN, GALINA 1101 S Arlington Ridge Rd#1006, Arlington, VA 22202 USA *Tel* 202-298-6565; 703-979-0144.
TL & SL English & Russian. **UDC** aesthetics, architecture, automotive, building/construction, communications, computers, data processing, documentation, electronics, engineering (chemical, civil, electrical, hydraulic, industrial, mechanical), industry, iron/steel industry, machine tools, metallurgy, patents/trademarks, petroleum, physics, telecommunications, welding.
Memb ATA, TG.

SWANEY, INES SZILARD 1223 Kearny St, San Francisco, CA 94133 USA *Tel* 415-982-2882
TL & SL English & Spanish. **UDC** architecture, art, banking/finance, biology, building/construction, chemistry, commerce, data processing, education, elections, engineering (civil, hydraulic, municipal, sanitary), food/nutrition, government, graphics, industry, law, legislation, medicine, music, petroleum, political science, printing, public administration, public health, recreation, sciences (medical), shipping, social services, taxation, technology.
Spanish Carlos Fernandez: *The Drawings of Juan Bautista Cuadra* (Univ of Calif, Berkeley, 1977). Also documents, business correspondence, academic papers, information pamphlets, candidates' statements, analysis of election issues, architectural floor plans, documents for California welfare hearings, laboratory manuals.
Memb NCTA.

SWART, INA One Wessex Gardens, London NW11, UK *Tel* (01) 455 3168.
TL English. **SL** Dutch. **UDC** agriculture, anthropology, art, art history, biochemistry, biology, botany, chemistry, dairy farming, ecology, education, film history, films, food/nutrition, genetics, geography, history, horticulture, linguistics/philology, literature (children's, criticism, drama, folklore, history, lyrics, poetry, prose, science fiction), natural history, political science, psychiatry, psychology, sociology, theater.
Dutch numerous articles for *Spectrum's Encyclopedia* (Spectrum, 1973).
Memb NGV, TA.

SWEETKO, MARJORIE 16 Mulberry Lane, Goring-by-Sea, Worthing, Sussex, UK *Tel* (0903) 47317.
TL English. **SL** French. **UDC** advertising, banking/finance, building/construction, commerce, economics.
Accred Univ of Montreal. **Memb** TG.

SZMIDT, A B 22 Belvedere Rd, Earlsdon, Coventry CV5 6PF, UK *Tel* (0203) 20863, 75847.
TL & SL English, German, Polish. **UDC** automotive, aviation, data processing, electronics, engineering (electrical, hydraulic, industrial, marine, mechanical), machine tools, telecommunications.
Affil The Coventry Translation Service. **Memb** TG.

TABI, UTE Two Lloydhaven Dr, Lloyd Harbor, NY 11743 USA *Tel* 516-673-0396.
TL & SL English & German. **UDC** aeronautics, aviation, banking/finance, chemistry, commerce, data processing, documentation, engineering (aerospace, mechanical), epidemiology, government, iron/steel industry, jurisprudence, law (international, property) legislation, linguistics/philology, medicine, metallurgy, paper/pulp, patents/trademarks, political economy/science, sciences (medical), sociology, transportation.
Memb ATA, Universitas.

TANNENBAUM, ARTHUR 280 Madison Ave, New York, NY 10016 USA *Tel* 212-679-1734.
TL English. **SL** French, German, Spanish. **UDC** banking/finance, building/construction, chemistry, commerce, communications, computers, copyright, ecology, economics, engineering (aerospace, chemical, civil, electrical, industrial, mechanical), fuel, jurisprudence, law (international), machine tools, metallurgy, patents/trademarks, photography, plastics, rubber technology, shipbuilding, taxation, textiles, welding.
French Haroun Tazieff: *Volcanoes* (Orion, 1961). Léopold Sédar Senghor and 18 African writers: "Who We Are and What We Stand For" (pending).
Memb ATA.

TAPELBAND, ESTHER AAGAARD 1910 Lucile Ave, Los Angeles, CA 90039 USA *Tel* 213-663-4955.
TL English. **SL** Danish. **UDC** aesthetics, art, athletics, bacteriology, banking/finance, business, copyright, dairy farming, education, genealogy, government, history, insurance, jurisprudence, law (international, maritime, property), legislation, library science, logic, microbiology, philately, philosophy, political economy/science, recreation, sciences (medical, natural), sociology, sports, theater, theology.
Accred Copenhagen Translator School. **Memb** CCIA.

TARKA, JOAN A 327 E Main St, Kutztown, PA 19530 USA *Tel* 215-683-5226.
TL English. **SL** French, German. **UDC** automotive, biochemistry, biology, biomedicine, brewing, chemistry, dentistry, ecology, education, engineering (chemical), food/nutrition, fuel, iron/steel industry, library science, medicine, metallurgy, microbiology, mineralogy, paper/pulp, patents/trademarks, petroleum, pharmacology, plastics, psychiatry, psychology, sciences (earth, life, medical, natural), textiles.
Memb ATA, DVTA.

TEAGUE, BEN PO Box 129, Athens, GA 30603 USA *Tel* 404-543-0860.
TL English. **SL** German, Russian. **UDC** chemistry, engineering (chemical), fuel, metallurgy, physics, sciences (applied, natural), technology.
Russian S N Postnikov: *Electrophysical and Electrochemical Phenomena in Friction, Cutting, and Lubrication* (Van Nostrand Reinhold, forthcoming).
Memb ATA, TRACT.

THOMAS, ANAMARÍA Apartado 67201, Caracas 106, Venezuela *Tel* 986 5981.
TL & SL English & Spanish. **UDC** commerce, finance, free trade export facilities, generators, industry, petroleum, turbines.
Accred/Memb Berlitz School of Interpreters (Ven), Interpretes y Traductores (Ven).

THORNTON, JOSEPHINE Mellon Bank, NA, Mellon Square, Pittsburgh, PA 15230 USA *Tel* 412-232-5751.
TL English. **SL** French, Portuguese, Spanish. **UDC** banking/finance, business, commerce, economics, iron/steel industry, law, taxation.
Affil Carnegie-Mellon Univ (Translation). **Memb** AIT, APT (founder and past pres), ATA (past pres).

THRESHMAN, CLARA I PO Box 463, South Norwalk, CT 06854 USA *Tel* 203-838-8168.
TL English. **SL** Spanish. **UDC** business, law enforcement, sociology, technical translations for management consultants.

TOURKOFF, E F 732 Maddux Dr, Colma, CA 94015 USA *Tel* 415-755-8224.
TL English. **SL** Russian. **UDC** architecture, building/construction, engineering (civil, electrical, hydraulic, industrial, marine, mechanical, municipal, sanitary), geodesy, machine tools, petroleum, railroads, shipbuilding, surveying, transportation, welding.
Russian M T Urazbayev, Yu R, Leyderman, et al: *Translations in Earthquake Engineering* (Earthquake Engineering Research Inst, 1960).

S Z Pogostin: *Economics and Organization of Chemical Industry* (US Govt, 1963–64). L S Boroditskiy & V M Spiridonov: *Reduction of Structural Noise in Ship Spaces* (US Dept of the Navy, 1975). A K Syrkov: *Modern Shipbuilding Yards* (US Dept of the Navy, 1978).
Memb ATA, NCTA.

TRANG, CLAIRE KIM-DUNG 1900 Columbia Pike #210, Arlington, VA 22204 USA *Tel* 703-521-5346.
TL & SL English & French. **UDC** agriculture, architecture, banking/finance, building/construction, commerce, communications, education, geography, government, human resources, medicine, military science, painting, pharmacology, philosophy, political economy, telecommunications.
Accred Georgetown Univ, Univ of Paris. **Memb** ATA.

TREANOR, PATRICK J 1744 Church St NW, Washington, DC 20036 USA *Tel* 202-667-7982.
TL English. **SL** Bulgarian, German, Russian, Serbo-Croatian. **UDC** biochemistry, chemistry, engineering (chemical), history, medicine, military science, patents/trademarks, transportation.
Affil Library of Congress.

TRIMBLE, RUSSELL F 1008 Walkup St, Carbondale, IL 62901 USA *Tel* 618-549-3405.
TL English. **SL** French, German, Italian, Russian. **UDC** chemistry (analytical, industrial, inorganic, organic, physical).
Accred/Memb ATA. **Affil** Southern Illinois Univ.

TUCK, DONALD S 31 St James Ave, Boston, MA 02116 USA *Tel* 617-426-6777.
TL & SL English & Spanish. **UDC** advertising, automotive, banking/finance, commerce, communications, data processing, economics, government, industry, information science, medicine, pharmacology, marketing, sales.
Memb TG.

TUNG, LOUISE WATANABE PO Box 9362, Austin, TX 78766 USA *Tel* 512-345-4475.
TL English. **SL** Japanese. **UDC** chemistry, engineering (chemical), fibers, food, iron/steel industry, paper/pulp, patents (main area of specialization), petroleum, plastics, textiles.
Memb ATA.

TYBULEWICZ, ALBIN Two Oak Dene, London W13 8AW, UK *Tel* (01) 997 8822.
TL English. **SL** Polish, Russian. **UDC** physics (solid-state and quantum electronics).
Russian V I Fistul: *Heavily Doped Semiconductors* (Plenum, 1969). Yu P Raiser: *Laser-induced Discharge Phenomena* (Consultants Bureau, 1977). S V Tyablikov: *Methods in the Quantum Theory of Magnetism* (Plenum, 1967). I S Zheludev: *Physics of Crystalline Dielectrics* (Plenum, 1971). Also more than 50 volumes.
Memb Aslib (Technical Translation Group, London), TG.

UNDERWOOD, DIANA MARY 27 ave des Cèdres, F-92410 Ville d'Avray, France *Tel* (01) 709 64 44.

TL English. **SL** French, German. **UDC** aeronautics, chemistry, electronics, engineering (aerospace, chemical, civil, electrical, hydraulic, mechanical), law (property), medicine, patents/trademarks, petroleum, pharmacology, plastics.
Memb TG, SFT.

VALENTI, BEATRICE Y 22331 SW 103 Ave Box 4, Miami, FL 33190 USA *Tel* 305-251-3467.
TL English. **SL** French, Spanish. **UDC** biology, business, documentation, engineering (mechanical), law (property), medicine, religion, sciences (medical).
Memb ATA.

VAN ABBÉ, DEREK MAURICE 40 Garden Close, Sutton, Ely, Cambs CB6 2RF, UK *Tel* (0353) 778 664.
TL English. **SL** Dutch, French, German. **UDC** astronomy, astrophysics, athletics, building/construction, commerce, electronics, engineering (civil, electric, industrial, mechanical, municipal), government, iron/steel industry, machine tools, metallurgy, military science, mineralogy, mining, missiles, photography, physics, plastics, political economy/science, public administration, public health, surveying, telecommunications, viniculture, welding.

VAN BOXELAER, MARC Bund 22, B-2070 Ekeren (Antwerp), Belgium *Tel* (031) 42 39 95.
TL Dutch. **SL** English, French, German, Russian. **UDC** banking/finance, commerce, computers, insurance, jurisprudence, literature (prose), medicine, navigation, philosophy, political economy/science, sciences (medical), shipping, taxation.
Memb CBTIP.

VAN BUREN, ROSA G 15900 W Ten Mile Rd #101, Southfield, MI 48075 USA *Tel* 313-559-7433.
TL English. **SL** Spanish. **UDC** automotive, banking/finance, commerce, communications, education, electronics, engineering (chemical, electrical, hydraulic, mechanical), food/nutrition, industry, recreation, social services.
Affil Gamboa School of Languages and Translations. **Memb** ATA.

VAN DAM, MAX 179 Beechwood Rd, Oradell, NJ 07649 USA *Tel* 201-265-6181.
TL English. **SL** Dutch, French, German. **UDC** most areas of science and technology.
Memb ATA.

VAN DAM, RUTH 179 Beechwood Rd, Oradell, NJ 07649 USA *Tel* 201-265-6181.
TL English. **SL** Dutch, French, German. **UDC** most areas of science and technology.

VANDENBRANDE, JEAN-PIERRE 1609 Rising Way, Westfield, NJ 07090 USA *Tel* 201-232-1787.
TL English. **SL** Dutch, French, Spanish. **UDC** most areas of industry, science, and technology, especially engineering.
Accred Inst of Translators & Interpreters (Antwerp). **Affil** General Electric Translation Dept.

VANDENBUSSCHE, EDDY R 147 Westheights Dr, Kitchener, ON N2N 1K2, Canada *Tel* 519-744-8335.
TL French. **SL** Dutch, English. **UDC** commerce, industry, insurance.
Memb CBTIP, STQ.

VAN HOORN-MULLER, C M Beatrixlaan 1, NL-3761 BB Soest, Netherlands *Tel* (02155) 17314.
TL Dutch. **SL** English. **UDC** computer applications, economics, film, industry, medicine, psychiatry, publicity translation.
Memb TG, NGV.

VAN MULDERS, ADOLF 50 rue Principale, Goetzange, Luxembourg *Tel* 30 91 84.
TL Dutch. **SL** English, French, German. **UDC** agriculture, commerce, documentation, economics, education, government, history, horticulture, linguistics/philology, political science, public administration, social services.
Affil European Parliament, Luxembourg (chief, Dutch Translation Div). **Memb** CBTIP.

VAN SANTEN, ANTHEA Katrinelundsvägen 21, S-722 19 Västerås, Sweden *Tel* (021) 123023.
TL English. **SL** Swedish. **UDC** computers, data processing, dentistry, engineering (mechanical, nuclear), literature (children's, prose), machine tools, music, patents/trademarks, theater.
Accred Swedish Chamber of Commerce. **Memb** FAT.

VARGAS, ALCEDO 33 Vermilyea Ave #4D, New York, NY 10034 USA *Tel* 212-942-4025.
TL Spanish. **SL** English. **UDC** insurance (policies and documents).
Memb ATA.

VASCONCELLOS, SYLVIO DE 1802 Corcoran St NW, Washington, DC 20009 USA *Tel* 202-667-7781.
TL English, French, Spanish. **SL** Portuguese **UDC** architecture, art history, building/construction, economics, engineering (civil), government, history, literature, mineralogy, mining, political economy, social sciences, urban development.
Affil Fed Univ of Minas Gerais, Brazil (emeritus). **Awards** 1978 NEH grant.

VÁSQUEZ-AYORA, GERARDO Watergate-at-Landmark #2-1712, 205 Yoakum Pkwy, Alexandria, VA 22304 USA *Tel* 703-751-8374.
TL & SL English, French, Portuguese. **UDC** art, art history, banking/finance, commerce, economics, education, ethics, food/nutrition, government, history, human resources, industry, information science, insurance, jurisprudence, law (international, maritime, property), legislation, linguistics/philology, literature (all areas), logic, philosophy, political economy/science, psychiatry, psychology, public administration, public health, sociology, theater, theology, translation theory and studies.
Author of *Introducción a la traductología* (Georgetown Univ, 1977). "La traducción de la nueva novela latinoamericana al inglés," (*Babel*, 24 no 1, 1978).
Memb AIT, ALTA, ATA.

VEGA, VALORIE JEAN 5050 Tamarus St #323, Las Vegas, NV 89109 USA *Tel* 702-737-1191; 386-4571.
TL & SL English & Spanish. **UDC** most areas of commerce, industry, and science.
Affil State Nevada Eighth Judicial Court (interpreter/translator). **Memb** CCIA, NTA.

VELA, JORGE 4601 N Park Ave #418, Chevy Chase, MD 20015 USA *Tel* 301-657-2245; 676-0297.
TL Spanish. **SL** English, Portuguese. **UDC** copyright, jurisprudence, law, legislation, political science, public administration.

VELLOSO, WILSON 7513 Westfield Dr, Washington, DC 20034 USA *Tel* 301-320-5979.
TL Portuguese, Spanish. **SL** English, French. **UDC** most areas of industry, science, and technology.
English Richard Wright: *Black Boy* (Editoria Nacional, 1946). George Orwell: *1984* (Editora Nacional, 1957). H G Wells: *The Time Machine* (Editora Brasiliense, 1946). Bertrand Russell: *Mysticism and Logic* (Editora Nacional, 1957). Also the works of Julien Benda, Pearl Buck, W Somerset Maugham, Charles Morgan, Ellery Queen, Evelyn Waugh, Lin Yutang.

VERMEIR, PAUL Provijnsstraat 5, B-3020 Herent, Belgium *Tel* (016) 237 554.
TL Dutch. **SL** English, French, German. **UDC** aesthetics, agriculture, anthropology, archeology, architecture, art, arts/crafts, athletics, automotive, banking, building/construction, commerce, communications, computers, copyright, data processing, documentation, economics, education, electronics, engineering (electrical), geography, history, human resources, information science, iron/steel industry, library science, linguistics/philology, photography, physics, political science, psychiatry, psychology, public health, recreation, social sciences, sociology, sports, telecommunications, veterinary medicine, welding, zoology.
English C B Bakker: *No Trespassing* (Nederlandsche, 1974). F Carpenter: *The Skinner Primer* (Nederlandsche, 1975). M Krantzler: *Creative Divorce* (Nederlandsche, 1974). G Bach & H Goldberg: *Creative Aggression* (Nederlandsche, 1974).
Memb CBTIP.

VINCKE, RONALD L Clos du Lievre 3, B-1490 Court St, Etienne, Belgium *Tel* (010) 61 43 37.
TL English. **SL** French. **UDC** banking/finance, business, insurance, management, marketing.
Memb CBTIP.

VOJTKO, MARGARET MARY PAULA 1110 Sylvan Ave, Homestead, PA 15120 USA *Tel* 412-462-5672.
TL English. **SL** French, Slovak. **UDC** engineering, literature (French), health professions, natural sciences, theology.
Czech Otakar Levy: *Baudelaire: His Esthetics and His Technique* (Univ of Alabama, forthcoming).
Affil Indiana Univ—Purdue Univ (Fort Wayne). **Memb** APT, ATA.

VOLLMER, LYDIA H 337 Smith Ave, Port Richey, FL 33568 USA *Tel* 813-868-2724.
TL English. **SL** Dutch, German. **UDC** economics, missiles/rocketry, military operations research.
Accred Monterey Inst of Foreign Studies. **Affil** US Dept of State (contract escort interpreter). **Memb** ATA, Concordiat.

VREELAND, ROY 5 Minschenden Crescent, Southgate, London N14 7EJ, UK *Tel* (01) 886 0569.
TL English. **SL** Danish, Dutch, French, German, Norwegian, Swedish. **UDC** chemistry, patents/trademarks, photography, sciences (applied), technology (general).
Memb TG.

WADE, SANDRA P The Balance, PO Box 914, Lower Lake, CA 95457 USA *Tel* 707-994-3022
TL English. **SL** French, German, Spanish. **UDC** agriculture, biochemistry, biology, business, ecology, horticulture, limnology, literature (children's, drama, poetry, prose), painting, psychology, sciences (natural), theater.
Memb TG.

WALLACE, L MACQUISTEN 63 Albemarle Rd, Beckenham, Kent BR3 3JG, UK *Tel* (01) 650 4778.
TL English. **SL** German. **UDC** communications, computers, cybernetics, electronics, engineering (electrical, hydraulic), sciences (natural), telecommunications, welding.
German Kurt Magnus: *Vibrations* (Blackie & Sons, 1965).
Memb Aslib (Specialist Translators' Panel).

WANTA, RAYMOND C PO Box 98, Bedford, MA 01730 USA *Tel* 617-470-0464.
TL English. **SL** Russian. **UDC** geophysics, meteorology, physics/mechanics, radio wave propagation, sciences (earth, environmental), statistics.
Russian M I Budyko: *Atmospheric Carbon Dioxide and Climate* (NASA).
Memb Word Guild.

WARDLE, E 81 Gloucester Ave, Grimsby, South Humberside DN34 5BU, UK *Tel* (0472) 77830.
TL English. **SL** Danish, Dutch, French, German, Italian, Norwegian, Portuguese, Russian, Spanish, Swedish. **UDC** banking/finance, commerce, economics, law, political economy, shipping, transportation.
Memb TG.

WAREHAM, PETER A 6 Gayhurst Close, Ernsford Grange, Coventry CV3 2GW, UK *Tel* (0203) 453 212.
TL English. **SL** German. **UDC** communications, electronics, engineering (chemical, electrical, mechanical), telecommunications.
Memb TG.

WEBB, A F 5 Firs Gate, Harrogate, Yorkshire HG2 9HE, UK *Tel* (0423) 872257.
TL English. **SL** French, German. **UDC** chemistry, engineering (chemical), medicine, pharmacology. Also experience in brewing, analysis of water, food and drugs, the manufacture of organic pharmaceuticals and food products.
Memb TG.

WEBSTER, PHILIP E 300 E 71 St, New York, NY 10021 USA *Tel* 212-744-3247.
TL English. **SL** French, Italian, Portuguese, Spanish. **UDC** banking/finance, business, commerce, government, industry, insurance, law, patents/trademarks, shipping.
Accred/Memb ATA.

WEDEKIND, ALMUTE M B 1330 Taney Ave #304, Frederick, MD 21701 USA *Tel* 301-662-0782.
TL English, German. **SL** French. **UDC** biology, literature (folklore, history, prose), medicine, physical therapy, sciences (life, medical, natural).
Affil Hood College. **Memb** ATA.

WEILL, PIERRE Résidence La Pastourelle, F-01630 Genis Pouilly, France *Tel* (50) 41 15 96.
TL French. **SL** English. **UDC** automotive, aviation, building/construction, business, commerce, communications, economics, electronics, geography, government, industry, insurance, iron/steel industry, law, military science, patents/trademarks, philately, plastics, public administration, standards, telecommunications, transportation.
Memb ATA, SFT.

WEISFELD, GLENN E 1334 E Joliet Pl, Detroit, MI 48207 USA *Tel* 313-393-2403.
TL English. **SL** French. **UDC** anthropology, bacteriology, biochemistry, biology, biomedicine, chemistry, genetics, medicine, microbiology, paleontology, parasitology, pharmacology, psychiatry, psychology, sciences (life, medical, natural, social), sociology, veterinary medicine, zoology.
French J Pommery: *Between Man and Beast* (Stein & Day, forthcoming); *What to do Till the Veterinarian Comes* (Chilton, 1976). Also the works of G Buttin (molecular biology), J Duplay et al (paleontology), Ramon y Cajal (neuroanatomy), others.
Affil Wayne State Univ.

WEISSMAN, RITA 12 Halevanon St, Tel Aviv, Israel *Tel* (03) 779 272.
TL Hebrew, Russian. **SL** English. **UDC** aeronautics, art, art history, aviation, engineering (civil, hydraulic), industry, literature (prose, science fiction), optics, physics, shipping, documentation, patents.
English G Green: *Travels with My Aunt* (Amarillo Library, 1975). A Cronin: *Beyond This World* (Amarillo Library, 1976). Also numerous scientific translations, articles, and documentation.

WEPPNER, EILEEN 1491 High St, Boulder, CO 80302 USA *Tel* 303-443-7933.
TL English. **SL** French, Russian. **UDC** astrophysics, atomic physics, brewing, computers, education, hydrology, linguistics, meteorology, mining, oceanography.
Russian V V Ivanov: *Transfer of Radiation in Spectral Lines* (US Govt Printing Office, 1973).
Accred/Memb ATA, CTA.

WERNER, ASTRID PO Box M-769, Hoboken, NJ 07030 USA *Tel* 201-792-5826.
TL English. SL German, Russian. UDC communications, computers, crystallography, electronics, geophysics, medicine, patents/trademarks, physics, polymers, telephony, pharmacology.
Affil Bell Laboratories. **Memb** ATA.

WHITE, EDWARD A 5307 Sangamore Rd, Washington, DC 20016 USA *Tel* 301-229-1932.
TL English. SL Russian. UDC agriculture, cybernetics, public health, sciences (medical).
Accred/Memb ATA.

WILSON, B ELISABETH 8774 Robles Way, San Diego, CA 92119 USA *Tel* 714-461-5943; 238-6869.
TL English. SL French, German. UDC aeronautics, aviation, engineering (compressor, electrical, hydraulic, industrial, mechanical, nuclear, turbine), fuel, metallurgy, metaphysics, physics (nuclear).
Affil Solar Turbines International (technical ed/translator). **Memb** ATA.

WINTERS, NANCY 1427½ Hampshire St, Quincy, IL 62301 USA *Tel* 217-224-8251.
TL English. SL French. UDC African affairs, birth control methods, cookery, economics, food/nutrition, horology, library science, literature (mysteries, science fiction), music, occultism, paper/pulp, political economy/science, printing, public administration, social services, sociology, witchcraft.
Memb ATA.

WOLF, GERDA R (Mrs John L) 5639 W Purdue, Dallas, TX 75209 USA *Tel* 214-352-9981.
TL English. SL French, German. UDC chemistry, geology, geophysics, engineering (chemical, industrial), patents/trademarks, petroleum, physics/mechanics, plastics/polymers, sciences (earth, life, medical, natural), technology.
Accred/Memb ATA.

WOLFE, CAROLE DYDA 609 W Cheyenne, Stillwater, OK 74074 USA *Tel* 405-377-0536.
TL & SL English & Russian. UDC agriculture, art, biology, botany, choreography (dance history), dairy farming, ecology, entomology, forestry, history, literature (prose), medicine (gynecology, obstetrics), music, parasitology, theater, veterinary medicine, zoology.

Author of translations for American Mathematical Society, East European Technical Translation Service, and Oklahoma State Univ.
Memb ATA.

WOODWORTH, LEWIS C 71 Moongale Dr, Carlisle, PA 17013 USA *Tel* 717-243-1194.
TL English. SL German, Russian. UDC building/construction, library science, linguistics/philology, literature (science fiction, songs) military science, music, philately, railroads, sciences (natural), transportation.
German the articles of Otto Arndt, Hilmar Barthel, Joachim Blady, Gerhard Fischer, Günter Heyden, Günter Knobloch, Rolf Opitz, Hans-Jürgen Röder, Hans Vielain. **Russian** the articles of Ye Davydov, A Gavrish, A Korobko, A Maslov & L Kropp, T Okhrimuk, numerous others.

WOROBEC, R B 1900 S Eads St #1228, Arlington, VA 22202 USA *Tel* 703-979-6758.
TL English. SL German, Polish, Russian, Ukrainian. UDC chemistry (inorganic, organic, pharmaceutical), sciences (medical).
Memb ATA, SFL, New York Acad of Med.

WREDE, J PETER Kirchweg 2, D-2361 Warder (Rohlsdorf), West Germany *Tel* (04559) 1034.
TL German. SL English, Spanish. UDC anthropology, commerce, copyright, documentation, education, government, history, jurisprudence, law (international), patents/trademarks, political economy, psychology, religion/scripture, theology.
Accred State of North Rhine (Westphalia). **Memb** TG.

WRIGHT, LELAND D, JR 243 Stanmary Dr, Berea, OH 44017 USA *Tel* 216-234-6345.
TL English. SL Portuguese, Spanish. UDC banking/finance, building/construction, engineering (industrial), fuel, iron/steel industry, law (international), machine tools, metallurgy, mineralogy, petroleum, technology, plastics/polymers, welding.
Spanish Daniel Ruzo: "The Authentic Testament of Nostradamus" (pending); Gerardo Vásquez-Ayora: "Introduction to Translatology" (pending).
Accred/Memb ATA. **Affil** Arthur G McKee and Co.

YANAI, MOSHE 18 Hayarmuk St, Ramat Hasharon, Israel *Tel* (03) 47 95 55.

TL Spanish. SL English, Hebrew. UDC aeronautics, automotive, aviation, banking/finance, business, documentation, economics, geography, government, history, information science, missiles/rocketry, political economy/science, sociology, technology.
Author of translations of technical handbooks, economic studies, and commercial reports.

YOHANNA, NICOLAS 212 Tamarack Dr, Berea, OH 44017 USA *Tel* 216-826-3199.
TL English. SL French, German, Italian, Portuguese, Rumanian, Russian, Spanish. UDC architecture, automotive, building/construction, engineering (all areas), geodesy, geography, industry, iron/steel industry, machine tools, metallurgy, optics, paper/pulp, physics/mechanics, standards, statistics, welding.
Accred/Memb ATA, NOTA.

YULE, MEERI 6600 NW Sweetbriar Lane, Kansas City, MO 64151 USA *Tel* 816-741-9441.
TL English. SL Finnish, Swedish. UDC commerce, dentistry, engineering (general), paper/pulp.
Memb ATA, MICATA.

ZACHARIA, NUHAD A 547 Woodward Dr, Huntingdon Valley, PA 19006 USA *Tel* 215-947-3548.
TL English. SL Arabic. UDC anthropology, archeology, banking/finance, engineering, law, patents/trademarks, petroleum.

ZOELLER, ANNELIESE V 600 S Lake Formosa Dr, Orlando, FL 32803 USA *Tel* 305-898-6652.
TL English. SL German. UDC aviation, engineering (aerospace, general), travel.
Accred Berlitz School of Languages (Heidelberg). **Memb** ATA.

ZOLONA, RIMA 69F Stadium Way, Allston, MA 02134 USA *Tel* 617-782-5269.
TL & SL English & Russian. UDC cosmology, hydrology, mathematics, oceanography, planetary physics, space science, theory of relativity.
English H Ray: *The Stars* (MIR, 1971). G Hawkins: *Stonehenge Decoded* (MIR, 1972). **Russian** *Handbook for Engineers on Building Materials* (MIR, 1977). M Budyko: *Climate Changes* (Amer Geophysical Union, 1977).
Memb NETA.

Industrial, Scientific & Technical Translators —Classified by Language

The translators in the preceding section have been classified here by target and source languages. The target language (language *into which* a translation is made) appears in boldface caps; source language (language *from which* a translation is made) appears in upper and lowercase boldface. Translators names, listed in alphabetical order under their specific target/source languages, are followed by the standard two-letter state abbreviations or abbreviated country name to identify regional accessibility. Emphasis is given here on English either as a source or target language.

Into ARABIC from:

English

Foz, F (NY)
Megalli, I Y (VA)

Into BURMESE from:

English

Khin, U (MD)

Into CATALAN from:

English

Foz, F (NY)

Into CHINESE from:

English

Liu, D Y (Taiwan)

Into CZECH from:

English

Let, N F (IL)

Into DANISH from:

English

Johannsen, H (UK)

Into DUTCH from:

English

Andriesse, E (NY, Neth)
Bogaert, D (Bel)
Bonnekamp, S M (UK)
Dierckx, M J (Bel)
Kagie, J L (Neth)
Moreau, J G M (Bel)
Nijk, H G (Isr)
Pauwels, P (Bel)
Penninckx, W (Bel)
Romeijn, H (Neth)
Van Boxelaer, M (Bel)
Van Hoorn-Muller, C M (Neth)
Van Mulders, A (Lux)
Vermeir, P (Bel)

Into DUTCH/FLEMISH from:

English

De Palmenaer, R (Bel)

Into ENGLISH from:

Afrikaans

Evans, W V (NY)

Arabic

Hanna, G M (NY)
Hasnain, Q (S Arab)
Irving, R A S (UK)
Kamal, S A (TN)
Mittelmann, G (UK)
Zacharia, N A (PA)

Bulgarian

Karriker, R J (OK)
Lebovitz, C H (IL)
Treanor, P J (DC)

Burmese

Khin, U (MD)

Castilian

Cardozo, M da S (DC)

Chinese

Broadbent, K P (Can)
Liu, D Y (Taiwan)
Mish, J L (NY)
Ridley, C P (CA)

Czech

Druck, K L (NJ)
Ehrlich, L (CA)
Jolly, S B (UK)
Lavoott, R (Isr)
Let, N F (IL)

Danish

Armstrong, J W (CA)
Bertsche, W I (NY)
Craddock, J T (UK)
Creutz, R T (MA)
Johannsen, H (UK)
Lund, J J (OR)
McIntyre, J (Ger)
Murray, S T (CA)
Schulemann, D F (VA)
Tapelband, E A (CA)
Vreeland, R (UK)
Wardle, E (UK)

Dutch

Akkerman, Fedde H (IN)
Bertsche, W I (NY)
Boer-Hoff, L E (Neth)
Bonnekamp, S M (UK)
Brown, G K (OH)
Butterworth, B (UK)

Devinney, M K (NJ)
De Vries, J (Bel)
Dierckx, M J (Bel)
Eichler, G P (CA)
Evans, W V (NY)
Gosden, A (Bel)
Griffith, R (NJ)
Guback, D I (IL)
Hardin, R (Isr)
Hasselriis, H (NY)
Hayward, S (UK)
Ilsink, Y Y (CA)
Kagie, J L (Neth)
Koenig, J (NY)
Kondor, R (Isr)
Kumin, J (MA)
Le Docte, E (Bel)
Leonard, I A (MA)
Lund, J J (OR)
McMillan, E N (DC)
Murray, S T (CA)
Nijk, H G (Isr)
Ordish, O (UK)
Pelz, T (Isr)
Ringold, J K (CA)
Robinson, E M (Bel)
Romeijn, H (Neth)
Schwarz, R A (DE)
Sinclair, D A (Can)
Smith, H A (UK)
Smuts, J (UK)
Swart, I (UK)
Van Abbé, D M (UK)
Van Dam, R & M (NJ)
Vandenbrande, J-P (NJ)
Vollmer, L H (FL)
Vreeland, R (UK)
Wardle, E (UK)

Finnish

Yule, M (MO)

Flemish

Evans, W V (NY)

French

Abileah, M M (Can)
Abilock, R (CA)
Adam, E W (NY)
Akkerman, Fedde H (IN)
Anacker, N M (CA)
Armstrong, J W (CA)
Balk, L R (NJ)
Barb, W G (UK)
Beck, C J (PA)
Bellagamba, M C (Pan)
Berger, S E (NY)
Berglund, A M (MA)

Bergmann, V (NY)
Berry, V E (NY)
Berson, A C (UK)
Bertsche, W I (NY)
Biggs, R R (UK)
Bolton, P L (NJ)
Bomse, M D (NY)
Bonning, H K (UK)
Borchardt, M (NY)
Bourgoin, E G (DC)
Brace, G (Fr)
Brodovikoff, L (Bel)
Brown, G K (OH)
Butcher, C H (MD)
Butterworth, B (UK)
Capaldo, S J (Can)
Cardozo, M da S (DC)
Carozzi, A V (IL)
Checketts, R J (UK)
Chevallier, M G (UK)
Chiapperini, F F (NY)
Chisman, A McG (VA)
Claff, C E, Jr (MA)
Clinquart (Fr)
Cohen, J E (NY)
Coles, D T (NY)
Conrad, I J (UK)
Corbyn, D R (UK)
Corcoran, N (UK)
Coutli, J M (MI)
Craddock, J T (UK)
Crafton, P (MA)
Crowley, C A (PA)
Crozy, A (UK)
Daly, M M (NY)
Dambergs, N (Can)
Davison, L S (CT)
Dell, K M (NY)
Deporte, P V (MD)
Derrick, F W (Fr)
De Vere, R (CA)
Devinney, M K (NJ)
De Vries, J (NY)
Diggs, N (OH)
Dilson, J (NY)
Dotzauer, H H (CA)
Druck, K L (NJ)
Du Bois, A E M (FL)
Dungan, S M (CA)
Eck, H Z (MI)
Egbert, S M (CA)
Ehrlich, L (CA)
Eisinger, E (NY)
Engle, E (NY)
Escobar, F J, Jr (TX)
Evans, G G (MA)
Everett, B H (MA)
Fairfield, F (MI)
Ferreira, M D (NJ)

Fforde, K (UK)
Fields, H A (UK)
Fisher, P L (MI)
Flinn, P A (PA)
Fontana, A (MA)
Forster, M P (Bel)
François, R R (CA)
Fraser, D A (UK)
Frey, H A (Switz)
Gardner, F H (UK)
Gawn, P (Can)
Gisbey, A E (Ger)
Goldblatt, H (MD)
Goldman, Y E (Isr)
Goldner, L R (NY)
Gordon, A A (CA)
Gosden, A (Bel)
Griffith, R (NJ)
Grimes, W J (MA)
Guback, D I (IL)
Gwirtsman, J J (NJ)
Habberton, A (CA)
Hajdu, M B (FL)
Hamilton, G C (CA)
Hammond, E (UK)
Hammond, R E (UK)
Hardin, R (Isr)
Hasselriis, H (NY)
Hausman, M J (RI)
Hawthorne, R E (CO)
Hayward, S (UK)
Heddy, M F (MA)
Hepner G D, III (PA)
Herman, F W (PA)
Herzer, I (VA)
Hirschhorn, H H (FL)
Hockelberg, W B (PA)
Horton, C W, Sr (TX)
Howell, W M, Jr (VA)
James, M (UK)
Jardine, D K (Fr)
Jebokji, K B (CA)
Jenks, R H (UK)
Jerison, I (CA)
Jones, I P (Lux)
Kaufman, H S (Can)
Kawecki, A T (NJ)
Kelly, W F (WA)
Kemendo, J P (TX)
Keogh, B T (UK)
King, B N (CA)
King, G & M (Fr)
King, S (Bel)
Kirk, K L (DC)
Koenig, J (NY)
Komorowicz, E (PA)
Kondor, R (Isr)
Kumin, J (MA)
Lambert, J L F (Can)
Lanniel, J M (PA)
Laporte, M A (TX)
Lawson, V (UK)
Leaman, L (MA)
Le Docte, E (Bel)
Leffler, D R (CA)
Leonard, I A (MA)
Leopold, C J (NY)
Light, L R (IA)
London, J E (NY)
Lynch, C A (IL)
McAllister, K J (TX)
McCarthy, M H P (UK)
McGee, L I (MA)
McGhee, J E (IL)
McIntyre, J (Ger)

McMillan, E N (DC)
McQuiston, H (CT)
Maddy, M C (OH)
Manstead, J (UK)
Marsh, A (UK)
May, J E (FL)
Megalli, I Y (VA)
Merrick, H (UK)
Milne, M (CA)
Morin, R (Can)
Naclerio, G (NY)
Neiden, M (OH)
Nowak, E V (MI)
O'Grady, L (NY)
Olechno, G (CA)
Ordish, G (UK)
Ordish, O (UK)
Orenstein, H S (VA)
O'Sullivan, A M (OR)
Paisley, H P (UK)
Parisi, A M (OH)
Patterson, L M (AL)
Pearcy, R (VA)
Pelz, T (Isr)
Pemberton, A E (UK)
Petrov, G R (DC)
Raikhlin-Eisenkraft, B (Isr)
Raïnof, A (CA)
Rajkay, L (MD)
Rastorfer, R (NY)
Reading-Leclercq, P (DC)
Rees, E S (CA)
Rehmus, E E (CA)
Ridley, C P (CA)
Ringold, J K (CA)
Robinson, E M (Bel)
Robinson, H L (UK)
Rodenas, M (DC)
Rose, W (UK)
Ryby, I J (NJ)
Saklad, M A (Fr)
Salmon, L J (CA)
Saussy, K W (SC)
Schechter, C (PA)
Schwarz, R A (DE)
Scott, J S (UK)
Sheehan, G D (NY)
Shevers, S D (OH)
Simpkin, R E (UK)
Sinclair, D A (Can)
Smith, H A (UK)
Snell, B M (UK)
Stacy, C M (TX)
Stanich, F S (NY)
Steenhagen, C L (CO)
Sterling, M (NY)
Stern, C M (NY)
Stocks, G R (UK)
Stratta, M C (NY)
Stuart, R A G (UK)
Sweetko, M (UK)
Tannenbaum, A (NY)
Tarka, J A (PA)
Thornton, J (PA)
Trang, C K-D (VA)
Trimble, R F (IL)
Underwood, D M (Fr)
Valenti, B Y (FL)
Van Abbé, D M (UK)
Van Dam, M (NJ)
Van Dam, R (NJ)
Vandenbrande, J-P (NJ)
Vasconcellos, S de (DC)
Vásquez-Ayora, G (VA)
Vincke, R L (Bel)

Vojtko, M M P (PA)
Vreeland, R (UK)
Wade, S P (CA)
Wardle, E (UK)
Webb, A F (UK)
Webster, P E (NY)
Wedekind, A M B (MD)
Weisfeld, G E (MI)
Weppner, E (CO)
Wilson, B E (CA)
Winters, N (IL)
Wolf, G R (TX)
Yohanna, N (OH)

German

Abileah, M M (Can)
Abilock, R (CA)
Adam, E W (NY)
Adams, J (CA)
Akkerman, Fedde H (IN)
Alex, K (IL)
Armstrong, J W (CA)
Balk, L R (NJ)
Barb, W G (UK)
Berger, S E (NY)
Berglund, A M (MA)
Bernays, H F (OH)
Bertsche, A (NY)
Bertsche, W I (NY)
Bick, W (UK)
Birdwood, G F B (UK)
Bolton, P L (NJ)
Bomse, M D (NY)
Bonning, H K (UK)
Bostwick, G L (CA)
Bradley, F (UK)
Broadbent, K P (Can)
Brown, G K (OH)
Butcher, C H (MD)
Butterworth, B (UK)
Butterfield, V (UK)
Carozzi, A V (IL)
Claff, C E , Jr (MA)
Coles, D T (NY)
Conrad, I J (UK)
Corbyn, D R (UK)
Corcoran, N (UK)
Craddock, J T (UK)
Crowley, C A (PA)
Crozy, A (UK)
Crummey, J A (CA)
Cunningham, D S (NJ)
Davison, L S (CT)
Devinney, M K (NJ)
Dickenson, U R (UK)
Diggs, N (OH)
Dilson, J (NY)
Dobes, R K (CA)
Dotzauer, H H (CA)
Drummond, H (UK)
Eck, H Z (MI)
Ehrlich, L (CA)
Ehrmann, R-H (IL)
Eichler, G P (CA)
Eliassaf, J (Isr)
Engle, E (NY)
Evans, G G (MA)
Fain, C A (CA)
Fainberg, A (UK)
Feldman, A A (WA)
Fenton, L (NY)
Ferreira, M D (NJ)
Fershee, S (MO)
Fforde, K (UK)
Fischer, H W (Ger)

Fisher, P L (MI)
Fitzgerald, B J (PA)
Flinn, P A (PA)
Fraser, D A (UK)
Frey, H A (Switz)
Gardner, F H (UK)
Gillmeier, I E (WI)
Gisbey, A E (Ger)
Glatz, E M (NY)
Goldman, Y E (Isr)
Goldner, L R (NY)
Gosden, A (Bel)
Griffith, R (NJ)
Grimes, W J (MA)
Guback, D I (IL)
Gwirtsman, J J (NJ)
Haas, G (ME)
Habberton, A (CA)
Hahn, M (MD)
Hajdu, M B (FL)
Hammond, E (UK)
Hanff, K Z (NY)
Hannemann, E (WI)
Hardin, R (Isr)
Harris, D (Ger)
Hasselriis, H (NY)
Hayes, J H (UK)
Hayward, S (UK)
Hellmann, U (CT)
Helmick, J G (OR)
Hepner, G D, III (PA)
Herman, F W (PA)
Herrmann, H H (NY)
Herzer, I (VA)
Hildebrandt, R H (IL)
Hirschhorn, H H (FL)
Horton, C W, Sr (TX)
Howe, K B (MA)
Hummel, J G (Ger)
Jerison, I (CA)
Johnston, I D (MI)
Jolly, S B (UK)
Jordan, D (Can)
Kandiner, H J (NJ)
Karkalas, O (PA)
Kellner, H M (NY)
Keogh, B T (UK)
Kidd, D L (TX)
King, I B (VA)
King, S (Bel)
Kittenbacher, P E (TX)
Knudsen, W (OH)
Koehler, H M (IL)
Koenig, H J (MN)
Koenig, J (NY)
Komorowicz, E (PA)
Kondor, R (Isr)
Krawutschke, P W (MI)
Kumin, J (MA)
Lakis, E A (NY)
Lambert, J L F (Can)
La Roche, M M S (MA)
Lawson, V (UK)
Leaman, L (MA)
Leffler, D R (CA)
Lieder, U E (CA)
Lindsey, D (AZ)
Loeffler, A G (Arg)
Lund, J J (OR)
McAllister, K J (TX)
McCarthy, M H P (UK)
McIndoo, T Q (WI)
McIntyre, J (Ger)
McMillan, E N (DC)
Maddy, M C (OH)

Martin, J (AZ)
May, J E (FL)
Mayer, E O (Bel)
Mecklenburg, S A (TX)
Merrick, H (UK)
Meyer, R G (UK)
Mitchell, I E (CO)
Mittelmann, G (UK)
Morehouse, K H (MA)
Murray, S T (CA)
Myrants, G (UK)
Nash, C W (MA)
Needles, R C (MO)
Neiden, M (OH)
Nekrassoff, V N (Can)
Niebauer, J J, Jr (MD)
Ordish, O (UK)
Paisley, H P (UK)
Pearcy, R (VA)
Pelz, T (Isr)
Pick, W (Gr)
Platz, A E (VA)
Polacek, J (Isr)
Raikhlin-Eisenkraft, B (Isr)
Rajkay, L (MD)
Rastorfer, R (NY)
Reeds, J A (MO)
Rehmus, E E (CA)
Reisenberger, R (UK)
Ritterskamp, M S (NY)
Robinson, E M (Bel)
Robinson, H L (UK)
Rodman, R B (MA)
Rose, W (UK)
Rosenberg, G (CA)
Ryby, I J (NJ)
Safonov, S H (CO)
Schoen, W (OH)
Schuldt, L M (OR)
Schulemann, D F (VA)
Schulte, J H (TX)
Schunk, C (TX)
Schwartz, L C A (OH)
Schwarz, R A (DE)
Scott, J S (UK)
Sheehan, G D (NY)
Simpkin, R E (UK)
Slater, T (Ger)
Smith, H A (UK)
Smith, M F (Ger)
Smith, R E (NY)
Smuts, J (UK)
Snell, B M (UK)
Spangler, P S (CA)
Stanich, F S (NY)
Sterling, M (NY)
Stern, C M (NY)
Stock, J W (OH)
Stocks, G R (UK)
Stoll, G C (FL)
Strickler, J A (MN)
Stuart, R A G (UK)
Stumpf, M L (CA)
Szmidt, A B (UK)
Tabi, U (NY)
Tannenbaum, A (NY)
Tarka, J A (PA)
Teague, B (GA)
Treanor, P J (DC)
Trimble, R F (IL)
Underwood, D M (Fr)
Van Abbé, D M (UK)
Van Dam, R & M (NJ)
Vollmer, L H (FL)
Vreeland, R (UK)

Wade, S P (CA)
Wallace, L M (UK)
Wardle, E (UK)
Wareham, P A (UK)
Webb, A F (UK)
Wedekind, A M B (MD)
Werner, A (NJ)
Wilson, B E (CA)
Wolf, G R (TX)
Woodworth, L C (PA)
Worobec, R B (VA)
Yohanna, N (OH)
Zoeller, A V (FL)

Greek

Helmick, J G (OR)
Pick, W (Gr)
Ponticas, E G (MD)

Hebrew

Goldman, Y E (Isr)
Jacoby, F R (NH)
Kapulski, I H (IL)
Lederman, D B (Isr)
Myers, G D (Isr)
Pelz, T (Isr)
Raikhlin-Eisenkraft, B (Isr)

Hindi

Iyer, M M (India)
Mittal, S C (India)

Hungarian

Geran, P (MI)
Gergay, P A (CA)
Goldman, Y E (Isr)
Hajdu, M B (FL)
Komorowicz, E (PA)
Kondor, R (Isr)
Rajkay, L (MD)

Indonesian

O'Bryan, T R (VA)
Smith, B D (UK)

Italian

Armstrong, J W (CA)
Bellagamba, M C (Pan)
Berger, S E (NY)
Berry, V E (NY)
Bertsche, W I (NY)
Bonning, H K (UK)
Butterworth, B (UK)
Cardozo, M da S (DC)
Conrad, I J (UK)
Cossu, F (CA)
Crozy, A (UK)
Dotzauer, H H (CA)
Escobar, F J, Jr (TX)
Everett, B H (MA)
Ferreira, M D (NJ)
Fields, H A (UK)
Fraser, D A (UK)
Goldman, Y E (Isr)
Gosden, A (Bel)
Grietti, M (CT)
Habberton, A (CA)
Hasselriis, H (NY)
Hayward, S (UK)
Hepner G D, III (PA)
Herzer, I (VA)
Interdonato-McNeil, R (MD)
Kawecki, A T (NJ)
Kemendo, J P (TX)
Kerr, L P (It)

Komorowicz, E (PA)
Kondor, R (Isr)
Leonard, I A (MA)
McAllister, K J (TX)
McIntyre, J (Ger)
Manstead, J (UK)
May, J E (FL)
Naclerio, G (NY)
Ordish, O (UK)
Parisi, A M (OH)
Pearcy, R (VA)
Pelz, T (Isr)
Pemberton, A E (UK)
Reading-Leclercq, P (DC)
Robinson, E M (Bel)
Robinson, H L (UK)
Rose, W (UK)
Santalesa, LA (NY)
Schechter, C (PA)
Schunk, C (TX)
Sheehan, G D (NY)
Sinclair, D A (Can)
Stocks, G R (UK)
Stratta, M C (NY)
Trimble, R F (IL)
Wardle, E (UK)
Webster, P E (NY)
Yohanna, N (OH)

Japanese

Davison, L S (CT)
Fraser, D A (UK)
Gorham, D C (MD)
Kawasaki, H (CA)
Kim, C-H (OH)
Kubota, H (TN)
Pearcy, R (VA)
Ridley, C P (CA)
Saganuma, M (Japan)
Sasaki, R S (NJ)
Tung, L W (TX)

Korean

Kim, C-H (OH)

Latin

Olechno-Huszcza, C (CA)

Latvian

Dambergs, N (Can)

Malay

O'Bryan, T R (VA)

Norwegian

Armstrong, J W (CA)
Bertsche, W I (NY)
Craddock, J T (UK)
Creutz, R T (MA)
Ellison, J A (UK)
Hawthorne, R E (CO)
Lund, J J (OR)
Murray, S T (CA)
Pelz, T (Isr)
Schulemann, D F (VA)
Vreeland, R (UK)
Wardle, E (UK)

Persian (Farsi)

Hasnain, Q (S Arab)

Polish

Gwirtsman, J J (NJ)
Hall, M J (NJ)
Hanff, K Z (NY)

Hummel, J G (Ger)
Jerison, I (CA)
Kawecki, A T (NJ)
Konstantin, A E (CT)
Lederman, D B (Isr)
Mish, J L (NY)
Mitchell, A D (CA)
Nowak, E V (MI)
Olechno-Huszcza, C (CA)
Orenstein, H S (VA)
Stuart, R A G (UK)
Szmidt, A B (UK)
Tybulewicz, A (UK)

Portuguese

Adam, E W (NY)
Adao, D M (CA)
Bellagamba, M C (Pan)
Bertsche, W I (NY)
Bourgoin, E G (DC)
Cardozo, M da S (DC)
Carrasco, A (OH)
Dears, P H (PA)
Du Bois, A E M (FL)
Eichler, G P (CA)
Engle, E (NY)
Ferreira, M D (NJ)
Fockens, R P (Brazil)
Habberton, A (CA)
Hasselriis, H (NY)
Hockelberg, W B (PA)
Howell, W M, Jr (VA)
Kapulski, I H (IL)
Labrada, E B (DC)
Langman, I K (NJ)
Leonard, I A (MA)
McMillan, E N (DC)
May, J E (FL)
Montero, B A (NJ)
Nunez, B (DC)
Ordás, R H (CA)
Ordish, G (UK)
Patterson, L M (AL)
Quiñones, M O (CA)
Robinson, H L (UK)
Santos, M B R (UK)
Schechter, C (PA)
Sheehan, G D (NY)
Spector, V C (FL)
Stacy, C M (TX)
Thornton, J (PA)
Vasconcellos, S de (DC)
Vásquez-Ayora, G (VA)
Wardle, E (UK)
Webster, P E (NY)
Wright, L D, Jr (OH)
Yohanna, N (OH)

Portuguese (Brazilian)

Bianco, C (NY)

Rumanian

Geran, P (MI)
Goldman, Y E (Isr)
Manstead, J (UK)
Raikhlin-Eisenkraft, B (Isr)
Yohanna, N (OH)

Russian

Adams, J (CA)
Agranov, I (VA)
Armstrong, J W (CA)
Beerbaum, M S (CA)
Berglund, A M (MA)
Berson, A C (UK)

Biderman, A (NY)
Blau, M R (OH)
Bolton, P L (NJ)
Brodovikoff, L (Bel)
Brown, G K (OH)
Burdick, D L (CA)
Cadmus, S P, Jr (CA)
Capaldo, S J (Can)
Conner, R M (TX)
Creutz, R T (MA)
Crozy, A (UK)
Crummey, J A (CA)
Dambergs, N (Can)
Davison, L S (CT)
Deporte, P V (MD)
Dilson, J (NY)
Dolberg, A (UK)
Druck, K L (NJ)
Eliassaf, J (Isr)
Engle, E (NY)
Evans, G G (MA)
Finch G K, II (MD)
Fraser, D A (UK)
Frentz L B, III (CA)
Geld, I (CA)
Gisbey, A E (Ger)
Graf, V (PA)
Grimes, W J (MA)
Gwirtsman, J J (NJ)
Haigh, B (UK)
Hall, M J (NJ)
Hammond, R E (UK)
Hanff, K Z (NY)
Hardin, R (Isr)
Herzer, I (VA)
Howe, K B (MA)
Iyer, M M (India)
Jerison, I (CA)
Jolly, S B (UK)
Kandiner, H J (NJ)
Karkalas, O (PA)
Karriker, R J (OK)
Kawecki, A T (NJ)
Kelly, W F (WA)
Kent, W, Jr (Can)
Keogh, B T (UK)
Komorowicz, E (PA)
Kondor, R (Isr)
Konstantin, A E (CT)
Lady, E L (HI)
Lavoott, R (Isr)
Leaman, L (MA)
Lebovitz, C H (IL)
Lederman, D B (Isr)
Leffler, D R (CA)
McAllister, K J (TX)
McCarthy, M H P (UK)
McConnaughey, W B (OR)
McGlothlin, W O (CA)
McQuiston, H (CT)
Maddy, M C (OH)
Marcinik, R L (DC)
Martin, J (AZ)
Mittal, S C (India)
Myers, G D (Isr)
Niebauer, J J, Jr (MD)
Olechno-Huszcza, C (CA)
Orenstein, H S (VA)
Patterson, L (MD)
Petrov, G R (DC)
Platt, J (IL)
Poch, W J (NJ)
Priest, P F H (IN)
Raikhlin-Eisenkraft, B (Isr)
Ringer, W C (CO)

Rodman, R B (MA)
Safonov, S H (CO)
Santalesa, L A (NY)
Silverman, R H (MA)
Sinclair, D A (Can)
Sobchak, P (CA)
Spangler, P S (CA)
Stackhouse, K (PA)
Stacy, C M (TX)
Stock, J W (OH)
Stuart, R A G (UK)
Sullivan, G (VA)
Teague, B (GA)
Tourkoff, E F (CA)
Treanor, P J (DC)
Trimble, R F (IL)
Tybulewicz, A (UK)
Wanta, R C (MA)
Wardle, E (UK)
Weppner, E (CO)
Werner, A (NJ)
White, E A (DC)
Wolfe, C D (OK)
Woodworth, L C (PA)
Worobec, R B (VA)
Yohanna, N (OH)
Zolina, R (MA)

Serbo-Croatian

Berger, S E (NY)
Davies, R F (MA)
Herzer, I (VA)
Lambert, J L F (Can)
Santalesa, L A (NY)
Treanor, P J (DC)

Slovak

Let, N F (IL)
Vojtko, M M P (PA)

Spanish

Adam, E W (NY)
Adao, D M (CA)
Ainsworth, C A (NY)
Albizu, E M (NY)
Arango, L E (VA)
Armstrong, J W (CA)
Banda, F C (DC)
Barraclough, F H (NY)
Beck, C J (PA)
Bellagamba M C (Pan)
Berriz, H A (FL)
Berry, V E (NY)
Berson, A C (UK)
Bertsche, W I (NY)
Bonning, H K (UK)
Bostwick, G L (CA)
Bourgoin, E G (DC)
Bours, J F (NY)
Butterworth, B (UK)
Carmell, P L (MO)
Checketts, R J (UK)
Chisman, A McG (VA)
Coles, D T (NY)
Conrad, I J (UK)
Cotta, H Z (Mex)
Craddock, J T (UK)
Crozy, A (UK)
Cruz, A (FL)
Dears, P H (PA)
Dell, K M (NY)
Deporte, P V (MD)
Diggs, N (OH)
Docal, S J (DC)
Dotzauer, H H (CA)

Druck, K L (NJ)
Du Bois, A E M (FL)
Dungan, S M (CA)
Dwin, A W (NJ)
Eichler, G P (CA)
Engle, E (NY)
Escobar, F J, Jr (TX)
Everett, B H (MA)
Evia, E Q de G (Mex)
Farber, C A (WA)
Ferreira, M D (NJ)
Fogarty, C M (IL)
Gaudy, C A (CA)
Genis, M (CR)
Gilboy, P T (Sp)
Gist, G S (FL)
Gómez, M F L (CA)
González, S G (PR)
Gordon, A A (CA)
Griffith, R (NJ)
Guback D I (IL)
Habberton, A (CA)
Hasselriis, H (NY)
Hayward, S (UK)
Hildebrandt, R H (IL)
Hirschhorn, H H (FL)
Hockelberg, W B (PA)
Howell, W M, Jr (VA)
Ilsink, Y Y (CA)
Intedonato-McNeil, R (MD)
Jacobs, R (NY)
Jones, I P (Lux)
Kapulski, I H (IL)
Kargleder, C L (AL)
Katzmark, J W (CA)
Kemendo, J P (TX)
Keogh, B T (UK)
Key, D B (VA)
King, I B (VA)
Kirk, K L (DC)
Kittenbacher, P E (TX)
Labrada, E B (DC)
Langman, I K (NJ)
Laporte, M A (TX)
Leffler, D R (CA)
Leonard, I A (MA)
Letourneaut, R (FL)
Lewis, E M (CO)
Li, P M (GA)
Loeffler, A G (Arg)
McAllister, K J (TX)
McGee, L I (MA)
McMillan, E N (DC)
Marzollini, P (OH)
May, J E (FL)
Mikkelson, H (CA)
Montero, B A (NJ)
Montero, S S (Mex)
Moore, W (VA)
Morales, R M (CA)
Naclerio, G (NY)
Neiden, M (OH)
Nunez, B (DC)
O'Grady, L (NY)
Ordás, R H (CA)
Ordish, G (UK)
Patterson, L M (AL)
Pearcy, R (VA)
Pelz, T (Isr)
Pemberton, A E (UK)
Peña, V (CT)
Platz, A E (VA)
Prada, A (OH)
Quiñones, M O (CA)
Raïnof, A (CA)

Ras, M F (NY)
Rastorfer, R (NY)
Rehmus, E E (CA)
Robinson, H L (UK)
Rock, E B (NC)
Rodenas, M (DC)
Santos, M B R (UK)
Schechter, C (PA)
Schulte, J H (TX)
Segura, V J (CA)
Sheehan, G D (NY)
Sherrill, S H (CA)
Shevers, S D (OH)
Silvera, F del C (CT)
Smith, R E (NY)
Snell, B M (UK)
Stacy, C M (TX)
Stern, C M (NY)
Stock, J W (OH)
Stocks, G R (UK)
Stratta, M C (NY)
Strong, C R (NY)
Swaney, I S (CA)
Tannenbaum, A (NY)
Thomas, A (Ven)
Thornton, J (PA)
Threshman, C I (CT)
Tuck, D S (MA)
Valenti, B Y (FL)
Van Buren, R G (MI)
Vandenbrande, J-P (NJ)
Vasconcellos, S de (DC)
Vega, V J (NV)
Wade, S P (CA)
Wardle, E (UK)
Webster, P E (NY)
Wright, L D, Jr (OH)
Yohanna, N (OH)

Swedish

Armstrong, J W (CA)
Bertsche, W I (NY)
Craddock, J T (UK)
Creutz, R T (MA)
Ellison, J A (UK)
Fleming, R (UK)
Gould, D E (UK)
Hawthorne, R E (CO)
Lund, J J (OR)
Miller, C J (Sw)
Murray, S T (CA)
Paul, D M & M (DC)
Schulemann, D F (VA)
Van Santen, A (Sw)
Vreeland, R (UK)
Wardle, E (UK)
Yule, M (MO)

Thai

Race, C (Thai)

Ukrainian

Karkalas, O (PA)
Kawecki, A T (NJ)
Konstantin, A E (CT)
Lebovitz, C H (IL)
Worobec, R B (VA)

Urdu

Hasnain, Q (S Arab)

Vietnamese

Balaban, J (PA)
Heddy, M F (MA)

Into FRENCH from:

English

Bellegarde, S (MD)
Binsfeld, G (Bel)
Borchardt, M (NY)
Brodovikoff, L (Bel)
Bronstein-Vinaver, B (Fr)
Chenail, J (Can)
Coriat, A (Ven)
Coutil, J M (MI)
Delisle, J (Can)
De Palmenaer, R (Bel)
Di Virgilio, L (Can)
Dube, B (Can)
Eisinger, E (NY)
Fairfield, F (MI)
Foz, F (NY)
François, R R (CA)
Girod, C (NY)
Halleux, N (Bel)
Hardy, C (MI)
James, M (UK)
Jebokji, K B (CA)
Jones-Daix, E (Lux)
King, G & M (Fr)
Kowalski-Nardone, A-M (It)
Lachmann, A D (VA)
Lambert, J L F (Can)
Laporte, M A (TX)
Lasquin, F (Fr)
Latortue, F (DC)
Light, L R (IA)
London, J E (NY)
Lottefier, P J (Bel)
McMath, A E L E (UK)
Moreau, J G M (Bel)
Morin, R (Can)
Noël, P (Bel)
Odiaux, P (NH)
Pauwels, P (Bel)
Pierson, G (Fr)
Rodenas, M (DC)
Salmon, L J (CA)
Saussy, K W (SC)
Sicaud, P (CA)
Simonnet, A (Fr)
Staljanssens, L (Bel)
Trang, C K-D (VA)
Vandenbussche, E R (Can)
Vasconcellos, S de (DC)
Vásquez-Ayora, G (VA)
Weill, P (Fr)

Into GERMAN from:

English

Adamson, U B (OH)

Alex, K (IL)
Balig, H (Bel)
Baumgart, A E (FL)
Bergmann, V (NY)
Binsfeld, G (Bel)
Bruch, K (Ger)
Cunningham, M (PA)
Delhey, L S (Peru)
Dickenson, U R (UK)
Fainberg, A (UK)
Feldmann, A A (WA)
Fershee, S (MO)
Fickau, B (WI)
Fischlin, J E (Switz)
Hannemann, E (WI)
Hayes, J H (UK)
Hellmann, U (CT)
Hermann, H H (NY)
Hertzer, W (IA)
Johnston, I D (MI)
Knudsen, W (OH)
Köhler, W (Ger)
Kondor, R (Isr)
La Roche, M M S (MA)
Lieder, U E (CA)
Linke, E (Ger)
Loeffler, A G (Arg)
Mayer, E O (Bel)
Pelz, T (Isr)
Pick, W (Ger)
Polacek, J (Isr)
Schulemann, D F (VA)
Schunk, C (TX)
Schwartz, L C A (OH)
Smuts, J (UK)
Staljanssens, L (Bel)
Szmidt, A B (UK)
Tabi, U (NY)
Wedekind, A M B (MD)
Wrede, J P (Ger)

Into GREEK from:

English

Ponticas, E G (MD)

Into HEBREW from:

English

Weissman, R (Isr)

Into HINDI from:

English

Iyer, M M (India)

Into HUNGARIAN from:

English

Samu, J (NY)

Into ITALIAN from:

English

Foz, F (NY)
Kowalski-Nardone, A-M (It)
Nardone, G (It)
Schunk, C (TX)
Vasquez-Ayora, G (VA)

Into JAPANESE from:

English

Kawasaki, H (CA)
Sakamoto, R K (NY)

Into POLISH from:

English

Baumgart, A E (FL)
Bronstein-Vinaver, B (Fr)
Gorski, J (OH)
Szmidt, A B (UK)

Into PORTUGUESE from:

English

Fockens, R P (Brazil)
Foz, F (NY)
Guise, M A de S (Brazil)
Labrada, E B (DC)
Pintocoelho, L C (MD)
Reis, D D (Brazil)
Selon, A (Brazil)
Spector, V C (FL)
Vásquez-Ayora, G (VA)
Velloso, W (DC)

Into RUSSIAN from:

English

Agranov, I (VA)
Brodovikoff, L (Bel)
Bronstein-Vinaver, B (Fr)
Mishelevich, B (PA)
Schneider, R (Isr)
Sullivan, G (VA)
Weissman, R (Isr)
Wolfe, C D (OK)
Zolina, R (MA)

Into SLOVAK from:

English

Let, N F (IL)

Into SPANISH from:

English

Ainsworth, C A (NY)
Albizu, E M (NY)
Alvarez, E A (MD)
Barraclough, F H (NY)
Baumgart, A E (FL)
Bramtot, J A (MD)
Burleigh, W A (MD)
Cháirez, J L (Mex)
Collazo, J L (NJ)
Coriat, A (Ven)
Cruz, A (FL)
Cuellar, B V de (Mex)
Delhey, L S (Peru)
Dieguez, I S (DC)
Docal, S J (DC)
Farber, C A (WA)
Foz, F (NY)
Garcia-Donoso, P (Ecua)
Gilboy, P T (Sp)
Gist, G S (FL)
Gómez, M F L (CA)
Guise, M A de S (Brazil)
Heeter, M C G R (VA)
Juncal, J A (DC)
Katzmark, J W (CA)
Labrada, E B (DC)
Laporte, M A (TX)
Lawton, D H (OH)
Loeffler, A G (Arg)
Montenegro, M A (VA)
Montero, S S (Mex)
Moore, W (VA)
Morales, R M (CA)
Peña, V (CT)
Rodrieguez, P (DC)
Ruiz, V M (CA)
Santos, M B R (UK)
Silvera, F del C (CT)
Swaney, I S (CA)
Thomas, A (Ven)
Tuck, D S (MA)
Vargas, A (NY)
Vasconcellos, S de (DC)
Vega, V J (NV)
Vela, J (MD)
Velloso, W (DC)
Yanai, M (Isr)

Into THAI from:

English

Race, C (Thai)

Humanistic/Literary Translators

Humanistic and literary translators are here identified as those who translate literature in its many forms and genres (children's, drama, folklore, poetry, fiction, science fiction, librettos, lyrics, songs, etc) and material within the areas commonly referred to as the humanities or humanistic disciplines. Each entry contains the following basic identifying professional designations: target language (s); source language(s); specialized subject fields of the translator's competence and/or preference; affiliation with academic institutions, international organizations, or government agencies; recognized accreditation from an association or translator-training program; and membership in a recognized professional association. These are, in most cases, accompanied by a selected bibliography of published translations arranged by source language, original author's name, English title, publisher's name, and year of publication. Where respondents have failed to provide an English title, the foreign title has been given.

It should be noted that in many instances these translators may also work with administrative, commercial, legal, industrial, scientific, or technical material, but because the major portion of their professional activity appears to be in the purely humanistic or literary areas, they have been listed in this section.

ADAIR, MONTE Domitianstr 4, D-6369 Nidderau 1, West Germany *Tel* (06187) 23775.
TL English. SL German. UDC economics, history, linguistics/philology, literature (drama, history, prose), philosophy, political economy/science, social sciences.
Memb ALTA, TG.

AHERN, MAUREEN 1438 E Williams St, Tempe, AZ 85281 USA *Tel* 602-966-8576; 965-7551.
TL English. SL Spanish. UDC education, history, linguistics/philology, literature (criticism, folklore, poetry, prose, science fiction), political science.
Spanish Antonio Cisneros: *The Spider Hangs Too Close to the Ground* (Jonathan Cape, 1970). Miguel Angel Asturias: *Guatemalan Sociology* (Arizona State Univ, Ctr for Latin American Studies, 1977); *Peru: The New Poetry* (London Magazine Editions, 1970). Rosario Castellanos: "Selected Poems" (pending). Also the works of Carlos German Belli, Cecilia Bustamante, Javier Heraud, Sebastian Salazar Bondy, Blanca Varela, Mario Vargas Llosa, Diane Wakowski, Carlos Zavaleta, numerous others.
Affil Arizona State Univ.

ALDAN, DAISY 743 Madison Ave, New York, NY 10021 USA *Tel* 212-744-6670; Unterdorfstr 23a, CH-4143 Dornach, Switzerland *Tel* 061 725674.
TL English. SL French, German. UDC aesthetics, astrology, communications, criticism, education, ethics/morals, linguistics/philology, literature (children's, drama, folklore, librettos, lyrics, poetry, songs), metaphysics, occultism, painting, philosophy, publishing, religion/scripture, sculpture/plastic arts, theater, theology.
French Stéphane Mallarmé: *A Throw of Dice Never Will Abolish Chance* (Tiber, 1959; Folder, 1978). German Albert Steffen: *Selected Poems* (Folder, 1968; St George, 1978). Rudolf Steiner: *The Calendar of the Soul* (Anthroposophic, 1974). Albert Steffen: *The Death Experience of Manes* (Folder, 1972). Also the works

of Arthur Adamov, Guillaume Apollinaire, Antonin Artaud, Charles Baudelaire, André Breton, Gabriel Celaya, Jean Grillet, Heinrich von Kleist, Christian Morgenstern, Artur Rimbaud, Jean Tardieu, Pierre Vidal, Herbert Witzenmann, numerous others.
Awards 1978 PEN Translation Citation.

ALEXANDER, LLOYD 1005 Drexel Ave, Drexel Hill, PA 19026 USA *Tel* 215-449-5569.
TL English. SL French. UDC literature (poetry, prose).
French Paul Eluard: *Uninterrupted Poetry* (New Directions, 1951). J-P Sartre: *The Wall and Other Stories* (New Directions, 1948); *Nausea* (New Directions, 1949). Also the works of Henri Michaux, Jacques Prévert, Paul Valéry, Paul Vialar.

AL-GHAZOULI, MOHAMMAD BM Alghazouli, c/o Scotts Office Services, 80 Queensway, London WC1V 6XX, UK *Tel* 01-2297511.
TL & SL Arabic & English. UDC computers, education, journalism, literature (criticism), political science, psychology, sociology.
Arabic George Orwell: "Animal Farm" (pending).
Memb TG.

ALPHONESE-FERERE, GERARD 215 Red Barn Rd, Willow Grove, PA 19090 USA *Tel* 215-657-3193.
TL & SL English, French, Spanish. UDC education, government, history, linguistics, navigation, literature (prose), social sciences, social services, sociology.
Memb AIT.

AMPHOUX, NANCY LIPE 1 rue Werinhar, F-67000 Strasbourg, France *Tel* 36 09 48.
TL English. SL French. UDC arts, education, history, literature (biography, drama).
French Henri Troyat: *Tolstoy* (Doubleday, 1967); *Pushkin* (Doubleday, 1970); *Divided Soul: The Life of Gogol* (Doubleday, 1973). Edmonde Charles-Roux: *Chanel* (Knopf, 1975). Costa de Loverdo: *Gods with Bronze Swords*

(Doubleday, 1970). Max Gallo: *With the Victors* (Doubleday, 1974).

ANDERS, PAUL 90 Summer St, Williamstown, MA 01267 USA *Tel* 413-458-8318.
TL English. SL French, German, Latin. UDC ancient Christianity, Greco-Roman history.

ANDRÉ, DESMET Markegemsestraat 70, B-8788 Wakken, Belgium *Tel* (056) 60 22 47.
TL Dutch. SL English, French. UDC commerce, economics, political economy.
Affil Belgian Office for Foreign Trade.
Memb CBTIP.

ARCE, CARMELO SAAVEDRA 4519 Traymore St, Bethesda, MD USA 20014 *Tel* 301-530-5394; 202-676-0299.
TL & SL English & Spanish. UDC literature (all areas).
English Rebecca West: *The Fountain Overflows* (Editorial Cumbre, 1958). John Steinbeck: *The Short Reign of Pippin IV* (Editorial Cumbre, 1957). Thomas B Costain: *Below the Salt* (Editorial Cumbre, 1958). James McGregor Burns: *Roosevelt: The Lion and the Fox* (Editorial Grijalbo, 1958). Also the works of Zsolt Arodi, Ladislas Farago, Hildegard Knef, John Masters, V S Naipul, Norman Vincent Peale, Ellery Queen, Desmond Stewart, numerous others.
Memb TAALS.

ARNO, PAULA von HAIMBERGER 299 Glen Ave, Sea Cliff, NY 11579 USA *Tel* 516-671-7994.
TL English. SL German. UDC literature (all areas).
German Frank Bahr: *Dr Bahr's Acu-Diet* (William Morrow, 1978). Ernst von Khuon: *The Invisible Made Visible* (NY Graphic Society, 1973).

ARROWSMITH, WILLIAM Rd 1, Lincoln, VT 05443 USA *Tel* 802-453-2298.
TL English. SL French, Greek (Classical),

Italian, Latin. **UDC** literature (poetry, prose, drama).

Greek (Classical) Euripides: *Cyclops, Bacchae, Heracles, Orestes, Hecuba,* in Grene & Lattimore, eds: *The Complete Greek Tragedies* (Univ of Chicago, 1960). Aristophanes: *The Birds* (Univ of Michigan, 1961). **Italian** Cesare Pavese: *Hard Labor* (Grossman/Viking, 1976); *Dialogues with Leucò* (Univ of Michigan, 1965); *Six Modern Italian Novellas* (Pocket Books, 1964). **Latin** *The Satyricon of Petronius* (Univ of Michigan, 1959; New American Library, 1961). Also numerous translations of poetic and dramatic works, published in academic journals and periodicals. Also the editor with Roger Shattuck of *The Craft and Context of Translation* (see Sec 6, Books).

ASBECK, HANS THEO Painbreitenstr 7, D-8022 Grünwald, West Germany *Tel* (089) 6411957.

TL German. **SL** English. **UDC** literature (all areas).

English Arnold J Toynbee: *Between Oxus and Jumna* (Kohlhammer-Verlag, 1963). Dennis Milner & Edward Smart: *The Loom of Creation* (Hermann Bauer-Verlag, 1977). Also the works of Jacques Barzun, John Buell, B J Chute, Ian Fleming, Margaret Forster, Owen Lattimore, Arnold Toynbee, Michael Young. **Memb** VDÜ.

AUBERT, JACQUES 16 rue de Tourvielle, F-69005 Lyon, France *Tel* (78) 25 51 42.

TL French. **SL** English. **UDC** literature.

English James Joyce: *The Dubliners* (Gallimard, 1974).

Affil Univ of Lyon (II). **Memb** ATLF.

AUERBACH, FRANK Platanenstr 96, D-8021 Taufkirchen, Munich, West Germany *Tel* (089) 612 58 91.

TL German. **SL** English. **UDC** literature (Commonwealth literature, poetry, prose).

English Okot p'Bitek: *Song of Ocol* (Rutten & Loening, 1978). Short stories and poems of 36 Australian writers in *Modern Stories of the World: Australia* (Erdmann Verlag, 1970). Short stories and poems of 27 New Zealand writers in *Modern Stories of the World: New Zealand* (Erdmann Verlag, 1972). Short stories, poems, and essays of 42 East African writers in *Modern Stories of the World: East Africa* (Erdmann Verlag, 1976). Also the works of Michael Beveridge, David Campbell, Henry Lawson, O E Middleton, Douglas Stewart, Alfred Lord Tennyson, Patrick White, William Wordsworth, others. **Memb** VDÜ.

AVELING, HARRY Murdoch Univ, Murdoch, Western Australia 6153.

TL English. **SL** Indonesian, Malay. **UDC** arts, biography, education, geography, history, literature (poetry, prose), religion, social sciences.

Indonesian Rendra: "Swan Song"; "Pickpocket's Message to His Mistress"; "Prostitutes of Jakarta, Unite!" (*Tenggara*, Oct, 1968). Pramoedya Ananta Toer: "Letter to a Friend from the Country" (*Quadrant*, 1969). Soe Hok Gie: "The Children of Independence" (*Quadrant*, 1969). Also the works of Utuy Tatang Sontani,

Rivai Apin, Toeti Heraty, Sapardi Djoko Damono, numerous others.

BABB, EMILIE ANN 1634 Mission Blvd, Fayetteville, AR 72701 USA *Tel* 501-521-1725.

TL English. **SL** French. **UDC** education, linguistics/philology, literature (children's, criticism, lyrics, poetry, prose, science fiction).

Affil Univ of Arkansas. **Memb** ALTA.

BACKUS, DAVID 4859 Sheboygan Ave, Madison, WI 53705 USA *Tel* 608-273-0897.

TL English. **SL** French. **UDC** banking/finance, economics, ethics, geography, government, history, linguistics/philology, literature (mainly 19th century French criticism, prose), music, philosophy, political economy/science, religion, theology, viniculture.

French the works of Henri Beyle (Stendhal), Ernest Renan, Auguste Sabatier, Albert Schweitzer.

Memb ATA.

BACON, THOMAS 3303 44 St, Lubbock, TX 79413 USA *Tel* 806-792-0089.

TL English. **SL** German. **UDC** literature (German criticism, poetry, prose).

Affil Texas Tech Univ. **Memb** ALTA.

BAIR, LOWELL PO Box 118, Woodstock, NY 12498 USA *Tel* 914-679-6656.

TL English. **SL** French. **UDC** literature (fiction, nonfiction), philosophy.

French Gustave Flaubert: *Madame Bovary* (Bantam, 1959). Stendhal: *The Red and the Black* (Bantam, 1958). Evelyn de Schmedt: *Lifearts* (St Martin's, 1977). Jean Rostand: *Humanly Possible* (Sat Rev Press, 1973). Also the works of Alain-Fournier, Honoré de Balzac, Paul Bodin, Giacomo Casanova, Jean-Pierre Conty, René Descartes, Alexandre Dumas, Victor Hugo, Roger de Lafforest, Guy de Maupassant, Alain Moury, Christiane Rochefort, Jean-Jacques Rousseau, Edouard de Segonzac, Jules Verne, Voltaire, Emile Zola, numerous others.

BARKO, CAROL 4501 Broadway #7C, New York, NY 10040 USA *Tel* 212-942-1911.

TL English. **SL** French. **UDC** aesthetics, anthropology, architecture, art, communications, education, human resources, literature (all areas), occultism, sculpture, witchcraft.

French Jean Chalon: *Portrait of a Seductress: The World of Natalie Barney* (Crown, 1979). H Cixous, M Gagnon, A Leclerc: "Coming to Writing" (pending).

Affil Oberlin College.

BARNES, JIM NE Missouri State Univ, Kirksville, MO 63501 USA.

TL English. **SL** Choctaw, French, German. **UDC** literature (modern French and German writers, poetry, prose).

French assistance in translating André Gide: *The Notebooks of André Walter* (Philosophical Library, 1968). **German** Gustav Shenk: "In the Lion's Den" (*Mundus Artium*, 8 no 2, 1975).

BARNSTONE, WILLIS 4930 E Heritage Woods Rd, Bloomington, IN 47401 USA *Tel* 812-339-2380.

TL English. **SL** French, Greek (Classical) Spanish. **UDC** literature (children's, criticism, poetry).

Greek (Classical) Sappho (Doubleday, 1966). *Greek Lyric Poetry* (Bantam, 1959; Schocken, 1972). **Spanish** St John of the Cross: *Poems* (New Directions, 1970). Pedro Salinas: *My Voice Because of You* (SUNY, 1976). Also the works of Angelos Sikelianos, Antonio Machado, Juan Ramon Jimenez, Fray Luis de Leon, Miguel Hernandez, Margarita Liberaki, Konstantinos Kavafis, San Juan de la Cruz, Plato, Jorge Guillen, Concha Zardoya, Claude Vigee, Marina Tsvetayeva, Vincente Aleixandre, Robert Creeley, Homero Aridjis, Marco Antonio de Montes de Oca, Manuel Vasquez Montalban, Sinopoulos, George Himonas, Nocanor Parra, Juan Ruiz, Mao Tsetung, Alfredo Silva Estrada, Andre Reszler, Horace, Eduardo Escobar, Jorge Luiz Borges, Rumi, numerous others.

Affil Univ of Indiana. **Memb** ALTA.

BAROLINI, HELEN 33 Ellis Pl, Ossining, NY 10562 USA *Tel* 914-941-6054.

TL English. **SL** Italian. **UDC** arts, biography, literature (poetry, prose), religion.

Italian Francesco Arcangeli: *Graham Sutherland* (Abrams, 1975). Antonio Barolini: *A Long Madness* (Pantheon, 1964). Bruno Brizzi: *Rome: The Fountains* (Colombo, 1973). Terisio Pignatti: *Painting: Through the Eighteenth Century* (Newsweek, 1974). Giancarlo Zizola: *The Utopia of Pope John* (Orbis, 1977). Also the works of Italo Calvino, Carlo Cassola, Eugenio Montale, Goffredo Parise, others.

BARROWS, ANITA 546 The Alameda, Berkeley, CA 94707 USA *Tel* 415-525-4899.

TL English. **SL** French, Italian. **UDC** literature (children's, criticism, drama, folklore, poetry, prose, history), social sciences.

French Didier Coste: *Sink Your Teeth in the Moon* (Calder & Boyars, 1973). Julia Kristeva: *About Chinese Women* (Urizen/Boyars, 1977). H Cixous: *Portrait of Dora* (Calder, 1977). **Italian** Felix Milani: *The Convict* (St Martin's/Joseph, 1978). Also the works of Roland Dubillard, Marguerite Duras, Anne-Marie Kegels, René de Obaldio, Cesare Pavese, Lalla Romano, Unberto Saba, G Ungaretti.

Memb ATA.

BARRY, RICHARD Little Place, Farringdon, Alton, Hampshire, UK *Tel* Tisted 26 (042 058).

TL English. **SL** French, German. **UDC** biography, current affairs, history, memoirs, military science.

French A Beaufre: *Introduction to Strategy* (Faber & Faber, 1965). **German** Heinz Höhne: *The Order of the Death's Head* (Secker & Warburg, 1969). Joseph Goebbels: *The Goebbels Diaries—The Last Days* (Secker & Warburg, 1978). Fritz Raddatz: *Karl Marx* (Weidenfeld & Nicolson, 1978). Also the works of Erwan Bergot, Dietrich Bracher, Hans Buchheim, Pierre Démaret, Peter Hoffmann, Werner Maser, Henri Michel, Kurt Schuschnigg, Eberhard Trumler, numerous others.

Memb TA. **Awards** 1970 Scott-Moncrieff Prize, 1972 Schlegel-Tieck Prize.

BARSTAD, NOEL K 144 Columbia Ave, Athens, OH 45701 USA *Tel* 614-592-2635.
TL English. SL German. UDC art/art history, literature (criticism, history, poetry, prose), music, philosophy, religion.
German Jean Gebser: *Origin and Presence: The Basis and Manifestations of Aperspectivity* (Ohio Univ Pr, forthcoming).
Accred ATA. Memb ALTA, ATA. Affil Ohio Univ (translation and translation theory).

BASA, ENIKO MOLNAR 707 Snider Lane, Silver Spring, MD 20904 USA *Tel* 301-384-4657.
TL English. SL Hungarian. UDC arts/crafts, history, literature (criticism, history, prose).
Hungarian the works of Agnes Nemes Nagy, Sandor Petöfi.
Affil Library of Congress. Memb SFL.

BAYBARS, TANER 69 Onslow Gardens, Muswell Hill, London N10 3JY, UK *Tel* (01) 444 8676.
TL English. SL Turkish. UDC literature (poetry, prose).
Turkish Nazim Hikmet: *Selected Poems* (Jonathan Cape, 1967); *The Moscow Symphony and Other Poems* (Rapp & Whiting, 1970); *The Day Before Tomorrow* (Carcanet, 1972). *Modern Poetry in Translation: Turkey* (MPT, 1972) Also the works of Oktay Rifat, Ahmet Hamdi Tanpinar, Orhan Veli.

BAYR, INGEBORG see **LINDT, INGE**

BECKER, STEPHEN Pine Hill Rd, Conway, MA 01341 USA *Tel* 413-625-6866.
TL English. SL French. UDC history, literature (prose), travel.
French Romain Gary: *The Colors of the Day* (Simon & Schuster, 1953). André Schwarz-Bart: *The Last of the Just* (Atheneum, 1961). André Malraux: *The Conquerors* (Holt, Rinehart & Winston, 1976). Louis Philippe, King of the French: *Diary of My Travels in America* (Delacorte, 1978). Also the works of Louis Carl, P-D Gaisseau, R Puissesseau, Elie Wiesel.

BEEKMAN, E M Univ of Massachusetts, Amherst, MA 01003 USA.
TL English. SL Dutch. UDC literature (drama, poetry, prose), philosophy.
Dutch Paul van Ostaijen: *Patriotism, Inc and Other Tales* (Univ of MA, 1971). Also numerous others.

BELITÍ, BEN Bennington College, Bennington, VT 05157 USA *Tel* 802-442-5956.
TL English. SL French, Italian, Spanish. UDC literature (criticism, drama, poetry, prose), philosophy, religion/scripture, theater.
Spanish Federico García Lorca: *Poet in New York* (Grove, 1955). Pablo Neruda: *Selected Poems* (Grove, 1961). Rafael Alberti: *Selected Poems* (Univ of California, 1966). Jorge Guillén: "Cántico: a Selection" (*Atlantic Monthly,* 1965). Also the works of Jorge Luis Borges, Arthur Rimbaud, Eugenio Montale, Antonio Machado, Juan de Mareina, numerous others. Also *Adam's Dream: A Preface to Translation* (Grove, 1978).

BENEDICT, REX 23 W 88 St, New York, NY 10024 USA *Tel* 212-724-0475.
TL English. SL Italian. UDC architecture, literature (all areas).
French Augusto Lunel: *The Polka Dot Twins* (Braziller, 1964). Italian A Midinola: *The Prayers of Man* (Obolensky, 1961). G Boccaccio: *Amorous Tales from The Decameron* (Fawcett-Crest, 1963). C Malaparte: *Those Cursed Tuscans* (Ohio Univ Pr, 1964). Also many Italian movie scripts, scenarios.

BENNANI, BEN M Comparative Literature, SUNY at Binghamton, NY 13901 USA *Tel* 607-798-4846.
TL English. SL Arabic. UDC literature (poetry, prose), philosophy.
Arabic Mahmoud Darweesh: *Splinters of Bone* (Greenfield Review Pr, 1974). Also numerous translations in periodicals: *Granite, Chelsea, Contemporary Literature in Translation, Journal of Arabic Literature, Mundus Artium, International Poetry Review.*

BERGER, DAVID 21-71 34 Ave, Long Island City, NY 11106 USA *Tel* 212-274-7614.
TL English. SL French, German. UDC art, literature (criticism, history, prose), political economy, psychiatry, psychology.
German A A Moll: *Libido Sexualis* (Amer Ethological Pr, 1935). French Eli Metchnikoff: *The Founders of Modern Medicine* (Walden, 1939). Also the works of Walter Benjamin, A M Fuchs, R Maria Rilke.
Memb ATA.

BERGER, JOSÉ 9 rue Quewée, B-6239 Pont-a-Celles, Belgium *Tel* (071) 84 68 47.
TL French. SL Dutch, English, German. UDC architecture, art, history, literature (prose), vulcanology.
English Maitland: *The Hamlyn Guide of Freshwater Fishes* (Elsevier, 1977).
Memb CBTIP.

BERGIN, THOMAS G 78 Wyndybrook Lane, Madison, CT 06443 USA *Tel* 203-245-7246.
TL English. SL Italian, Latin, Provençal (Old), Spanish. UDC biography, history, literature (poetry, prose).
Italian Dante: *Divine Comedy* (Appleton-Century-Crofts, 1959; Grossman/Orion, 1969). *Autobiography of G B Vico,* co-translated with M Fisch (Cornell Univ, 1944, rev 1963). Machiavelli: *The Prince* (Appleton-Century-Crofts, 1947). *The New Science of G B Vico,* co-translated with M Fisch (Cornell Univ, 1948). Latin Petrarch: *Sonnets and Odes of Petrarch* (Appleton-Century-Crofts, 1966); *Bucolicum Carmen* (Yale Univ, 1974). Numerous others.
Awards 1972 Poet Lorc Translation Prize.

BERISCH, KARL Kreuznacher Str 36, D-1000 Berlin 33, West Germany *Tel* (303) 821 07 94.
TL German. SL English. UDC aesthetics, archeology, art, history, human resources, literature (criticism, drama, history, librettos, poetry, prose), psychology, sculpture, theater.
English Lord Moran: *Churchill—The Struggle for Survival* (Droemer-Knaur, 1967). Kenneth Clark: *Piero della Francesca* (Phaidon, 1969). Lawrence Williams: *James McNeil*

Whistler (Wunderlich, 1974). Vincent Cronin: *Katharina die Grosse* (Claassen, 1978).
Memb VDÜ.

BERNSTEIN, JEROME S Spanish & Portuguese, Univ of California, Los Angeles, CA 90024 USA *Tel* 213-825-1036; 657-7551.
TL English. SL Spanish. UDC art, education, history, literature (criticism, history, poetry, prose), music, philosophy, theater.
Spanish Camilo José Cela: *Mrs Caldwell Speaks to Her Son* (Cornell Univ Pr, 1968). Gabriel García Márquez: *No One Writes to the Colonel and Other Stories* (Harper & Row, 1968). José Ruibal: *The Begging Machine* (Modern International Drama, 1976). Octavio Paz: *Claude Lévi-Strauss: An Introduction* (Cornell Univ Pr, 1970). Also the works of Enrique Lafourcade, X R de Ventós.
Memb ALTA.

BHAKTIVEDANTA, A C (SWAMI PRABHUPADA) The International Society for Krishna Consciousness, 3764 Watseka Ave, Los Angeles, CA 90034 USA *Tel* 213-871-0717.
TL English. SL Bengali, Sanskrit. UDC philosophy, religion.
Bengali & Sanskrit translations and commentaries of religious classics of India.

BIEBER, KONRAD F PO Box 208, Port Jefferson, NY 11777 USA *Tel* 516-473-0036.
TL English, French. SL French, German. UDC history, literature (all areas), political science, theater.
Affil SUNY at Stony Brook.

BIGUENET, JOHN 26 Bluebird St, New Orleans, LA 70124 USA *Tel* 504-283-4140.
TL English. SL French. UDC literature (poetry, prose).
French translations of works of Blaise Cendrars, Max Jacob, André Pieyre de Mandiargues, Henri Michaux. Also ed of *Foreign Fictions: 24 Contemporary Stories from Canada, Europe, Latin America* (Vintage, 1978).
Affil Loyola Univ, *New Orleans Review* (associate ed). Memb ALTA.

BIRD, PAMELA G 11 Library Lane, Old Lyme, CT 06371 USA *Tel* 203-434-8860.
TL & SL English, Portuguese, Spanish. UDC art, architecture, archeology, literature (all areas), occultism, painting, sculpture, theater, witchcraft.
English Niles W Bond: *Elegos* (Martins Editôra, 1967); *The Enchanted Egret* (Teatro de Juventude, 1966). Portuguese José J Veiga: *The Misplaced Machine & Other Stories* (Knopf, 1970); *The Three Trials of Manirema* (Knopf, 1970). Also the works of Marcos Leal, numerous poets.
Affil US Dept of State (contract). Memb ATA.

BIRD, THOMAS E PO Box 189, Little Neck, NY 11363 USA *Tel* 212-520-7587.
TL English. SL Byelorussian, Russian. UDC literature (criticism, poetry), political science, theology.
Russian the works of George Fedotov, Itsik Feffer, Georges Florovsky, Vyacheslav Ivanov,

Kastus Kalinouski, Anton Kartashev, Vladimir Lossky, Anatol Vyartsinski.
Affil Queens College of CUNY. **Memb** ATA.

BIRRELL, ANNE MARGARET Kent Hall 407, Columbia Univ, New York, NY 10027 USA.
TL English. **SL** Chinese, Japanese. **UDC** literature (Medieval Chinese poetry).

BISHOP, MARYANN B 846 Hawkeye Pk, Iowa City, IA 52240 USA *Tel* 319-354-7284.
TL English. **SL** French. **UDC** anthropology, data processing, economics, education, linguistics, literature, medicine, painting, political science, psychology, sociology.
Affil Univ of Iowa. **Memb** ATA.

BISSETT, JUDITH ISHMAEL 3526 E North Lane, Phoenix, AZ 85028 USA *Tel* 602-996-1290.
TL English. **SL** Portuguese, Spanish. **UDC** library science, literature (drama, folklore, history, prose, science fiction), theater.
Spanish Efraím Cardozo: *America at the Crossroads: Parthenon, Yes; Firing Squad, No* (Ctr for Latin Amer Studies, Arizona State Univ, 1974).

BJORK, ROBERT E 14801 Sherman Way #401, Van Nuys, CA 91405 USA *Tel* 213-988-3282.
TL English. **SL** Swedish. **UDC** aesthetics, history, literature (all areas).
Swedish Birger Sjöberg: "Frida's Book" (pending).
Affil Univ of California. **Memb** ALTA.

BLAAS, ERIKA Elsenheimstr 14/12, Salzburg, A-5020 Austria *Tel* (06222) 21 17 63.
TL German. **SL** English. **UDC** literature (children's, poetry, prose).
Memb ATA.

BLACK, KITTY 16 Brunswick Gardens, London W8 4AJ, UK *Tel* (01) 229 0931.
TL English. **SL** French. **UDC** biography, literature (drama, history, librettos, prose).
French J-P Sartre: *Crime Passionnel* (Hamilton/Knopf). Jean Anouilh: *The Rehearsal* (Methuen); *Point of Departure* (Methuen). Evelyne Coquet: *Riding to Jerusalem* (John Murray, 1978). Also the works of Jean Cocteau, Jacques de Launay, Fritz Hochwaelder, Felicien Marceau, Georges Simenon.
Memb TG.

BLADES, WILLIAM M 57 Forest Dr, Pennsville, NJ 08070 USA *Tel* 609-299-3361.
TL English. **SL** Spanish. **UDC** art, linguistics, literature (criticism), religion.
Spanish Luis Mario Schneider: "The Resurrection of Clotilde Gõni."
Memb ATA.

BLECHER, LONE & GEORGE 125 E 93 St, New York, NY 10028 USA *Tel* 212-427-4620.
TL Danish, English. **SL** Danish, English, German, Norwegian, Swedish. **UDC** art, history, literature (all areas).
Danish Franz Berliner: *The Lake People*

(Putnam, 1973). **German** Eleonore Schmid: *Tonia* (Putnam, 1974). **Swedish** Rose Lagercrantz: *Tulla's Summer* (Harcourt Brace Jovanovich, 1977). Carl Larsson & Lennart Rudstrom: *A Home* (Putnam, 1974).
Affil Lehman College of CUNY. **Memb** ALTA.

BOGIN, MEG 172 W 79 St #5G, New York, NY 10024 USA *Tel* 212-362-7667.
TL English. **SL** Catalan, French, Italian, Provençal, Spanish. **UDC** anthropology, art, literature (drama, librettos, lyrics, poetry, prose), music, painting, philosophy, sociology, theater.
French Serge Bramly: *Macumba* (St Martin's, 1977). Dominique St Alban: *Déja-Vu* (St Martin's, 1978). **Provençal** various women troubadours: *The Women Troubadours* (Paddington, 1976). Also the works of Jean Cocteau, Salvador Dali, Salvador Esprin, Federico García Lorca, Juan Ramón Jiménez, Guillaume de Machaut, Netzhualcoyotl.
Awards 1978 Columbia Univ Translation Center.

BONEY, ELAINE E 9357 De Camp Dr, La Mesa, CA 92041 USA *Tel* 714-463-2282.
TL English. **SL** German. **UDC** literature.
German R M Rilke: *Duinesian Elegies* (Univ of N Carolina, 1975).
Affil San Diego State Univ. **Memb** ATA.

BORN, ANNE 14 Hawkswell Gardens, Oxford OX2 7EX, UK *Tel* (0865) 56335.
TL English. **SL** Danish, Norwegian, Swedish. **UDC** architecture, art, literature (children's, criticism, folklore, poetry, prose), logic, painting, philosophy, witchcraft.
Danish Gustav Henningsen: *The Witches' Advocate* (Univ of Nevada, 1978–79). Lise Bek: "Axiality and the Patterning of Roleplay in Architecture" (pending). Frithiof Brandt: *Søren Kierkegaard* (Det Danske Selskab, 1963). Paul Vad: *Erik Thommesen* (Munksgaard, 1964). Also the works of Benny Andersen, Birthe Arnrak, Tove Ditlevsen, Marisa Henningsen, Arild Hvidtfeldt, Vagn Nielsen, Henrik Nordbrandt, others.
Memb TA, TG.

BORNEMANN, EVA see **GEISEL, EVA**

BOSKY, JULIA I 313 Second Ave #4, San Francisco, CA 94118 USA *Tel* 415-387-0752.
TL French, Russian. **SL** English. **UDC** archeology, art, literature (prose), painting, philosophy, theater.
English Margaret Kreig: *Green Medicine* (Nauka, 1968).
Affil Univ of California at Berkeley. **Memb** NCTA.

BOUIS, ANTONINA W 212 E 48 St #2C, New York, NY 10017 USA *Tel* 212-688-4946.
TL English. **SL** Russian. **UDC** literature (prose).
Russian Boulat Okudjava: *Nocturne* (Harper & Row, 1978). Chinghiz Gusseinov: *Mohamed, Mahmed, Mamish* (Macmillan, 1979). Valentin Rasputin: *Live and Remember* (Macmillan, 1978). Arkady & Boris Strugatsky: *Roadside Picnic* (Macmillan, 1977). Also the works of

Dmitri Bilenkin, Mikhail Emtsev & Fremei Parnov, Grigori Gerenstein, Yuri Kuper, Mstislav Rostropovich, Andrei Sakharov, Efraim Sevela, Gavriil Troyepolsky.

BOURKE, LEON H 1304 N Central Ave, Indianapolis, IN 4620-2 USA *Tel* 317-632-2116.
TL English. **SL** French. **UDC** art, history, literature (prose), religion/scripture.
Affil Indiana—Purdue Univ. **Memb** ATA.

BOUYGUES, CLAUDE P 4214 W 15 Ave, Vancouver, BC V6R 3A6, Canada *Tel* 604-228-1261, 2879.
TL French. **SL** English. **UDC** anthropology, education, ethnography, genealogy, geography, government, history, linguistics/philology, literature (all areas), philosophy, psychology, theater, viniculture.
Affil Univ of British Columbia (dir, translation program).

BOYER, MILDRED VINSON Spanish & Portuguese, Univ of Texas, Austin, TX 78712 USA *Tel* 512-471-1882.
TL English. **SL** Spanish. **UDC** literature (poetry, prose).
Spanish the works of Manuel García-Blanco, Enrique Arnal, Jorge Luis Borges, Miguel Enguídanos, Medardo Fraile, Juan Goytisolo in *Texas Quarterly*.

BOYLE, JOHN ANDREW 266 Rye Bank Rd, Manchester, M21 1LY UK *Tel* (061) 881 1161.
TL English. **SL** Arabic, Armenian, Persian (Farsi), Turkish. **UDC** history, literature.
Persian (Farsi) Farid al-Din 'Attar: *Ilahinama or Book of God* (Manchester Univ, 1977). 'Ata-Malik Juvaini: *History of the World-Conqueror* (Manchester Univ, 1958). Rashid al-Din: *Successors of Genghis Khan* (Columbia Univ, 1971).
Affil Univ of Manchester (UK). **Memb** TA.
Awards Order & Decoration of Sepass (Iran).

BRACHER, ULRICH Kappisweg 1, D-7000 Stuttgart 1, West Germany *Tel* (0711) 25 29 51.
TL German. **SL** English, Swedish. **UDC** archeology, education, linguistics/philology, political science.
English Charles A Beard: *An Economic Interpretation of the American Constitution* (Suhrkamp, 1974). Also the works of Norman H Baynes, T B Bottomore, John Dewey.
Affil Werkschule A L Merz (Stuttgart). **Memb** VDÜ.

BRADY, TERESA 4414 Pearson Ave, Philadelphia, PA 19114 USA *Tel* 215-338-5927.
TL English. **SL** Spanish. **UDC** public relations.
Memb ATA.

BRAÏNIN, PERRY 147 W 95 St, New York, NY 10025 USA *Tel* 212-865-8661.
TL English. **SL** Chinese. **UDC** anthropology, ethnography, history, linguistics/philology, literature (all areas), painting, political economy/science, social sciences, sociology.

BRALEY, ALAN 93 London Rd, Knebworth, Herts, UK *Tel* (0438) 813 155.

TL English. SL French, German. UDC biography, history, literature (poetry, prose), political economy/science, religion.

French Georges-André Fiechter: *Brazil Since 1964* (Macmillan, 1976). Denis de Rougemont: *The Meaning of Europe* (Sidgwick & Jackson, 1965). Pierre Moussa: *The Underprivileged Nations* (Sidgwick & Jackson, 1962). **German** Erich Körlin: *Profit Centered Sales Management* (Business Books, 1976).

Memb TA, TG.

BRERETON, GEOFFREY Cork House, Fairlight, Hastings, Sussex, UK *Tel* Pett 2184.

TL English. SL French, French (Old). UDC literature (drama, history, poetry, prose).

French Charles Perrault: *Fairy Tales* (Penguin, 1957). *Penguin Book of French Verse* (Penguin, 1958); A Adamov: *Paolo Paoli* (Calder, 1959). **French (Old)** Jean Froissart: *Chronicles* (Penguin, 1968, rev 1978).

Memb TA.

BREWSTER, ROBERT R Box 56, Earlham College, Richmond, IN 47374 USA *Tel* 317-962-6561, 2748.

TL English. SL German. UDC art, history, library science, literature, music, philosophy, political science, psychology, publishing, religion/Scripture.

Memb ATA.

BRIFFAULT, HERMA 137 W 12 St, New York, NY 10011 USA *Tel* 212-243-6323.

TL English. SL French, Italian, Spanish. UDC arts, biography, geography, history, literature (poetry, prose), philosophy, religion, science (applied), theology.

French Colette: *Earthly Paradise* (Farrar, Straus & Giroux, 1966); *The Pure and the Impure* (Farrar, Straus & Giroux, 1966-67); *The Ripening Seed* (Farrar, Straus & Cudahy, 1955). Marguerite Duras: *The Sea Wall* (Pellegrini & Cudahy, 1952). Also the works of Hervé Bazin, Paul Bodin, André Brincourt, José Cabanis, Yves Congar, José De Broucker, Jean Giraudoux, Joseph Kessell, Charles Kunstler, Jean Malaquais, Françoise Mallet-Joris, Albert Maquet, François Mauriac, Marcel Migeo, Molière, Monique Nathan, Guy Ponce de Leon, Racine, Leonard Rosenthal, St Paulien, Jean Sainteny, Antoine de Exupéry, Jean-Paul Sartre, Michel Siffre. **Spanish** the works of Isabel Alvarez, José Camilo Cela, Bartolomé de Las Casas, Alejandro Nuñez-Alonzo, Miguel de Salabert, Ramón Sender, numerous articles on various aspects of her translations.

BRISCOE, PETER 23249 Washington St, Colton, CA 92324 USA *Tel* 714-825-6672.

TL English. SL French. UDC library science, literature (poetry, prose), viniculture.

French José Cabanis: "Night Games" (pending).

BRITT, CHRISTA W 4609 W Country Gables Dr, Glendale, AZ 85306 USA *Tel* 602-938-1264.

TL English. SL German. UDC art, economics, history, law, literature (criticism, history, prose), painting, political science, theater.

Affil Amer Grad School of International Management. **Memb** ATA.

BRØNNER, HEDIN 112 Indian Springs Rd #3C, Williamsburg, VA 23185 USA *Tel* 804-229-2198.

TL English. SL Danish, Faroese, Norwegian. UDC archeology, geography, history, literature, mythology, theater.

Danish William Heinesen: *The Kingdom of the Earth* (Twayne, 1974); "The Man from Malta and Other Stories" (pending). **Faroese** *Faroese Short Stories* (Twayne, 1972). Also the works of Johan Bojer.

BROVENDER, JACQUELINE 11 Ray Hill Dr, Chelmsford, MA 01824 USA *Tel* 617-256-7542.

TL & SL English & French. UDC education, history, literature (criticism, drama, history, prose), painting, philosophy, political science, religion, theater.

French Jean Starobinski: "The Accuser and the Accused" (*Daedelus*, Summer, 1978).

Affil Tufts Univ. **Memb** ATA, Word Guild.

BROWN, ASHLEY English, Univ of South Carolina, Columbia, SC 29208 USA *Tel* 803-799-8535.

TL English. SL Portuguese (Brazilian). UDC literature (poetry, prose).

Portuguese Elizabeth Bishop, ed: *Anthology of Twentieth-Century Brazilian Poetry*, (Wesleyan Univ Pr, 1972). Also the works of Vinicius de Moraes, Joâo Cabral de Melo Neto, Graciliano Ramos, in *Shenandoah* 16, 1965 and *Latin American Writing Today* (Penguin, 1967).

BROWN, MARÍA C PO Box 13612, Santurce, PR 00908 *Tel* 809-783-5782.

TL English. SL Spanish. UDC art, history, human resources, literature (poetry, prose).

Spanish the works of Agostini de del Río, Gabriel Fernández Román, Miguel A Morales, Luis Nieves Falcón, Luis Roberto, Piñero, others.

Memb Asociación Profesional de Traductores de Puerto Rico, ATA.

BROWNJOHN, J MAXWELL Orchard House, Marnhull, Dorset, DT10 1PS, UK *Tel* (025) 882 438.

TL English. SL French, German, Portuguese. UDC art, literature (history, drama, prose), political science.

German Willy Brandt: *People and Politics* (Collins/Little, Brown, 1978). Lothar-Günther Buchheim: *U-Boat* (Collins, 1974). Heinz Höhne: *Canaris* (Secker/Doubleday, 1978). Hans Hellmut Kirst: *The Night of the Generals* (Collins/Harper & Row, 1963). Also the works of Frank Arnau, Romain Gary, Hans Habe, Otto Klemperer, Alfred Speer, Robert Stoll, numerous others.

Memb TA (past chairperson).

BROWNSBERGER, SUSAN C 25 Russell Ave, Watertown, MA 02172 USA *Tel* 617-926-3130.

TL English. SL Russian. UDC literature (criticism, drama, prose), medicine.

Russian Vasily Aksenov: *The Steel Bird and Other Stories* (Ardis, 1978). Also the works of Boris Gofman, M Saltykov-Shchedrin (pending).

Memb ATA.

BRUCE, LENNART 1815 Jones St, San Francisco, CA 94109 USA *Tel* 415-776-7099.

TL English. SL Swedish. UDC literature (aphorisms, poetry).

Swedish Vilhelm Ekelund: *Agenda, An Anthology* (Cloud Marauder, 1976).

Memb Swedish Writers' Association. **Awards** 1977 Swedish Academy poetry prize.

BRUEHL, EDELGARD H 19 Wood Lane, Locust Valley, NY 11560 USA *Tel* 516-676-4909.

TL English. SL German. UDC literature (children's, poetry).

German James Kruess: *My Great Grandfather and I* (Atheneum, 1966). Katherine Allfrey: *Golden Island* (Doubleday, 1966). Gina Ruck-Pauquèt: *The Most Beautiful Place* (Dutton, 1965). **Author of** "The Publication of Translated Children's Books in the US" (thesis).

BRUZINA, RONALD C Univ of Kentucky, Lexington, KY 40506 USA.

TL English. SL French. UDC philosophy.

French Kostas Axelos: *Alienation, Praxis, and Techné in the Thought of Karl Marx* (Univ of Texas, 1977).

BRYSON, JOSETTE SAINT-AGNE 411 West Ave #42, Los Angeles, CA 90065 USA *Tel* 213-225-1129.

TL English. SL French. UDC literature (all areas).

French Georges Dumézil: "Myth and Epic (III)" (pending). Also the works of Louis Aragon, Alain Bousquet, Andrée Chedid, Mohammed Dib, others.

BULL, GEORGE ANTHONY c/o 116 Pall Mall, London SW1, UK *Tel* 642 2470; 839 1233.

TL English. SL French, Italian. UDC literature.

Italian Cellini: *Autobiography* (Penguin, 1956). Machiavelli: *The Prince* (Penguin, 1961). Vasari: *The Lives of the Artists* (Penguin, 1965). Aretino: *Letters* (Penguin, 1976).

Memb Soc of Authors.

BURANELLI, ANN 27 Cold Soil Rd, Lawrenceville, NJ 08648 USA *Tel* 609-896-2180.

TL English. SL French. UDC art, literature (drama, history, songs), music, painting, sculpture, theater.

French Charles de Tolnay: *Religious Conceptions in the Painting of Piero della Francesco* (Schocken, forthcoming); *The Art and Thought of Michelangelo* (Pantheon, 1964).

BURLS, MICHAEL Otto-Hahn-Str 16, D-6501 Saulheim 2, West Germany *Tel* (06732) 7628.

TL English. SL Chinese, German. UDC literature (prose).

Affil Inst of Linguists.

BURTON, THOMAS, E 15 Sq Goldschmidt, B-1050 Brussels, Belgium *Tel* (02) 649 79 12.

TL English. SL French, German, Russian, Spanish. UDC archeology, art, history, literature (drama, history, prose, science fiction), painting, sculpture.

French Pierre du Bourguet: *Early Christian*

Art (Morrow, 1972). Anatole Kopp: *Town and Revolution: Soviet Architecture and City Planning, 1917–35* (Braziller, 1970). **German** Konrad Wachsmann: *The Turning Point of Building* (Reinhold, 1961). **Spanish** José Gudiol: *The Arts of Spain* (Doubleday, 1964).

Memb ATA, TAALS, Belgian Assn of Translators.

CAMPBELL, JANICE L 1129 First #23, Monterey, CA 93940 USA.

TL English. **SL** Spanish. **UDC** art/art history, athletics, communications, education, food/nutrition, government, human resources, jurisprudence, law, legislation, linguistics/philology, literature (history), political science, public administration, social services.

Accred Monterey Inst of Foreign Studies. **Memb** ATA, Concordiat.

CAMPBELL, JOHN LORNE Isle of Canna, Scotland, UK.

TL English. **SL** Scottish Gaelic. **UDC** oral tradition.

Scottish Gaelic Alexander MacDonald et al: *Highland Songs of the '45* (John Grant, 1933). Angus MacLellan: *The Furrow behind Me* (Routledge & Kegan Boyd, 1962). Donald MacCormick: *A Collection of Waulking Songs* (Oxford Univ, 1969). Annie Johnston et al: *Hebridean Folksongs,* I and II (Oxford Univ, 1977).

Memb Soc of Authors.

CARDOZO, MANOEL DA SILVEIRA The Catholic Univ of America, Washington, DC 20064 USA *Tel* 202-832-5392.

TL English. **SL** Castilian, French, Italian, Portuguese. **UDC** biography, literature (drama, poetry, prose), religion, theology.

Portuguese *Poesia Brasileira Moderna, A Bilingual Anthology,* co-edited with José Neistein (Brazilian-American Cultural Inst, 1972).

CARME, CLAUDE 40 quai Blanqui, F-94140 Alfortville, France *Tel* 375 21 79.

TL French. **SL** English, Italian, Spanish. **UDC** archeology, art, astrology, history, literature (history, poetry, science fiction), occultism, religion, witchcraft.

English Francis King: *Ritual Magic in England* (Denoel, 1972). Benjamin Lee Whorf: *Language, Thought, and Reality* (Denoel, 1969). Also the works of Isaac Asimov, David Ben Gurion, Martin Wells.

Memb ATLF.

CARPENTER, JOHN & BOGDANA 2409 E Roanoke St, Seattle, WA 98112 USA *Tel* 206-324-3441.

TL English. **SL** French, Polish. **UDC** literature (poetry, prose).

Polish Zbigniew Herbert: *Selected Poems* (Oxford Univ, 1978).

Awards 1978 Islands and Continents Translation Award (honorable mention).

CARR, RICHARD J 201 Massachusetts Ave NE, Washington, DC 20002 USA *Tel* 202-547-7251.

TL English. **SL** Spanish. **UDC** literature (poetry).

Spanish Nicolas Guillen: *Tengo* (Broadside, 1974).

Affil Library of Congress.

CARROLL, BONNIE L 5513 Brooklyn Ave NE, Seattle, WA 98105 USA *Tel* 206-525-5927.

TL English. **SL** Spanish. **UDC** literature (criticism, folklore, history, poetry, prose).

Affil Conference on Translation, Instituto Allende, Mexico.

CARYNNYK, MARCO Canadian Inst of Ukrainian Studies, 126 Evelyn Crescent, Toronto, ON M6P 3E2, Canada *Tel* 416-769-7037.

TL English. **SL** Polish, Russian, Ukrainian. **UDC** biography, history, linguistics, literature (poetry, prose).

Ukrainian Alexander Dovzhenko: *The Poet as Filmmaker, Selected Writings* (MIT, 1973). Mykhaylo Osadchy: *Cataract* (Harcourt Brace Jovanovich, 1976). *The USSR versus Dr. Mikhail Stern: An Ordinary Trial in the Soviet Union* (Urizen, 1977). Also numerous others.

CASARIL, GUY la Chevallerie F-27820 Chennebrun, France *Tel* (32) 321704.

TL French. **SL** English, Italian, Spanish. **UDC** anthropology, history, literature (children's, prose, science fiction), philosophy, political science/economy, religion, theater.

English Eric Ambler: *Send No More Roses* (Humanoïdes, 1977). Carlos Castaneda: *The Ring of Power* (Gallimard, 1978). Ross Terrill: *The Future of China* (Flammarion, 1978). Also the works of Richard Bach, Len Deighton, Harlan Ellison, Egon Larsen.

Memb ATLF.

CASERTA, ERNESTO G Romance Languages, Duke Univ, Durham, NC 27706 USA *Tel* 919-684-3706.

TL English. **SL** French, Italian, Spanish. **UDC** literature (poetry, prose), philosophy.

Italian Giacomo Leopardi: *The War of the Mice and the Crabs* (Univ of North Carolina, 1976). Also the works of Carlo Betocchi, Dino Campana, Alfredo de Palchi, Mario Luzi, Rossana Ombres, Enzo Paci.

CASEWIT, CURTIS, W PO Box 19039, Denver, CO 80219 USA *Tel* 303-935-0277.

TL English. **SL** German. **UDC** history, literature (prose), sports, travel.

German Karl Schranz: *The Karl Schranz 7-Day Ski System* (Macmillan, 1973).

Affil Colorado Univ.

CASSELL, ANTHONY K 716 S Lynn, Champaign, IL 61820 USA *Tel* 217-359-2561.

TL English. **SL** French, German, Italian, Latin. **UDC** literature (Italian medieval, poetry, prose). **Italian** Giovanni Boccaccio: *The Corbaccio* (Univ of Illinois, 1975).

CASTERA-KAHN, MARCEL 14 rue des Arbustes, F-75014 Paris, France.

TL French. **SL** English, Spanish. **UDC** archeology, architecture, literature (children's, folklore, poetry, prose), occultism.

English Carlos Castaneda: *The Teachings of Don Juan* (Soleil Noir, 1972); *Voir* (Gallimard, 1973); *Journey to Ixtlan* (Gallimard, 1975). Frank Waters: *Book of the Hopi* (Payot, 1978).

Memb ATLF.

CAWS, MARY ANN 140 E 81 St, New York, NY 10028 USA *Tel* 212-988-5967.

TL English. **SL** French. **UDC** literature (criticism, poetry).

French René Char: *Poems* (Princeton Univ, 1966). Tristan Tzara: *Approximate Man and Other Works* (Wayne State Univ, 1974). André Breton: *Poems* (Univ of Texas, forthcoming). Robert Desnos: *The Surrealist Voice* (Univ of Massachusetts, 1977). Also the works of Louis Aragon, Paul Eluard, Benjamin Péret.

Affil CUNY, Graduate School.

CEREA, DORIS 822½ N Seward St, Los Angeles, CA 90038 USA *Tel* 213-466-7052; 550-8700.

TL Italian. **SL** English, French. **UDC** anthropology, history, literature (all areas), metaphysics, motion pictures (outlines, screenplays, treatments), philosophy, psychology, social sciences, sociology, theater.

English Colin Wilson: *The Space Vampires* (Mondadori, 1978).

Affil Dino de Laurentiis Corp, Associazione Italiana Giornalisti.

CHAMBERS, ANTHONY H Fisk Hall, Wesleyan Univ, Middletown, CT 06457 USA *Tel* 203-347-9411.

TL English. **SL** Japanese. **UDC** literature (modern Japanese drama, fiction, poetry).

CHAMBERS, LELAND H English, Univ of Denver, Denver, CO 80210 USA *Tel* 303-753-2266.

TL English. **SL** Spanish. **UDC** literature (criticism, history, lyrics, poetry, prose).

Spanish Baltasar Gracián: *The Mind's Wit and Art* (Univ Microfilms, 1962).

CHAMBERS, RICHARD 2104 Glen Forest, Plano, TX 75023 USA *Tel* 214-596-1837; 235-7770.

TL English. **SL** Spanish. **UDC** communications. literature (poetry, prose), photography, TV & film scripts.

Spanish the works of Juan Liscano, Eugenio Montejo, Ramón Palomares.

Memb ALTA.

CHANDRA, G S SHARAT English, Washington State Univ, Pullman, WA 99163 USA *Tel* 509-567-6561.

TL English. **SL** Hindi, Kannada, Tamil, Telugu, Urdu. **UDC** art, literature (poetry, prose).

Kannada *Offsprings of Servagna,* with a foreword by the translator (Writers Workshop, Calcutta, 1975).

CHAPPEL, ALLEN HARRIS 1202 Dauphine St, New Orleans, LA 70116 USA *Tel* 504-523-4723.

TL English. **SL** German. **UDC** literature (poetry, prose).

Affil Univ of New Orleans. **Memb** ALTA.

CHEVALIER, HAAKON M 19 rue du Mont-Cenis, F-75018 Paris, France *Tel* 076 44 29.

TL English. **SL** French. **UDC** art, economics, education, history, literature, painting, philosophy, sculpture.

French André Malraux: *Man's Fate, Days of Wrath* (Smith & Haas, 1934–36). Louis Aragon: *The Bells of Basel, Residential Quarter, Holy Week* (Harcourt, Brace, 1936). Stendhal: *Roman Journal* (Orion, 1957). Salvador Dali: *The Secret Life of Salvador Dali, Hidden Faces* (Dial, 1943–44).

Memb AIIC, ATLF, SFT.

CHNEOUR, JACQUELINE FRANÇOISE 11 rue de la Pierre Levée, F-75011 Paris, France *Tel* 806 03 47.

TL French. **SL** English. **UDC** drama, folklore (Eastern European Jewish), psychology, theater.

English June Goodfield: *Cancer Under Siege* (Arthaud, 1977). Peter Ustinov: *Dear Me* (Stock, 1978). Isaac B. Singer: *A Crown of Feathers* (Stock, 1976). Donald Woods: *Steve Biko* (Stock, 1978).

Memb ATLF.

CHOSET, CHARLES 90 Bedford St, New York, NY 10014 USA *Tel* 212-243-0035.

TL English. **SL** German, Portuguese (Brazilian), Spanish. **UDC** archeology, choreography, logic, music, painting, philosophy, sculpture, theater.

German Renate Dolz: *Porcelain* (Popular Library, 1977). Bircher-Benner Clinic: *Handbook for Multiple Sclerosis Patients* (Jove, 1979); *Handbook for Heart Disease Patients* (Jove, 1978). **Portuguese (Brazilian)** Machado de Assis: *The Psychiatrist* (Dell, 1968).

CHRISTENSEN, NADIA 127 E 73 St, New York, NY 10021 USA *Tel* 212-879-9779.

TL English. **SL** Danish, Norwegian, Spanish. **UDC** literature (all areas).

Danish Anders Bodelsen: *Consider the Verdict* (Harper & Row, 1976); *Straus* (Harper & Row, 1974). Henrik Nordbrandt: *Selected Poems* (Curbstone, 1978). Klaus Rifbjerg: *Selected Poems* (Curbstone, 1976). Also the works of Cecil Bødker, Karin Boye, Orla Bundgaard-Povlsen, Tove Ditlevsen, Elsa Gress, Gunvor Hofmo, Per Højholt, Hulda Lutken, Peter Seeberg, Lise Sørensen, Ole Wivel, numerous others.

CLAUDEL, CALVIN A PO Box 1083, Chalmette, LA 70044 USA *Tel* 504-271-4209.

TL English. **SL** French, Spanish. **UDC** folklore (religious), linguistics/philology, literature (all areas).

Affil Delgado College.

CLINE, RUTH HARWOOD 5315 Oakland Rd, Chevy Chase, MD USA *Tel* 301-652-2505.

TL English. **SL** French (Old). **UDC** economics, government, literature (drama, poetry, prose).

French (Old) Chrétien de Troyes: *Yvain; or, The Knight with the Lion* (Univ of Georgia, 1975).

Accred Georgetown Univ (1978). **Memb** ATA.

CLOUTIER, DAVID Copper Beech Press, Box 1852, Brown Univ, Providence, RI 02912 USA *Tel* 401-863-2392.

TL English. **SL** French. **UDC** poetry, tribal poetry.

French Claude Esteban: *White Road: Selected Poems* (Charioteer, 1978). Also the

works of Yvonne Caroutch, René Daumal, Paul Éluard, Jean Follain, Jean Paul Guibbert, Jean Laude, Pierre Reverdy.

COETZEE, JOHN M English, Univ of Cape Town, Rondebosch, South Africa.

TL English. **SL** Dutch. **UDC** linguistics, literature (criticism, poetry, prose).

Dutch Marcellus Emants: *A Posthumous Confession* (Twayne, 1976). Also the works of Gerrit Achterberg, Hans Faverey, Sybren Polet, Leo Vroman.

COHEN, JONATHAN PO Box 25, Setauket, NY 11733 USA *Tel* 516-751-4978.

TL English. **SL** Spanish. **UDC** literature (poetry).

Spanish Enrique Lihn: *The Dark Room and Other Poems* (New Directions, 1978). Also the works of Rafael Alberti, Ernesto Cardenal, Javier Heraud.

Memb ALTA, Islands and Continents.

COLCHIE, THOMAS 187 Pinehurst Ave, New York, NY 10033 USA *Tel* 212-927-6993.

TL English. **SL** Portuguese, Spanish. **UDC** literature (children's, criticism, poetry, prose, science fiction), political science.

Portuguese Oswaldo França Júnior: *Jorge, from Brazil* (Dutton, 1979). Marcio Souza: *Galvez: Emperor of the Amazon* (Avon, forthcoming). Murilo Rubião: *The Ex-Magician* (Harper & Row, 1979). **Spanish** Manuel Puig: *Kiss of the Spider Woman* (Knopf, 1979). Also the works of Francisco Alvim, Oswald de Andrade, Manuel Bandeira, João Cabral de Melo Neto, Pero Vaz de Caminha, Fidel Castro, Carlos Drummond de Andrade, Gregório de Matos, Fernando Morais, Wander Piroli, Ary Quintella, Graciliano Ramos, Cassiano Ricardo, Armindo Trevisan, Antônio Vieira.

COLLINS, J RAPHAELLE Foxella, Matfield, Tonbridge, Kent, UK *Tel* 892-72-2463.

TL English. **SL** German, Greek. **UDC** history, literature (children's, criticism, drama, folklore, prose), travel.

Memb Ctr for Translation and Interpretation (Greece).

COLOMER, GLORIA I 719 51 St, Brooklyn, NY 11220 USA *Tel* 212-436-7941.

TL Spanish. **SL** English. **UDC** business, history.

COMEAU, PAUL T 1023 Avondale Dr, Las Cruces, NM 88001 USA *Tel* 505-523-4318.

TL English. **SL** French. **UDC** art, ethics, history, literature (criticism, drama, history, poetry, prose) music, philosophy, religion.

Affil New Mexico State Univ. **Memb** ALTA, ATA.

COOK, GEOFFREY PO Box 18274, San Francisco, CA 94118 USA *Tel* 415-567-0691.

TL English. **SL** Latin. **UDC** literature (poetry).

Latin Gaius Valerius Catullus: *Love & Hate: Selected Translations from the Carmina* (Outrigger, 1975).

COPPOTELLI, ARTHUR 25 W 68 St, New York, NY 10023 USA *Tel* 212-427-3407.

TL English. **SL** Italian. **UDC** art, film scripts, literature (drama, poetry, prose).

Italian Alberto Arbasino: *Brothers of Italy* (Grove, forthcoming). Pope John XXIII: *Social Teachings* (Grosset, 1967). Marco Valsecchi: *Landscape Painting of the 19th Century* (New York Graphic Soc, 1970). Marinetti: *An Anthology* (Farrar, Straus & Giroux, 1973). Also the works of Alberto Moravia, Pier Paolo Pasolini.

CORMIER, RAYMOND J 761 Millbrook Lane, Haverford, PA 19041 USA *Tel* 215-896-0216.

TL English. **SL** French, French (Old), German, Italian, Latin, Irish (Old), Spanish. **UDC** literature (criticism, folklore, history, prose).

French Jean Frappier: *Chrétien de Troyes— The Man and His Works* (Indiana Univ, 1979). **French (Old)** Anon: *Three Tales of Antiquity; The Romance of Brutus*.

Affil Temple Univ.

COWOOD, JOHN PHILIP 4 Ave Vanden Thoren, B-1160 Brussels, Belgium *Tel* 219-35-10.

TL English. **SL** French, German. **UDC** law.

Affil Commission of the European Communities (head, Legal Translation Group).

CROW, MARY English, Colorado State Univ. Ft Collins, CO 80523 USA *Tel* 303-491-6843.

TL English. **SL** Spanish. **UDC** literature (poetry).

Spanish "Anthology of Latin American Women Poets" (pending). Selections of Latin American women poets for *Colorado State Review*; selection of recent Latin American poetry for *Gumbo*.

CZARNECKI, MARK 54 Cecil St #3, Toronto, ON, Canada *Tel* 416-598-3361.

TL English. **SL** French. **UDC** economics, literature (prose), navigation, theater.

French Guy Joron: *Minimum Salary: $1 Million* (General, 1978). Nik Kebedgy: *Sailing* (Collier-Macmillan, 1975).

Memb ATIO, Literary Translators Assn of Canada.

CZERNICKI, KARL-OTTO von Wolfratshauserstr 70d, D-8023 Pullach, West Germany *Tel* (089) 793 0647.

TL German. **SL** English. **UDC** archeology, art, history, military science, philately, science fiction.

English Morris L West: *The Salamander* (Droemer, 1974); *Harlequin* (Droemer, 1975). John Kenneth Galbraith: *Ambassador's Journal* (Droemer, 1976). Abba Eban: *My Country, The Story of Modern Israel* (Droemer, forthcoming). Also the works of Cyril Abraham, N Amosow, John Howlett, Robert Lacey, Mary McCarthy, John Quigley, William Wingate, numerous others.

Memb VDÜ.

DAGENAIS, JOHN Box 2991 Sta A, Champaign, IL 61820 USA.

TL English. **SL** Catalan, French, Latin, Spanish. **UDC** art, history, history of science &

medicine, information science, library science, linguistics/philology, literature (all areas).

Latin Sesto Prete: *Studies in Latin Poets of The Quattrocento* (Univ of Kansas, 1978). Also the works of Antonio Costanzi, Aeneas Silvius Piccolomini (Pius II), Tito Vespasiano Strozzi.

Memb ALTA.

DAILLIE, RENÉ ISSIRAC F-30330 Pont-Saint-Esprit, France *Tel* (66) 82 17 14.

TL French. **SL** English, German, Italian. **UDC** literature (criticism, poetry, prose).

English Henry James: *The Princess Casamassima* (Denoël, 1974).

Memb ATLF, SFT.

DALVEN, RAE 11 Fifth Ave, New York, NY 10003 USA *Tel* 212-254-7391.

TL English. **SL** French, Greek. **UDC** biography, history, literature (poetry, prose).

Greek Joseph Eliyia: *Poems* (Jannina, 1944). Iefcros Anthias: *A Trip to the Sun* (Flame, 1954). *Modern Greek Poetry, An Anthology* (Gaer/Russell & Russell, 1949, 1971). Constantine P Cavafy: *Complete Poems* (Harcourt Brace Jovanovich, 1961). Yannis Ritsos: *The Fourth Dimension* (Godine, 1976). Katina Papa: "The House of Strati Gazia" (*Mundus Artium*, 1971).

DANA, KATHLEEN OSGOOD Nether Wallop Hollow, RFD 1, Northfield, VT 05663 USA *Tel* 802-485-8687.

TL English. **SL** Finnish. **UDC** history, literature (folklore, history).

Finnish Väinö Linna: "Here Under the Northern Stars" (pending).

DANALD, RUTH M 11 New Durham St, Westville, IN 46391 USA *Tel* 219-785-4044.

TL Spanish. **SL** English. **UDC** literature (criticism, drama, history, prose).

Memb ATA.

DANIELS, GUY 416 E 65 St, New York, NY 10021 USA *Tel* 212-879-7886.

TL English. **SL** French, Russian. **UDC** ethics/morals, history, human rights, literature (all areas), political economy/science, psychiatry, psychology, religion/scripture, social sciences, sociology.

French Stendhal: *Racine and Shakespeare* (Crowell-Collier, 1962). **Russian** Vladimir Mayakovsky: *The Complete Plays* (Simon & Schuster, 1968). Mikhail Lermontov: *A Lermontov Reader* (Macmillan, 1965). *Russian Comic Fiction* (New American Library, 1970). Also book-length translations of the works of Alfred Adler, Erich Auerbach, Honoré de Balzac, Ivan Bunin, André Castelot, Valery Chalidze, Anton Chekhov, Alexander Demidov, Leo Kovalev, Ivan Krylov, Nikolai Leskov, Pierre Louÿs, Roy Medvedev, Sergei Mikhalkov, Henry de Montherlant, Collete Portal, Sergei Prokofiec, Evgeny Riabchikov, Andrei Sakharov, Sergei Shtemenko, Leo Tolstoy, Valentin Turchin, Alexander Voronel.

Affil New York Univ (adjunct faculty). **Awards** 1978 Columbia Univ Translation Center grant.

DANIELSON, J DAVID 56 Scott Dr, Bloomfield, CT 06002 USA *Tel* 203-242-2344.

TL English. **SL** French, Spanish. **UDC** history, linguistics/philology, literature (criticism, history, poetry, prose), general competence in the humanities and social sciences.

Affil Univ of Hartford. **Memb** ALTA.

DAVIS, LUISE KATHARINA 1517 E Oak Ave, Lompoc, CA 93436 USA *Tel* 805-736-2023.

TL & SL English & German. **UDC** art, education, history, literature (all areas), political science, theater.

English Nathaniel Benchley: *Only Earth and Sky Last Forever* (Beltz & Gelbert/Weinheim, forthcoming). **German** *Hilton in Deutschland* (Verlag Kunst & Wissen, 1974). Also articles for *Sport and Mode* and *Sport Lexicon 1974* (trilingual periodical).

Memb ATA.

DAVIS, WILLIAM MYRON Modern Languages, Stephen F Austin State Univ, Nacogdoches, TX 75961 USA *Tel* 713-569-0035.

TL English. **SL** Spanish. **UDC** literature (children's, criticism, drama, folklore, history, poetry, prose, science fiction).

Spanish *Anthology of Spanish Poetry from Garcilaso to García Lorca* (Modern Library, 1966). L F de Moratín: *When a Girl Says Yes in Spanish Drama* (Bantam, 1962). Also the works of Yehuda Amihai, Peire Cardenal, Guido Cavalcanti, Miguel de Cervantes y Saavedra, Rubén Darío, García de Paiva, Manuel González Prada, numerous others.

DAY, JOHN 3 rue Geoffroy L'Angevin, F-75004 Paris, France *Tel* 278 3545.

TL English. **SL** French, Italian. **UDC** history.

French Emmanuel Le Roy Ladurie: *The Peasants of Languedoc* (Univ of Illinois, 1974); "*Motionless History*" (*Social Science History*, 1, 1977). Jean Glénisson: *Handbook of Contemporary Development in Historical Studies: French* (Greenwood, forthcoming).

Affil Univ of Paris (VII), National Ctr for Scientific Research.

DEBRECZENY, PAUL Slavic Languages, Univ of North Carolina, Chapel Hill, NC 27514 USA *Tel* 919-933-3977.

TL English. **SL** Hungarian, Russian. **UDC** literature.

Russian *Literature and National Identity: A Collection of 19th-Century Russian Critical Essays* (Univ of Nebraska, 1970).

Awards 1978 NEH grant (for an annotated translation of Pushkin's prose works).

DEES, COLETTE JOLY José de Cadalso 15, E-Madrid 24, Spain *Tel* 218 32 27.

TL English, French. **SL** Spanish. **UDC** architecture, art, ethics, history, literature (criticism, history, prose) metaphysics, philosophy, sociology, theology.

Spanish Claudio-Sanchez Albornoz: *Spain, a Historical Enigma* (Fundación Universitaria Española, 1976); *The Drama of the Formation of Spain and of Spaniards* (Fundación Universitaria Española, 1978).

Memb ATLF.

DE GÁMEZ, TANA PO Box 4048, Key West, FL 33040 USA *Tel* 305-294-7812.

TL & SL English & Spanish. **UDC** art, history, lexicography, literature (history, poetry, prose), music, painting, philosophy, sculpture, theater.

English Tana de Gámez: *Like a River of Lions* (Pleamar, 1964). **Spanish** Ricardo Alonso: *The Candidate* (Pocket Books, 1972). Carlos Franqui: *The Twelve* (Lyle Stuart, 1968). Andrés Segovia: *Autobiography* (Macmillan, 1976).

DE GARZA, HILDA Q Rub 10 Col Pedregal, Garza Garcia, Nuevo Léon, Mexico *Tel* 56 13 10.

TL English. **SL** Spanish. **UDC** communications, education, history, literature (children's, prose), social sciences.

Memb ATA.

DE GRAAF, KASPER 276 Monument Rd, Edgbaston, Birmingham B16 8XF, UK *Tel* (021) 454 4612.

TL English. **SL** Dutch. **UDC** education, legislation, literature (drama, history, prose), political science.

Dutch Jelte Rep: *The England Game* (Dent & Sons, 1979).

Memb TA.

DEJLIDKO, BARBARA 9 Gipsy Hill, London SE19 1QG, UK *Tel* (01) 670 1942.

TL English. **SL** Polish. **UDC** architecture, art, music, shipbuilding.

Polish J Golos & E Smulikowska: "Polish Organs and Organ Music" (pending). E Watala & W Woroszylski: "Life of Sergei Yesenin" (pending).

Memb TA.

DELAHAYE, ALAIN 26 ave d'Amsterdam, F-59300 Valenciennes, France.

TL French. **SL** English. **UDC** literature.

English John Hawkes: *The Blood Oranges* (Denoël, 1973). Jean Pasqualini: *Prisoner of Mao* (Gallimard, 1974). Arthur Koestler: *The Heel of Achilles* (Calmann-Lévy, 1975). Patricia Highsmith: *Edith's Diary* (Calman-Lévy, 1978). Also the works of Robert Coover, W S Merwin, Kenneth White.

Memb ATLF.

DEL CARO, ADRIAN 659 NE Pierce St, Minneapolis, MN 55413 USA *Tel* 612-379-7734.

TL English. **SL** German. **UDC** ethics, literature (poetry, prose), philosophy, sensory physiology.

German Friedrich Nietzsche: "The Dionysus Dithyrambs" (pending).

Affil Univ of Minnesota. **Memb** ALTA.

DE OLIVEIRA, CELSO Foreign Languages, Univ of South Carolina, Columbia, SC 29208 USA *Tel* 803-777-8477.

TL English. **SL** Portuguese. **UDC** literature (criticism, poetry, prose).

Portuguese Graciliana Ramos: *Childhood* (Peter Owen, 1979).

DERIS, NUR Abdülhakhamit Cad 70/6, Taksim-Istanbul, Turkey.

TL & SL English & Turkish. **UDC** archeology, architecture, law, legislation, linguistics/

philology, literature (children's, criticism, drama, folklore, history), political economy/science, theater.

English Thomas Hardy: *Jude the Obscure* (Altin Kitaplar, 1968). R Hooker: *MASH* (E Yayinlari, 1973). Christopher Cfudwell: "Studies in a Dying Culture" (pending). Edgar Snow: *The Long Revolution* (Yücel Yayinlari, 1974). Also the works of Katherine Mansfield, Frank O'Brien.
Memb ACIT.

DETIERE, DOROTHY JEAN 48 W 87 St #A, New York, NY 10024 USA *Tel* 212-580-8570.
TL & SL English & French. **UDC** anthropology, art/art history, economics, education, ethics, food/nutrition, geography, government, history, human resources, literature (history), music, philosophy, political economy/science, psychology, sociology.

DeVOLLD, WALTER L 1823 Crinella Dr, Saint Helena, CA 94574 USA *Tel* 707-963-9378.
TL English. **SL** German. **UDC** art, education, ethics, linguistics, literature (criticism, drama, history, poetry, prose), theater, viniculture.
German Fritz Engelmann: *Der Dachshund*, summary translation (Menninger, 1949). Also articles on high frequency radio tubes, oscillating gyroscopes for the science departments of Texas A & M Univ and Kent State Univ.
Memb ATA, NCTA.

DEWEES, ALETHA REED 5317 Montrose Dr, Dallas, TX 75209 USA *Tel* 214-352-9535.
TL English. **SL** French. **UDC** literature (drama, poetry, prose).
Memb ALTA.

DICK, ERNST S 910 W 29 St, Lawrence, KS 66044 USA *Tel* 913-843-5224.
TL & SL English & German. **UDC** anthropology, ethics, history, linguistics, literature (all areas), metaphysics, philosophy.

DIEHL, PATRICK SIDNEY English, Univ of California, Berkeley, CA 94720 USA *Tel* 415-763-4388; 642-2377.
TL English. **SL** French, Greek, Latin. **UDC** literature (poetry).
Italian Dante Alighieri: *Rime* (Princeton Univ/Lockert, 1979). Also the works of St Thomas Aquinas, Pierre Corneille, Hildegard of Bingen, John Mauropus, numerous medieval Latin and Greek poets.

DIRKS, MARY DOUGLAS 73 Broadway, Ossining-on-Hudson, NY 10562 USA *Tel* 914-941-2426.
TL English. **SL** French. **UDC** literature (criticism, drama), theater.
French Adolphe Appia: *Music and the Art of the Theater* (Univ of Miami, 1962). Paul Valéry: "My Faust" (play). Beaumarchais: "The Marriage of Figaro" (pending). Also the works of Marcel Achard, Emile Augier, Jean Giraudoux, Thomas Mann.

DIXON, ADRIENNE 20 Wavell Ave, Colchester, Essex, UK *Tel* (0206) 78031.

TL English. **SL** Dutch. **UDC** literature (all areas).
Dutch Louis Paul Boon: *Chapel Road* (Twayne, 1972). Harry Mulisch: *The Stone Bridal Bed* (Abelard-Schuman, 1962). Gerard Walschap: *The Man Who Meant Well* (Panther, 1975). Jan Wolkers: "The Dodo" (pending). Also the works of J F Bernlef, Hugo Claus, Maria Dermout, Jef Geeraerts, Ivo Michiels, Hugo Raes, Herman Vos, Beb Vuyk, numerous others.
Awards 1974 Martinus Nijhoff Prize.

DORIAN, MARGUERITE 210 Laurel Ave, Providence, RI 02906 USA *Tel* 401-751-0070.
TL English. **SL** French, German, Rumanian. **UDC** art, botany, literature (children's, criticism, drama, poetry, prose, Rumanian folklore).
Rumanian Ion Caraion: "Selected Poems" (pending); "Selected Poems" (*Mundus Artium*, 7 no 2, 1975). Veronica Porumbacu & Gabriela Melinescu: "Selected Poems" (*Mundus Artium*, 7 no 2, 1974).
Memb ALTA.

DOYLE, LOUIS 150 West End Ave, New York, NY 10023 USA *Tel* 212-874-7025.
TL English. **SL** French, Italian. **UDC** history, horticulture, medicine, music.
French Bernard Gavoty: *Chopin* (Scribners, 1977). **Italian** Gian Paolo Mondino: *Flowering Trees and Shrubs in Color* (Ottenheimer/Doubleday, 1972). Anon: *Rock Gardens and Water Plants in Color* (Ottenheimer/Doubleday, 1972).
Memb ATA.

DUBOIS, ROCHELLE HOLT 59 Sandra Circle #A3, Westfield, NJ 07090 USA *Tel* 201-232-7224.
TL English. **SL** Spanish. **UDC** art, graphics, literature, (drama, librettos, poetry, prose, songs), painting, photography, theater.
Spanish Leonora Carrington: *The Oval Lady* (Capra, 1975).

DUKAS, VYTAS 6152 Mary Lane Dr, San Diego, CA 92115 USA *Tel* 714-582-0249.
TL English. **SL** German, Lithuanian, Russian. **UDC** literature (poetry, prose, science fiction, songs), political science.
Russian Tokareva Gorin et al: *Twelve Contemporary Russian Stories* (Fairleigh Dickinson Univ, 1977). L Martynov, E Vinokurov, et al: *Thought in Poetry* (Prentice-Hall, 1973).
Affil San Diego State Univ. **Memb** ALTA.

DURAND, GUY & JEAN Chalet "Los Carlines," Sevrier F-74410 France *Tel* (51) 45 46 20.
TL French. **SL** English. **UDC** literature (poetry, prose), philosophy.
English Lewis Mumford: *The City in History* (du Seuil, 1963). Ludwig Wittgenstein: *The Blue and Brown Books* (Gallimard, 1965). John Fowles: *The French Lieutenant's Woman* (du Seuil, 1971). Thomas Sanchez: *Rabbit Boss* (du Seuil, 1977). Also the works of Hannah Arendt, Arthur Basham, Erich Jacoby, Marshall McLuhan, Peter Matthiessen, Gunnar Myrdal, Alan Silitoe, Susan Sontag, Dylan Thomas, numerous others.
Memb ATLF.

DuVAL, CHARLES 78 Bedford St, New York, NY 10014 USA *Tel* 212-243-0430; 586-6300.
TL French. **SL** English. **UDC** film dubbing and post-synchronization.
Memb ATA.

DuVAL, JOHN TABB 1903 Melrose Dr, Albany, GA 31707 USA *Tel* 912-883-4409.
TL English. **SL** French (Modern & Old). **UDC** literature (Old French, poetry, especially Old French fabliau).
French (Old) Anon: "The Medieval Fabliau" (pending). Also the works of Jean Bodel, Eustace D'amiens, Owrand, Guerin.
Memb ALTA. **Awards** 1974, 1975 Dudley Fitts Award in Translation.

EBER, IRENE Inst of Asian and African Studies, Hebrew Univ, Jerusalem, Israel.
TL English. **SL** Chinese, German. **UDC** history, literature (prose).
German Richard Wilhelm: *Essays on the I Ching: Constancy and Change* (Princeton Univ, 1979).

EBNER, JEANNIE Schlossgasse 3/8, A-1050 Vienna, Austria *Tel* (0222) 55 84 875.
TL German. **SL** English. **UDC** literature (lyrics, poetry, prose).
English Salvador de Madariaga: *Don Quixote* (Molden, 1967). N Scott Momaday: *House Made of Dawn* (Ullstein, 1971). J B Priestley: *Snoggle* (Georg Bitter, 1973). Larry Woiwode: *Beyond the Bedroom Wall* (Ullstein, 1979). Also the works of Cynthia Asquith, Richard Bach, Ludwig Bemelmans, Derek Lambert, Doris Lessing, Walter Macken, Edna O'Brien, Flannery O'Connor, numerous others.
Memb VDÜ. **Awards** 1975 Austrian State Prize for Children's Literature.

ELIASBERG, GEORG Beth Zera, PO Emek Hayarden, Israel 15135 *Tel* (067) 502 3516.
TL German, Hebrew. **SL** English, Hebrew. **UDC** history, literature (children's, history, prose), political economy/science, social sciences, sociology.

ELLIOTT, WILLIAM ISAAC Linfield College, McMinnville, OR 97128 USA *Tel* 503-472-4121.
TL English. **SL** Japanese. **UDC** literature (poetry, prose).
Japanese Shintarō Ishihara: *Ambush* (Praeger/Penguin, 1972–73). Shuntarō Tanikawa: *With Silence My Companion* (Prescott Street, 1975). Anon: *Festive Wine* (Weatherhill Walker, 1969); *Wind and Pines* (Image Gallery, 1977). Also the works of Chang Chi, Ishihara Shintarō, Ishikawa Michio, Kitagawa Fuyuhiko, Kuroda Saburo, Nishiwaki Junzaburo, Sato Haru, Takamatsu Fumiki, Tanikawa Shuntarō, Yamamura Bocho.
Affil Linfield College. **Memb** ALTA.

EPP, ROBERT C 1738 Armacost Ave #209, Los Angeles, CA 90025 USA *Tel* 213-825-3445.
TL English. **SL** Japanese. **UDC** history, literature (children's poetry).
Japanese Tsubota Jōji: *Children in the Wind* (Tuttle, forthcoming). Also the works of Etō Jun, Fujita Shōzō, Hagiwara Sakutarō, Horiguchi Daigaku, Ito Mitsuharu, Kawashima

Takeyoshi, Kikuchi Masanori, Kinoshita Yūji, Maruyama Kaoru, Matsumoto Sannosuku, numerous others.
Affil Univ of California.

ERICSON, MARC Ctr for Japanese Social & Political Studies, 2-8-8 Nishinogawa, Komaeshi, Tokyo 201, Japan *Tel* (03) 489-2175.
TL English. **SL** Japanese. **UDC** political science, social science.
Affil *The Japan Interpreter.*

ÉRTAVY-BARÁTH, JOSEPH M 1041 Stephenson Rd, Stone Mountain, GA 30087 USA *Tel* 404-377-2600; 469-0231.
TL English. **SL** Hungarian. **UDC** literature (poetry, prose).
Hungarian "14 Hungarian Poets" (*Modern Poetry Studies,* 1969).
Affil Georgia State Univ College (East European & Slavic); *Modern Poetry Studies* (assoc ed).

ÉVRARD, LOUIS Editions Gallimard, 5 rue Sébastien-Botein, Paris VIIᵉ, France *Tel* 544 39 19.
TL French. **SL** English. **UDC** anthropology, art, economics, history, history of religions, literature (criticism, history, poetry, prose), music, theology.
English Thorstein Veblen: *The Theory of the Leisure Class* (Gallimard, 1970). E E Evans-Pritchard: *The Nuer* (Gallimard, 1970). R van Gulik: *Sexual Life in Ancient China* (Gallimard, 1971). Hans Jonas: *The Gnostic Religion* (Flammarion, 1978). Also the works of George Jackson, David S Landes, Karl Marx, C Northcote Parkinson, Bertrand Russell.
Memb ATLF.

FAHNESTOCK (LEGGETT), LEE 520 E 89 St, New York, NY 10028 USA *Tel* 212-879-9263.
TL English. **SL** French, Italian. **UDC** literature (criticism, poetry).
French Francis Ponge: *The Making of the Pré* (Univ of Missouri, 1978). Paul Fournel: *Little Girls Breathe the Same Air As We Do* (Braziller, 1979). Also the works of Michel Butor, Martine de Courcel, Alexis Lefrançois, Roger Munier, Cesare Pavese, Geneviève Serrau, Christian Zimmer.
Memb ALTA, ATA.

FALLA, P S 63 Freelands Rd, Bromley, Kent BR1 3HZ, UK *Tel* (01) 460 4995.
TL English. **SL** Czech, French, German, Polish, Russian, Slovak.
German J Bauer: *Kafka in Prague* (Phaidon, 1971). Dahm: *History of Indonesia* (Pall Mall, 1969). **Polish** Raczynski: *In Allied London* (Weidenfeld, 1962). **Russian** Evgenia Ginzburg: *Into the Whirlwind,* co-translated with M Harari (Collins-Harville/Harcourt, Brace, 1967).
Memb TG. **Awards** 1972 Scott-Moncrieff translation prize.

FARMER, MARY WILLIX 1733 Red Barn Rd, Encinitas, CA 92024 USA *Tel* 714-436-1121.
TL English. **SL** Spanish. **UDC** art, astrology, choreography/dance, education, food/nutrition, history, linguistics/philology, literature (all areas), occultism, philosophy, psychiatry, psychology, social sciences, sociology.
Affil Univ of California. **Memb** ATA, CCIA.

FAWCETT, CAROLYN RUTH 334 Harvard St #D6, Cambridge, MA 02139 USA *Tel* 617-864-8293.
TL English. **SL** French, Italian, Latin. **UDC** aesthetics, philosophy, philosophy of science and medicine.
French George Canguilhem: *The Normal and the Pathological* (Reidel, 1978).
Affil Widener Library (Harvard Univ).

FEENEY, MARY Howlett Hill Rd, Marcellus, NY 13108 USA *Tel* 315-673-2593.
TL & SL English & French. **UDC** art (painting), cooking, literature (lyrics, poetry, prose), wine & food.
French Jean Follain: *Prose Poems,* co-translated with William Matthews (Grilled Flowers, 1978); *Removed from Time,* co-translated with William Matthews (Tideline, 1977); *Initiation* (Bieler, 1978); *Twelve Poems* (Grilled Flowers, 1977).

FELDMAN, RUTH 221 Mt Auburn St, Cambridge, MA 02138 USA *Tel* 617-491-7229.
TL English. **SL** Italian. **UDC** literature (Italian poetry, prose).
Italian Lucio Piccolo: *Collected Poems* (Princeton Univ, 1972). Andrea Zanzotto: *Selected Poetry* (Princeton Univ, 1975). Primo Levi: *Shema: Collected Poems* (Menard, 1976). Rocco Scotellaro: *Day Breaks* (Princeton Univ, 1979). Also the works of Raffaele Aversa, Luigi Ballerini, Pietro Cimatti, Luciano Erba, Giovanni Giudici, Mario Lunetta, Luigi Malerba, Elsa Morante, Alberto Mario Moriconi, Nelo Risi, Umberto Saba, Maria Luisa Spaziani, numerous others. All translations with Brian Swann.
Memb ATA. **Awards** 1977 John Florio Prize (with Brian Swann).

FELTEN, GRETE Pippinplatz 6, D-8035 Ganting b Munich, West Germany *Tel* (089) 850 32 32.
TL German. **SL** English. **UDC** archeology, architecture, art/art history, education, history, literature (history, prose), psychology.
English John Kenneth Galbraith: *Economics, Peace and Laughter* (Droemarsche, 1972). Michael Grant: *The Twelve Caesars* (C H Beck'sche, 1975). Laurie Lee: *Cider with Rosie* (Kindler, 1964). C P Snow: *The Two Cultures: and A Second Look* (Ernst Klett, 1967). Also the works of N K Chadwick, Robert Coles, Lucy Freeman, Gerald Leach, John O'Hara, Jean Rhys, Barbara Tuchman.

FERGUSON, CHARLES A Box 44, East Vassalboro, ME 04935 USA *Tel* 207-923-3781.
TL English. **SL** French, Italian. **UDC** arts/crafts, automotive, education, ethics, linguistics, literature (drama, history, prose), music, organology, theater.
French François Bédos de Celles: *The Organ-Builder* (Sunbury, 1977).
Affil Colby College. **Memb** ATA.

FICKERT, KURT J 33 Kensington Pl, Springfield, OH 45504 USA *Tel* 513-399-5983.
TL English. **SL** German. **UDC** literature (criticism, drama, lyrics, poetry, prose).
Affil Wittenberg Univ. **Memb** ALTA.

FIELD, EDWARD 463 West St, New York, NY 10014 USA *Tel* 212-675-6430.
TL English. **SL** Danish. **UDC** literature (poetry).
Danish *Eskimo Songs and Stories* (Delacorte, 1973).

FIELD, FERN 13935 Tahiti Way #147, Marina Del Rey, CA 90291 USA *Tel* 213-821-8533.
TL English. **SL** French, Italian, Russian, Spanish. **UDC** business, literature (children's, drama), motion picture scripts and dialogue, occultism, painting, philosophy, photography, psychiatry, psychology, telecommunications, theater, witchcraft.
Memb ATA.

FIENE, DONALD MARK 2215 Clinch Ave, Knoxville, TN 37916 USA *Tel* 615-524-0987.
TL English. **SL** Russian. **UDC** linguistics, literature (criticisim, poetry, prose, both fiction and nonfiction).
Russian Vasily Shukshin: *Snowball Berry Red* (Ardis, 1978). Mikhail A Osorgin: *A Reintroduction: Selected Stories, Reminiscences, Essays* (Ardis, 1979). Also the works of Vladimir R Maramzin, A I Solzhenitsyn, Vladimir N Voinovich.
Affil Univ of Tennessee (German & Slavic). **Memb** ALTA.

FITZ, EARL EUGENE Spanish, Italian, Portuguese, N-357 Burrowes Bldg, Penn State Univ, Univ Park, PA 16802 USA *Tel* 814-865-1188.
TL English. **SL** Portuguese, Spanish. **UDC** biography, history, literature (children's, criticism, prose).
Portuguese Lima Barreto: *Clara dos Anjos* (Hall, 1979). Enrique Lefevre: *The Panama Scandal: Why They Hate Us* (Pageant Poseidon, 1976). Clarice Lispector: "White Water" (pending); "The Woman Who Killed the Fish" (pending). Also the works of Mario Benedetti, Haraldo de Campos, Jorge de Lima, Nélida Piñon, Maria Luis Ramos.
Memb ATA.

FLEISHER, LISA 2720 N Swan Rd #7D, Tucson, AZ 85712 USA *Tel* 602-325-8966.
TL English. **SL** German. **UDC** library science, literature (children's, lyrics, prose), music.
German Herbert Rosendorfer: *The Wall* (Dimension, 1979).
Affil Tucson Public Library. **Memb** ALTA.

FLINT, ROBERT W 8 Irving Terr, Cambridge, MA 02138 USA *Tel* 617-864-9323.
TL English. **SL** Italian. **UDC** literature (all areas).
Italian Cesare Pavese: *Selected Works* (Farrar, Straus & Giroux, 1968). F T Marinetti: *Selected Writings* (Farrar, Straus & Giroux, 1971).

FLOURNOY, LILIANE 45 ave de Champel, CH-1206 Geneva, Switzerland *Tel* (022) 46 22 49.

TL French, Italian. SL English. UDC history, journalism, literature (history, prose).

English Ernest Jones: *The Life and Work of Sigmund Freud Vol 3* (French Univ, 1969). P Tompkins & Ch Bird: *The Secret Life of Plants* (Robert Laffont, 1973). Lucienne Lanson: *From Woman to Woman* (Robert Laffont, 1975). Carter Brown: *The Pornbroker* (Gallimard, 1973). Also the works of Gil Brewer, Harrison E Salisbury, René A Spitz.

Memb ATLF.

FON, MINCIO 24 Man Ying St, Kowloon, Hong Kong *Tel* 3-305402.

TL Chinese. SL English. UDC commerce, education, history, philosophy, political economy, public administration, social services, sociology, theater.

Chinese Feng Meng Lung & Ling Mong Chu: *Classical Short Stories of China* (Translation & Publication Centre, 1978). **English** Jane Austen: *Pride and Prejudice* (China Publishing, 1955). George Eliot: *The Mill on the Floss* (China Publishing, 1955).

Memb TG.

FORTUNE, CHRISTOPHER R 2721 Burdick Ave, Victoria, BC V8R 3L8, Canada *Tel* 604-592-9263.

TL English. SL Russian. UDC literature (criticism, poetry, prose).

Affil Univ of Victoria. **Memb** ALTA.

FOUQUES DUPARC, ROBERT 21 rue de Verneuil, F-75007 Paris, France *Tel* 261 44 49.

TL French. SL English, Russian, Spanish. UDC linguistics/philology, literature (children's, prose, science fiction).

English André Brink: *Looking on Darkness* (Stock, 1976). James Clavell: *Shogun* (Stock, 1977). Carson McCullers: *The Mortgaged Heart* (Stock, 1977). Walker Percy: *Lancelot* (Seuil, 1979). Also the works of Neville Randall, Anne Tylor, Alan Watts, Donald Woods.

Memb ATLF.

FOX, ELLEN 878 West End Ave, New York, NY 10025 USA *Tel* 212-222-0128.

TL English. SL French, Spanish. UDC ecology, education, ethics, ethnography, government, history, linguistics/philology, literature (children's, criticism, drama, folklore, history, poetry, prose, science fiction), medicine, sociology.

French Charles Baudelaire: *Artificial Paradise* (Herder & Herder, 1971). Stefan Wul: *The Temple of the Past* (Seabury, 1973).

FOX, HENRY Three Chimneys, Farley Hill, nr Reading, Berks RG7 IUA, UK *Tel* (0734) 73 31 89.

TL English. SL Czech, French, German. UDC biography, political science, travel.

French Paul-Henri Spaak: *The Continuing Battle* (Weidenfeld & Nicholson, 1971). Guy Hermet: *The Communists in Spain* (Saxon House/Lexington, 1974). **German** Rene Gardi: *Sahara* (Kummerly & Frey, 1970). Franz Josef Strauss: *Challenge and Response* (Weidenfeld & Nicholson, 1969). Also the works of Jean-

Jacques Barloy, Werner Buchholtz, Hugo Portisch.

Affil British Broadcasting Corp. **Memb** TA.

FRAME, DONALD M 401 W 118 St, New York, NY 10027 USA *Tel* 212-749-5755.

TL English. SL French. UDC literature (French drama, prose).

French Molière (Jean-Baptiste Poquelin): *The Misanthrope and Other Plays* (New American Library, 1968); *Tartuffe and Other Plays* (New American Library, 1967). Michel de Montaigne: *Complete Works* (Stanford Univ, 1957). Abbé Antoine-François Prévost: *Manon Lescaut* (New American Library, 1961). Voltaire (François-Marie Arouet): *Candide, Zadig, and Selected Stories* (New American Library, 1961).

Affil Columbia Univ.

FRASER, DOUGLAS ATHOL 22 Gresley Rd, London N19 3JZ, UK *Tel* (01) 272 5664.

TL English. SL French, German, Italian, Japanese, Russian. UDC literature, philosophy, religion (Eastern).

Memb TG.

FRATTI, MARIO 145 W 55 St #15D, New York, NY 10019 USA *Tel* 212-582-6697.

TL & SL English & Italian. UDC dialogue, drama, films, television.

English Reginald Rose: "Sacco and Vanzetti" (Italian RAI-TV, 1964). Barrie Stavis: *Joe Hill Is Not Dead* (Sipario, 1966). Also the works for television by R O Hirson, J P Miller, Thomas W Phipps, David Shaw.

FREELAND, SISTER JANE PATRICIA St Andrew's School, St Andrew's, TN 37372 USA *Tel* 615-598-0503.

TL English. SL French, Latin (Medieval). UDC literature (poetry, prose), religion.

Latin (Medieval) Pope Leo I: *Sermons* (Catholic Univ of America). Peter Abelard: "The Hymns" (pending).

Memb ALTA.

FREEMAN, CHRISTINE 203B Satterfield Hall, Kent State Univ, Kent, OH 44242 USA *Tel* 216-672-3647.

TL English. SL Spanish. UDC literature (criticism, poetry, prose).

Memb ALTA.

FRENAYE, FRANCES 15 W 67 St, New York, NY 10023 USA *Tel* 212-724-4730.

TL English. SL French, Italian. UDC history, literature (prose), sociology.

French Jean Duvignaud: *Change at Shebika* (Pantheon, 1970). Elie Wiesel: *Dawn* (MacGibbon & Kee, 1961). **Italian** Benedetto Croce: *History of the Kingdom of Naples* (Univ of Chicago, 1971). Carlo Scarfoglio: *The True Cross* (Pantheon, 1956). Also the works of Dante Arfelli, Robert Aron, Honoré de Balzac, Jean Bloch-Michel, Georges Blond, Henri Bordeaux, Jean Caran, Francis Carco, Claude Cattaert, Arthur Conte, Assia Djébar, François Ribadeau Dumas, Natalia Ginzburg, Edouard Glissant, Armand Lanoux, Carlo Levi, Isa Mari, Giuseppe Marotta, André Maurois, Anna-Maria Ortese, Maurice Pons, Françoise

Sagan, Ignazio Silone, Henri Troyat, Etio Vittorini, Emile Zola, numerous others.

Awards 1952 Clairouin Prize, 1975 John Florio Prize.

FRIEDBERG, MAURICE Slavic Languages & Literatures, Univ of Illinois, Urbana, IL 61801 USA *Tel* 217-333-0680.

TL English. SL Polish, Russian. UDC history, literature (criticism, history, prose), political science, theater.

Russian *A Bilingual Collection of Russian Short Stories* (Random House, 1964). Leon Trotsky: *The Young Lenin* (Doubleday, 1972). Also the works of Isaac Babel, Vyacheslav Ivanov, Venyamin Kaverin, Boris Pilnyak, Yuri Tynyanov.

FRIEND, ROBERT 13 Jabotinsky St, Jerusalem, Israel *Tel* 02 34998.

TL English. SL Hebrew. UDC literature (poetry).

Hebrew Leah Goldberg: *Selected Poems* (Panjandrum, 1976). Natan Alterman: *Selected Poems* (Hakibbut, Hameuchad, 1978).

Affil The Hebrew Univ.

FRIERSON, JAMES WRIGHT & ELEANOR B 1070 Mokulua Dr, Kailua, HI 06734 USA *Tel* 808-262-8704.

TL English. SL French. UDC anthropology, art, choreography, education, history, literature (criticism, lyrics, poetry, prose), philosophy.

French Pierre Loti (Julien Viaud): *The Marriage of Loti* (Univ Press of Hawaii, 1976).

Affil Univ of Hawaii & Chaminade Univ. **Memb** Pacific Translators (Honolulu).

FRIIS, ERIK J 19 Shadow Lane, Montvale, NJ 07645 USA *Tel* 201-391-8970.

TL English. SL Danish, Norwegian, Swedish. UDC biography, geography, government, history, literature (drama, history, prose), political science.

Danish William Heinesen: *The Lost Musicians* (Twayne, 1971). **Norwegian** Alfred Hauge: *Cleng Peerson* (Twayne, 1975). Helge Ingstad: *Westward to Vinland* (St Martin's, 1969). **Swedish** Hans Granqvist: *The Red Guard—A Report on Mao's Revolution* (Praeger, 1967). Also the works of K Arne Blom, R Broby-Johansen, Olaf Rynning-Tönnesen, Liv Ullmann.

GÁLER, RAÚL 144-12 Village Rd #B, Jamaica, NY 11435 USA *Tel* 212-969-3841.

TL & SL English & Spanish. UDC business, economics, government, jurisprudence, law (international), legislation, literature (drama, prose), political economy/science, public administration, theater.

English Bruno Fischer: *Murder in the Raw* (Gral Fabril, 1958). Also numerous translations of executive reports, manuals, monthly bulletins of the Alexander Hamilton Inst.

Affil UN. **Memb** AIIC, TAALS.

GAL-OR, GIDEON H Jerusalem 92509, Israel *Tel* 02 64684.

TL German. SL English, Hebrew. UDC humanities (all areas), political science, social sciences.

GALT, ALAN B German, Univ of Cincinnati, Cincinnati, OH 45221 USA *Tel* 513-475-2752.
TL English. **SL** German. **UDC** history, linguistics/philology, literature (criticism, folklore, poetry, prose), music, religion/scripture.
Memb ATA.

GARCÍA, GONZALO PO Box 905, Glendale, CA 91209 USA *Tel* 213-243-6144.
TL Spanish. **SL** English. **UDC** arts, business, communications, copyright, ecology, economics, education, ethics, history, jurisprudence, law, literature (poetry, prose), music, philosophy, plastic arts, political science, religion, sculpture, sociology, theater.
English the works of R Critfied, Angie Debo, John Dance, Grace Halsell, Lamar Herring, Wayne Powell, Donald P West.
Affil Polylanguages Inst. **Memb** ALTA, ATA (S California chapter).

GARREAU, JOSEPH E 8 Dakota Dr, Chelmsford, MA 01824 USA *Tel* 617-256-9602.
TL English. **SL** French, Spanish. **UDC** linguistics/philology, literature (history), religion/scripture, theology.
Spanish Fernando Diaz-Plaja: "Another History of Spain" (pending).
Memb NETA, Word Guild.

GARRIN, STEPHEN HOWARD Germanic Languages, Univ of Texas, Austin, TX 78712 USA *Tel* 512-471-4422.
TL English. **SL** German, Yiddish. **UDC** literature (all areas).
German novellas of Stefan Zweig. **Yiddish** poetry of Izak Manger.

GAVRONSKY, SERGE 525 West End Ave, New York, NY 10024 USA *Tel* 212-787-7068.
TL English. **SL** French. **UDC** poetry.
French Ponge et al: *Poems and Texts* (October House, 1969). Francis Ponge: *The Sun Placed in the Abyss and Other Texts* (SUN, 1977); *Francis Ponge and the Power of Language with Translations* (Univ of California, 1979).
Affil Barnard College. **Awards** 1978 NEH grant for "Translation: Access to Cultural Communication."

GEISEL, EVA (Eva Bornemann) A-4612 Scharten, Austria *Tel* 07275 235.
TL & SL English & German. **UDC** biography, literature (all areas).
Affil *Der Übersetzer* (ed). **Memb** BDÜ, TA, VDÜ, VS.

GELLY, ALEXANDER English & Comparative Literature, Univ of California, Irvine, CA 92717 USA *Tel* 714-833-6714.
TL English. **SL** German. **UDC** aesthetics, art, literature (criticism, history, poetry, prose), philosophy.
German Thomas Mann & Karl Kerényi: *Mythology and Humanism, The Correspondence of Thomas Mann and Karl Kerényi* (Cornell Univ, 1975).

GETHING, THOMAS W Indo-Pacific Languages, Univ of Hawaii, Honolulu, HI 96822 USA *Tel* 808-948-8948, 8672.
TL English. **SL** Thai. **UDC** anthropology, education, linguistics.
Thai "The Rām Khamhāēng Inscription" (*The World of Southeast Asia*, Harper & Row, 1967).

GETSI, LUCIA CORDELL English, Stevenson Hall, Illinois State Univ, Normal-Bloomington, IL 61761 USA *Tel* 309-828-0959.
TL English. **SL** German. **UDC** literature (all areas, especially poetry).
German Georg Trakl: *Poems* (Mundus Artium Press, 1973).
Memb ALTA.

GHITESCU, MICAELA (Mrs. Ionescu-Stoian) Str Cobalcescu 50, 70768 Bucharest, Rumania *Tel* 14 67 62.
TL Rumanian. **SL** English. **UDC** documentation, education, library science, linguistics/philology, literature (poetry, prose), pharmacology.
English Henry Fielding: *Joseph Andrews* (Univers, Bucharest, 1966). Also the works of Stephen Leacock.
Memb ATLF, Rumanian Writers Union.

GHOSSEIN, MIRENE 170 Overlook Circle, New Rochelle, NY 10804 USA *Tel* 914-632-1580.
TL English. **SL** Arabic, French. **UDC** literature (poetry, prose), philosophy.
Arabic *The Blood of Adonis,* co-translated with Samuel Hazo (Univ of Pittsburgh, 1971).

GIACOMELLI, ELOAH F 310-2416 W Third Ave, Vancouver, BC V6K 1L8, Canada *Tel* 604-731-4301.
TL English. **SL** Portuguese. **UDC** art, history, literature (children's, criticism, history, prose, short fiction).
Portuguese short stories and poetry of contemporary Brazilian writers: Lygia Fagundes Telles, Hilda Hilst, Murilo Mendes, Clarice Lispector, Moacyr Scliar, Autran Dourado, Carlos Drummond de Andrade, in *Antigonish Review, Prism International, Malahat Review, Contemporary Literature in Translation, Mundus Artium, The Literary Review,* others.

GIBBONS, REGINALD Creative Writing Program, Princeton Univ, 185 Nassau St, Princeton, NJ 08540 USA *Tel* 609-452-4712.
TL English. **SL** Spanish. **UDC** literature (criticism, history, poetry, prose).
Spanish Luis Cernuda: *Selected Poems* (Univ of California, 1978). Jorge Guillen: *Guillen on Guillen: The Poetry and the Poet* (Princeton Univ, 1979).
Award 1977 Denver Quarterly Translation Award.

GILBERT, CLAUDE 27 blvd de Rochechouart, F-75009 Paris, France *Tel* 1 526 88 50.
TL French. **SL** English. **UDC** economics, government, history, literature (history, prose, science fiction), political economy/science, psychiatry, social sciences, witchcraft (esotericism).
English Gerald A Browne: *Slide* (Presses de la Cité, 1977). David Horowitz: *From Yalta to Vietnam* (Union Générale, 1973). Jane Kramer: *Allen Ginsberg in America* (Union Générale 1972). H P Lovecraft & A Derleth: *The Lurker at the Threshold* (Christian Bourgois, 1971). Also the works of Alexander Bland, John Brunner, Robert Browning, Talbot Mundy, Douglas Reeman, numerous others.
Memb ATLF.

GILL, EVALYN PIERPOINT 8 Morven Pl, Princeton, NJ 08540 USA *Tel* 609-924-6764.
TL English. **SL** French. **UDC** literature (poetry).
French the works of Guillaume Apollinaire, Pierre Béarn, Jean Breton, Paul Élouard, Jean Follain, Jean Orizet, Jules Supervielle in *Southern Poetry Review, Paintbrush, International Poetry Review.*
Affil *International Poetry Review* (ed). **Memb** ALTA.

GILLESPIE, GERALD Stanford Univ, Stanford, CA 94305 USA *Tel* 415-497-0416, 3266.
TL English. **SL** French, German, Spanish. **UDC** literature.
German Anon: *The Night Watches of Bonaventura* (Univ of Texas, 1972). Ludwig Tieck: *Puss-in-Boots* (Edinburgh Univ/Univ of Texas, 1974). **Spanish** Ramón María del Valle-Inclán: *Bohemian Lights* (Edinburgh Univ/Univ of Texas, 1976). Julio Matas: "It Is the Realm of the Sun" (*Mundus Artium*, 4 no 7, Winter, 1970).

GINSBURG, MIRRA 150 W 96 St, New York, NY 10025 USA *Tel* 212-222-7172.
TL English. **SL** Russian, Yiddish. **UDC** literature (children's, criticism, drama, folklore, prose, science fiction).
Russian Yevgeny Zamyatin: *The Dragon: Fifteen Stories* (Random House, 1966); *We* (Viking/Bantam Books, 1972). Mikhail Bulgakov: *The Master and Margarita* (Grove, 1967). Fyodor Dostoyevsky: *Notes from the Underground* (Bantam, 1972). Also the works of Chingiz Aitmatov, Vera Alexandrova, Henrik Altov, Gleb Anfilov, Isaac Babel, Vladlen Bakhnov, Dmitry Bilenkin, Kirill Bulychev, Korney Chukovsky, Anatoly Dneprov, Sever Gansovsky, Gennady Gor, Roman Goul, M Greshnov, Vladimir Grigoriev, Ilya Ilf, Valentin Katayev, Yury Kazakov, Mikhail Koltsov, Victor Kolupayev, Nina Kosterina, L Lagin, Olga Larionova, Andrey Platonov, Alexey Remizov, Isaac Bashevis Singer, Valentina Zhuravleva, Mikhail Zoshchenko, numerous others.
Memb ALTA. **Awards** 1967 National Translation Ctr, 1972 Lewis Carroll Shelf Award, 1975–76 Guggenheim Fellowship.

GIRODAY, VÉRONIQUE DE LA 320 W 19 St, New York, NY 10011 USA *Tel* 212-255-6638.
TL French, German. **SL** English. **UDC** literature.
Author of *Die Übersetzertätigkeit des Münchner Dichterkreises* (Athenaion, Wiesbaden, 1978).
Accred Univ of Geneva (diploma). **Affil** Marymount Manhattan College. **Memb** ATA.

GLASNOVIC, ROSARIO 36 Villa Maria Dr, West Seneca, NY 14224 USA *Tel* 716-674-8018.

TL English. SL Croatian. UDC geography, history, literature (children's, criticism, folklore, history, prose), music.

Croatian Meša Salimović: "The Dervish and Death" (pending); "The Fortress" (pending). Vladimir Nazor: "Stories from Childhood" (pending). Also the works of Ivo Andrić, Mirko Vidović, Joseph Vrbić.

Affil Cleveland Hill School. **Memb** ALTA, ATA.

GODNEFF, NINA 193 ave Jean Jaurès, F-93300 Aubervilliers, France *Tel* Paris 833 19 82.

TL French. SL English, Russian. UDC art, history, literature (criticism, history, prose), political economy/science, psychology.

English Erik Erikson: *Young Man Luther* (Flammarion, 1968): *Insight and Responsibility* (Flammarion, 1971). Rudolf Arnheim: *Toward a Psychology of Art* (Seghers, 1973). Graham Hughes: *The Art of Jewelry* (Calmann Levy, 1973). Also the works of Dee Brown, J P Harrison, Liv Ullmann, B Kouznetsov, E M Meletinsky.

Memb ATLF.

GOGOL, JOHN M 8744 SE Rural, Portland, OR 97266 USA *Tel* 503-771-8540.

TL English. SL German, Polish, Russian. UDC ethnography, literature (folklore, lyrics, poetry, prose).

German, Polish, Russian the works of Anna Akhmatova, Johannes Bobrowski, Paul Celan, Zbigniew Herbert, Reiner Kunze, Osip Mandelstam, Tadeusz Rozewicz, Alexandr Solzhenitsyn.

GOLDGAR, HARRY 938 Philip St, New Orleans, LA 70130 USA *Tel* 504-522-1917.

TL English. SL French. UDC literature (criticism, poetry, prose).

GOLDSTEIN, STEVEN 527 Merritt Ave, Oakland, CA 94610 USA.

TL & SL English & French. UDC magic.

Memb ATA, NCTA.

GÖMÖRI, GEORGE Darwin College, Cambridge, UK.

TL English. SL Hungarian, Polish, Russian. UDC literature (criticism, poetry, prose).

Hungarian László Nagy: *Love of the Scorching Wind* (Oxford Univ, 1973). Miklós Radnóti: *Poems* (Carcanet, 1979). **Polish** *Modern Polish Poets* (Occidental, 1979). **Russian** Boris Pasternak: *Post-1945 Poetry* (Occidental, 1965). Also the works of Sándor Csoóri, István Csurka, Zbigniew Herbert, Elemér Horváth, Czeslaw Milosz, numerous others.

Awards 1972 Jurzykowski Prize.

GOYNE, MINETTA ALTGELT 1205 Sherwood Dr, Arlington, TX 76013 USA *Tel* 817-275-4095.

TL English. SL German. UDC art, history, literature (all areas), theater.

GRAHAM, HELGA R 8022 Candlewood Dr, Alexandria, VA 22306 USA *Tel* 703-768-6931.

TL & SL English & German. UDC literature (children's, folklore, history, prose).

Memb ATA.

GRANDLE, LYNN HACKMAN 141 Wilderness Rd, Hampton, VA 23669 USA *Tel* 804-851-8433.

TL English. SL French, German. UDC aesthetics, anthropology, art, education, ethics, food/nutrition, genealogy, geography, history, linguistics/philology, literature (history, lyrics, poetry, prose, songs), metaphysics, music, philosophy, theater.

Memb ATA.

GREEN, PETER MORRIS Classics, Univ of Texas, Austin, TX 78712 USA *Tel* 512-471-5742.

TL English. SL French, Greek (Classical & Modern), Italian, Latin. UDC ancient history, archeology, art history (Greek & Roman), biography, literature (poetry, prose), numismatics.

French Simone de Beauvoir: *The Prime of Life* (World, 1962). Zoë Oldenburg: *Destiny of Fire* (Gollancz, 1961). **Italian** Fosco Maraini: *Where Four Worlds Meet* (Hamish Hamilton, 1964). **Latin** D Iunius Iuvenalis: *Juvena: The Sixteen Satires* (Penguin, 1967). Also the works of Luciana d'Arad, Giovanni Arpino, Claude Aveline, Collete Audry, Ranuccio Bianchi Bandinelli, Mongo Beti, Laura Breglia, R Christophe, Petru Dumitriu, Enrico Emmanuelli, Paul Guimard, F Mallet-Joris, Gusztav Rab, numerous others.

Memb ALTA, TA.

GREGORY, PATRICK BOLTON 36 Butler Pl, Northampton, MA 01060 USA *Tel* 413-586-4571.

TL English. SL French. UDC anthropology, art, athletics, history, literature (all areas), philosophy, theology.

French René Girard: *Violence and the Sacred* (Johns Hopkins Univ, 1977). Pasca Pia: *Baudelaire* (Grove, 1959). Jaime Sabartés: *Picasso: Toreros* (Braziller, 1961). Also the works of Romain Gary, André Gide, Henri Michaux.

Affil Boston Univ.

GREINKE, ERIC PO Box 2662, Grand Rapids, MI 49501 USA *Tel* 616-532-6471.

TL English. SL French, Spanish. UDC literature (poetry).

French Arthur Rimbaud: *The Drunken Boat & Other Poems* (Free Books, 1976).

GRESSET, MICHEL ALBERT LOUIS 10 ave de Paris F-78000 Versailles, France *Tel* 950 41 55.

TL French. SL English. UDC aesthetics, ethics, literature (criticism, prose), philosophy, psychology.

English Heather Ross Miller: *The Edge of the Woods* (Gallimard, 1967); *Gone a Hundred Miles* (Gallimard, 1970). William Faulkner: *Flags in the Dust*; *Sanctuary* (Gallimard, 1977). Also the works of Fred Chappell, Flannery O'Connor, John Cowper Powys, Reynolds Price, William Styron, Kenneth White.

Affil Univ of Sorbonne. **Memb** ATLF.

GRIFFIN, PETER 3536 Garnet St #18, Torrance, CA 90503 USA *Tel* 213-542-7802.

TL English, Spanish. SL Catalan, English, Portuguese, Spanish. UDC linguistics/philol-

ogy, literature (children's, folklore, history, prose).

Memb ATA.

GRINDROD, MURIEL KATHLEEN 45 Lancaster Grove, London NW3, UK *Tel* (01) 794 3786.

TL English. SL Italian. UDC economics, government, history, Italian affairs, political economy.

Italian Carlo Falconi: *The Popes in the Twentieth Century* (Weidenfeld & Nicolson, 1967); *Pope John and His Council* (Weidenfeld & Nicolson, 1964). Federico Chabod: *A History of Italian Fascism* (Weidenfeld & Nicolson, 1961). Arrigo Levi: *Journey among the Economists* (Alcove, 1973). Also the works of Guido Artom, Giovanni Carandente, Bruno Molajoli, Luigi Parett.

Memb TA. **Award** 1968 John Florio Prize.

GROLMES, SAMUEL B & YUMIKO T see TSUMURA, YUMIKO

GROSS, ALEX 1292 Lamouree Rd, Saugerties, NY 12477 USA *Tel* 914-246-9692; 212-777-7609.

TL English. SL French, German, Italian, Spanish. UDC literature (drama).

German Peter Weiss: "The Investigation" (play). Friedrich Dürrenmatt: "The Meteor" (play); "Hercules and the Augean Stables" (play). Also the works of Jacques Audiberti, Carlo Goldoni, Hans Günter Michelsen, Marcel Mithois, Eckhart Peterich.

GROSSMAN, EDITH 800 West End Ave, New York, NY 10025 USA *Tel* 212-666-7396.

TL English. SL Spanish. UDC literature (criticism, poetry, prose).

Spanish Manuel Scorza: *Drums for Rancas* (Harper & Row, 1977). Also the works of Guillermo Cabrera Infante, Julio Cortázar, Jorge Edwards, Macedonio Fernández, Jean-Michel Fossey, Gustavo Alvarez Gardeazabal, Salvador Garmendia, Luis Gusman, Hector Libertella, Silvina Ocampo, Nicanor Parra, Antonio Skarmeta.

Affil Dominican College of Blauvelt.

GUADARRAMA, ARGELIA ARIZPE 908 S 16, Edinburg, TX 78539 USA *Tel* 512-383-6928.

TL & SL English & Spanish. UDC education (bilingual/bicultural teaching materials, especially for Spanish-speaking children of the Southwest).

English Carolyn Penn: *Reflections for Living Values—Curriculum for Adults* (Harris County, Dept of Education, 1978). "Bilingual Science Series K–3" (filmstrips), "Bilingual Math Series K–3" (filmstrips) (Region I Education Ctr, 1977).

Memb ATA.

GUENTHER, CHARLES 2935 Russell Blvd, St Louis, MO 63104 USA *Tel* 314-664-2384.

TL English. SL French, Italian, Spanish. UDC art/art history, literature (poetry, prose).

French *Paul Valéry in English* (Olivant, 1970). *Selected Poems of Alain Bousquet* (New Directions/Lippincott, 1963). *Voices in the*

Dark (The Printery, 1974). **Italian** *Modern Italian Poets* (Inferno, 1961). Also the works of Maria Celeste Achille Todde, Rafael Alberti, Vincente Aleixandre, Octavio Amortegui, Guillaume Appolinaire, Augustin Lopez Arciega, Hans Arp, Jean Arp, Antonin Artaud, Jacques Baron, Nino Bellassai, Luc Beremont, László Berenczey, Attilio Bertolucci, Carlo Betocchi, Yves Bonnefoy, Jean Bourdeillette, René-Guy Cadou, Raffaele Carrieri, Aime Cesaire, René Char, Jean Cocteau, Arnaut Daniel, Ruben Dario, Edgar Degas, Ala Delfino, Blas de Otero, Jacques Dupin, Esteban Borrero Echeverria, Paul Eluard, Pierre Emmanuel, Alfonso Gatto, Pierre Jean Jouve, Giacomo Leopardi, Mario Luzi, Antonio Machado, Stéphane Mallarmé, Francesco Petrarca, Pablo Picasso, Jacques Prevert, Salvatore Quasimodo, Rainer Maria Rilke, Jules Romain, Jean Rousselot, Georges Senechal, Léopold Sédar Senghor, Maria Luisa Spaziani, Jules Supervielle, Giuseppe Ungaretti, Paul Verlaine, Jean Wahl, Suwa Yu, numerous others. Also numerous essays, reviews.
Memb ALTA. **Awards** 1971 St Louis Poetry Center Translation Prize.

GUGELBERGER, GEORG H Literatures & Languages, Univ of California, Riverside, CA 92502 USA *Tel* 714-784-1923; 787-4522.
TL German. **SL** English, French, Latin. **UDC** literature (French), poetry (German).
English Helmut Maria Soik: *Rimbaud under the Steel Helmet* (Red Hill Pr, 1976). Also the works of Kieseritzky, Sarah Kirsch, Kunert, Kunze, numerous other East German poets in E G Petry: *Micromegas* (1973).
Memb ALTA.

GUGLI, WILLIAM V French & Italian, Univ of Massachusetts, Amherst, MA 01002 USA.
TL English. **SL** French. **UDC** literature (criticism, history, prose).
French André Chouraqui: *Letter to an Arab Friend* (Univ of MA, 1972); *The People and the Faith of the Bible* (Univ of MA, 1975).

GUIBERT, RITA 301 E 78 St, New York, NY 10021 USA *Tel* 212-861-3891.
TL Spanish. **SL** English. **UDC** art, biology, biomedicine, communications, education, food/nutrition, government, graphics, literature (children's, criticism, drama, folklore, history, prose), painting, philosophy, printing, psychiatry, psychology, public administration, public hèalth, sculpture, sociology, telecommunication, theater.
English Robert Kraus: *Milton the Early Riser* (Dutton/Windmill, 1977). William Steig: *Sylvester and the Magic Pebble* (Dutton/Windmill, 1977). Also preface and chapter introductions of *Seven Voices* (Novaro Mexico, 1972).

GUICHARNAUD, JUNE 195 Bishop St, New Haven, CT 06511 USA *Tel* 203-562-7187.
TL English. **SL** French. **UDC** art, biography, history, literature (drama, prose), philosophy, psychology.
French André Malraux: *Picasso's Masks* (Holt, Rinehart & Winston, 1976). Robert Courtine: *Feasts of a Militant Gastronome* (Morrow, 1974). Gisèle Freund: *The World in*

My Camera (Harcourt Brace Jovanovich, 1974). José Cabanis: *The Joyless Years* (Prentice-Hall, 1971). Also the works of Simone Berteaut, Germaine Brée, Jean Delay, André Gide, Jacques Guicharnaud, Daniel Halévy, Pierre-Jakez Hélias, Philippe Auguste Villiers de L'Isle-Adam, Jules Laforgue, Paul Mus, Agnes Raymond, Auguste Toussaint, Paul Valéry.

HAASL, EDWARD J Vaarstraat 59, B-3000 Leuven, Belgium *Tel* (016) 228 254.
TL English. **SL** Dutch, French. **UDC** economics, ethics/morals, law, philosophy, theology.
Dutch Carlos G Steel: *The Changing Self: A Study of the Soul in Later Neoplatonism* (Belgian Royal Academy, 1973). Eugeen Roosens: *"Crazytown:" Geel, Belgium* (Sage, 1979). **French** *Becoming a Catholic Christian* (Sadlier, 1978). **French & Dutch** Antoine Vergote: *Parental Images and the Representation of God* (Leuven Univ/Toronto Univ, 1979). Also the works of J De Ploey, H Degreef, A Dooms-Goosens, L Missotten, E Roosens, H Van der Wee, numerous others.
Memb CBTIP.

HACKEN, RICHARD German, Univ of Kansas, Lawrence, KS 66045 USA *Tel* 913-843-2456.
TL English. **SL** Dutch, German. **UDC** genealogy, literature (criticism, poetry, prose), religion/scripture.
Dutch O M Brouwer-Van Vetthoven: "Luigi Malerba and the *nouveau roman* in Italy" (*Criticism in Translation*, 1 no 1, 1976).

HAHN, MARIE 808 N Market St, Frederick, MD 21701 USA *Tel* 301-662-1598.
TL English. **SL** German. **UDC** literature, sciences (natural).
German Samuel Urlsperger, ed: *Detailed Reports on the Salzburger Emigrants who Settled in America, Vol III, 1736* (Univ of Georgia, 1972).
Affil Hood College.

HALEY, ALBERT W, JR 14 Wethersfield St, Rowley, MA 01969 USA *Tel* 617-948-2525.
TL English. **SL** Anglo-Saxon. **UDC** literature (poetry).
Anglo-Saxon numerous anonymous poems and riddles published in periodicals, journals, collections.

HALL, MICHAEL B 200 Robin St, Rome, GA 30161 USA *Tel* 404-291-2248.
TL English. **SL** German. **UDC** cinema, literature (drama, librettos, lyrics, poetry, prose, songs), music, theater.
German Gerhart Hauptmann: "The Bow of Odysseus" (pending).
Accred SUNY at Binghamton (Certificate in Translation). **Affil** Berry College. **Memb** ALTA, ATA.

HALMAN, TALAT SAIT 333 E 30 St, New York, NY 10016 USA *Tel* 212-725-4803.
TL English. **SL** Turkish. **UDC** aesthetics, anthropology, archeology, architecture, art, communications, education, ethics/morals, ethnography, government, history, linguistics/

philology, literature (children's, criticism, drama, folklore, history, poetry, prose, songs), metaphysics, music, painting, philosophy, political economy/science, psychiatry, psychology, religion, sculpture, social sciences, sociology, theater, theology.
Turkish Fazil Hüsnü Daglarca: *Selected Poems* (Pittsburgh Univ, 1969). Orhan Veli Kanik: *I am Listening to Istanbul, Selected Poems* (Corinth, 1971). Yunus Emre: *The Humanist Poetry of Yunus Emre* (RCD Cultural Inst, 1972).
Affil Princeton Univ (Near Eastern Program).

HAMBURGER, MICHAEL Marsh Acres, Middleton, Saxmundham, Suffolk, UK *Tel* (0728) 73 247.
TL English. **SL** French, German, Italian. **UDC** literature (poetry).
French Baudelaire: *20 Prose Poems* (Poetry/Jonathan Cape/Grossman, 1946–68). **German** *German Poetry 1910–1975* (Urizen/Carcanet, 1976–78). Beethoven: *Letters, Journals & Conversations* (Thames & Hudson/Jonathan Cape/Greenwood/Pantheon/Anchor, 1960–78). Friedrich Hölderlin: *Poems, Selected Verse, Poems & Fragments* (Penguin/Routledge & Kegan Paul/Pantheon/Univ of Michigan, 1943–66).
Awards 1961–63, 1965–66 Bollingen Foundation Awards, 1966 Deutsche Akademie für Sprache und Dichtung Translation Prize, 1970 Levinson Prize, 1978 Schlegel-Tieck Prize.

HANNAH, RICHARD W German Studies, Stanford Univ, Stanford, CA 94305 USA.
TL English. **SL** German. **UDC** intellectual history, linguistics, literature (fiction), lyrics.
German Wilhelm von Humboldt: "Universal Aspects of Linguistic Structure" (pending).
Memb ALTA.

HANNAHER, WILLIAM 6374 Wingate St, Alexandria, VA 22312 USA *Tel* 703-354-3762.
TL English. **SL** Serbo-Croatian. **UDC** aesthetics, anthropology, archeology, architecture, art, banking/finance, commerce, geography, history, law, legislation, linguistics/philology, literature (criticism, drama, folklore, history, librettos, lyrics, poetry, prose, songs), music, philosophy, political science, sociology, theater.
Serbo-Croatian Danilo Kis: *Garden, Ashes* (Harcourt Brace Jovanovich, 1975). Also the works of Mihajlo Mihajlov, Danilo Pejovic, Karlo Štajner, Rudi Supek, Predrag Vranicki.

HANNUM, HUNTER G RD 5, Old Lyme, CT 06371 USA *Tel* 203-434-8425.
TL English. **SL** German. **UDC** art, education, government, history, literature (criticism), medicine, philosophy, psychiatry, psychology, sociology, theater.
German Katia Mann: *Unwritten Memories* (Knopf, 1975).
Memb ATA.

HANSEN, KURT HEINRICH Kieselweg 1, D-2 Hamburg 65, West Germany *Tel* (040) 602 72 22.
TL German. **SL** English. **UDC** art, geography, history, linguistics/philology, literature

(drama, folklore, history, poetry, prose), painting, philosophy, photography, religion, sculpture, theater.

English Wystan Hugh Auden: *The Age of Anxiety* (Limes, 1949). William Faulkner: *A Fable* (Scherz & Goverts, 1955). John Updike: *A Month of Sundays* (Rowohlt, 1976). Richard Wright: *Black Boy; American Hunger* (Kiepenheuer & Witsch, 1978–79). Also the works of Conrad Aiken, Truman Capote, Sean O'Casey, E E Cummings, Emily Dickinson, Robinson Jeffers, James Joyce, Jerzy Kosinski, Archibald MacLeish, Muriel Spark, Wallace Stevens, Jonathan Swift, Tennessee Williams, William Carlos Williams, William Butler Yeats.

Memb VDÜ.

HARCOURT, FELICE Willow Cottage, Colwell Chine Rd, Colwell Bay, Isle of Wight, UK *Tel* (0983 83) 3126.

TL English. **SL** French. **UDC** history, literature (criticism, history, prose), travel.

French Marquise de la Tour du Pin: *Memoirs of Madame de la Tour du Pin* (Harvill, 1970). Shahbanou d'Iran Farah: *My Thousand and One Days* (Allen, 1978).

HARKINS, WILLIAM E 10 Monroe Pl, Brooklyn, NY 11201 USA *Tel* 212-624-1616.

TL English. **SL** Czech, Russian. **UDC** literature (criticism, poetry).

Czech Edward Bass: *Umberto's Circus* (Farrar, Straus, 1951). **Russian** Alexander Pushkin: *Three Comic Poems—Gavriiliada, Count Nulin, The Little House* (Ardis, 1977). Also the works of Josef & Karel Čapek, N M Karamzin, Jindrich Jiři Kolář, Josef Šlejhar, A P Sumarokov, Evgeny Zamyatin, Alexander Zinoviev.

Affil Columbia Univ (Slavic Lang & Lit).

HARRINGTON, NAIDA Nairobi Peace Corps, c/o Dept of State, Washington, DC 20520 USA *Tel* Nairobi, Kenya 582 551.

TL English. **SL** Spanish. **UDC** literature (children's, criticism, drama, folklore, history, prose, science fiction), religion, sociology, theater, theology.

Memb ATA.

HARRIS, BRIAN LA MONT 658 S Reed Ct #M-31, Lakewood, CO 80226 USA *Tel* 303-934-1914.

TL English. **SL** German. **UDC** literature (all areas), philosophy, photography, theater.

German Hugo Ball: "Critique of the German Mind" (PhD diss). Also the works of Ilse Aichinger, Johannes Bobrowski, Günter Eich, Peter Uwe Hohendahl, Christoph Meckel, others.

Memb ALTA.

HARTMANN, JOHN F Foreign Languages & Literatures, Northern Illinois Univ, DeKalb, IL 60115 USA *Tel* 815-753-1501.

TL English. **SL** Thai. **UDC** law, linguistics, literature, political science.

Memb ATA.

HARVEY, ANNE-CHARLOTTE HANES 2242 Lawton Dr, Lemon Grove, CA 92045 USA *Tel* 714-461-4926.

TL English. **SL** Danish, Norwegian, Swedish. **UDC** aesthetics, art, choreography, literature (all areas except folklore and science fiction), musical theater, textiles.

Affil San Diego State Univ. **Memb** ATA.

HEIM, MICHAEL HENRY Slavic Languages, Univ of California, Los Angeles, CA 90024 USA *Tel* 213-825-2676.

TL English. **SL** Czech, Russian. **UDC** linguistics, literature (criticism, drama, prose), music, theater.

Czech Bohumil Hrabal: *The Death of Mr. Baltisberger* (Doubleday, 1975). **Russian** A P Chekhov: *Letters* (Harper & Row, 1973). Also the works of Arbuzov, Roshchin.

HEIN, RUTH 707 Orange St, New Haven, CT 06511 USA *Tel* 203-865-1491.

TL English. **SL** German. **UDC** aesthetics, anthropology, archeology, art, choreography, education, ethics, history, human resources, linguistics/philology, literature (criticism, drama, history, librettos, prose, science fiction), metaphysics, music, painting, philosophy, political science, printing, psychology, sociology, theater.

German Oskar Anweiler: *The Soviets* (Pantheon, 1975). Hans Buchheim: *Totalitarian Rule* (Wesleyan Univ, 1968). Sandra Paretti: *Tenants of the Earth* (Evans, 1976). Also the works of Theodor W Adorno, Bertolt Brecht, Heimito von Doderer, Ernst Fischer, Max Frisch, Günter Grass, Joachim Kaiser, Alexander Kluge, Raphael Lenne, Anna Seghers, Karlheinz Stockhausen, Philipp Vandenberg, numerous others. Also uncredited revision of translations of works of Heinrich Böll, Peter Handke, Monica Mann.

Affil Ctr for Independent Studies, New Haven, CT.

HELMAN, EDITH 3 Concord Ave #31, Cambridge, MA 02138 USA.

TL English. **SL** Spanish. **UDC** literature (poetry).

Spanish Pedro Salinas: *Reality and the Poet in Spanish Poetry* (Johns Hopkins Univ, 1937); *To Live in Pronouns* (Norton, 1974).

HEMSCHEMEYER, JUDITH English, Douglass College, New Brunswick, NJ 08903 USA *Tel* 201-932-9777.

TL English. **SL** French, Russian. **UDC** literature (poetry).

HENNESSY, DANIEL 550 Alta Vista Way, Laguna Beach, CA 92651 USA *Tel* 714-494-7651.

TL English. **SL** German. **UDC** aesthetics, art, education, ethics, linguistics, literature (children's, criticism, drama, folklore, history, librettos, lyrics, poetry, prose, songs), philosophy, psychology, theater.

Memb ATA.

HENNESSY, EILEEN B 5 Shaker Hollow Rd, Setauket, NY 11733 USA *Tel* 516-941-3815.

TL English. **SL** French, German, Spanish. **UDC** art, commerce, ethics/morals, law, literature (prose), patents/trademarks.

French Edgar de Bruyne: *The Esthetics of the Middle Ages* (Ungar, 1968). Pierre Couperie et al: *A History of the Comic Strip* (Crown, 1968).

Maurice Daumas, ed: *A History of Technology and Invention* (Crown, 1969). Jean Selz: *Nineteenth-Century Drawings and Watercolors* (Crown, 1968). Also the works of Jacques Bergier, Denys Chevalier, Raymond Cogniat, Gaston Diehl, Jacques Sadoul, numerous others.

Memb ATA.

HENRIQUES, EUNICE RIBEIRO 115-A Stinson St, Chapel Hill, NC 27514 USA *Tel* 919-942-2589.

TL & SL English & Portuguese. **UDC** education, linguistics, literature (criticism, drama, poetry, prose, science fiction), psychiatry, psychology, social sciences, theater.

HERMSTEIN, RUDOLF Thomastr 15, D-8204 Brannenburg, West Germany *Tel* (08034) 2428.

TL German. **SL** English. **UDC** economics, geography, literature (prose, science fiction, songs), photography.

English Brian W Aldiss: *Best Science Fiction Stories* (Insel, 1972). Jimmy Breslin: *The Gang That Couldn't Shoot Straight* (Zsolnay, 1972). Doris Lessing: *Memoirs of a Survivor* (S Fischer, 1978). Robert M Pirsig: *Zen and the Art of Motorcycle Maintenance* (S Fischer, 1976). Also the works of Peter Cowan, Salvador Dali, W W Davenport, Robert Elegant, Virginia Kidd, Warren Leslie, Desmond Morris, John Postgate, Theodore Sturgeon, Bryce S Walker, Robert Wood, numerous others.

Memb VDÜ.

HERNÁNDEZ, FRANCES PO Box 3196, Las Cruces, NM 88003 USA *Tel* 505-524-3809; 915-747-5731.

TL English. **SL** Spanish. **UDC** aesthetics, anthropology, ecology, education, ethnography, geography, history, human resources, literature (all areas), occultism, social sciences, sociology.

Spanish E C Menéndez: *Only the Wind: Legends of the Onas of Tierra del Fuego* (Pajarito, 1978). Francisco de Moncada: *The Catalan Chronicle* (Texas Western, 1975). Ramón Sender: "Chronus and the Lady with a Tail" (pending).

Affil Univ of Texas at El Paso. **Memb** ATA.

HERSH, ELLEN E Box 204, Bradford, NH 03221 USA *Tel* 603-938-2196.

TL English. **SL** French, German. **UDC** history, literature (all areas, especially poetry), religion, theater.

French Boris Vian: "Red Grass' (pending). **Memb** ALTA.

HESSELING, CHRISTINA G 1642-D Mitchell Ave, Waterloo, IA 50702 USA *Tel* 319-233-3060.

TL English. **SL** Dutch. **UDC** business, commerce, literature (all areas), medicine, music. **Memb** ATA.

HEURCK, JAN van 28 Hilton Ave, East Haven, CT 06512 USA *Tel* 203-468-0338.

TL English. **SL** French, German, Spanish. **UDC** art, literature (all areas), popular science, religion.

German Hoimar von Ditfurth: *Children of*

the Universe (Atheneum, 1974). Vitus B Dröscher: *They Love and Kill: Sex, Sympathy, and Aggression in Courtship* (Allen/Dutton, 1976). Jozsef Cardinal Mindszenty: *Memoirs* (Macmillan, 1974). Monika Schwinn & Bernhard Diehl: *We Came to Help* (Harcourt Brace Jovanovich, 1976). Also the works of F L Boschke, Hermann Hesse, others.

HIBBETT, HOWARD S Japanese, Harvard Univ, EALC, 2 Divinity Ave, Cambridge, MA 02138 USA *Tel* 617-495-2754.
   TL English. **SL** Japanese. **UDC** literature (prose).
   Japanese Tanazaki Jun'ichiro: *The Key* (Knopf, 1961); *Diary of a Mad Old Man* (Knopf, 1965); *Seven Japanese Tales* (Knopf, 1963). Kawabata Yasunari: *Beauty and Sadness* (Knopf, 1974). Takeyama Michio: *The Harp of Burma* (Tuttle, 1966). Stories and poems in Donald Keene, ed: *Anthology of Japanese Literature* (1955). *Contemporary Japanese Literature: An Anthology of Fiction, Film, and Other Writing since 1945* (Knopf, 1977).

HOCHMAN, STANLEY 34 Gramercy Park E, New York, NY 10003 USA *Tel* 212-982-2860.
   TL English. **SL** French, Italian. **UDC** history, literature (criticism, drama, history, prose), theater.
   French Louis Pergaud: *War of the Buttons* (Walker, 1968). Jules Renard: *Poil de Carotte and Other Plays* (Ungar, 1977). Emile Zola: *Germinal* (New American Library, 1970). **Italian** Vitaliano Brancati: *Bell'Antonio* (Ungar, 1978). Also the works of Pierre Barbet, Claude Chabrol, Colette, Moyshe Dayan, Réné Dumont, Francois Giroud, Jean Larteguy, Konrad Lorenz, Ugo Pirro, Eric Rohmer.

HOEGL, JUERGEN K 1382 W Pershing Rd, Decatur, IL 62526 USA *Tel* 217-875-0220.
   TL English. **SL** German. **UDC** literature (criticism, prose), semiotics.
   Memb ALTA.

HOEKSEMA, THOMAS JAY Box 3671, Univ Park, NM 88001 USA *Tel* 505-523-4896.
   TL English. **SL** Spanish. **UDC** literature (poetry, prose).
   Spanish Isabel Fraire: *Only This Light: Selected Poems* (Mundus Artium Pr, 1975).
   Affil New Mexico State Univ. **Memb** ALTA.

HOFFMAN, STANLEY B 3112 Eighth St, Boulder, CO 80302 USA *Tel* 303-447-8335.
   TL English. **SL** German, Indonesian. **UDC** musicology.
   Indonesian Poerbatjaraka: *Prince Inu Plays Gamelan: Sources for Explanation of the Word "Patet"* (Univ of Michigan, 1977). Purbodiningrat: *Gamelan* (Univ of Michigan, 1977). Ki Sinooesawarno: *Explanation of the Word "Patet"* (Univ of Michigan, 1977). Sulaiman Gitosaprodjo: *Summary of the Theory of Singing* (Univ of Michigan, 1977), numerous others.

HOHENSTEIN, A K 261 Cypress St, Providence, RI 02906 USA *Tel* 401-357-4269.
   TL English **SL** Catalan, Spanish. **UDC** graphics, history, literature (criticism, history, lyrics, poetry, prose).

Catalan Montserrat Puig: *Rough on Parts* (Bingo Chow/Loose Art, 1978). Also the works of J Arreola, A Somers.
   Affil Brown Univ. **Memb** ALTA.

HOLD, OLGA 801 Pan American Bank Bldg, Orlando, FL 32801 USA *Tel* 305-843-7877.
   TL English. **SL** French, German, Spanish. **UDC** advertising, business, commerce, copyright, economics, finance, law, patents/trademarks.
   Memb ATA.

HOLLAND, MICHAEL E 1302 N Ctr St, Bloomington, IL 61701 USA.
   TL English. **SL** German, Russian. **UDC** agriculture, literature (prose), music, philately, philology, religion, sciences (life).
   Memb ATA.

HOLLAND, MUHTAR The Islamic Foundation, 223 London Rd, Leicester LE2 IZE, UK *Tel* (0533) 700725.
   TL English. **SL** Arabic, French, Russian. **UDC** ethics/morals, history, law (Islamic), literature (Islamic), philosophy, religion/scripture.
   Arabic al-Ghazali: *The Duties of Brotherhood* (Latimer, 1975; Overlook, 1977).
   Accred Civil Service Commission Interpretership (Russian).

HOLOCH, GEORGE 3 Storrs Ave, Middlebury, VT 05753 USA *Tel* 802-388-7788.
   TL English. **SL** French. **UDC** history, literature (prose), philosophy, social sciences.
   French Bernard-Henri Lévy: *Barbarism with a Human Face* (Harper & Row, 1979). Jean Lacouture: *Léon Blum* (New Republic, 1979). Robert Jaulin: *White Peace* (Urizen, 1979).

HOLT, MARION PETER 133 W 71 St #7B, New York, NY 10023 USA *Tel* 212-362-6876.
   TL English. **SL** Spanish. **UDC** literature (criticism, drama, librettos, prose), theater.
   Spanish José López Rubio: "The Blindfold" (*The Modern Spanish Stage: Four Plays*, (Hill & Wang, 1970). Also the works of Antonio Buero-Vallejo, Alejandro Casona, Victor Ruiz Iriarte.
   Memb ATA.

HOLTON, WILLIAM MILNE English, Univ of Maryland, College Park MD 20742 USA *Tel* 301-454-2525; 202-547-8052.
   TL English. **SL** Macedonian, Polish. **UDC** literature (drama, poetry, prose).
   Macedonian *The Big Horse and Other Stories of Modern Macedonia* (Univ of Missouri, 1974). *Reading the Ashes: An Anthology of the Poetry of Modern Macedonia*, co-translated with Graham W Reid (Univ of Pittsburgh, 1977). **Polish** *The New Polish Poetry: A Bilingual Collection*, co-translated with Paul Vangelisti (Univ of Pittsburgh, 1978).
   Memb ALTA.

HONIG, EDWIN English, Box 1852, Brown Univ, Providence, RI 02912 USA *Tel* 401-521-0545; 863-2393.
   TL English. **SL** Portuguese, Spanish. **UDC** literature (poetry, prose).

Portuguese Fernando Pessôa: *Selected Poems* (Swallow, 1971). **Spanish** Federico García Lorca: *Divan and Other Writings* (Copper Beech, 1977). Pedro Calderon de la Barca: *Life Is a Dream* (Hill & Wang, 1970); *Calderon: Four Plays* (Hill & Wang, 1961). Also the works of Jorge Luis Borges, Miguel Hernandez, Ramón Sender, Lope de Vega, others.
   Affil Brown Univ. **Awards** 1966 National Inst of Arts & Letters citation, 1975 NEH grant.

HOWER, ALFRED 71 SW 32 St, Gainesville, FL 32607 USA *Tel* 904-372-6855.
   TL English. **SL** Portuguese. **UDC** literature (drama, history, prose).
   Portuguese Antonio Olavo Pereira: *Marcorê* (Univ of Texas, 1970).
   Affil Univ of Florida (Romance Langs).

HRUBÝ, OLGA S 545 W 111 St #3A, New York, NY 10025 USA *Tel* 212-663-6771.
   TL English. **SL** Czech, Slovak. **UDC** religion, theology.
   Affil Research Ctr for Religion & Human Rights.

HUBERMAN, EDWARD 33 Hickory Dr, Maplewood, NJ 07040 USA *Tel* 201-762-3143.
   TL English. **SL** Spanish. **UDC** literature (all areas).
   Spanish Antonio Robles Soler: *Tales of Living Playthings* (Modern Age, 1938); *Merry Tales from Spain* (Winston, 1939); *The Refugee Centaur* (Twayne, 1952). Also the works of Emilia Pardo Bazan, Pedro Calderón, Maruxa Vilalta, numerous others.
   Affil Rutgers Univ.

HUGGINS, EDWARD NORTON Willow Lake Resort, Butte Falls, OR 97522 USA *Tel* 503-865-3229,
   TL English. **SL** Latvian, Russian. **UDC** literature (all areas).
   Latvian *Blue and Green Wonders and Other Latvian Tales* (Simon & Schuster, 1971). **Russian** Boris Pasternak: "Doctor Zhivago" (pending).

HULICK, ELIZABETH C 501 E 85 St, New York, NY 10028 USA *Tel* 212-744-3456.
   TL English. **SL** French, Russian, Spanish. **UDC** literature (poetry), theater.
   Russian the works of Nikolai Gogol, Alexander Pushkin.
   Awards 1961 Pushkin Prize for Verse Translations.

HURST, GEORGE CAMERON, III History, Univ of Kansas, Lawrence, KS 66045 USA *Tel* 913-864-3878.
   TL English. **SL** Japanese, Korean. **UDC** history, literature (prose), social sciences.
   Japanese Yukichi Fukuzawa: *An Outline of a Theory of Civilization* (Sophia Univ, 1973).

HUTTER, CATHERINE 2 Philo Ave, Glens Falls, NY 12801 USA *Tel* 518-792-3756.
   TL English. **SL** German. **UDC** art, literature (children's, drama, folklore, history, prose), painting, theater.

HVIDONOV, ANNELI 4 Dwight Lane, Great Neck, NY 11024 USA *Tel* 516-487-9140.

TL English. SL Finnish, Swedish. UDC literature (prose), philately.

Finnish *Stamp Catalogue* (Suomen Postimerkkeily, 1977). Mikko Ossa: *Forgeries of Finnish Postage Stamps* (Lape Oy, 1977). Herbert Oesch: *Collecting 1875 Finnish Stamps* (Scandinavian Contact, 1976). Also articles from Finnish philatelic publications for American-Scandinavian philatelic magazines.

HYDE, LEWIS 8 Donnell St, Cambridge, MA 02138 USA *Tel* 617-661-2565.

TL English. SL Spanish. UDC literature (poetry).

Spanish Vicente Aleixandre: *A Longing for the Light: Selected Poems* (Harper & Row, 1979).

IMPEY, MICHAEL HOWARD 1033 Hawthorne, Bloomington, IN 47401 USA *Tel* 812-336-2641; 606-258-2551.

TL English. SL Italian, Rumanian. UDC aesthetics, literature (criticism, folklore, librettos, poetry, prose).

Rumanian Tudor Arghezi: *Selected Poems* (Princeton Univ, 1976). Tristan Tzara: *First Poems* (New Rivers, 1976). Also the works of Ana Blandiana, Nicolae Bretan, Constanta Buzea, Nina Cassian, Gabriela Melinescu.

Affil Univ of Kentucky.

IONESCU-STOIAN, MRS see **GHITESCU, MICAELA**

IRIBARNE, LOUIS Slavic Languages & Literatures, Univ of Toronto, 21 Sussex Ave, Toronto, ON M5S 1A1, Canada *Tel* 416-978-3419, 4895.

TL English. SL Polish, Russian. UDC literature (drama, poetry, prose, science fiction).

Polish Witold Gombrowicz: *The Marriage* (Grove/Caldar & Boyars, 1970); *Operetta* (Caldar & Boyars, 1971). Stanislaw Ignacy Witkiewicz: *Insatiability* (Univ of Illinois, 1977). Stanislaw Lem: *The Chain of Chance* (Harcourt Brace Jovanovich, 1978). Also the works of Leszek Kolakowski, Czeslaw Milosz, Jan Potocki.

Affil Univ of Toronto. **Awards** 1966 Univ of California Center for East European Studies Translation Award, 1967 National Translation Center Fellowship, 1969 Translator-in-Residence, National Translation Ctr.

ISBELL, HAROLD 1346 Roxbury Rd, Salt Lake City, UT 84108 USA *Tel* 801-582-7427; 534-6063.

TL English. SL Latin. UDC literature (Latin).

Latin *The Last Poets of Imperial Rome* (Penguin, 1971). Ovid: "The Heroides" (poems). Virgil: "The Georgics" (poems). Also the works of Alcuin, Ausonius, Boethius, Claudian, Columba, Namatianus, Nemesianus, Paulinus of Pella, Prudentius.

JACKIW, SHARON EDWARDS 5806 Murrayhill Pl, Pittsburgh, PA 15217 USA *Tel* 412-665-1559.

TL English. SL German. UDC literature (children's, criticism, history, poetry, prose).

Affil Chatham College. **Memb** ALTA.

JACKSON, KENNETH DAVID Spanish & Portuguese, Univ of Texas, Austin, TX 78712 USA *Tel* 512-471-5401; 451-3255.

TL English. SL Portuguese. UDC art, history, literature (all areas), music.

JANVIER, ELISABETH 28 rue Daubenton, F-75005 Paris, France *Tel* 535 22 95.

TL French. SL English. UDC literature (children's, drama, poetry, prose), theater.

English Edward Albee: *Zoo Story* (Laffont, 1963). James Joyce: *Critical Writings* (Gallimard, 1966). Anaïs Nin: *Winter of Artifice* (Editions des Femmes, 1976). Constantin Stanislavski: *An Actor Prepares* (Perrin, 1958). Also the works of Brendan Behan, M Chekhov, Ira Levin, Wole Soyinka.

Memb ATLF.

JANY, HILDEGARD Mülhauser Str 3a, D-5 Cologne, West Germany *Tel* (0221) 17 52 78.

TL German. SL English, French. UDC literature (prose), military policy, political science.

English Martin Luther King, Jr: *Where Do We Go from Here?* (Econ, 1968). Mary Stolz: *Pray Love, Remember* (Franckh'sche, 1964); *Rosemary* (Franckh'sche, 1966). Also the works of Renata Bournazel.

Memb VDÜ.

JENKINS, M F O Angelo State Univ 1332 S Madison, San Angelo, TX 76901 USA *Tel* 915-655-7012.

TL English. SL French. UDC biography, history, literature (drama, prose).

French Augustin Thierry: *Tales of the Early Franks* (Univ of Alabama, 1977).

JOHNSON, LESLIE MARIA 191 Milbank Ave, Greenwich, CT 06830 USA *Tel* 203-869-2936.

TL English. SL German. UDC art, commerce, law (international), literature (drama, poetry, prose, songs), theater.

German the works of Günter Grass, Martin Walser.

Memb ALTA, ATA. **Awards** 1976 Excellence in Translation (Univ of Kansas).

JONES, GEORGE FENWICK 3931 Cloverhill Rd, Baltimore, MD 21218 USA *Tel* 301-235-2693.

TL English. SL German. UDC history, literature (history).

German John Martin Boltzius: *Detailed Reports of the Georgia Salzburgers*, Vols I–IV (Univ of Georgia, 1968–74).

Affil Univ of Maryland. **Awards** 1977 Concordia Historical Society.

JOUVENEL, RENAUD DE Poste restante, F-06400 Cannes, France.

TL French. SL English. UDC literature (criticism, drama, poetry, prose).

English Mark Twain: *Roughin' It* (Françáis Réunis, 1958). Tennessee Williams: *In the Hell of the Cities* (Seghers, 1963). Also the works of Howard Fast, Alexander Saxton, Agnes Smedley and numerous American poets: E E Cummings, Edgar Lee Masters, Carl Sandburg, Walt Whitman, William Carlos Williams.

Memb ATLF.

JUDGE, FRANK 50 Inglewood Dr, Rochester, NY 14619 USA *Tel* 716-436-0178; 434-8633.

TL English. SL Italian. UDC education, law, literature (poetry, prose), psychology.

Italian an anthology of contemporary Italian poetry in a special issue of the *Vanderbilt Poetry Review* (Summer, 1974).

Affil SUNY at Binghamton. **Memb** ALTA.

JURGSON, THELMA 10 Mitchel Pl, White Plains, NY 10601 USA *Tel* 914-948-6206.

TL English. SL French. UDC literature.

Affil Empire State College, SUNY.

KABDEB, THOMAS 6 Albion Rd, Manchester, UK *Tel* (061) 224-3007.

TL & SL English & Hungarian. UDC communications, history, library science, linguistics/philology, literature (all areas), sports.

Hungarian Attila Jozsef: *Poems* (Danubia, 1966). Ferenc Mora: *Chimneysweep Giraffes* (Chatto & Windus, 1970). Bela Rajki: *Teaching How to Swim* (Corvina, 1978). Gyula Illyes: *Selected Poems* (Chatto & Windus, 1971).

Affil Univ of Manchester.

KANES, EVELINE L 101 Alta Vista Dr, Santa Cruz, CA 95060 USA *Tel* 408-426-2962.

TL English. SL German. UDC literature (criticism, contemporary poetry, prose).

German Henry Jacoby: *The Bureaucratization of the World* (Univ. of California, 1973). Also the works of Wilhelm Dilthey, Iwan Goll, Peter Huchel, Marie Luise Kaschnitz.

Memb ALTA.

KANO, TSUTOMU Ctr for Japanese Social & Political Studies, 2-8-8 Nishinogawa, Komaeshi, Tokyo, 201 Japan *Tel* (03) 489-2175.

TL & SL English & Japanese. UDC political science, social science.

Affil *The Japan Interpreter.*

KAPLAN, ROGER FRANCIS SOLON 61 E 95 St, New York, NY 10028 USA *Tel* 212-722-3280.

TL & SL English & French. UDC literature (history, poetry, prose).

English Irwin Shaw: *Evening in Byzantium* (Les Presses de la Cité, 1974). **French** Blaise Cendrars: *The Prose of the Trans-Siberian Railroad and the Little Jehanne of France* (Chicago Review, 1973). Julien Freund: *German Sociology in the Time of Max Weber* (Basic Books, 1978).

KARPOV, LENA 601 N Fifth, Ann Arbor, MI 48106 USA.

TL & SL English & Russian. UDC aesthetics, library science, linguistics/philology, literature (all areas), philosophy, printing, theater.

English Mark Twain: *The Mysterious Stranger* (Soviet Progress, 1970). **Russian** Leonid Grossman: *Balzac and Dostoyevsky* (Ardis, 1972). N Polevoi: *Siberian Notebook* (Four Continents, 1973). A Bek: *Convoy* (Mouton, 1976). Also the works of B Akhmadulina, Edward Albee, A Bely, Joseph Heller, A Pushkin, John Updike, V Zhirmunsky.

Award 1970 Pushkin Prize (Moscow Philological Inst).

KARR, PHYLLIS ANN Rte 1, Box 136, Hiawatha Pk, Rice Lake, WI 54868 USA *Tel* 715-234-3398.
TL English. **SL** French, Russian. **UDC** literature (children's, drama, folklore, history, poetry, prose), nontechnical science fiction and fantasy, songs.
French the works of Yves-Marie Rudel. **Russian** the works of Alexander Volkov.

KARVONEN, HILJA J 707 N Harrison, Alpine, TX 79830 USA.
TL English. **SL** Finnish. **UDC** history, immigration history, literature (children's, criticism, drama, folklore, history, prose).
Finnish the works of Minna Canth, Anni Swan (pending).
Affil Mankato State Univ (emeritus). **Memb** ALTA.

KEELEY, EDMUND 185 Nassau St, Princeton Univ, Princeton, NJ 08540 USA *Tel* 609-452-4711.
TL English. **SL** Greek. **UDC** literature (criticism, poetry, prose).
Greek CP Cavafy: *Collected Poems* (Princeton Univ, 1975). George Seferis: *Collected Poems, 1924–1955* (Princeton Univ, 1967). Cavafy et al: *Six Poets of Modern Greece* (Knopf, 1961). Yannis Ritsos: *Ritsos in Parentheses* (Princeton Univ, 1979). Also the works of Anagnostakis, Lina Kasdagli, Lorenzatos, Solomos, Vassilikos.
Affil Princeton Univ. **Memb** ALTA. **Awards** 1973 National Book Award in Translation.

KEELEY, MARY 140 Littlebrook Rd, Princeton, NJ 08540 USA *Tel* 609-921-9290.
TL English. **SL** Greek. **UDC** literature (drama, prose).
Greek Vassilis Vassilikos: *The Plant, the Well, and the Angel*, co-translated with Edmund Keeley (Knopf, 1964); *The Monarch* (Bobbs-Merrill, 1976). Katy Katsoyanis: *Dmitri Mitropoulos: A Correspondence with Katy Katsoyanis* (Science Press/Martin Dale, 1973). Also the works of Manolis Anagnostakis, Lina Kasdagli, George Seferis.

KEENE, DONALD 407 Kent Hall, Columbia Univ, New York, NY 10027 USA *Tel* 212-222-1449.
TL English. **SL** Japanese. **UDC** literature (drama, history, prose).
Japanese Yoshida Kenkō: *Essays in Idleness* (Columbia Univ). Chikamatsu Monzaemon: *Major Plays* (Columbia Univ). Yukio Mishima: *After the Banquet* (Knopf). Osamu Dazai: *The Setting Sun* (New Directions).

KEITH, HENRY HUNT 79 Central Ave, San Francisco, CA 94117 USA *Tel* 415-863-9853; 861-4785.
TL English. **SL** French, Portuguese, Spanish. **UDC** art, business, government, history, literature (poetry, prose), political economy/science.
Portuguese Cecilia Meireles: *Poems in Translation* (Brazilian-American Cultural Inst, 1977). *Studies in Honor of the Bicentennial of American Independence* (Gulbenkian Foundation/Fulbright Commission, 1976).

KELERTAS, VIOLETA 700 Sunny Lane, Richland Ctr, WI 53581 USA *Tel* 608-647-2704.
TL English. **SL** Lithuanian. **UDC** literature (criticism, drama, folklore, prose).
Affil Univ of Wisconsin. **Memb** ALTA.

KELLY, LYNDA L 1927 Stoney Brook, Houston, TX 77063 USA *Tel* 713-789-6794.
TL English. **SL** French. **UDC** aesthetics, architecture, art, history, linguistics, literature.
Affil Houston Community College. **Memb** ATA.

KEMP, LYSANDER 814 E 30 St, Austin, TX 78705 USA *Tel* 512-471-5551.
TL English. **SL** Spanish. **UDC** anthropology, art, ecology, history, literature (criticism, drama, poetry, prose).
Spanish Octavio Paz: *The Labyrinth of Solitude: Life and Thought in Mexico* (Grove, 1961). Juan Rulfo: *Pedro Páramo* (Grove, 1959). Mario Vargas Llosa: *The Time of the Hero* (Grove, 1966). Miguel León-Portilla, ed: *The Broken Spears: The Aztec Account of the Conquest of Mexico* (Beacon, 1959). Also the works of Rubén Darío, Xavier Domingo, Ricardo Pozas.
Affil Latin American Studies, Univ of Texas-Austin.

KERN, GARY 545 Highlander Dr, Riverside, CA 92507 USA *Tel* 714-682-3738.
TL English. **SL** Russian. **UDC** literature (children's, criticism, drama, history, poetry, prose, science fiction).
Russian Boris Eikhenbaum: *The Young Tolstoi* (Ardis, 1972). Mikhail Zoshchenko: *Before Sunrise* (Ardis, 1974). *The Serapion Brothers: A Critical Anthology of Stories & Essays* (Ardis, 1975). Velimir Khlebnikov: *Snake Train: Poetry and Prose* (Ardis, 1976). Also the works of Alexander Blok, Anton Chekhov, Konstantin Fedin, Leonid Grossman, Vsevolod Ivanov, Lev Kopelev, Aleksei Remizov, Evgeny Zamyatin, numerous others.

KING, J FANNIN Clark Univ, Worcester, MA 01610 USA *Tel* 617-793-7234.
TL English. **SL** French, Spanish. **UDC** communications, education, history, linguistics, literature, music, philosophy.

KING, MARTHA J 3431 N Hills Dr #307, Austin, TX 78731 USA *Tel* 512-345-0794.
TL English. **SL** Italian. **UDC** literature (criticism, poetry, prose).
Affil Univ of Texas-Austin. **Memb** ALTA.

KIRBERG, GISELA 92 Chevening Rd, London NW6, UK *Tel* (01) 969 6204.
TL German. **SL** English. **UDC** literature (prose, especially with an Irish interest).
English Christy Brown: *A Shadow on Summer* (Fischer, forthcoming). Christian Barnard: *The Unwanted* (Scherz, 1976). Jack London: *The Game* (Büchergilde Gutenberg, 1979). Sumner Locke Elliott: *Water under the Bridge* (Ullstein, forthcoming). Also the works of Catherine Gaskin, Patricia Highsmith, Carola Salisbury.
Memb VS.

KLIN, GEORGE Atlantic Community College, Mays Landing, NJ 08330 USA.
TL English. **SL** French, Spanish. **UDC** art, history, humanities, literature (criticism), social sciences.
French Charles C Lehrmann: *The Jewish Element in French Literature* (Fairleigh Dickinson Univ, 1971); *Jewish Influences on European Thought* (Fairleigh Dickinson Univ, 1976).
Memb ATA.

KLINE, GEORGE L 632 Valley View Rd, Ardmore, PA 19003 USA *Tel* 215-642-0946.
TL English. **SL** German, Russian. **UDC** literature (poetry), philosophy.
Russian Joseph Brodsky: *Selected Poems* (Penguin/Harper & Row, 1973, 1974). V V Zenkovsky: *A History of Russian Philosophy*, 2 vols (Columbia Univ/Routledge & Kegan Paul, 1953).
Affil Bryn Mawr College.

KLOTH, FRIEDRICH A Grasredder 33, D-2050 Hamburg 80, West Germany *Tel* (040) 724 37 00.
TL German. **SL** English. **UDC** literature (prose), political science.
English Edward Luttwak: *Coup d'Etat* (Rowohlt, 1969). Conor Cruise O'Brien: *The United Nations: Sacred Drama* (Rowohlt, 1971). Also the works of Eldridge Cleaver, Bernadette Devlin, Frederic Golden, James Herriot, Jack Lindsay.
Memb VDÜ.

KNIGHT, MAX 760 Grizzly Peak Blvd, Berkeley, CA 94709 USA *Tel* 415-524-5624.
TL English. **SL** German. **UDC** history, law (international), literature (drama, lyrics, poetry, songs), mountaineering, political science.
German Bertolt Brecht: *Schweyk in the Second World War*, co-translated with Joseph Fabry (Random House, 1974). Hans Kelsen: *The Pure Theory of Law* (Univ of California, 1967). Christian Morgenstern: *Gallows Songs* (Univ of California, 1963). *A Confidential Matter: Letters of Richard Strauss and Stefan Zweig* (Univ of California, 1977). Also the works of Heinrich Heine, Karl Kraus, Johann Nestroy.
Affil Univ of California Press.

KOBLICK, DAVID B 2617 Hyde St, San Francisco, CA 94109 USA *Tel* 415-885-1488.
TL English. **SL** German. **UDC** biography, literature (prose, science fiction), medicine, occultism, orthopedic surgery.
German Peter Krassa: *Erich von Däniken: Disciple of the Gods* (Allen, 1978).
Memb ATA.

KOHN, DENA J One University Pl #9C, New York, NY 10003 USA *Tel* 212-674-9024.
TL English. **SL** Spanish. **UDC** aesthetics, art, business, communications, documentation, education, government, history, law (civil, criminal, international), linguistics, literature (all areas), music, philosophy, political science, psychiatry, psychology, sociology, theater.
Spanish "European and Common Market Patents" (pending).
Memb ASI, ATA.

KOLOVAKOS, GREGORY M 760 West End Ave #5C, New York, NY 10025 USA *Tel* 212-222-0348.

TL English. **SL** Spanish. **UDC** literature (children's, criticism, prose).

Spanish Mario Vargas Llosa: *Captain Pantoja and the Special Service,* co-translated with Ronald Christ (Harper & Row, 1978). José Donoso: *The Boom in Spanish American Literature* (Columbia Univ, 1977). Also the works of Romulo Betancourt, José Bianco, J L Borges, Julio Cortázar, Juan García Ponce, E Rodríguez Monegal, others.

Affil Ctr for Inter-American Relations, Brooklyn College of CUNY Summer Translation Workshop.

KORNFELD, MELVIN Rehov Beilis 8, Haifa, Israel *Tel* (04) 89512.

TL English. **SL** German. **UDC** literature (criticism, history, prose).

German Jurek Becker: *Jacob the Liar* (Harcourt Brace Jovanovich, 1975).

Affil Univ of Haifa.

KOTTA, SUSAN 33 Littleworth Lane, Sea Cliff, NY 11579 USA *Tel* 516-676-6619.

TL English. **SL** French. **UDC** arts, linguistics, literature (prose).

French Paul-Jacques Bonzon: *The Runaway Flying Horse* (Parents Magazine Pr, 1976).

KOZLOVSKY, VLADIMIR 164 E 33 St #19, New York, NY 10016 USA *Tel* 212-686-3654.

TL Russian. **SL** English, Hindi, Ukrainian, Urdu. **UDC** anthropology, art, education, ethics, ethnography, government, history, jurisprudence, legislation, linguistics/philology, military science, philosophy, political economy/science, psychiatry, psychology, religion, sociology, theater, theology.

English Richard Pipes: "Russian under the Old Regime" (pending). Stephen H Cohen: *Bukharin and the Russian Revolution,* with co-translators (Strathcona, 1979). Also the works of Katherine Anne Porter, John Updike.

KRAUSSKOPF, KARIN S 10 rue du Général Camou, F-75007 Paris, France *Tel* 551 62 98.

TL German. **SL** English, French. **UDC** astrology, history, literature (children's, history, librettos, lyrics, poetry, prose, songs), metaphysics, psychiatry, psychology, religion.

English Robert D Atkins: *Diet Revolution* (Goverts Krüger Stahlberg, 1974). Charles Berlitz: *The Mystery of Atlantis* (Paul Zsolnay, 1975). Jonathan Black: *Oil* (Alfred Scherz, 1975). Victoria Holt: *The Queen's Confession* (Goverts Krüger Stahlberg, 1970). Also the works of Mary Ann Crenshaw, Catherine Gaskin, Harrison E Salisbury, Rebecca West.

Memb VS.

KRISPYN, EGBERT Rte 2, Box 113A, Comer, GA 30629 USA *Tel* 404-783-5628.

TL English. **SL** Dutch, German. **UDC** literature (drama, poetry, prose).

Dutch Joost van den Vondel: *Brethren* (Twayne, forthcoming); *Gysbrecht van Amstel* (Twayne, forthcoming).

Affil Univ of Georgia. **Memb** ALTA.

KRUUSE, ELSA 334 Riverside Dr, New York, NY 10025 USA *Tel* 212-222-9741.

TL English. **SL** French, Swedish. **UDC** history, literature (all areas).

Swedish Arvid Albrektson: *Tariro* (Muhlenberg, 1959). Gustaf Bolinder: *We Dared the Andes: Three Journeys into the Unknown* (Abelard-Schuman, 1959). Nicholas Fokker: *No Roses Grow in Sawdust* (Kärnekull, 1973). Olov Hartman: *The Sudden Sun* (Fortress, 1964).

KRYNSKI, MAGNUS JAN 1004 W Markham Ave, Durham, NC 27701 USA *Tel* 919-682-6886.

TL English. **SL** Polish, Russian. **UDC** literature (criticism, drama, prose).

Polish Tadeusz Rózewicz: *The Survivor and Other Poems* (Princeton Univ, 1976). Also the works of St Baranczak, H Jasiczek, E Lipska, M Piechal, A Swirszczynska, W Szymborska.

Affil Duke Univ.

KUBY, ALEXANDER 4070 Park Fulton Oval #1122, Cleveland, OH 44144 USA *Tel* 216-661-5860.

TL & SL Czech, English, Slovak. **UDC** art/art history, arts/crafts, library science, literature, medicine, painting, pharmacology.

English Alfred Hitchcock: *My Favorites in Suspense* (Slovenský spisovatel', 1969); *Stories That Scared Even Me* (Slovenský spisovatel', 1970). Also the works of Pearl Buck, Agatha Christie, Graham Greene, Katherine Mansfield, Somerset Maugham, Dorothy Parker.

Accred/Memb ATA, NOTA. **Affil** Cleveland Museum of Art.

KUDIAN, MISCHA 111 Marylebone High St #2, London W1, UK.

TL English. **SL** Armenian. **UDC** literature (children's, drama, folklore, history, poetry, prose), religion.

Armenian Vahan Totovents: *Scenes from an Armenian Childhood* (Oxford Univ, 1962). Hovannes Toumanian: *The Bard of Loree* (Mashtots, 1970). *Soviet Armenian Poetry* (Mashtots, 1974). Grigor Narekatsi: *Lamentations of Narek* (Mashtots, 1977). Also the works of Hagop Baronian, Yeghishe Charents, Gevorg Emin, Avetik Issahakian, Parvir Sevak, numerous others.

Memb TA.

KUHNER, HERBERT Gentgasse 14/4, A-1180 Vienna, Austria *Tel* 34 80 952.

TL English. **SL** French, German. **UDC** literature (drama, poetry, prose).

German Peter Paul Wiplinger: *Borders/Grenzen* (Cross-Cultural Communications, 1977). Also the works of Margarethe Herzele, numerous Austrian, Hungarian, Rumanian, Russian, Yugoslav poets and dramatists.

Memb ALTA, ATA.

KULCHYCKY, GEORGE Arts & Sciences, Youngstown State Univ, Youngstown, OH 44555 USA.

TL English. **SL** Ukrainian. **UDC** history.

Ukrainian M I Braichevskyi: *Annexation or Reunification: Critical Notes on One Conception* (Ukrainisches Institut für Bildungspolitik, 1974).

KUSSI, PETER 118-45 Metropolitan Ave, Kew Gardens, NY 11415 USA *Tel* 212-441-2446.

TL English. **SL** Czech, German. **UDC** linguistic/philology, literature (criticism, poetry, prose), medicine.

Czech Milan Kundera: *Life Is Elsewhere* (Knopf, 1974); *The Farewell Party* (Knopf, 1976). Arne Novák: *Czech Literature:* (Michigan Slavic Publications, 1976). T G Masaryk: *The Meaning of Czech History* (Univ of N Carolina, 1974). Also the works of Jaroslav Hašek, Josef Koenigsmark, Antonin Liehm, Jan Prochazka, Josef Škvorecky.

Affil Columbia Univ. **Awards** National Translation Ctr grant.

LACY, ALAN F 11909 Watertown Plank Rd, Wauwatosa, WI 53226 USA *Tel* 414-476-9905.

TL English. **SL** German. **UDC** history, law, linguistics/philology, popular science.

German Günter Paul: *The Satellite Spin-Off* (Robert Luce, 1975).

Affil Marquette Univ. **Memb** ATA.

LAERMANN, KLAUS Konstanzer Str 56, D-1000 Berlin 31, West Germany *Tel* (030) 883 5678.

TL German. **SL** English, French, Italian, Spanish. **UDC** aesthetics, literature (criticism), philosophy, psychiatry, psychology, sociology.

English Otto Fenichel: *Psychoanalytic Theory of Neurosis* (Walter, 1974–77). B F Skinner: *About Behaviorism* (Rowohlt, 1978). George Herbert Mead: *Collected Papers* (Suhrkamp, 1979).

Memb VS.

LA FARGE, SHEILA 158 Mount Auburn St, Cambridge, MA 02138 USA *Tel* 617-876-3448.

TL English. **SL** Danish, Norwegian, Swedish. **UDC** aesthetics, anthropology, archeology, arts, astrology, heraldry, history, literature (children's, drama, folklore, librettos, poetry, prose), occultism, painting, psychiatry, psychology, religion, sculpture, theater.

Danish Cecil Bødker: *Silas and the Black Mare* (Delacorte/Seymour Lawrence, 1978). Inger Christensen: *It* (Curbstone, 1979). **Swedish** Bo Carpelan: *Bow Island* (Delacorte/Seymour Lawrence, 1971). Maria Gripe: *The Glassblower's Children* (Delacorte/Seymour Lawrence, 1973). Also the works of Björn Berglund, Elsa Beskow, Nils O Jacobson, Alf Löfgren, Bengt Martin, Swami Janakananda Saraswati, Edith Södergran.

Memb Word Guild. **Awards** 1978 IBBY Honor List.

LAMONT, ROSETTE C 260 W 72 St, New York, NY 10023 USA *Tel* 212-799-5512.

TL English. **SL** French, Russian. **UDC** literature (drama, poetry, prose).

French Eugene Ionesco: "Slime" (*Evergreen Review*); "The Gap" (*Massachusetts Review*). Charlotte Delbo: "Phantoms, My Faithful Ones" (*Massachusetts Review,* 1973). Also the works of Amos Kenan, Luisa Valenzuela, Alexander Voronel, Nina Voronel.

Affil Graduate Center of CUNY.

LANG, SUSANNA 3524 N Broadway #3N, Chicago, IL 60657 USA *Tel* 312-935-1788.

TL English. **SL** French. **UDC** art, literature (criticism, poetry, prose).

French Yves Bonnefoy: *Words in Stone* (Univ of Massachusetts, 1976); "In the Lure of the Threshold" (pending); *The Origin of Language and Other Poems* (George Nama, forthcoming). Andréi Boris Nakov: *Russian Pioneers: At the Origins of Non-Objective Art* (Annely Juda Fine Art, 1976). Also the works of Bernard Collins, René Depestre.

LAROCHE, SYLVIE 10 rue Vandrezanne, F-75013 Paris, France *Tel* (1) 580 43 20.
   TL French. **SL** English, Italian. **UDC** anthropology, archeology, art, engraving, ethnography, literature (prose), painting, psychology, social sciences.
   English Norman Cohn: *Europe's Inner Demons* (Payot, forthcoming). Theodore Reik: *The Compulsion to Confess* (Payot, 1973). Geza Roheim: *The Riddle of the Sphinx* (Payot, 1976). Alvin Toffler: *Future Shock* (Denoël, 1971). Also the works of Eric Berne, Erich Fromm, John Kenneth Galbraith, G Murdock, others.
   Memb ATLF.

LAST, REX WILLIAM German, Hull Univ, HU6 7RX, UK *Tel* (0482) 46311.
   TL English. **SL** German. **UDC** history, literature, politics.
   German Willy Brandt: *In Exile* (Wolff, 1971). J Braun: *Gustav Heinemann: The Committed President* (Wolff, 1972). U M Schneede: *The Essential Max Ernst* (Thames & Hudson, 1972). R Taëni: *Rolf Hochhuth* (Wolff, 1977). Also the works of Hans Arp, Michael Freund, Georg Kaiser, Beatrix Kempf.
   Memb TA.

LATIMER, RENATE Foreign Languages, Auburn Univ, Auburn, AL 36830 USA *Tel* 205-826-4345.
   TL English. **SL** German. **UDC** literature (drama, prose).
   German Adalbert Stifter: "Indian Summer" (pending).

LATTIMORE, RICHMOND 123 Locust Grove Rd, Rosemont, PA 19010 USA *Tel* 215-525-1618.
   TL English. **SL** Greek (Classical). **UDC** literature (poetry).
   Greek (Classical) Aeschylus: *The Oresteia* (Univ of Chicago, 1953). Homer: *The Iliad* (Univ of Chicago, 1951); *The Odyssey* (Harper & Row, 1967). Pindar: *The Odes* (Univ of Chicago, 1947). Also the works of Alcaeus, Archilochus, Bacchylides, Cavafy, Daniel, Du Bellay, Euripides, Hesiod, Leconte de Lisle, Ronsard, Sappho.
   Awards 1962 Bollingen.

LAUGHLIN, JAMES PO Box 606, Norfolk, CT 06058 USA *Tel* 203-542-5388.
   TL English. **SL** French, German, Italian. **UDC** literature (drama, poetry, prose).
   French numerous works of French poetry for the New Directions' Anthologies. **German** Goethe: *Faust*, Part I, co-translated with C F MacIntyre (New Directions, 1941). Martin Walser: *Marriage in Phillipsburg*, co-translated with Eva Figes (New Directions, 1961). **Italian** Eugenio Montale: *New Poems*, co-translated with G Singh (New Directions, 1976).
   Affil New Directions (ed). **Memb** ALTA.

LAUGHMAN, PAUL S 872 Sunbury Dr, Fayetteville, NC 28301 USA *Tel* 919-488-0409.
   TL English. **SL** Laotian, Portuguese (Brazilian). **UDC** history, literature (history), military science, religion.
   Affil US Army. **Memb** ATA.

LAWRENCE, MARLOYD LUDINGTON 102 Chestnut St, Boston, MA 02108 USA *Tel* 617-523-5895.
   TL English. **SL** French. **UDC** literature (children's, prose), psychiatry, psychology.
   French Balzac: *Eugenie Grandet; The Curé of Tours* (Houghton Mifflin, 1964). Flaubert: *Madame Bovary* (Houghton Mifflin, 1969). Claude Mauriac: *The Dinner Party* (Braziller, 1960). Marie-Claire Blais: *Mad Shadows* (Little, Brown, 1960). Also the works of Geneviève Dormann, Pierre Gascar, Claude Mauriac, Anne Philipe, Francis Ponge.
   Memb ATA.

LAYERA, RAMON Spanish, Univ of Texas, Austin, TX 78712 USA *Tel* 512-471-1554.
   TL English. **SL** Spanish. **UDC** literature (drama, history, prose).
   Spanish Jesús Campos García: "The Marriage of Drama and Censorship" (*Modern International Drama*, 8 no 1, 1974). Sergio Vodanovic: "Same As Ever" (*Modern International Drama*, 1978).
   Affil *Latin American Literary Review* (translation ed). **Memb** ALTA, ATA.

LEACH, VICKIE L 84 Havemeyer Lane, Old Greenwich, CT 06870 USA *Tel* 203-637-5349.
   TL English. **SL** Spanish. **UDC** business, human resources, literature (prose), metaphysics, philosophy, religion, sociology, theology.
   Spanish José Miguéz Bonino: *Space To Be Men* (Fortress, 1978).
   Memb ATA.

LEDOUX, FRANCIS 21 rue du Cherche-Midi, F-75006 Paris, France *Tel* 548 40 68.
   TL French. **SL** English. **UDC** literature (prose).
   English J R R Tolkien: *The Lord of the Rings* (Bourgois, 1972–73). Henry Fielding: *Tom Jones* (Pléïade, 1964). Daniel Defoe: *Novels* (Pléïade, 1959–69). Herman Melville: *Israel Potter* (Gallimard, 1956). Also the works of Charlotte Brontë, Ivy Compton-Burnett, Robert Craft, Charles Dickens, Edgar Allan Poe, Frederic Morton, William Shakespeare, Igor Stravinsky, Horace Walpole, Tennessee Williams, Maurice Zolotow, numerous others.
   Memb ATLF.

LEFEVERE, ANDRE German, Univ of Antwerp, B-2610 Universiteitsplein 1, Wilrÿk, Belgium *Tel* (031) 30 89 82.
   TL English. **SL** Dutch, French, German, Greek (Classical), Latin. **UDC** literature (criticism, drama, poetry, prose).
   French Philippe Jaccottet: *Seed-Time* (New Directions, 1976). **German** Peter Hacks: *Omphale* (Dimension, 1973). Günter Herburger: *Exhibition or a Struggle for Rome* (Dimension, 1972). **Greek (Classical)** *Classical Epigrams: Love and Wit* (Studio Vista, 1970). Also the works of Guido Bachmann, Kurt Bartsch, F Delius, Peter Hacks, Peter Henisch, Denise Le-

vertov, Charles Olson, Charles Reznikoff, Karel von De Woestyne, numerous others.
   Memb ALTA.

LEONARD, BYRON 1757 Meadowlark Ct, St Paul, MN 55122 USA *Tel* 612-452-4345; 647-7476.
   TL English. **SL** French. **UDC** art, cinema, communications, literature (children's, criticism, history, poetry, prose), photography.

LESSER, RIKA 133 Henry Street #5, Brooklyn, NY 11201 USA *Tel* 212-852-1163.
   TL English. **SL** German, Swedish. **UDC** archeology (Etruscology), art, biology, botany, literature (children's, criticism, drama, folklore, history, poetry, prose), music, painting.
   German Hermann Hesse: *Hours in the Garden and Other Poems* (Farrar, Straus & Giroux, 1979). Rainer Maria Rilke: *Holding Out* (Abattoir, 1976). **Swedish** Gunnar Ekelöf: "Guide to the Underworld" (pending). Also the works of C J L Almquist, Hugo von Hofmannsthal, Conrad Ferdinand Meyer, Edith Södergran, Tomas Tränstromer.
   Awards 1974–75 Fulbright-Hays grant, 1974–75 Thord-Gray Memorial Fund Scholar Incentive Award, 1976 Columbia Univ Translation Ctr grant.

LEVENTOGLU, FÜSUN 1414 E 59 St #310, Chicago, IL 60637 USA *Tel* 312-753-0072.
   TL English. **SL** Turkish. **UDC** history, linguistics/philology, literature (children's, drama, history, prose), theater.

LEVESQUE, RAY PO Box 297, Monitor, WA 98843 USA *Tel* 509-884-2804.
   TL & SL English & Spanish. **UDC** public health, religion, sciences (medical), theology.
   Affil Washington Language Service.

LEVINE, PHILIP 4549 N Van Ness, Fresno, CA 93704 USA *Tel* 209-226-3361.
   TL English. **SL** Spanish. **UDC** literature (poetry).
   Spanish Jaime Sabines: *Tarumba: Selected Poems* (Twin-Peaks, 1978).
   Affil California State Univ.

LEVINE, SUZANNE JILL 350 W 12 St, New York, NY 10014 USA *Tel* 212-255-1738.
   TL English. **SL** Spanish. **UDC** literature (prose).
   Spanish Manuel Puig: *Betrayed by Rita Hayworth* (Dutton, 1971); *Heartbreak Tango* (Dutton, 1973). Severo Sarduy: *From Cuba with a Song* (Dutton, 1972). Julio Cortázar: *All Fires the Fire* (Pantheon, 1973). Adolfo Bioy Casares: *A Plan for Escape* (Dutton, 1975). Also the works of Guillermo Cabrera Infante, José Donoso, Carlos Fuentes, Gustavo Sainz, Juan Carlos Onetti, Mario Benedetti, Felisberto Hernandez, Fray Servando Teresa de Mier. Also numerous articles on translation in anthologies and contemporary literary journals: *Mundus Artium, Triquarterly, Translation, Review*.
   Affil Tufts Univ.

LEVITIN, ALEXIS 106 Chapin Pl, Granville, OH 43023 USA *Tel* 614-587-4717.
   TL English. **SL** Portuguese, Portuguese (Brazilian). **UDC** literature (poetry, prose).

Portuguese the works of Eugenio de Andrade, Mario Cesariny, Manuel de Fonseca, Antonio Ramos Rosa, Miguel Torga, others. **Portuguese (Brazilian)** the works of Carlos Drummond de Andrade, Manuel Bandeira, Plinio Cabral, Raul Caldas Filho, Gilberto Freyre, Clarice Lispector, Carlos Nejar, Nelida Pinon, others. Translations of these comprise the Brazilian section of *Latin American Literature Today* (New Directions).
Affil Denison Univ.

LEVITON, MARK 212 Buena Vista Dr, Claremont, CA 91711 USA *Tel* 714-624-2552.
TL English. **SL** Spanish. **UDC** literature (poetry).
Spanish Juan Ramon Jimenez: "Three Poems" (*Webster Review,* 3 no 4, 1977).

LEWINTER, ROGER 31 rue du Fort-Barreau, CH-1201 Geneva, Switzerland *Tel* (4122) 34 45 17.
TL French. **SL** English, German. **UDC** literature (poetry), psychoanalysis.
English Marion Milner: *The Hands of the Living God* (Gallimard, 1974).
Memb ATLF.

LICH, GLEN ERNST Sturdy Oak Farm, Comfort, TX 78013 USA *Tel* 512-995-3961.
TL English. **SL** German. **UDC** genealogy, history, literature (children's, criticism, folklore, prose).
German the works of Harald Groehler, Guenter Guben, Guenter Kunert, Otto Walter.
Affil Southwest Texas State Univ. **Memb** ALTA.

LIMA, ROBERT Pennsylvania State Univ, University Park, PA 16802 USA *Tel* 814-865-1140, 4252.
TL English. **SL** Spanish. **UDC** aesthetics, archeology, literature (criticism, drama, folklore, poetry, prose), metaphysics, occultism, theater, witchcraft.
Spanish Ana María Barrenechea: *Borges the Labyrinth Maker* (New York Univ, 1965). Ramón del Valle-Inclán: "The Lamp of Marvels: Spiritual Exercises" (pending). Also the works of Vicente Aleixandre, Silvia Barros, J L Borges, Olga Casanova-Sanchez, Nicolás Guillen, Juana de Ibarbourou, Gloria Stolk, César Vallejo, numerous others.

LINDT, INGE (Ingeborg Bayr) Hellbrunn 20, Salzburg, A-5034 Austria *Tel* 06222-42373.
TL German. **SL** English, French. **UDC** history.
English Bertram D Wolfe: *Drie Männer, die Welterschütterten* (Forum-Verlag, 1954). James Gould Cozzens: *Kinder und andere Leute* (Sigbert Mohn, 1966). Frederick Rolfe: *Hadrian VII* (Ullstein, 1970). Wilkie Collins: *Der Monddiammant* (Munich, 1973). Also the works of Charity Blackstock, Max Catto, Brian Glanville, Robert L Heilbroner, James Michener, Herbert Read, Oscar Wilde.

LIVINGSTON, KRIEMHILDE I R 357 Sullivan Ave, Akron, OH 44305 USA *Tel* 216-733-9234.
TL & SL English & German. **UDC** art history, education, genealogy, history, political science, religion, sociology, social sciences.

Affil The Univ of Akron. **Memb** ATA, LDF, NOTA.

LOCKIE, DAVID McNAUGHT chemin de la Panouche, Sainte-Anne, F-06130 Grasse, France *Tel* (93) 364 293.
TL English. **SL** French. **UDC** archeology, art, education, genealogy, history, literature (all areas), music, painting, religion, theater, theology, witchcraft.
French Victor-L Tapié: *France in the Age of Louis XIII and Richelieu* (Macmillan/Praeger, 1974).
Memb TA. **Awards** 1974 Scott-Moncrieff Prize.

LONGLAND, JEAN R 490 West End Ave #2D, New York, NY 10024 USA *Tel* 212-877-2952.
TL English. **SL** Portuguese. **UDC** literature (poetry).
Portuguese *Selections from Contemporary Portuguese Poetry* (Harvey House, 1966). Also the works of Antonio Machado, Rafael Alberti, Maria Enriqueta, Rufino Blanco-Fombona, Fernando Pessôa, Francisco de Sousa, Almeida Garrett, Airas Nunes, Joaquim Cardozo, Oswald de Andrade, Cassiano Ricardo, numerous others, in *Anthology of 20th-Century Brazilian Poetry, Translations from Hispanic Poets, Journal of the American Portuguese Society, The Literary Review, Modern Poetry in Translation, The Malahat Review,* other anthologies and journals.
Affil The Hispanic Society of America (curator of the library). **Memb** ALTA, ATA. **Awards** 1973 Portugal Prize of the International Poetry Assn (Rome).

LOOS, DOROTHY SCOTT Stonecroft, RFD #3, Brattleboro, VT 05301 USA *Tel* 802-254-2781.
TL English. **SL** French, Portuguese, Spanish. **UDC** literature (children's, poetry, prose).
Spanish Alfonsina Storni: "Selected Poems" (pending). Gloria Fuertes: "Selected Poems" (pending). Also six poems of A Storni in *Poetry Today* (Translation Issue, Spring, 1979).
Memb ALTA.

LÓPEZ-MORILLAS, FRANCES M 90 Brown St, Providence, RI 02906 USA *Tel* 401-751-6170.
TL English. **SL** French, Spanish. **UDC** arts, biography, history, literature (prose), philosophy, religion, social sciences, theology.
Spanish Camilo José Cela: *Journey to the Alcarria* (Univ of Wisconsin, 1964). Bartolomé Arzáns de Orsúa y Vela: *Tales of Potosí* (Brown Univ, 1975). Julián Marías: *Miguel de Unamuno* (Harvard Univ, 1966). Also the works of Jaime Vicens Vives, Luis Suárez Fernández, Juan Torres Fontes, José Maria Font y Rius, Juan Ainaud de Lasarte, Juan Beneyto Pérez, numerous others.

LOVELL, EMILY KALLED PO Box 26013, Tempe, AZ 85282 USA *Tel* 602-968-4928.
TL & SL Arabic & English. **UDC** history, literature (history, prose).
Affil Arizona State Univ.

LOWCOCK, PETER HARRY 146 S Virginia Ave, Falls Church, VA 22046 USA.

TL English. **SL** German, Russian. **UDC** agriculture, government, history, human resources, literature (history), political science, public health, social sciences, sociology, sports.
Accred/Memb ATA (Russian).

LOWE, ELIZABETH 26 Grand View Blvd, Yonkers, NY 10710 USA *Tel* 914-779-3720; Apartado Aéreo 16192, Bogotá, DE, Colombia.
TL English. **SL** Portuguese, Spanish. **UDC** literature (all areas).
Portuguese the works of Demetrio Aguilera-Malta, Roberto Drummond, Rubem Fonseca, Victor Giudice, Clarice Lispector, Nelida Piñon, Samuel Rawet, Murilo Rubião.
Memb ALTA.

LOWE, PATRICIA TRACY 665 Rte 9W, Grandview, South Nyack, NY 10960 USA *Tel* 914-359-2296.
TL English. **SL** French, Italian. **UDC** literature (children's, folk tales, poetry, prose).
Italian Alexander Pushkin: *Tale of the Czar Saltan* (Crowell, 1975). Bruno Munari: *A Flower with Love* (Crowell, 1975); *The Circus in the Mist* (Crowell, 1968).

LUCCARELLI, LUIGI 25480 Halton Rd, Carmel, CA 93923 USA *Tel* 408-624-4287.
TL English. **SL** Spanish. **UDC** architecture, art, arts/crafts, ceramics, economics, literature (poetry, prose), sculpture.
Memb ALTA, NCTA, Concordiat (pres).

LUCCIONI, JEAN MATHIEU 7 bis, rue des Moulins, F-93370 Montfermeil, France *Tel* 936 5885.
TL French. **SL** English. **UDC** archeology, botany, literature (Greek and Latin classics, poetry, science fiction), philology, philosophy, psychology, physics.
English Grinker & Robbins: *Psychosomatic Case Book* (Presses Universitaires, 1957). Browne & Cohn: *The Function of Leadership* (PUF, 1963). Rudolf Carnap: *The Philosophical Foundations of Physics* (Armand Colin, 1973). Malcolm Lowry: *Selected Poems* (La Différence, 1976).
Affil Univ of Paris X (Nanterre).

LUNDE, DAVID 205 Newton St, Fredonia, NY 14063 USA *Tel* 716-672-5627.
TL English. **SL** French. **UDC** literature (poetry).
Affil SUNY at Fredonia.

LYDAY, LEON F 317 Hartswick Ave, State College, PA 16801 USA *Tel* 814-237-3613.
TL English. **SL** Portuguese, Spanish. **UDC** literature (drama).
Portuguese Dias Gomes: "The Cradle of the Hero" (*Modern International Drama,* 1978).
Spanish Antonio Martínez Ballesteros: "The Straw Men" (*Modern International Drama,* 1969).
Affil Penn State Univ.

LYKIARD, ALEXIS Tillworth Cottage, Hawkchurch, Axminster, Devon, UK *Tel* (029) 77 317.
TL English. **SL** French. **UDC** literature (criticism, poetry, prose).
French Comte de Lautrémont: *Maldoror*

(Crowell, 1972). Emmanuelle Arsan: *Laure* (Mayflower/Granada, 1977): *Néa—A Young Emmanuelle* (Mayflower/Granada, 1978). Isidore Ducasse: *Poetry & Complete Miscellenea* (Allison & Busby, 1978).
Memb TA.

LYMAN, HENRY 6 Fort Hill Terr, Northampton, MA 01060 USA *Tel* 413-586-3850.
TL English. **SL** Estonian, French, German, Russian. **UDC** literature (poetry, prose).
Estonian Alexis Rannit: *Cantus Firmus* (Elizabeth Press, 1978). Also individual poems in *Baltic Literature, The Literary Review, New Directions, Yale Magazine and Journal,* other publications.

McAULEY, ALMUT 624 Lincoln, Cheney, WA 99004 USA *Tel* 509-235-8725.
TL & SL English & German. **UDC** literature (all areas).
German Thomas Bernhard: "4 Prose Pieces: The Cashier, The Pastor's Sister, The Professor, The Chimneysweep" (*Malahat Review,* 1976). Christian Morgenstern: "The Authorities" (*International Poetry Review,* 1976). Brigitte Röttgers: "Fraud/Dampness/Plain Facts/Conquest" (*Dimension,* 1976). Karin Kiwus: "Splitting/Trapdoors" (*New Orleans Review,* 1978). Also the works of Wolf Biermann, Johannes Bobrowski, Bertolt Brecht, Volker Braun, Georg Maurer, others.
Memb ALTA.

McBRIDE, CATHRYN ANN 319 W 105 St #3R, New York, NY 10025 USA *Tel* 212-749-3535.
TL English. **SL** French, Spanish. **UDC** aesthetics, anthropology, archeology, data processing, education, film, literature (criticism, folklore, prose, songs), planetary atmospheres, psychology, theater.
Spanish David Vinas: "The Fallen" (pending).
Memb ATA.

McCARTHY, SISTER MARY FRANCES Emmanuel College, Boston, MA 02115 USA *Tel* 617-277-9346.
TL English. **SL** German. **UDC** linguistics/philology, literature (prose), religion, theology.
German Paul Konrad Kurz: *On Modern German Literature* (Univ of Alabama, 1970–73). Georg Siegmund: *Buddhism and Christianity* (Univ of Alabama, forthcoming).

McCONNELL-DUFF, ALAN BRIAN The British Council, 9 rue de Constantine, F-75007 Paris, France.
TL English. **SL** French, Hungarian, Serbo-Croatian. **UDC** art, education, ethics, history, literature (all areas), music, painting, philosophy, political science, psychology (child), theater.
Serbo-Croatian *Poets of Vojvodina* (Stražilovo, 1975). Krste Misirkov: "On Macedonian Matters" (*Macedonian Review,* 1974). *The Big Horse and Other Stories of Modern Macedonia* (Univ of Missouri, 1974). Dragan Taškovski: "Bogomilism in Macedonia" (*Macedonian Review,* 1975). Also the works of numerous writers.
Memb TA, TG, Serbian Literary Translators Assn.

McDERMOTT, C Philosophy, Univ of New Mexico, Albuquerque, NM 87131 USA.
TL English. **SL** Latin, Sanskrit, Tibetan. **UDC** linguistics, philosophy, religion.
Sanskrit Ratnakirti: *An Eleventh Century Buddhist Logic of "Exists"* (Reidel-Dordrecht, 1969).

MacDONALD, SANDY 333 Western Ave, Cambridge, MA 02139 USA *Tel* 617-864-0863.
TL English. **SL** French, Italian, Spanish. **UDC** aesthetics, archeology, feminism, literature (drama, poetry, prose), psychology, theater.
French Andre Pochan: *Mysteries of the Great Pyramid* (Avon, 1977). Simone Weisbard: *Machu Picchu* (Avon, 1979). Also the works of Louis Aragon, Fernando Arrabal, Roland Barthes, Ruth Escobar, Lucien Goldman, Alexandro Jodorowsky, Nelly Kaplan, Françoise Kourilsky, Dacia Maraini, Franco Quadri, Danielle Rapoport, Simone Weisbard.
Memb ALTA, NETA.

MacDONALD, LESLEY & WEISSEN-BORN, HELLMUTH 7 Harley Gardens, London SW10 9SW, UK *Tel* (01) 373 5244.
TL English. **SL** German. **UDC** literature (Baroque German).
German H J C von Grimmelshausen: *Simplicius Simplicissimus* (John Calder, 1964).

McDOUGALL, RICHARD 214 E 88 St #1A, New York, NY 10028 USA.
TL English. **SL** French. **UDC** aesthetics, art, history, literature (all areas), painting, sculpture, theater.
French *The Very Rich Hours of Adrienne Monnier,* collected essays from several books (Scribner, 1976).

McEWAN-ALVARADO, ANGELA 15325 Lodosa Dr, Whittier, CA 90605 USA *Tel* 213-693-7673.
TL & SL English & French. **UDC** archeology, commerce, communications, education, literature (children's, criticism, drama, folklore, history, poetry, prose), travel/tourism.
Memb ATA, CCIA.

McINTYRE, ALICE 444 E 58 St #2C, New York, NY 10022 USA *Tel* 212-753-2274.
TL English. **SL** French. **UDC** literature (poetry).

MACKLER, MARY 325 W 77 St #9C, New York, NY 10024 USA *Tel* 212-362-2936.
TL English. **SL** Russian. **UDC** aesthetics, anthropology, archeology, art, biology, botany, food/nutrition, genetics, geography, history, literature (prose), medicine, paleontology, political economy/science, sociology, theater.
Russian Leonid Grossman: *Dostoyevsky, A Biography* (Bobbs-Merrill, 1975). Nguyen Dinh Thi: "Under Fire, a North Vietnamese Novel" (*Atlas Magazine,* 1966). Marc Raeff, ed: *Catherine the Great, A Profile* (Hill & Wang, 1972). Also the works of F Abramov, S Bakhrushin, V Bogomolov, A Kuznyetsov, Nina Popva, others.

MACKWORTH, CECILY 6 rue des Coutures-Saint-Gervais, F-75003 Paris, France *Tel* 887 32 43.

TL English. **SL** French. **UDC** art/history, poetry.
French Daniel Cordier: *Jean Dubuffet* (Braziller, 1960).

McMAHON, JAMES V German, Emory Univ, Atlanta, GA 30322 USA *Tel* 404-329-6439.
TL English. **SL** German. **UDC** aesthetics, biology, ethics, food, government, history, linguistics, literature, music, philosophy, theater, theology.
Memb AAIT, ATA.

McMASTER, MARIAN B 605 S 800 E, Orem, UT 84057 USA *Tel* 801-225-2568.
TL Spanish. **SL** English. **UDC** education, genealogy, history, literature (all areas), religion, theology (Mormon).
English Andrew & Edward Kimball: *Spencer W Kimball* (APAK International, 1979).
Accred/Memb ATA. **Affil** Brigham Young Univ (Translation Program).

MacSHANE, FRANK Brandt & Brandt, 101 Park Ave, New York, NY 10017 USA *Tel* 212-280-4391.
TL English. **SL** Spanish. **UDC** literature (general, including fiction).
Spanish Miguel Serrano: *C G Jung and Hermann Hesse: A Record of Two Friendships* (Routledge/Kegan Paul, 1966); *El/Ella* (Harper & Row/Routledge, 1962, 1972, 1973); *The Serpent of Paradise* (Rider/Routledge/Harper & Row, 1962, 1972, 1973); *The Ultimate Flower* (Routledge/Schocken/Harper & Row, 1969, 1970, 1972). Also the works of Miguel Angel Asturias.
Affil Columbia Univ.

MAGAL, MIRIAM PO Box 22316, Tel Aviv, Israel *Tel* (03) 45 95 85.
TL German. **SL** English, French, Hebrew, Spanish. **UDC** anthropology, archeology, architecture, art, business, commerce, ecology, economics, ethnography, history, literature (folklore, history), political economy/science, psychology, religion, sociology.
English Geoffrey Hindley: *Saladin* (Brockhaus, 1978). *Israeli Humor and Satire* (Sadan & Kindler, 1976).

MAHEUX, GUY 7705 blvd l'Acadie #101, Montreal, PQ H3N 2W1, Canada *Tel* 514-272-3256; 277-4990.
TL French. **SL** English, Hindi (Nagali), Hindoustani. **UDC** art, astrology, computers, education, human resources, literature (poetry, prose), occultism, philosophy, psychology, witchcraft.
English David J Schwartz: *The Magic of Thinking Big* (Presses Select, 1977). Thomas Harris: *Black Sunday* (Presses Select, 1977). Martin Ebon: *The Riddle of the Bermuda Triangle* (Presses Select, 1976). Also the works of Ronald Cooke, Xaviera Hollander, John Kesson.
Memb ALTA.

MALMBERG, CARL Rte 1, Warner, NH 03278 USA *Tel* 603-456-3395.
TL English. **SL** Danish, Norwegian, Swedish. **UDC** literature (drama, prose).
Danish Leif Panduro: *Kick Me in the Tradi-*

tions (Eriksson-Taplinger, 1961). Carl Erik Soya: *Seventeen* (Eriksson, 1961). Jacob Paludam: *Jórgen Stein* (Univ of Wisconsin, 1966). Tom Kristensen: *Havoc* (Univ of Wisconsin, 1968). Also the works of Hans Christian Andersen, Tove Ditlevsen, Kristian Gestrin, Jens Kruuse, Ottar Raastad, Jens August Schade, numerous others in *The American-Scandinavian Review*, 1963–74.

MANDEL, OSCAR Humanities, California Inst of Technology, Pasadena, CA 91125 USA *Tel* 213-795-6811.
TL English. SL French, German, Spanish. UDC literature (drama).
French Marivaux: *Seven Comedies* (Cornell Univ, 1968). *Five Comedies of Medieval France* (Dutton, 1970). **German** Ludwig Tieck: *The Land of Upside Down* (Fairleigh Dickinson Univ, 1978). **Spanish** Tirso de Molina: *The Playboy of Seville* (Univ of Nebraska, 1963).

MANNING, MIMI 875 E Broadway, Stratford, CT 06497 USA *Tel* 203-378-0152.
TL English. SL French, German, Spanish. UDC ethics, history, literature (children's, criticism, history, prose), philosophy, sociology.
Memb ATA.

MÁRQUEZ, ROBERT 307 Middle St, Amherst, MA 01002 USA.
TL English. SL Spanish. UDC aesthetics, Caribbean and Latin American literature, ethnography, history, literature (criticism, folklore, history, poetry, prose).
Spanish Nicolás Guillén: *Patria o Muerte: The Great Zoo and Other Poems* (Monthly Review Pr, 1972); *Man-Making Words: Selected Poems* (Univ of Massachusetts, 1972). *Latin American Revolutionary Poetry* (Monthly Review Pr, 1974). Also the works of Jorge Enrique Adoum, Edmundo Aray, Igor Calvo, Ernesto Cardenal, Norberto Codina, others.
Affil Hampshire College. **Memb** ALTA.

MARRACINO, PAOLA 290 Riverside Dr, New York, NY 10025 USA *Tel* 212-749-6184.
TL English. SL Italian, Spanish. UDC aesthetics, art, business, commerce, communications, education, literature, theater.
Spanish Florencia Varas & José Manuel Vergara: *Operation Chile* (Stein & Day).

MARSH, GWEN 35 Tanza Rd, London NW3 2UA, UK *Tel* (01) 435 7715.
TL English. SL French, German. UDC literature (children's).
French René Guillot: *Sirga* (Oxford Univ, 1953); *The Children of the Wind* (Oxford Univ, 1964). **German** Hans Baumann: *Katzimir the Greatest* (Dent & Sons, 1977). Walter Kreye: *The Ragamuffin King* (Dent & Sons, 1978). Also the works of Willy Baum, Philippe Dumas, Michael Ende, Sigrid Heuck, Michèle Kahn, Mira Lobe, Emanuele Luzzati.
Memb TA.

MARSHALL, TRAUTE M 5643 S Drexel, Chicago, IL 60637 USA *Tel* 312-947-0706.
TL & SL English & German. UDC art history, education, history, linguistics, literature (criticism, history), music, psychology.

German Edward E Lowinsky: *The Antwerp Motet Book of Orlando di Lasso* (Univ of Chicago, forthcoming). Hermann Abert: *W A Mozart* (Univ of Chicago, forthcoming).
Accred/Memb ATA.

MARTIN, PEDRO Rivadavia 3789, piso 4, dto B, 1204 Buenos Aires, Argentina *Tel* 812-6891.
TL Spanish. SL English. UDC economics, law (international), logic, philosophy, political economy/science.
English Gerhard Masur: *Simón Bolívar*: (Grijalbo, 1960). Herbert Hyman: *Survey Design and Analysis, Principles, Cases, and Procedures* (Amorrortu, 1971). Also the works of John M Henderson, William Foote White.
Memb AIT.

MATHES, DAVID L 4708 Pierre St, Columbia, MO 65201 USA *Tel* 314-474-6470.
TL English. SL Portuguese, Spanish,. UDC art/art history, athletics, communications, history, literature (all areas), photography, sports.
Memb ATA.

MAUROC, DANIEL 15 rue Berthollet, F-75005 Paris, France *Tel* 331 51 72.
TL French. SL English. UDC literature (drama, poetry, prose).
English John Cowper Powys: *The Inmates* (Seuil, 1976). Tom Wolfe: *The Electric Kool Aid Acid Test* (Seuil, 1975). Robert Coover: *The Public Burning* (Seuil, 1979). Gertrude Stein: *Ida* (Seuil, 1978). Also the works of Hal Bennett, David Dalton, Vina Delmar, David Divine, Emmett Grogan, Mark Steadman, Oscar Wilde.
Memb ATLF.

MEAD, A DENNIS Tannenweg 8, D-6368 Bad Vilbel, West Germany *Tel* 842 87.
TL English. SL French, Norwegian, Russian. UDC history, linguistics/philology, literature (criticism, history, prose), religion.
Affil The Church of Jesus Christ of Latter-Day Saints. **Memb** ATA.

MERCADO, BENJAMIN E 21000 NW Miami Ct, Miami, FL 33169 USA *Tel* 305-652-0398.
TL Spanish. SL English. UDC education, geography, government, history, literature (prose), religion/scripture, theology.
English Myer Pearlman: *Knowing the Doctrines of the Bible* (Vida, 1958). Peter Wagner: *Latin American Theology* (Vida, 1969). Nicky Cruz: *The Corruptors* (Vida, 1974); *The Cross and the Switchblade* (Vida, 1965). Also the works of Katheryn Kuhlman, others.
Accred Cordoba Univ (Argentina). **Affil** Vida Publishers. **Memb** ATA.

MERELLO, BARBARA SHELBY ICA, 1425 K St NW #870, Washington, DC 20547 USA *Tel* 202-523-4286.
TL English. SL Portuguese, Spanish. UDC literature (all areas).
Portuguese Jorge Amado: *Terena Batista, Home from the Wars* (Knopf, 1975). Antônio Callado: *Quarup* (Knopf, 1969). Gilberto Freyre: *Mother & Son: A Brazilian Tale*

(Knopf, 1966). João Guimarães Rosa: *The Third Bank of the River* (Knopf, 1967).
Affil International Communication Agency.
Memb ALTA.

MERIVALE, ALEXANDER Box 536, Carmel, CA 93921 USA *Tel* 408-624-4680.
TL English. SL Russian. UDC literature (Russian poetry).
Russian A S Pushkin: *Ruslan & Ludmila—Three Fairy Tales* (Carlton, 1978).
Memb ALTA.

MEROWITZ, MORTON J 71 N Maplemere Rd, Buffalo, NY 14221 USA *Tel* 716-631-5684.
TL English. SL Hebrew. UDC education, history, library science, literature (folklore), philosophy, religion/scripture.
Hebrew Nahman Krochmal: "Moreh Nebukhei Hazeman" (pending).

METZGER, ANNE French Inst, Ambassade de France, Beyoglu, Istanbul, Turkey *Tel* 44 33 27.
TL French. SL English. UDC archeology, art, literature (children's, poetry, prose, songs), music, religion/scripture.
English Anaïs Nin: *Ladders to Fire* (Stock, 1970); *A Spy in the House of Love* (Stock, 1972); *Seduction of the Minotaur* (Stock, 1974). Piotrovsky: *Ourartou* (Nagel, 1974).
Memb ATLF.

MEYER, PETER 13 Chelsea Sq, London SW3, UK *Tel* (01) 351 0531.
TL English. SL French. UDC theater.
French Alfred de Musset: *Seven Plays* (Hill & Wang, 1962). Georges Feydeau: *Three Farces* (BBC, 1974); *Better Late* (Samuel French, 1976). Arthur Adamov: *Professor Taranne* (John Calder, 1964).
Memb TA.

MICHAEL, MAURICE Chucks Cottage, Partridge Green, Horsham, Sussex, UK *Tel* 710 412.
TL English. SL French, Norwegian, Polish, Swedish. UDC archeology, history, history of sport.
Norwegian Agnar Mykle: *Lasso Round the Moon* (Barrie & Rockliffe). **Polish** *A Polish Anthology* (Duckworth). **Swedish** Harry Martinson: *The Road* (Jonathan Cape).
Memb TA.

MIDDLETON, CHRISTOPHER Univ of Texas, Rt 8, Box 168, Austin, TX 78746 USA *Tel* 512-263-2313.
TL English. SL German. UDC literature (poetry, prose).
German Robert Walser: *The Walk and Other Stories* (Calder, 1957). *German Writing Today* (Penguin, 1967). *Modern German Poetry 1910–60*, co-translated with Michael Hamburger (Grove, 1962). Friedrich Nietzsche: *Selected Letters* (Chicago Univ, 1969). Elias Canetti: *Kafka's Other Trial* (Schocken, 1974).

MIHAILOVICH, VASA D 821 Emory Dr, Chapel Hill, NC 27514 USA *Tel* 919-942-5261.
TL English. SL Macedonian, Russian, Serbo-Croatian, Slovenian. UDC literature (criticism, drama, history, poetry, prose).

Macedonian, Serbo-Croatian, Slovenian *Contemporary Yugoslav Poetry* (Univ of Iowa, 1977). Also the works of numerous Macedonian, Russian, Serbo-Croatian, and Slovenian writers.
Affil Univ of North Carolina.

MIKIĆ-MITCHELL, DUŠKA 251 Dean St, Brooklyn, NY 11217 USA *Tel* 212-271-8010.
TL English. **SL** Serbo-Croatian. **UDC** literature.
Serbo-Croatian Danilo Kiš: *A Tomb for Boris Davidovich* (Harcourt Brace Jovanovich, 1978).
Affil Graduate Center of CUNY.

MIKRIAMMOS, PHILIPPE 56 rue de Turenne, F-75003 Paris, France *Tel* 271 1226.
TL French. **SL** Dutch, English, German. **UDC** literature (criticism, poetry, prose, songs).
English William S Burroughs: *Port of Saints* (Flammarion, 1977). Allen Ginsberg: *Indian Journals* (Christian Bourgois, 1977). Tom Robbins: *Even Cowgirls Get the Blues* (France Adel-Balland, 1978). Hunter S Thompson: *Fear and Loathing in Las Vegas* (1977). Also the works of Angela Carter, J Cott, L Ferlinghetti, Jack Kerouac, Kurt Vonnegut, others.
Memb ATLF.

MILETICH, IVO 618 Exchange Ave, Calumet City, IL 60409 USA *Tel* 312-868-4884; 995-2245.
TL English. **SL** Bulgarian, Macedonian, Serbo-Croatian, Slovenian. **UDC** Balkan history and culture, bibliography, dialects of the Croatian language, Southern Slavic linguistics.
Accred/Memb ATA. **Affil** Chicago State Univ; Cosmopolitan Translation Bureau.

MILLER, BARBARA STOLER Oriental Studies, Barnard College, New York, NY 10027 USA *Tel* 212-280-5416, 5417.
TL English. **SL** Sanskrit. **UDC** literature (drama, lyrics, poetry).
Sanskrit Jayadeva: *Love Song of the Dark Lord* (Columbia Univ, 1977). Bilhana: *Phantasies of a Love-Thief* (Columbia Univ, 1971). Bhartrihari: *Poems* (Columbia Univ, 1967).

MILLER, JIM WAYNE 1512 Eastland Dr, Bowling Green, KY 42101 USA *Tel* 502-842-0049.
TL & SL English & German. **UDC** linguistics/philology, literature (criticism, drama, folklore, history, lyrics, poetry, prose).
German Emil Lerperger: *The Figure of Fulfillment* (Green River, 1975). Also the works of Christine Busta, J G Schütze.
Affil Western Kentucky Univ. **Awards** 1972 Translation Prize, Green River Review.

MILLER, JOAN M 1418 Pearce Pk #5, Erie, PA 16502 USA *Tel* 814-838-1966.
TL English. **SL** French. **UDC** philosophy, psychology, religion, social sciences, theology.
French A de Waelhens: "A Philosophy of Ambiguity" (pending). G van Riet: "The Problem of God in Hegel" (*Philosophy Today*, 1967). Varia in *Social Compass* (Belgium).
Affil Villa Maria College. **Memb** ATA.

MITCHELL, BEVERLY CC 333, Univ of Arkansas, Fayetteville, AR 72701 USA *Tel* 501-521-6422.
TL English. **SL** French, Spanish. **UDC** art, anthropology, ethnography, literature (poetry, prose), theater.
Memb ALTA.

MITCHELL, BREON Comparative Literature, BH 402, Indiana Univ, Bloomington, IN 47401 USA *Tel* 812-337-7070.
TL English. **SL** German. **UDC** literature (children's, drama, lyrics, poetry, prose).
German Rüdiger Kremer: *The Time in V* (Dimension, 1974); *The List* (New Directions Annual 27, 1973); *Pegasus* (New Directions Annual 33, 1976).
Affil Indiana Univ. **Memb** ALTA.

MITCHELL, JOHN M 76 S Mains Rd, Milngavie, Glasgow G62, UK *Tel* (041) 956 2536.
TL English. **SL** German. **UDC** current affairs/politics in Germany, education (German), 20th-Century German history.
German Hanns Werner Schwarze: *The GDR Today* (Oswald Wolff, 1973).
Affil Jordanhill College of Education (Modern Languages).

MONAHAN, PATRICK A 1517 E Oak, Lompec, CA 93436 USA *Tel* 805-736-2023.
TL & SL English & German. **UDC** art, education, government, history, literature (all areas), political economy/science, theater.
English Nathaniel Benchley: *Only Earth and Sky Last Forever* (Beltz & Gelbert, forthcoming).
Memb ATA.

MONAS, SIDNEY Slavic Languages, Univ of Texas, Austin, TX 78712 USA.
TL English. **SL** German, Russian. **UDC** biography, history, literature (drama, poetry, prose).
Russian Mikhail Zoshchenko: *Scenes from the Bath House* (Ann Arbor Paperbacks, 1963). F Dostoyevsky: *Crime and Punishment* (Signet/Mentor, 1968). "The Tale of Igor's Men," co-translated with Burton Raffell (*Delos* 6, 1970). Osip Mandelstam: *Selected Essays* (Univ of Texas, 1977).

MOORE, MARIAN H PO Box 652, Crossett, AR 71635 USA *Tel* 501-364-6100.
TL English. **SL** Spanish (Galician). **UDC** literature.
Accred Univ of Arkansas (MFA in Translation).

MORGAN, EDWIN 19 Whittingehame Ct, Glasgow G12 OBG, UK *Tel* (041) 339-6260.
TL English. **SL** Anglo-Saxon French, Italian, Russian. **UDC** literature (poetry).
Anglo-Saxon *Beowulf: A Verse Translation into Modern English* (Hand & Flower Press, 1952; Univ of California, 1962). **Italian** Eugenio Montale: *Poems* (Univ of Reading, 1959). Various authors; *Rites of Passage: Selected Translations* (Carcanet, 1976). *Sovpoems* (Migrant/Ventura, 1961).
Affil Univ of Glasgow. **Awards** 1972 Magyar PEN Memorial Medal.

MORGAN, WILLIAM A 231 Lurgan Ave, Shippensburg, PA 17257 USA *Tel* 717-532-7519.
TL English. **SL** Spanish. **UDC** literature (history, prose), road machinery.
Accred/Memb ATA. **Affil** Shippensburg State College.

MORRISON, R H 21 Glenunga Ave, Glenunga, South Australia 5064 *Tel* (08) 79 1084.
TL English. **SL** French, Italian, Russian, Spanish. **UDC** literature (poetry).
French *Some Poems of Verlaine* (Hawthorn, 1972). **Russian** *America's Russian Poets* (Ardis, 1975). A S Pushkin: *Lyrics from Pushkin* (Meanjin, 1951). Also the works of Lydia Alexeyeva, Nona Belavina, Ivan Burkin, Lydia Daleka, Afanasi Fet, Oleg Ilyinsky, Oleg Kozin, Iraida Legkaya, Nikolai Morshen, Iryna Narizna, Boris Nartsissov, Vsevolod Pugachev, Vasili Reznikov, Ivan Smal-Stotsky, Tania Voloschka, Vasili Zhukovsky, numerous others.

MOSBACHER, ERIC Trellis Cottage, Grove Pl, London NW3 1JR, UK *Tel* (01) 435 7017.
TL English. **SL** French, German, Italian. **UDC** literature (all areas).
German Sigmund Freud: *The Origins of Psycho-Analysis* (Imago, 1954). **Italian** Fosco Maraini: *Meeting with Japan* (Hutchinson, 1959). Ignazio Silone: *Fontamara* (Methuen, 1934). Giovanni Verga: *The House by the Medlar Tree* (Weidenfeld & Nicolson, 1950). Also the works of I Aichinger, L Biancardi, M Bonaparte, S Ferenczi, Witold Gombrowicz, B Nicolaievsky, V Pratolini, E Vittorini, numerous others.
Memb TA. **Awards** 1963 John Florio Prize, 1970 Schlegel-Tieck Prize.

MOSSIKER, FRANCES 3601 Turtle Creek Blvd, Dallas, TX 75219 USA *Tel* 214-528-4493.
TL English. **SL** French. **UDC** history, literature (children's, history).
French *The Queen's Necklace*, historical source material (Simon & Schuster, 1961). Various authors: *Napoleon and Josephine, Biography of a Marriage* (Simon & Schuster, 1964). Various authors: *The Affairs of the Poisons* (Knopf, 1969).
Memb ALTA.

MÜHRINGER, DORIS Goldeggasse, 1, A-1040 Vienna, Austria *Tel* (0222) 65 30 405.
TL German. **SL** English. **UDC** literature (children's, poetry, prose).
English Dana & Ginger Lamb: *Quest for the Lost City* (Pallas, 1956). Walt Disney: *The Aristocats* (Styria, 1972). Carl Sandburg: *Rootabaga Stories* (Georg Bitter, 1974). Also the works of George Bruce, Allen Ginsberg, Gary Snyder, Alice Utley, Jade Snow Wong.
Memb VDÜ.

MUKHERJEE, P 20 rue le Dantec, F-75013, Paris, France *Tel* 589 47 11.
TL English. **SL** Bengali, French. **UDC** education, history, linguistics/philology, literature (all areas), music, political science, printing, psychology, social sciences, sociology.
Bengali *Poems of Bangla-Desh* (Publications

Orientalistes, 1974). **English** Halldor Laxness: *Independent People* (Manmohan, 1963). **French** Saint-John Perse: *Bengali: Brittanta* (Manmohan, 1961). Also the works of Sri Aurobindo, Albert Camus, Ezra Pound, John Steinbeck, Ranbindranath Tagore.
Memb ATLF.

MURAD, TIMOTHY Foreign Languages, Univ of Arkansas, Fayetteville, AR 72701 USA *Tel* 501-575-2951.
TL English. **SL** Spanish. **UDC** literature (poetry, prose).
Memb ALTA.

MURPHY, SISTER MARY BENEDICT RSHM 2807 N Glebe Rd, Arlington, VA 22207 USA *Tel* 703-524-2500.
TL English. **SL** French, Portuguese. **UDC** commerce, education, history, law, medicine, psychology, religion, sciences (medical), sociology.
French Henri Dumery: *Faith and Reflection* (Herder & Herder, 1969). **Portuguese** Sister Maria de Chantal: *Lives Aglow with the Spirit* (private, 1978).
Memb ATA.

MURRAY, PATRICIA Ctr for Japanese Social & Political Studies, 2-8-8 Nishinogawa, Komae-shi, Tokyo 201, Japan *Tel* (03) 489-2175.
TL English. **SL** Chinese, French, Japanese. **UDC** political science, social science.
Affil *The Japan Interpreter*.

MUSMANN, KLAUS 1351 E Calaveras St, Altadena, CA 91001 USA *Tel* 213-797-0680; 629-3531.
TL English. **SL** German. **UDC** history, information science, jurisprudence, legislation, library science, literature (criticism, history, poetry, prose).
German Bircher-Benner Clinic Staff: *Bircher-Benner Nutrition Plan for Liver and Gallbladder Problems* (Nash, 1972).
Memb ATA.

MYRSIADES, KOSTAS 370 N Malin Rd, Newtown Square, PA 19073 USA *Tel* 215-353-5720.
TL English. **SL** Greek. **UDC** literature (criticism, drama, lyrics, poetry, prose).
Greek Yannis Ritsos: *Scripture of the Blind* (Ohio State Univ, 1979); *Selected Poems, 1938-1975* (Falcon, Mansfield State College, 1978). Also the works of Katerina Anghelaki-Rock, Yannis Kondos, Antonios Mollas, Takis Papatsonis, Lefteris Poulios, Markos Xanthos.
Memb ALTA.

NABIL, SALLY ADKISSON 1203B E Harding, Urbana, IL 61801 USA *Tel* 217-367-5559.
TL English. **SL** Spanish. **UDC** business, history, literature (drama, history, prose), religion.
Memb ATA.

NARDROFF, ELLEN von 48 Woodland Ave, East Orange, NJ 07017 USA *Tel* 201-675-0765.
TL English. **SL** German. **UDC** astronomy, economics, history, literature (criticism, drama, history, prose), political science.

Accred Univ of Saarbrücken. **Affil** Upsala College. **Memb** ATA.

NATIONS, ELLEN PO Box 91 Postal Sta B, Toronto, ON M5T 2T3, Canada *Tel* 416-366-0533.
TL English. **SL** Norwegian. **UDC** art, literature (drama, poetry, prose), psychiatry, psychology, sociology.
Norwegian Jon Michelet: *Orion's Belt* (Liberator, 1979).
Memb ALTA.

NÉTILLARD, SUZANNE 24 rue Ferdinand Jamin F-92340 Bourg La Reine, France *Tel* (1) 665-23 17.
TL French. **SL** English. **UDC** literature.
English Henry Fielding: *The Adventures of Joseph Andrews* (Français Réunis, 1955). John Cowper Powys: *Wolf Solent* (Gallimard, 1967). Mark Twain: *Huckleberry Finn* (Français Réunis, 1948). Patrick White: *The Eye of the Storm* (Gallimard, 1978). Also the works of Russel Braddon, Carter Brown, Frank Conroy, Nicholas Morley, Richard Stark, Angus Wilson.
Memb ATLF.

NEUGROSCHEL, JOACHIM 855 West End Ave, New York, NY 10025 USA *Tel* 212-866-6734.
TL English. **SL** French, German, Yiddish. **UDC** literature (all areas).
German Reiner Kunze: *The Wonderful Years* (Braziller, 1977). Hans Heinrich Ziemann: *The Explosion* (St Martin's, 1978). Gerhard Roth: *Winter Voyage* (Farrar, Straus & Giroux, 1979). Hans Magnus Enzensberger: *Mausoleum* (Urizen, 1976). Also the works of Uwe Ahrens, Jean-Paul Alata, Jean Arp, Corradio Augias, Georges Bataille, Lialiana Betti, Bertolt Brecht, Alain Bosquet, Antoine Bourseiller, Martin Buber, Elias Canetti, Paul Celan, Anton Chekhov, Jean Daive, Ovsei Driz, Jean Dubuffet, Ilya Ehrenburg, Fischer-Dieskau, Klaus Dörner, Andreas Franzke, Ivo Frenzel, Hans J Fröhlich, Jean Hamburger, Rolf Hochhuth, Richard Huelsenbeck, Alfred Jarry, Henry Kolarz, Jean Laude, Maurice Leblanc, Max Lüscher, Hans Jörg Martin, Molière, Miodrag Pavlovich, Racine, Edmond Rostand, Jean Rousselot, Claude Roy, Manes Sperber, Dolf Sternberger, André Thirion, Johann Willsberger. Also translations into German.
Award 1978 Goethe House-PEN Translation Prize.

NICHOLS, JAMES MANSFIELD Univ of Michigan, 4901 Evergreen Rd, Dearborn, MI 48128 USA *Tel* 313-593-5208.
TL English. **SL** Arabic, French, Spanish. **UDC** history, linguistics/philology, literature (criticism, history, poetry, prose).
Memb ATA.

NISETICH, FRANK J Classics, Harbor Campus, Univ of Massachusetts, Boston, MA 02125 USA *Tel* 617-287-1900; 641-0424.
TL English. **SL** French, German, Greek (Classical), Latin. **UDC** literature (English, Greek, and Latin poetry).
Greek (Classical) *Pindar's Victory Songs:*

The Odes of Pindar (Johns Hopkins Univ, forthcoming).
Awards 1978 Columbia Univ Translation Ctr grant.

NODARSE, CONNIE Box 35-0206, Riverside Sta, Miami, FL USA *Tel* 305-649-8043.
TL Spanish. **SL** English. **UDC** banking/finance, business, history, law, philosophy, psychiatry, psychology, public administration, public health, religion/scripture, social services, sociology, theater.
English Willard Cantelon: *The Day the Dollar Dies* (Vida, 1975). Philip Guerin: *Just Married or About To Be* (Claretian, 1977). Charles E Miller, C M: *Love in the Language of Penance* (Alba House, 1976). Pope Paul VI: *This Is Progress* (Claretian, 1978).
Memb AIT, ATA.

NOËL, BERNARD Mauregny-en-Haye, F-02820 Saint-Erme, France *Tel* (23) 23 35 43.
TL French. **SL** English. **UDC** literature (poetry, prose).
English Robert Maguire: *Lunatics I–XXIX* (Flammarion, 1973). William Shakespeare: *Timon of Athens* (Club Français, 1960).
Memb ATLF.

NOËL, CLAUDE 5 rue Charles-Dickens F-75016 Paris, France *Tel* 527 13 75.
TL French. **SL** English. **UDC** art/art history, literature (prose), sculpture/plastic arts, theater.
English C P Snow: *The Two Cultures* (Pauvert, 1968). Angus Wilson: *England* (Braun, 1971). Rudolf Arnheim: *Visual Thinking* (Flammarion, 1976). Carlos Baker: *Ernest Hemingway: A Life Story* (Robert Laffont, 1971).
Memb ATLF (pres).

NOONAN, FREDERICK W 525 Hudson St, New York, NY 10014 USA *Tel* 212-989-6387.
TL English. **SL** German. **UDC** literature (folklore, prose), music.
German E S von Kamphoevener: *Caravan Campfires* (Great Ocean, 1979).

NOWELL, JOHN 3 York Pl, York Ave, Hove, Sussex, BN3 1PN UK *Tel* (0273) 77 69 74.
TL English. **SL** German. **UDC** literature (biography, drama, prose).
German Richard Friedenthal: *Goethe: His Life and Times* (Weidenfeld & Nicolson, 1965); *Luther* (Weidenfeld & Nicolson, 1970). Albert Paris Gütersloh: *The Fraud* (Peter Owen, 1965). Klaus Völker: *Bertolt Brecht: A Biography* (Marion Boyars, 1978).
Memb TA.

NYERGES, ANTON N 201 Langford Ct, Richmond, KY 40475 USA *Tel* 606-623-7153.
TL English. **SL** Hungarian. **UDC** literature (poetry, prose).
Hungarian Endre Ady: *Poems* (Hungarian Cultural Foundation, 1969). Sandor Petofi: *Poems and Prose* (Historical Cultural Foundation, 1973). Attila Jozsef: *Poems and Prose* (Hungarian Cultural Foundation, 1973). Janos Arany: *Epics of the Hungarian Plain* (Anton Nyerges, 1976).
Affil Eastern Kentucky Univ.

O'CONNELL, MATTHEW JOSEPH RD 2, Aqueduct Rd, Peekskill, NY 10566 USA *Tel* 914-739-1290.

TL English. **SL** French, German, Italian, Spanish. **UDC** history, philosophy, religion/scripture, theology.

French Edmond Barbotin: *The Humanity of Man* (Orbis, 1975). Jacques Ellul: *The Betrayal of the West* (Seabury, 1978). Lucien Deiss: *God's Word and God's People* (Liturgical Press, 1976). Eloi Leclerc: *The Canticle of Creatures: Symbols of Union* (Franciscan Herald, 1977)

O'CONNELL, RICHARD English, Temple Univ, Philadelphia, PA 19122 USA *Tel* 215-787-1778.

TL English. **SL** Greek (Classical), Irish, Latin, Portuguese, Spanish. **UDC** literature (poetry).

Greek (Classical) Sappho: *Selected Poems* (Atlantis, 1975). **Irish** *Irish Monastic Poems* (Atlantis, 1975). **Latin** Martial: *Epigrams* (Perivale, 1976). **Spanish** Federico García Lorca: *Selected Poems* (Atlantis, 1976).

ODIO, ARNOLD 2627 Wyman Rd, Fayetteville, AR 72701 USA *Tel* 501-443-5914.

TL & SL English & Spanish. **UDC** literature (criticism, drama, poetry, prose).

Affil Univ of Arkansas. **Memb** ALTA.

ODIO, ELENA BACA 2627 Wyman Rd, Fayetteville, AR 72701 USA *Tel* 501-443-5014; 575-4301.

TL English. **SL** French, German, Spanish. **UDC** aesthetics, art history, business, communications, education, geography, history, literature (children's, criticism, drama, history, poetry, prose), occultism, psychology, religion, social sciences.

Spanish Arnaldo Rascovsky: "The Slaughter of Our Young" (pending).

Affil Univ of Arkansas. **Memb** ALTA.

O'FLAHERTY, JAMES CARNEAL 2164 Faculty Dr, Winston-Salem, NC 27106 USA *Tel* 919-723-0936.

TL English. **SL** German. **UDC** literature (criticism, prose), philosophy, theology.

German Johann Georg Hamann: *Socratic Memorabilia* (Johns Hopkins, 1967). Wilhelm Raabe: *Else von der Tanne* (Univ of Alabama, 1972).

Affil Wake Forest Univ.

OHLENDORF, SHEILA MACFARLANE Rte 2, Box 30B, Elgin, TX 78621 USA *Tel* 512-285-4232.

TL English. **SL** French, Spanish. **UDC** biography, history.

French M J Eugène Daumas: *The Horses of the Sahara* (Univ of Texas, 1968); *The Ways of the Desert* (Univ of Texas, 1971). **Spanish** Elías L Torres: *Twenty Episodes in the Life of Pancho Villa* (Encino Pr, 1973).

Affil Univ of Texas.

OLIVIER, DARIA 2D ave Brezin, F-92380 Garches, France *Tel* (33) 1 970 05 42.

TL French. **SL** English, Russian. **UDC** archeology, art history, history, literature (criticism, prose), painting, plastic arts, theology.

English Han Suyin: *A Many-Splendored Thing* (Stock). Also the works of Mikhail

Bakhtine, Nicolas Berdiaeff, Alexander Herzen, Leo Tolstoy, numerous others.

Memb ATLF, SFT.

OPPENHEIMER, DOROTHEA 866 United Nations Plaza, New York, NY 10017 USA *Tel* 212-421-3789.

TL English. **SL** German. **UDC** biography, history, literature (prose).

German Dieter Wellershoff: *A Beautiful Day* (Harper & Row, 1972).

ORTZEN, LEN Ivy Cottage, Leonard Stanley, Stonehouse, Glos, UK *Tel* Stonehouse 2045.

TL English. **SL** French. **UDC** literature (prose), naval history, wartime resistance (intelligence, military, Napoleonic).

French Oriss Chraibi: *Heirs to the Past* (Heinemann, 1971). Jacques Mordal: *25 Centuries of Sea Warfare* (Souvenir/Clarkson Potter, 1965). Gilles Perrault: *The Secrets of D-Day* (Arthur Barker/Little, Brown, 1965). Jorge Semprun: *The Second Death of Ramon Mercader* (Weidenfeld/Grove, 1973). Also the works of Michel Bar-Zohar, Françoise de Bernardy, Claude Cattaert, Robert Christophe, Alain Decaux, Henri Queffelec, numerous others.

Memb TA.

OSERS, EWALD 33 Reades Lane, Sonning Common, Reading, Berks, UK *Tel* (073525) 3196.

TL English. **SL** Czech, German. **UDC** current affairs, geography, literature (poetry, prose), military science, political economy/science.

Czech Jaroslav Seifert: *The Plague Column* (Terra Nova, 1979). **German** H von Hosmannsthal & Richard Strauss: *Correspondence* (Collins/Random House/Vienna House, 1961). *The Secret Conferences of Dr Goebbels 1939-43* (Weidenfeld & Nicolson/Dutton, 1970). Kurt Waldheim: *The Austrian Example* (Weidenfeld & Nicolson, 1972). Also the works of Rose Ausländer, Antonín Bartusek, Paul Carell, Hans Habe, Hans Hass, Wolfgang Leonhard, Ondra Lysohorsky, Jiří Mucha, others.

Memb BDÜ, TA, TG. **Awards** 1971 Schlegel-Tieck Prize, 1977 C B Nathorst/FIT Prize.

PACHMUSS, TEMIRA A 2013 Vawter St, Urbana, IL 61801 USA *Tel* 217-344-3761.

TL English. **SL** Russian. **UDC** literature (criticism, lyrics, poetry, prose).

Russian Zinaida Hippius: *Selected Works* (Univ of Illinois, 1972); *Between Paris and St Petersburg: Selected Diaries* (Univ of Illinois, 1975). *Women Writers in Russian Modernism* (Univ of Illinois, 1978). "A Russian Cultural Renaissance" (pending).

Affil Univ of Illinois.

PADDON, HILARY ELIZABETH One Shirlock Rd #9, London NW3, UK *Tel* (01) 267 6364.

TL English. **SL** French, Spanish. **UDC** African studies, anthropology, art/art history, economics, linguistics, social sciences.

French Jacques Lethève: *Daily Life of French Artists in the Nineteenth Century* (Allen & Unwin, 1972).

Memb TA.

PADGETT, RON 342 E 13 St #6, New York, NY 10003 USA *Tel* 212-477-4472.

TL English. **SL** French. **UDC** literature (poetry, prose).

French Guillaume Appolinaire: *The Poet Assassinated* (Holt, Rinehart & Winston, 1968). Blaise Cendrars: *Kodak* (Adventures in Poetry, 1976). Marcel Duchamp & Pierre Cabanne: *Dialogues with Marcel Duchamp* (Viking, 1971). Valery Larbaud: *The Poems of A O Barnabooth* (Mushinsha, 1977). Also the works of Max Jacob, Francis Picabia, Pierre Reverdy, Raymond Roussel.

Affil St Mark's Poetry Project. **Awards** 1977 Columbia Univ Translation Ctr.

PALLADINO, JOSEPH G 2472 Grand Ave, Bronx, New York, NY 10768 USA *Tel* 212-295-9280.

TL English. **SL** French, Italian, Spanish. **UDC** library science, linguistics/philology, literature (history).

Memb ATA.

PALLISTER, JANIS L 211 State St, Bowling Green, OH 43402 USA *Tel* 413-353-9513.

TL English. **SL** French, Italian, Portuguese, Spanish. **UDC** business, literature (all areas), theater.

French Bolamba: *Esanzo* (Naaman, 1977). Claudel: "100 Fan Poems" (pending). Pallister: *Confrontations,* bilingual edition (Westbury Assn, 1977). Also the works of Diopi Birago, Aimé Cesaire, René Depestre, Anne Hebert, A Nanto, M A F de Oliveira, Ungaretti, numerous others.

Affil Bowling Green State Univ. **Memb** ALTA.

PAOLUCCI, ANNE 166-25 Powells Cove Blvd, Beechhurst, NY 11357 USA *Tel* 212-767-8380.

TL English. **SL** French, German, Italian. **UDC** astronomy, literature (criticism, drama, history, lyrics, poetry, prose, songs).

Italian Pirandello: "Storia del Teatro Italiano" in *Genius of the Italian Theater,* Eric Bentley, ed, (Mentor, 1964). *Machiavelli's Mandragola* (Bobbs-Merrill, 1957). Virginia Aganoor Pompili: "Two Poems" (*Ararat,* 1968).

Affil St John's Univ.

PARISOT, HENRI GEORGES ROBERT 28 rue de la Marne, F-92330 Sceaux, France *Tel* 702 95 52.

TL French. **SL** English. **UDC** literature (poetry, prose, puns), music (jazz), theater.

English Lewis Carroll: *Alice's Adventures in Wonderland* (Flammarion, 1968). S T Coleridge: *Poems* (Aubier/Flammarion, 1975). Edgar Allan Poe: *Poems* (Aubier/Montaigne, 1978). Edward Lear: *Nonsense Poems* (Aubier/Flammarion, 1974). Also the works of Leonora Carrington, Nathaniel Hawthorne, Allan Lomax.

Memb ATLF.

PAROUTAUD, MARGARET (Mrs Henri) 36 Wellings Pl, Monterey, CA 93940 USA *Tel* 408-372-6196.

TL & SL English & French. **UDC** agriculture, art, arts/crafts, commerce, forestry, horticulture, law, literature (all areas except science

fiction), medicine, music, oceanography, painting, philosophy, photography, psychology, religion, sculpture, sports, theology.
French the works of Père de Breboeuf, Antoine du Saix.
Affil Monterey Inst of Foreign Studies. **Memb** TG.

PARRENT, PATRICIA S PO Box 8177, Univ Sta, Austin, TX 78712 USA *Tel* 512-452-9167.
TL English. **SL** Spanish. **UDC** architecture, art, civil engineering, commerce, linguistics/philology, painting, sculpture.
Spanish J R Buendía: *A Basic Guide to the Prado Museum* (Silex, 1973). F Marías: *Bosch* (Silex, 1975). J M Pita Andrade: *Goya* (Silex, 1975); *Velázquez* (Silex, 1972).
Memb APETI, TRACT.

PARTRIDGE, FRANCES 16 W Halkin St SW1, London UK *Tel* (01) 235 6998.
TL English. **SL** French, Spanish. **UDC** aesthetics, art, arts/crafts, botany, ethics, history, literature (criticism, drama, history, prose), logic, metaphysics, philosophy, psychiatry, psychology, sociology.
French Gilbert Martineau: *Madame Mère: Napoleon's Mother* (John Murray, 1978). **Spanish** Blasco Ibañez: *Blood and Sand* (Elek). Miguel Angel Asturias: *The President* (Gollancz, 1963). Alejo Carpentier: *Reasons of State* (Gollancz, 1976). Also the works of Mercedes Ballesteros, Raymond Cogniet, Gabrielle Estivals, Joseph Kessel, Carmen Laforet, Octavio Paz, numerous others.
Memb TA.

PATRICK, BERT E & LURA LARSSON 120 E Lindburg, Pittsburgh, KS 66762 USA *Tel* 316-231-8989.
TL English. **SL** French, Spanish. **UDC** archeology, art, arts/crafts, history, literature (criticism, drama, folklore, history, poetry, prose, science fiction). paleontology, philately, sculpture, social sciences, sociology, sports, theater.
Spanish Sergio Galindo: *Rice Powder* (Perivale, 1978).
Affil Pittsburgh State Univ.

PATT, RICHARD A 87 Texas Way, Fayetteville, AR 72701 USA *Tel* 503-521-7103.
TL English. **SL** French, Italian, Russian. **UDC** international affairs (Russian area affairs), linguistics/philology, literature (all areas), political science.
Affil Univ of Arkansas. **Accred** Univ of Arkansas (MFA in Translation). **Memb** ALTA.

PAUL, DAVID 11 Pandora Rd, W Hampstead, London NW6 1TS, UK *Tel* (01) 435-9059.
TL English. **SL** French. **UDC** literature (criticism, drama, lyrics, poetry, prose).
French Paul Valéry: *Poems* (Princeton Univ, 1971); *Idee Fixe* (Pantheon, 1965); *My Faust* (Pantheon, 1960). *Poison and Vision: Poems and Prose of Baudelaire, Rimbaud, Mallarmé* (Random House, 1974). Also the works of René Char, Giuseppe Dessi.
Memb TA.

PAUL, DAVID MEL & MARGARETA 4912 W St NW, Washington, DC 20007 USA *Tel* 202-337-2575.
TL English. **SL** Swedish. **UDC** literature (poetry, prose).
Swedish Rolf Edberg: *At the Foot of the Tree* (Univ of Alabama, 1974). Per C Jersild: *The Animal Doctor* (Pantheon/Random, 1975).

PAVESI, JULIE 1 rue de Mirbel, F-75005 Paris, France *Tel* 331 44 80.
TL French. **SL** English, Spanish. **UDC** literature (children's, criticism, prose).
English Cetin Altan: *Whisky* (Flammarion, 1976–77). Caroline Blackwood: *The Stepdaughter/Great Granny Webster* (Flammarion, 1978). Also the works of Elizabeth Packard, Virginia Woolf.
Memb ATLF.

PAYNE, ROBERT 2 W 67 St, New York, NY 10023 USA.
TL English. **SL** Chinese, Danish, Russian. **UDC** literature.
Chinese *The White Pony: An Anthology of Chinese Poetry* (Allen & Unwin/John Day, 1949) **Danish** Søren Kierkegaard: *Fear and Trembling* (Oxford Univ, 1939, 1946). **Russian** Boris Pasternak: *Childhood* (private, 1941). Yuri Olyesha: *Love and Other Stories* (Washington Square, 1967).
Affil/Memb Columbia Univ Translation Ctr (dir).

PEARCE, BRIAN LEONARD 42 Victoria Rd, New Barnet, Herts, UK.
TL English. **SL** French, Russian. **UDC** economics, history, political economy/science, sociology.
French Maxime Rodinson: *Islam and Capitalism* (Allen Lane/Penguin, 1974). Fernando Claudin: *The Communist Movement; From Comintern to Cominform*, Part 1 (Penguin/Harmondsworth, 1975). **Russian** E A Preobrazhensky: *The New Economics* (Clarendon/Oxford, 1965). *Congress of Peoples of the East, Baku, Sept, 1920*, minutes of proceedings (New Park Publications, 1977). Also the works of Samir Amin, Charles Bettelheim, Arghiri Emmanuel, Maurice Godelier, Robert Mandrou, Roland Mousnier, Leon Trotsky, others.
Memb TA. **Award** 1975 Scott-Moncrieff Prize.

PEDEN, MARGARET SAYERS Romance Languages, Univ of Missouri, Columbia, MO 65211 USA *Tel* 314-882-4874.
TL English. **SL** Spanish. **UDC** literature (criticism, drama, poetry, prose).
Spanish Faustino González Aller: *Niña Huanca* (Seaver/Viking, 1977). Emilio Carballido: *The Norther* (Univ of Texas, 1958). Jorge Díaz: *Topography of a Nude* (Mundus Artium, 1972). Carlos Fuentes: *Terra Nostra* (Farrar, Straus & Giroux, 1976); *The Hydra Head* (Farrar, Straus, & Giroux, 1978). Pablo Neruda: *The Elemental Odes* (Farrar, Straus & Giroux, forthcoming). Also numerous works of Elsa Cross, Vicente Leñero, Octavio Paz, Horacio Quiroga, Juan Tovar, Egon Wolff, others.
Memb ALTA, ATA, MICATA.

PENDRY, DE ANN 1102 Hughes St #2, Fayetteville, AR 72701 USA *Tel* 501-521-4276.
TL English. **SL** Portuguese, Spanish. **UDC** most areas of the humanities, literature, sciences.
Affil Univ of Arkansas (Translation Workshop). **Memb** ALTA.

PENGLASE, WILLIAM O, JR 415 W 22 St #2, New York, NY 10011 USA *Tel* 212-989-8306.
TL English. **SL** French, Spanish. **UDC** linguistics, literature.
Affil Hispanic Soc of America.

PENMAN, BRUCE 123 Upper Woodcote Rd, Caversham, Reading, UK.
TL English. **SL** French, German, Italian. **UDC** art, evolution, geography, history, literature (drama, prose), religion, travel, zoology.
Italian *Five Italian Renaissance Comedies* (Penguin, 1978). Alessandro Manzoni: *The Betrothed* (Penguin, 1972). Lidia Storoni Mazzolani: *The Idea of the City in Roman Thought* (Hollis & Carter, 1970). Silvio Micheli: *Mongolia: in Search of Marco Polo and Other Adventures* (Hollis & Carter, 1967). Also the works of d'Annunzio, Ariosto, Boccaccio, Capuana, Grazzini, Storoni.
Memb TA. **Awards** 1973 Italian Inst of Culture.

PEPIN, ROBERT MAURICE 11 rue des Laitières, F-94300 Vincennes, France *Tel* (1) 365 03 52.
TL French. **SL** English. **UDC** literature (drama, poetry, prose).
English Richard Brautigan: *Willard and His Bowling Trophies* (Christian Bourgois, 1978). Samuel Taylor Coleridge: *Shakespearian Criticism* (Rencontre, 1970). Robert Graves: *Goodbye To All That* (Stock, 1965). Kurt Vonnegut, Jr: *God Bless You, Mr Rosewater* (Le Seuil, 1976). Also the works of Max Hart, Malcolm Boden Lowry, Mary Nicholson, Victor Price.
Memb ATLF.

PÉREZ, LAURA LEE CRUMLEY DE Apartado Aereo 020641, Cali, Columbia *Tel* 584 821.
TL & SL English & Spanish. **UDC** business, commerce, literature (criticism, folklore, history, prose).
English Glenn A Welsch: *Budgeting: Profit Planning and Control,* co-translated with Carlos Perez Alegría (Prentice-Hall, 1979).
Accred/Memb ATA.

PERRY, THOMAS AMHERST 214 Brookhaven Terr, Commerce, TX 75428 USA *Tel* 214-886-6333.
TL English. **SL** Rumanian, Spanish. **UDC** literature (criticism, poetry, prose).
Rumanian the works of Tudor Arghezi, Ion Barbu. **Spanish** the works of Jose Gautier Benítez, Manrique Carbrera, Manuel Corchado, Virgilio Dávila, Concepción Meléndez, Jose Padilla, Lola Rodríguez de Tió, Manuel Sama, Luis Llorens Torres, Santiago Vidarte.
Affil East Texas State Univ. **Memb** ALTA.

PETERSON, PAUL W Gannon College, Erie, PA 16501 USA *Tel* 814-456-7523.

TL English. **SL** German. **UDC** anthropology, biomedicine, linguistics/philology, literature (folklore).
Accred/Memb ATA.

PEVEAR, RICHARD 463 West St #D1015. New York, NY 10014 USA *Tel* 212-691-0393.
TL English. **SL** French, Italian, Spanish. **UDC** aesthetics, archeology, architecture, art, history, literature (criticism, drama, folklore, history, prose), painting, philosophy, religion, sculpture, shipbuilding, theater, theology.
French Alain: *The Gods* (New Directions, 1974). Marie-Rose Seguy: *The Miraculous Journey of Mahomet* (Braziller, 1977). José Vicente Ortuño: *Bitter Roots* (Pomerica, 1978); *Ethiopian Magic Scrolls* (Braziller, forthcoming).

PICARD, ANDRÉE R 2 bis, villa Logerais, F-92270 Bois-Colombes, France *Tel* (33 1) 242 40 91.
TL French. **SL** English, German. **UDC** education, literature (criticism, history, prose).
English Richard Wright: *Black Boy* (Gallimard, 1947). John K Galbraith: *The Affluent Society* (Calmann-Lévy, 1960). Patrick White: *The Solid Mandala* (Gallimard, 1973). Also the works of Carlos Baker, Ian Gray, Emery Jones, Erich Kuby, Anya Seton, Dalton Trumbo, Irving Wallace, Richard Whalen.
Memb ATLF.

PINKHAM, JOAN 737 Bay Rd, Amherst, MA 01002 USA *Tel* 413-256-6644.
TL English. **SL** French. **UDC** literature (nontechnical nonfiction, prose,).
French J-P Sartre & Paul Nizan: *Aden Arabie* (Monthly Review Pr, 1968). Pierre Vallières: *White Niggers of America* (Monthly Review Pr, 1971). Lucien Israël; *Conquering Cancer* (Random House, 1978). Henri Troyat: *Catherine the Great* (Dutton, forthcoming). Also the works of Samir Amin, Charles Bettelheim, Aimé Césaire.

PITTHAN, INGEBORG MARIA 13B Escondido Village, Stanford, CA 94305 USA *Tel* 415-321-8367.
TL German. **SL** English, Polish, Russian. **UDC** bacteriology, linguistics, medicine, political economy, technology (balancing).
Affil Stanford Univ.

PITZ, CATHERINE M 6828 Creston Rd, Edina, MN 55435 USA *Tel* 612-922-3959.
TL English. **SL** Spanish. **UDC** art history, documentation, education, history, law, linguistics/philology, psychology.
Affil Univ of Minnesota. **Memb** ATA.

POHORYLES, BERNARD M Eight Stuyvesant Oval, New York, NY 10009 USA *Tel* 212-285-3433; 673-2639.
TL & SL English & German. **UDC** art, commerce, education, history, literature (all areas), theater.
English Peter Fingesten: *The Meaning of the Concept of the Symbol in Modern Art* (Valentin Koerner, 1976); *The Craft of Creation* (Antaios, 1968). **German** Emil Fröschels: "The Language of Children and Aphasia" (pending). Also the works of Heinrich Heine, Friedrich Hölderlin.
Affil Pace Univ. **Memb** ATA, SFL.

POLAČKOVÁ-HENLEY, KÁČA 78 Hutchison Ave, Elliott Lake, ON P5A 1W5, Canada *Tel* 705-848-2480.
TL English. **SL** Czech, Slovak. **UDC** aesthetics, art, arts/crafts, communications, education, film subtitles, human resources, information sciences, literature (all areas).
Czech Ludvik Vaculík: *The Guinea Pigs* (Third Press, 1973; Penguin, 1975). Josef Škvorecký: *The Bass Saxophone* (Anson Cartwright, 1977; Chatto & Windus, 1978). A J Liehm: *Closely Watched Films* (International Arts & Sciences, 1973). Pavel Kohout: *Hangwoman* (Putnam, 1979). Also the works of Ludvík Aškenazy, J Brodský, Ladislav Fuks, Václav Havel, Jiří Hochman, Vladimír Holan, Miroslav Holub, Franz Kafka, Arnošt Lustig, Jan Potočka, Ivan Sviták, numerous others.

POLGAR, STEVEN 432 W Ellet St, Philadelphia, PA 19119 USA *Tel* 215-843-0774.
TL English. **SL** German, Hungarian. **UDC** literature (poetry, prose).
Hungarian Miklós Radnóti: *Clouded Sky* (Harper & Row, 1972).

POLLAK, FELIX 3907 Winnemac Ave, Madison, WI 53711 USA *Tel* 608-238-8147.
TL English. **SL** German. **UDC** literature (poetry, prose).
German the works of Rainer Brambach, Wilhelm Busch, Hilde Domini, Karl Krolow, Robert Musil, Alfred Palgar, Rainer Maria Rilke, Marbin Steiner, George Trakl, others.
Affil Univ of Wisconsin (emeritus). **Memb** ALTA.

POLLER, NIDRA 139 blvd St Germain, F-Paris VIe, France *Tel* 633 93 49.
TL English. **SL** French. **UDC** literature (all areas), with special competence in French West Indies writers and contemporary American writers.
French Michael McClure: *Jaguar Skies*, co-translated with Georges Louisy (Christian Bourgois, 1978). Also excerpts from the works of Natalia Ginsburg, Edouard Glissant, Jean-Luc Godard, Jeanne Hyvrard, Xavier Orville, Francis Paul.
Affil Editions Cimarron.

PONTIERO, GIOVANNI 3 The Grove, Didsbury, Manchester M/R 208RG, UK *Tel* (061) 455-2935.
TL English. **SL** Italian, Portuguese, Spanish. **UDC** literature (all areas).
Italian Guido Noccioli: "On Tour with Eleanora Duse" (pending). **Portuguese** Clarice Lispector: *Family Ties* (Univ of Texas, 1972). Manuel Bandeira: *Lyric Poems* (New Directions, 1968). Nélida Piñon: "The House of Passion" (pending). Also the works of Carlos Drummond de Andrade, Carlos Martínez Moreno, Renata Pallomini, Lydia Fagundes Telles.
Affil Univ of Manchester. **Awards** 1968 Camoens Prize.

PORTINHO, WALDIVIA I M Rua Gen Barbosa Lima/406, Copacabana, Rio de Janeiro, Brazil *Tel* (021) 256-8416.
TL Portuguese. **SL** English, French, Spanish. **UDC** business administration, communications, history of Brazil, literature (history, prose), social sciences.
English Warren Dean: *Rio Claro: A Brazilian Plantation System 1820–1920* (Paz e Terra, 1977). Mary Parker Follet: *Dynamic Administration* (Fund Escola Serv Público, forthcoming). Janice E Perlman: *The Myth of Marginality: Urban Politics in Rio de Janeiro* (Paz e Terra, 1977). Paul Sweezy et al: *The Transition from Feudalism to Capitalism* (Paz e Terra, 1978). Also numerous articles, papers, proceedings of conferences.
Memb ABRATES, AIT.

POULIN, A, JR 92 Park Ave, Brockport, NY 14420 USA *Tel* 716-637-3844.
TL English. **SL** French, German. **UDC** literature (poetry).
French Rainer Maria Rilke: *Saltimbanques: French Prose Poems* (Graywolf, 1978); *The Roses and The Windows* (Graywolf, 1978). **German** Rainer Maria Rilke: *Duino Elegies and the Sonnets to Orpheus* (Houghton Mifflin, 1977). Also the works of Charles Baudelaire, Jean Follain, Saint Denys Garneau, Roland Giguére, Alain Grandbois, Anne Hébert, Gilles Hénault, Gatien Lapointe.
Affil SUNY at Brockport. **Memb** ALTA. **Awards** 1976 Columbia Univ Translation Ctr.

PREISSER, DOROTHY CURRIER 133 Georgetown Rd, Annapolis, MD 21403 USA *Tel* 301-263-5560.
TL English. **SL** French, Spanish. **UDC** education, linguistics/philology, literature (drama, music, prose), psychology, social services.
Memb ATA.

PRINGLE, NORMA Box 234, Columbia, MO 65205 USA *Tel* 314-474-7556.
TL & SL English & Spanish (specialized knowledge of dialects of southern Spain). **UDC** banking/finance, commerce, electronics, literature (criticism, drama, folklore, history, poetry, prose), viniculture.
Accred/Memb ATA, MICATA. **Affil** Columbia College.

PUSEY, WILLIAM W, III, Tucker Hall, Washington & Lee Univ, Lexington, VA 24450 USA *Tel* 703-463-9111.
TL English. **SL** German. **UDC** literature (criticism, prose).

RAABE, GERHARD Fichtestr 1, D-3000 Hannover, West Germany *Tel* (0511) 550 979.
TL German. **SL** English, French. **UDC** anthropology, ethics/morals, history, literature (criticism, drama, history, prose), metaphysics, military science, philosophy, political science, religion/scripture, theology.
English F F Bruce: *New Testament History* (Brockhaus, 1975–76). W K C Guthrie: *Greek Philosophers from Thales to Aristotle* (Vandenhoeck & Ruprecht, 1960). S H Steinberg: *The Thirty Years' War and the Conflict for European Hegemony 1600–1660* (Vandenhoeck & Ruprecht, 1967). Also the works of Jay E Adams, C Barnett, G Cornfeld, A Singer, Arnold J Toynbee, Chaim Wirszubski, others.
Memb VDÜ.

RABASSA, GREGORY 36 Red Creek Rd, Hampton Bays, NY 11946 USA *Tel* 516-728-2304.

TL English. **SL** Portuguese, Spanish. **UDC** literature (criticism, drama, history, poetry, prose).

Portuguese Osman Lins: *Avalovara* (Knopf, 1979). **Spanish** Julio Cortázar: *Hopscotch* (Pantheon, 1966). Gabriel García Márquez: *One Hundred Years of Solitude* (Harper & Row, 1970); *The Autumn of the Patriarch* (Harper & Row, 1976). Also book-length translations of the works of Demetrio Aguilera-Malta, Miguel Angel Asturias, Afrânio Coutinho, Juan Goytisolo, José Lezama Lima, Clarice Lispector, Manuel Mujica-Lainez, Dalton Trevisan, Mario Vargas Llosa.

Affil Queens College and Graduate Ctr of CUNY. **Memb** ALTA, ATA. **Awards** 1967 National Book Award in Translation, 1977 PEN Translation Prize.

RABIN, BATYA B PO Box 7158, Jerusalem, Israel *Tel* (02) 39974.

TL English. **SL** German, Hebrew. **UDC** archeology, education, history, literature (children's, history, prose), political science, religion/scripture.

Hebrew Shin Shalom: *Storm over Galilee* (Vallentine, Mitchell, 1967). Yigael Yadin: *The Scroll of the War of the Sons of Light against the Sons of Darkness* (Oxford Univ, 1962). Benjamin Mazar, ed: *Patriarchs: The World History of the Jewish People* (Massada, 1970); *Judges: The World History of the Jewish People* (Rutgers Univ, 1971).

RAFFEL, BURTON 765 Harrison St, Denver, CO 80206 USA *Tel* 303-377-7073.

TL English. **SL** Catalan, French, German, Indonesian, Russian, Spanish, Vietnamese. **UDC** literature (poetry, prose), theater.

Catalan Salvador Espriu: *The Bull-Hide* (Writers Workshop, 1977). **Indonesian** *The Complete Poetry and Prose of Chairil Anwar* (State Univ of NY, 1970). **Russian** *Russian Poetry Under the Tsars* (State Univ of NY, 1971). **Vietnamese** *From the Vietnamese: Ten Centuries of Poetry* (October House, 1968). Also works on translation: *The Forked Tongue: A Study of the Translation Process* (Mouton, 1971); *Why Re-Create?* (Chandler & Sharp, 1973); *Guide to Paperback Translations in the Humanities* (National Humanities Faculty, 1976).

Affil Univ of Denver (English).

RALEY, HAROLD Foreign Languages, Oklahoma State Univ, Stillwater, OK 74074 USA.

TL English. **SL** French, Spanish. **UDC** literature (poetry, prose), philosophy.

Spanish Julián Marías: *Generations: A Historical Method* (Univ of Alabama, 1970).

RAMSEY, PAUL Poet-in-Residence, Univ of Tennessee, Chattanooga, TN 37403 USA *Tel* 615-755-4238.

TL English. **SL** Greek (Classical), Italian, French, Latin. **UDC** literature (poetry).

Memb ALTA (Text Committee for revision of Episcopal Hymnal).

RANUM, PATRICIA M 208 Ridgewood Rd, Baltimore, MD 21210 USA *Tel* 301-467-4841.

TL English. **SL** French. **UDC** demography, history (17th-18th Century Europe), history of "mentalities."

French *Selections from the "Annales, E S C"* (Johns Hopkins Univ, 1975). Philippe Aries: *Western Attitudes toward Death* (Johns Hopkins Univ, 1974). Fernand Brundel: *Afterthoughts On* (Johns Hopkins Univ, 1977). Alain Besançon: *The Soviet Syndrome* (Harcourt Brace Jovanovich, 1978).

RATNER, ROCHELLE 50 Spring St, New York, NY 10012 USA *Tel* 212-226-8333.

TL English. **SL** French. **UDC** literature (poetry, prose, songs).

French Paul Colinet: "Selected Prose Poems" (*Clown War*, 1975). Anon: *Songs of the Women of Fes* (Tiresias, forthcoming). Also the works of René Magritte, Francis Picabia, Renée Vivien.

RAULET, GÉRARD 1 Mail du Bois-Brûlé, F-78380 Bougival, France *Tel* (1) 969 19 80.

TL French. **SL** English, German. **UDC** linguistics/philology, literature (criticism, lyrics, poetry), metaphysics, philosophy, political science, social sciences, sociology, theology.

German the works of Ernst Bloch, Jürgen Habermas, Herbert Marcuse, Karl Marx, Joachim Ritter, others.

Memb ATLF (secy general).

RAY, SUSAN H 275 Central Park W, New York, NY 10024 USA *Tel* 212-724-1489.

TL English. **SL** German. **UDC** education, ethics/morals, film, graphology, librettos, psychiatry, psychology.

German Cornelia Gerstenmaier: *The Voices of the Silent* (Hart, 1972). Ludwig Liegle: *The Family's Role in Soviet Education* (Springer, 1975). Gerhard Prause: *School Days of the Famous* (Springer, 1978). Günter Ammon: *Psychoanalysis and Psychosomatics* (Springer, 1978). Also the works of Walter Noder, Lene Riefenstahl, Rudolph Schanzer & Ernst Welisch, Fritz Schweighofer, Herbert Weiner, numerous articles of a general nature on literature, medicine, philately, mathematics, law.

Accred/Memb ATA. **Affil** Fordham Univ.

READ, RALPH R, III PO Box 7939, Austin, TX 78712 USA *Tel* 512-471-4123.

TL English. **SL** German. **UDC** literature (criticism, drama, lyrics, poetry, prose).

German Horst Bienek: *Bakunin: An Invention* (Gollancz, 1976); *The First Polka* (Gollancz, 1977). Also the works of Karlhans Frank, Uwe Friesel, Rolf Hädrich, Günter Herburger, Hans Mayer, Christa Reinig, Paul Schalluck, Heinz Schwitzke, Heinrich Vormweg, numerous others.

Affil Univ of Texas (Germanic Langs). **Memb** ALTA.

REEVE, F D Phyllis Seidel Agency, 164 E 93 St, New York, NY 10028 USA.

TL English. **SL** Russian. **UDC** aesthetics, art, choreography, history, literature (all areas), logic, occultism, painting, philately, philosophy, printing, psychology, public health, recreation, sciences (applied, earth, life, medical, natural, social), sports, theater.

Russian Ivan S Turgenev: *Five Short Novels* (Bantam, 1961). *Anthology of Russian Plays*, Vol 1 (Vintage, 1962). *Anthology of Russian Plays*, Vol 2 (Vintage, 1963). A I Solzhenitsyn: *Nobel Lecture* (Noonday, 1972).

REGEHR, LYDIA 6339 34 St SW #413, Seattle, WA 98126 USA *Tel* 206-937-0217.

TL & SL English, German, Russian. **UDC** humorous quatrains, hymns, literature (children's, drama, folklore, librettos, lyrics, poetry, prose, songs).

German Anna Ilgenstein Katterfeld: *The Morning Star of Wittenberg* (Review & Herald, 1956); *The Story of Martin Luther for Young People* (Eerdmans, 1955). **Russian** *Finist the Falcon Prince,* (Carolrhoda, 1973). Also the works of J von Eichendorff, Hoffmann von Fellersleben, Heinrich Heine, G von Hünefeld, J W von Goethe, Ivan Krylov, A S Pushkin, Ivan S Turgenev, numerous others.

Memb ATA.

REICHENBACH, BODO 23 Vista Circle, Arlington, MA 02174 USA *Tel* 617-646-8982.

TL English. **SL** German. **UDC** literature (all areas), metaphysics, philosophy, religion.

German Bô Yin Râ: *The Wisdom of St John* (Kober, 1975); *About My Books, Concerning My Name, and Other Texts* (Kober, 1977); *The Book on Life Beyond* (Kober, 1978).

Accred/Memb ATA. **Affil** Boston Univ, Harvard Univ.

REID, ALASTAIR The New Yorker Magazine, 25 W 43 St, New York, NY 10036 USA *Tel* 212-840-3700.

TL English. **SL** Spanish. **UDC** literature (children's, librettos, poetry, prose, songs).

Spanish Pablo Neruda: *Extravagaria* (Cape, 1972; Farrar, Straus & Giroux, 1973). Jorge Luis Borges: *Personal Anthology,* co-translated with Anthony Kerrigan (Grove, 1967; Cape, 1968). Mario Vargas Llosa: *Sunday Sunday* (Bobbs-Merrill, 1973). *Mother Goose in Spanish,* co-translated with Anthony Kerrigan (Crowell, 1967). Also the works of Jean Cocteau, Jorge Guillen, José Hierro, Guillermo Cabrera Infante, Pablo Neruda (additional volumes), José Emilio Pacheco, Suetonius, numerous others. Also numerous books, articles, editorial comment, reviews, reportage on poetry and prose.

REIK, MIRIAM M 760 West End Ave, New York, NY 10025 USA *Tel* 212-222-5495.

TL English. **SL** German. **UDC** literature (poetry, prose), medicine.

REISS, KATHARINA Hiltensperger Str 80, D-8000 Munich, West Germany *Tel* (089) 300 8737.

TL German. **SL** English, Spanish. **UDC** education, ethnography, geography, history, linguistics, literature (criticism, history, prose), political science.

Memb BDÜ, VDÜ.

REMY-ZEPHIR, JACQUES 17 blvd des Batignolles, F-75008 Paris, France *Tel* 292 00 38.

TL French. **SL** English, Spanish. **UDC** anthropology, archeology, art history, dentistry, documentation, ethnography, history, linguistics/philology, literature (folklore, history,

prose, science fiction), navigation, paleontology, psychology, sociology, sports.
Memb ATLF.

REUTER, JAS Corina 117 A-12, Coyoacan, Mexico 21, DF Mexico *Tel* 549-49 50.
TL Spanish. **SL** English, German. **UDC** aesthetics, anthropology, art/art history, economics, history, music, psychology.
English Donald Schneider: *Psychoanalysis and the Artist* (Fondo de Cultura Económica, 1975). Also the works of numerous German writers.
Memb AIT.

REYNOLDS, G EDWARD 3532 Hamlet Pl, Chevy Chase, MD 20015 USA *Tel* 301-652-6505.
TL English. **SL** French, German. **UDC** economics, international relations, literature (prose), political science.
German Arthur Schnitzler: *The Little Comedy* (Ungar, 1977). Gerhart Hauptmann: "Wanda" (pending). Martin Walser: "A Runaway Horse" (pending).
Memb ALTA, ATA.

RICHARDSON, ELIZABETH ANN 2120 Shad Court, Naples, FL 33942 USA *Tel* 813-774-1204.
TL English. **SL** French. **UDC** literature (poetry, prose).
Memb ALTA.

RICHARTZ, WALTER E Otto-Kämper-Ring 33, D-6072 Dreieich-Buchschlag, West Germany *Tel* (06103) 68505.
TL German. **SL** English. **UDC** chemistry, literature (children's, drama, poetry, prose), sciences (natural).
English Lewis Carroll: *The Tangled Tale* (Insel, 1978); *The Nursery Alice* (Diogenes, 1977). Raymond Chandler: *The Little Sister* (Diogenes, 1976). F Scott Fitzgerald: *The Vegetable* (Diogenes, 1973). Also the works of Stephen Crane, D Hammett, Nathaniel Hawthorne, H L Mencken, H D Thoreau.
Memb VS.

RICHMAN, LARRY L 250 B-34, Brigham Young Univ, Provo, UT 84602 USA *Tel* 801-374-1211.
TL & SL Cakchiquel, English, Spanish. **UDC** communications, education, genealogy, linguistics, religion/scripture, theology.
Cakchiquel Larry Richman, ed: "Cakchiquel Stories, Legends, and Myths" (pending). **English** *Selections from the Book of Mormon* (Church of Jesus Christ of LDS, 1978); *Organizational Guidebooks* (Church of Jesus Christ of LDS, 1978). **Spanish** Reinaldo Alfaro Palacios: "My First Friend" (pending).
Accred Brigham Young Univ Translation Certificate. **Affil** Translation Services Dept.
Memb ATA.

RIGGS, LYNNE Ctr for Japanese Social & Political Studies, 2-8-8 Nishinogawa, Komaeshi, Tokyo 201, Japan *Tel* (03) 489-2175.
TL English. **SL** Japanese. **UDC** political science, social science.
Affil *The Japan Interpreter.*

RISCHIN, RUTH S 350 Arballo Dr #9J, San Francisco, CA 94132 USA *Tel* 415-585-2167.
TL English. **SL** Russian. **UDC** art history, horticulture, literature (children's, criticism, drama, folklore, history, librettos, poetry, prose), music, theater.
Russian Leonid P Grossman; *Confession of a Jew* (Arno, 1975). V N & Z K Klimenko: *Roses* (San Francisco Rose Society, 1979). Ivan Shmelov: "Selected Stories" (pending). V Shukshin: "Selected Stories" (pending). Also the works of Mikhail Bargman, Anton Rubinstein, Moses Stern.

ROBERTS, SPENCER E Modern Languages, Brooklyn College of CUNY, Brooklyn, NY 11210 USA *Tel* 780-5451, 5452.
TL English. **SL** Russian. **UDC** history, literature (all areas), music, philosophy, theater.
Russian Vasily Rozanov: *Dostoevsky and the Legend of The Grand Inquisitor* (Cornell Univ, 1972); *Four Faces of Rozanov: Christianity, Sex, Jews, and the Russian Revolution* (Philosophical Library, 1978). *Essays in Russian Literature: The Conservative View* (Ohio Univ, 1968). Lev Shestov: *Dostoevsky, Tolstoy, and Nietzsche* (Ohio Univ, 1969).

ROBERTS, WILLIAM H & MARY M 808 Wellesley Dr SE, Albuquerque, NM 87106 USA *Tel* 505-265-9606.
TL English. **SL** French, Portuguese, Spanish. **UDC** literature (poetry, prose).
Spanish Juan Ramón Jiménez: *Platero and I* (Dolphin/Oxford, 1956; New American Library, 1961).
Affil Univ of New Mexico.

ROBERTSON, EDWIN H 9 Porchester Gardens, London W2 4DB, UK *Tel* (01) 727 0979.
TL English. **SL** German. **UDC** communications, ethics/morals, history, philosophy, psychology, religion/scripture, telecommunications, theology.
German Dietrich Bonhoeffer: *Christ the Center; Christology* (Collins, 1977); *Selected Works* (Collins/Harper & Row, 1965–73). Paul Schneider: *The Pastor of Buchenwald* (SCM Pr, 1954). Jan Milič Lochman: *Encountering Marx* (Christian Journals, 1976). Also the works of Jan Christoph Hampe, Helmut Künneth, Ernst Lange, Helmuth Thielicke.
Memb TA.

ROCHE, PAUL The Stables, The Street, Aldermaston, Berkshire, UK *Tel* Woolhampton 3242.
TL English. **SL** Greek (Classical), Latin. **UDC** cooking, drama, film scripts, gardening, meditation, poetry.
Greek (Classical) Sophocles: *The Oedipus Plays* (New American Library, 1958). Aeschylus: *The Orestes Plays* (New American Library, 1962). Euripides: *Three Plays: Alcestis, Medea, The Bacchae* (Norton, 1974). **Latin** Plautus: *Three Plays: Amphitryon, Miles Gloriosus, Captivi* (New American Library, 1968).
Affil The Arvon Foundation. **Memb** TA.

RODRÍGUEZ, JEANNE M 1412 Los Padres Way, Sacramento, CA 95831 USA *Tel* 916-421-9065.
TL English. **SL** Spanish. **UDC** education, government, literature (prose), social welfare.

Affil State Dept of Social Services (translation of government documents, regulations, state planning designs).

RÖMER, KARL Rehweg 16, D4830 Gütersloh 11, West Germany *Tel* (05241) 77419.
TL German. **SL** English. **UDC** history, political science.
English Zbigniew K Brzezinski: *The Soviet Bloc* (Kiepenheuer & Witsch, 1962). Merle Fainsod: *How Russia Is Ruled* (Kiepenheuer & Witsch, 1965). J P Nettl: *Rosa Luxemburg* (Kiepenheuer & Witsch, 1967). Chalmers Johnson: *Revolutionary Change* (Kiepenheuer & Witsch, 1971). Also the works of M Brecher, R V Daniels, B B Fall, Henry A Kissinger, K von Klemperer, Leopold Labedz.
Affil Verlagsgruppe Bertelmann. **Memb** VDÜ.

ROMERO, HECTOR R 33129 Twickingham Dr, Sterling Heights, MI 48077 USA *Tel* 313-264-0504.
TL English. **SL** Spanish. **UDC** automotive, chemistry, literature (all areas).
Affil Wayne State Univ. **Memb** ATA.

ROMERO, ILSE W 605 W 113 St #81, New York, NY 10025 USA *Tel* 212-663-3923.
TL English, German. **SL** French. **UDC** art/art history, history, literature (all areas), philosophy, psychiatry, psychology, social sciences, sociology, theater.
Accred/Memb ATA.

ROODA, ANTOINETTE W M Sunsetlane, Martinsville, NJ 08836 USA *Tel* 201-356-5908.
TL English. **SL** Dutch, German. **UDC** art, business, ceramics, literature (children's, history, songs), medicine, patents/trademarks, sculpture.
Affil Rutgers Preparatory School (Somerset). **Memb** ATA.

ROOT, WAYNE Ctr for Japanese Social & Political Studies, 2-8-8 Nishinogawa, Komaeshi, Tokyo 201, Japan *Tel* (03) 489-2175.
TL English. **SL** Japanese. **UDC** political science, social science.
Affil *The Japan Interpreter.*

ROSACKER, HORST DIETER Bahnhofstr 32, D-8031 Eichenau, Germany *Tel* (08141) 70427.
TL German. **SL** English. **UDC** aesthetics, anthropology, archeology, architecture, art/art history, education, ethics/morals, logic, metaphysics, philosophy, psychiatry, psychology, social sciences, sociology.
English Hans Jürgen Eysenick: *The Inequality of Man* (Paul List, 1975). Calvin S Hall & Gardner Lindzey: *Theories of Personality* (C H Becksche, 1978–79).
Memb VDÜ/VS.

ROSE, MARILYN GADDIS 4 Johnson Ave, Binghamton, NY 13905 USA *Tel* 607-772-1634; 798-6763.
TL English. **SL** French, German, Spanish. **UDC** art history, ethics, history, linguistics, literature (history, prose), music history, painting, philosophy, theater.
French Villiers de l'Isle-Adam: *Axel* (Dol-

men, 1970). Also the works of Roger Ikor, Franco Tonelli, Aurielu Weiss.

Affil SUNY at Binghamton (chairperson, translation program). **Memb** ATA.

ROSENBERG, JAMES L Drama, Carnegie-Mellon Univ, Pittsburgh, PA 15213 USA *Tel* 412-578-2404.

TL English. **SL** English (Middle), French, German. **UDC** literature (drama, poetry, prose).

English (Middle) Anon: *Sir Gawain and the Green Knight* (Rinehart, 1959). **French** Molière: *Tartuffe* (Chandler, 1962). **German** Max Frisch: *The Chinese Wall* (Hill & Wang, 1961); *Three Plays* (Hill & Wang, 1964). Also the works of Tankred Dorst, Günter Grass, George Trakl.

ROSENFELD, MAX 322 E Wadsworth Ave, Philadelphia, PA 19119 USA *Tel* 215-242-2870.

TL English. **SL** Yiddish. **UDC** literature (drama, poetry, prose).

Yiddish Sholem Shtern: *The White House* (Warbrooke, 1974). *Pushcarts and Dreamers,* an anthology (Yoseloff, 1969). Hayim Sloves: *Haman's Downfall* (Fairleigh Dickinson Univ, 1975). Shmuel Eisenstadt: *The Prophets* (Yiddisher Kultur Farband, 1971). Also the works of Sholem Aleichem, Sholem Asch, Yehuda Elberg, Leon Korbin, Peretz Markish, Moishe Nadir, Isaac Raboi, Abraham Reisen, Morris Rosenfeld, David Seltzer, others.

ROUILLER, ANNA GLORIA F 429 Third Ave SW, Glen Burnie, MD 21061 USA *Tel* 301-768-1568.

TL English. **SL** Italian. **UDC** literature. **Memb** ATA.

ROYALL-MANACH, COLETTE Y 4210 Tideland Dr, Bridgeton, MO 63044 USA *Tel* 314-739-5835.

TL & SL English & French. **UDC** art/art history, biology, education, geography, history, jurisprudence, law, linguistics, literature (criticism, history, poetry, prose), patents/trademarks, philosophy, recreation, religion, sociology.

Affil Pacific High School. **Memb** ATA.

ROZENBAUM, WLODZIMIERZ Liberal Arts, Clark College, 1840 N Meridian, Indianapolis, IN 46202 USA *Tel* 317-923-3933.

TL & SL English & Polish. **UDC** political science, social sciences.

English scientific translations for the Central Inst for Scientific, Technical, and Economic Information, Warsaw.

Affil Amer Assn for the Advancement of Slavic Studies.

RUDOLF, ANTHONY 23 Fitzwarren Gardens, London N19 3TR, UK.

TL English. **SL** French, Hungarian, Russian. **UDC** literature (all areas).

French Yves Bonnefoy: *Selected Poems* (Jonathan Cape/Grossmans, 1969). **Hungarian** Eugene Heimler: *The Storm* (Menard, 1976). **Russian** Alexander Tvardovsky: *Tyorkin and the Stovemakers* (Carcanet, 1974). Yevgenii Vinokurov: *The War Is Over: Selected Poems*

(Carcanet, 1976). Also the works of Françoise Basch, Edmond Jabes, Ana Novac, Petru Popescu, others.

RUKEYSER, MURIEL c/o Monica McCall, ICM, 40 W 57 St, New York, NY 10019 USA *Tel* 212-691-4870.

TL English. **SL** French, German, Spanish, Swedish. **UDC** literature (poetry, prose).

German Bertolt Brecht: *Uncle Eddie's Moustache* (Pantheon, 1975); *Poems 1913–1956* (Methuen, 1976). **Spanish** Octavio Paz: *Selected Poems* (Indiana Univ, 1963); *Sun Stone* (New Directions). **Swedish** Gunnar Ekelöf: *Selected Poetry* (Twayne, 1967).

SAKURAI, EMIKO 3027 Pualei Circle #212, Honolulu, HI USA 96815 *Tel* 808-922-4861.

TL & SL English & Japanese. **UDC** literature (criticism, drama, history, poetry, prose).

Memb Japanese-English Interpreters & Translators Assn, Univ of Hawaii.

SALAZAR, PAULA S 112 Lugar de Oro, Santa Fe, NM 87501 USA *Tel* 505-983-3190.

TL Spanish. **SL** English. **UDC** commerce, economics, education, history, literature (children's, history, prose, science fiction), political science.

Accred Monterey Inst of Foreign Studies. **Memb** Concordiat.

SALEMSON, HAROLD J 12 Brookdale Rd, Glen Cove, NY 11542 USA *Tel* 516-676-2894.

TL English. **SL** French. **UDC** art, communications, copyright, film, history, literature (French), Marxism, political science, printing, social sciences, telecommunications.

French Pierre Cabanne: *Pablo Picasso, His Life and Times* (William Morrow, 1977). Henri Guillemin: *Joan, Maid of Orléans* (Saturday Review Pr, 1973). Serge Groussard: *The Blood of Israel* (William Morrow, 1975). André Parinaud: *The Unspeakable Confessions of Salvador Dali* (William Morrow/Allen, 1976). Also the works of Michel Bataille, Jacques Bergier, Roger Bourgeon, Catherine Breillat, Ricciotto Canudo, Jean Cocteau, Frederico Fellini, Henri Fesquet, Maurice Ghnassia, Jean Giraudoux, Jacques Graven, Henri Jeanson, Roger Peyrefitte, Jean Renoir, Jules Romains, Philippe Soupault, Jules Verne, Roger Vitrac.

SALINGER, HERMAN 3444 Rugby Rd, Durham, NC 27707 USA *Tel* 919-489-5140.

TL English. **SL** French, German. **UDC** literature (criticism, poetry, prose).

French the works of Francis Jammes, Charles d'Orleans, Marcel Proust, Paul Valéry, Paul Verlaine. **German** Heinrich Heine: *Germany: A Winter's Tale* (Fischer, 1944). Rudolf Hagelstange: *Ballad of the Buried Life* (Univ of N Carolina, 1962–63). *Twentieth-Century German Verse: A Selection* (Princeton Univ, 1952). Karl Krolow: *Poems Against Death* (Charioteer, 1969). Also the works of Erich Fitzbauer, Hermann Hesse, Hans Egon Holhusen, Kurt Loop, Rainer Maria Rilke, Nelly Sachs, Georg Trakl, J W von Goethe, August von Platen, Wolfgang Weyrauch, numerous others.

Affil Duke Univ.

SALWAY, LANCE 4 Westbridge Park, Sherborne, Dorset DT9 6AW, UK *Tel* (093 581) 4853.

TL English. **SL** Afrikaans, Dutch. **UDC** literature (children's).

Dutch Annie M G Schmidt: *The Island of Nose* (Methuen, 1977). Gertie Evenhuis: *What About Me?* (Kestrel, 1974); *The School at Schellebelle* (Kestrel, 1975). Johan Fabricius: *The Devil in the Tower: Seven Diabolical Tales* (Longman Young Books, 1973). Also the works of Margriet Heymans, Paul Hulshof.

Memb TA.

SAMELSON, WILLIAM Languages, San Antonio College, San Antonio, TX 78284 USA *Tel* 512-734-7311.

TL English. **SL** French, German, Polish, Spanish. **UDC** history, literature (drama, folklore, history, poetry, prose), political science.

Accred Univ of Heidelberg. **Memb** ATA.

SAMPAIO, ADOVALDO FERNANDES Rua Joaquim Antônio Teixeira 63, Pires do Rio-Goiás, Brazil *Tel* 490.

TL & SL English, Portuguese, Spanish. **UDC** communications, linguistics/philology, literature (poetry).

Portuguese A F Sampaio: *Time of Brazilian Poetry* (Bloom Press, 1977). Lupe Cotrim Garaude, Cecilia Meireles, Bruna Lombardi, Marly de Oliveira: *Four Brazilian Women Who Make Poetry* (Poets & Poetry, 1975). Also the works of numerous Portuguese and Spanish writers and poets.

SANDBACH, MARY 2 Hedgerley Close, Cambridge CB3 0EW, UK *Tel* (0223) 53152.

TL English. **SL** Swedish. **UDC** literature (children's, drama, prose).

Swedish August Strindberg: *Inferno* (Hutchinson, 1962); *Getting Married* (Gollancz, 1972). Eyvind Johnson: *1914* (Adam, 1970). Per Olof Sundman: *The Flight of the Eagle* (Secker & Warburg, 1970). Also the works of Ingmar Bergman (films), Sven Fagerberg, Ingemar Fjell, Henrik Tikkanen, Viola Wahlstedt.

Memb TA.

SANDSTROEM, YVONNE L English, Southeastern Massachusetts Univ, North Dartmouth, MA 02747 USA *Tel* 401-272-2638.

TL English. **SL** Danish, Norwegian, Swedish. **UDC** literature (all areas), psychology, religion.

Swedish Lars Gustafsson: *Warm Rooms and Cold* (Copper Beech Pr, 1975). Augustin Mannerheim: *Rounded with a Sleep* (Patmos Press, 1978). Also the works of Bengt Anderson-Kent Bratt, Werner Aspenström, Gunnar Ekelöf, Harry Martinsson, Kjell Sundberg, Tomas Tranströmer, Karl Vennberg.

Memb ALTA.

SAUMONT, ANNIE 9 villa St Georges, F-92160 Antony, France *Tel* (1) 666 10 95.

TL French. **SL** English, Spanish. **UDC** literature (drama, poetry, prose).

English Pearl S Buck: *Mrs Stoner and the Sea* (Pierre Belfond, 1978). John Fowles: *The Magus* (Albin Michel, 1977); *The Ebony Tower* (Albin Michel, 1978). Robert Silveberg: *The*

Gate of Worlds (Robert Laffont, 1977). Also the works of Anthony Burgess, Edna O'Brien. **Accred** ESIT. **Memb** ATLF.

SAVORY, TÉO PO Box 309, West Stockbridge, MA 01266 USA.
TL English. **SL** French, German, Latin, Spanish. **UDC** literature (poetry, prose).
French Guillevic: *Selected Poems* (Penguin, 1974). **German** Günter Eich: *Selected Poems* (Unicorn, 1971). Horst Bienek: *The Cell* (Unicorn, 1972). Also the works of Hans (Jean) Arp, Aloysius Bertrand, B Brecht, Tristan Corbière, Pablo Antonio Cuadra, Paul Eluard, García Lorca, Katrina v Hutten, Francis Jammes, numerous others.
Affil Unicorn Pr (ed). **Memb** ALTA.

SAX, BORIA 137 W Winspear, Buffalo, NY 14214 USA *Tel* 716-837-7224.
TL English. **SL** German. **UDC** literature (all areas), painting, religion/scripture.
Affil SUNY at Buffalo, *Terra Poetica* (ed). **Memb** ALTA.

SAYERS, RAYMOND S 2018 Madison St, Madison, WI 53711 USA *Tel* 608-257-7999.
TL English. **SL** Portuguese, Spanish. **UDC** literature (history, poetry, prose), social sciences.
Portuguese *The Poetry of Cecilia Meireles* (Brazilian Cultural Soc, 1977). Also the works of Lino Novás Calvo, Jorge de Sena.
Affil Queens College of CUNY (emeritus).

SCAMMELL, MICHAEL Clemath Cottage, St John's Rd, Woking, Surrey, UK *Tel* (04862) 65260.
TL English. **SL** Russian, Serbo-Croatian. **UDC** literature (drama, poetry, prose).
Russian Fyodor Dostoyevsky: *Crime and Punishment* (Pocket Books, 1963). Leo Tolstoy: *Childhood, Boyhood, and Youth* (McGraw-Hill, 1964). Vladimir Nabokov: *The Gift* (Putnam, 1963). Anatoly Marchenko: *My Testimony* (Dutton, 1965). Also the works of Isaac Babel, Vladimir Bukovsky, Konstantin Fedin, Julian Semyonov, Alexander Solzhenitsyn, Valery Tarsis.
Memb TA.

SCHADE, DOROTHY ANN Tintoretto Str 4/II, D-8000 Munich 19, West Germany *Tel* (089) 178 1976.
TL German. **SL** English, French. **UDC** archeology, art/art history, ecology, horticulture, literature (children's, prose).
English Peter Dobereiner: *Stroke, Hole, or Match* (Kless-Böker, 1977). Also translations for German Agency for Technical Cooperation, Deutscher Kunstverlag Munich.
Accred Univ of Geneva (translator's diploma). **Memb** AIT, BDÜ.

SCHEER, LINDA 242 Garfield Pl, Brooklyn, NY 11215 USA *Tel* 212-965-3513.
TL English. **SL** Spanish. **UDC** literature (poetry, prose).
Spanish Carlos Isla, Robert Bonazzi, C W Truesdale: *Domingo*, bilingual edition (Latitudes, 1974). Also the works of Juan José Arreola, José Carlos Becerra, Marco Antonio Campos, Marvin Cohen, Salvador Elizondo,

Miguel Flores Ramírez, Ulalume González de León, numerous others.
Memb ALTA.

SCHMIDT, HENRY J German, Ohio State Univ, 1841 Millikin Rd, Columbus, OH 43210 USA *Tel* 614-422-8639.
TL English. **SL** German. **UDC** literature, theater.
German Georg Büchner: *Woyzeck* (Avon, 1969); *Danton's Death* (Avon, 1971); *The Complete Collected Works* (Avon, 1977).
Memb ALTA.

SCHMITZ, SIEGFRIED Wettersteinstr 8, D-8031 Puchheim, West Germany *Tel* (089) 802362.
TL German. **SL** English. **UDC** biology, literature (children's, poetry, prose), zoology.
English Theodore Besterman: *Voltaire* (Winkler, 1971). Howard Loxton: *Elsevier's Guide to the Cats of the World* (BLV, 1976). Lionel Tiger & Robin Fox: *The Imperial Animal* (Bertelsmann, 1973). Oscar Wilde: *Complete Dramatic Works* (Winkler, 1971). Also the works of S Berggren, B Bova, E Bowen, Byron, R Davies, Charles Dickens, E Dudley, Nathaniel Hawthorne, Edgar Allan Poe, L Sterne, B Stonehouse, numerous others.
Memb VDÜ.

SCHNEEWIND, ELIZABETH HUGHES 234 Berkeley Pl, Brooklyn, NY 11217 USA *Tel* 212-857-1729.
TL English. **SL** German. **UDC** philosophy, social services, sociology.
German Franz Brentano: *The Origin of Our Knowledge of Right and Wrong* (Routledge & Kegan Paul, 1969); *The Foundation and Construction of Ethics* (Routledge & Kegan Paul, 1973). Hans Reichenbach: *Selected Writings*, 2 vols (Reidel, forthcoming). Viktor Kraft: *Foundations for a Scientific Analysis of Value* (Reidel, forthcoming).
Accred ATA. **Memb** ATA, TA.

SCHNEIDER, LOUISE E 1850 Taft Ave #8, Los Angeles, CA 90028 USA *Tel* 213-467-2333.
TL German. **SL** English. **UDC** art/art history, history, law, literature (all areas), medicine, theater.

SCHOENMAN, HELEN BENEDEK & THEODORE 2000 El Camino de la Luz, Santa Barbara, CA 93109 USA *Tel* 805-962-4643.
TL English. **SL** German, Hungarian. **UDC** history, literature (children's, folklore).
Hungarian János Xantus: *Letters from North America* (Wayne State Univ, 1975); *Travels in Southern California* (Wayne State Univ, 1976). Farkas Bölöni Sándor: *Journey in North America* (Amer Philosophical Soc, 1977). György Gaal: *Hungarian Folktales* (Urizen, 1978). Also the works of Agoston Haraszthy, Kálmán Mikszáth, Jenö Tersánszky.

SCHRAPS-POELCHAU, MARIA Klostertieg 20, D-2000 Hamburg 13, West Germany *Tel* (040) 44 92 45.
TL German. **SL** English. **UDC** art history, horses/riding, psychoanalysis.
English Diana Hirsch: *The World of Turner*

1775–1851 (Time/Life International, 1973). Fosco Moraini: *Tokyo* (Time/Life International, 1976). Robert J Stoller: *Perversion: The Erotic Form of Hatred* (Rowohlt, 1979). Yigael Yadin: *Hazor: The Rediscovery of a Great Citadel of the Bible* (Hoffmann & Camp, 1976). Also the works of Peter S Feibleman, John R Hale, William Harlan Hale, Robert Owen & John Bullock, Theodore Rowland-Entwistle.
Memb BDÜ.

SCHULMAN, GRACE One University Place, New York, NY 10003 USA *Tel* 212-533-0235.
TL English. **SL** Spanish. **UDC** literature (poetry).
Spanish the works of Julia de Burgos and Pablo Antonio Cuadra in *The Nation,* and *The Hudson Review.*
Affil *The Nation* (poetry ed).

SCHULTE, RAINER Univ of Texas at Dallas, Box 688, Richardson, TX 75080 USA *Tel* 214-690-2092.
TL English. **SL** French, German, Spanish. **UDC** literature (drama, poetry, prose).
French, German, Spanish the works of Gottfried Benn, Heinrich Böll, Ivan Goll, Roberto Juarroz, Karl Krolow, Juan Liscano, Ramon Palomares, Jules Supervielle. **Author of** "Literary Translation in the West: A Struggle for Recognition" (*World Literature Today,* Spring, 1978); "Bringing a New Focus to Literary Translation" (*Translation Review,* 1, 1978).
Affil Translation Ctr, Univ of Texas (dir), *Translation Review* (ed), *Mundus Artium* (ed). **Memb** ALTA (co-founder).

SCHÜRENBERG, WALTER Hasselfelder Weg 2, D-1000 Berlin 45, West Germany *Tel* (030) 772 11 74.
TL German. **SL** English, French. **UDC** literature (criticism, prose).
English E M Forster: *Aspects of the Novel* (Suhrkamp, 1949). Joseph Conrad: *Victory* (S Fischer, 1963). F Scott Fitzgerald: *The Great Gatsby* (Lothar Blanvalet, 1953). John Fowles: *The Magus* (Ullstein, 1969). Also the works of Carlo Coccioli, Lawrence Durrell, Rose Macaulay, Patrick Modiano, Frank Norris, Jean Schlumberger, Charles Wertenbaker, Duke of Windsor.
Memb VDÜ.

SCHWEIER, JÜRGEN Hugo-Wolf-Weg 5, D-7312 Kircheim/Teck, West Germany *Tel* (07021) 2804.
TL German. **SL** English. **UDC** literature (folklore, poetry, science fiction).
English Peter S Beagle: *The Last Unicorn* (Klett, 1976). Frederick S Perls: *In & Out of the Garbage Pail* (Klett, 1979). Evangeline Walton: *The Four Branches of the Mabinogion* (Klett, 1979). Sinclair Lewis: *The Post-Mortem Murder* (Wunderlich, 1977).
Memb VS.

SCOTT, JOHN ANTHONY 3902 Manhattan College Pkwy, Bronx, NY 10471 USA *Tel* 212-548-1464.
TL English. **SL** French. **UDC** history, law, literature (poetry), political science.
French François Noël Babeuf: *Defense of*

Gracchus Babeuf Before the High Court of Vendôme (Gehenna, 1964; Univ of Massachusetts, 1967).
Affil Rutgers Univ.

SEBASTIANI, NANCY A 3600 Montrose #1009, Houston, TX 77006 USA *Tel* 713-529-7146.
TL & SL English & Spanish. **UDC** art, athletics, ecology, education, ethics, history, linguistics/philology, literature (all areas), painting, political science, printing, recreation, sociology, sports, theater.
Spanish Rafael Catala: *Roads* (Las Américas, 1973). Emilio Díaz-Valcárce: *Schemes in the Month of March* (Bilingual, 1979).
Affil Univ of Houston. **Memb** ALTA.

SEBBA, HELEN 1088 Lullwater Rd, Atlanta, GA 30307 USA *Tel* 404-378-2041.
TL English. **SL** French, German. **UDC** art history, literature (criticism, poetry), sociology.
French Roger Bastide: *The African Religions of Brazil* (Johns Hopkins Univ, 1978). **German** Wilhelm Fraenger: *Hieronymus Bosch* (Putnam, forthcoming). Heinz Lippmann: *Honecker and the New Politics* (Macmillan, 1972). Käte Hamburger: *From Sophocles to Sartre* (Ungar, 1969). Also the works of Karl Bednarik, Bodo Cichy, Sabine Cotté, Jean Cuisenier, Horst Frenz, Klaus Gallwitz, Nahum Goldmann, H E Holthusen, G Jean-Aubry, Hans Georg Meyer, Leo Pollmann, numerous others.
Affil Language Bank, Atlanta Council for International Visitors (dir). **Memb** AAIT.

SEESLEN, UTE Herzogstr 40, D-8000 Munich, West Germany *Tel* (089) 139 6482.
TL German. **SL** English. **UDC** anthropology, education, literature (prose, science fiction), psychology, sociology.
English Agatha Christie: *Curtain* (Scherz, 1976). Ann F Neel: *Theories of Psychology: A Handbook* (Kindler, 1974). Carl R Rogers: *Therapist and Client* (Kindler, 1977). Arthur G Nikelly: *Techniques for Behavior Change* (Kindler, 1978). Also the works of Poul Anderson, Anthony Burgess, D MacKenzie, Patricia Moyes, Theodore Sturgeon, others.
Memb VS.

SEIDENSTICKER, EDWARD 407 Kent Hall, Columbia Univ, New York, NY 10027 USA *Tel* 212-280-2589.
TL English. **SL** Japanese. **UDC** literature (Japanese prose).
Japanese Murasaki Shikibu: *The Tale of Genji* (Knopf). Kawabata Yasunari: *Snow Country* (Knopf, 1956); *The Sound of the Mountain* (Knopf, 1970). Tanizaki Junichiro: *The Makiuki Sisters* (Knopf, 1957). Also numerous others.
Awards 1970 National Book Award in Translation.

SEILER, CHRISTIANE I 2927 Westbrook Dr #6/320, Fort Wayne, IN USA *Tel* 219-484-7098.
TL English. **SL** German. **UDC** literature (lyrics, poetry, prose), music, painting, technical texts, theater.
German the works of Michael Guttenbrun-

ner, G W Hegel, H C Hölty, Wolfgang Koeppen, Ilse Fischer-Reitböck, Hannelies Taschau in *Zeitschrift für Deutsch-amerikanische Literatur* (Cincinnati) and *Dimension* (Univ of Texas).
Affil Indiana Univ; Purdue Univ (Fort Wayne). **Memb** ALTA.

SELIGMAN, JANET 19 Oakhill Rd, Putney, London SW15, UK *Tel* (01) 874 8400.
TL English. **SL** French, German. **UDC** architecture, art, arts/crafts, arts of the book, engraving/prints, painting, sculpture.
French Jean Boisselier: *Thai Painting* (Kodansha, 1976). **German** Gertrud Schiller: *Iconography of Christian Art*, 2 vols (Lund Humphries/Graphic Soc, 1971–72). Hans Jürgen Hansen, ed: *Architecture in Wood* (Faber & Faber, 1971). Ann Berendsen, ed: *Tiles: A General History* (Faber & Faber, 1967). Also the works of H Brunner, Theo van Doesburg, W Eichhorn, Werner Hoffmann, Hermann Mathesius, Laszlo Moholy-Nagy, G Weiss, numerous articles by French and German art historians in *The Burlington Magazine*.
Memb TA, TG.

SELLNER, TIMOTHY FREDERICK PO Box 7353, Reynolda Sta, Winston-Salem, NC 27109 USA *Tel* 919-761-5362.
TL English. **SL** German. **UDC** literature (prose), philosophy, sociology.
German three articles in *Studies in Nietzsche and the Classical Tradition* (Univ of N Carolina, 1976). Theodor Gottlieb von Hippel: *On Improving the Status of Women* (Wayne State Univ, 1978). Also the works of Max L Baeumer, Karl Schlechta, Hedwig Wingler.
Affil Wake Forest Univ.

SEMAAN, K I SUNY at Binghamton, NY 13901 USA *Tel* 798-2000.
TL & SL Arabic & English. **UDC** biography, history, linguistics, literature (poetry, prose), religion.
Arabic Salah Abd- al-Sabur: *Murder in Bagdad* (Leiden: Brill, 1972). **English** Burnham: *The Coming Defeat of Communism* (Dahran, 1956–57). Eastman: *The Failure of Socialism*, co-translated with Edward Kalian (Dahran, 1956–57). Also numerous other works.

SEYMOUR, MENTON 2641 Basswood St, Newport Beach, CA 92660 USA *Tel* 714-644-1021.
TL English. **SL** Spanish. **UDC** literature (prose).
Affil Univ of California (Irvine).

SHAHNAZARIAN, GEORGE 111-45 76 Ave #41B, Forest Hills, NY 11375 USA *Tel* 212-544-3674.
TL English. **SL** Persian (Farsi). **UDC** anthropology, banking/finance, commerce, economics, education, ethics, ethnography, food/nutrition, geography, government, history, literature (all areas), philosophy, political economy/science, religion, theology.
Memb ALTA, ATA, SFL.

SHAPIRO, NORMAN R 214 High St, Middletown, CT 06457 USA *Tel* 203-344-0059; 347-9411.

TL English. **SL** French. **UDC** literature (all areas).
French Georges Feydeau: *Four Farces* (Univ of Chicago, 1970). *Negritude: Black Poetry from Africa and the Caribbean,* anthology (October House, 1970). Anne Hébert: *Kamouraska* (Crown, 1973). Jean Raspail: *The Camp of the Saints* (Scribners, 1975). Also the works of Allais, Alphonse, Robert de Blois, Léon Damas, René Depestre, David Diop, Malick Fall, Marie de France, Jean Froissart, Léon Laleau, Guilaume de Machaut, Joseph Majault, Colin Muset, Charles d'Orléans, Léopold Sédar Senghor, Guy Tirolien, others.
Affil Wesleyan Univ. **Awards** 1967–68 National Translation Ctr grant.

SHARMA, ARVIND Univ of Queensland, Brisbane, Australia 4067 *Tel* 377-3010.
TL English. **SL** Hindi, Sanskrit. **UDC** religion/scripture.
Sanskrit Abhinavagupta: "Commentary on the Bhagavad Gītā" (PhD diss).

SHATTUCK, ROGER French, Univ of Virginia, Charlottesville, VA 22903 USA *Tel* 804-924-7157.
TL English. **SL** French. **UDC** literature (all areas), painting.
French Apollinaire: *Selected Writings* (New Directions, 1949). René Daumal: *Mount Analogue* (Pantheon, 1959; Penguin, 1973). Alfred Jarry: *Works,* co-translated with Simon W Taylor (Grove, 1964). Paul Valéry: *Occasions,* co-translated with Frederick Brown (Bollingen/Princeton Univ, 1970). Also the co-editor with William Arrowsmith of *The Craft and Context of Translation* (see Sec 6, Books).

SHAW, GISELA KLARA 57 Westbury Rd, Bristol BS9 3AS, UK *Tel* (0272) 62 95 78.
TL German. **SL** English. **UDC** philosophy.
English K T Fann: *Wittgenstein's Conception of Philosophy* (List, 1971). Stephan Körner: *What Is Philosophy?* (List, 1970). Noel Minnis, ed: *Linguistics at Large* (List, 1974). Hans S Reiss: *Kant's Political Thought* (Peter Lang, 1977).
Affil Bristol Polytechnic. **Memb** VS.

SHELDON, RICHARD Russian, Dartmouth College, Hanover, NH 03755 USA *Tel* 603-646-3404.
TL English. **SL** Russian. **UDC** literature (prose).
Russian Viktor B Shklovsky: *A Sentimental Journey* (Cornell Univ, 1970); *Zoo or Letters Not About Love* (Cornell Univ, 1971); *Third Factory* (Ardis, 1977).

SHEPLEY, JOHN 308 E 90 St, New York, NY 10028 USA *Tel* 212-831-0716.
TL English. **SL** French, Italian. **UDC** arts, history, literature (poetry, prose), psychology, social sciences.
Italian Mario Bussagli et al: *Oriental Architecture* (Abrams, 1975). Oriana Fallaci: *Letter to a Child Never Born* (Simon & Schuster, 1977); *Interview with History* (Liveright, 1976). Guido Piovene: *In Search of Europe* (St Martin's, 1975). Also the works of Umbro Apollonio, Giuseppe De Logu, Indro Montanelli, Franco Russoli, Emilio Servadio, Tiziano Terzani, Lorenza Trucchi.

SHEVRIN, ALIZA 2021 Vinewood, Ann Arbor, MI 48104 USA *Tel* 313-769-6343.
TL English. SL Yiddish. UDC literature (all areas).
Yiddish Isaac Bashevis Singer: *Enemies: A Love Story* (Farrar, Straus & Giroux, 1972). "The Letter Writer" (*The Seance,* Farrar, Straus & Giroux, 1968). Sholem Aleichem: *8 Children's Stories* (Scribner, forthcoming).

SHIRLEY, JANET 2A Gotham Lawn Rd, Bristol BS6 6DU, UK *Tel* (0272) 30815.
TL English. SL French, French (Old). UDC education, history, literature (criticism), religion.
French Guernes de Pont-Ste-Mayence: *Garnier's Becket* (Phillimore, 1975). Jean Richard: *The Latin Kingdom of Jerusalem* (North-Holland, 1978). **French (Old)** Anon: *A Parisian Journal, 1405-1449* (Clarendon, 1968).
Memb TA.

SHORE, MICHAEL 63A Maple Tree Ave, Stamford, CT 06906 USA *Tel* 203-324-0799; 212-285-7178.
TL English. SL French, Spanish. UDC art/art history, astrology, banking/finance, business, education, literature (drama, poetry, prose), occultism, theater, witchcraft.
French the works of Charles Baudelaire, Albert Camus, Jean Giraudoux, Marcel Proust, Antoine de Saint-Exupery.

SHUB, ELIZABETH 185 West End Ave, New York, NY 10023 USA *Tel* 212-724-2135.
TL English. SL German, Yiddish. UDC literature (children's, folklore).
German The Brothers Grimm: *Of Wise Men and Simpletons, Twelve Tales* (Macmillan, 1971). Theodor Fontane: *Sir Ribbeck of Ribbeck of Havelland* (Macmillan, 1969). Wilhelm Hauff: *The Adventures of Little Mouk* (Macmillan, 1974). **Yiddish** Isaac Bashevis Singer: *Zlateh, the Goat, and Other Stories* (Harper & Row, 1966). Also the works of Sholem Aleichem, Antonella Bolliger-Savelli, Achim Bröger, Ursula Konopka, Gerlinne Schneider.

SIDDAL, ABIGAIL T (Mrs W R) 1616 Beechwood Terr, Manhattan, KS 66502 USA *Tel* 913-539-1660.
TL English. SL French. UDC archeology, aviation, history, literature (criticism, drama, prose), music, sciences (natural), theater.
French André Corvisier: *Armies and Societies in Europe, 1494-1789* (Indiana Univ, 1978).

SIMMERMANN, ULF 206 E Second St, Northfield, MN 55057 USA *Tel* 507-645-8909.
TL English. SL German. UDC literature (criticism, prose).
German Theodor Fontane: *Jenny Treibel* (Ungar, 1976). Also the works of Walter Benjamin, Herman Lins.
Memb ALTA.

SIMMS, RUTH L C 102 N Sterling Blvd, Sterling, VA 22170 USA *Tel* 703-430-1570.
TL English. SL Spanish. UDC aesthetics, agriculture, architecture, art, education, ethics, history, human resources, library science, literature (all areas), occultism, painting, philosophy, public health, recreation, religion, sociology, theology.
Spanish Jorge Luis Borges: *Other Inquisitions 1937-1952* (Univ of Texas, 1964). Elena Garro: *Recollections of Things to Come* (Univ of Texas, 1969). José Clemente Orozco: *The Artist in New York* (Univ of Texas, 1974). Octavio Paz: *The Bow and the Lyre* (Univ of Texas, 1973). Also the works of Adolfo Bioy Casares.

SIMPSON, MICHAEL Bard College, Annandale-on-Hudson, NY 12504 USA *Tel* 914-758-6822, 5297.
TL English. SL Greek (Classical), Latin. UDC languages and literatures (Classical).
Greek (Classical) Apollodorus: *Gods and Heroes of the Greeks: The Library of Apollodorus* (Univ of Massachusetts, 1976).

SINGLETON, CHARLES S Princeton Univ Pr, Princeton, NJ 08540 USA.
TL English. SL Italian. UDC literature.
Italian Dante Alighieri: *The Divine Comedy: Inferno, Purgatorio, Paradiso,* 6 vols (Princeton Univ).

SISSON, C H Moorfield Cottage, The Hill, Langport, Somerset TA10 9PU, UK *Tel* (STD 0458) 250 845.
TL English. SL French, Italian, Latin. UDC literature (poetry).
Italian Dante: *The Divine Comedy* (Carcanet, 1979). **Latin** Catullus: *Poetry* (MacGibbon & Kee, 1966; Viking, 1969). Lucretius: *The Poem on Nature* (Carcanet, 1976). Horace: *The Poetic Art* (Carcanet, 1975).

SITA, JOHN B 3204 PO Box, Univ Sta, Moscow, ID 83843 USA *Tel* 208-882-0439; 885-7312.
TL English. SL Croatian, French, Italian, Russian, Spanish. UDC archeology, art, engraving/prints, entomology, ethics, ethnography, linguistics/philology, literature (all areas), religion.
Croatian Nevjestic et al: *Active Immunization in the Prophylaxis of Enzootic Abortion of the Ovines* (Univ of Idaho, 1973). **Russian** Spasskiy et al: *Helminths of the Pikas of the Pre-Baikal,* collection of articles (Univ of Idaho, 1970-71).
Affil Univ of Idaho (Langs & Lits). **Memb** ATA.

SJÖBERG, LEIF T 15 Claremont Ave, New York, NY 10027 USA *Tel* 212-662-2531.
TL English. SL Danish, Norwegian, Swedish. UDC aesthetics, architecture, art, literature (criticism, poetry, prose).
Swedish Gunnar Ekelöf: *Selected Poems,* co-translated with W H Auden (Penguin/Pantheon, 1971-72). Pär Lagerkvist: *Evening Land,* co-translated with W H Auden (Wayne State Univ/Souvenir, 1975-76). Tomas Tranströmer: *Windows and Stones,* co-translated with May Swenson (Pittsburgh Univ, 1973). Artur Lundkvist: *Agadir,* co-translated with William Jay Smith (International Poetry Forum/Ohio Univ, 1978). Also the works of Aspenström, Edfelt, Hammarskjold, Hillbäck, Lindegren, Strindberg, Vennberg.
Affil SUNY at Stony Brook.

SKELTON, GEOFFREY 49 Downside, Shoreham, Sussex BN4 6HF UK *Tel* (07917) 2985.
TL English. SL German. UDC literature (drama, librettos, prose), music, theater.
German Max Frisch: *Sketchbook, (1) 1946-49, (2) 1966-71* (Harcourt Brace Jovanovich, 1974, 1977). Robert Lucas: *Frieda Lawrence* (Secker & Warburg/Viking, 1973). Cosima Wagner: *The Diaries,* Vol 1: 1869-1877, Vol II: 1878-1883 (Harcourt Brace Jovanovich/Collins, 1978). Peter Weiss: *The Persecution and Assassination of Marat as Performed by the Inmates of the Asylum of Charenton under the Direction of the Marquis de Sade,* co-translated with Adrian Mitchell (John Calder/Atheneum, 1965). Also the works of Bertolt Brecht, Georg Britting, Erich Fried, Friedrich Heer, Günther Herburger, Ernst Krenek, Michael Meschke & György Ligeti, Johann Nestroy, Ferdinand Raimund, Theodor Storm, Richard Wagner, Wieland Wagner, others.
Memb TA. **Awards** 1966 PEN Translation Prize (with Adrian Mitchell), 1973 Schlegel-Tieck Prize.

SLAVOV, ATANAS VASILEV PO Box 4877, Washington, DC 20008 USA *Tel* 202-689-8876.
TL & SL Bulgarian & English. UDC literature (drama, lyrics, poetry, prose).
English Charles Dickens: *Bleak House* (Otechestven Front, 1959). Graham Greene: *Our Man in Havana* (Otechestven Front, 1960). Sean O'Casey: *I Knock at the Door* (Narodna Kultura, 1962). William Saroyan: *My Name Is Aram* (Narodna Mladezh, 1961). Also the works of Francis Beaumont, Robert Burns, Erskine Caldwell, Langston Hughes, Hugh McDiarmid, Carl Sandburg, Dylan Thomas, Walt Whitman, others. Also numerous articles and reviews on translations, translation theory and practice for leading Bulgarian literary periodicals.

SLOBIN, GRETA NACHTAILER 3 Brainerd Ave, Middleton, CT 06457 USA *Tel* 203-344-0649.
TL English. SL Polish, Russian. UDC arts, philology, literature (drama, poetry, prose), psychology.
English Tony Connor: "Journal of Bad Time," (*Życie Literackie,* 1975). **Russian** Viktor M Beliaev: *Central Asian Music* (Wesleyan Univ, 1975). Also the works of Vasilij Aksenov, A G Aslanov, A Bitov.
Affil Yale Univ.

SMALL, RICHARD B 1169 Yellowstone Rd, Cleveland Heights OH 44121 USA *Tel* 216-381-8490.
TL English. SL French. UDC commerce, economics, education, literature (criticism, history, prose), sociology.
Affil Cleveland State Univ. **Memb** ATA, NOTA.

SMITH, DAVID Wilhelminasingel 35, NL-Pijnacker, the Netherlands *Tel* (01736) 4601.
TL English. SL Dutch, German. UDC literature (prose), transportation.
Dutch Ward Ruyslinck: *Golden Ophelia* (Peter Owen, 1975); *The Reservation* (Peter Owen, 1978).

SMITH, DAVID CARLSON 249 Pine St, Philadelphia, PA 19106 USA *Tel* 215-922-1186.
TL English. SL Spanish. UDC literature (poetry, prose).
Spanish Cesár Vallejo: *Trilce* (Grossman-Mushinsha/Viking, 1973).

SMITH, DEBRA JEANNE United Nations #1223, New York, NY 10017 USA *Tel* 212-754-6705; 243-6623.
TL English. SL French, Russian. UDC art, education, history, literature (criticism, drama, folklore, history, lyrics, poetry, prose), music, political science, psychology, theater.
Russian N S Leskov: *The Cathedral Folk*, co-translated with Wm Edgerton (Indiana Univ, 1979).
Memb ATA.

SMITH, HENRY A Eikhof 18, D-2053 Fuhlenhagen, West Germany *Tel* (04156) 596.
TL English. SL German. UDC literature (poetry, prose).
German Gertrud Kolmar: *Dark Soliloquy* (Seabury, 1975). Ulrich Becher: *Woodchuck Hunt* (Crown, 1977).

SMITH, NORMAN DAVID 27 Constitution Hill, Norwich NR3 4HA, UK *Tel* (0603) 46424.
TL English. SL Dutch, French, German. UDC aesthetics, archeology, architecture, aviation, economics, linguistics, music, philosophy, sociology, theology.
Dutch A Kraal: *The Income Bond: An Undervalued Financial Instrument* (Univ of Leiden, 1977). Huub Oosterhuis: *Your Word Is Near* (Paulist Pr, 1968). **French** Roland de Vauz: *The Early History of Israel* (Darton, Longman & Todd, 1978). **German** Wolfgang Wickler: *The Biology of the Ten Commandments* (McGraw-Hill, 1972). Also the works of Robert Adolfs, Hans Ausenhammer, Ladislaus Boros, Paul Haschek, F J Heggen, Corinne van Moorselaar, numerous others.
Memb TA.

SMITH, WILLIAM JAY 1675 York Ave #20K, New York, NY 10028 USA *Tel* 212-860-2576.
TL English. SL French, Hungarian, Italian, Russian, Spanish, Swedish. UDC literature (children's, criticism, drama, lyrics, poetry, prose), theater.
French Jules Laforgue: *Selected Writings* (Greenwood, 1956; Grove, 1971). Valery Larbaud: *Poems of a Multimillionaire* (Bonacio & Saul/Grove, 1955). **Hungarian** Miklós Vajda, ed: *Modern Hungarian Poetry* (Columbia Univ, 1977). **Russian** Andrei Voznesensky, Vera Dunham & Max Hayward, eds: *Nostalgia for the Present* (Doubleday, 1978). Also the works of Louis Aragon, Charles Bertin, Roger Caillois, René Char, Kornei Chukovsky, Yvan Goll, Anna Hajnal, Lyula Illyés, Federico García Lorca, Artur Lundkvist, Adam Mickiewicz, Ottó Orbán, János Pilinszky, Pierre Reverdy, Pierre Seghers, József Tornai, Paul Valéry, István Vas, Sándor Weöres, Szbolcs Várady.
Affil Hollis College. **Memb** Columbia Univ Translation Ctr (Board of Dirs); *Translation* (ed). Awards 1978 Gold Medal of Labor, Presidential Council of Hungarian People's Republic (for translation of modern Hungarian poetry), 1978 NEH grant.

SOCEANU-VAMOS, MARA 2 King St #4A, New York NY 10012 USA *Tel* 212-242-4590.
TL English. SL French, Rumanian. UDC literature (criticism, drama, prose), philosophy.
French Brissot de Warville: *New Travels to the United States, 1788* (Harvard Univ, 1964). **Rumanian** Ecaterina Oproiu: "I Am Not the Eiffel Tower" (play).
Affil Fairleigh Dickinson Univ. **Memb** ALTA.

SOKOLINSKY, MARTIN 383 Pearl St, Brooklyn, NY 11201 USA *Tel* 212-855-2143.
TL English. SL French, German, Spanish. UDC literature (drama, history, prose).
French Joseph Joffe: *A Bag of Marbles* (Houghton Mifflin, 1974). Jacques Chessex: *A Father's Love* (Bobbs-Merrill, 1975). Roger Riou: *The Island of My Life* (Delacorte, 1975). Robert Merle: *The Virility Factor* (McGraw-Hill, 1977). Also the works of Bernard Gavoty, Caroline Gayet, Albert Kantof, Fred Kassak, Omar Sharif, Albert Spaggiari, Jacques Thiroloix.

SOLOMON, SAMUEL 51 Hollycroft Ave, London NW3 7QJ, UK *Tel* (01) 435 2866.
TL English. SL French, German. UDC literature (drama, lyrics, poetry, prose).
French Corneille: *Seven Plays* (Random House, 1969). Racine: *The Complete Plays* (Random House/Weidenfeld & Nicolson, 1968, 1969). **German** Franz Grillparzer: *Plays on Classic Themes* (Random House, 1970). Also the works of Charles Baudelaire, Heinrich Heine, Jose Maria de Heredia, Victor Hugo, Leconte de Lisle, Paul Verlaine, numerous others.
Memb TA.

SOLYN, PAUL 725 S Ford #3, McMinnville, OR 97128 USA *Tel* 503-472-1219, 4121.
TL English. SL German. UDC literature (poetry).
German the works of Jürgen Becker, Günter Eich, Ernst Jandl, Helga M Novak, Nelly Sachs, Annette von Droste-Hülshoff.
Affil Linfield College.

SOMMERSTEIN, ALAN HERBERT Classics, Univ of Nottingham, Nottingham, UK *Tel* (0602) 56101.
TL English. SL Greek (Classical). UDC linguistics, literature (drama).
Greek (Classical) Aristophanes: *Lysistrata and Other Plays* (Penguin, 1973); *The Birds and Other Plays*, co-translated with David Barrett (Penguin, 1978).

SONNENFELD, MARION 27 Carol Ave, Fredonia, NY 14063 USA *Tel* 716-673-1953.
TL English. SL German. UDC literature (drama, poetry, prose).
German Hebbel: *Three Plays* (Bucknell Univ, 1974). Kleist: *Amphitryon* (Ungar, 1962). C F Meyer: *Complete Narrative Prose* (Bucknell Univ, 1976). Also the works of Stefan Zweig.
Affil SUNY at Fredonia.

SORA, MARIANNE Mauerkircherstr 3 D-8000 Munich 80, West Germany *Tel* (4989) 980 181.
TL German. SL English, French, Rumanian. UDC literature (criticism, prose), philosophy.
Accred State Examination (Bucharest). **Memb** VDÜ, Writers Union of Rumania.

SOUSA, RONALD W Spanish & Portuguese, 4 Folwell Hall, Univ of Minnesota, Minneapolis, MN 55455 USA *Tel* 612-373-7998.
TL English. SL Portuguese. UDC economics, history, literature (criticism, history, lyrics, poetry, prose), sociology.

SPACKMAN, DENNIS M 109 Peterborough St #19, Boston, MA 02215 USA *Tel* 617-262-8641.
TL English. SL Japanese. UDC history, literature (criticism, history, lyrics, poetry, prose, science fiction), philosophy.
Japanese the works of Hagiwara Sakutarō, Muroo Saisei, Nakano Shigeharu, Kiyooka Takayuki in *International Poetry Review* (Asian Issue, Fall 1978).
Affil Harvard Univ. **Memb** ALTA.

SPIEGEL, MOSHE PO Box 1003, Philadelphia, PA 19105 USA.
TL English. SL Russian, Yiddish. UDC history (Jewish), literature (prose).
Russian Simon Dubnov: *History of the Jews*, 5 Vols (Yoseloff, 1967–73). **Yiddish** Itzhok Laibush Peretz: *In This World and the Next, A Reader* (Yoseloff, 1958). Mendele Mocher S'forim: *The Nag* (Beechhurst, 1955). Zalman Shneour: *Restless Spirit, A Reader* (Barnes, 1963). Also the works of Sholem Aleichem, Sholem Asch, Isaac Babel, David Bergelson, Ilya Ehrenburg, Maxim Gorky, Itzik Manger, K Paustovsky, numerous others.
Affil Inst for Jewish Research.

SPINGARN, LAWRENCE P c/o Perivale Pr, 13830 Erwin St, Van Nuys, CA 91401 USA *Tel* 213-785-4671.
TL English. SL Portuguese. UDC literature (poetry, prose).
Portuguese the works of Saul Dias, Gomes Leal, Camilo Pessanha, Fernando Pessôa, Mario Sa-Cerneiro, Cesario Verde.
Affil Los Angeles Valley College **Memb** ALTA.

SPINK, REGINALD 6 Deane Way, Eastcote, Ruislip, Middlesex HA4 8SU, UK *Tel* (01) 866-6899.
TL English. SL Danish, Norwegian, Swedish. UDC literature (children's, criticism, drama, folklore, history, prose).
Danish H C Andersen: *Fairy Tales and Stories* (Dent/Dutton, 1960). Ludvig Holberg: *Three Comedies* (Heinemann/Theater Arts, 1957). Carl Nielsen: *My Childhood* (Hutchinson/Wilhelm Hansen, 1953). **Swedish** Bengt Danielsson: *Gauguin in the South Seas* (Allen & Unwin/Doubleday, 1965).
Memb TA.

SPRICK, CLAUS G Waldsaum 6, D-4300 Essen, West Germany *Tel* (0)201 441819.
TL German. SL English, French. UDC law

(international), literature (prose), shortwave amateur radio & Citizens Band (CB).

English Graham T Allison et al: *Reader on Bureaucratic Politics* (Klett, 1979). John A Fairlie: *The Nature of Political Representation* (Wissenschaftliche Buchgesellschaft, 1968). Arthur L Corbin: *The Law and the Judges* (Wissenschaftliche Buchgesellschaft, 1979). Also the works of Daniel Boulanger, Dimitri S Constantopoulos, Morton H Halperin. **Memb** VDÜ.

STAFFORD, WILLIAM English, Lewis & Clark College, Portland, OR 97219 USA *Tel* 503-244-6161.

TL English. **SL** Spanish. **UDC** literature (poetry).

STANKOVIC, JUDITH A 9545 M Sylvan Still Rd, Laurel, MD 20810 USA.

TL English. **SL** French, Spanish. **UDC** literature (children's, prose).

French A M Besnard: *Your Name is Written in Heaven* (Dimension, 1978).

Accred ATA, St Mary-of-the-Woods College. **Memb** ATA.

STANLEY, PATRICIA HAAS 5660 Rustic Dr, Tallahassee, FL 32303 USA *Tel* 904-385-0840.

TL English. **SL** German. **UDC** literature (criticism, drama, prose).

German the works of Wolfgang Hildesheimer in *Dimension* and *Gargoyle*.

Affil Florida State Univ. **Memb** ALTA.

STARK, MILTON 1642 Ocean Ave, Santa Monica, CA 90401 USA *Tel* 213-395-9344.

TL English. **SL** Lithuanian. **UDC** literature (prose).

Lithuanian Liudas Dovydenas: *The Brothers Domeika* (Lithuanian Encyclopedia, 1976). Vincas Ramonas: *Crosses* (Lithuanian Days, 1953).

Memb ALTA.

STASI, SUSAN L 771 Pronto Dr, San Jose, CA 95123 USA *Tel* 408-226-8854.

TL English. **SL** Spanish. **UDC** literature (criticism).

Affil San Jose State Univ. **Memb** ATA (student).

STEFANILE, FELIX 103 Waldron St, West Lafayette, IN 47906 USA *Tel* 317-743-1991.

TL English. **SL** Italian. **UDC** literature (poetry).

Italian Umberto Saba: *31 Poems* (Elizabeth, 1978). Also the works of Govoni, Marinetti, Palazzeschi, others.

Affil Purdue Univ. **Memb** ALTA.

STEIN, MURRAY 342 Custer Ave, Evanston, IL 60202 USA *Tel* 312-869-9232.

TL English. **SL** German. **UDC** mythological studies, mythology, psychology (Jungian), religion (history), theology (comparative).

German Karl Kerényi: *Hermes: Guide of Souls* (Spring Pub, 1976); *Athene: Virgin and Mother in Greek Religion* (Spring Pub, 1978); *Daughters of Sun and Moon* (Spring Pub, 1979). Adolf Guggenbühl-Craig: *Marriage—*

Dead or Alive (Spring Pub, 1977). Also the works of Aniela Jaffe, Rivkah Kluger, Rene Malamud.

Memb ALTA.

STEVENS, JOAN 42 Wensleydale Rd, Hampton, Middlesex, UK *Tel* (01) 979 1837.

TL English. **SL** French. **UDC** film, literature.

Memb TG.

STEWART, JEAN (Mrs Jean Pace) Malting Cottage, Malting Lane, Cambridge CB3 9HF, UK *Tel* (0223) 65382.

TL English. **SL** French. **UDC** art/art history, literature (criticism, history, prose).

French Louis Aragon: *Henri Matisse* (Collins, 1972). Jacques Bergue: *Egypt, Imperialism and Revolution* (Faber & Faber, 1972). E Delacroix: *Selected Letters, 1813-1863* (Eyre & Spottiswoode, 1971). Jean Guignet: *Virginia Woolf and Her Works* (Hogarth, 1965). Also the works of M Brion, M Butor, M Chadourne, Jacques Cousteau, Pierre Gascar, F Geoffrey, others.

Awards 1968 & 1971 (shared) Scott-Moncrieff Prize. **Memb** TA.

STIEHL, HERMAN Reichsforststr 7, D-6000 Frankfurt/Main, West Germany *Tel* (0611) 672235.

TL German. **SL** English, French, Spanish. **UDC** literature (prose).

English William Golding: *Lord of the Flies* (S Fischer, 1956). John C Gardner: *The Sunlight Dialogues* Rowohlt (1977).

Memb VDÜ.

STONE, BARBARA ROSE 5560 Lakewood Dr, La Mesa, CA 92041 USA *Tel* 714-463-1558.

TL English. **SL** German. **UDC** art history, banking, communications, economics, literature, painting, photography, political economy/science, sculpture, social services, theater.

STRACHAN, WALTER JOHN 10 Pleasant Rd, Bishop's Stortford CM23 2SJ, UK *Tel* (0279) 54493.

TL English. **SL** French, German, Italian. **UDC** architecture, art, engraving, graphics, literature (poetry, prose), painting, sculpture.

French Julien Gracq: *Dark Stranger* (Peter Owen/New Directions, 1950). **German** Hermann Hesse: *Demian* (Peter Owen/Panther, 1960, 1969). **Italian** Cesare Pavese: *The Comrade* (Peter Owen, 1959); *The House on the Hill* (Peter Owen, 1957, 1977). Also the works of George Bernanos, Marcel Bron, Vera Cacciatore, Jacques Chardonne, Jean Cocteau, Enrico Emannuelli, Maurice Gindertael, André Lhote, others.

Memb TA.

STRAWN, RICHARD R Wabash College, Crawfordsville, IN 47933 *Tel* 317-362-1400.

TL English. **SL** French, Italian, Russian. **UDC** art/art history, library science, linguistics/philology, literature (criticism, drama, history, librettos, prose, songs), stylistics.

French Francis Ponge: "A Bias for Things" (pending). Claude Debussy: *"Pelléas and Melisande"* (libretto). **Russian** Nicolai Rimsky-

Koraskov: "Christmas Eve," co-translated with Peteris Silins (libretto). Also the works of Samuel Beckett, Pierre Gascar, Jacques Lacarrière, Gianfrancesco Malipiero.

Memb ALTA.

STRONG, ROBERT L, JR Fermier Rd, RFD, Willington, CT 06279 USA *Tel* 203-429-6685.

TL English. **SL** Russian. **UDC** aesthetics, art, athletics, commerce, documentation, economics, education, engineering (hydraulic), ethics, government, heraldry, history, human resources, library science, linguistics/philology, literature (all areas), logic, music, occultism, painting, philosophy, political economy/science, printing, psychology, public administration, railroads, recreation, religion, social sciences, sciences (applied), shipbuilding, shipping, sociology, sports, theater, theology, transportation, witchcraft.

Russian various articles in *Great Soviet Encyclopedia* (Macmillan, 1972–79).

Affil Macmillan Educational Corp. **Memb** ATA.

STRYK, LUCIEN English, Northern Illinois Univ, DeKalb, IL 60115 USA *Tel* 815-753-0611

TL English. **SL** Chinese, French, Japanese. **UDC** literature (poetry), philosophy.

Chinese *The Penguin Book of Zen Poetry* (Allen Lane/Penguin, 1977). *Zen Poems of China and Japan: The Crane's Bill* (Doubleday/Anchor, 1973). **Japanese** Shinkichi Takahashi: *Afterimages: Zen Poems* (Swallow, 1970). Zen: *Poems, Prayers, Sermons, Anecdotes, Interviews* (Doubleday/Anchor, 1965).

Awards 1978 Islands and Continents Translation Award.

SUMMER, SUSAN COOK 228 W 82 St #4, New York, NY 10024 USA *Tel* 212-799-3230.

TL English. **SL** French, Russian. **UDC** art/art history, ballet, choreography, dance, history, linguistics/philology, literature (criticism, librettos, prose), music, painting, theater.

Russian André Levinson: "The Old and the New Ballet" (*Dance Horizons*, in press). Vera Krasovskaya: "Russian Ballet Theater at the Beginning of the 20th Century" (*Dance Horizons*, in press). Mikhail Bulgakov: *The Capital in a Notebook* (Russian Literary Triquarterly, 1978).

SŪRMANIS, BIRUTA 42-48 81 St, Elmhurst, NY 11373 USA *Tel* 212-779-0691.

TL Latvian. **SL** English, German. **UDC** literature (children's, folklore, history), music, sociology.

Latvian L Apkalns: *Latvian Music* (Breitkopf & Haertel, 1977). Also articles for Radio Liberty, Baltic Appeal to the United Nations, Frank C Farnham Co.

SUSSDORF, ANGELA Schroedersweg 27, D-Hamburg 61, West Germany *Tel* (040) 58 14 06.

TL & SL English & German. **UDC** anthropology, documentation, ethnography, literature (children's, drama, librettos, lyrics, prose), music, painting, sculpture, theater.

English Richard E Leakey & Roger Lewin:

Origins (Hoffmann & Campe, 1978). **German** Hilla & Max Jacoby: *The Land of Israel* (Thames & Hudson, 1978). Also the works of Sean O'Faolain, André Picot, Louis C Thomas, Hugh Wickham.

SUTHERLAND, JOAN ITEN 639 Pier Ave, Santa Monica, CA 90405 USA.
TL English. **SL** Chinese. **UDC** anthropology, art/art history, geography, history, literature (all areas), philosophy, religion/scripture.
Memb ALTA, OARS.

SVOBODA, TERESE 116 W Houston St, New York, NY 10012 USA *Tel* 212-473-6947.
TL English. **SL** Nuer (African). **UDC** literature (poetry).
Awards 1975 Columbia Univ Translation Ctr Fellowship, 1978–79 NEH.

SWANN, BRIAN Humanities, Cooper Union, Cooper Sq, New York, NY 10003 USA *Tel* 212-254-6300.
TL English. **SL** Italian. **UDC** literature (poetry).
Italian Lucio Piccolo: *Collected Poetry,* co-translated with Ruth Feldman (Princeton Univ, 1972). Andrea Zanzotto: *Selected Poems,* co-translated with Ruth Feldman (Princeton Univ, 1974). Primo Levi: *Shema: Collected Poems of Primo Levi,* co-translated with Ruth Feldman (Menard, 1976). Rocco Scotellaro: *Selected Poems,* co-translated with Ruth Feldman (Princeton Univ, forthcoming).
Awards 1976 John Florio Prize (shared with Ruth Feldman).

SWIETLICKI, ALAIN 1209 Subella Dr, Columbia, MO 65201 USA *Tel* 314-445-7996; 882-2030.
TL English. **SL** Polish, Spanish. **UDC** agriculture, business, history, literature (prose).
Spanish Ezequiel Martinez Estrada: *X-ray of the Pampa* (Univ of Texas, 1971).
Accred/Memb ATA. **Affil** Univ of Missouri.

SYROP, KONRAD 15 St German's Pl #5, London SE3 ONN, UK *Tel* (01) 858 4892.
TL English. **SL** Polish. **UDC** literature (history, prose), political science.
Polish Jerzy Andrzejewski: *The Inquisitors* (Weidenfeld & Nicolson/Knopf, 1960). Slawomir Mrozek: *The Elephant* (Macdonald/Grove, 1962); *The Ugupu Bird* (Macdonald/Grove, 1968).
Memb TA.

SZELL, TIMEA K 157 Hudson Ave, Tenafly, NJ 07670 USA *Tel* 201-569-7883.
TL English. **SL** French, Hungarian, Russian. **UDC** aesthetics, anthropology, archeology, architecture, art, brewing, choreography, dairy farming, documentation, education, engraving, ethics, ethnography, food/nutrition, forestry, genealogy, genetics, heraldry, history, horticulture, human resources, linguistics/philology, literature (children's, criticism, drama, history, lyrics, poetry, prose), logic, music, painting, philosophy, psychiatry, religion, sculpture, theater, theology.
Hungarian Agnes Gergely: "The Interpreter" (pending).
Affil SUNY at Stony Brook.

SZENDREY, THOMAS 655 W Eighth St, Erie, PA 16502 USA *Tel* 814-455-9575.
TL English. **SL** Hungarian. **UDC** history, philosophy, religion.
Hungarian Cs Malyusz, ed: *The Role of the Theater in the Development of National Consciousness in East Central Europe* (Hungarian Cultural Foundation, 1978).
Affil Gannon College.

TAKECHI, MANABU Ctr for Japanese Social and Political Studies, 2-8-8 Nishinogawa, Komae-shi, Tokyo 201, Japan *Tel* (03) 489-2175.
TL & SL English & Japanese. **UDC** political science, social science.
Affil *The Japan Interpreter.*

TALAMANTES, FLORENCE WILLIAMS 5225 Trojan Ave #39, San Diego, CA 92115 USA *Tel* 714-286-7107.
TL English. **SL** Spanish. **UDC** literature (prose).
Spanish Alfonsina Storni: *Poemas de Amor,* (Costa-Amic, 1977). José María de Pereda: *Selections from Sotileza and Peñas Arriba* (Univ Pr of Amer, 1977).

TALBOT, KATHRINE The Old Cottage, Bexley Hill, Lodsworth, Petworth, Sussex GU28 9EA, UK *Tel* (079) 85 338.
TL English. **SL** German. **UDC** art/art history, literature (children's, drama, prose), painting.
German Manfred Bieler: *The Three Daughters* (St Martin's, 1977–78). Bernhard Borchert: *Miro* (Faber & Faber, 1958). Ulf Miehe: *Puma* (St Martin's, 1978). H H Parrs: *Pictures in Peril* (Faber & Faber, 1957). Also the works of Siegfried Lenz, Hans Erich Nossack, Rolf Schroers, Gabriele Wohmann.

TALBOT, TOBY 180 Riverside Dr, New York, NY 10024 USA.
TL English. **SL** Spanish. **UDC** arts, biography, literature (prose).
Spanish José Ortega y Gasset: *On Love* (Meridian, 1957). Benito Pérez Galdós: *Compassion* (Ungar, 1968). Felix Marti Ibánez: *Ariel* (MD Publications, 1969). Don Juan Manuel: *Count Lucanor's Tales* (Dial, 1970).
Affil John Jay College, New School for Social Research.

TANASESCU, GREGORIUS 7104 Calea Victoria 214, Bucharest, Rumania *Tel* 50 32 19.
TL English, Rumanian. **SL** French, German, Latin. **UDC** literature (criticism), history.
French *Ancient and Medieval Science* (Scientifica, 1970). **German** E R Curtius: *Balzac* (Minerva, 1974). A Schopenhauer: *The World as Will and Representation* (Scientifica, 1974). **Latin** *Anthology of Latin Poetry* (Albatros, 1973). Also the works of André Chénier, Ernst Robert Curtius, others.
Memb VDÜ.

TASCHIAN, JOAN PO Box 5112, Berkeley, CA 94705 USA *Tel* 415-848-5023.
TL English. **SL** Russian. **UDC** art, ballet, computers, music, sciences, theater.

TATE, JOAN 36 Kennedy Rd, Shrewsbury SY3 7AB, UK *Tel* (0743) 56105.
TL English. **SL** Danish, Norwegian, Swedish. **UDC** literature.
Danish, Norwegian, Swedish over 50 book-length translations of leading Scandinavian writers.

TAYLOR, MARTHA R 5110 S Kenwood Ave #709, Chicago, IL 60615 USA *Tel* 312-667-6946.
TL English. **SL** French, Russian. **UDC** linguistics/philology, literature (poetry, science fiction), recreation/games.
Affil Univ of Chicago.

TAYLOR, MICHAEL ANTHONY 166 blvd du Montparnasse, F-75014 Paris, France *Tel* 326 3057.
TL English. **SL** French. **UDC** art/art history, history, literature (criticism, history, poetry, prose), painting.
French Christian Metz: *Film Language* (Oxford Univ, 1974). Cècile Beurdeley: *L'Amour Bleu* (Office du Livre, 1978). Victor Segaley: "The Major Poems" (pending). Also the works of Georges Lougrée, Pierre Nora.

TEAL, THOMAS A 365 West End Ave #502, New York, NY 10024 USA *Tel* 212-580-0983.
TL English. **SL** Danish, Norwegian, Swedish. **UDC** arts, biography, history, literature (drama, prose).
Swedish Hans Axel Holm: *The Other Germans: Report from an East German Town* (Pantheon, 1970). Per Wästberg: *The Air Cage* (Delacorte/Seymour Lawrence, 1972). Maj Sjöwall & Per Wahlöö: *The Abominable Man* (Pantheon, 1972). Karl-Erik Fichtelius & Sverre Sjölander: *Smarter than Man? Intelligence in Whales, Dolphins and Humans* (Pantheon, 1972). Also the works of Mats Andersson, Suzanne Brøgger, Robert Danielsson, Stig Ericson, Tove Jansson, Theodor Kallifatides, Tore Zetterholm.
Affil *The New Yorker.*

TEELE, NICHOLAS J PO Box 247, Georgetown, TX 78626 USA *Tel* 512-863-3461.
TL English. **SL** Chinese, Japanese. **UDC** aesthetics, anthropology, art, ceramics, education, ethics, ethnography, history, literature (all areas), philosophy, theology.
Japanese Giji Shono: *Meadow of Stars,* co-translated with Roy E Teele & Yoko Sugiyama (Rironsha, 1970). Also the works of Fujiwara No Kinto, Kino Tsurayuki, Onono Komachi, Miruno Tadamine, numerous others.
Affil Univ of Texas (English). **Memb** ALTA.

TERSTEGGE, SISTER GEORGIANA St. Mary-of-the-Woods College, St Mary-of-the-Woods, IN 47876 USA *Tel* 812-535-4141.
TL English. **SL** French. **UDC** art/art history, communications, education, genealogy, heraldry, history, literature (history), philosophy.
French Abbé Besnard: *Your Name Is Written in Heaven* (Thos Coffey/Dimension, 1976).
Accred/Memb ATA. **Awards** 1973 Les Bois Award (St Mary-of-the-Woods College).

THALER, WILLY Reichsapfelgasse 14, A-1150 Vienna, Austria *Tel* (0222) 83 18 774; (02231) 39 0 34.
   TL German. **SL** English, French. **UDC** art history, business, ecology, history, literature, music, politics.
   English Arthur Koestler: *Act of Creation* (Scherz); *Trail of the Dinosaur* (Scherz). Walter Lacquer: *Europe in Crisis* (Kindler). Leon Uris: *Trinity* (Kindler). Also the works of R Adams, A Comfort, Ian Fleming, James Jones, Henry Moore, Henry Robbins.

TOLMAN, JON M Modern & Classical Languages, Univ of New Mexico, Albuquerque, NM 87131 USA *Tel* 505-277-4310.
   TL Portuguese, Spanish. **UDC** literature (criticism, poetry, prose).
   Portuguese H de Campos et al: *Theory of Concrete Poetry* (Whitston, forthcoming).

TOMKINSON, MICHAEL 36 Oakdale, London N14 5RE, UK.
   TL English. **SL** Arabic, French, German. **UDC** anthropology, archeology, architecture, art, ethics, geography, history, linguistics/philology, music, painting, photography, printing, recreation/games, zoology.
   Memb TG.

TOMLINS, JACK E Modern & Classical Languages, Univ of New Mexico, 2933 Camila Rd NE, Albuquerque, NM 87111 USA *Tel* 505-292-2018.
   TL English. **SL** Portuguese, Spanish. **UDC** literature (poetry, prose).
   Portuguese Mário de Andrade: *Hallucinated City* (Vanderbilt Univ, 1968). Wilson Martins: *The Modernist Idea* (New York Univ, 1970).

TOOL, DENNIS CASLER 33 W Prospect, Fayetteville, AR 72701 USA *Tel* 501-443-2617.
   TL English. **SL** French, Italian. **UDC** education, linguistics/philology, literature (all areas), music, philosophy, psychiatry, psychology, sociology, surveying, theater, theology.
   Affil Univ of Arkansas. **Memb** ALTA. **Awards** 1978 Dudley Fitts Award in Translation.

TRAHAN, ELIZABETH WELT 79 Via Ventura, Monterey, CA 93940 USA *Tel* 408-372-7931.
   TL English. **SL** German, Russian. **UDC** literature (criticism, drama, history, prose), teaching and materials development for teaching translation and interpretation.
   Author of "Translation and Interpretation Techniques for Advanced Language Study" (*ADFL Bulletin*, 9 no 3, March, 1978).
   Affil Monterey Inst of Foreign Studies. **Memb** ALTA, ATA.

TRASK, WILLARD R 233 E 33 St, New York, NY 10016 USA *Tel* 212-725-2133.
   TL English. **SL** French, German, Portuguese, Spanish. **UDC** art history, literature (history, poetry, songs), religion (history).
   French Giacomo Casanova: *History of My Life* (Harcourt Brace Jovanovich, 1966–71). **German** Erich Auerbach: *Mimesis* (Princeton Univ, 1953). Ernst Robert Curtius: *European Literature and the Latin Middle Ages* (Bol-

lingen/Pantheon, 1953). **Spanish** José Ortega y Gasset: *Man and People* (Norton, 1957). Also the works of Mircea Eliade, Thomas Mann, Ramón Sender, Georges Simenon, Fritz von Unruh.
   Affil Columbia Univ Translation Ctr. **Memb** ATA. **Awards** 1966 National Book Award in Translation, 1978 Columbia Univ Gold Medal.

TREITEL, RENATA 1503 E 27 St, Tulsa, OK 74114 USA *Tel* 918-743-0748.
   TL English. **SL** Italian, Spanish. **UDC** business, literature (criticism, history, poetry, prose).
   Memb ALTA, ATA.

TREVINO, VICTORIA S Priv San Martin Nte #348, Monterrey, Nuevo Léon, Mexico *Tel* 40 81 46.
   TL English. **SL** Spanish. **UDC** art/art history, astrology, ecology, education, linguistics, literature (prose), music, theater.
   Accred/Memb ATA.

TSUMURA, YUMIKO (Samuel B Grolmes & Yumiko T Grolmes) 3494 Cowper St, Palo Alto, CA 94306 USA *Tel* 415-493-7934.
   TL English. **SL** Japanese. **UDC** literature (children's, drama, folklore, poetry, prose).
   Japanese Yumiko Kurahashi: "Bridge of Dreams" (pending); *The Ugly Devils; Partei; The Boy Who Became An Eagle* (New Directions, 1972–1974). Ryuichi Tamura: *The World Without Words* (New Directions, 1970).
   Affil Foothill College, College of San Mateo, West Valley College. **Memb** ALTA.

TUCKER, EVA 63B Belsize Pk Gardens, London NW3, UK *Tel* (01) 722 9010.
   TL English. **SL** German. **UDC** literature (biography, poetry, prose).
   German Joseph Roth: *The Radetzkymarch* (Allen Lane, 1974). Jara Ribnikar: *I and You and She* (Calder & Boyars, 1972).
   Memb TA.

TURNELL, MARTIN 37 Smith St, Chelsea, London SW3 4EP UK *Tel* (01) 352 7229.
   TL English. **SL** French, Spanish. **UDC** literature (criticism, French writers and dramatists).
   French Jean Steinmann: *Pascal* (Burns & Oates, 1965). Marcel Jouhandeau: *Monsieur Godeau Marié; Chroniques Maritales; Nouvelles Chroniques Maritales; Chronique d'une Passion; Ménagerie Domestique; L'Imposteur; Elise Architecte* (Pantheon, 1953; Longmans, Green & Co, 1955). Jean-François Revel: *On Proust* (Hamish Hamilton, 1972). Jean-Paul Sartre: *Baudelaire* (Hamish Hamilton, 1949). Also the works of Guy de Maupassant, Blaise Pascal.

TURNER, DOROTHY E 2300 Bonita, Austin, TX 78703 USA *Tel* 512-472-2374; 475-3856.
   TL English. **SL** Spanish. **UDC** art, communications, education, literature, philosophy, psychology, social services.
   Affil Texas Dept of Human Resources. **Memb** ATA.

TURNER, PAUL Linacre College, Oxford, UK *Tel* (0865) 57275.

   TL English. **SL** Greek (Classical), Latin. **UDC** literature (poetry, prose).
   Greek (Classical) Longus: *Daphnis and Chloe* (Penguin, 1956). Lucian: *Satirical Sketches* (Penguin, 1961). **Latin** Sir Thomas More: *Utopia* (Penguin, 1965). Ovid: *The Technique of Love* (Panther, 1968). Also the works of John Barclay, E T A Hoffmann, Xenophon of Ephesus.
   Affil Oxford Univ. **Memb** TA.

TUTTLE, LYNN Box 9, Marlboro, VT 05344 USA *Tel* 802-254-2876.
   TL English. **SL** Spanish. **UDC** linguistics, literature (children's, criticism, folklore, history, poetry, prose).
   Spanish the works of Pablo Neruda, Octavio Paz, José Revueltas, Josefa Rivas.
   Memb ALTA, ATA.

TVEITE, A E c/o Chr Michelsens Institutt, Fantoftvegen 38, N-5036 Fantoft (Bergen), Norway *Tel* 47 5 28 58 23.
   TL English. **SL** Norwegian. **UDC** anthropology, archeology, economics, religion/scripture.
   Norwegian Torstein Eckhoff: *Justice: Its Determinants in Social Interaction* (Rotterdam Univ, 1974). All numerous documents for the Norwegian ministries and other government institutions, generally of an economic nature.
   Memb TG.

TWOREK, JOHN 1601 Oakmont Dr #5, Walnut Creek, CA 94595 USA *Tel* 415-937-0516.
   TL English. **SL** Polish, Russian. **UDC** economics, education, government, history, legislation, literature (history, prose), political economy/science, public administration.
   Affil JPRS, US Dept of State.

TYLER, LILIANE S 1116 Swanston Dr, Sacramento, CA 95818 USA *Tel* 916-444-2450.
   TL English. **SL** Dutch, French, **UDC** commerce, communications, ecology, education, government, history, law, linguistics, literature (all areas except songs), medicine, philately, political economy/science, religion, social science, sciences (life).
   Memb ATA.

UNDERWOOD, JOHN K 65 blvd Hippolyte Marques, F-94200 Ivry-sur-Seine, France *Tel* (1) 670 49 76.
   TL English. **SL** French. **UDC** ecology, economics, government, history, literature (children's, criticism, drama, history, Judaica, librettos, poetry, prose), music.

UNGER, ALFRED H 27 Daleham Gardens, London NW3 UK *Tel* 435-4350.
   TL German. **SL** English. **UDC** theater.
   English Terence Rattigan: *The Winslow Boy* (Kurt Desch, 1948). Charles Morgan: *The Burning Glass* (Ahn & Simrock, 1955). Peter Ustinov: *Blow Your Own Trumpet* (Felix Bloch Erben, 1956). Benjamin Britten & E M Forster: *Billy Budd*, based on the novel by Herman Melville (Boosey & Hawkes, 1960). Also other plays by Terence Rattigan, Peter Ustinov, others.
   Memb TA, VDÜ.

UNGER, DAVID 517 W 113 St #65, New York, NY 10025 USA *Tel* 212-866-9052.
TL English. SL Spanish. UDC anthropology, literature (all areas), political science.
Spanish Enrique Lihn: *The Dark Room and Other Poems* (New Directions, 1978). Vicente Aleixandre: *The World Alone* (Penman, forthcoming). Also the works of Isaac Goldemberg, Vicente Huidobro, José Kozer, Nicanor Parra, others.
Affil New School for Social Research, College of New Rochelle. **Awards** 1978 Columbia Univ Translation Ctr grant, 1978 Islands and Continents Translation Award.

UNWIN, GEORGE Harold's Hill, Churt, Farnham, Surrey GU10 2JN, UK *Tel* (025125) 3193.
TL English. SL French, German. UDC copyright, history, literature (history), music.
French Claude Manceron: *Austerlitz* (Allen & Unwin, 1966); *Napoleon Recaptures Paris* (Allen & Unwin, 1968). **German** Hans Jensen: *Sign, Symbol, and Script* (Allen & Unwin, 1970). Joachim Kaiser: *Great Pianists of Our Time* (Allen & Unwin, 1971). Also the works of Ole Klindt-Jensen, Jean Meyer, Zoltan Toth.
Memb TA.

UPTON, JOHN 988 Doud Ave, Monterey, CA 93940 USA *Tel* 408-375-2061.
TL English. SL Spanish. UDC arts, biography, history, literature (poetry, prose), philosophy, social sciences.
Spanish Ramón Díaz Sánchez: *Cumboto* (Univ of Texas, 1969). Ramón Beteta: *Jarano* (Univ of Texas, 1970). Luis González: *San José de Gracia: Mexican Village in Transition* (Univ of Texas, 1974). Fernando Benítez: *In the Magic Land of Peyote* (Univ of Texas, 1975). Also the works of Juan José Arreola, Luis de Góngora y Argote, Fernando Henrique Cardoso.

URDANG, ELLIOTT B 57 Dana St, Providence, RI 02906 USA *Tel* 401-274-2315.
TL English. SL French, Spanish, Rumanian. UDC literature (poetry, prose), psychiatry.
Rumanian Ion Caraion: *Selected Poems,* co-translated with Marguerite Dorian (Mundus Artium, 1976). Veronica Porumbacu, Gabriela Melinescu: *Selected Poems,* co-translated with Marguerite Dorian (Mundus Artium, 1974). Also the works of Mikhail Lermontov.
Memb ALTA.

URQUIDI, MARJORY MATTINGLY 1625½ 19 St NW #E, Washington, DC 20009 USA.
TL English. SL French, Spanish. UDC anthropology, banking/finance, demography, economics, history, political economy/science, sociology, social sciences.
Spanish Daniel Cosío Villegas et al: *A Compact History of Mexico* (El Colegio de México, 1974). Aldo Ferrer: *The Argentine Economy* (Univ of California, 1967). Ramiro Guerra y Sánchez: *Sugar and Society in the Caribbean* (Yale Univ, 1964). José Carlos Mariátegui: *Seven Interpretive Essays on Peruvian Reality* (Univ of Texas, 1971). Also the works of Carlos Aguirre Anaya, Gustavo Cabrera, Roberto Campos, Antonio Carillo Flores, Jorge Castañeda, Fernando Henrique Cardoso,

Carlos Díaz Alejandro, Eduardo Frei, Celso Furtado, Alfonso García Robles, Héctor Hurtado, Enrique Iglesias, Fernando Kusnetzoff, Ricardo Lagos Escobar, José López Portillo, Carlos Lleras Restrepo, Rolando Mellafe, Jean Meyer, Carmen Miró, Raúl Prebisch, Alfred Sauvy, Léon Tabah, Víctor Urquidi.
Memb ATA, TAALS. **Awards** 1977–78 NEH grant.

VAN DER SCHALIE, FRANZISKA B 1704 Oakmount Rd, South Euclid, OH 44121 USA *Tel* 216-382-7997.
TL English. SL French, German. UDC art/art history, literature (children's, criticism, folklore), medicine, music, philosophy, public health. sciences (medical).
Affil Cuhayoga County Public Library. **Memb** ATA, NOTA.

VAN VESSEM, DIETS Catharijnesingel 124, NL-3511 GX Utrecht, the Netherlands *Tel* (30) 31 73 59.
TL Dutch. SL English, French, German. UDC law, philosophy, wine.
English Richard Cavendish, ed: *Encyclopedia of the Unexplained* (Elsevier, 1975). Pamela Vandyke Price: *The Taste of Wine* (Elsevier, 1976). Michael Broadbent: *Wine Tasting* (Elsevier, 1978). K Kuypers: *The Relation between Knowing and Making as an Epistemological Principle* (SUNY at Buffalo, 1974).
Memb NGV, TA, TG.

VASCONCELLOS, MURIEL 1802 Corcoran St NW, Washington, DC 20009 USA *Tel* 202-667-7781.
TL English. Sl Portuguese, Spanish. UDC architecture, art, biomedicine, data processing, economics, history, natural resources, public health, social sciences.
Portuguese Sylvio de Vasconcellos: *The Baroque in Brazil* (OAS, 1974). **Spanish** Lorenzo Meyer: *Mexico and the United States in the Oil Controversy* (Univ of Texas, 1977). Luis Vera: *Agricultural Land Inventory Techniques* (OAS, 1964). *OAS: Social Survey of Latin America: 1962* (OAS, 1964). Also numerous unsigned translations of published articles and documents done in staff capacity for OAS and PAHO since 1963. Numerous unsigned translations, including literary pieces for *Américas* magazine.
Affil PAHO, Georgetown Univ. **Memb** SFL, TAALS. **Awards** 1978 NEH.

VENNEWITZ, LEILA 401-710 Chilco St, Vancouver, BC V6G 2P9, Canada *Tel* 604-688-9706.
TL English. SL French, German. UDC literature (prose).
German Heinrich Böll: *The Clown* (McGraw-Hill, 1965); *Group Portrait with Lady* (McGraw-Hill, 1973). Uwe Johnson: *Anniversaries* (Harcourt Brace Jovanovich, 1974). Ernst Nolte: *Three Faces of Fascism* (Holt, Rinehart & Winston, 1966). Also the works of Fritz Rudolf Fries, Franz Fühmann, Walter Hinderer, Klaus, Alexander Kluge, Mehnert, Emil Staiger, Martin Walser, numerous other works of Heinrich Böll, French literary scholars such as Diéguez, Martini.
Memb TA. **Awards** 1968 Schlegel-Tieck Prize.

VENRICK, BRUCE B 2572 Olentangy River Rd #B12, Columbus, OH 43202 USA *Tel* 614-267-7798.
TL English. SL French, Russian. UDC economics, international affairs, linguistics/philology, literature (prose), political science, social sciences, sciences (natural).
Accred ATA (Russian), Ohio State Univ.

VICTOR-ROOD, JULIETTE 1350 Knox Dr, Boulder, CO 80303 USA.
TL English. SL German. UDC anthropology, art/art history, astrology, computers, data processing, ecology, history, linguistics/philology, literature (criticism, drama, folklore, history, poetry, prose), music, psychology, social sciences, theater.
German the works of Johannes Bobrowski, Anna Hajnal, Hans Manz, Arpád Toth, Sándor Weöres.

VIRTANEN, JOHN O 2116 NE 18 Ave, Portland, OR 97212 USA *Tel* 503-282-1383.
TL & SL English & Finnish. UDC literature (biography, prose), sports.
Finnish Paavo Karikko & Mauno Koski: *Paavo Nurmi, Still King of the Runners* (Continental, 1978). Sulo Kolkka & Helge Nygren: *Paavo Nurmi; The Flying Finn* (Continental, 1978). Lassi Sinkkonen: *Solveig's Song* (Continental, 1978).

VIVIAN, KATHARINE (Mrs Anthony Ashton) Quarry Field, Stonewall Hill, Presteigne, Powys, LD8 2HB, UK *Tel* (054-44) 447.
TL English. SL French, Georgian. UDC literature (history, poetry, prose).
French Alain-Fournier: *Le Grand Meaulnes* (Folio Soc, 1979). K Salia, ed: *Georgia: An Introduction* (Salia, 1975). **Georgian** Shota Rustaveli: *The Knight in Panther Skin* (Folio Soc, 1977). Also the works of Guy de Maupassant (pending).
Memb TA.

VON KOSKULL, HANS JÜRGEN Neubürgerstr 2, D-8203 Oberandorf, West Germany *Tel* (08033) 1374.
TL German. SL English. UDC archeology, art, ethics, geography, government, history (modern), literature (biography, prose), military science, philosophy, political science, religion (non-Christian, Indian & Chinese).
English Michael Grant: *Saint Paul* (Gustav Lübbe, 1978). Alan Palmer: *Napoleon in Russia* (Fischer, 1967). Harrison E Salisbury: *The 900 Days, The Siege of Leningrad* (S Fischer, 1970). Albert Seaton: *The Russo-German War 1941–45* (Bernard & Graefe, 1973). Also the works of Gordon Brook-Shepherd, Richard Cavendish, Charles Chaplin, Robert Claiborne, Virginia Cowles, Andrew Duncan, Edmund Hillary, George Kennan, Rose Kennedy, Ronald Lewin, Norman Lewis, Montgomery of Alamein, Leonardi Mosely, John Toland, Harold Wilson, numerous others.

VON WIESE, URSULA Beckhammer 25 or Postfach 121, CH-8057 Zürich, Switzerland *Tel* 60 39 95.
TL German. SL English, French, Danish, Norwegian, Swedish. UDC literature (children's, drama, prose), psychology, sociology, zoology.

English Upton Sinclair: *Dragon's Teeth* (Alfred Scherz). James M Barrie: *Peter Pan* (Hoch, 1964). Morris L West: *The Shoes of the Fisherman* (Kurt Desch, 1963). Also the works of James Aldridge, H C Andersen, Louis Bromfield, Pearl S Buck, A J Cronin, Patrick Dennis, Gerald Durrell, Ben Hecht, Richard Hutchinson, Richard Llewellyn, Compton Mackenzie, Grace Metalious, Katherine Pinkerton, Nevil Shute, numerous others. **Memb** VDÜ. **Awards** 1975 Kanton Zürich Translation Prize.

VOSTEEN, THOMAS R 42 Forest View Ct, Iowa City, IA 52240 USA *Tel* 319-337-4205.
TL English. **SL** French. **UDC** art, government, literature (criticism, history, prose).
Affil Univ of Iowa.

WALDROP, ROSMARIE 71 Elmgrove Ave, Providence, RI 02906 USA *Tel* 401-351-0015.
TL English. **SL** French, German. **UDC** literature (criticism, drama, poetry, prose).
French Edmond Jabès: *The Book of Questions/The Book of Yukel/Return to the Book*, 2 vols (Wesleyan Univ, 1976–77). **German** Peter Weiss: *Bodies and Shadows* (Delacorte, 1969). Konrad Bayer et al: *Five Poets from Vienna* (Transgravity, 1979).
Awards 1978 Columbia Univ Translation Ctr grant.

WALEY, PAMELA JOAN 24 Park Rd #5, London NW1 4SH, UK *Tel* (01) 402 6234.
TL English. **SL** Catalan, French, Italian, Spanish. **UDC** archeology, architecture, art, heraldry, history, literature (history, prose), painting, political science, sculpture, theater.
Italian Giovanni Botero: *The Reason of State* (Routledge & Kegan Paul, 1956). Paolo Verzone: *From Theodoric to Charlemagne* (Methuen, 1967). Terisio Pignatti: *Pietro Longhi* (Phaidon, 1969). Giuliano Briganti: *The Viewpainters of Europe* (Phaidon, 1970). Also the works of Jean-Louis Bory, Flavio Conti, Giorgio Spini.
Affil Univ of London (Theory and Practice of Literary Translation). **Memb** TA.

WALSH, DONALD D PO Box 881, Madison, CT 06443 USA *Tel* 203-245-2944.
TL English. **SL** Spanish. **UDC** aesthetics, education, government, linguistics/philology, literature (criticism, drama, folklore, history, poetry, prose), philosophy, theater.
Spanish Julio Alvarez del Vayo: *Give Me Combat: The Memoirs* (Little, Brown, 1973). Ernesto Cardenal: *In Cuba* (New Directions, 1974). Angel Gonzalez: *Harsh World and Other Poems* (Princeton Univ, 1977). Pablo Neruda: *Residence on Earth* (New Directions, 1973).
Memb ALTA. **Awards** 1973 Chicago Review Poetry Prize.

WANG, HUI-MING Greenfield Rd, Montague, MA 01351 USA *Tel* 413-367-2314.
TL & SL Chinese & English. **UDC** anthropology, art, arts/crafts, engraving/prints, graphics, literature (all areas), painting, photography, printing, sculpture.
Chinese Mao Tse-tung: *Ten Poems and Lyrics* (Univ of Massachusetts, 1975). Tang Poets (12): *The Boat Untied and Other Poems* (Barre,

1971). Also the works of Taishan Hermit, Wang Wei, Chang Chiu Nin, Tu Mu, Tu Fu, Chia Chih, Li Po, Szu Kung Shu, James Purdy, William Stafford.
Affil Univ of Massachusetts.

WARD, DAVID J 1505 Alegria, Austin, TX 78757 USA *Tel* 512-454-8573.
TL English. **SL** German. **UDC** literature (children's, criticism, drama, prose).
German the works of Hans Bender, Thomas Brasch, Bertolt Brecht, Hans Magnus Enzensberger, Manfred Peter Hein, Günter Herburger, Eberhard Hilscher, Heinrich Vormweg, Christian Wallner, Gerhard Zwerenz in *Dimension: Contemporary German Arts & Letters*.
Affil Univ of Texas at Austin, *Dimension* (asst ed). **Memb** ALTA.

WARNICK, MARIANNE C 11 Ross Dr, Londonderry, NH 03053 USA *Tel* 603-434-5332.
TL English. **SL** French, Spanish. **UDC** art/art history, biology, history, medicine, music, patents/trademarks, sociology.
Memb ATA, NETA.

WAUTIER, ANDRÉ 18 rue Fréd Pelletier, B-1040 Brussels, Belgium *Tel* (02) 734-61-04.
TL French. **SL** English. **UDC** astrology, ethics, history, jurisprudence, law, linguistics/philology, sociolinguistics, literature (criticism, poetry), philosophy, political science, public administration, religion.
Memb CBTIP.

WEAVER, ELENA B 5 Redcoat Lane, Lexington, MA 02173 USA *Tel* 617-861-9351.
TL & SL English, French, Italian. **UDC** history, linguistics/philology, literature (children's, criticism), nutrition.
Accred Univ of Geneva. **Memb** ATA.

WEAVER, HELEN Abbey Road, Mt Tremper, NY 12457 USA *Tel* 914-679-9136.
TL English. **SL** French. **UDC** arts, literature (prose), philosophy, psychology, religion, social sciences.
French Raymond Aron: *An Essay on Freedom* (New Amer Library, 1967); *Main Currents in Sociological Thought*, 2 vols (Basic Books, 1965–67); *Marxism and the Existentialists* (Harper & Row, 1969). Antonin Artaud: *The Peyote Dance* (Farrar, Straus & Giroux, 1976); *Selected Writings* (Farrar, Straus & Giroux, 1976). Also the works of Paul Claudel, Didier Decoin, Joseph Kessel, Violette Leduc, Robert Merle, Jacques Merleau-Ponty, Bruno Morando, Georges Michel, Jean Piaget, Bärbel Inhelder, Monique Wittig, Georges Balandier, François Clement, Pierre Teilhard de Chardin, Jacques Ellul, Gustave Flaubert, Jules Isaac, Sebastian Japrisot, Marquis de Sade, Jean-François Steiner, numerous others.

WEBER, SISTER MARY CHAMINADE 4545 College Rd, S Euclid, OH 44121 USA *Tel* 216-381-1680.
TL English. **SL** French. **UDC** art, education, literature (criticism, prose), philosophy, theology, translation theory.
Accred ATA. **Affil** Notre Dame College. **Memb** ATA, NOTA.

WEBER, WILHELM-KARL 425 Van Buren St, Monterey, CA 93940 USA *Tel* 408-649-3113.
TL French, German. **SL** Dutch, English. **UDC** all areas.
Accred Univ of Geneva. **Affil** Monterey Inst of Foreign Studies (dir, Translation & Interpretation Program). **Memb** AIIC (former exec secy).

WEBSTER, MAREE THERESE 35 Galloupes Point, Swampscott, MA 01907 USA *Tel* 617-581-3290.
TL English. **SL** French, German, Italian. **UDC** literature (drama, prose).

WEIGHTMAN, J G & J D 13 Weech Rd, London NW6 1DL, UK *Tel* 794 6035.
TL English. **SL** French. **UDC** anthropology, ethics, ethnography, history, linguistics, literature (drama, prose), theater.
French Henry de Montherlant: *Selected Essays* (Weidenfeld & Nicolson, 1960). Roger Bordier: *The Golden Plain* (Gollancz, 1963). Jean Guehenno: *Jean-Jacques Rousseau* (Routledge & Kegan Paul/Columbia Univ, 1966). Claude Lévi-Strauss: *Triste Tropiques* (Jonathan Cape/Penguin, 1973); "Mythologiques" (pending).
Memb TA. **Awards** 1967, 1974 Scott-Moncrieff Prize.

WEINBERGER, ELIOT The Montemora Foundation, Box 336, Cooper Sta, New York, NY 10003 USA *Tel* 212-255-2733.
TL English. **SL** Spanish. **UDC** literature (poetry, prose).
Spanish Homero Aridjis: *Exhaltation of Light* (Boa, 1979). Octavio Paz: *Eagle or Sun?* (New Directions, 1976); *New Poems* (New Directions, 1979). Also the works of Macedonio Fernández, Olivero Girondo, Roberto Juarroz, Guillermo Sucre, José Juan Tablada, Idea Vilariño, Ulalume González de León, anonymous street songs from Quito.
Awards 1977 Columbia Univ Translation Ctr grant.

WEISS, GASPARD E PO Box 284, Arcata, CA 95521 USA *Tel* 707-822-6623.
TL French. **SL** English, German, Greek (Classical), Latin. **UDC** art/art history, law (international), paleontology, philosophy, religion.
Affil Humboldt State Univ (professor emeritus). **Memb** ATA, NCTA, Monterey Inst of Foreign Studies (founder, pres emeritus).

WEISS, JASON 618 S Detroit St #2, Los Angeles, CA 90036 USA *Tel* 213-933-3418.
TL English. **SL** Spanish. **UDC** art/art history, literature (criticism, drama, poetry, prose).

WEISSBORT, DANIEL Comparative Literature, Univ of Iowa, Iowa City, IA 52242 USA *Tel* 319-353-6734.
TL English. **SL** French, Russian. **UDC** literature (children's, drama, poetry, prose), political science.
Russian Nikolai Zabolotsky: *Scrolls, Selected Poems* (Cape/Grossman, 1970). Natalya Gorbanevskaya: *Selected Poems*, with a tran-

script of her trial and papers relating to her detention in a prison psychiatric hospital (Carcanet/Dufour, 1972). Andrei Amalrik: *Nose! Nose? No-Se! and Other Plays* (Harcourt Brace Jovanovich, 1972). Various authors: *Post-War Russian Poetry* (Penguin, 1974), numerous others.
Memb ALTA, TA.

WEISSENBORN, HELLMUTH, see Mac-**DONALD, LESLEY**

WEITBRECHT, BRIGITTE Fraasstr 12 A, D-7000 Stuttgart 1, West Germany *Tel* (0711) 243 548.
TL German. **SL** English, French. **UDC** architecture, art/art history, ethics, history, literature (history, prose, science fiction), religion.
English Frederic Spotts: *The Churches and Politics in Germany* (Deutsche Verlags-Anstalt, 1976). Nadia Benois Ustinov: *Klop and the Ustinov Family* (Deutsche Verlags-Anstalt, 1975). Also the works of Isaac Asimov, Bruno Bettelheim, Maurice Chandler, Iris Dornfeld, Harold Loukes, David Mackay, Terence Maloney, Daniel Olivier, Rex Stout, Paul White, numerous others.
Memb VDÜ.

WELLWARTH, GEORGE E Theater, SUNY at Binghamton, NY 13901 USA *Tel* 607-798-2704.
TL English. **SL** Catalan, French, German, Spanish. **UDC** literature (drama).
Catalan Manuel de Pedrolo: "Cruma" in *3 Catalan Dramatists* (Engendra, 1974). **French** Eugene Ionesco: "The Picture" in *Modern French Theatre* (Dutton, 1964). **German** Siegfried Melchinger: *Concise Encyclopedia of the Modern Drama* (Horizon, 1964). **Spanish** Eduardo Quiles: "The Refrigerator" in *New Generation Spanish Drama* (Engendra, 1974). Also the works of Walter Hasenclever, Georg Kaiser, Jean Tardieu, Jordi Teixidor, Kurt Tucholsky.

WELSH, DAVID 3026 Modern Languages, Univ of Michigan, Ann Arbor, MI 48109 USA *Tel* 313-764-5337.
TL English. **SL** Polish. **UDC** literature (prose).
Polish Boleslaw Prus: *The Doll* (Twayne, 1972). Tadeusz Konwicki: *Dreambook for Our Time* (MIT, 1970). Stanislaw Dygat: *Cloak of Illusion* (MIT, 1970). Leopold Buczkowski: *Black Torrent* (MIT, 1970). Also the works of Jerzy Andrzejewski, Kazimierz Brandys, Stanislaw Korbonski, Wlodzimierz Odojewski, Leopold Tyrmand.

WENSINGER, ARTHUR STEVENS 178 Wesleyan Univ Sta, Middletown, CT 06457 USA *Tel* 203-347-9411.
TL English. **SL** German. **UDC** art/art history, literature (criticism, drama, poetry, prose), theater.
German G C Lichtenberg et al: *Hogarth on High Life* (Wesleyan Univ, 1970). W Gropius et al: *The Theater of the Bauhaus* (Wesleyan Univ, 1961). *Modern European Poetry* (Bantam, 1966). Also the works of Johannes Bobrowski, Hermann Hesse, Heinrich von Kleist, Georg Christoph Lichtenberg, Farkas Molnar,

Rainer Maria Rilke, Luise Rinser, Nelly Sachs, others.
Memb ATA.

WHALEY, JOHN 53 Danson Rd, Bexleyheath, Kent, UK *Tel* (01) 303 7180.
TL English. **SL** German. **UDC** government, literature (lyrics, poetry, prose), public administration.
German J Wolfgang Goethe: *West-Eastern Divan* (Oswald Wolff, 1974).

WHITE, IAIN 55 Acrefield Dr, Cambridge, UK *Tel* (0223) 50157.
TL English. **SL** French, German. **UDC** anthropology, ethnography, history, literature (criticism, folklore, prose, history of early science fiction, popular literature of the 19th Century), history of 19th Century radical movements, the "fin de siècle" (c 1880–1914) in all its aspects, religion.
French, German Gunnar Brandell: *Freud—A Man of His Century* (Harvester/Humanities, 1979). Also the works of Alphonse Allais, Charles Baudelaire, J-L Fougeret de Monbron, J O de la Meltrie, Jean Ray, Maurice Renard, numerous others.
Memb TA.

WHITEHILL, SAMUEL ROBERT 5907 Nasco Dr, Austin, TX 78757 USA *Tel* 512-451-6632.
TL English. **SL** Hebrew. **UDC** literature (all aspects).
Hebrew Hanoch Bartov: "The Impersonator" (pending). Yitzhok Ben-Ner: *Rustic Sunset* (Inst for Translation of Hebrew Literature, 1979). Aharon Megged: "The Bat" (pending); "The Richter File" (pending). Also the works of S Y Agnon, Amir Gilboa, Yossi Gamzu, Zvi Luz.
Memb ALTA, Histadruth Ivrith. **Awards** 1976 PEN Translation grant.

WHITMAN, DANIEL F 401 Wayland Ave, Providence, RI 02906 USA *Tel* 401-272-6541.
TL English. **SL** French. **UDC** anthropology, art, business, education, ethnography, literature, government, history, law, music, political science, public administration, social services, theater.
Accred US Dept of State (consecutive & simultaneous interpretation). **Affil** Brown Univ.

WHITMAN, RUTH 1559 Beacon St, Brookline, MA 02146 USA *Tel* 617-734-2361.
TL English. **SL** French, Greek, Yiddish. **UDC** literature (poetry).
French Alain Bosquet: *Selected Poems* (New Directions, 1963). **Yiddish** Jacob Glatstein: *Selected Poems* (October House, 1972). *An Anthology of Modern Yiddish Poetry* (October House, 1966). Also the works of Oddeseus Elytis, Michel Sachtouris, George Seferis, Jules Supervielle.
Awards 1972 N Chanin Award in Translation.

WHITTALL, MARY 10 Woodway Crescent, Harrow HA1 2NQ, UK.
TL English. **SL** German. **UDC** aesthetics, archeology, architecture, art, arts/crafts, his-

tory, literature (criticism, drama, folklore, history, librettos), music, painting, theater.
German Otto Demus: *Romanesque Mural Painting* (Thames & London, 1970). Hubert Faensen & Vladimir Ivanov: *Early Russian Architecture* (Paul Elek, 1975). Curt von Westernhagen: *The Forging of "The Ring"*, co-translated with Arnold Whittall (Cambridge Univ, 1976); *Wagner: A Biography* Vol 1: 1813–64, Vol 2: 1864–83 (Cambridge Univ, 1979). Stefan Kozakiewicz: *Bernardo Bellotto* (Paul Elek, 1972). Also the works of Ferdinand Anton, Margarete Baur-Heinhold, Carl Dahlhaus, Wolf-Dieter Dube, Walter Koschatzky, ·Edith Rothe, numerous others. Also anthologies, symposia, periodical articles on art, music history.
Memb TA.

WIEMKEN, CHRISTEL Julius Vosseler-Str 149, D-2000 Hamburg 54, West Germany *Tel* (040) 56 78 65.
TL German. **SL** English. **UDC** art/art history, botany, history (cultural), horticulture, literature (children's, prose), medicine, painting.
English Lee Edson: *How We Learn* (Time-Life International, 1976). MacDonald Harris: *The Balloonist* (Rowohlt, Reinbeck, 1977). Gay G Luce: *Body Time* (Hoffmann & Campe, 1973). Margery Sharp: *Rosa* (Claassen, 1972). Also the works of Dale Brown, Erskine Caldwell, George Constable, Charles Higham, Richard Schickel, Jay Williams, numerous others.
Memb VS.

WIEMKEN, HELMUT Julius Vosseler-Str 149, D-2000 Hamburg 54, West Germany *Tel* (040) 56 78 65.
TL German. **SL** English. **UDC** literature (prose).
English Anon: *Everyman* (Philipp Reclam, 1970). Edgar Allan Poe: *Tales* (Carl Schünemann, 1960). Mark Twain: *Short Stories* (Carl Schünemann, 1960). Herman Wouk: *Youngblood Hawke* (Kindler, 1964). Also the works of Walter Allen, John Howard Griffin, Evan Hunter, Douglas Kiker, Peggy Mann, Elizabeth Mann Borgese.
Memb VS.

WIENIEWSKA, CELINA (Mrs Janson-Smith) 7 North End House, London W14 ORS, UK *Tel* (01) 603 7849.
TL English. **SL** French, German, Polish. **UDC** literature (all areas).
English Margaret Mitchell: *Gone with the Wind* (Czytelnik, 1939, 1957, 1976, 1977). **Polish** Bruno Schulz: *Cinnamon Shops* (Walker, 1963); *Sanatorium under the Sign of the Hourglass* (Walker, 1978). Julian Stryjkowski: *The Inn* (Harcourt Brace Jovanovich, 1972). Also the works of Jerzy Andrzejewski, Kazimierz Brandys, Jaroslaw Iwaszkiewicz, Czeslaw Milosz.
Accred Univ of Warsaw. **Awards** 1963 Roy Prize.

WILCOX, KENNETH P Germanic Languages, Indiana Univ, Bloomington, IN 47401 USA *Tel* 812-337-7611.
TL English. **SL** German. **UDC** literature (criticism, prose).

German Ulrich Plenzdorf: *The New Sufferings of Young W* (Ungar, 1979).
Memb ALTA.

WILKIE, EVERETT C, JR Box E, Brown Univ, Providence, RI 02912 USA *Tel* 401-845-3910.
TL English. **SL** French, Spanish. **UDC** architecture, information science, library science, literature (drama, poetry, prose), medieval texts, printing.
French Anon: *The Palatine and Autun Passions, with the Sion Fragment* (Univ Microfilms, 1977).
Memb ALTA.

WILKINS, SOPHIE 211 W 106 St #11C, New York, NY 10025 USA *Tel* 212-222-3560.
TL English. **SL** German. **UDC** archeology, art/art history, literature (criticism, drama, folklore, poetry, prose), religion/scripture.
German Thomas Bernhard: *The Lime Works* (Knopf, 1973); *Correction* (Knopf, 1979). C W Ceram: *Gods, Graves and Scholars* (Knopf, 2nd rev ed, 1963). Friedrich Schiller: *Mary Stuart* (Barron, 1959). Botho Strauss: *Devotion* (Farrar, Straus & Giroux, 1979). Ernst Fuchs: *Fuchs on Fuchs* (Abrams, forthcoming). Also the works of Martin Buber, Romain Gary, Oskar Maria Graf, Erich von Däniken, Franz Kafka, Rudolf Pörtner, Robert Musil, Christian Morgenstern, Klaus Wagn, Esther Vilar, Katia Mann, numerous others.
Awards 1974 Goethe-House-PEN Translation Prize.

WILKINSON, NATASHA 633 Kirkham St, San Francisco, CA 94122 USA *Tel* 415-566-9982.
TL English. **SL** Russian. **UDC** literature (poetry, prose), medicine, patents/trademarks, psychiatry.

WILLEN, DRENKA Harcourt Brace Jovanovich, Inc, 757 Third Ave, New York, NY 10017 USA *Tel* 212-754-3100.
TL English. **SL** Serbo-Croatian. **UDC** literature (prose).
Serbo-Croatian Dragoslav Mihailović: *When Pumpkins Blossomed* (Harcourt Brace Jovanovich, 1971). Ivo Andrić: *The Vizier's Elephant* (Harcourt Brace Jovanovich, 1962). Milovan Djilas: *Memoir of a Revolutionary* (Harcourt Brace Jovanovich, 1973). Ivan Kusan: *The Mystery of a Stolen Painting* (Harcourt Brace Jovanovich, 1975). Also the works of Matija Becković, Mihailo Lalić.

WILLIAMS, JEAN FRANTZ 10709 E 83 Terrace, Raytown, MO 64138 USA *Tel* 816-358-1957.
TL English. **SL** French. **UDC** aesthetics, art/art history, biology, botany, choreography, education, genealogy, heraldry, linguistics/philology, literature (drama, prose), painting, theater.
Memb MICATA.

WILLIAMS, MILLER Creative Writing & Translation, English, Univ of Arkansas, Fayetteville, AR 72701 USA *Tel* 501-575-4301; 521-2934.
TL English. **SL** Italian, Spanish. **UDC** literature (drama, poetry, prose).

Spanish Nicanor Parra: *Poems and Antipoems* (New Directions, 1966); *Emergency Poems* (New Directions, 1972). *Chile: An Anthology of New Writers* (Kent State Univ, 1968). Also the works of Miguel Arteche, Ephrain Barquero, G G Belli, Horst Bienek, Jacques Brel, Rolando Cardenas, Carlos Cortinez, Poli Delano, Lucienne Desnoues, Franco Fortini, Luisa Johnson, Jules Laforgue, Enrique Lihn, Antonio Machado, Christoph Meckel, Andreas Okopenko, Antonia Porta, Rainer Maria Rilke, Pedro Salinas, Alberto Rubio, Raul Ruiz, Jorge Teillier.
Memb ALTA.

WILLIAMS, ROSALIE H 750 Jeronimo Dr, Coral Gables, FL 33146 USA *Tel* 305-448-1054.
TL English. **SL** French, Russian, Spanish, Ukrainian. **UDC** jurisprudence, law, legislation, literature (prose, science fiction), medicine, sciences (medical).
Russian Yuri Dolgushin: "Generator of Miracles" (pending).

WILLSON, A LESLIE PO Box 7032, Austin, TX 78712 USA *Tel* 512-471-4123.
TL English. **SL** German. **UDC** literature (children's, drama, poetry, prose).
German Günter Grass: *The Wicked Cooks* (Harcourt Brace Jovanovich, 1967); *Max*, cotranslated with Ralph Manheim (Harcourt Brace Jovanovich, 1972). Also the works of Jurek Becker, Jürgen Becker, Hans Bender, Thomas Bernhard, Peter Bichsel, Rolf Dieter Brinkmann, Hubert Fichte, Karlhans Frank, Dieter Fringeli, Max Frisch, Harald Gröhler, Wolfgang Hildesheimer, Walter Höllerer, Uwe Johnson, Hans Peter Keller, Hans Kroliczak, Günter Kunert, Jürg Laederach, Reinhard Lettau, Friederike Mayröcker, Helga Novak, Fritz von Opel, Fritz Pratz, Gerhard Roth, Peter Rühmkorf, Mathias Schreiber, Jürgen Theobaldy, Fred Viebahn, Martin Walser, Wolfgang Weyrauch, Paul Wiens, Christa Wolf, Wolf Wondratschek.
Affil Univ of Texas at Austin. **Memb** ALTA (pres), ATA.

WILSON, CLOTILDE 6262 Vassar Ave NE, Seattle, WA 98115 USA *Tel* 206-525-9729.
TL English. **SL** French, Portuguese, Spanish. **UDC** literature (prose).
Portuguese Machado de Assis: *Philosopher or Dog?* (Noonday, 1954). Gustavo Corcão: *Who If I Cry Out* (Univ of Texas, 1967); *My Neighbor as Myself* (Longmans, Green, 1957).
Affil Univ of Washington (emeritus). **Memb** ALTA.

WILSON, DON D 121 Central Ave, Stirling, NJ 07980 USA *Tel* 201-647-5318.
TL English. **SL** Anglo-Saxon, Greek, Latin, Spanish. **UDC** literature (poetry).
Author of *Spied from the Other Side, Verse from 27 Languages, 27 Countries* (FAS, 1976); *Singular Speech, Verse from Old Babylonian to Vietnamese Now* (Triton, 1977); *Bread for All Roses for All, 5000 Years of Verse from 30 Languages* (FAS, 1977); *Spring Is Almost Gone, Verse from Alcaeus to Brecht* (Lorrah & Hitchcock, 1978).
Memb ALTA.

WILSON, LAWRENCE PATRICK ROY Three Chimneys, Fittleworth nr Pulborough, West Sussex, UK *Tel* Fittleworth 400.
TL English. **SL** French, German. **UDC** autobiography, biography, history, literature (children's, drama, prose), military science, psychiatry, religion.
German J M Bauer: *As Far As My Feet Will Carry Me* (André Deutsch, 1957). Ludwig Reiners: *Frederick the Great* (Oswald Wolff, 1960). Franz Jetzinger: *Hitler's Youth* (Hutchinson, 1960). Harald Busch: *U-Boats at War* (Putnam, 1955). Also the works of W Bergengruen, H Heiber, E von Hornstein, H v Kleist, H Mann, H Reitsch, H Rothfels, D. Schmidt, numerous others.

WINN, MARIE 194 Riverside Dr, New York, NY 10025 USA *Tel* 212-799-1994.
TL English. **SL** Czech, Russian. **UDC** literature (drama, poetry, prose).
Czech Zdena Salivarova: *Summer in Prague* (Harper & Row, 1973). **Russian** Puntaleimon Romanov: "Without Bird-Cherry Blossoms" (*Great Soviet Short Stories*, Dell, 1962). Valentin Katayev: "Our Father Who Art in Heaven" (*Great Soviet Short Stories*, Dell, 1962). Boris Bedny: "Mosquitos" (*Great Soviet Short Stories*, Dell, 1962).

WINSTON, KRISHNA 655 Bow Lane, Middletown, CT 06457 USA *Tel* 203-347-9082.
TL English. **SL** German. **UDC** education, literature (children's, criticism, drama, history, prose), psychology, theater.
German Gunilla Bergsten: *Thomas Mann's "Doctor Faustus": The Sources and Structure of the Novel* (Univ of Chicago, 1969). Heike Doutiné: *German Requiem* (Scribner, 1975). Aniela Jaffé: *C G Jung: Word and Image* (Princeton Univ/Bollingen, 1979). Oskar Schlemmer: *Letters and Diaries* (Wesleyan Univ, 1972). Also the works of Karl Christ, Odön von Horváth, Erich Kahler, Herman Meyer, Günther Pflug, Manès Sperber.
Affil Wesleyan Univ (German Lang & Lit).

WINSTON, RICHARD & CLARA Duino Farm via Jacksonville Stage, Brattleboro, VT 05301 USA *Tel* 802-368-7119.
TL English. **SL** German. **UDC** astronomy, history, literature (all areas), paleontology, philosophy, theology.
German Heimito von Doderer: *The Demons* (Knopf, 1961). Hermann Hesse: *The Glass Bead Game* (Holt, Rinehart & Winston, 1969). Franz Kafka: *Letters to Friends, Family and Editors* (Schocken, 1977). Thomas Mann: *Letters 1889–1955* (Knopf, 1971). Over 150 book-length translations of the works of Konrad Adenauer, Achmed Amba, Alfred Andersch, Hannah Arendt, Hans Baumann, Emery Bekessy, Margot Benary-Isbert, Ernst Benz, Thomas Bernhard, C W Ceram, Hermann Dembeck, Otto Dietrich, Vitus B Dröscher, Friedrich Dürrenmatt, Alice Ekert-Rotholz, Gerhart Ellert, Horst Fanger, Joachim Fest, Viktor E Frankl, Alexander M Frey, René Fülöp-Miller, Heinz Gartmann, Uwe George, Hans Bernd Gisevius, Martin Gregor-Dellin, Ida Friederike Goerres, Adolf Haller, Willi Heinrich, Hans Herlin, Rolf Hochhuth, H E Jacob, Henry Jaeger, Uwe Johnson, C G Jung, Erich Kahler, Werner Keller, Hellmut Kirst, J Klein-Harapash, Ludwig Koch-Isenberg,

Kaethe Kollwitz, Erich Kuby, A Lernet-Holenia, Gunnel Linde, Elinor Lipper, Karl Loewenstein, Edgar Maass, Valeriu Marcu, Walter Mehring, József Cardinal Mindszenty, Johanna Moosdorf, Walter Nigg, Joseph Pieper, Theodore Plievier, Hermann Rauschning, Theodor Reik, Ludwig Reiners, Erich Maria Remarque, Luise Rinser, Hans Sahl, Erich Schenk, Ernst Schnabel, Hans-Joachim Scoeps, Walter Schoenstedt, Otto Schrag, Hermann & George Schreiber, Albert Schweitzer, Paul Sethe, Johannes Mario Simmel, Albert Speer, Ethelberg Stauffer, Elsa Steinmann, Rudolf Thiel, Jürgen Thorwald, Herbert Wendt, Simon Wiesenthal, Harry Winterfeld, Hans-Georg Wunderlich, Reiner Zimnik, Carl Zuckmayer.

Memb ATA. **Awards** 1966 Alexander Gode Medal (ATA), 1971 American PEN Translation Prize, 1978 National Book Award in Translation.

WINTER, ELSE Marschalkenstr 77, CH-4054 Basel, Switzerland *Tel* (061) 38 84 49.

TL German. **SL** English, French. **UDC** music, musical history, musical instruments.

English Leonard Bernstein: *The Infinite Variety of Music* (Rainer Wunderlich, 1969); *Young People's Concerts* (Rainer Wunderlich, 1969). Gerald Moore: *Am I Too Loud?; The Schubert Song Cycles* (Rainer Wunderlich, 1963, 1975). Yehudi Menuhin: *Violin* (Albert Müller/Ruschlikon, 1973). Also the works of Leon Gossens, Gregor Piatigorsky, Edwin Roxburgh, Percy A Scholes, Douglas Sutherland, Henry Temianka.

Memb ASTI, VDÜ.

WINTERS, ANNE 22 Robinson St, Cambridge, MA 02138 USA; c/o Princeton Univ Pr, Princeton, NJ 08540 USA.

TL English. **SL** French. **UDC** literature (poetry).

French Robert Marteau: *Salamander: Selected Poems* (Princeton Univ, 1979).

WITRIOL, JOSEPH 63 Mayfield Ave, London N12 9JG, UK *Tel* (01) 445 2422.

TL English. **SL** French, German, Hebrew, Yiddish. **UDC** law, literature (prose), linguistics, medicine, military science.

German Max Brod: *Heinrich Heine* (Vallentine Mitchell, 1956). **Hebrew** Beno Rotherberg: *God's Wilderness* (Thames & Hudson, 1961).

Memb TG.

WOLF, PATRICIA 221 Bungalow Ave, San Rafael, CA 94901 USA *Tel* 415-453-1381.

TL English. **SL** French. **UDC** art/art history, history, literature (history, librettos, prose), painting.

French Jean Orieux: *Talleyrand* (Knopf, 1974). Claude Manceron: *Twilight of the Old Order* (Knopf, 1977). Jacques Ellul: *Autopsy of Revolution* (Knopf, 1971). Philippe Erlanger: *Richelieu* (Stein & Day, 1968). Also the works of Pierre Boulle, Jean Lacouture, Patrick Modiano, Maurice Pons.

WOODRUFF, MARGARET S 115 W 32 St, Austin, TX 78705 USA *Tel* 512-474-1396.

TL English. **SL** German. **UDC** aesthetics, art history, communications, documentation, education, ethics, history, library science, linguistics/philology, literature (all areas), philosophy, psychology, social sciences, theater.

German the works of Carola Benninghoven, Elias Canetti, Robert Kahn, Christoph Meckel, Thomas Velentin, Gabriele Wohmann.

Accred/Memb ALTA, ATA, TRACT.

WOOLSEY, WALLACE 619 Grove St, Denton, TX 76201 USA *Tel* 817-387-1103.

TL English. **SL** Spanish. **UDC** economics, education, history, literature (poetry, prose), sociology.

Spanish Adolfo Bécquer: *The Witch of Trasmoz and Other Tales* (Olympic, 1965). Fernando Rojas: *La Celestina* (Las Américas, 1969). Francisco de Quevedo: *Dreams* (Barron's, 1976). Lorenzo de Zavala: *Journey to the United States of North America* (Shoal Creek, forthcoming).

Affil Texas Woman's Univ (emeritus). **Memb** ALTA.

YALON, JUDITH 13b Menuha Venahala St, Rehovot, Israel.

TL English. **SL** French, Hebrew. **UDC** cookery, Israel and the Arab world, Judaica, jurisprudence, law (international, maritime, property), legislation, literature (children's, history, poetry, prose), Middle Eastern affairs, military science, political economy/science, psychology, public administration, shipping, sociology, Zionist history.

Hebrew Arie Lova Eliav: *Land of the Hart* (Jewish Publications Soc of Amer, 1974). Also the works of Uri Dan, Yerahmiel Weingarten.

Accred Tel Aviv Interpreters School. **Affil** Tel Aviv Translators' Pool.

YATES, DONALD A Romance Languages, Michigan State Univ, 537 Wells Hall, East Lansing, MI 48824 USA *Tel* 517-351-1997.

TL English. **SL** Spanish. **UDC** literature (drama, criticism, poetry, prose).

Spanish Jorge Luis Borges: *Labyrinths* (New Directions, 1962). Marco Denevi: *Rosa at Ten O'Clock* (Holt, Rinehart & Winston, 1964). Adolfo Bioy Casares: *Diary of the War of the Pig* (McGraw-Hill, 1972). Manuel Peyrou: *Thunder of the Roses* (Herder & Herder, 1972). Also the works of Velmiro Ayala Gauna, Enrique Anderson Imbert, Alfonso Ferrari Amores, Hernando Téllez, Gregorio López y Fuentes, numerous others.

Memb ALTA.

YOSHIDA, YOSHIO Ctr for Japanese Social & Political Studies, 2-8-8 Nishinogawa, Komae-shi, Tokyo 201, Japan *Tel* (03) 489-2175.

TL & SL English & Japanese. **UDC** political science, social science.

Affil The Japan Interpreter.

ZATZ, ASA Amsterdam 212-8, Mexico 11, DF, Mexico *Tel* 905-564-1186.

TL English. **SL** Spanish. **UDC** aesthetics, anthropology, art/art history, business, economics, law, medicine, theater.

Spanish Alonso Aguilar: *Pan Americanism: From Monroe to the Present* (Monthly Review, 1968). Luis Cardoza y Aragón: *Mexican Art Today* (Fondo de Cultura Económico, 1966).

Antonio Rodríguez: *Posada: The Man Who Portrayed an Epoch* (Domés, 1978). Also the works of Enrique Alvarez del Castillo, Ferdinand Bruckner, José Luis Cuevas, numerous others.

Memb AIT.

ZDANYS, JONAS 2151 Berlin Turnpike, Newington, CT 06111 USA *Tel* 203-666-6735.

TL English. **SL** Lithuanian. **UDC** literature (all areas).

Lithuanian *Selected Post-War Lithuanian Poetry* (Manyland, 1978). Leonardas Andriekus: *Eternal Dream: Selected Poems* (Manyland, 1978). Sigitas Geda: *Songs of Autumn* (Slow Loris, 1978). Also the works of Jonas Aistis, Kazys Boruta, Jurgis Gliauda, Kotryna Grigaityte, Kostas Kubilinskas, Algimantas Mackus, numerous others.

Memb Lithuanian Writers Assn in Exile.

ZINS, CÉLINE 13 rue de Thorigny, F-75003 Paris, France *Tel* 271 07 47.

TL French. **SL** English, Spanish. **UDC** literature (drama, prose).

English Philip Roth: *Goodbye Columbus* (Gallimard, 1962). Oscar Lewis: *The Children of Sanchez* (Gallimard, 1963). Also the works of Donald Barthleme, Alan Burns, Paul Bowles, Truman Capote, Robert Creeley, Sean O'Casey, Douglas Woolf, numerous others.

Memb ATLF. **Awards** 1963 Prix du Meilleur Livre Étranger.

ZIPSER, RICHARD A German & Russian, Oberlin College, Oberlin, OH 44074 USA *Tel* 216-775-8659.

TL English. **SL** German. **UDC** literature (criticism, prose).

German the works of Jurek Becker, Tankred Dorst, Ulrich Plenzdorf.

Memb ALTA.

ZOHN, HARRY 48 Davis Ave, West Newton, MA 02165 USA *Tel* 617-969-9324.

TL English. **SL** German. **UDC** art history, education, history, linguistics, literature (criticism, history, librettos, poetry, prose, songs), music, philosophy, political science, psychiatry, psychology, religion, sociology, theater.

German Theodor Herzl: *Complete Diaries*, 5 vols (Herzl/Yoseloff, 1960–61). Kurt Tucholsky: *The World Is a Comedy* (Sci-Art, 1957). Walter Benjamin: *Illuminations* (Harcourt Brace, 1968). Marianne Weber: *Max Weber, A Biography* (Wiley & Sons, 1975). Also the works of Hannah Arendt, Raoul Auernheimer, Ilse Blumenthal-Weiss, Max Brod, Martin Buber, Jacob Burckhardt, Franz Theodor Csokor, Vera Ferra-Mikura, Z F Finot, Sigmund Freud, Erich Fried, Albrecht Goes, Giora Josephthal, Erich Kästner, Rudolf Kayser, Hermann Kesten, Karl Kraus, Else Lasker-Schüler, Mira Lobe, Heinrich Mann, Zenta Maurina, Eugen Relgis, Nelly Sachs, Arthur Schnitzler, Oskar Jan Tauschinski, Walter Toman, Christian Wallner, Robert Weltsch, Ernst Wiechert, Hugo Zuckermann, Friderike Maria Zweig, Stefan Zweig. Also articles on translation for *The Word Guild Magazine*.

Affil Brandeis Univ. **Memb** ALTA, ATA.

ZUCKERMAN, MARVIN S 555 Marquette St, Pacific Palisades, CA 90272 USA *Tel* 213-454-4081; 781-1200.

TL English. **SL** Yiddish. **UDC** aerospace, anthropology, engineering, ethics, ethnography, geography, government, history, linguistics/philology, literature (all areas), music, philosophy, political science, social sciences, sociology, theater.

Yiddish Ignaz Bernstein: *Yiddish Sayings Mama Never Taught You* (Perivale, 1975). Also the works of Moishe L Halpern, H Leivick, Mendl Mann, Avrom Reisin, Isaac E Ronch, Abraham Sutskever.

Affil Los Angeles Valley College.

ZUR NEDDEN PFERDEKAMP, MODESTE Schuetzenweg 1, D-7840 Muellheim 11, West Germany *Tel* (07631) 2463.

TL German. **SL** English. **UDC** aesthetics, art, art/crafts, astrology, ethics, history, human resources, literature (drama, prose), occultism, painting, philosophy, religion, social sciences, sculpture, theater.

English Arnold J Toynbee: *Experiences* (List, 1970). Carleton S Coon: *Story of Man* (Kiepenheuer & Witsch, 1970). Gunter W Remmling: *Road to Suspicion* (Ferdinand Enke, 1975). H H Ben Sasson: *A History of the Jewish People* (Beck'sche, 1979). Also the works of J P Balsdon, Nicholas Gage, Lancelot

Lengyel, Ralph Linton, Talcott Parsons, Arthur Schweitzer, Helen Webster, others.

Memb VDÜ.

ZWEIFEL, HEINRICH M Kanzleistr 115, CH-8004 Zurich, Switzerland *Tel* (01) 241 61 30.

TL German. **SL** English, French, Japanese. **UDC** aesthetics, archeology, art history, arts/crafts, economics, ethnography, government, history, linguistics/philology, literature (criticism, history, poetry, prose), painting, philosophy, political economy/science, psychology, sciences (applied), sociology, textiles, theater.

Memb ATA.

Humanistic/Literary Translators
—Classified by Language

Translators are classified here by target and source languages. The target language (language *into which* a translation is made) appears in boldface caps; source language (language *from which* a translation is made) appears in upper and lowercase boldface. Translators' names, in alphabetical order under their specific target/source languages, are followed by the two-letter state abbreviations or abbreviated country name to identify regional accessibility. Emphasis is given here on English either as a source or target language.

Into ARABIC from:

English

Al-Ghazouli, M (UK)
Lovell, E K (AZ)
Semaan, K I (NY)

Into BULGARIAN from:

English

Slavoc, A V (DC)

Into CHINESE from:

English

Fon, M (Hong Kong)
Wang, H-M (MA)

Into CZECH from:

English

Kuby, A (OH)

Into DANISH from:

English

Blecher, L & G (NY)

Into DUTCH from:

English

André, D (Bel)
Van Vessem, D (Neth)

Into ENGLISH from:

Afrikaans

Salway, L (UK)

Anglo-Saxon

Haley, A W, Jr. (MA)
Morgan, E (UK)
Wilson, D D (NJ)

Arabic

Al-Ghazouli, M (UK)
Bennani, B M (NY)
Boyle, J A (UK)
Ghossein, M (NY)
Holland, M (UK)
Lovell, E K (AZ)
Nichols, J M (MI)
Semaan, K I (NY)
Tomkinson, M (UK)

Armenian

Boyle, J A (UK)
Kudian, M (UK)

Bengali

Bhaktivedanta, A C (CA)
Mukherjee, P (Fr)

Bulgarian

Miletich, I (IL)
Slavov, A V (DC)

Byelorussian

Bird, T E (NY)

Castilian

Cardozo, M da S (DC)

Catalan

Bogin, M (NY)
Dagenais, J (IL)
Griffin, P (CA)
Hohenstein, A K (RI)
Raffel, B (CO)
Waley, P J (UK)
Wellwarth, G E (NY)

Chinese

Birrell, A M (NY)
Braïnin, P (NY)
Burls, M (Ger)
Eber, I (Isr)
Murray, P (Japan)
Payne, R (NY)
Stryk, L (IL)
Sutherland, J I (CA)
Teele, N J (TX)
Wang, H-M (MA)

Choctaw

Barnes, J (MO)

Croatian

Glasnovic, R (NY)
Sita, J B (ID)

Czech

Falla, P S (UK)
Fox, H (UK)
Harkins, W E (NY)
Heim, M H (CA)
Hrubý, O S (NY)
Kuby, A (OH)
Kussi, P (NY)
Osers, E (UK)

Poláčková-Henley, K (Can)
Winn, M (NY)

Danish

Blecher, L & G (NY)
Born, A (UK)
Brønner, H (VA)
Christensen, N (NY)
Field, E (NY)
Friis, E J (NJ)
Harvey, A-C H (CA)
La Farge, S (MA)
Malmberg, C (NH)
Payne, R (NY)
Sandstroem, Y L (MA)
Sjöberg, L T (NY)
Spink, R (UK)
Tate, J (UK)
Teal, T (NY)

Dutch

Beekman, E M (MA)
Coetzee, J M (S Afr)
De Graaf, K (UK)
Dixon, A (UK)
Haasl, E J (Bel)
Hacken, R (KS)
Hesseling, C G (IA)
Krispyn, E (GA)
Lefevere, A (Bel)
Rooda, A W M (NJ)
Salway, L (UK)
Smith, D (Neth)
Smith, N D (UK)
Tyler, L S (CA)

English (Middle)

Rosenberg, JL (PA)

Estonian

Lyman, H (MA)

Faroese

Brønner, H (VA)

Finnish

Dana, K O (VT)
Hvidonov, A (NY)
Karvonen, H J (TX)
Virtanen, J O (OR)

French

Aldan, D (NY)
Alexander, L (PA)
Alphonese-Ferere, G (PA)
Amphoux, N L (Fr)
Anders, P (MA)
Arrowsmith, W (VT)
Babb, E A (AR)
Backus, D (WI)
Bair, L (NY)
Barko, C (NY)
Barnes, J (MO)
Barnstone, W (IN)
Barrows, A (CA)
Barry, R (UK)
Becker, S (MA)
Belitt, B (VT)
Bieber, K F (NY)
Biguenet, J (LA)
Bishop, M B (IA)
Black, K (UK)
Bogin, M (NY)
Bourke, L H (IN)
Braley, A (UK)
Brereton, G (UK)
Briffault, H (NY)
Briscoe, P (CA)
Brovender, J (MA)
Brownjohn, J M (UK)
Bruzina, R C (KY)
Bryson, J S-A (CA)
Bull, G A (UK)
Buranelli, A (NJ)
Burton, T E (Bel)
Cardozo, M da S (DC)
Carpenter, J & B (WA)
Caserta, E G (NC)
Cassell, A K (IL)
Caws, M A (NY)
Chevalier, H M (Fr)
Claudel, C A (LA)
Cline, R H (MD)
Cloutier, D (RI)
Comeau, P T (NM)
Cormier, R J (PA)
Cowood, J P (Bel)
Czarnecki, M (Can)
Dagenais, J (IL)
Dalven, R (NY)
Daniels, G (NY)
Danielson, J D (CT)
Day, J (Fr)
Dees, C J (Sp)
Detiere, D J (NY)
Dewees, A R (TX)
Diehl, P S (CA)
Dirks, M D (NY)
Dorian, M (RI)
Doyle, L (NY)
DuVal, J T (GA)
Fahnestock (Leggett), L (NY)
Falla, P S (UK)

Fawcett, C R (MA)
Feeney, M (NY)
Ferguson, C A (ME)
Field, F (CA)
Fox, E (NY)
Fox, H (UK)
Frame, D M (NY)
Fraser, D A (UK)
Freeland, Sr J P (TN)
Frenaye, F (NY)
Frierson, J W & E B (HI)
Garreau, J E (MA)
Gavronsky, S (NY)
Ghossein, M (NY)
Gill, E P (NJ)
Gillespie, G (CA)
Goldgar, H (LA)
Goldstein, S (CA)
Grandle, L H (VA)
Green, P M (TX)
Gregory, P B (MA)
Greinke, E (MI)
Gross, A (NY)
Guenther, C (MO)
Gugli, W V (MA)
Guicharnaud, J (CT)
Haasl, E J (Bel)
Hamburger, M (UK)
Harcourt, F (UK)
Hemschemeyer, J (NJ)
Hennessy, E B (NY)
Hersh, E E (NH)
Heurck, J van (CT)
Hochman, S (NY)
Hold, O (FL)
Holland, M (UK)
Holoch, G (VT)
Hulick, E C (NY)
Jenkins, M F O (TX)
Jurgson, T (NY)
Kaplan, R F S (NY)
Karr, P A (WI)
Keith, H H (CA)
Kelly, L L (TX)
King, J F (MA)
Klin, G (NJ)
Kotta, S (NY)
Kruuse, E (NY)
Kuhner, H (Aust)
Lamont, R C (NY)
Lang, S (IL)
Laughlin, J (CT)
Lawrence, M L (MA)
Lefevere, A (Bel)
Leonard, B (MN)
Locke, D M (Fr)
Loos, D S (VT)
López-Morillas, F M (RI)
Lowe, P T (NY)
Lunde, D (NY)
Lykiard, A (UK)
Lyman, H (MA)
McBride, C A (NY)
McConnell-Duff, A B (Fr)
MacDonald, S (MA)
McDougall, R (NY)
McEwan-Alvarado, A (CA)
McIntyre, A (NY)
Mackworth, C (Fr)
Mandel, O (CA)
Manning, M (CT)
Marsh, G (UK)
Mead, A D (Ger)
Meyer, P (UK)
Michael, M (UK)

Miller, J M (PA)
Mitchell, B (AR)
Morgan, E (UK)
Morrison, R H (Austral)
Mosbacher, E (UK)
Mossiker, F (TX)
Mukherjee, P (Fr)
Murphy, Sr M B (NY)
Murray, P (Japan)
Neugroschel, J (NY)
Nichols, J M (MI)
Nisetich, F J (MA)
O'Connell, M J (NY)
Odio, E B (AR)
Ohlendorf, S M (TX)
Ortzen, L (UK)
Paddon, H E (UK)
Padgett, R (NY)
Palladino, J G (NY)
Pallister, J L (OH)
Paolucci, A (NY)
Paroutaud, M (CA)
Partridge, F (UK)
Patrick, B E & L L (KS)
Patt, R A (AR)
Paul, D (UK)
Pearce, B L (UK)
Penglase, W O, Jr (NY)
Penman, B (UK)
Pevear, R (NY)
Pinkham, J (MA)
Poller, N (Fr)
Poulin, A, Jr (NY)
Preisser, D C (MD)
Raffel, B (CO)
Raley, H (OK)
Ramsey, P (TN)
Ranum, P M (MD)
Ratner, R (NY)
Reynolds, G E (MD)
Richardson, E A (FL)
Roberts, W H & M M (NM)
Romero, I W (NY)
Rose, M G (NY)
Rosenberg, J L (PA)
Royall-Manach, C Y (MO)
Rudolf, A (UK)
Rukeyser, M (NY)
Salemson, H J (NY)
Salinger, H (NC)
Samelson, W (TX)
Savory, T (MA)
Schulte, R (TX)
Scott, J A (NY)
Sebba, H (GA)
Seligman, J (UK)
Shapiro, N R (CT)
Shattuck, R (VA)
Shepley, J (NY)
Shirley, J (UK)
Shore, M (CT)
Siddall, A T (KS)
Sisson, C H (UK)
Sita, J B (ID)
Small, R B (OH)
Smith, D J (NY)
Smith, N D (UK)
Smith, W J (NY)
Soceanu-Vamos, M (NY)
Sokolinsky, M (NY)
Solomon, S (UK)
Stankovic, J A (MD)
Stevens, J (UK)
Stewart, J (UK)
Strachan, W J (UK)

Strawn, R R (IN)
Stryk, L (IL)
Summer, S C (NY)
Szell, T (NJ)
Tanasescu, G (Rum)
Taylor, M A (Fr)
Taylor, M R (IL)
Terstegge, Sr G (IN)
Tomkinson, M (UK)
Tool, D C (AR)
Trask, W R (NY)
Turnell, M (UK)
Tyler, L S (CA)
Underwood, J K (Fr)
Unwin, G (UK)
Urdang, E B (RI)
Urquidi, M M (DC)
Van der Schalie, F B (OH)
Vennewitz, L (Can)
Venrick, B B (OH)
Vivian, K (UK)
Vosteen, T R (IA)
Waldrop, R (RI)
Waley, P J (UK)
Warnick, M C (NH)
Weaver, E B (MA)
Weaver, H (NY)
Weber, Sr M C (OH)
Webster, M T (MA)
Weightman, J G & J D (UK)
Weissbort, D (IA)
Wellwarth, G E (NY)
White, I (UK)
Whitman, D F (RI)
Whitman, R (MA)
Wieniewska, C (UK)
Wilkie, E C, Jr (RI)
Williams, J F (MO)
Williams, R H (FL)
Wilson, C (WA)
Wilson, D D (NJ)
Wilson, L P R (UK)
Winters, A (NJ)
Witriol, J (UK)
Wolf, P (CA)
Yalon, J (Isr)

French (Old)

DuVal, J T (GA)
Shirley, J (UK)

Georgian

Vivian, K (UK)

German

Adair, M (Ger)
Aldan, D (NY)
Anders, P (MA)
Arno, P van H (NY)
Bacon, T (TX)
Barnes, J (MO)
Barry, R (UK)
Barstad, N K (OH)
Berger, D (NY)
Bieber, K F (NY)
Blecher, L & G (NY)
Boney, E E (CA)
Braley, A (UK)
Brewster, R R (IN)
Britt, C W (AZ)
Brownjohn, J M (UK)
Bruehl, E H (NY)
Burls, M (Ger)
Burton, T E (Bel)

Casewit, C W (CO)
Cassell, A K (IL)
Chappel, A H (LA)
Choset, C (NY)
Collins, J R (UK)
Cormier, R J (PA)
Cowood, J P (Bel)
Davis, L K (CA)
Del Caro, A (MN)
DeVolld, W L (CA)
Dick, E S (KS)
Dorian, M (RI)
Dukas, V (CA)
Eber, I (Isr)
Falla, P S (UK)
Fickert, K J (OH)
Fleisher, L (AZ)
Fox, H (UK)
Fraser, D A (UK)
Galt, A B (OH)
Garrin, S H (TX)
Geisel, E (Aust)
Gelly, A (CA)
Getsi, L C (IL)
Gillespie, G (CA)
Gogol, J M (OR)
Goyne, M A (TX)
Graham, H R (VA)
Grandle, L H (VA)
Gross, A (NY)
Hacken, R (KS)
Hahn, M (MD)
Hall, M B (GA)
Hamburger, M (UK)
Hannah, R W (CA)
Hannum, H G (CT)
Harris, B L M (CO)
Hein, R (CT)
Hennessy, D (CA)
Hennessy, E B (NY)
Hersh, E E (NH)
Heurck, J van (CT)
Hoegl, J K (IL)
Hoffman, S B (CO)
Hold, O (FL)
Holland, M E (IL)
Hutter, C (NY)
Jackiw, S E (PA)
Johnson, L M (CT)
Jones, G F (MD)
Kanes, E L (CA)
Kline, G L (PA)
Knight, M (CA)
Koblick, D B (CA)
Kornfeld, M (Isr)
Krispyn, E (GA)
Kuhner, H (Aust)
Kussi, P (NY)
Lacy, A F (WI)
Last, R W (UK)
Latimer, R (AL)
Laughlin, J (CT)
Lefevere, A (Bel)
Lesser, R (NY)
Lich, G E (TX)
Livingston, K I R (OH)
Lowcock, P H (VA)
Lyman, H (MA)
McAuley, A (WA)
McCarthy, Sister M F (MA)
MacDonald, L &
   H Weissenborn (UK)
McMahon, J V (GA)
Mandel, O (CA)
Manning, M (CT)

Marsh, G (UK)
Marshall, T M (IL)
Middleton, C (TX)
Miller, J W (KY)
Mitchell, B (IN)
Mitchell, J M (UK)
Monahan, P A (CA)
Monas, S (TX)
Mosbacher, E (UK)
Musmann, K (CA)
Nardroff, E von (NJ)
Neugroschel, J (NY)
Nisetich, F J (MA)
Noonan, F W (NY)
Nowell, J (UK)
O'Connell, M J (NY)
Odio, E B (AR)
O'Flaherty, J C (NC)
Oppenheimer, D (NY)
Osers, E (UK)
Paolucci, A (NY)
Penman, B (UK)
Peterson, Paul W (PA)
Pohoryles, B M (NY)
Polgar, S (PA)
Pollak, F (WI)
Poulin, A, Jr, (NY)
Pusey W W, III (VA)
Rabin, B B (Isr)
Raffel, B (CO)
Ray, S H (NY)
Read, R R, III (TX)
Regehr, L (WA)
Reichenbach, B (MA)
Reik, M M (NY)
Reynolds, G E (MD)
Robertson, E H (UK)
Rooda, A W M (NJ)
Rose, M G (NY)
Rosenberg, J L (PA)
Rukeyser, M (NY)
Salinger, H (NC)
Samelson, W (TX)
Savory, T (MA)
Sax, B (NY)
Schmidt, H J (OH)
Schneewind, E H (NY)
Schoenman, H B & T (CA)
Schulte, R (TX)
Sebba, H (GA)
Seiler, C I (IN)
Seligman, J (UK)
Sellner, T F (NC)
Shub, E (NY)
Simmermann, U (MN)
Skelton, G (UK)
Smith, D (Neth)
Smith, H A (Ger)
Smith, N D (UK)
Sokolinsky, M (NY)
Solomon, S (UK)
Solyn, P (OR)
Sonnenfeld, M (NY)
Stanley, P H (FL)
Stein, M (IL)
Stone, B R (CA)
Strachan, W J (UK)
Sussdorf, A (Ger)
Talbot, K (UK)
Tanasescu, G (Rum)
Tomkinson, M (UK)
Trahan, E W (CA)
Trask, W R (NY)
Tucker, E (UK)
Unwin, G (UK)

Van der Schalie, F B (OH)
Vennewitz, L (Can)
Victor-Rood, J (CO)
Waldrop, R (RI)
Ward, D J (TX)
Webster, M T (MA)
Wellwarth, G E (NY)
Wensinger, A S (CT)
Whaley, J (UK)
White, I (UK)
Whittall, M (UK)
Wieniewska, C (UK)
Wilcox, K P (IN)
Wilkins, S (NY)
Willson, A L (TX)
Wilson, L P R (UK)
Winston, K (CT)
Winston, R & C (VT)
Witriol, J (UK)
Woodruff, M S (TX)
Zipser, R A (OH)
Zohn, H (MA)

Greek
Collins, J R (UK)
Dalven, R (NY)
Diehl, P S (CA)
Green, P M (TX)
Keeley, E (NJ)
Keeley, M (NJ)
Myrsiades, K (PA)
Nisetich, F J (MA)
Whitman, R (MA)
Wilson, D D (NJ)

Greek (Classical)
Arrowsmith, W (VT)
Barnstone, W (IN)
Green, P M (TX)
Lattimore, R (PA)
Lefevere, A (Bel)
O'Connell, R (PA)
Ramsey, P (TN)
Roche, P (UK)
Simpson, M (NY)
Sommerstein, A H (UK)
Turner, P (UK)

Hebrew
Friend, R (Isr)
Merowitz, M J (NY)
Rabin, B B (Isr)
Whitehill, S R (TX)
Witriol, J (UK)
Yalon, J (Isr)

Hindi
Chandra, G S S (WA)
Sharma, A (Austral)

Hungarian
Basa, E M (MD)
Debreczeny, P (NC)
Értavy-Baráth, J M (GA)
Gömöri, G (UK)
Kabdeb, T (UK)
McConnell-Duff, A B (Fr)
Nyerges, A N (KY)
Polgar, S (PA)
Rudolf, A (UK)
Schoenman, H B & T (CA)
Smith, W J (NY)
Szell, T (NJ)
Szendrey, T (PA)

Indonesian
Aveling, H (Austral)
Hoffman, S B (CO)
Raffel, B (CO)

Irish
O'Connell, R (PA)

Irish (Old)
Cormier, R J (PA)

Italian
Arrowsmith, W (VT)
Barolini, H (NY)
Barrows, A (CA)
Belitt, B (VT)
Benedict, R (NY)
Bergin, T G (CT)
Bogin, M (NY)
Briffault, H (NY)
Bull, G A (UK)
Cardozo, M da S (DC)
Caserta, E G (NC)
Cassell, A K (IL)
Coppotelli, A (NY)
Cormier, R J (PA)
Day, J (Fr)
Doyle, L (NY)
Fahnestock (Leggett), L (NY)
Fawcett, C R (MA)
Feldman, R (MA)
Ferguson, C A (ME)
Field, F (CA)
Flint, R W (MA)
Fraser, D A (UK)
Fratti, M (NY)
Frenaye, F (NY)
Green, P M (TX)
Grindrod, M K (UK)
Gross, A (NY)
Guenther, C (MO)
Hamburger, M (UK)
Hochman, S (NY)
Impey, M H (IN)
Judge, F (NY)
King, M J (TX)
Laughlin, J (CT)
Lowe, P T (NY)
MacDonald, S (MA)
Marracino, P (NY)
Morgan, E (UK)
Morrison, R H (Austral)
Mosbacher, E (UK)
O'Connell, M J (NY)
Palladino, J G (NY)
Pallister, J L (OH)
Paolucci, A (NY)
Patt, R A (AR)
Penman, B (UK)
Pevear, R (NY)
Pontiero, G (UK)
Ramsey, P (TN)
Rouiller, A G F (MD)
Shepley, J (NY)
Singleton, C S (NJ)
Sisson, C H (UK)
Sita, J B (ID)
Smith, W J (NY)
Stefanile, F (IN)
Strachan, W J (UK)
Strawn, R R (IN)
Swann, B (NY)
Tool, D C (AR)
Treitel, R (OK)

Waley, P J (UK)
Weaver, E B (MA)
Webster, M T (MA)
Williams, M (AR)

Japanese

Birrell, A M (NY)
Chambers, A H (CT)
Elliott, W I (OR)
Epp, R C (CA)
Ericson, M (Japan)
Fraser, D A (UK)
Hibbett, H S (MA)
Hurst, G C, III (KS)
Kano, T (Japan)
Keene, D (NY)
Murray, P (Japan)
Riggs, L (Japan)
Root, W R (Japan)
Sakurai, E (HI)
Seidensticker, E (NY)
Spackman, D M (MA)
Stryk, L (IL)
Takechi, M (Japan)
Teele, N J (TX)
Tsumura, Y (CA)
Yoshida, Y (Japan)

Kannada

Chandra, G S S (WA)

Korean

Hurst, G C, III (KS)

Laotian

Laughman, P S (NC)

Latin

Anders, P (MA)
Arrowsmith, W (VT)
Bergin, T G (CT)
Cassell, A K (IL)
Cook, G (CA)
Cormier, R J (PA)
Dagenais, J (IL)
Diehl, P S (CA)
Fawcett, C R (MA)
Green, P M (TX)
Isbell, H (UT)
Lefevere, A (Bel)
McDermott, C (NM)
Nisetich, F J (MA)
O'Connell, R (PA)
Ramsey, Paul (TN)
Roche, P (UK)
Savory, T (MA)
Simpson, M (NY)
Sisson, C H (UK)
Tanasescu, G (Rum)
Turner, P (UK)
Wilson, D D (NJ)

Latin (Medieval)

Freeland, Sr J P (TN)

Latvian

Huggins, E N (OR)

Lithuanian

Dukas, V (CA)
Kelertas, V (WI)
Stark, M (CA)
Zdanys, J (CT)

Macedonian

Holton, W M (MD)
Mihailovich, V D (NC)
Miletich, I (IL)

Malay

Aveling, H (Austral)

Norwegian

Blecher, L & G (NY)
Born, A (UK)
Brønner, H (VA)
Christensen, N (NY)
Friis, E J (NJ)
Harvey, A-C H (CA)
La Farge, S (MA)
Malmberg, C (NH)
Mead, A D (Ger)
Michael, M (UK)
Nations, E (Can)
Sandstroem, Y L (MA)
Sjöberg, L T (NY)
Spink, R (UK)
Tate, J (UK)
Teal, T (NY)
Tveite, A E (Nor)

Nuer (African)

Svoboda, T (NY)

Persian (Farsi)

Boyle, J A (UK)
Shahnazarian, G (NY)

Polish

Carpenter, J & B (WA)
Carynnyk, M (Can)
Dejlidko, B (UK)
Falla, P S (UK)
Friedberg, M (IL)
Gogol, J M (OR)
Gömöri, G (UK)
Holton, W M (MD)
Iribarne, L (Can)
Krynski, M J (NC)
Michael, M (UK)
Rozenbaum, W (IN)
Samelson, W (TX)
Slobin, G N (CT)
Swietlicki, A (MO)
Syrop, K (UK)
Tworek, J (CA)
Welsh, D (MI)
Wieniewska, C (UK)

Portuguese

Bird, P G (CT)
Bissett, J I (AZ)
Brownjohn, J M (UK)
Cardozo, M De S (DC)
Colchie, T (NY)
De Oliveira, C (SC)
Fitz, E E (PA)
Giacomelli, E F (Can)
Griffin, P (CA)
Henriques, E R (NC)
Honig, E (RI)
Hower, A (FL)
Jackson, K D (TX)
Keith, H H (CA)
Longland, J R (NY)
Loos, D S (VT)
Lowe, E (NY, Col)
Lyday, L F (PA)

Mathes, D L (MO)
Merello, B S (DC)
Murphy, Sr M B (NY)
O'Connell, R (PA)
Pallister, J L (OH)
Pendry, D A (AR)
Pontiero, G (UK)
Rabassa, G (NY)
Roberts, W H & M M (NM)
Sampaio, A F (Brazil)
Sayers, R S (WI)
Sousa, R W (MN)
Spingarn, L P (CA)
Tolman, J M (NM)
Tomlins, J E (NM)
Trask, W R (NY)
Vasconcellos, M (DC)
Wilson, C (WA)

Portuguese (Brazilian)

Brown, A (SC)
Choset, C (NY)
Laughman, P S (NC)
Levitin, A (OH)

Provençal

Bogin, M (NY)

Provençal (Old)

Bergin, T G (CT)

Rumanian

Dorian, M (RI)
Impey, M H (IN)
Perry, T A (TX)
Soceanu-Vamos, M (NY)
Urdang, E B (RI)

Russian

Bird, T E (NY)
Bouis, A W (NY)
Brownsberger, S C (MA)
Burton, T E (Bel)
Carynnyk, M (Can)
Daniels, G (NY)
Debreczeny, P (NC)
Dukas, V (CA)
Falla, P S (UK)
Field, F (CA)
Fiene, D M (TN)
Fortune, C R (Can)
Fraser, D A (UK)
Friedberg, M (IL)
Ginsburg, M (NY)
Gogol, J M (OR)
Harkins, W E (NY)
Heim, M H (CA)
Hemschemeyer, J (NJ)
Holland, M (UK)
Holland, M E (IL)
Huggins, E N (OR)
Hulick, E C (NY)
Iribarne, L (Can)
Karpov, L (MI)
Karr, P A (WI)
Kern, G (CA)
Kline, G L (PA)
Krynski, M J (NC)
Lamont, R C (NY)
Lowcock, P H (VA)
Lyman, H (MA)
Mackler, M (NY)
Mead, A D (Ger)
Merivale, A (CA)
Mihailovich, V D (NC)

Monas, S (TX)
Morgan, E (UK)
Morrison, R H (Austral)
Pachmuss, T A (IL)
Patt, R A (AR)
Payne, R (NY)
Pearce, B L (UK)
Raffel, B (CO)
Reeve, F D (NY)
Regehr, L (WA)
Rischin, R S (CA)
Roberts, S E (NY)
Rudolf, A (UK)
Scammell, M (UK)
Sheldon, R (NH)
Sita, J B (ID)
Slobin, G N (CT)
Smith, D J (NY)
Smith, W J (NY)
Spiegel, M (PA)
Strawn, R R (IN)
Strong, R L, Jr (CT)
Summer, S C (NY)
Szell, T (NJ)
Taschian, J (CA)
Taylor, M R (IL)
Trahan, E W (CA)
Tworek, J (CA)
Venrick, B B (OH)
Weissbort, D (IA)
Wilkinson, N (CA)
Williams, R H (FL)
Winn, M (NY)

Sanskrit

Bhaktivedanta, A C (CA)
McDermott, C (NM)
Miller, B S (NY)
Sharma, A (Austral)

Scottish Gaelic

Campbell, J L (UK)

Serbo-Croatian

Hannaher, W (VA)
McConnell-Duff, A B (Fr)
Mihailovich, V D (NC)
Mikić-Mitchell, D (NY)
Miletich, I (IL)
Scammell, M (UK)
Willen, D (NY)

Slovak

Falla, P S (UK)
Hrubý, O S (NY)
Kuby, A (OH)
Poláčková-Henley, K (Can)

Slovenian

Mihailovich, V D (NC)
Miletich, I (IL)

Spanish

Ahern, M (AZ)
Alphonese-Ferere, G (PA)
Arce, C S (MD)
Barnstone, W (IN)
Belitt, B (VT)
Bergin, T G (CT)
Bernstein, J S (CA)
Bird, P G (CT)
Bissett, J I (AZ)
Blades, W M (NJ)
Bogin, M (NY)

Boyer, M V (TX)
Brady, T (PA)
Briffault, H (NY)
Brown, M C (PR)
Burton, T E (Bel)
Campbell, J L (CA)
Carr, R J (DC)
Carroll, B L (WA)
Caserta, E G (NC)
Chambers, L H (CO)
Chambers, R (TX)
Choset, C (NY)
Christensen, N (NY)
Claudel, C A (LA)
Cohen, J (NY)
Colchie, T (NY)
Cormier, R J (PA)
Crow, M (CO)
Dagenais, J (IL)
Danielson, J D (CT)
Davis, W M (TX)
Dees, C J (Sp)
De Gámez, T (FL)
De Garza, H Q (Mex)
Dubois, R H (NJ)
Farmer, M W (CA)
Field, F (CA)
Fitz, E E (PA)
Fox, E (NY)
Freeman, C (OH)
Gáler, R (NY)
Garreau, J E (MA)
Gibbons, R (NJ)
Gillespie, G (CA)
Greinke, E (MI)
Griffin, P (CA)
Gross, A (NY)
Grossman, E (NY)
Guadarrama, A A (TX)
Guenther, C (MO)
Harrington, N (DC)
Helman, E (MA)
Hennessy, E B (NY)
Hernández, F (NM)
Heurck, J van (CT)
Hoeksema, T J (NM)
Hohenstein, A K (RI)
Hold, O (FL)
Holt, M P (NY)
Honig, E (RI)
Huberman, E (NJ)
Hulick, E C (NY)
Hyde, L (MA)
Keith, H H (CA)
Kemp, L (TX)
King, J F (MA)
Klin, G (NJ)
Kohn, D J (NY)
Kolovakos, G M (NY)
Layera, R (TX)
Leach, V L (CT)
Levesque, R (WA)
Levine, P (CA)
Levine, S J (NY)
Leviton, M (CA)
Lima, R (PA)
Loos, D S (VT)
López-Morillas, F M (RI)
Lowe, E (NY, Col)
Luccarelli, L (CA)
Lyday, L F (PA)
McBride, C A (NY)
MacDonald, S (MA)
MacShane, F (NY)
Manning, M (CT)

Márquez, R (MA)
Marracino, P (NY)
Mathes, D L (MO)
Merello, B S (DC)
Mitchell, B (AR)
Morgan, W A (PA)
Morrison, R H (Austral)
Murad, T (AR)
Nabil, S A (IL)
Nichols, J M (MI)
O'Connell, M J (NY)
O'Connell, R (PA)
Odio, A (AR)
Odio, E B (AR)
Ohlendorf, S M (TX)
Paddon, H E (UK)
Palladino, J G (NY)
Pallister, J L (OH)
Parrent, P S (TX)
Partridge, F (UK)
Patrick, B E & L L (KS)
Peden, M S (MO)
Pendry, D A (AR)
Penglase, W O, Jr (NY)
Pérez, L L C de (Col)
Perry, T A (TX)
Pevear, R (NY)
Pitz, C M (MN)
Pontiero, G (UK)
Preisser, D C (MD)
Pringle, N (MO)
Rabassa, G (NY)
Raffel, B (CO)
Raley, H (OK)
Reid, A (NY)
Richman, L L (UT)
Roberts, W H & M M (NM)
Rodríguez, J M (CA)
Romero, H R (MI)
Rose, M G (NY)
Rukeyser, M (NY)
Samelson, W (TX)
Sampaio, A F (Brazil)
Savory, T (MA)
Sayers, R S (WI)
Scheer, L (NY)
Schulman, G (NY)
Schulte, R (TX)
Sebastiani, N A (TX)
Shore, M (CT)
Simms, R L C (VA)
Sita, J B (ID)
Smith, D C (PA)
Smith, W J (NY)
Sokolinsky, M (NY)
Stafford, W (OR)
Stankovic, J A (MD)
Stasi, S L (CA)
Swietlicki, A (MO)
Talamantes, F W (CA)
Talbot, T (NY)
Tolman, J M (NM)
Tomlins, J E (NM)
Trask, W R (NY)
Treitel, R (OK)
Trevino, V S (Mex)
Turnell, M (UK)
Turner, D E (TX)
Tuttle, L (VT)
Unger, D (NY)
Upton, J (CA)
Urdang, E B (RI)
Urquidi, M M (DC)
Vasconcellos, M (DC)
Waley, P J (UK)

Walsh, D D (CT)
Warnick, M C (NH)
Weinberger, E (NY)
Weiss, J (CA)
Wellwarth, G E (NY)
Wilkie, E C, Jr (RI)
Williams, M (AR)
Williams, R H (FL)
Wilson, C (WA)
Wilson, D D (NJ)
Woolsey, W (TX)
Yates, D A (MI)
Zatz, A (Mex)

Spanish (Galician)

Moore, M H (AR)

Swedish

Bjork, R E (CA)
Blecher, L & G (NY)
Born, A (UK)
Bruce, L (CA)
Friis, E J (NJ)
Harvey, A-C H (CA)
Hvidonov, A (NY)
Kruuse, E (NY)
La Farge, S (MA)
Lesser, R (NY)
Malmberg, C (NH)
Michael, M (UK)
Paul, D M & M (DC)
Rukeyser, M (NY)
Sandbach, M (UK)
Sandstroem, Y L (MA)
Sjöberg, L T (NY)
Smith, W J (NY)
Spink, R (UK)
Tate, J (UK)
Teal, T (NY)

Tamil

Chandra, G S S (WA)

Telugu

Chandra, G S S (WA)

Thai

Gething, T W (HI)
Hartmann, J F (IL)

Tibetan

McDermott, C (NM)

Turkish

Baybars, T (UK)
Boyle, J A (UK)
Deris, N (Tur)
Halman, T S (NY)
Leventoglu, F (IL)

Ukrainian

Carynnyk, M (Can)
Kulchycky, G (OH)
Williams, R H (FL)

Urdu

Chandra, G S S (WA)

Vietnamese

Raffel, B (CO)

Yiddish

Garrin, S H (TX)
Ginsburg, M (NY)
Neugroschel, J (NY)

Rosenfeld, M (PA)
Shevrin, A (MI)
Shub, E (NY)
Spiegel, M (PA)
Whitman, R (MA)
Witriol, J (UK)
Zuckerman, M S (CA)

Into FINNISH from:

English

Virtanen, J O (OR)

Into FRENCH from:

English

Alphonese-Ferere, G (PA)
Aubert, J (Fr)
Berger, J (Bel)
Bieber, K F (NY)
Bosky, J I (CA)
Bouygues, C P (Can)
Brovender, J (MA)
Carme, C (Fr)
Casaril, G (Fr)
Castera-Kahn, M (Fr)
Chneour, J F (Fr)
Daillie, R I (Fr)
Dees, C J (Sp)
Delahaye, A (Fr)
Detiere, D J (NY)
Durand, G & J (Fr)
Duval, C (NY)
Évrard, L (Fr)
Feeney, M (NY)
Flournoy, L (Switz)
Fouques Duparc, R (Fr)
Gilbert, C (Fr)
Giroday, V de le (NY)
Godneff, N (Fr)
Goldstein, S (CA)
Gresset, M A L (Fr)
Janvier, E (Fr)
Jouvenel, R de (Fr)
Kaplan, R F S (NY)
Laroche, S (Fr)
Ledoux, F (Fr)
Lewinter, R (Switz)
Luccioni, J M (Fr)
McEwan-Alvarado, A (CA)
Maheux, G (Can)
Mauroc, D (Fr)
Metzger, A (Tur)
Mikriammos, P (Fr)
Nétillard, S (Fr)
Noël, B (Fr)
Noël, Claude (Fr)
Olivier, D (Fr)
Parisot, H G R (Fr)
Paroutaud, M (CA)
Pavesi, Julie (Fr)
Pepin, R M (Fr)
Picard, A R (Fr)
Raulet, G (Fr)
Remy-Zephir, J (Fr)
Royall-Manach, C Y (MO)
Saumont, A (Fr)
Wautier, A (Bel)
Weaver, E B (MA)
Weber, W-K (CA)
Weiss, G E (CA)
Zins, C (Fr)

Into GERMAN from:

English

Asbeck, H T (Ger)
Auerbach, F (Ger)
Berisch, K (Ger)
Blaas, E (Aust)
Bracher, U (Ger)
Czernicki, K-O von (Ger)
Davis, L K (CA)
Dick, E S (KS)
Ebner, J (Aust)
Eliasberg, G (Isr)
Felten, G (Ger)
Gal-Or, G H (Isr)
Geisel, E (Aust)
Giroday, V de le (NY)
Graham, H R (VA)
Gugelberger, G H (CA)
Hansen, K H (Ger)
Hermstein, R (Ger)
Jany, H (Ger)
Kirberg, G (UK)
Kloth, F A (Ger)
Krausskopf, K S (Fr)
Laermann, K (Ger)
Lindt, I B (Aust)
Livingston, K I R (OH)
McAuley, A (WA)
Magal, M (Isr)
Marshall, T M (IL)
Miller, J W (KY)
Monahan, P A (CA)
Müchringer, D (Aust)
Pitthan, I M (CA)
Pohoryles, B M (NY)
Raabe, G (Ger)
Regehr, L (WA)
Reiss, K (Ger)
Richartz, W E (Ger)
Römer, K (Ger)
Romero, I W (NY)
Rosacker, H D (Ger)

Schade, D A (Ger)
Schmitz, S (Ger)
Schneider, L E (CA)
Schraps-Poelchau, M (Ger)
Schürenberg, W (Ger)
Schweier, J (Ger)
Seeslen, U (Ger)
Shaw, G K (UK)
Sora, M (Ger)
Sprick, C G (Ger)
Stiehl, H (Ger)
Sussdorf, A (Ger)
Thaler, W (Aust)
Unger, A H (UK)
Von Koskull, H J (Ger)
Von Wiese, U (Switz)
Weber, W-K (CA)
Weitbrecht, B (Ger)
Wiemken, C (Ger)
Wiemken, H (Ger)
Winter, E (Switz)
zur Nedden Pferdekamp, M (Ger)

Into HEBREW from:

English
Eliasberg, G (Isr)

Into HUNGARIAN from:

English
Kabdeb, T (UK)

Into ITALIAN from:

English
Cerea, D (CA)
Flournoy, L (Switz)

Fratti, M (NY)
Weaver, E B (MA)

Into JAPANESE from:

English
Kano, T (Japan)
Sakurai, E (HI)
Takechi, M (Japan)
Yoshida, Y (Japan)

Into LATVIAN from:

English
Surmanis, B (NY)

Into POLISH from:

English
Rozenbaum, W (IN)

Into PORTUGUESE from:

English
Bird, P G (CT)
Henriques, E R (NC)
Portinho, W I M (Brazil)
Sampaio, A F (Brazil)

Into RUMANIAN from:

English
Ghitescu, M (Rum)

Into RUSSIAN from:

English
Bosky, J I (CA)

Karpov, L (MI)
Kozlovsky, V (NY)
Regehr, L (WA)

Into SLOVAK from:

English
Kuby, A (OH)

Into SPANISH from:

English
Alphonese-Ferere, G (PA)
Arce, C S (MD)
Bird, P G (CT)
Colomer, G I (NY)
Danald, R M (IN)
De Gámez, T (FL)
Gáler, R (NY)
García, G (CA)
Griffin, P (CA)
Guadarrama, A A (TX)
Guibert, R (NY)
Levesque, R (WA)
McMaster, M B (UT)
Martin, P (Arg)
Mercado, B E (FL)
Nodarse, C (FL)
Odio, A (AR)
Pérez, L L C de (Col)
Pringle, N (MO)
Reuter, J (Mex)
Salazar, P S (NM)
Sampaio, A F (Brazil)
Sebastiani, N A (TX)

Into TURKISH from:

English
Deris, N (Tur)

Conference Translators

Conference translators work exclusively at large multilingual international meetings and like their colleagues, conference interpreters, form an integral part of any such conference, working from written rather than oral texts and preparing translated written rather than orally interpreted texts. Both conference translators and conference interpreters are primarily members of three professional societies: International Association of Conference Translators (AITC), International Association of Conference Interpreters (AIIC), and The American Association of Language Specialists (TAALS). Since all three bodies use special rating systems to identify the linguistic proficiency of their membership, their classifications have been maintained and partially adapted to conform to the overall system used in this section.

AITC refers to a target language as one's "mother tongue" and classifies source languages as "working languages," either primary (A), or secondary (B).

An explanation of the rating systems for AIIC and TAALS will be found in the section on Conference Interpreters. It should be noted that conference translators who are also interpreters may be located in the Conference Interpreters section with an asterisk preceding the name to identify their dual translation role.

ABDALLA, ZARIF ABDALLA 2 passage Du-Guesclin, F-75015 Paris, France *Tel* 577 16 10; 567 65 48.
TL Arabic. **SL** English (A), French (A). **Memb** AITC.

ABDEL-AZIZ, FOUAD KAMEL 18 rue no 87, Maadi, Cairo, Egypt *Tel* 35 166.
TL Arabic. **SL** English (A), French (A). **Memb** AITC.

ABENSOUR, PASCAL SALOMON 6 rue de Bellechasse, F-75007 Paris, France *Tel* 551 82 09.
TL French. **SL** English (A), German (A). **Memb** AITC.

ABRIAL, GENEVIÈVE 153 bis, rue Tahère, F-92210 Saint-Cloud, France *Tel* (1) 771 88 64.
TL French. SL Spanish (A), Portuguese (A).
Memb AITC.

ACHKAR, MAURICE 41 rue du XXXI-Décembre, CH-1207 Geneva, Switzerland *Tel* 36 78 93.
TL Arabic. SL English (A), French (A).
Memb AITC.

AGOSTINI, YVETTE c/o Señor Agostini, Casilla 2353, Santiago, Chile.
TL French. SL English (A), Spanish (A); German (B), Portuguese (B).
Memb AITC.

ALBRECHT, NICHOLAS 60 rue Franklin, F-92400 Courbevoie, France *Tel* 788 60 56.
TL English. SL French (A), Russian (A); Spanish (B).
Memb AITC.

ALSOP, MARJORIE HOSKEN Les Ecrins 71, 9 ave du Bijou, F-01210 Ferney-Voltaire, France *Tel* (50) and (023) 41 32 54.
TL English. SL French (A), Spanish (A); German (B), Italian (B), Russian (B).
Memb AITC.

AMACKER, JEAN-MICHEL 79 ave du Bois-de-la-Chapelle, CH-1213 Onex, Switzerland *Tel* (022) 93 17 25.
TL French. SL English (A), Spanish (A); German (B).
Memb AITC.

ARIAS, GONZALO Juan Abelló 25 b, San Lorenzo del Escorial, E-Madrid, Spain *Tel* 896 19 17.
TL Spanish. SL English (A), French (A).
Memb AITC.

AUBERT, CATHERINE 63 ch du Périmètre, F-74000 Annecy, France *Tel* 23 17 67.
TL French. SL English (A); German (B), Spanish (B).
Memb AITC.

AUDOUX, MARGUERITE 25 rue Paul-Barruel, F-75015 Paris, France *Tel* 842 06 43.
TL French. SL English (A); Spanish (B).
Memb AITC.

BAILLEUL, ANNIE Weimarerstr 61/6, A-1180 Vienna, Austria *Tel* 34 93 79.
TL French. SL English (A), Spanish (A); German (B).
Memb AITC.

BARBIER-MOKOBODZKI, NICOLE 10 rue Raynouard, F-75016 Paris, France *Tel* 527 03 46.
TL French. SL English (A), Spanish (A); Catalan (B), Portuguese (B).
Memb AITC.

BARRAU, GENEVIÈVE Commission du Pacifique Sud, BP D 5 Nouméa Cedex, New Caledonia.
TL French. SL English (A).
Memb AITC.

BAYAN-BAÏEFF, HÉLÈNE 5 rue Lekain, F-75016 Paris, France *Tel* 527 70 39.
TL French. SL English (A), Russian (A); German (B).
Memb AITC.

BAZINET, GENEVIÈVE 43 bis, rue Madeleine-Michelis, F-92200 Neuilly s/Seine, France *Tel* 624 62 11.
TL French. SL English (A).
Memb AITC.

BERESNIKOFF, ALEXANDRE 18 ave Dumas, CH-1206 Geneva, Switzerland *Tel* 46 02 83.
TL French. SL English (A), Russian (A); German (B), Spanish (B).
Memb AITC.

BERGER-BOSTOCK, ANNA 65 rte de Mategnin, CH-1217 Meyrin, Switzerland.
TL English. SL German (A), Russian (A).
Affil UN, Geneva. Memb AITC.

BERKELEY, CLAUDE Travellers Club, Pall Mall, London SW1, UK *Tel* 930 8688.
TL English. SL French (A); German (B), Italian (B), Spanish (B).
Memb AITC.

BERNARD, EILEEN 17 St Paul's Square, Bromley, Kent BR2 OXH, UK *Tel* 464 6092.
TL English. SL French (A), Spanish (A); Italian (B), Portuguese (B).
Memb AITC.

BETHENOD, BETTY 11 rue de Boulainvilliers, F-75016 Paris, France *Tel* 224 51 32.
TL English. SL French (A); German (B), Italian (B).
Memb AITC.

BLANCHARD, GEORGES Fontbedeau, F-17200 Royan, France *Tel* (46) 38 05 38.
TL French. SL English (A), Spanish (A).
Memb AITC.

BLANCO, CARLOS 41 ave de Budé, CH-1202 Ginebra, Switzerland *Tel* 34 02 54.
TL Spanish. SL English (A), French (A).
Memb AITC.

BLOCH-MICHEL, JEAN 60 rue Mazarine, F-75006 Paris, France *Tel* 326 71 73.
TL French. SL English (A).
Memb AITC.

BONET-MAURY, CLAUDE 3 rue Frédéric-Bastiat, F-75008 Paris, France *Tel* 225 19 17.
TL French. SL English (A); German (B).
Memb AITC.

BORDONOVE, HUGUETTE 18 Les Terrasses-de-Cassis, F-13260 Cassis, France *Tel* (91) 01 04 50.
TL French. SL English (A).
Memb AITC.

BOURDARIAT, ROLAND 2 rue de Gribeauval, F-75007 Paris, France *Tel* 544 20 23.

TL French. SL English (A), Italian (A), Spanish (A).
Memb AITC.

BOYADJIAN, MARIE-ANNE 126-132 blvd de la République, F-92210 Saint-Cloud, France *Tel* (1) 602 05 22.
TL French. SL English (A), German (A).
Memb AITC.

BROUSSE-DONDENNE, PASCALE 38 ave de Vaudagne, CH-1217 Meyrin, Switzerland *Tel* (022) 82 85 35.
TL French. SL English (A), German (A); Italian (B).
Accred EIT. Memb AITC.

CANAVAN, EUNICE 84 rue du Cherche-Midi, F-75006 Paris, France *Tel* 222 87 06.
TL English. SL French (A), Russian (A); Italian (B), Spanish (B).
Memb AITC.

CARAGIALE, ELSIE 23 rue Vaneau, F-75007 Paris, France *Tel* 705 83 73.
TL English. SL French (A), Spanish (A); Portuguese (B).
Memb AITC.

CARRÈRE, ALBERT DANIEL Le Patriarche, 34 ch de la Planche-Brûlée, F-01210 Ferney-Voltaire, France.
TL French. SL English (A); Spanish (B).
Memb AITC.

CARTANAS, MONIQUE 7 rue de Savoie, F-74160 St-Julien-en-Genevois, France.
TL French. SL English (A), Spanish (A).
Memb AITC.

CHÉRIF, FERIDA 11 rue Erard, F-75012 Paris, France *Tel* 345 30 89.
TL French. SL English (A), Italian (A); Arabic (B).
Memb AITC.

CHESNERAYE DE LA, HUGUES-CHARLES Aux bons soins de Mme Claudine Chonez, 87 ave du Maine, F-75014 Paris, France *Tel* 322 09 48.
TL French. SL English (A), Spanish (A), Italian (A).
Author of *Dictionnaire Anglais-Français de Mots et d'Expression Difficiles* (ECAFE, 1970).
Memb AITC.

CHOSSUDOVSKY, EUGENIA c/o IMCO, 101-104 Piccadilly, London W1V OAE, UK.
TL French. SL English (A); German (B), Russian (B), Spanish (B).
Memb AITC.

COROMINAS DE MOLIST, MONTSERRAT Avenida Generalissimo Franco 672, E-Barcelona, Spain *Tel* 203 07 54.
TL Spanish. SL English (A), French (A); Italian (B), Portuguese (B), Russian (B).
Memb AITC.

COUTURIER, HÉLÈNE 47 rte de Saint-Loup, CH-1290 Versoix, Switzerland *Tel* (022) 55 14 47.

TL French. SL English (A), German (A); Italian (B), Spanish (B).
Affil UN. **Memb** AITC.

COVENEY, JAMES 40 Westfield Close, Bath, Avon, UK.
TL English. SL French (A), German (A), Spanish (A).
Author of *Glossary of French and English Management Terms,* jointly (Longman, 1972); *Glossary of German and English Management Terms,* jointly (Longman, 1977); *Glossary of Spanish and English Management Terms,* jointly (Longman, 1978); "Training Translators for International Organizations" (*Aslib Technical Translation Bulletin,* 17 no 1, 1971); "The Bath University Postgraduate Diploma in Language Studies" (*Babel* 17 no 2, 1971); "Training Linguists for Europe and UNO" (*Times Educational Supplement,* Oct 31, 1975).
Memb AITC, CIUTI.

COWX, KENNETH 3 Simmondley Hall, Simmondley, Glossop, Derbyshire SK13 9LS, UK *Tel* (4574) 3660.
TL English. SL French (A), Russian (A), Spanish (A); German (B).
Memb AITC.

CREN, MONIQUE 7 ave de Miremont, CH-1206 Geneva, Switzerland *Tel* 46 12 13.
TL French. SL English (A); Italian (B), Spanish (B).
Memb AITC.

CROMBIE, JOHN 13 rue de la Grande-Chaumière, F-75006 Paris, France.
TL English. SL French (A), German (A); Spanish (B).
Memb AITC.

CUISINE, JEAN-ROBERT Atelier du Pin, Bois de Cancé, Rivières, F-81600 Gaillac, France.
TL French. SL English (A), Swedish (A); German (B), Spanish (B).
Memb AITC.

DANIEL, CARMEN RIVAS DE 3 rue Schaub, CH-1202 Ginebra, Switzerland *Tel* 34 82 93.
TL Spanish. SL English (A), French (A); German (B), Russian (B).
Memb AITC (vice pres, ed of AITC Bulletin).

DARWALL, RICHARD c/o John Matthews, 30 ch de la Gradelle, CH-1224 Chêne-Bougeries, Switzerland *Tel* (022) 48 42 00.
TL English. SL French (A), Italian (A).
Memb AITC.

DAURÉ, BERNARD PO Box 20, Grand Central Station, New York, NY 10017 USA.
TL French. SL English, French, Spanish.

DAVID, ALAIN 15 bis, ave du Mail, CH-1205 Geneva, Switzerland *Tel* 28 49 03.
TL French. SL English (A), German (A); Spanish (B).
Memb AITC.

DAVIDSON, JENNIFER 17 Parr's Pl, Hampton, Middlesex TW12 2NJ, UK *Tel* 979 9129.
TL English. SL French (A), Spanish (A); Portuguese (B).
Memb AITC.

DECLERCQ, SUZANNE 28 rue des Saules, F-75018 Paris, France *Tel* 254 21 83.
TL French. SL English (A), Italian (A), Spanish (A).
Memb AITC.

DEEKS, JOSLIN STEWART 13 rue van Grootven, B-1350 Limal, Belgium *Tel* (010) 41 44 22.
TL English. SL French (A), German (A), Spanish (A).
Memb AITC.

DELATTRE, JULES 4 rue des Délices, CH-1203 Geneva, Switzerland *Tel* 44 07 89.
TL French. SL English (A); Dutch (B), German (B), Spanish (B).
Memb AITC.

DELPIERRE, MARIE-ALICE 92 blvd de la République, F-92210 Saint-Cloud, France.
TL French. SL English (A), Spanish (A).
Memb AITC.

DESEILLIGNY, MARTHE-ANNIE 53 Kensington Ct, London W8, UK *Tel* 937 7887.
TL French. SL English (A).
Memb AITC.

DORRELL, DAPHNE MARY 19a Bateman St, Cambridge CB2 1NB, UK *Tel* 31 26 06.
TL English. SL Czech (A), French (A), German (A); Russian (B), Spanish (B).
Memb AITC.

DUBUCQ, BERNADETTE 18 rte de Veyrier, CH-1227 Carouge, Switzerland *Tel* (022) 43 60 03.
TL French. SL English (A), Spanish (A); Dutch (B).
Memb AITC.

DUMAYNE, RÉGINE 32 ch des Crêts-de-Champel, CH-1206 Geneva, Switzerland *Tel* 47 99 08.
TL French. SL English (A), Spanish (A).
Memb AITC.

EAST, KATHLEEN MABEL 20 Somerset Rd, Salisbury, Wilts SP 13BN, UK *Tel* (722) 20963.
TL English. SL French (A); Russian (B), Spanish (B).
Memb AITC.

EL GUEBALY, AHMED 113 rue Port-Said, Alexandria, Egypt. Chez M Echallon, Laiz, F-01290 Pont-de-Veyle, France.
TL Arabic. SL English (A), French (A).
Memb AITC.

EL-MOUELHY, KHALIL Via S Giovanni Bosco, I-10024 Moncalieri (Turin), Italy *Tel* (011) 668382, 668392.
TL Arabic. SL French (A); English (B).
Memb AITC.

ENAN, MONA 7 rue Chackour, Koubbeh Gardens, Cairo, Egypt *Tel* 82 35 08.
TL Arabic. SL English (A), French (A).
Memb AITC.

ESTINEL, MARTIN 2 Grand-Montfleury, CH-1290 Versoix, Switzerland *Tel* (022) 55 20 98.
TL English. SL French (A), German (A), Italian (A), Portuguese (A), Spanish (A).
Accred Holborn College of Law. **Memb** AITC.

EWALD, PIERRE 14 ave des Amazones, CH-1224 Chêne-Bougeries, GE, Switzerland *Tel* (022) 48 24 27.
TL French. SL English (A); German (B), Spanish (B).
Affil International Telecommunication Union. **Memb** AITC.

EYDOUX, LAURENCE 17 quai Augagneur, F-69003 Lyon, France.
TL French. SL English (A); Spanish (B).
Memb AITC.

FAWZY, DIDAR Chez Mme Nevine Homery, Cessy-sur-Ville, F-01170 Gex, France *Tel* 41 66 96.
TL French. SL English (A); Arabic (B).
Memb AITC.

FEATHERSTONE, BRIAN ROBERT 04 Simiane la Rotonde, France.
TL English. SL French (A), Russian (A).
Memb AITC.

FERRON, MAURICE 27 rue Escudier, F-92100 Boulogne s/Seine, France *Tel* 605 84 77.
TL French. SL English (A).
Memb AITC.

FINEBERG, MICHAEL 6 rue Jean-Moulin, F-94300 Vincennes, France *Tel* 328 68 00.
TL English. SL French (A); Spanish (B).
Memb AITC.

FRY, DAVID GEORGE Eagle House, Ivyleaf Hill, Bush near Bude, Cornwall, UK *Tel* Kilkhampton (028 882) 365.
TL English. SL French (A), Russian (A).
Memb AITC.

GAGNAIRE, JOSEPH 2 rue du Champ-des-Oiseaux, F-17200 Royan, France *Tel* 05 45 71.
TL French. SL English (A), Czech (A), Spanish (A).
Memb AITC.

GAMARD, JEAN 1 ave de la République, F-74100 Annemasse, France *Tel* 38 21 61, 39 60 96.
TL French. SL English (A), Spanish (A); Dutch (B), German (B).
Memb AITC.

GARCIA-ABBOTT, JUNE 89 Bleecker St #6A, New York, NY 10012 USA. United Nations #1223, New York, NY 10017 USA *Tel* 212-754-6705. 20 Cotswold Gardens, Newcastle-upon-Tyne 7, UK.

TL English. **SL** French (A), Italian (A), Portuguese (A), Spanish (A).
Memb AITC.

GARDNER, JEAN 42 Tudor Hill, Sutton Coldfield, West Midlands, UK *Tel* 021 354 1144.
TL English. **SL** French (A), Spanish (A); German (B).
Memb AITC.

GARVIE, FRANCISCA ANNE c/o Barclays Bank Ltd. 93 Baker St, London W1, UK.
TL English. **SL** French (A), German (A).
Memb AITC.

GENTY, FRANÇOISE 64 rue Rennequin, F-75017 Paris, France *Tel* 754 0355.
TL French. **SL** English (A), Spanish (A).
Memb AITC.

GILSON, BERNARD 9 Villa Virginie, F-75014 Paris, France *Tel* 540 53 23.
TL French. **SL** English (A), German (A); Russian (B).
Memb AITC.

GOLAY, MICHÈLE 18 rue Daubin, CH-1203 Geneva, Switzerland *Tel* 44 94 12.
TL French. **SL** English (A), Spanish (A).
Memb AITC.

GOODMAN, DAVID Chemin de la Clairière, CH-1261 Gingins, Switzerland *Tel* (022) 69 18 17.
TL English. **SL** French (A), German (A), . Russian (A), Spanish (A).
Memb AITC (Chairperson, Negotiating & Liaison Committee).

GOURMOUX, DENISE La Pommeraie, 24 rte de Genève, F-01210 Ferney-Voltaire, France *Tel* (50) 40 73 83, (023) 40 73 83.
TL French. **SL** English (A); German (B).
Memb AITC.

GREENSTONE, MARGUERITE 10 South Villas #8, Camden Square, London NW1, UK *Tel* 267 3955.
TL English. **SL** French (A), Spanish (A).
Memb AITC.

GRIFFITHS, R STUART 74 rue de Sèvres, F-75007 Paris, France *Tel* 567 68 62.
TL English. **SL** French (A), Italian (A), Spanish (A).
Memb AITC.

GUILLON, ARLETTE Linke Wienzeile 14/23, A-1060 Vienna, Austria.
TL French. **SL** English (A), German (A), Spanish (A).
Affil IAEA. **Memb** AITC.

HALL, SHEILA Red Lodge, Grange Rd, Ryton-on-Tyne NE40 3LU, UK *Tel* 422 2596.
TL English. **SL** French (A), Spanish (A).
Memb AITC.

HARTLEY, ERIC CHASTEL Woodspring, The Twitten, Crowborough, Sussex, UK *Tel* (08926) 61486.
TL English. **SL** Danish (A), French (A), German (A), Russian (A).
Memb AITC.

HENNEQUIN, SIMONE 22 rue de la Py, F-75020 Paris, France *Tel* 797 94 16.
TL French. **SL** English (A), German (A), Spanish (A).
Memb AITC.

HOORIN, ALEXANDER Fir Trees, Cliff End, Fairlight, Sussex, UK *Tel* Pett 3445.
TL English. **SL** French (A), Spanish (A); Italian (B), Portuguese (B).
Memb AITC.

HOORIN, GERALDINE Fir Trees, Cliff End, Fairlight, Sussex, UK *Tel* Pett 3445.
TL English. **SL** French (A), Portuguese (A), Spanish (A); Dutch (B), German (B), Russian (B).
Memb AITC.

HORVATH, ELISABETH Haydnstr 7/14, A-2103 Langenzersdorf, Austria *Tel* (2244) 33 882.
TL German. **SL** English (A), French (A); Spanish (B).
Memb AITC.

INTRATOR, MIRA 20 ave des Amazones, CH-1224 Geneva, Switzerland *Tel* 48 72 24.
TL English. **SL** French (A), Russian (A); German (B), Spanish (B).
Memb AITC.

ISORÉ, JEAN-PIERRE Case postale 162, CH-1217 Meyrin, Switzerland *Tel* (022) 41 40 42.
TL French. **SL** English (A); German (B), Spanish (B).
Memb AITC.

ISORÉ, PIERRE 15 ch des Bossons, 01 Ferney-Voltaire, France *Tel* (50) and (023) 41 34 26.
TL French. **SL** English (A); German (B), Spanish (B).
Memb AITC.

ISRAÉLI, GENIA 8 ave du Maine, F-75015 Paris, France *Tel* 544 22 05.
TL French. **SL** English (A), Russian (A).
Memb AITC.

JACKSON, DAWSON 5A Wellington Pl, London NW8 7PB, UK *Tel* 722 3644.
TL English. **SL** French (A), Russian (A).
Memb AITC.

JACKSON, JEFFREY 3 Hazelmere Ave, Melton Park, Newcastle-upon-Tyne NE3 5QL, UK *Tel* Wideopen 2658.
TL English. **SL** Danish (A), Dutch (A), French (A), German (A), Italian (A), Norwegian (A), Portuguese (A), Russian (A), Spanish (A), Swedish (A); Bulgarian (B), Serbo-Croatian (B).
Memb AITC.

JAN-DUBARRY, ANAÏK 6 rue Guy de Maupassant, F-75016 Paris, France *Tel* 503 12 07.
TL French. **SL** English (A), German (A).
Memb AITC.

JAWORSKI, MICHEL 3 rue des Granges, CH-1204 Geneva, Switzerland *Tel* 24 71 41.
TL French. **SL** English (A), Spanish (A).
Memb AITC.

JENNINGS, SHIRLEY Villa Beausoleil, F-01170 Florimont-sur-Gex, France *Tel* (50) or (023) 41 56 00.
TL English. **SL** French (A), German (A), Russian (A); Italian (B), Spanish (B).
Memb AITC.

JOHNSTONE, JOHN MICHAEL Plaza Regino Mas 8, pta 17, E-Ciudad Fallera, Valencia 15, Spain *Tel* 378 64 35.
TL English. **SL** French (A), Russian (A), Spanish (A); Italian (B), Portuguese (B).
Author of "The Language Barrier" (*Electrical Review*, Apr 7, 1967); "Translation Problems" (*Financial Times*, Feb 19, 1968).
Memb AITC.

JUANARENA, MARIO Case Postale 114, Ch-1211 Geneva, Switzerland.
TL Spanish. **SL** English (A), French (A); Russian (B).
Memb AITC.

KAMEL-SALEH, ROCHDI 4 rue Ibn-Ayas, Manshiet-el-Bakry, Cairo, Egypt *Tel* 82 86 34.
TL Arabic. **SL** French (A).
Memb AITC.

KARARA, MOHAMED rue du Premier-Juin, CH-1207 Geneva, Switzerland *Tel* 35 25 01.
TL Arabic. **SL** French (A); English (B).
Memb AITC.

KATZ, MONIQUE 6 rue du Général-de-Castelnau, F-75015 Paris, France *Tel* 734 43 66.
TL French. **SL** English (A); Spanish (B).
Memb AITC.

KEANE, DENIS MICHAEL 10 St Stephens Ave, St Albans, Herts, UK *Tel* (0727) 50522.
TL English. **SL** French (A), German (A), Greek (A), Russian (A), Spanish (A); Italian (B), Portuguese (B).
Affil IAEA. **Memb** AITC.

KERAUDREN, CLAUDE 20 ch Rieu, CH-1208 Geneva, Switzerland *Tel* 47 84 09.
TL French. **SL** English (A), Spanish (A); German (B).
Memb AITC.

KHALIAF, MOURAD 15 rue Georges-Pitard, F-75015 Paris, France *Tel* 531 67 17.
TL Arabic. **SL** English (A); French (B).
Memb AITC.

KHALIL AHMED, MOHAMED Villa M Khalil, rue 284, Smouha, Alexandria, Egypt *Tel* 73 783.

TL Arabic. SL English (A), French (A); Spanish (B).
Memb AITC.

KHAW, DENISE 26a, ch de Pont-Céard, CH-1290 Versoix, Switzerland Tel (022) 55 34 52.
TL French. SL English (A), Spanish (A).
Memb AITC.

KOESTER, FRANCINE 23 blvd de Montmorency, F-75016 Paris, France Tel 525 68 38.
TL Spanish. SL English (A), French (A).
Memb AITC.

KOLOKOLTZOFF, GEORGES 34 ch François-Lehmann, CH-1218 Grand-Saconnex, Switzerland.
TL French.
Affil UN. Memb AITC.

KOSELEFF, ELISABETH 7 rue Lhomond, F-75005 Paris, France Tel 325 07 90.
TL German. SL Spanish (A); English (B), French (B).
Memb AITC.

KOSMANN, CLAUDE 20 rue de Varize, F-75016 Paris, France Tel 651 45 32; 608 14 56.
TL French. SL English (A), Spanish (A); Dutch (B).
Memb AITC.

LAMON, FRANÇOISE 332 rue Lecourbe, F-75015 Paris, France Tel 250 53 06; 250 48 14.
TL French. SL English (A), Spanish (A).
Memb AITC.

LAMUNIÈRE, CHARLOTTE 115 rue de Lausanne, CH-1202 Geneva, Switzerland Tel 32 72 45.
TL French. SL English (A), Spanish (A); Italian (B).
Memb AITC.

LANGLEY, JUDITH 3630 Merrick, Houston, TX 77025 USA.
TL English. SL French (A), Spanish (A).
Memb AITC.

LAPOUGE, CHANTAL DE 209 rue de Tolbiac, F-75013 Paris, France Tel 588 33 97.
TL French. SL English (A).
Memb AITC.

LAROCHE, NICOLE a/c Hortensia Salas, Calle de Certificados 24-6, Mexico 13, DF, Mexico.
TL French. SL English (A), Spanish (A); German (B), Russian (B).
Memb AITC.

LEFEBVRE, DANIELLE 10 rue des Marronniers, F-75016 Paris, France Tel 527 70 14.
TL French. SL English (A), Spanish (A); German (B).
Memb AITC.

LEHMANN, ALFRED L 11 Crêts-de-Champel, CH-1206 Geneva, Switzerland Tel 46 51 02.

TL English. SL French (A), German (A), Spanish (A).
Memb AITC.

LÉONTIDOU, JEANNE 22 rue des Asters, CH-1202 Geneva, Switzerland Tel 33 22 45.
TL French. SL English (A), Greek (A); German (B).
Memb AITC.

LEVICK, MARGARET ENSOR 40 bis, rue de Sévigné, F-75003 Paris, France Tel 272 75 58.
TL English. SL French (A), Italian (A), Spanish (A); Portuguese (B).
Memb AITC (pres).

LEWIS, EDINA 13 Talbot House, 98 St Martin's Lane, London WC2, UK Tel 836 7072, 405 8657.
TL English. SL French (A), Spanish (A).
Memb AITC.

LIMÁN RUBIO, PILAR CH-1261 Chavannes-de-Bogis, Ginebra, Switzerland.
Memb AITC.

LLOYD, JOHN EDWARDES ROGERS Ffin-y-Llannau, Harlech, Merioneth, Wales, UK Tel Harlech 461.
TL English. SL French (A), German (A), Russian (A); Spanish (B).
Memb AITC.

LOESCH, CARL von Ulrichstr 41, D-6000 Frankfurt/Main 50, West Germany Tel 52 45 62.
TL English, German. SL French (A); Spanish (B).
Memb AITC.

MACKAY, VIVIEN C M 8 rue de l'Exposition, F-75007 Paris, France Tel 555 43 78. 78.
TL English. SL French (A); German (B), Spanish (B).
Memb AITC.

McLAUGHLIN, PATRICK 38 ave de Saturne, B-1180 Brussels, Belgium Tel 374 94 02.
TL English. SL French (A), Italian (A), Spanish (A).
Memb AITC.

MacNEALY-ROBERT, ROLANDE 29D, ch de Grange-Canal, CH-1208 Geneva, Switzerland Tel 36 83 16.
TL French. SL English (A); German (B), Spanish (B).
Memb AITC.

MARCUSE, JEANNE Les Bruyères, Résidence des Quatre-Saisons, Moens-Prévessin, F-01210 Ferney-Voltaire, France Tel (023) 42 52 62 and 40 61 19.
TL French. SL English (A); German (B), Italian (B), Spanish (B).
Memb AITC.

MARIE, RAYMONDE 56 rue de la Py, F-75020 Paris, France Tel 361 11 57.

TL French. SL English (A), Spanish (A); Italian (B).
Memb AITC.

MARILLIER, JEAN 16 ch de la Paumière, CH-1231 Conches, Switzerland Tel (022) 47 05 36.
TL French. SL English (A), Spanish (A).
Memb AITC.

MARLIÈRE, THAN-TU CES, 105 rue Aristide-Briand, F-92120 Montrouge, France Tel (1) 253 47 21.
TL French. SL English (A), Vietnamese (A).
Memb AITC.

MARZUK, SIMONE 24 ave des Cottages, F-92340 Bourg-la-Reine, France Tel (1) 660 72 87.
TL French. SL English (A); Italian (B), Spanish (B).
Memb AITC.

MEARES, BERNARD 9 Ashburnham Ave, Harrow, Middlesex 2HA 1JQ, UK Tel (01) 427 0050.
TL English. SL French (A), Russian (A); German (B), Italian (B), Serbo-Croatian (B), Spanish (B).
Memb AITC.

MÉNDEZ-HERRERA, JOSÉ Capitán Haya 22, E-Madrid, Spain Tel 455 43 78.
TL Spanish. SL English (A), French (A); Italian (B).
Memb AITC.

MESNET, MARIE-BÉATRICE 5 place de l'Alma, F-75008 Paris, France Tel 359 23 39.
TL French. SL English (A).
Memb AITC.

MEYER, PHILIPPE 20 ch de Drize, CH-1256 Troinex, Switzerland Tel (022) 42 24 55.
TL French. SL English (A); Spanish (B).
Memb AITC.

MICÓ, JOSÉ 18 ave Tournay, CH-1292 Chambésy, Switzerland Tel (022) 58 10 92.
TL French. SL English (A), Italian (A); Spanish (B).
Memb AITC.

MOLIAN, MICHAEL 44 Brunswick Square #3, Hove, Sussex, UK.
TL English. SL Arabic (A), French (A), German (A), Italian (A), Russian (A), Spanish (A).
Memb AITC.

MOURAVIEFF-APOSTOL, ANDREW 31 rue de l'Athénée, CH-1206 Geneva, Switzerland Tel 47 12 36; 46 36 88.
TL English. SL French (A), Portuguese (A), Spanish (A); German (B), Russian (B).
Memb AITC.

MOWBRAY, MOSTYN 75 blvd de Charonne, F-75011 Paris, France Tel 370 02 96.
TL English. SL French (A). UDC econom-

ics, engineering (civil), finance, public works, tourism/travel, Third World development problems and projects, transportation.
Memb AITC.

NARISHKIN, ARIADNA 11 ave de Richelien, CH-1290 Versoix, Switzerland *Tel* (022) 55 12 81.
TL Russian. **SL** English (A), French (A).
Memb AITC.

NAVARRO, CLAUDE 47 rue Liancourt, F-75014 Paris, France *Tel* 566 44 25.
TL French. **SL** English (A); Spanish (B).
Memb AITC.

NICOLAS, PIERRE 31 rue Letellier, F-75015 Paris, France *Tel* 575 15 90.
TL French. **SL** English (A), German (A); Spanish (B).
Affil UN (London), US Embassy (Paris), Les Editions Mondiales. **Memb** AITC.

NORTIER, HUBERT Les Merlettes, 18 ouest, rue du Brouaz, F-74100 Annemasse, France *Tel* (023) or (50) 38 68 90.
TL French. **SL** English (A), Spanish (A).
Memb AITC.

NOVI, CARLOS IMCO, 101-104 Picadilly, London W1V OAE, UK.
Memb AITC.

OGIER, KENNETH NOEL 1 rue de l'Université, F-75007 Paris, France *Tel* 261 78 15.
TL English. **SL** French (A), Spanish (A); German (B).
Memb AITC.

OLIVES, GONZALO DE Quadrado 36, Ciudadela (Menorca), Spain.
TL Spanish. **SL** English (A), French (A).
Memb AITC.

PACTEAU, LOUIS 11 rue de la Porte Jaune, 92 Garches, France *Tel* 970 33 36.
TL French. **SL** English (A).
Memb AITC.

PAENSON, ISAAC 45 rte de Colovrex, CH-1218 Grand-Saconnex, Switzerland *Tel* (022) 98 42 02.
TL Russian. **SL** English (A), French (A); German (B).
Author of *English/French/Spanish/Russian Systematic Glossary of Selected Economic and Social Terms* (Oxford Univ/Pergamon Pr, 1964); *Manual of the Terminology of Public International Law and International Organizations* (Ets E Bruylant, forthcoming); *English/French/Spanish/Russian Systematic Glossary of Environmental Terms* (Pergamon Pr, forthcoming).
Memb AITC.

PARKER, MICHAEL Hotel Rembrandt, Tangier, Morocco *Tel* 34292.
TL English. **SL** French (A), German (A); Danish (B), Spanish (B).
Memb AITC.

PENNEY, MARY 40 Bassett Rd, London W10, UK *Tel* 969 2081.
TL English. **SL** French (A), Spanish (A); Portuguese (B).
Memb AITC.

PERL, ERNST 5 ch du Calot, CH-1290 Richelien-sur-Versoix, Switzerland *Tel* (022) 55 21 98.
TL English. **SL** French (A), German (A), Russian (A); Danish (B), Italian (B), Spanish (B).
Memb AITC.

PERLSTEIN, NICOLE 14 rue Pestalozzi, F-75005 Paris, France *Tel* 707 89 28.
TL French. **SL** English (A); Spanish (B).
Memb AITC.

PHILIBERT, GILLES 44 rue Perronet, 92 Neuilly-sur-Seine, France *Tel* 624 29 66.
TL French. **SL** Bengali (A), English (A), Russian (A); German (B), Hindi (B).
Memb AITC.

PICKERING, ROBERT EASTON F-07150 Lagorce, France.
TL English. **SL** French (A), Russian (A), Spanish (A); German (B).
Memb AITC.

PINARD, ANDRÉE 2 La Petite-Vie, F-01630 Saint-Genis-Pouilly, France *Tel* (50) 42 13 35 and 42 13 70, (023) 42 13 35 and 42 13 70.
TL French. **SL** English (A), Spanish (A).
Memb AITC.

PIQUET, MIREILLE 10 rue Duvivier, F-75007 Paris, France; Résidence Sibilli, 83 Saint-Tropez, France *Tel* 97 14 11.
TL French. **SL** English (A); Spanish (B).
Memb AITC.

PLUMLEY, DAMIAN Las Negras (Rodalquilar), Almería, Spain.
TL English. **SL** French (A), Spanish (A); Portuguese (B).
Memb AITC.

PRÉVOST, SONIA 64 rue St Louis-en-l'Ile, F-75004 Paris, France *Tel* 633 58 80.
TL French. **SL** English (A), Italian (A), Spanish (A).
Memb AITC.

RAAB, ANDRÉE 19 rue Ribéra, F-75016 Paris, France *Tel* 16-1-2245209.
TL French. **SL** English (A), German (A).
Memb AITC.

RENS, DANIÈLE-ANNE 6 ch Dami, CH-1212 Grand-Lancy, Switzerland *Tel* (022) 42 66 22.
TL French. **SL** Spanish (A); German (B).
Memb AITC.

RETBI, SYLVAIN PO Box 8145, Jerusalem, Israel *Tel* (02) 61935.
TL French. **SL** English (A); Spanish (B).
Memb AITC.

ROBINSON, JOHN BARNARD Cheserex-sur-Nyon, CH-Vaud, Switzerland *Tel* (022) 69 18 26.
TL English. **SL** French (A), German (A), Spanish (A); Italian (B), Portuguese (B).
Memb AITC.

RODRÍGUEZ ARANDA, LUIS "Taormina," Punta de la Mona, E-La Herradura (Granada), Spain.
TL Spanish. **SL** English (A), French (A), Italian (A); German (B).
Memb AITC.

ROFÉ, HUSEIN c/o Hang Seng Bank Ltd, 18 Carnarvon Rd, Kowloon, Hong Kong.
TL English. **SL** Arabic (A), Dutch (A), French (A), German (A), Indonesian (A), Italian (A), Persian (A), Portuguese (A), Spanish (A), Turkish (A); Chinese (B), Russian (B).
Memb AITC.

ROJAS, BARBARA BRYAN PO Box 2171, Trenton, NJ 08607 USA *Tel* 989 8817.
TL English. **SL** Russian (A), Spanish (A); Portuguese (B).
Memb AITC.

ROLAND-GOSSELIN, CHARLES Gli Eucalipti, I-00069 Trevignano-Romano, Italy.
TL French. **SL** English (A), Italian (A); Spanish (B).
Memb AITC.

ROSENBAUM, LISE 5 rue Chalgrin, F-75016 Paris, France.
TL French. **SL** English (A), Italian (A); Russian (B), Spanish (B).
Memb AITC.

ROSSINGTON, SUSAN Les Dorthes, F-13630 Eyragues, France *Tel* (90) 94 17 45.
TL English. **SL** French (A), Spanish (A).
Memb AITC.

SABRY, OMAR HASSAN 22a rue Taha-Hussein, Zamalek, Cairo, Egypt *Tel* 80 44 45.
TL Arabic. **SL** English (A), French (A).
Memb AITC.

SALCH, ABDEL HAMID 45 ave du Jura, F-01210 Ferney-Voltaire, France *Tel* (023) or (50) 40 61 52; Case postale 804, Geneva, CH-1211 Switzerland.
TL Arabic. **SL** English (A), French (A).
Memb AITC.

SANTA ANA, VIOLAINE IVONNE DE 15 ch de l'Erse, CH-1218 Grand-Saconnex, Ginebra, Switzerland *Tel* (022) 98 12 92.
TL Spanish. **SL** English (A), French (A); Italian (B), Portuguese (B).
Author of *Ecumenical Terminology* (World Council of Churches, 1975).
Memb AITC.

SAUL, JOHN DEREK GILBERT 53 Bolsover St, London W1P 7HL, UK *Tel* (01) 387 8171.
TL English. **SL** French (A), Italian (A),

Spanish (A). **UDC** law (international & municipal).
Memb AITC.

SAVARY, JENNIFER 145 Fourth Ave, New York, NY 10003 USA *Tel* 212-982-8112.
TL English. **SL** French (A), Spanish (A).
Memb AITC.

SAVVIN, VICTOR 3 Graveney Dr, Caversham, Reading, Berks RG4 7EG, UK *Tel* 734 47 60 36.
TL Russian. **SL** English (A); French (B).
Memb AITC.

SCHUTTE, THÉRÈSE Chemin Vy-des-Mores, CH-1299 Commugny, Switzerland *Tel* (022) 76 13 51.
TL French. **SL** English (A); Spanish (B).
Memb AITC.

SCHWARZ, ROBERT P 17 ch de Roches, CH-1208 Geneva, Switzerland *Tel* 35 11 75.
TL French, German. **SL** English (A), French (A); Italian (B), Spanish (B).
Memb AITC.

SEGUIN, CHARLES 3 rue de Valence, F-75005 Paris, France *Tel* 331 39 81.
TL French. **SL** English (A).
Memb AITC.

SELKE, RUDOLF 3 ave du Bijou, F-01210 Ferney-Voltaire, France *Tel* (023) or (50) 41 34 66.
TL German. **SL** English (A), French (A), Russian (A), Spanish (A).
Memb AITC.

SHARAF, TAREK 18 ch François-Lehmann, CH-1218 Grand-Saconnex, Switzerland *Tel* (022) 98 51 16.
TL Arabic. **SL** English (A), French (A).
Memb AITC.

SIRGES, HORST Bäckerkamp 25, D-483 Gutersloh 1, West Germany *Tel* (5241) 38 173; 11 rue du Jura, F-74100 Ambilly, France *Tel* (023) or (50) 38 29 52.
TL German. **SL** English (A), French (A).
Memb AITC.

SMITH, HANS ABRAM 99 North End Rd, London NW11 7TA, UK *Tel* 458 7353.
TL English. **SL** Dutch (A), French (A), German (A); Russian (B), Spanish (B).
Memb AITC.

SOUDAN, ROBERT 3 rue Samuel-Constant, CH-1201 Geneva, Switzerland *Tel* 45 84 71.
TL French. **SL** English (A), Spanish (A); Dutch (B), Italian (B).
Memb AITC.

STENERSEN, CHRISTIAN 15 rue de la Dôle, CH-1203 Geneva, Switzerland *Tel* 45 36 28.
TL French. **SL** English (A), Spanish (A); Danish (B), Norwegian (B), Swedish (B).
Memb AITC.

STEWART, ELSA Caixa postal 1723, Luanda, Angola.

TL English. **SL** French (A), Portuguese (A), Spanish (A); German (B).
Memb AITC.

STROVER, ANTHONY JAMES 217 Chelsea Cloisters, Sloane Ave, London SW3 3DS, UK *Tel* 584 3701.
TL English. **SL** French (A), German (A), Russian (A), Spanish (A); Portuguese (B).
Memb AITC.

SUCHENKO, ALEXANDRA **von** Casella Postale 749, I-00100 Rome, Italy.
TL English. **SL** French (A), Italian (A), Russian (A), Spanish (A).
Memb AITC.

SULZER, HENRI-GUY 10 blvd Emile Augier, F-75016 Paris, France *Tel* 520 40 72.
TL French. **SL** Dutch (A), English (A), Italian (A), Spanish (A); German (B), Russian (B). **UDC** accounting, chemistry, computers, data processing, economics, electricity, electronics, law, mathematics, physics, telecommunications.
Memb AITC, SFT.

TAALAB, FARID MOSTAFA 6 Abul-Saurour-el-Bakry St, Manshiet-el-Bakry, Cairo, Egypt *Tel* 83 61 65.
TL Arabic. **SL** English (A); French (B).
Memb AITC.

TERRASA, JUAN 86 rue de la Fédération, F-75015 Paris, France.
TL Spanish.
Memb AITC.

TESSIER, MARC Chemin de St-Jean, F-13420 Gemenos, France *Tel* (42) 82 25 24.
TL French. **SL** English (A), Italian (A).
Memb AITC.

TOUTCHKOV, PAUL Lascombes, Montagnac-sur-Auvignon, F-47600 Nérac, France *Tel* (58) 65 00 29.
TL French. **SL** English (A), Russian (A); Spanish (B).
Memb AITC.

TRONEL, HÉLÈNE 9 bis, rue Labie, F-75017 Paris, France *Tel* 574 81 05.
TL French. **SL** English (A), Spanish (A).
Memb AITC.

TRUFFAULT, ANNE 26 rue Brillat-Savarin, F-75013 Paris, France *Tel* (1) 581 52 54; Atelier du Pin, Rivières, F-81600 Gaillac, France *Tel* (63) 57 31 42.
TL French. **SL** English (A), Russian (B), Spanish (B).
Memb AITC.

VAUDOYER, ANDRÉ Le Mé Viollet-de-Duc, F-78350 Jouy-en-Josas, France *Tel* 946 40 36.
TL French. **SL** English (A).
Memb AITC.

VEILLET-LAVALLÉE, FRANCIS 98 rue de Longchamp, F-75016 Paris, France *Tel* 727 90 63.
TL French. **SL** English (A); Spanish (B).
Memb AITC.

VERNIZY, GUILLAUME DE 26 ch François-Lehmann, CH-1218 Grand-Saconnex, Switzerland *Tel* (022) 98 48 43.
TL French. **SL** English (A), Spanish (A).
Memb AITC.

VEYSSIÈRE, GUY PIERRE La Châtelaine, Rte de Commugny, CH-1296 Coppet, Switzerland.
TL French.
Memb AITC.

VOIGT, IRÈNE Hilton Wien, Am Stadtpark, A-1030 Vienna, Austria *Tel* 75 42 26.
TL German. **SL** English (A), French (A).
Affil Dolmetsch-Center Irene Voigt. **Memb** AITC.

WARDROPER, PAT 60 St Paul's Rd, London N1, UK *Tel* 226 7767.
TL English. **SL** French (A), Spanish (A); Italian (B).
Memb AITC.

WEGMAN, DENISE 7 rue des Canettes, F-75006 Paris, France *Tel* 326 83 45.
TL French. **SL** English (A), Spanish (A).
Memb AITC.

WEISER, ERIC 74 bis, rue du Rôle, F-91800 Brunoy, France *Tel* (1) 046 95 37.
TL German. **SL** English (A), French (A).
Memb AITC.

WERTH, ALINE 13 rue Hérold, F-75001 Paris, France *Tel* 236 16 49.
TL English. **SL** French (A), Italian (A), Russian (A); Spanish (B).
Memb AITC.

WETENHALL, WILLIAM JAMES "Meiga," Oxhey Lane, Pinner, Middlesex HA5 4AN, UK *Tel* (01) 428 7286.
TL English. **SL** French (A), German (A), Spanish (A); Danish (B), Norwegian (B), Russian (B), Swedish (B).
Memb AITC.

WOURGAFT, ELIZABETH 9 Résidence Beausoleil, F-92210 Saint-Cloud, France *Tel* (1) 771 68 77.
TL English. **SL** French (A); Russian (B), Spanish (B).
Memb AITC.

YATES, SYLVIA Chemin d'Eysins, 24 bis, CH-1260 Nyon, Switzerland.
TL English. **SL** French (A).
Affil World Health Organization. **Memb** AITC.

ZALESZCZANSKA, OLGA 11 ch du Champs d'Anier, CH-1209 Geneva, Switzerland *Tel* 98 09 92.
TL French. **SL** English (A); Russian (B).
Memb AITC.

ZREIKAT, IBRAHIM Case postale 370, CH-1217 Meyrin, Switzerland *Tel* (022) 41 91 01.
TL Arabic. **SL** English (A), French (A).
Memb AITC.

Conference Translators
—Classified by Language

Target language (language *into which* a translation is made) appears in boldface caps; source language (language *from which* a translation is made) appears in upper and lowercase boldface. Conference translators are entered in alphabetical order under their specific target/source languages followed by the standard two-letter state abbreviations or abbreviated country name to identify regional accessibility. Please note that in the following only the primary (A) source languages for each translator have been classified.

Into ARABIC from:

English

Abdalla, Z A (Fr)
Abdel-Aziz, F K (Egypt)
Achkar, M (Switz)
El Guebaly, A (Egypt, Fr)
Enan, M (Egypt)
Khaliaf, M (Fr)
Khalil Ahmed, M (Egypt)
Sabry, O H (Egypt)
Salch, A H (Fr, Switz)
Sharaf, T (Switz)
Taalab, F M (Egypt)
Zreikat, I (Switz)

French

Abdalla, Z A (Fr)
Abdel-Aziz, F K (Egypt)
Achkar, M (Switz)
El Guebaly, A (Egypt, Fr)
El-Mouelhy, K (It)
Enan, M (Egypt)
Kamel-Saleh, R (Egypt)
Karara, M (Switz)
Khalil Ahmed, M (Egypt)
Sabry, O H (Egypt)
Salch, A H (Fr, Switz)
Sharaf, T (Switz)
Zreikat, I (Switz)

Into ENGLISH from:

Arabic

Molian, M (UK)
Rofé, H (Hong Kong)

Czech

Dorrell, D M (UK)

Danish

Hartley, E C (UK)
Jackson, J (UK)

Dutch

Jackson, J (UK)
Rofé, H (Hong Kong)
Smith, H A (UK)

French

Albrecht, N (Fr)
Alsop, M H (Fr)
Berkeley, C (UK)
Bernard, E (UK)
Bethenod, B (Fr)
Canavan, E (Fr)
Caragiale, E (Fr)
Coveney, J (UK)

Cowx, K (UK)
Crombie, J (Fr)
Darwall, R (Switz)
Davidson, J (UK)
Deeks, J S (Bel)
Dorrell, D M (UK)
East, K M (UK)
Estinel, M (Switz)
Featherstone, B R (Fr)
Fineberg, M (Fr)
Fry, D G (UK)
Garcia-Abbott, J (NY)
Gardner, J (UK)
Garvie, F A (UK)
Goodman, D (Switz)
Greenstone, M (UK)
Griffiths, R S (Fr)
Hall, S (UK)
Hartley, E C (UK)
Hoorin, A (UK)
Hoorin, G (UK)
Intrator, M (Switz)
Jackson, D (UK)
Jackson, J (UK)
Jennings, S (Fr)
Johnstone, J M (Sp)
Keane, D M (UK)
Langley, J (TX)
Lehmann, A L (Switz)
Levick, M E (Fr)
Lewis, E (UK)
Lloyd, J E R (UK)
Loesch, C von (Ger)
Mackay, V C M (Fr)
McLaughlin, P (Bel)
Meares, B (UK)
Molian, M (UK)
Mouravieff-Apostol, A (Switz)
Mowbray, M (Fr)
Ogier, K N (Fr)
Parker, M (Mor)
Penney, M (UK)
Perl, E (Switz)
Pickering, R E (Fr)
Plumley, D (Sp)
Robinson, J B (Switz)
Rofé, H (Hong Kong)
Rossington, S (Fr)
Saul, J D G (UK)
Savary, J (NY)
Smith, H A (UK)
Stewart, E (Arg)
Strover, A J (UK)
Suchenko, A von (It)
Wardroper, P (UK)
Werth, A (Fr)
Wetenhall, W J (UK)
Wourgaft, E (Fr)
Yates, S (Switz)

German

Berger-Bostock, A (Switz)
Coveney, J (UK)
Crombie, J (Fr)
Deeks, J S (Bel)
Dorrell, D M (UK)
Estinel, M (Switz)
Garvie, F A (UK)
Goodman, D (Switz)
Hartley, E C (UK)
Jackson, J (UK)
Jennings, S (Fr)
Keane, D M (UK)
Lehmann, A L (Switz)
Lloyd, J E R (UK)
Loesch, C von (Ger)
Molian, M (UK)
Parker, M (Mor)
Perl, E (Switz)
Robinson, J B (Switz)
Rofé, H (Hong Kong)
Smith, H A (UK)
Strover, A J (UK)
Wetenhall, W J (UK)

Greek

Keane, D M (UK)

Indonesian

Rofé, H (Hong Kong)

Italian

Darwall, R (Switz)
Estinel, M (Switz)
Garcia-Abbott, J (NY)
Griffiths, R S (Fr)
Jackson, J (UK)
Levick, M E (Fr)
McLaughlin, P (Bel)
Molian, M (UK)
Rofé, H (Hong Kong)
Saul, J D G (UK)
Suchenko, A von (It)
Werth, A (Fr)

Norwegian

Jackson, J (UK)

Persian

Rofé, H (Hong Kong)

Portuguese

Estinel, M (Switz)
Garcia-Abbott, J (NY)
Hoorin, G (UK)
Jackson, J (UK)
Mouravieff-Apostol, A (Switz)
Rofé, H (Hong Kong)
Stewart, E (Ang)

Russian

Albrecht, N (Fr)
Berger-Bostock, A (Switz)
Canavan, E (Fr)
Cowx, I (UK)
Featherstone, B R (Fr)
Fry, D G (UK)
Goodman, D (Switz)
Hartley, E C (UK)
Intrator, M (Switz)
Jackson, D (UK)
Jackson, J (UK)
Jennings, S (Fr)
Johnstone, J M (Sp)
Keane, D M (UK)
Lloyd, J E R (UK)
Meares, B (UK)
Molian, M (UK)
Perl, E (Switz)
Pickering, R E (Fr)
Rojas, B B (NJ)
Strover, A J (UK)
Suchenko, A von (It)
Werth, A (Fr)

Spanish

Alsop, M H (Fr)
Bernard, E (UK)
Caragiale, E (Fr)
Coveney, J (UK)
Cowx, K (UK)
Davidson, J (UK)
Deeks, J S (Bel)
Estinel, M (Switz)
Garcia-Abbott, J (NY)
Gardner, J (UK)
Goodman, D (Switz)
Greenstone, M (UK)
Griffiths, R S (Fr)
Hall, S (UK)
Hoorin, A (UK)
Jackson, J (UK)
Johnstone, J M (Sp)
Keane, D M (UK)
Langley, J (TX)
Lehmann, A L (Switz)
Levick, M E (Fr)
Lewis, E (UK)
McLaughlin, P (Bel)
Molian, M (UK)
Mouravieff-Apostol, A (Switz)
Ogier, K N (Fr)
Penney, M (UK)
Pickering, R E (Fr)
Plumley, D (Sp)
Robinson, J B (Switz)
Rofé, H (Hong Kong)
Rojas, B B (NJ)
Rossington, S (Fr)

Saul, J D G (UK)
Savary, J (NY)
Stewart, E (Ang)
Strover, A J (UK)
Suchenko, A von (It)
Wardroper, P (UK)
Wetenhall, W J (UK)

Swedish

Jackson, J (UK)

Turkish

Rofé, H (Hong Kong)

Into FRENCH from:

Bengali

Philibert, G (Fr)

Czech

Gagnaire, J (Fr)

Dutch

Sulzer, H-G (Fr)

English

Abensour, P S (Fr)
Agostini, Y (Chile)
Amacker, J-M (Switz)
Audoux, M (Fr)
Bailleul, A (Aust)
Barbier-Mokobodzki, N (Fr)
Barrau, G (N. Cal)
Bayan-Baïeff, H (Fr)
Bazinet, G (Fr)
Beresnikoff, A (Switz)
Blanchard, G (Fr)
Bloch-Michel, J (Fr)
Bonet-Maury, C (Fr)
Bordonove, H (Fr)
Bourdariat, R (Fr)
Boyadjian, M-A (Fr)
Brousse-Dondenne, P (Switz)
Carrère, A D (Fr)
Cartanas, M (Fr)
Chérif, F (Fr)
Chesneraye, H-C (Fr)
Chossudovsky, E (UK)
Couturier, H (Switz)
Cren, M (Switz)
Cuisine, J-R (Fr)
David, A (Switz)
Declercq, S (Fr)
Delattre, J (Switz)
Delpierre, M-A (Fr)
Deseilligny, M-A (UK)
Dubucq, B (Switz)
Dumayne, R (Switz)
Ewald, P (Switz)
Eydoux, L (Fr)
Fawzy, D (Fr)
Ferron, M (Fr)
Gagnaire, J (Fr)
Gamard, J (Fr)
Genty, F (Fr)
Gilson, B (Fr)
Golay, M (Switz)
Gourmoux, D (Fr)
Guillon, A (Aust)
Hennequin, S (Fr)

Isoré, J-P (Switz)
Isoré, P (Fr)
Israéli, G (Fr)
Jan-Dubarry, A (Fr)
Jaworski, M (Switz)
Katz, M (Fr)
Keraudren, C (Switz)
Khaw, D (Switz)
Kosmann, C (Fr)
Lamon, F (Fr)
Lamunière, C (Switz)
Lapouge, C de (Fr)
Laroche, N (Mex)
Lefebvre, D (Fr)
Léontidou, J (Switz)
MacNealy-Robert, R (Switz)
Marcuse, J (Fr)
Marie, R (Fr)
Marillier, J (Switz)
Marlière, T-T (Fr)
Marzuk, S (Fr)
Mesnet, M-B (Fr)
Meyer, P (Switz)
Micó, J (Switz)
Navarro, C (Fr)
Nicolas, P (Fr)
Nortier, H (Fr)
Pacteau, L (Fr)
Perlstein, N (Fr)
Philibert, G (Fr)
Pinard, A (Fr)
Piquet, M (Fr)
Prévost, S (Fr)
Raab, A (Fr)
Retbi, S (Isr)
Roland-Gosselin, C (It)
Rosenbaum, L (Fr)
Schutte, T (Switz)
Schwarz, R (Switz)
Seguin, C (Fr)
Soudan, R (Switz)
Stenersen, C (Switz)
Sulzer, H-G (Fr)
Tessier, M (Fr)
Toutchkov, P (Fr)
Tronel, H (Fr)
Truffault, A (Fr)
Vaudoyer, A (Fr)
Veillet-Lavallée, F (Fr)
Vernizy, G de (Switz)
Wegman, D (Fr)
Zaleszczanska, O (Switz)

German

Abensour, P S (Fr)
Boyadjian, M-A (Fr)
Brousse-Dondenne, P (Switz)
Couturier, H (Switz)
David, A (Switz)
Gilson, B (Fr)
Guillon, A (Aust)
Hennequin, S (Fr)
Jan-Dubarry, A (Fr)
Nicolas, P (Fr)
Raab, A (Fr)

Greek

Léontidou, J (Switz)

Italian

Barbier-Mokobodzki, N (Fr)

Bourdariat, R (Fr)
Chérif, F (Fr)
Chesneraye, H-C (Fr)
Declercq, S (Fr)
Mico, J (Switz)
Prevost, S (Fr)
Roland-Gosselin, C (It)
Rosenbaum, L (Fr)
Sulzer, H-G (Fr)
Tessier, M (Fr)

Portuguese

Abrial, G (Fr)

Russian

Bayan-Baïeff, H (Fr)
Beresnikoff, A (Switz)
Israeli, G (Fr)
Philibert, G (Fr)
Toutchkov, P (Fr)

Spanish

Abrial, G (Fr)
Agostini, Y (Chile)
Aubert, C (Fr)
Amacker, J-M (Switz)
Bailleul, A (Aust)
Barbier-Mokobodzki, N (Fr)
Blanchard, G (Fr)
Bourdariat, R (Fr)
Cartanas, M (Fr)
Chesneraye, H-C (Fr)
Declercq, S (Switz)
Delpierre, M-A (Fr)
Dubucq, B (Switz)
Dumayne, R (Switz)
Gagnaire, J (Fr)
Gamard, J (Fr)
Genty, F (Fr)
Golay, M (Switz)
Guillon, A (Aust)
Hennequin, S (Fr)
Jaworski, M (Switz)
Keraudren, C (Switz)
Khaw, D (Switz)
Kosmann, C (Fr)
Lamon, F (Fr)
Lamunière, C (Switz)
Laroche, N (Mex)
Lefebvre, D (Fr)
Marie, R (Fr)
Marillier, J (Switz)
Nortier, H (Fr)
Pinard, A (Fr)
Prevost, S (Fr)
Rens, D (Switz)
Soudan, R (Switz)
Stenevsen, C (Switz)
Sulzer, H-G (Fr)
Tronel, H (Fr)
Vernizy, G de (Switz)
Wegman, D (Fr)

Swedish

Cuisine, J-R (Fr)

Vietnamese

Marliere, T-T (Fr)

Into GERMAN from:

English

Horvath, E (Aust)
Loesch, C von (Ger)
Schwarz, R-P (Switz)
Selke, R (Fr)
Sirges, H (Ger, Fr)
Voigt, I (Aust)
Weiser, E (Fr)

French

Horvath, E (Aust)
Loesch, C von (Ger)
Schwarz, R-P (Switz)
Selke, R (Fr)
Sirges, H (Ger, Fr)
Voigt, I (Aust)
Weiser, E (Fr)

Russian

Selke, R (Fr)

Spanish

Koseleff, E (Fr)
Selke, R (Fr)

Into RUSSIAN from:

English

Narishkin, A (Switz)
Paenson, I (Switz)
Savvin, V (UK)
Toutchkov, P (Fr)

French

Narishkin, A (Switz)
Paenson, I (Switz)
Toutchkov, P (Fr)

Into SPANISH from:

English

Arias, G (Sp)
Blanco, C (Switz)
Corominas de Molist, M (Sp)
Daniel, C R de (Switz)
Juanarena, M (Switz)
Koester, F (Fr)
Méndez-Herrera, J (Sp)
Olives, G de (Sp)
Rodríguez Aranda, L (Sp)
Santa Ana, V I de (Switz)

French

Arias, G (Sp)
Blanco, C (Switz)
Corominas de Molist, M (Sp)
Daniel, C R de (Switz)
Juanarena, M (Switz)
Koester, F (Fr)
Méndez-Herrera, J (Sp)
Olives, G de (Sp)
Rodríguez Aranda, L (Sp)
Santa Ana, V I de (Switz)

Italian

Rodríguez Aranda, L (Sp)

Conference Interpreters

The largest and most prestigious international society of conference interpreters (as distinguished from conference translators), servicing the European and international communities—Commission of the European Communities, United Nations, and the numerous professional organizations and both inter- and intra-governmental bodies—is the Geneva-based International Association of Conference Interpreters (AIIC). The classification of its membership is based upon working performance in 31 languages and covers three categories:

A   mother tongue: the main active (i.e., target) language of the members, normally used for both simultaneous and consecutive interpretation;

B   active (i.e., target) languages other than the mother tongue, in which proficiency is fully adequate to the needs of understanding;

C   passive (i.e., source) languages: those into which members do *not* interpret but of which they have a complete understanding and *from* which they interpret *into* their active (target) languages.

The language classification employed by TAALS, the Western Hemisphere's largest and most prestigious group of conference interpreters, rates its membership according to the following language classifications:

A   principal active language(s), i.e., target language(s), into which members translate or interpret;

B   other active language(s), i.e., target language(s), into which they translate or interpret;

C   language(s), from which they translate or interpret, i.e., source language(s), regardless of difficulties of terminology or idiom.

Members of Association Suisse des Traducteurs et Interprètes (ASTI) and the American Society of Interpreters (ASI) are classified according to their target (or mother tongue) language(s), and A, B, and C categories are not used.

Rather than attempt to adapt the various rating codes of these associations into one system, membership in each association has been identified within each entry so that the user may turn to the above explanation of each association's specific rating codes for further clarification of an interpreter's language proficiency.

Members of AIIC, ASI, ASTI, and TAALS are automatically assumed to be accredited by their associations.

In the entries which follow, an asterisk preceding a name identifies an interpreter as a conference translator also.

AABERG-DAVIDS, HANNELORE Kildevej 27, DK-2960 Rungsted-Kyst, Copenhagen, Denmark *Tel* (02) 863720.
TL German (A); English (B). **SL** Danish (C), French (C.)
Memb AIIC.

ABATE-KRAHE, ILSE 6 av de la Pinede. B 1180 Brussels, Belgium *Tel* 358 42 30.
TL Italian (A). **SL** Dutch (C), French (C), German (C).
Memb AIIC.

ABDEL SAYED, SAMIRA 12 rue Soliman-el-Halaby (ex Doubré) #29, Cairo, Egypt *Tel* 41 884.
TL English (A). **SL** Arabic (C), French (C).
Arabic G Lattin: *Modern Hotel Management* (Franklin).
Memb AIIC.

ABOU-ZAHR, OMAR Les Gouthethés, rue du Lac, CH-1296 Coppet, Switzerland *Tel* 76 35 55.
TL Arabic (A); English (B). **SL** French (C).
Affil UN (Geneva). **Memb** AIIC.

* ADELO, ABDALLAH SAMUEL 320 Galisteo St #401, Santa Fe, NM 87501 USA *Tel* 505-983-9285; 988-8905.
TL Spanish (A); English (B), Portuguese (B). **SL** Italian (C).
Affil Gulf Companies. **Memb** TAALS.

AKBELEN, HASAN Postakutusu 1234, Karaköy, Istanbul, Turkey *Tel* (00-90-11) 45 74 30, 63 62 93 *Cable* AKBELEN-ISTANBUL.
TL Turkish (A). **SL** English (C), French (C).
Memb AIIC.

* ALARCÓN, SERGIO M CDA Rincón de Tlacopac 61, Tlacopac San Angel, Mexico 20, DF, Mexico *Tel* (905) 550-4713.
TL Spanish (A); English (B). **SL** French (C).
UDC biochemistry, chemistry.
Memb TAALS.

ALLAIN, JEAN-PIERRE 8 rue Carqueron, CH-1220 Geneva, Switzerland *Tel* (022) 971723.
TL English (A), Spanish (A). **SL** French (C), German (C), Portuguese (C).
Memb AIIC.

ALLPORT, CHARLES A c/o IFAL, Nazas 43, Mexico 5, DF, Mexico *Tel* 566 07 77.
TL French (A). **SL** English (C), Spanish (C).
Memb AIIC.

AMBROSO RUBERL, LIANA Via Moisé Loria 75, I-20144 Milan, Italy *Tel* 49 89 196.
TL Italian (A); English (B). **SL** French (C).
Memb AIIC.

ANCELOT, CLAUDIA 16 bis, rue Gustave-Robin. F-92290 Châtenay-Malabry, France *Tel* 661 26 78.

TL French (A); English (B), German (B). **SL** Czech (C).
French Karel Čapek: *La Guerre des Salamandres* (Marabout-Gérard, 1969). Jaroslav Hašek: *Les Nouvelles Aventures du Brave Soldat Chveïk* (Gallimard, 1971). *Josef Škvorecký: Miracle en Bohême* (Gallimard, 1978).
Memb AIIC.

ANDERSON, MRS E E Great Myth Manor, Great Lyth, GB-Shrewsbury, UK *Tel* (01) 935 9838; Bayston Hill 3327.
TL English (A); German (B). **SL** Italian (C).
Memb AIIC.

ANDERSON, TINA 214 Kemah Rd, Ridgewood, NJ 07450 USA *Tel* 201-444-0815.
TL Russian (A); English (B). **SL** French (C).
Memb TAALS.

ANDERSON, VALÉRIE 33 Amherst Rd, GB-London W13 8LX, UK *Tel* (01) 998-3103.
TL English (A). **SL** French (C), Spanish (C).
Memb AIIC.

ANDRESCO, IRÈNE 10 chemin de la Tourelle, CH-1209 Geneva, Switzerland *Tel* (022) 98 58 33.
TL Spanish (A). **SL** English (C), French (C), Russian (C).
Memb AIIC.

ANDRONIKOFF, CONSTANTIN 16 rue de Condé, F-75006 Paris, France *Tel* 326-09 35.
  TL & SL French (A), Russian (A); English (B).
  French the works of Berdiayevm, Bulgakov, Florensky, Kluchevsky, Merezhkovsky, and Zenkovsky.
  Memb AIIC (founder & honorary pres).

ANSLEV, AKSEL A Skovledet 15, DK-2830 Virum, Denmark *Tel* (02) 85 74 08.
  TL Danish (A); English (B), Norwegian (B). **SL** German (C), Swedish (C).
  Memb AIIC.

ARDITI, MIREILLE Via Volturno 31, I-20124 Milan, Italy *Tel* 688 17 26.
  TL French (A), Italian (A). **SL** English (C). **UDC** anthropology, education, psychoanalysis, psychology, social sciences.
  Memb AIIC.

ARDITI, SHOSHANA Rehov Habanim 76, Ness-Ziona, Israel *Tel* 054-73766.
  TL Spanish (A). **SL** English (C), French (C), Hebrew (C), Yiddish (C).
  Memb AIIC.

ARIDJIS, NERI 111 ave Paul Hymans, Bte 7, B-1200 Brussels, Belgium *Tel* 771 59 94; (00 31 10) 19 45 79.
  TL French (A); English (B). **SL** German (C), Greek (C).
  Memb AIIC.

AYERS, LANA H 66 Pacific Ave, Toronto, ON M6P 2P4, Canada *Tel* 416-762-8993.
  TL English (A). **SL** French (C), Russian (C). **Memb** AIIC, TAALS.

BABURKOVA, DITA Sultysova 9, Prague 6, Brevnov, Czechoslovakia *Tel* 35 00 94.
  TL Czech (A). **SL** English (C), German (C).
  Memb AIIC.

BACK, JEAN-HUGUES 34 ave Krieg, CH-1208 Geneva, Switzerland *Tel* (022) 47 75 84.
  TL French (A); English (B). **SL** German (C), Spanish (C).
  Memb AIIC.

BACK-SOLE, ROBERTA Im Krähenwinkel 7, D-5060 Bergisch Gladbach 1, West Germany *Tel* (02204) 5 56 26.
  TL English (A), Italian (A). **SL** French (C), German (C).
  Memb AIIC.

BAER-NAGGAR, MARILYN 903 Park Ave, New York, NY 10021 USA *Tel* 212-861-8357.
  TL English (A). **SL** French (C), Italian (C). **Memb** AIIC, TAALS.

BAILLIEUX, FRANCINE 18 Royal Crescent, GB-London W11 4SL, UK *Tel* (01) 603-9649.
  TL French (A). **SL** English (C), German (C).
  Memb AIIC.

BAND, KARIN 88 Ditton Rd, GB-Surbiton, Surrey, UK *Tel* (01) 399 1778, 5590.
  TL & SL German (A); English (B).
  Memb AIIC.

*BARBAJOSA, ALEJANDRO Rio Guadalquivir 48-5, Mexico 5, DF, Mexico *Tel* 563-8911; 525-3427.
  TL Spanish (A); English (B). **SL** French (C). **Memb** AIIC, TAALS.

*BARNABE, MARTHE Yamandú Rodriguez 1326, Montevideo, Uruguay *Tel* 50 33 53.
  TL French (A), Spanish (A). **SL** English (C), Italian (C), Portuguese (C).
  Memb AIIC, TAALS.

BARRAU, GENEVIEVE Commission du Pacifique Sud, BI D5, Noumea Cedex, New Caledonia *Tel* 26 20 00.
  TL & SL French (A); English (B).
  Memb AIIC, AITC.

BATAILLE, LÉON 112 ter ave de Suffren. F-75015 Paris, France *Tel* 567 09 35; 326 81 04.
  TL & SL French (A); English (B), Spanish (B).
  Memb AIIC.

BAUDON-BLANCHET, MADELEINE c/o Mekong Secretariat, ESCAP, Bangkok 2, Thailand *Tel* 282 9161; 391 1413 *Telex* ESCAP-BANGKOK.
  TL & SL French (A); English (B).
  Memb AIIC.

*BAYO, ILMA NIEDERHEITMANN 18 Calle 3-75, Zona 14, Guatemala City, Guatemala, Central America *Tel* 68-2746.
  TL English (A), Spanish (A). **SL** French (C), German (C).
  Memb AIIC, TAALS.

BECK, JULIAN 46 rue de la Réforme, B-1060 Brussels. Belgium *Tel* 345 14 20.
  TL English (A). **SL** French (C), Italian (C). **Memb** AIIC.

BELCHER, MARILA Amcongen, Rio de Janeiro, Brazil. APO Miami, FL 34030 USA.
  TL Spanish (A); English (B), Portuguese (B). **SL** French (C).
  Memb ASI, TAALS.

BELISLE, ESTELLE 8817 Cooper Rd, Alexandria, VA 22309 USA *Tel* 703-780-6297.
  TL English (A); French (B). **SL** Spanish (C).
  Memb TAALS.

*BELLAGAMBA, MARIA CAROLINA c/o CIAT, Apartado 2129, Panama 9A, Panama *Tel* 26-7227; 64-3766/64-0437.
  TL English (A), Spanish (A). **SL** French (C), Italian (C), Portuguese (C).
  Author of "Papers and Proceedings of the First General Assembly in Panama, 1967, of the Inter-American Center for Tax Administrators," *Newsletter*, (CIAT, 1975–78); *English-Spanish Glossary of Tax Terms* (CIAT Studies Series, 1974).
  Memb AIIC, TAALS.

BENEDEK, MARISA 64 rue Emeriau, F-75015 Paris, France *Tel* 578 78 16; 522 05 40.
  TL Italian (A); French (B), German (B). **SL** English.
  Memb AIIC.

*BENNATON, ANN Apartado Postal 1739, Guatemala, Central America *Tel* 20 564; 46 122 *Telex* BENST-GUATEMALA.
  TL English (A), Spanish (A). **SL** German (C).
  Memb AIIC, TAALS.

BERGER, ELÈNE Cologny-Parc 9B, Plateau de Frontenex, CH-1208 Geneva, Switzerland *Tel* (022) 36 18 61.
  TL English (A), French (A). **SL** Dutch (C), German (C).
  Memb AIIC.

BERNSTEIN, ALEXANDRE 32 rue Dareau, F-75014 Paris, France *Tel* 331 89 37.
  TL English (A), French (A), Russian (A). **SL** German (C), Spanish (C).
  Affil IAEA, UN. **Memb** AIIC (pres).

BERTELSEN, SOPHIE 15 rue Gazan, F-75014 Paris, France *Tel* 588 55 74; 734 55 72.
  TL English (A); French (B). **SL** Danish (C), Italian (C), Spanish (C).
  Memb AIIC.

BERTONE, LAURA E 1 quai de Montebello, F-75005 Paris, France *Tel* 326 54 85; 326 81 04.
  TL Spanish (A); English (B). **SL** French (C), Portuguese (C).
  Memb AIIC.

BIASS, CECIL Via Francesco Belloni 52, I-00147 Rome, Italy *Tel* 512 69 20 *Telex* FOODAGRI ROME.
  TL English (A), French (A). **SL** Spanish (C). **Affil** Food & Agriculture Organization (FAO). **Memb** AIIC.

BIASS-MALUCELLI, MARIA-PAOLA 3 rte de Meyrin, CH-1202 Geneva, Switzerland *Tel* (022) 34 89 84.
  TL Italian (A); English (B). **SL** French (C). **Accred** Univ of Geneva (1972). **Memb** AIIC.

BIEGEL-HARTZELL, SUSAN Villa de Beauverd, CH-1296 Coppet, Switzerland *Tel* (022) 76 34 85.
  TL English (A). **SL** French (C), German (C).
  Accred Univ of Geneva (1964). **Memb** AIIC.

BINZER, JOHN J 6 Nannasvej, DK-Svendborg 5700, Denmark *Tel* (09) 21 33 35.
  TL English (A), Danish (A); Norwegian (B). **SL** German (C), Swedish (C).
  Memb AIIC.

BLAUENSTEIN, REIKO 3d rue de Moillebeau, CH-1209 Geneva, Switzerland *Tel* (022) 34 69 94.
  TL Japanese (A); English (B). **SL** French (C).
  Memb AIIC.

BLONDEAU, SIMONE 36 Le May Ave, Grove Park, London SE12 9SU, UK *Tel* (01) 857-0503.
  TL French (A); Spanish (B). **SL** English (C), Portuguese (C).
  Memb AIIC.

BO BRAMSEN, MICHELE Esperance Alle 11, 2920 Charlottenlund, Copenhagen Ø, Denmark *Tel* (01) 61 01 23.
  TL & SL French (A); English (B).
  Memb AIIC.

BOCK-MICHEL, GISELA Bertholdstr 1, D-1 Berlin 37, West Germany *Tel* (030) 817 30 65; 802 79 18.
  TL German (A); English (B). **SL** French (C).
  Memb AIIC.

BOERO, RAUL Maldonado 1565, Montevideo, Uruguay *Tel* 49 57 41.
  TL English (A), Spanish (A). **SL** French (C), Portuguese (C).
  Memb AIIC.

BOKOWNEX, JOY 70 rue des Plantes, F-75014 Paris, France *Tel* 539 67 43; 306 89 41.
  TL English (A); French (B). **SL** German (C).
  Memb AIIC.

BOLOMEY, MARTINE 137 E 36 St, Carlton Regency North, New York, NY 10016 USA *Tel* 212-679-4791.
  TL French (A); Spanish (B). **SL** English (C). **Affil** UN. **Memb** AIIC.

BORCHARDT, MARGUERITE 345 E 54 St #5H, New York, NY 10022 USA *Tel* 212-355-0135.
  TL English, French. **SL** German.
  Memb ASI (vice pres & dir for public relations and information).

BOROVSKI, ALEKSEI Schwalbenweg 61, D-6900 Heidelberg, West Germany *Tel* (06221) 7-5900.
  TL English (A); French (B). **SL** Russian (C).
  Accred School of Interpreters & Translators (Paris). **Memb** AIIC.

* BORST, KONRAD Aaraustr 26, D-741 Reutlingen, West Germany.
  TL German (A). **SL** English (C), French (C).
  Memb TAALS.

BOSMAN-DELZONS, PATRICK-ALEXIS Wagenaarweg 20, NL-The Hague, The Netherlands *Tel* (070) 55 00 44.
  TL & SL English (A), French (A).
  Affil UN. **Memb** AIIC.

BOTERO-BROWNING, SOCORRO British Residency, Vila, New Hebrides *Tel* 359 Santo *Telex* BRITRES-SANTO.
  TL Spanish (A). **SL** English (C), French (C).
  Memb AIIC.

BOULADON, VALÉRIE "Chantoiseau," 2 chemin Megard, CH-1290 St-Loup, Versoix, Switzerland *Tel* (022) 55 24 39.
  TL English (A); French (B). **SL** Spanish (C).
  Memb AIIC.

BOURDELET-GOFFINET, ANTOINETTE 52 ave de Boissy, F-94370 Sucy-en-Brie, France *Tel* (1) 902 35 68.
  TL & SL English (A), French (A).
  Memb AIIC.

BOURGEOIS, DENISE 2505 Edouard-Montpetit #106, Montreal, PQ H3T IJ5, Canada *Tel* 514-731-2896.
  TL & SL French (A), English (A). **UDC** law, medicine, unionism.
  Memb AIIC, ATIO.

BOUVERAT, COLLETE Hausdorffstr 35, D-5300 Bonn, West Germany *Tel* (02221) 21 13 86.
  TL German (A); French (B), Italian (B). **SL** English (C).
  Accred Univ of Geneva (1946). **Memb** AIIC.

BOUYGES, CLAUDE 4214 W 15 Ave, Vancouver, BC V6R 3A6, Canada *Tel* 604-228-1261.
  TL & SL French, English.
  Memb ASI.

*BOWEN, DAVID 628 S 25 St, Arlington, VA 22202 USA *Tel* 703-684-7497. c/o H Bloksberg, Singerstr 28/5, A-1010 Vienna, Austria *Tel* 52 78 85.
  TL English (A). **SL** French (C), Spanish (C).
  Affil Georgetown Univ. **Memb** AIIC, TAALS.

*BOWEN, MARGARETA 628 S 25 St, Arlington, VA 22202 USA *Tel* 703-684-7497. c/o H Bloksberg, Sirgerstr 28/5, A-1010 Vienna, Austria *Tel* 52 78 85.
  TL French (A), German (A). **SL** English (C), Italian (C).
  Affil Georgetown Univ. **Memb** AIIC, TAALS.

BOYCE, CRISTINA 94 Sutherlands Grove, GB-London SW 18, UK *Tel* (01) 789 1613.
  TL Italian (A); English (B). **SL** French (C).
  Memb AIIC.

BOYDE, BERNADETTE 100 Lofting Rd, GB-London N1 1JB, UK *Tel* (01) 607 52 13; (01) 858 4187.
  TL French (A). **SL** English (C), German (C).
  Memb AIIC.

BRAUNSTEIN, ALICIA Sybelstr 44, D-1 Berlin 12, West Germany *Tel* 323 14 67.
  TL Spanish (A); German (B). **SL** English (C).
  Memb AIIC.

BRISSA-BENCKERT, KATHARINA 21 rue de l'Athénée, CH-1206 Geneva, Switzerland *Tel* (022) 46 16 30. Turnerstr 12, D-69 Heidelberg, West Germany *Tel* (06221) 3 36 15.
  TL German (A); English (B). **SL** French (C), Italian (C), Russian (C).
  Memb AIIC.

BROOK, MARIE-CLAIRE Wah Kwong Cliff A3, 200 Victoria Rd, Pokfulam, Hong Kong *Tel* 5-871484.
  TL Spanish (A). **SL** English (C), French (C).
  Memb AIIC.

BROS-BRANN, ELIANE 31 rue des Charmes, F-93100 Montreuil, France *Tel* 858 55 65.
  TL English (A); French (B). **SL** German (C).
  Accred Univ of Paris (1961). **Memb** AIIC.

BUCKLEY, PAULITA 30 av Krieg, CH-1208 Geneva, Switzerland *Tel* (022) 47 75 48.
  TL English (A); Spanish (B). **SL** French (C), Italian (C).
  Memb AIIC.

BUENDIA, MARÍA TERESA 13 Hollybranch Ct, Baltimore, MD 21057 USA *Tel* 301-592-8075.
  TL Spanish (A); English (B). **SL** French (C).
  Memb ASI, TAALS.

BÜHLER, HANNS HERMANN Doktorberg 16/13, A-2391 Kaltenleutgeben, Austria *Tel* (02238) 481.
  TL German (A); English (B). **SL** French (C).
  Accred Univ of Georgetown (1957), Univ of Vienna (1962), diploma. **Memb** AIIC.

BURNET, DOROTHY 24 rue Léon Frot, F-75011 Paris, France *Tel* 371 43 37; 555 17 56.
  TL & SL English (A); French (B), German (B).
  Memb AIIC.

CALIXTO, NEIF 85 Kenmare St, New York, NY 10012 USA *Tel* 212-226-5548.
  TL English, Portuguese. **SL** Spanish.
  Memb ASI.

CAMBIEN, RAOUL 14 av des Eglantiers, B-1860 Meise, Belgium *Tel* (02) 269 13 58. BIOC, 14-16 rue Willems #209, B-1040 Brussels, Belgium *Tel* 02 218 65 97; 217 46 87.
  TL Dutch (A), French (A); English (B). **SL** German (C).
  Memb AIIC.

CAMICI, GIORGIO 21 place Dauphine, F-75001 Paris, France *Tel* 633 77 42; 522 06 40.
  TL Italian (A); French (B). **SL** English (C).
  Memb AIIC.

CAMPAGNOLA, MASSIMO 31 rue Lecourbe, F-75015 Paris, France *Tel* 578 71 31; 326 81 04.
  TL Italian (A); French (B). **SL** English (C), German (C).
  Memb AIIC.

CAMPOS, FRANCISCO 3705 George Mason Dr #2407S, Falls Church, VA 22041 USA *Tel* 703-379-8291.
  TL Spanish. **SL** English, Italian, Portuguese.
  Memb ASI.

CANIN LAMIELLE, ELISABETH 94 rue de la Tour, F-75016 Paris, France *Tel* 504 34 52.
  TL French (A); English (B). **SL** Spanish (C).
  Memb AIIC.

CAPLAN, FLORA 78 Leeside Cresc, GB-London NW11 OLA, UK *Tel* (01) 455 7129.
TL English (A). SL French (C), German (C).
Memb AIIC.

CARDENAS, MARIA ELENA 49 E 96 St, New York, NY 10028 USA *Tel* 212-722-6565.
TL English, Spanish. SL French.
Memb ASI.

***CARDOSO, PABLO** Case postale 105, CH-1217 Meyrin 1, Switzerland *Tel* (Geneva) 82-8625; 31-0231.
TL Spanish (A); English (B). SL French (C), Portuguese (C).
Affil ICITO/GATT. Memb AIIC.

CARTER, ISOBEL 16 Pembroke Pl, GB-London W8 6ET, UK *Tel* (01) 937-5318.
TL English (A); French (B). SL Russian (C).
Memb AIIC.

CARTER, PEERS Holgate, GB-Balcombe, Sussex RH 17 6LL, UK *Tel* (044) 483 205.
TL & SL English (A); French (B).
Memb AIIC.

CAVANNA, SERGE Jungfrudansen 14, 7 tr, S-171 56 Solna, Sweden *Tel* (08) 730 29 71. Sveriges Exportraad, Box 5513 Storgatan 19, S-114 85 Stockholm, Sweden *Tel* (08) 63 05 80 *Telex* 19620 EXPORTS.
TL English (A), Italian (A); French (B), Swedish (B). SL Spanish (C).
Memb AIIC.

CEREBROG, JEFIN 31 W 71 St #201, New York, NY 10023 USA *Tel* 212-362-3626; 799-2802.
TL Russian. SL English, French, Spanish.
Memb ASI.

CHABERT, VÉRA 82 blvd St Denis, F-92400 Courbevoie, France *Tel* 788 87 88; 522 06 40.
TL French (A), German (A). SL English (C).
Memb AIIC.

CHALANDON, MICHELE 40 rue de Paris, F-92100 Boulogne, France *Tel* 825 06 48; 555 17 56.
TL French (A); English (B). SL Spanish (C).
Memb AIIC.

CHENAIS-MONJOL, ANNE 11 rue St-Martin, F-74160 St-Julien-en-Genevois, France *Tel* (050) 49 00 87; (022) 33 75 29.
TL French (A); English (B). SL Italian (C).
Memb AIIC.

CHENNAULT, CLAIRE LEE CH-1261 Chavannes-de-Bogis, Switzerland *Tel* (022) 76 18 24.
TL English (A). SL French (C), Spanish (C).
Memb AIIC.

CHEVASSUS, JO 5 rue Jules-Ferry, BP 285, Dakar, Senegal *Tel* 235 50. 9 rue Dupin, F-75006 Paris, France *Tel* 548-3905.
TL & SL French (A); English (B).
Memb AIIC.

CHILDS, BELITA Gothic House, 53 Maze Hill, Greenwich, GB-London SE 10, UK *Tel* 858 98 57; 399 5590.
TL & SL English (A); French (B), Spanish (B).
Memb AIIC.

CHLEPNER, NADIA Clos des Vergers, 19 av du Jura, F-01210 Ferney-Voltaire, France *Tel* (023) 40 65 47.
TL French (A); English (B). SL Italian (C), Spanish (C).
Memb AIIC.

CHOI, MIRELLA 3 rue de Fribourg, CH-1201 Geneva, Switzerland *Tel* 32 06 41.
TL Italian (A). SL French (C), German (C).
Memb AIIC.

CLARENS, JEANNIE DE 39 quai de Grenelle, F-75015 Paris, France *Tel* 577 39 09; 326 54 52.
TL French (A); English (B). SL Spanish (C).
Memb AIIC.

CLAVEL, MARIE MICHELLE 70 rue de Miromesnil, F-75008 Paris, France *Tel* 522 97 56.
TL French (A); Spanish (B). SL English (C).
Memb AIIC.

COGLIATI, BEATRIZ ELSA Billinghurst 2402, 1425 Buenos Aires, Argentina *Tel* 824-2130.
TL Spanish (A); Portuguese (B). SL English (C), French (C), Italian (C).
Memb AIIC.

COLE-EGAN, HAZEL 569 Chelsea Crescent, Beaconsfield, PQ H9W 4N4, Canada *Tel* 514-695-5922.
TL English (A); French (B). SL German (C).
Accred ESIT, Univ of Paris. Memb AIIC.

CORAY, FRANK Russenweg 12, CH-8008 Zurich, Switzerland *Tel* (01) 53 71 73.
TL English. SL French, German, Spanish.
Memb ASTI.

CORSINI-PASSI, CATERINA S Felice, Torre 4, I-20090 Segrate, Milan, Italy *Tel* (0039-2) 753 13 85.
TL English (A), Italian (A); Portuguese (B). SL French (C).
Memb AIIC.

CORY-JAMES, ANTONY 41 rue Verte Bte 8, B-1950 Cranheim, Belgium *Tel* (02) 731 57 59.
TL & SL English (A), French (A).
Affil NATO. Memb AIIC.

COTE, MICHEL 54 Rochester, Ottawa, ON K1R 7L5, Canada *Tel* 613-233-6894.
TL & SL English, French.
Memb ASI.

COULTER, HARRIS L 4221 45 St NW, Washington, DC 20016 USA *Tel* 202-362-3185.
TL English (A). SL French (C), Russian (C).
Memb AIIC, TAALS.

CREDAZZI SALVI, MAXIMILIEN Via di Monteverde 162, I-00151 Rome, Italy *Tel* 531 10 54. 18 rue de Trèves, B-1040 Brussels, Belgium *Tel* 511 25 59; 500 51 54.
TL & SL Italian (A); French (B).
Memb AIIC.

CRU, ANTONY ROBERT 50 ch Ami-Argand, CH-1290 Versoix, Switzerland *Tel* (022) 55 10 64.
TL & SL English (A), French (A).
Memb AIIC.

CUNY-FRANZ, JUTTA KARIN F-88460 Docelles, France *Tel* (1529) 66 21 79; 66 26 76.
TL German (A); French (B). SL English (C).
Memb AIIC.

CURTIS, MICHEL 46 av du Bois-de-Verrières, F-92160 Antony, France *Tel* 666 02 59; 326 54 52.
TL & SL French (A); English (B).
Memb AIIC.

CUSUMANO, CAROLL Reisnerstr 18/21, A-1030 Vienna, Austria *Tel* 222 75 37 232.
TL French (A); English (B). SL Spanish (C).
Memb AIIC.

DAGUERRE-MASSIEU, CHRISTINE 4099 Isabella, Montreal, PQ H3T 1N5, Canada *Tel* 514-731-5285.
TL Spanish (A); French (B). SL English (C).
Memb AIIC.

DANA, MARIE-JOSÉE 515 François, Nuns' Island, Montreal, PQ H3E 1G5, Canada *Tel* 514-766-3877.
TL French (A). SL English (C), Russian (C).
Memb AIIC.

DECHAMPS, PIERRE 62 blvd Louis-Schmidt, B-1040 Brussels, Belgium *Tel* (02) 733-83-03.
TL & SL English (A), French (A).
Affil NATO. Memb AIIC.

DECOSTER-BERRY, ANNE 30 rue Croix-Bosset, F-92310 Sèvres, France *Tel* 534 34 63.
TL & SL French (A); English (B).
Affil Organization of Economic and Cooperative Development (OECD). Memb AIIC.

DEJEAN LE FEAL, KARLA 28 rue Montrosier, F-92200 Neuilly, France *Tel* 722 71 00; 306 89 41.
TL German (A); French (B). SL English (C).
Affil ESIT. Memb AIIC.

DE LA VEGA, MARÍA ISABEL Carrera 6a, No 67-63, Bogatá, Colombia *Tel* 49-3449.
TL Spanish (A); French (B). SL English (C), Portuguese (C).
Memb TAALS.

DELLI ZOTTI, MARIA Résidence Fuchsias, 5 clos des Acacias, B-1150 Brussels, Belgium *Tel* 762 48 76.
TL French (A); English (B). SL German (C), Italian (C).
Affil NATO. Memb AIIC.

DELLMANN, RENATE 1026 Gaskill Dr, Ames, IA 50010 USA *Tel* 515-232-6020.
TL & SL German (A); English (B).
Memb AIIC.

DELPEUT DE LEMOS, FRANÇOISE Viale Aspromonte 5/2, I-16128 Genova, Italy *Tel* (0039-10) 58 22 33 *Telex* 270060 PP DE A PER SEMINODO.
TL French (A), Portuguese (A); Italian (B). **SL** English (C), Spanish (C).
Accred Conseil International de la Langue Française. **Memb** AIIC.

DENIS-FLOCK, HANNA 6 place Possoz, F-75016 Paris, France *Tel* 870 64 35; 266 17 76.
TL German (A); French (B). **SL** English (C).
Accred Univ of Geneva (1953) (parliamentary interpretation). **Memb** AIIC.

DERGUINE-VARSAVSKY, MRS T "Le Clos des Vergers," F-01210 Ferney-Voltaire, France *Tel* (50) 40 68 30.
TL Russian (A); English (B), German (B). **SL** French (C).
Author of *Russian-English Dictionary of Metallurgy and Allied Sciences* (Frederick Ungar, 1962); *Basic Russian-English Geological Dictionary* (The Amer Soc of Mechanical Engineering, 1959); *Transliteration of Soviet Geographical Terms* (Val Talberg, 1959).
Memb AIIC.

DESBONNET, ERIKA 52 Appletree Lane, Roslyn Heights, NY 11577 USA *Tel* 516-621-3530.
TL English (A); French (B), Polish (B). **SL** Russian (C).
Memb AIIC.

DESROSIERS, EVA F 3436 Washington Dr, Falls Church, VA 22041 USA *Tel* 703-820-3645.
TL English, Spanish. **SL** German, Portuguese.
Memb ASI.

DIEHL, ERIKA 4 rampe de Chavant, CH-1232 Confignon, GE, Switzerland *Tel* (022) 57 41 78.
TL German (A). **SL** Dutch (C), French (C).
Memb AIIC.

DIEPHAUS-ALTENKIRCH, ODINA Bienhornhöhe 23, D-54 Koblenz-Pfaffendorf, West Germany *Tel* (0261) 77 694.
TL German (A); French (B). **SL** English (C), Italian (C).
Memb AIIC.

DIEZ, ASTRID 2 Tudor City Pl, New York, NY 10017 USA *Tel* 212-697-5706.
TL Spanish (A). **SL** English (C), French (C).
Affil UN. **Memb** AIIC.

DOBLE-GESSENEY, MARINETTE Rte de la Plaine 73, CH-1249 La Plaine, Switzerland *Tel* (22) 54 14 89; 33 75 29.
TL French (A); English (B). **SL** German (C), Russian (C).
Memb AIIC.

DOBOSZ, IRENA 12 ch de Castelver, CH-1255 Veyrier, Switzerland *Tel* (022) 43 05 45.
TL Polish (A); English (B), Russian (B). **SL** French (C).
Memb AIIC.

DOCAL, SONIA 2947 Tilden St NW, Washington, DC 20008 USA *Tel* 202-362-2459.
TL English, Portuguese. **SL** Spanish.
Memb ASI.

DOEMPKE, BURCKHARD 5 rue du Canal, B-1000 Brussels, Belgium *Tel* (02) 217 93 42.
TL German (A); English (B). **SL** French (C).
Accred Central London Polytechnic. **Memb** AIIC.

DOLDER, LYDIA 30 av E Parmentier, B-1150 Brussels, Belgium *Tel* 770 87 09.
TL Dutch (A); English (B), Spanish (B). **SL** French (C), German (C), Italian (C), Portuguese (C).
Affil EEC. **Memb** AIIC.

DOUEK, RAYMOND IBRAHIM 53 rue des Peupliers, F-92100 Boulogne, France *Tel* 608 30 89; 577 16 10.
TL Arabic (A); French (B). **SL** English (C).
Affil UN (Paris). **Memb** AIIC, SFT.

DRAPIER, AGNES IRIS 33834 Tidewater Ct, Olney, MD 20832 USA *Tel* 301-459-0610.
TL Portuguese. **SL** English, Spanish.
Memb ASI.

DROWSKI, JÜRGEN 41 rue de l'Eglise, F-75015 Paris, France *Tel* 578 11 67; 306 89 41.
TL German (A); English (B), French (B). **SL** Italian (C).
Memb AIIC.

DUCROUX, COLETTE 7 ch des Tulipiers, CH-1208 Geneva, Switzerland *Tel* (022) 35 38 44.
TL French (A). **SL** English (C), Spanish (C).
Memb AIIC.

DUCROUX, MONIQUE 3 place des Charmilles, CH-1203 Geneva, Switzerland *Tel* (022) 44 12 03.
TL French (A); Spanish (B). **SL** English (C).
Memb AIIC.

DU JARDIN, JEAN-LOUIS Via Friggeri 35, I-00136 Rome, Italy *Tel* (06) 341861.
TL French (A). **SL** English (C), Italian (C), Spanish (C).
Memb AIIC.

DUNAND, GEORGES 5 chemin des Prés-Courts, CH-1222 Vésenaz, Switzerland *Tel* (022) 52 23 57.
TL French (A); English (B). **SL** German (C), Italian (C), Portuguese (C), Spanish (C).
Memb AIIC.

DURAN, RAQUEL Homero 1911, Dpto 1101, Mexico 10, DF, Mexico *Tel* 5 57 92 27.
TL Spanish (A); English (B). **SL** French (C).
Memb AIIC.

DURKOP, GERTRUD 11 rue Diderot, F-78110 Le Vésinet, France *Tel* 976 08 35; 326 54 52.
TL German (A), Spanish (A); English (B). **SL** French (C), Italian (C).
Memb AIIC.

DUTTWEILER-BILANEY, ANITA Hauptstr 117, CH-4416 Bubendorf (BL), Switzerland *Tel* (061) 95 24 45.
TL English (A); French (B). **SL** German (C).
Accred Univ of Geneva (1967). **Memb** AIIC.

DYNER, RICHARD 17 E 96 St, New York, NY 10028 USA *Tel* 212-831-9248.
TL & SL English, French.
Memb ASI.

EDWARDS, NORMAN 13 Christchurch Rd, GB-Winchester (Hants), UK *Tel* (0962) 2687.
TL English (A); French (B). **SL** Spanish (C).
Memb AIIC.

EMDE BOAS, MAGDA van Stadionweg 80, NL-1077 SP Amsterdam, The Netherlands *Tel* (020) 79 05 80; 76 49 41.
TL German (A); Czech (B), Dutch (B). **SL** English (C), French (C), Italian (C).
Memb AIIC.

ERBA-SAIN, MARIA GIUSEPPINA Via Giason Del Maino 16, I-Milan, Italy *Tel* 49 74 08.
TL Italian (A); English (B). **SL** French (C). **Memb** AIIC.

ERICHSEN, BIRGIT Strandvaenget 2, DK-2791 Dragør, Denmark *Tel* (01) 53 88 73.
TL Danish (A); French (B). **SL** English (C).
Memb AIIC.

ESCOBAR-BUDGE, MARIA TERESA Av Vicuña Mackenna 3 #1702, Santiago, Chile *Tel* 384944.
TL English (A), Spanish (A). **SL** French (C), Portuguese (C).
Memb AIIC.

ETCHEGORRY, ANA MARIA 31 chemin des Palettes, Case postale 73, CH-1212 Grand-Lancy 1, Geneva, Switzerland *Tel* (022) 94 86 17.
TL & SL Spanish (A); English (B), French (B), Portuguese (B).
Affil ILO. **Memb** AIIC.

EUSTACE-WERKNER, KRISTINA Ballyfolan, Brittas, Co Dublin, Ireland *Tel* 582266.
TL German (A); English (B), French (B). **SL** Italian (C), Spanish (C).
Memb AIIC.

FAGAN, THEODORE 1042 Paradise Way, Palo Alto, CA 94306 USA *Tel* 415-493-7319.
TL English (A), Spanish (A); French (B). **SL** Italian (C), Portuguese (C).
Memb AIIC, TAALS.

FAILLACE-GINDRE, LINDE Azulinas 6, E-Madrid 16, Spain *Tel* 458 0355; 458 64 33.

TL English (A); Italian (B), Spanish (B). **SL** French (C).
Memb AIIC.

FALCON-PICKERING, JUANITA 8718 Arlington Blvd, Fairfax, VA 22030 USA *Tel* 703-560-5996.
TL English, French, Spanish. **SL** Italian, Portuguese.
Memb ASI.

FARCOT, MARIE-CHRISTINE 4 rue de St Quentin, F-67000 Strasbourg, France *Tel* (88) 61 65 44.
TL & SL French (A); English (B).
Memb AIIC.

FARRELL, PETER Via E Besta 5, I-00167 Rome, Italy *Tel* 622 49 48; 623 29 47.
TL English (A). **SL** French (C), Italian (C).
Memb AIIC.

FEDRIGHINI, DONATELLA Via Tripoli 142, I-10137 Turin, Italy *Tel* 32 28 47.
TL & SL Italian (A); English (B), French (B).
Memb AIIC.

FERAT-GAIN, CAROL 52 blvd Pasteur, F-75015 Paris, France *Tel* 320 65 95; 326 54 52.
TL French (A); English (B). **SL** Spanish (C).
Memb AIIC.

FERNANDEZ DE CORDOBA, DIEGO PO Box 6923, Panama 5, Panama *Tel* 64 5960, 2102.
TL & SL Spanish (A); English (B).
Memb AIIC.

*FERRUA, PIETRO Foreign Languages, Lewis & Clark College, Portland, OR 97219 USA *Tel* 503-244-6161.
TL French (A), Italian (A); Portuguese (B). **SL** English (C), Spanish (C).
Memb AIIC, TAALS.

FIEVET, PAMELA 37 rue Borghèse, F-92200 Neuilly, France *Tel* 624 93 18.
TL English (A), German (A). **SL** French (C), Spanish (C).
Memb AIIC.

FISCHER, MARGARITA Cra 3-A, No 57-84, Bogotá, Colombia *Tel* 35 31 92.
TL English (A), Spanish (A). **SL** French (C).
Memb AIIC, TAALS.

FISHBOURNE, LESLY 159 rue Théodore-Decuyper Bte 37, B-1200 Brussels, Belgium *Tel* 762 43 42.
TL English (A). **SL** French (C), German (C).
Memb AIIC.

*FISHKIN, MADELEINE 5012 Dodson Dr, Annandale, VA 22003 USA *Tel* 703-354-2362; 202-488-2378.
TL French (A); English (B). **SL** Spanish (C).
Affil INTELSAT. **Memb** TAALS.

FOLCH, SIMONE Rio Amazonas 57-201, Mexico 5, DF, Mexico *Tel* 535 64 66.
TL French (A). **SL** English (C), Spanish (C).
Memb AIIC.

FORSTER-TURPIN, FRANÇOISE c/o Conference Interpreters Group, 26 Leonard Ct, Edwardes Sq, GB-London W8 6NN, UK *Tel* (01) 602 6218.
TL French (A); English (B). **SL** Spanish (C).
Memb AIIC.

FOSTER, PATRICIA 41 ave des Alpes, CH-Montreaux, Switzerland.
TL English (A); French (B). **SL** German (C).
Memb AIIC.

FOURNIER-LLUHI, SOLANGE Cerrada la Perpetua 20, Dept 9, San José Insurgentes, Mexico, DF Mexico *Tel* 524 04 17.
TL French (A). **SL** English (C), Spanish (C).
Memb AIIC.

FRADIER, MARY 13 rue Baudin, F-94160 St-Mandé, France *Tel* 328 97 99; 326 54 52.
TL & SL English (A); French (B).
Memb AIIC.

FRANK, WOLFE "La Rouve," La Celle-Les Bordes, 78720 Dampierre, France *Tel* 485-2288; 326-5452.
TL English (A), German (A). **SL** French (C).
Memb AIIC.

FREICHELS, BRIGITTE Cronstettenstr 37, D-6 Frankfurt/Main, West Germany *Tel* 59 85 13.
TL German (A); English (B). **SL** French (C).
Memb AIIC.

FREUDENSTEIN, KARL Buchfinkenweg 34, D-5300 Bonn, West Germany *Tel* 62 36 76.
TL & SL German (A); English (B), French (B), Portuguese (B).
Affil Ministry of Defense. **Memb** AIIC.

FRIESE, RALF Veilchenstr 12, D-7560 Gaggenau, West Germany *Tel* (07225) 5 922.
TL & SL German (A); English (B).
Memb AIIC.

FRITSCH, GERTRUDE 15/17, allée Tissot, F-92240 Malakoff, France *Tel* 735 64 91.
TL German (A); French (B). **SL** English (C).
Memb AIIC.

FROST, BATIA Gotlieb 10, Tel Aviv, Israel *Tel* 249 903.
TL Hebrew (A); English (B). **SL** French (C), German (C).
Affil Bar-Ilan Univ (Tel Aviv). **Memb** AIIC.

FUCHS-VIDOTTO, LETIZIA Meerfeldstr 30, D-5 Cologne-Longerich, West Germany *Tel* (0221) 599 19 05.
TL German (A), Italian (A); French (B). **SL** English (C).
Memb AIIC.

GAIN, MALCOLM 52 blvd Pasteur, F-75015 Paris, France *Tel* 320 65 95; 326 54 52.
TL English (A); French (B). **SL** German (C).
Accred Univ of Paris. **Memb** AIIC.

*GÁLER, RAÚL 144-12 Village Rd #B, Jamaica, NY 11435 USA *Tel* 212-969-3841.
TL Spanish (A); English (B). **SL** French (C).
Affil UN. **Memb** AIIC, TAALS.

GALLANT-BAUER, CHRISTEL 45 Rockland Dr, Moncton, NB E1A 3T2, Canada *Tel* 506-855-5075.
TL German (A); French (B). **SL** English (C).
Affil Univ of Moncton (Translation & Lang). **Memb** AIIC.

GALVAN, ALVARO 800 Fourth St NW #S102, Washington, DC 20024 USA *Tel* 202-554-8149.
TL English, Spanish. **SL** French, Portuguese.
Memb ASI (dir for professional relations and standards).

GARCÍA-LANDA, MARIANO lla rue Copernic-Bte 2, B-1180 Brussels, Belgium.
TL Spanish (A). **SL** English (C), French (C), German (C), Italian (C).
Memb AIIC, TAALS.

*GARRIDO, OLGA 2601 Woodley Place NW, Washington DC 20008 USA *Tel* 202-332-4819; 387-0314.
TL Spanish (A); English (B). **SL** Portuguese (C).
Memb TAALS.

GARTNER, KARL 14 ch des Roulets, CH-1228 Plan-les-Ouates, Geneva, Switzerland *Tel* (022) 94 18 74.
TL German (A); French (B). **SL** English (C).
Accred Univ of Geneva. **Memb** AIIC.

GAUTIER, MAX 12201 River Rd, Potomac, MD 20854 USA *Tel* 301-299-2049, 3346; 202-381-8611.
TL French. **SL** English, Portuguese, Spanish.
Memb ASI.

GELDART, GRAHAM rue des Epouses 140, CH-1700 Fribourg, Switzerland *Tel* (037) 22 96 14.
TL English. **SL** French, Spanish.
Memb ASTI.

GEUZENDAM, ANNETTETEN 94 ave des Camélias, B-1150 Brussels, Belgium *Tel* 7710228.
TL Dutch (A); French (B). **SL** German (C).
Memb AIIC.

GIANNINI, ANNE 15 rue des Aulnes, F-92330 Sceaux, France *Tel* 350 12 28; 326 54 52.
TL English (A), French (A). **SL** Italian (C).
Memb AIIC.

GILLMAN, RODERICK Enrumvej 8A, DK-2942 Skodsborg, Denmark *Tel* 289 34 27.
    TL English (A); French (B). **SL** Danish (C).
Memb AIIC.

GIOSSAN, INGRID 188 Stanley Ave, Ottawa, ON K1M 1P3, Canada *Tel* 613-741-3075.
    TL & SL English (A); French (B), Spanish (B).
Memb AIIC.

GIROT, MADELEINE 4 rue des-Fosses-St-Marcel, F-75005 Paris, France *Tel* 337 81 87; 336 81 04.
    TL & SL French (A); English (B), Spanish (B).
Memb AIIC.

GITAI, SHLOMO 11 Rehov Israëls, Jérusalem 94548, Israel *Tel* (02) 22 54 93.
    TL & SL Spanish (A); French (B), Hebrew (B).
Memb AIIC.

GLEMET, ROGER 9 rue Henri-Spiess, CH-1208 Geneva, Switzerland *Tel* (022) 36 07 57.
    TL English (A), French (A). **SL** Spanish (C).
Memb AIIC.

GLEMSER, HELGA 6 cité Alma, F-75007 Paris, France *Tel* 705 80 67.
    TL German (A); French (B). **SL** English (C).
Memb AIIC.

GOEHRING, HEINZ Wolfsbrunnensteige 13, D-69 Heidelberg 1, West Germany *Tel* (06221) 80 21 93.
    TL German (A); Spanish (B). **SL** English (C), French (C).
    Affil Univ of Mainz (Applied Linguistics).
Memb AIIC.

GOISCHKE, URSULA Lise-Meitner-Weg 2, D-7514 Eggenstein-Leop, West Germany *Tel* (07247) 2378.
    TL & SL German (A); French (B).
Memb AIIC.

*GOMEZ, BARBARA Liverpool 149-102, Mexico 6, DF, Mexico *Tel* 533 38 29.
    TL English (A). **SL** French (C), Portuguese (C), Spanish (C).
Memb AIIC, TAALS.

*GÓMEZ, JOAN FABLING DE a/c Familia Noriega, Apartado 4828, Panama 5, Panama *Tel* 23-9411.
    TL English (A), Spanish (A). **SL** Portuguese (C).
Memb AIIC.

GÓMEZ DE SILVA, GUIDO PO Box 20, Rm 2494, Grand Central Sta, New York, NY 10017 USA *Tel* 212-754-6487; 889-2863.
    TL Spanish (A). **SL** English (C), French (C), Italian (C).
Memb AIIC, TAALS.

GONZALEZ, ANNABELLA 333 E 49 St #1H, New York, NY 10017 USA *Tel* 212-751-8932; 840-1234.
    TL English (A); Spanish (B). **SL** French (C).
Memb TAALS.

GRAEBER, CHRISTINE 31 av Général-de-Gaulle, B-1050 Brussels, Belgium *Tel* 640 39 20.
    TL German (A); French (B). **SL** English (C).
Memb AIIC.

GRANDMAISON-ORSUCCI, FRANCE DE 40 blvd Ornano, F-75018 Paris, France *Tel* 0768742.
    TL French (A); German (B). **SL** Dutch (C), English (C).
Memb AIIC.

GREN, NIKOLAI DE 6 parc Château-Banquet, CH-1202 Geneva, Switzerland *Tel* (022) 31 65 73.
    TL English (A). **SL** French (C), German (C), Russian (C), Spanish (C).
Memb AIIC.

GRIFFITH, JENNIFER 44 rue Geiler, F-67000 Strasbourg, France *Tel* 61 65 49.
    TL English (A); French (B). **SL** German (C).
Memb AIIC.

GRIFFITHS, JILL 74 rue de Sèvres, F-75007 Paris, France *Tel* 567 68 62.
    TL & SL English (A); French (B).
Memb AIIC.

GROSS, JEAN-PIERRE 13 ave Boileau, B-1040 Brussels, Belgium *Tel* (0634) 4 9320.
    TL English (A), French (A). **SL** German (C).
Memb AIIC.

GROSSETÊTE-VILLEROUX, MARIE-THÉRESE "Les Jardinières" esc 2, 18 cours des Juilliotes, F-94700 Maisons-Alfort, France *Tel* (1) 376 78 42; (1) 520 0221.
    TL French (A); Spanish (B). **SL** English (C).
Memb AIIC.

*GUTIÉRREZ-SUÁREZ, EMMA E DE Cerro del Dios del Hacha 25, Coyoacán, Mexico 21, DF, Mexico *Tel* 905-554-1416.
    TL English (A), Spanish (A). **SL** French (C), Portuguese (C).
Memb TAALS.

GUZMAN-PABON, MARIA TERESA 3127-2 University Blvd W, Kensington, MD 20795 USA *Tel* 301-933-0870; 530-0084.
    TL Spanish. **SL** English.
    Memb ASI (dir for membership).

HAMAD, SALWÁ 157 rue du 26-Juillet, Cairo, Egypt *Tel* 801 703. 3 bis, rue Moillebeau, CH-1209 Geneva, Switzerland *Tel* 33 30 28.
    TL & SL Arabic (A), French (A); English (B).
Memb AIIC.

HANNARD, JIMMY De Kranssen 11, NL-Waalre, The Netherlands *Tel* (0) 4904-4666; (0) 40-756487.
    TL French (A). **SL** Dutch (C), English (C). **UDC** automotive, aviation, computers, electronics, radiology, sports, typewriters.
Memb AIIC.

HARE, CECILIA 15 rue Jussieu, F-75005 Paris, France *Tel* (01) 535 32 16; 326 54 52.
    TL Spanish (A); English (B). **SL** French (C).
Memb AIIC.

*HARWAY, MONIQUE 3518 Williamsburg Lane NW, Washington, DC 20008 USA *Tel* 202-362-9443.
    TL & SL French (A); English (B).
Memb TAALS.

HASS-HUERNI, BETTINA S c/o Th Huerny, Alexandraweg 9, CH-3006 Bern, Switzerland *Tel* (031) 44 30 30. 4277-B S 35 St #B1, Arlington, VA 22206 USA *Tel* 703-931-2876.
    TL German (A). **SL** English (C), French (C).
    Accred Univ of Geneva (1965, 1967, diploma).
Memb AIIC.

HASZARD, JOHN PO Box 1, Virgin Gorda, British Virgin Islands, West Indies *Tel* Tortola 55320.
    TL English (A). **SL** French (C), Spanish (C).
Memb AIIC.

HEIDELBERGER, BERNARD 52 A rue des Sept-Arpents, L-Luxembourg *Tel* 479894.
    TL French (A); German (B). **SL** Italian (C).
    Affil European Parliament. **Memb** AIIC.

HENCHOZ STAFANOVICH, ANNIE Kepler 143-901, Mexico 5, DF Mexico *Tel* 531 6138.
    TL & SL French (A); Spanish (B).
Memb AIIC.

HERSCHBERG, HADASSAH Rhijngeesterstraatweg 157 C, NL-2343 BV Oegstgeest, The Netherlands *Tel* (071) 154 614; (070) 24 44 55.
    TL Dutch (A); English (B), French (B). **SL** German (C), Hebrew (C), Yiddish (C).
Memb AIIC.

HERZENSTEIN, GUIDO Vicolo Moroni 39, I-00153 Rome, Italy *Tel* 589 1760.
    TL & SL French (A), Italian (A); English (B).
Memb AIIC.

HESPEL, DIDIER Schoonzichtlaan 110, B-3009 Winksele (Herent), Belgium *Tel* (016) 48 01 08.
    TL French (A); Dutch (B). **SL** English (C), German (C).
    Affil EEC. **Memb** AIIC.

HEYMANS, JOHN 11 av du Général de Gaulle, F-67000 Strasbourg, France *Tel* (88) 61 14 61.
    TL English (A), French (A). **SL** Dutch (C).
    Affil Council of Europe. **Memb** AIIC, TG.

HEYSCH, DANIELLE 30 rue Aubry-et-Rau, F-67000 Strasbourg, France *Tel* (88) 61 09 14.
TL French (A); English (B). SL German (C).
Affil Council of Europe. Memb AIIC.

*HOLMES, TAMARA 301 S Carolina Ave SE, Washington, DC 20003 USA *Tel* 202-544-1644.
TL English (A), Russian (A). SL Portuguese (C).
Memb TAALS.

HORAK, RENATE Laskegasse 35/4, A-1120 Vienna, Austria *Tel* 85 81 68.
Tl German (A); French (B). SL English (C), Italian (C).
Memb AIIC.

HORINE, RUTH 110 ch des Mollies, CH-1293 Belleuve/GE, Switzerland *Tel* (022) 74 11 53.
TL English (A); French (B), German (B). SL Spanish (C).
Memb AIIC.

HORN, MAURICE C One Fifth Ave, New York, NY 10003 USA *Tel* 212-982-2933.
TL & SL English, French.
Memb ASI.

HORN, PIERRE L 1006 Stonybrook Tr, Fairborn, OH 45324 USA *Tel* 513-879-1258.
TL & SL English, French.
Memb ASI.

HOROWITZ, DORON 425 Palmerston Blvd, Toronto, ON M6G 2N7, Canada *Tel* 416-534-7786.
TL English (A); French (B), Hebrew (B). SL German (C), Yiddish (C).
Memb AIIC, TAALS.

HORSPOOL, MARGOT 4 Milbrook, GB-Esher, Surrey, UK *Tel* (78) 62411.
TL English (A), Dutch (A); German (B). SL French (C).
Memb AIIC.

*HOWARD, ELENA 510 E 23 St #1G, New York, NY 10010 USA *Tel* 212-475-2763; 754-6487.
TL English (A), Spanish (A). SL French (C), Portuguese (C).
Affil UN. Memb TAALS.

HOWARD-NEUMARK, MONIQUE 51 Sderoth Chen, Tel Aviv, Israel *Tel* (03) 224 702. 24 ave Ledru-Rollin, F-75012 Paris, France *Tel* 343 81 69; 734 55 72.
TL & SL French (A); English (B).
Memb AIIC.

HUFFMAN, SANDA M 520 Chestnut St, Ithaca, NY 14850 USA *Tel* 607-272-6049.
TL English (B), French (B). SL Rumanian (C), Spanish (C).
Affil Cornell Univ. Memb TAALS.

HUNTER, CICELY 20 ave du Mail, CH-1205 Geneva, Switzerland *Tel* (022) 21 53 85; (022)

33 75 29. 1522 K St NW #400, Washington, DC USA *Tel* 202-347-7953.
TL English (A). SL French (C), German (C), Russian (C).
Accred Central London Polytechnic.

*HUTCHINSON, INGE 309 Towerview Rd, Dayton, OH 45429 USA *Tel* 513-434-3491.
TL German (A); English (B). SL French (C).
Memb TAALS.

IACOVELLA, YOLANDE 19 rte des Gardes, F-92190 Meudon, France *Tel* 634 52 49; 522 06 40.
TL French (A); Italian (B). SL English (C).
Memb AIIC.

IAROVICI, EDITH 8 Str Semilunei, 70229 Bucharest, Rumania *Tel* 12 88 56.
TL English (A). SL Rumanian (B).

ILLIN-BORCK, BORIS Ave José-Antonio 13, E-Madrid 14, Spain *Tel* 221 35 85.
TL Russian (A); Spanish (B). SL English (C), French (C).
Memb AIIC.

INFANTE, ALFREDO 2601 Woodley Pl NW, Washington, DC 20008 USA *Tel* 202-244-0754.
TL English, Spanish. SL Portuguese.
Memb ASI.

JAGGERS, BARRY 21 rue Parmentier F-77780 Bourron-Marlotte, France *Tel* (1) 326 5452.
TL & SL English (A); French (B).
Memb AIIC.

JAGGERS, CLAUDINE 21 rue Parmentier, F-77780 Bourron-Marlotte, France *Tel* (1) 326 5452.
TL & SL French (A); English (B).
Memb AIIC.

JONES, IAN PETER 7 rue Dante, Luxembourg-Ville, Luxembourg *Tel* 442 540.
TL English (A); French (B). SL Spanish (C).
Memb TAALS.

JUAN, MARCELA DE General Mola, E-85 Madrid 6, Spain.
TL Spanish (A); French (B). SL Chinese (C), English (C).
Memb AIIC.

JUMPELT, WALTER Nachtigallenweg 29, D-5307 Wachtberg-Pech, West Germany *Tel* Bonn (02221) 35 72 72.
TL German (A); English (B). SL French (C).
Memb AIIC.

KAHANE, EDUARDO 181 Princes Gardens, GB-London W3 OLT, UK *Tel* (01) 992 3218; 602 4155.
TL Spanish (A). SL English (C), French (C).
Affil Polytechnic of Central London. Memb AIIC.

KARARA-ROHN, SIGRUN 3 rue du Premier-Juin, CH-1207 Geneva, Switzerland *Tel* (022) 35 25 01.
TL German (A); French (B). SL English (C).
Memb AIIC.

KARWINSKY, NIKOLAUS Av Gal Rondon 30, 11400 Guarujà, SP, Brazil *Tel* 0055 132 86 3032.
TL French (A); English (B). SL German (C), Portuguese (C), Spanish (C).
Accred Brazilian Assn of Translators; São Paulo Assn of Conference Interpreters. Memb AIIC.

KATZ, JEAN-DANIEL 155 Rayvithi Rd, Bangkok 3, Thailand *Tel* 281 22 93 *Cable* c/o Language Services UNESCAP, Bangkok.
TL French (A); English (B). SL Spanish (C).
Memb AIIC.

KATZ, WILLI 3 bis, rue Léon-Jost, F-75017 Paris, France *Tel* 924 20 06.
TL French (A), German (A). SL English (C), Spanish (C).
Memb AIIC.

KEISER, WALTER 142 ave de Mai, B-1200 Brussels, Belgium *Tel* (02) 770 02 41.
TL French (A), German (A); English (B). SL Italian (C).
Memb AIIC.

KELIS, JAROSLAV U starého hrbitova 8, 110 00 Prague 1, Czechoslovakia *Tel* 629 82 *Telex* 122 824.
Memb AIIC.

KELLER, BORIS DE 21 bis, rue Leconte-de-Lisle, F-75016 Paris, France *Tel* 527 77 04. "La Cadeniere" D 11, Le Tignet, F-06530 Peymeinade, France *Tel* (93) 36 82 20.
TL French (A), Russian (A). SL English (C).
Memb AIIC.

KEMMERLING, MARC GEORGES 11 Quai Kléber, F-67000 Strasbourg, France *Tel* (88) 32 83 87.
TL French (A). SL Dutch (C), English (C), Italian (C).
Memb AIIC.

KENDREW, PHILIP 47 Mollestraat, F2, B-1700 Asse, Belgium *Tel* (02) 452 70 46.
TL English (A). SL French (C), German (C).
Affil Commission of European Communities. Memb AIIC.

KENGEN, KAJA 159 Drève des Gendarmes, B-1180 Uccle, Brussels, Belgium *Tel* 374 31 27.
TL French (A), German (A). SL Dutch (C), English (C).
Memb AIIC.

KHAN, EBRAIMA B BP 3243, Addis Ababa, Ethiopia.
TL & SL English (A), French (A).
Memb AIIC.

KHAN-GMUR, ANITA 23 ave de Budé, CH-1202 Geneva, Switzerland *Tel* (022) 34 20 33.
TL German (A); French (B). SL English (C), Russian (C), Spanish (C).
Memb AIIC.

KIEFFER, NADINE Centre Culturel Français, S/C Ambassade de France, 20, JL Thamrin, Djakarta, Indonesia *Tel* 82 284 *Cable* Ambafrance.
TL French (A). SL English (C), German (C).
Memb AIIC.

KIKEL, INGRID 15 rue Gracieuse, F-75005 Paris, France *Tel* 331 85 99; 326 81 04.
TL German (A); French (B). SL English (C).
Memb AIIC.

KIRILOFF, NIKITA 27 Best Way, Kanata, Ottawa, ON K2K 1C5, Canada *Tel* 613-592-4321; 997-2551.
TL Russian (A); French (B). SL English (C), German (C).
Affil Canadian Govt. Memb TAALS.

KLEBES, HEINRICH 9 rue de Londres, F-67000 Strasbourg, France *Tel* (88) 61 33 79; 61 49 61.
TL German (A); English (B). SL French (C).
Memb AIIC.

KLEBES, MARIE-LOUISE 9 rue de Londres, F-67000 Strasbourg, France *Tel* (88) 61 33 79.
TL German (A); French (B). SL English (C).
Memb AIIC.

KLOSE, REINHARD K Fack, S-220 03 Lund, Sweden *Tel* (046) 14 90 01 *Cable* POLYLENGUAS.
TL German (A). SL English (C), Spanish (C), Swedish (C).
Memb AIIC.

KOCH, RITA Schwarzenbergstr 8, A-1010 Vienna, Austria *Tel* 52 87 40.
TL German (A), Hebrew (A), Italian (A); English (B). SL French (C).
Memb AIIC.

KOCH-ELLES, ANNE-MARIE 63 ave Raymond-Poincaré, F-75116 Paris, France *Tel* 553 91 41.
TL & SL French (A); English (B), Spanish (B).
Memb AIIC.

KOLMER, HERBERT Mexikoplatz 25/12, A-1020 Vienna, Austria *Tel* 24 63 94.
TL & SL German (A); English (B).
Accred Univ of Vienna (1948). Memb AIIC.

KOMATSU, TATSUYA 7-16-Chome, Miharadai, Nerima-Ku, Tokyo 177, Japan *Tel* (03) 921-5595; 582-4224.
TL & SL Japanese (A); English (B).
Memb TAALS.

KONOPKA, JEAN & SUZANNE Case postale 5, CH-1292 Chambésy/Geneva, Switzerland *Tel* (022) 58 15 68.
TL & SL English, French, German.
Memb ASTI.

*KONUK, ERIKA R 6510 Fairlawn Dr, McLean, VA 22101 USA *Tel* 703-893-5614.
TL German (A); English (B). SL Spanish (C).
Memb TAALS.

KOSCHITZKY, BEATE von Hof Röndahl, D-2125 Salzhausen, West Germany *Tel* (04172) 600.
TL German (A). SL English (C), French (C), Italian (C).
Memb AIIC.

KOY, MARTIN Steinacker 9, D-53 Bonn 3, West Germany *Tel* (02221) 48 13 35.
TL & SL German (A); Russian (B).
Affil Federal Ministry of Economics. Memb AIIC.

KRAFFT, REMCO 304 E 81 St, New York, NY 10028 USA *Tel* 212-535-2694.
TL French (A); English (B). SL Dutch (C), Spanish (C).
Memb TAALS.

KRAKOWSKY, BARBARA 898 24 Ave, San Francisco, CA 94121 USA *Tel* 415-387-0784, 6192.
TL French (A), Spanish (A); English (B). SL Portuguese (C).
Memb TAALS.

KRAMER-MEYN, MARIE-HORTENSE Bundesratufer 4, D-1 Berlin 21, West Germany *Tel* (030) 39 11 473.
TL & SL French (A); German (B).
Memb AIIC.

KRAUSHAAR-FRANQUET, NELLY 4801 de Maisonneuve W, Westmount, Montreal, PQ H3Z 1M4, Canada *Tel* 514-935-5000.
TL French (A). SL English (C).
Memb AIIC.

KRIVOCHEINE, NIKITA c/o OMCI, Conference Service, Piccadilly 101-104, GB-London W1V OAE, UK *Tel* (01) 499 90 40.
TL French (A), Russian (A). SL English (C).
Accred Polytechnic of Central London. Affil Intergovernmental Maritime Navigation Organization. Memb AIIC.

KUNTE, ANURADHA Ctr of French Studies, Jawaharlal Nehru Univ, New Mehrauli Rd, New Delhi, India *Tel* 675102; 652282.
TL & SL English (A), French (A), Marathi (A).
Accred Univ of Sorbonne. Memb AIIC.

KURZ, INGRID Braungasse 10, A-1170 Vienna, Austria *Tel* 46 53 97.
TL & SL German (A); English (B).
Memb AIIC.

KUSTERER, HERMANN Birkenweg 4, D-5307 Wachtberg-Niederbachem, West Germany *Tel* Bonn (02221) 34 50 69.
TL & SL German (A); English (B), French (B).
Accred Johannes Gutenberg Univ (1949). Memb AIIC.

LA BONTE, JOHN CHRISTOFER Peter-Paul-Althausstr 9 b, D-Munich 40, West Germany *Tel* (089) 36 92 60.
TL & SL English (A), German (A).
Memb AIIC.

LABRADA, EMILIO B 8364 Glastonbury Ct, Annandale, VA 22003 USA *Tel* 703-256-1398.
TL English (A), Spanish (A). SL French (C), Portuguese (C).
Affil OAS. Memb TAALS.

LACHOW-BUDEEV, VALENTINE c/o Simon, 4601 N Park Ave #1417, Chevy Chase, MD 20015 USA *Tel* 301-986-1542. 3810 Liggett Dr, San Diego, CA 92106 USA.
TL English (A); Spanish (B). SL French (C).
Accred Georgetown Univ. Memb AIIC.

LADEN, SIGRID von der Beltweg 12, D-Munich 40, West Germany *Tel* 361 2992.
TL German (A); English (B). SL French (C).
Memb AIIC.

LAFFOREST, JEAN DE c/o Transla Ltd, 29 Villiers St, Strand, GB-London WC2N 6ND, UK *Tel* (01) 930 2971; 839 5821 *Cable* LAFFOREST LONDON WC2.
TL & SL French (A); English (B).
Memb AIIC.

*LAMON, FRANÇOISE 332 rue Lecourbe, F-75015 Paris, France *Tel* 250 53 06; 250 48 14.
TL & SL French (A); English (B), Spanish (B).
Memb AIIC, AITC, TAALS.

LANDA, MARIE-THÉRÈSE DE via Costantino Beltrami 10, I-00154 Rome, Italy *Tel* 577 26 77.
TL French (A), Spanish (A). SL English (C).
Affil Food and Agriculture Organization (FAO). Memb AIIC.

LANZ, ANDRÉ-NOËL 97 Townshend Ct, McKennal St, GB-London NW8 6LD, UK *Tel* (01) 722-6040.
TL French (A). SL English (C), Spanish (C).
Memb AIIC.

LARRAURI, AGUSTIN A "Taillevent," F-78580 Bazemont, France *Tel* 090 83 24.
TL French (A), Spanish (A). SL English (C), Italian (C).
Affil UNESCO (Paris). Memb AIIC.

*LATEINER DE BRY, JEANNINE 6040 Blvd E #12K, West New York, NJ 07093 USA *Tel* 201-869-5112.
TL French (A); English (B). SL Italian (C), Spanish (C).
Memb AIIC, TAALS.

LAURENT, MARIE-CLAUDE 32 av Ed Lacomblé, B-1040 Brussels, Belgium *Tel* (02) 771 25 35.
TL French (A). SL English (C), Italian (C). **Memb** AIIC.

LEDERER, MARIANNE 30 rue des Blagis, F-92340 Bourg la Reine, France *Tel* 702 91 53; 306 89 41.
TL French (A); English (B). SL German (C).
Affil Univ of Paris. **Memb** AIIC.

LEFCADITI, ANNA MARIA Odos Demokritou 34-36, GR-Athens 136, Greece *Tel* (0030-1) 36 00 518.
TL Greek (A); English (B), German (B). SL French (C).
Memb AIIC.

LEHMANN, ROLF Neckarhamm 45, D-69 Heidelberg, West Germany *Tel* (06221) 82 837; 24 073.
TL German (A); English (B). SL Dutch (C), Spanish (C).
Accred Heidelberg Univ. **Memb** AIIC.

LEISING, RODOLPHE 24B rue Lamartine, CH-1203 Geneva, Switzerland *Tel* (022) 44 19 00; 32 76 58.
TL French (A). SL English (C), German (C), Spanish (C).
Memb AIIC.

LENFERT, WOLF DIETER 23 ave Gustave Mesureur, F-78170 La Celle Saint Cloud, France *Tel* (1) 969 73 10; 326 81 04.
TL German (A); French (B). SL English (C).
Accred Univ of Paris. **Memb** AIIC.

LEVY, MARGOT Rodsundavägen 19, S-171 52 Solna, Sweden *Tel* (08) 83 48 63.
TL Swedish (A); English (B), German (B). SL Danish (C), Norwegian (C).
Memb AIIC.

* **LEWIS-BONACCORSI, ELVIRA** 942 Youngsford Rd, Gladwyne, PA 19035 USA *Tel* 215-649-0122.
TL & SL Italian (A); English (B), French (B).
Accred Univ of Geneva. **Memb** AIIC, TAALS.

LINDEMANN, HELMUTH ANDRE Schläflirain 3, CH-3013 Bern, Switzerland *Tel* (031) 42 83 31.
TL & SL English, French, German.
Memb ASTI.

LIPCOVICH, TAMARA 5290 Louis-Colin, Montreal, PQ H3T 1T3, Canada *Tel* 514-731-6269.
TL English (A), Spanish (A). SL French (C), German (C).
Memb AIIC.

LOMBRASSA-D'ORO, PAOLA Via Giuseppe Gorio 9, I-22100 Como, Italy *Tel* (031) 26 56 56.
TL Italian (A). SL English (C), French (C).
Affil EEC. **Memb** AIIC.

LONGLEY, PATRICIA E 4L Portman Mansions, Chiltern St, GB-London W1, UK *Tel* (01) 486 65 82 *Cable* DUOCON LONDON W1.
TL & SL English (A); French (B).
Accred Polytechnic of Central London. **Memb** AIIC.

LOTFY, R L 14A ave Ernest, Pictet, CH-1203 Geneva, Switzerland.
TL Arabic (A); English (B). SL French (C).
Affil UN (Arabic Translation Service). **Memb** AIIC.

LUCIANI, BERNARD 270 Somerset St W #201, Ottawa, ON K2P OJ7, Canada *Tel* 613-234-7210; 996-1001.
TL French (A); English (B). SL Spanish (C).
Affil Canadian Govt. **Memb** AIIC.

* **LUKIANOFF, BASIL** 15 Hillside St, Danbury, CT 06810 USA *Tel* 203-743-4884.
TL Russian (A); English (B). SL German (C), Italian (C).
Memb TAALS.

LUND, HELGA 19A, The Little Boltons, GB-London SW10 9LJ, UK *Tel* (01) 373 4919; (Brussels) 649 67 00.
TL English (A); German (B). SL French (C).
Memb TAALS.

McFARLANE, MALCOLM 119 rue de l'Université, F-75007 Paris, France *Tel* 556 19 87; 326 54 52.
TL English (A); French (B). SL Spanish (C), Portuguese (C).
Memb AIIC.

MACHEREZ, EDITH 252 E 33 St, New York, NY 10016 USA *Tel* 212-754-6487.
TL French (A); English (B), Spanish (B). SL Russian (C).
Affil UN. **Memb** TAALS.

* **McMILLAN, E NORMAN** The Savoy #1009, 1101 New Hampshire Ave NW, Washington, DC 20037 USA *Tel* 202-659-2390; 676-0276.
TL English (A). SL Dutch (C), French (C), German (C), Portuguese (C), Spanish (C).
Affil World Bank. **Memb** ATA, TAALS.

MAFFRE-MALLET, ELISABETH F-83145 Port-Cros, France *Tel* (94) 71 91 21; 65 20 73.
TL French (A); German (B). SL English (C).
Memb AIIC.

MAGEE, RICHARD A 2194 Golf Course Dr, Reston, VA 22091 USA *Tel* 703-620-3256; 202-554-6428.
TL English (A), French (A). SL Spanish (C).
Affil INTELSAT. **Memb** TAALS.

MAJOR, JENNIFER 28 quai Rouget-de-l'Isle, F-6700 Strasbourg, France *Tel* (88) 35 11 91; (1) 734 55 72.
TL English (A); French (B). SL Italian (C).
Memb AIIC.

MAKARIUS, RAOUL 146 rue de Chevaleret, F-75013 Paris, France *Tel* 585 24 05.
TL English (A); French (B). SL Arabic (C).
Memb AIIC.

MALOT, JACQUELINE 19 rue de Boulainvilliers, F-75016 Paris, France *Tel* 525 05 94; 326 81 04.
TL & SL French (A); English (B).
Memb AIIC.

* **MARCUSE, GISELA** 6611 16 St NW, Washington, DC 20012 USA *Tel* 202-726-3736; 632-8917.
TL German (A); English (B). SL Russian (C).
Memb TAALS.

MÄRKL-JAENISCH, BRIGITTE Lukastr 2, D-4047 Dormagen, West Germany *Tel* (02106) 37 86; 71686.
TL & SL German (A); English (B), French (B).
Memb AIIC.

MARLE, ILONA van c/o van Marle, 3 rue de Cronstadt, F-06000 Nice, France *Tel* (93) 82 07 75. Largo della Gancia 1, I-00195 Rome, Italy *Tel* 359 59 15.
TL English (A), Italian (A); French (B). SL German (C).
Memb AIIC.

MARLOW, VERONICA 102 Downs Rd, GB-Coulsdon, Surrey CR 3 1 AE, UK *Tel* Downland 53294.
TL & SL German (A); English (B).
Memb AIIC.

MARQUEZ, ANGELICA Edificio Paiclas Apto 1-B, Terrazas de Santa Ines 106, Caracas 106, Venezuela *Tel* 92 76 16.
TL English (A), Spanish (A). SL French (C), Portuguese (C).
Memb AIIC.

* **MARTIN, NATALY** 3509 McKinley St NW, Washington, DC 20015 USA *Tel* 202-244-3361; 376-4799.
TL English (A), Russian (A). SL Spanish (C).
Affil DOE. **Memb** TAALS.

MARTIN-PREVEL, RENÉ Av Victor Gilsoul 110, Bte 4, B-1200 Brussels, Belgium *Tel* 771 81 74.
TL French (A). SL German (C), Italian (C).
Affil Commission of European Communities. **Memb** AIIC.

MARTINEZ-SMITH, MARIA 23 square Montsouris, F-75014 Paris, France *Tel* 589 16 19.
TL Spanish (A); French (B). SL English (C).
Accred Univ of Paris. **Memb** AIIC.

MARTORANI, SUSANA United Nations, Rm 1740, New York, NY 10017 USA *Tel* 212-754-6492; 759-6770.
TL Spanish (A); English (B). SL French (C), Italian (C).
Affil UN. **Memb** AIIC.

MASSIEU, JORGE 4099 Isabella, Montreal, PQ H3T 1N5, Canada *Tel* 514-731-5285.
TL Spanish (A). SL French (C).
Memb TAALS.

MATSUO, KAZUYUKI 3-14-16 Hisagi, Zushi-shi, Kanagawa 249, Japan.
TL & SL Japanese (A); English (B).
Memb TAALS.

MATTERN, NANZA 51 blvd Gén Wahis, B-1040 Brussels, Belgium.
TL English (A); German (B). SL French (C).
Memb AIIC.

MAYER, BEATRICE H Patricio Sanz 748-5, Mexico, DF, Mexico *Tel* (905) 523-16-75.
TL & SL English (A), Spanish (A).
Memb TAALS.

MEISTER, ELISABETH CH-3145 Oberscherli, Berne, Switzerland *Tel* (031) 84 00 27.
TL French (A); English (B). SL German (C), Spanish (C).
Memb AIIC.

MELERO, FRANCISCA 28 rue Le Titien, B-1040 Brussels, Belgium *Tel* 734 7917; 513 8583. Calle Malaga 9, E-Madrid 3, Spain *Tel* 441 7948.
TL German (A); English (B). SL French (C), Italian (C), Spanish (C).
Accred Univ of Heidelberg (1944). Memb AIIC.

MENG-GUBLER, ANNELISE Oberwilstr 24, CH-8330 Pfäffikon, Zurich, Switzerland *Tel* (01) 950 24 39; 950 10 96.
TL German (A); French (B). SL English (C), Italian (C).
Memb AIIC.

MERAL, FRANÇOISE c/o Laurent, 32 rue Moillebeau, CH-1209 Geneva, Switzerland *Tel* 33 75 29.
TL French (A); English (B). SL Spanish (C).
Memb AIIC.

* MERTVAGOS, CONSTANTINE 8308 Britton Ave, Elmhurst, NY 11373 USA *Tel* 212-426-8142.
TL English (A), Russian (A). SL French (B), German (B); Italian (C).
Memb TAALS.

METHORST, HENRI W Van Boshuizenstraat 13, NL-1054 GA-Amsterdam, The Netherlands *Tel* 42 62 94; 83 22 92 *Cable* METHORSTINTER Amsterdam.
TL & SL Dutch (A), French (A); English (B), German (B).
Memb AIIC.

MEURICE, PIERRE 5290 Louis Colin, Montreal, PQ H3T 1T3, Canada *Tel* 514-731-6269.
TL & SL French (A); English (B).
Accred Translators Soc of Quebec. Memb AIIC.

MEYER, ANN 10 ave du Général-de-Gaulle, F-67000 Strasbourg, France *Tel* 61 69 09.
TL & SL English (A); French (B).
Memb AIIC.

MEYER, LINA 3801 Rodman St NW #D4, Washington, DC 20016 USA *Tel* 202-244-0754.
TL Portuguese. SL English, Spanish.
Memb ASI.

MICHAELI, BELLA 13 rue Shamai, Jerusalem 94631, Israel *Tel* (9722) 225 931 *Telex* 03 2470 COIN-IL.
TL English (A), Hebrew (A); Yiddish (B). SL French (C).
Memb AIIC.

MICHEL, M BROOKS 10561 NE 2 Pl, Miami Shores, FL 33138 USA *Tel* 305-758-1391.
TL English (A); Spanish (B). SL French (C), Portuguese (C).
Memb TAALS.

* MIGONE, RAÚL Azcuenaga 1038, Buenos Aires, Argentina *Tel* 83 79 60; 83 06 12. Callao 1442, Buenos Aires, Argentina *Tel* 44 05 32.
TL Spanish (A). SL Portuguese (C).
Memb TAALS.

MILEV, GABRIEL 2 rue A Tchekhov, 1113 Sofia, Bulgaria *Tel* 72 77 70.
TL Bulgarian (A), French (A). SL English (C), Russian (C).
Memb AIIC.

MINDER-MAGALOFF, WANDA 17 chemin François-Lehmann, CH-1218 Graɪ d-Saconnex, Geneva, Switzerland *Tel* (022) 98 34 83.
TL French (A); English (B). SL Russian (C).
Accred Univ of Geneva (1964). Memb AIIC.

MINNS, PHILIP 30 rue Croix-Bosset, F-92310 Sèvres, France *Tel* 534 34 63; 326 54 52.
TL English (A); French (B). SL German (C).
Memb AIIC.

MIZNE, SUZANA R Sgto Gilberto Marcondes Machado 270, 05683 Sao Paulo, Brazil *Tel* 61 51 55.
TL Portuguese (A); English (B), French (B). SL German (C), Spanish (C).
Memb AIIC.

MOGGIO, LILIANA Via Fratelli Bronzetti 28, I-20129 Milan, Italy *Tel* 72 37 31.
TL Italian (A); French (B). SL English (C), German (C).
Memb AIIC.

MONGWA, TENING c/o Service Linguistique, Présidence de la République, Yaounde, Cameroon *Tel* 22-37-28; 22-24-96.
TL & SL English (A), French (A), Pinyin (A).
Memb AIIC.

MONTALTE, DAVID DE 9 ave Hoche, F-75008 Paris, France *Tel* 485 20 72; 766 04 00; 227 62 62.
TL & SL English (A); French (B).
Memb AIIC.

MONTECINO, MARCELO 2151 Connecticut Ave NW #303, Washington, DC 20008 USA *Tel* 202-483-4682.
TL Spanish. SL English.
Memb ASI.

MONTERISI, DONATELLA 41 rue du Cherche-Midi, F-75006 Paris, France *Tel* 544 68 19; 326 81 04. Viale Parioli 93, I-00197 Rome, Italy *Tel* 87 52 20.
TL Italian (A). SL English (C), French (C), Spanish (C).
Memb AIIC.

* MORAYTA, ITALIA DE Cascada 206, Pedregal de San Angel, Mexico 20, DF, Mexico *Tel* 905-568-0003; 4732; 548-1119; 550-0170.
TL English (A), Spanish (A). SL French (C), Portuguese (C).
Memb TAALS.

MORIARTY-EDMONDS, FRANCES One Lindfield Gardens, Hampstead, London, NW3 6PX UK *Tel* (01) 435 0277; (0606) 74 306.
TL English (A). SL French (C), Italian (C).
Memb AIIC.

MOSTAFA, SHAWKI 65 Strathcona Dr, Town of Mount Royal, PQ H3R 1E5, Canada *Tel* 514-341-1469.
TL Arabic (A); English (B). SL French (C).
Affil International Civil Aviation Organization. Memb AIIC.

MULDER-BERRY, WIETTY 10 Taunton Pl, Ottawa, ON K1J 7J6, Canada *Tel* 613-746-8439.
TL Dutch (A); French (B). SL English (C), German (C).
Affil Canadian Govt Memb AIIC.

MÜLLER, ULRICH F Rösslstr 17, D-8026 Ebenhausen, Munich, West Germany *Tel* (081-78) 41 11.
TL & SL German (A); French (B).
Memb AIIC.

MULLER, URSULA 4 rue de Bragance, L-Luxembourg *Tel* 47 22 78.
TL Italian (A); German (B). SL French (C).
Memb AIIC.

MULLER DE ABADAL, CONCEPCIÓN Balmes 182 pral, E-Barcelona 6, Spain *Tel* 217 78 72.
TL Catalan (A), Spanish (A); French (B). SL English (C).
Memb AIIC.

MÜLLER-HOLDINGHAUSEN, GERTRUD Vorbeckweg 6, D-2 Hambourg 52, Gr Flottbek, West Germany *Tel* (040) 82 62 67.
TL German (A); English (B). SL French (C).
Memb AIIC.

MULLER-VIERIN, GODELIEVE Graaf willem de oude laan 56, NL-1412 AV Naarden (NH), The Netherlands *Tel* (02159) 45586.
TL Dutch (A). SL English (C), French (C), German (C).
Memb AIIC.

MURAMATSU, MASUMI 186-32 Nishi-Shiba, Kanazawa-ku, 236 Yokohama, Japan *Tel* (045) 783-1711; (03) 582-4224. *Cable* SIMULCONFER TOKYO.
TL & SL English (A), Japanese (A).
Memb TAALS.

NEAMAN, ODÈDA 94a route de Valavran, CH-1294 Genthod, Geneva, Switzerland *Tel* (022) 74 20 87 *Cable* ODEMAN Geneva.
TL & SL English (A), French (A).
Memb AIIC.

* NEDELCOVIC, BOSCO 6001 N 18 St, Arlington, VA 22205 USA *Tel* 703-536-7710; 202-693-8023.
TL Spanish (A); English (B), Italian (B), Serbo-Croatian (B). SL Portuguese (C).
Affil Inter American Defense Board. Memb TAALS.

NEGRONI COUCKE, MARIA ROLANDA 89 Begijnhoflaan, B-9000 Ghent, Belgium *Tel* (091) 23 86 45.
TL Italian (A). SL English (C), French (C).
Memb AIIC.

NERCESSIAN, MICHEL 21 rue Fontaine, F-75009 Paris, France *Tel* 974 71 75.
TL French (A); Russian (B). SL English (C).
Memb AIIC.

NEUENSCHWANDER-HESS, BÉATRICE Wendschatzstr 3, CH-3006 Bern, Switzerland *Tel* (31) 44 92 20.
TL German (A); French (B). SL English (C).
Memb AIIC.

NEUPREZ, JEAN 31 rue Dancet, CH-1205 Geneva, Switzerland. *Tel* 20 84 85.
TL French (A); English (B). SL Spanish (C).
Memb AIIC.

NOUARI, URSULA Parc de Villeroy, 40 rue des Bouvreuils, F-91540 Mennecy, France *Tel* 499 73 01; 306 89 41.
TL German (A); French (B). SL English (C).
Memb AIIC.

NOVERRAZ-DIEULANGARD, JACQUE-LINE 72 rue Amiral-Roussin, F-75015 Paris, France *Tel* (1) 533 42 65. 178 rue Maréchal-Oudinot, F-54000 Nancy, France *Tel* (83) 51 55 32.
TL French (A). SL English (C), Spanish (C).
Memb AIIC.

NUROCK, ELLA 22 ave du Bouchet, CH-1209 Geneva, Switzerland *Tel* (022) 33 30 89.
TL Russian (A); English (B). SL French (C), German (C), Hebrew (C).
Memb AIIC.

OFRI, NOEMI c/o Laurent, 32 rue Moillebeau, CH-1209 Geneva, Switzerland *Tel* (022) 33 75 29.
TL Spanish (A); English (B), Hebrew (B). SL French (C), Yiddish (C).
Memb AIIC.

OLIVER, JEAN "La Damaz" CH-1162 St-Prex, Switzerland *Tel* (021) 76 12 90; 76 10 54.
TL English (A); French (B), German (B). SL Spanish (C).
Memb AIIC.

ORGLMEISTER, E INGRID Caixa Postal 550, 06700 Cotia, São Paulo, Brazil *Tel* (011) 429-2522.
TL German (A), Portuguese (A); English (B). SL Italian (C), Spanish (C).
Memb TAALS.

OSTERHOLZ-LEBLOND, BARBARA 112 Irvine Ave, Montreal, PQ H3Z 2K2, Canada *Tel* 514-937-3164.
TL German (A). SL English (C), French (C), Italian (C).
Memb AIIC.

OSWALD, SIGRID Katangabinnenhof 1, B-1980 Tervuren, Belgium *Tel* (02) 767 42 31.
TL German (A). SL English (C), French (C), Italian (C).
Memb AIIC.

OUIMET, CARO LEMAN 7 ave Ainslie, Outremont, PQ H2V 2Y2, Canada *Tel* 514-272-9225.
TL & SL French (A); English (B).
Memb AIIC.

OVERMAN, GLADES PO Box 213, Gettysburg, PA 17325 USA *Tel* 717-334-7979. 5415 Connecticut Ave NW #235, Washington, DC 20008 USA *Tel* 202-966-2893.
TL English, Portuguese. SL Spanish.
Memb ASI.

PANDY, CALMAN DE Strandvägen 37, S-11456 Stockholm, Sweden *Tel* 62 64 16.
TL Hungarian (A), Swedish (A); English (B), German (B). SL Danish (C), French (C), Norwegian (C).
Memb AIIC.

PANETH, EVA 47 Netherhall Gardens, GB-London NW3, UK *Tel* (01) 435 2942.
TL German (A); English (B). SL French (C).
Memb AIIC.

PANSINI, FREDDY 18 rte de Diekirch, L-Lintgen, Luxembourg *Tel* 32 87 31.
TL Italian (A), Spanish (A). SL English (C), French (C).
Memb AIIC.

PARRA-IDREOS, VIVIANE calle Yucatan 3, Colonia Veracruz, Las Rozas, E-Madrid, Spain *Tel* 637-08-73.
TL English (A); French (B). SL Spanish (C).
Memb AIIC.

PATTON, SUSAN 12 rue de Soufflenheim, F-67000 Strasbourg-Robertsau, France *Tel* 31 31 91.
TL English (A); German (B). SL French (C).
Memb AIIC.

PEDRONI, SILVANO 22 rue Rambuteau, Cité Noel, F-75003 Paris, France *Tel* 278 25 50.
TL Italian (A). SL English (C), French (C), German (C).
Memb AIIC.

PEGNA, VERA via S Salvator 22, I-09058 Sestu (Cagliari), Italy *Tel* 070 23345; 23100 *Cable* PEGNA TF 23345 Sestu.
TL & SL French (A), Italian (A); English (B).
Memb AIIC.

PELICHET, HELGA Im Rebacher 3, CH-8122 Pfaffhausen, Zurich, Switzerland *Tel* (01) 825 37 53; (081) 39 25 30.
TL & SL German (A); French (B).
Memb AIIC.

PERKHOFER, ELFI via Flaminia Nouva 249, I-00191 Rome, Italy *Tel* (06) 327 19 36. via Secondo Orticello 10, I-04029 Sperlonga, (LT), Italy *Tel* (0771) 54238.
TL Italian (A); French (B). SL English (C), German (C), Spanish (C).
Memb AIIC

PETROFF, ALEXANDRE c/o N Guillenstein, 30 rue de Vermont, CH-1202 Geneva, Switzerland *Tel* (05022) 33 72 23; (022) 33 41 79.
TL Russian (A); English (B), French (B). SL German (C).
Memb AIIC.

PICARD, ALICE L 32 Broadway, New York, NY 10004 USA *Tel* 212-425-5540.
TL & SL French, English.
Memb ASI.

PIDGEON, DIANA MARY 12 rue Jean-Violette, CH-1205 Geneva, Switzerland *Tel* (022) 20 64 85.
TL English (A). SL French (C), Spanish (C).
Accred Polytechnic of Central London (1972). Memb AIIC.

PINHAS, RENÉ 117 blvd Exelmans, F-75016 Paris, France *Tel* 651 94 51; (93) 83 93 32.
TL French (A); English (B). SL Spanish (C).
Affil Catholic Univ of Paris. Memb AIIC.

PINKNEY, MARISA 35 Bird-in-Hand Lane, GB-Bickley, Kent, UK *Tel* (01) 464 95 64.
TL Spanish (A); English (B). SL French (C).
Memb AIIC.

PINSONNAUX MEJIAS, JACQUELINE 485 Victoria Ave, Montreal, PQ H3Y 2R3, Canada *Tel* 514-937-1200.
TL English, French. SL Spanish.
Memb ASI.

PONETTE, BERNARD 3106 Wessynton Way, Alexandria, VA 22309 USA *Tel* 703-360-3613.
TL French. SL English, Italian, Portuguese, Spanish.
Memb ASI.

PORRET, DANIELLE 9 rue Joseph-Pasquier, CH-1203 Geneva, Switzerland *Tel* (022) 44 96 76; (038) 25 42 92.
TL French (A). SL English (C), Spanish (C). Memb AIIC.

POSEWITZ, RÉKA 7 chemin Valérie, CH-1292 Chambésy, Switzerland *Tel* (022) 58 13 85.
TL Spanish (A); English (B), German (B). SL French (C). Memb AIIC.

PRATT-HIRIDJEE, NANCY PO Box 8, Carlsbad Springs, ON KOA 1KO, Canada *Tel* 613-822-0485.
TL English (A); French (B). SL Spanish (C). Accred ESIT (1972). Memb AIIC.

QUIGLEY, PATRICIA 174 blvd Pereire, F-75017 Paris, France *Tel* 380 68 05, 555 17 56.
TL English (A). SL French (C), Italian (C). Memb AIIC.

* RAMLER-VAISBERG, MONICA PO Box 75933, Caracas 107, Venezuela *Tel* 514591, 512417.
TL Spanish (A); English (B), French (B). SL German (C). Memb AIIC, TAALS.

RAMSAY, MICHAEL 2, ave des Prisonniers-Politiques, B-1150 Brussels, Belgium *Tel* 770 28 30.
TL & SL English (A); French (B). Memb AIIC.

RAS, MANUEL 163-07 21 Ave, Whitestone, Queens, New York, NY 11357 USA *Tel* 212-352-8493.
TL Spanish. SL English, French, Italian, Portuguese. Memb ASI.

RAS-ALLARD, MICHAEL 259 Noroton Ave, Darien, CT 06820 USA *Tel* 203-655-4585.
TL French. SL English, Portuguese, Spanish. Memb ASI.

RASO, GIANNI Pedro Berro 1087, Ap 504, Montevideo, Uruguay *Tel* 298188; 986145.
TL Italian (A); Spanish (B). SL French (C). Memb AIIC.

RAUTENBERG, WERNER Im Hermesgarten 20, D-5307 Wachtberg-Gimmersdorf, West Germany *Tel* (02221) 341312.
TL German (A); French (B), Italian (B). SL Dutch (C), English (C), Spanish (C). Memb AIIC.

REICHENBACH-DESQUAND, SOLANGE 255 blvd Saint-Denis, F-92400 Courbevoie, France *Tel* 788 67 79; 555 17 56.
TL French (A); English (B). SL Spanish (C). Memb AIIC.

REIGERSBERG, FERNANDO van 6957 Duncraig Ct, McLean, VA 22101 USA *Tel* 703-356-7294.
TL English (A), Spanish (A). SL French (C), Portuguese (C).
Affil INTELSAT (Language Services). Memb AIIC.

REINERT, DAVID 53 ave des Tritons, B-1170 Brussels, Belgium *Tel* 672 18 49.
TL German (A), Italian (A); English (B), French (B). SL Spanish (C). Memb AIIC.

REIS LEAL, MARIA AUGUSTA Quinta de Carreira, Lote 52, P-São João do Estoril, Portugal *Tel* 268 15 75.
TL English (A), Portuguese (A). SL French (C), Italian (C), Spanish (C). Memb AIIC.

REMEDIOS, SOFIA ave des Acacias 10, P-Monte Estoril, Portugal *Tel* (268) 04 65, 18 10.
TL English (A), Portuguese (A). SL French (C), Spanish (C). Memb AIIC.

REPELLIN, ANNICK Eisencherstr 13, D-1000 Berlin 30, West Germany *Tel* 211 53 50.
TL French (A); English (B). SL German (C). Memb AIIC.

RICHTER-WILDE, EVA 1805 rue du Bocage, Saint-Bruno, PQ J3V 4M7, Canada *Tel* 514-653-3469.
TL English (A). SL French (C), German (C). Memb AIIC.

RINGLER, SUZANNE 11a rue Copernic Bte 2, B-1180 Brussels, Belgium
TL French (A); English (B). SL Spanish (C). Memb TAALS.

* RIVAS, ISABEL DE Diagonal 73, 1-01 Int 3, Bogotá, DE 2, Colombia *Tel* 557550.
TL Spanish (A); English (B). SL French (C). Memb AIIC, TAALS.

ROCHA, ANNE 16 rue La Condamine, F-75017 Paris, France *Tel* 293 46 76; 326 54 52.
TL French (A); English (B), Portuguese (B). SL Spanish (C). Memb AIIC.

ROCHA, NANCY 3395 N Knoll Dr, Los Angeles, CA 90068 USA *Tel* 213-876-4666.
TL English (A), Spanish (A). SL French (C). Memb AIIC, TAALS.

* RODITI, EDOUARD H Tour Ravenne #3163, 130 blvd Masséna, F-75013 Paris, France *Tel* 583-0227.
TL English (A), French (A); German (B). SL Italian (C), Portuguese (C), Spanish (C). Memb TAALS.

RODRIGUEZ, EVELYN B DE Apt 68434 Altamira, Caracas, Venezuela *Tel* 979-8658 *Cable* ROGUEZ.
TL English (A), Spanish (A). SL French (C), Portuguese (C). Memb AIIC.

RODRIGUEZ, MARIA Nicolás San Juan 1328, Mexico 12, DF, Mexico *Tel* 575 02 63.
TL & SL English (A), Spanish (A). Memb AIIC.

RODRIGUEZ-DELGADO, RAFAEL Dr Gómez Ulla 4, E-Madrid 28, Spain *Tel* 256 51 55.
TL Spanish (A). SL English (C), French (C), Italian (C). Memb AIIC.

ROHATYN, JEANNETTE 1125 Park Ave, New York, NY 10028 USA *Tel* 212-722-6574.
TL English (A); French (B). SL Spanish (C). Memb AIIC.

ROHR, EVA von 48 rue Schaub, CH-1202 Geneva, Switzerland *Tel* (022) 33 36 69; (021) 61 21 73.
TL French (A); English (B). SL German (C). Memb AIIC.

ROMANINI-RODA, ISABELLA Vicolo del Cinque 47, I-00191 Rome, Italy *Tel* 589 49 51.
TL Italian (A); French (B). SL German (C), Portuguese (C). Memb AIIC.

ROOS, IRINA 120 chemin des Mollies, CH-1293 Bellevue-Geneva, Switzerland *Tel* (022) 74 18 83.
TL German (A), Russian (A). SL English (C), Finnish (C), French (C), Italian (C), Swedish (C). Memb AIIC.

ROSSHANDLER, LEO 89 Milton St, Montreal, PQ H2X 1V2, Canada.
TL English, German, Spanish. SL Dutch, French. Memb ASI.

ROSSI-VALSECCHI, FRANCA 438 ave Louise, B-1050 Brussels 5, Belgium *Tel* 649 73 69.
TL Italian (A); German (B). SL French (C). Memb AIIC.

ROTHERMANN, H F BROCH de 245 E 80 St, New York, NY 10021 USA *Tel* 212-734-7242.
TL & SL English, French, German. Memb ASI (pres).

RUBINI-HEILMANN, IRMHILD via Washington 29, I-20146 Milan, Italy *Tel* 46 95 214.
TL German (A). SL French (C), Italian (C). Memb AIIC.

RUCKHAUS, KARIN Apartado 61 811, Caracas, Venezula *Tel* 77 00 08 *Cable* PLASQUIM Caracas.
TL Spanish (A); English (B). SL French (C). Memb AIIC, TAALS.

RÜHL, MILITZA 55 ave Th Gautier, F-75016 Paris, France *Tel* 525 71 24; 326 54 52.
TL & SL French (A); English (B). Memb AIIC.

RUSSELL-AUGUSTIN, IDA 32 rue de la Clef, F-75005 Paris, France *Tel* 331 96 10; 326 81 04.
  TL German (A); French (B). **SL** English (C).
  Memb AIIC.

RUTGERS-SOLLBERGER, VERENA 5106 Westport Rd, Chevy Chase, MD 20015 USA *Tel* 301-656-9524.
  TL English, French, German. **SL** Dutch, Spanish.
  Memb ASI.

RUTHERFORD, ALAIN 194A ave Tervueren, Btes 1 & 2, B-1150 Brussels, Belgium *Tel* (02) 771 74 82; 767 44 31.
  TL & SL English, French.
  Affil EUROCONTROL. **Memb** AIIC.

* SAGASTI-HOCHHAUSLER, ELSA 2030 N Adams St #1207, Arlington, VA 22201 USA *Tel* 703-527-2449.
  TL Spanish (A); English (B). **SL** German (C), Portuguese (C).
  Affil Inter American Defense Board. **Memb** AIIC, TAALS.

SAITO, YOSHIHIRO 1280 21 St NW, Washington, DC 20036 USA *Tel* 202-659-8849.
  TL & SL Japanese (A); English (B).
  Memb TAALS.

SALZMANN, VITAL HAYIM 18 Remetta (Veyrier), CH-1227 Carouge/Geneva, Switzerland *Tel* (022) 42 82 97.
  TL French (A). **SL** English (C), Russian (C).
  Memb AIIC.

* SAXON-FORTI, ANNA 395 Riverside Dr #11B, New York, NY 10025 USA *Tel* 212-865-0183.
  TL Italian (A). **SL** French (C).
  Memb TAALS.

SCHAEFER-BAZELLI, GINETTE 80 Dorfstr, CH-8037 Zurich, Switzerland. *Tel* (01) 42 34 00.
  TL French (A), German (A); English (B), Italian (B). **SL** Spanish (C).
  Memb AIIC.

SCHAI, DENISE ANNE Im Rebberg 43, CH-8104 Weiningen/Zurich, Switzerland *Tel* (041) 94 29 48.
  TL French (A); German (B). **SL** English (C).
  Memb AIIC.

SCHALIT, RITA 1 rue du Pont-Levis Bte 6, B-1200 Brussels, Belgium *Tel* (02) 762 07 50.
  TL English (A). **SL** Danish (C), French (C), Italian (C).
  Accred Holborn College of Law (Languages, & Commerce). **Memb** AIIC.

SCHARFENBERGER, ANNETTE 61 ave de Champel, CH-1206 Geneva, Switzerland *Tel* (022) 47 35 81.
  TL German (A); English (B). **SL** French (C).
  Memb AIIC.

SCHERMAN, LEO 14 Morpeth Mansions, Morpeth Terrace, GB-London SW1, UK *Tel* (01) 834 5971; 602 4155 *Cable* CONFINTERPRET-London W8.
  TL & SL French (A); English (B).
  Memb AIIC.

SCHIMMEL-BIGGS, ELISABETH Wormserstr 119, "Stubenwald" D-614 Bensheim/Bergstr, West Germany *Tel* (06251) 6713; (06252) 71542.
  TL German (A); French (B). **SL** English (C).
  Memb AIIC.

SCHIRMER, UTE Lietzernsee-Ufer 5, D-1000 Berlin 19, West Germany *Tel* (030) 321 40 09.
  TL German (A). **SL** English (C), Spanish (C).
  Memb AIIC.

SCHLUCKBIER, NEDRA Casilla 4892, Miraflores, Lima 18, Peru *Tel* 47 57 39.
  TL & SL English (A); Spanish (B).
  Memb AIIC.

SCHMITT-ARNO, FRANCA Rte Gouvernementale, B-1150 Brussels, Belgium *Tel* 731 58 09.
  TL Italian (A); French (B). **SL** English (C), German (C).
  Memb AIIC.

SCHÜTZ, IRMENTRAUD Waldstr 72, D-6 Frankfurt 71, West Germany *Tel* (0611) 67 36 10.
  TL German (A); Italian (B). **SL** English (C).
  Memb AIIC.

SCHWABECHER, BRIGITTE DIANA Mühlebachstr 26, CH-8800 Thalwil, Switzerland *Tel* (01) 720 48 62.
  TL & SL English, French, German, Italian.
  Memb ASTI.

SCHWAMBERGER, KURT 9 rue Darius-Milhaud, F-78370 Plaisir, France *Tel* (1) 050 24 60.
  TL German (A); French (B). **SL** English (C).
  Memb AIIC.

SCHWARZ, EDITH Nassau Dillenburgstraat 37, 2596 AC The Hague, The Netherlands *Tel* (070) 24 66 60.
  TL Dutch (A); French (B), German (B). **SL** English (C).
  Memb AIIC.

SELESKOVITCH, DANICA 2 rue Georges Lafenestre, F-92340 Bourg-la-Reine, France *Tel* 660 23 06.
  TL French (A); English (B), German (B). **SL** Serbo-Croatian (C).
  Affil Univ of Sorbonne. **Memb** AIIC.

* SELO-FRALIN, MARYLOU 15 W 72 St #21N, New York, NY 10023 USA *Tel* 212-877-0232; 686-7600.
  TL Dutch (A); English (B), German (B). **SL** French (C), Spanish (C).
  Accred Univ of Geneva, Georgetown Univ.
  Memb ASI, TAALS.

SERRANO, GUSTAVO 4 ave Peschier, CH-1206 Geneva, Switzerland *Tel* (022) 47 16 78, 33 75 29.
  TL Spanish (A). **SL** English (C), French (C), Italian (C).
  Memb AIIC.

SETHI, RANJIT B-337, New Friends Colony, New Delhi, India *Tel* 63 44 33.
  TL & SL Chinese (A), English (A), French (A).
  Affil Indian Foreign Service. **Memb** AIIC.

SEYDEL-REHERS, VERONIKA Klausinweg 4, D-8000 Munich 40, West Germany *Tel* (089) 309504.
  TL German (A); English (B). **SL** Spanish (C).
  Memb AIIC.

SHIMONI, MIRIAM Ramat Hayahal, PO Box 13051, Tel Aviv, Israel *Tel* (03) 47 93 34.
  TL English (A). **SL** Hebrew (C).
  Memb AIIC.

SHIOMI, KAZUKO.19 E 82 St, New York, NY 10028 USA *Tel* 212-483-9796.
  TL & SL English (A), Japanese (A).
  Memb AIIC.

SHIRAI, CLAUDE RYO 2001 N Adams St #709, Arlington, VA 22201 USA *Tel* 703-525-0347; 202-293-6958.
  TL & SL English, Japanese.
  Memb ASI.

SIEBER, IDY Ackerstein 180, CH-8049 Zurich, Switzerland *Tel* (01) 56 26 49.
  TL English. **SL** German.
  Memb ASTI.

SIEGENTHALER, FREDERIC United Nations, Interpretation Service, Box 20, GCPO, New York, NY 10017 USA *Tel* 212-754-6487.
  TL French (A); English (B). **SL** German (C), Russian (C), Spanish (C).
  Affil UN. **Memb** AIIC.

* SIERRA, ANTHONY D 7011 Flint Hill Rd, Owings, MD 20836 USA *Tel* 301-855-7654; 202-632-3476.
  TL English (A), Spanish (A). **SL** French (C).
  Affil US Dept of State. **Memb** TAALS.

SIEVEKING, ANTONIA 17 rue Cavour, CH-1203 Geneva, Switzerland *Tel* (022) 45 10 87.
  TL English (A); French (B). **SL** Spanish (C).
  Memb AIIC.

SIMHA, ERIC R Villa Mikael, 17 chemin Pierre-à-Bochet, CH-1226 Thônex/GE, Switzerland *Tel* (022) 48 67 32 *Cable* SIMINTER.
  TL English (A); French (B). **SL** German (C), Greek (C), Spanish (C).
  Accred Univ of Geneva. **Affil** World Health Organization. **Memb** AIIC.

SIMMONS, PETER 52 rue Moillebeau, CH-1209 Geneva, Switzerland *Tel* (022) 33 94 52.
  TL English (A). **SL** French (C), German (C), Italian (C), Spanish (C).
  Memb AIIC.

SIMON, BARBARA 4601 N Park Ave #1417, Chevy Chase, MD 20015 USA *Tel* 301-986-1542.
TL Spanish (A); English (B). SL French (C), Portuguese (C).
Memb ASI, TAALS.

SIMOND, YVETTE 14 rue de la Poterie, CH-1202 Geneva, Switzerland *Tel* (022) 44 98 78.
TL French (A). SL English (C), Spanish (C).
Affil UN. **Memb** AIIC.

SKUNCKE, MARIE-FRANCE 31 chemin des Palettes, CH-1212 Grand-Lancy, Switzerland *Tel* (022) 94 75 73; 21 13 13.
TL & SL French (A), Polish (A); English (B).
Memb AIIC.

SLIVKO-SMESMAN, DENISE 39 rue Colonel-Chaltin, B-1180 Brussels, Belgium *Tel* (02) 374 37 72.
TL Dutch (A), French (A); English (B). SL German (C).
Memb AIIC.

SOLE-LERIS, AMADEO La Vigna, via di Marino Campagna 73, I-00040 Rocca di Papa, Rome, Italy *Tel* (06) 57 97; 91 70.
TL Catalan (A), English (A), Spanish (A). SL French (C), German (C), Italian (C).
Affil Food & Agriculture Organization (FAO). **Memb** AIIC.

SPITZ, RUDOLPH 83 Berrylands, GB-Surbiton, Surrey, UK *Tel* (01) 399 3017.
TL & SL German (A); English (B).
Memb AIIC.

STEUDEMANN, IRMELA Vaudagne 37, CH-1217 Meyrin, Switzerland *Tel* (022) 41 02 44.
TL & SL English, French, German.
Memb ASTI.

STEURS, SIMONE 11 rue des Floralies, B-1200 Brussels, Belgium *Tel* 762 18 91; 345 76 65.
TL & SL French (A); English (B), Spanish (B).
Memb AIIC.

STEVENS, EDWIN SPENCER Myrtenweg 27, CH-3018 Bern, Switzerland *Tel* (031) 55 19 32.
TL English. SL German.
Memb ASTI.

STJERNVALL, NICOLAS DE 1 chemin des Clochettes, CH-1206 Geneva, Switzerland *Tel* (022) 46 61 49.
TL French (A), Russian (A). SL English (C), Finnish (C), Swedish (C).
Memb AIIC.

SWETYE, IDETTE One Holmes Ct, Darien, CT 06820 USA *Tel* 203-357-7609. TL English (A), Spanish (B). SL French (C)
Accred Georgetown Univ (1970). **Memb** AIIC, TAALS.

SYRPIS, VASSILIKI 150 Copse Hill, GB-Winbledon, London SW20, UK *Tel* (01) 947 2739.
TL French (A). SL English (C), Greek (C), Spanish (C).
Memb AIIC.

TAYLOR, NANCY 64 Effingham Rd, GB-Long Ditton, Surrey, KT6 5LB, UK *Tel* (01) 398 2393.
TL & SL English (A); French (B).
Affil Western European Union. **Memb** AIIC.

TELL, BEATRIZ GONZÁLEZ-COSIO DE 816 Daley Ct, Mississauga, ON L5J 1E6, Canada *Tel* 416-822-7045.
TL Spanish (A); English (B). SL French (C).
Memb TAALS.

TEMPÉ, JANINE 2 ave Léopold-II, F-75016 Paris, France *Tel* 527 26 38.
TL & SL French (A); German (B). SL English (C).
Memb AIIC.

TEMPINI, JEAN via Sapeto 1, I-20123 Milan, Italy *Tel* (02) 837 36 63.
TL & SL English (A), Italian (A); French (B), Spanish (B).
Memb AIIC.

TEMPLETON, JOYCE via Pergolesi 6, I-20124 Milan, Italy *Tel* 2 716 147.
TL English (A); Italian (B). SL French (C).
Memb AIIC.

TERRA, DIANE DE 26 Leonard Ct, Edwarde Sq, London W8, UK *Tel* 602-4155 *Cable* CONFINTERPRET London W8. Box 1990, East-West Center, 1777 East-West Rd, Honolulu, Hawaii 96848 USA *Tel* 808-948-8395 *Cable* EASWESCEN.
TL English (A); French (B). SL Spanish (C).
Memb AIIC.

THELLUNG-FONTANA, ANNA 26 Piazza della Torretta, I-00186 Rome, Italy *Tel* (00396) 679 82 26; 678 35 48.
TL Italian (A); French (B). SL English (C).
Memb AIIC.

THIER, ADRINA 8 ave Baden-Powell, Bte 13, B-1200 Brussels, Belgium *Tel* 762 19 32.
TL Dutch (A). SL English (C), French (C).
Memb AIIC.

THIERY, CHRISTOPHER rue de Chaumont, Chambors, F-60240 Chaumont-en-Vexin, France *Tel* (33-1) 326 54 52.
TL & SL English (A), French (A).
Memb AIIC.

THIESS, HELMUT E 1834 Lamont St NW, Washington, DC 20010 USA *Tel* 202-265-9439.
TL & SL English, German.
Memb ASI (dir for special projects).

THYGESEN, JORGEN C 53 rue de Steinsel, L-Hünsdorf, Luxembourg *Tel* 333 06.

TL Danish (A); English (B). SL French (C), German (C), Norwegian (C), Swedish (C).
Memb AIIC.

TIGGES, IRMELIN via della Fonte di Fauno 5, I-00153 Rome, Italy *Tel* 577 20 77.
TL German (A); Italian (B). SL French (C).
Memb AIIC.

TOLEDANO-SABBATUCCI, ELSA 74 ave Franklin Roosevelt, B-1050 Brussels, Belgium *Tel* 649 11 93.
TL French (A), Italian (A). SL English (C), Spanish (C).
Memb AIIC.

TOLNAY, CLAIRE 12 chemin de Malombré, CH-1206 Geneva, Switzerland *Tel* (022) 46 65 75.
TL English (A); French (B), Spanish (B). SL German (C).
Memb AIIC.

TOLSTOY, PAUL Col Interprétation, UNESCO, 9 place Fontenoy, F-75700 Paris, France *Tel* 577 16 10.
TL English (A), Russian (A). SL French (B).
Affil UNESCO. **Memb** AIIC.

TORRENTS DELS PRATS, ALFONSO 39 rue de St-Jean, CH-1203 Geneva, Switzerland *Tel* 44 60 63.
TL Spanish (A); English (B). SL French (C), Russian (C).
Affil UN. **Memb** AIIC.

TOVAR, ALMA ROSA Cleveland 14-302, Colonia Napoles, Mexico 18, DF, Mexico *Tel* 915-563-8911.
TL Spanish (A); English (B). SL French (C).
Memb AIIC.

TRANIER, PIERRE 333 E 30 St #18K, New York, NY 10016 USA *Tel* 212-889-3148.
TL French (A). SL English (C), Spanish (C).
Affil UN. **Memb** AIIC.

TREIDELL, FRÉDÉRIC C 61 quai d'Orsay, F-75007 Paris, France *Tel* 551 59 83; 566 56 50.
TL English (A), French (A). SL German (C), Italian (C).
Memb AIIC.

TREVISAN-CSERGO, CLARA 1 A Falkland Rd, GB-London NW5, UK *Tel* (01) 267 8259.
TL Italian (A); English (B). SL French (C), German (C), Spanish (C).
Memb AIIC.

TULIAN, MARIE C El Retiro, Edif Jardin del Avila Apto 14, Alta-Florida, Caracas 105, Venezuela *Tel* 746226.
TL & SL French (A), Spanish (A).
Memb AIIC.

* TUNIK, GALINA 2033 F St NW, Washington, DC 20006 USA *Tel* 202-638-2970; 632-7752.
TL English (A), Russian (A). SL German (C).
Affil US Dept of State. **Memb** TAALS.

UDOVICKI, DANILO FRANÇOIS YVO 469 Fourth St #2L, Brooklyn, NY 11215 USA *Tel* 212-499-2232.
TL French (A), Serbo-Croatian (A); Spanish (B). **SL** English (C), Italian (C), Portuguese (C).
Memb AIIC.

UMANSKY, ELYANE Parc Eiffel, F-93210 Sèvres, France *Tel* 027 09 87.
TL & SL French (A); English (B).
Memb AIIC.

UMANSKY, JOSEPH Parc Eiffel, F-92310 Sèvres, France *Tel* 027 09 87.
TL French (A); English (B), German (B). **SL** Russian (C).
Accred/Memb AIIC. **Affil** Organization for Economic Cooperation and Development.

* URQUIAGA, HÉCTOR C Edificio Diez Canesco 434, Depto 302, Miraflores, Lima 18, Peru *Tel* 46 9590. Casilla 5002, Miraflores, Lima 18, Peru.
TL English (A), Spanish (A). **SL** Portuguese (C).
Memb TAALS.

* VALDIVIA-MENDOZA, LIDIA 1 rte de Sauverny #63, CH-1290 Versoix, Geneva, Switzerland *Tel* (022) 55 33 59.
TL Spanish (A); English (B). **SL** French (C).
Memb AIIC, TAALS.

VALERO-BOVET, MAITE 7 rue des Eaux-Vives, CH-1207 Geneva, Switzerland *Tel* (022) 35 49 52.
TL Spanish (A); English (B). **SL** Catalan (C), French (C).
Memb AIIC.

VALK, WILLIAM 44 rue Geiler, F-67000 Strasbourg, France *Tel* 61 65 49.
TL English (A); French (B). **SL** German (C).
Memb AIIC.

* VALYIOVA, LISA 225 E 57 St #3R, New York, NY 10022 USA *Tel* 212-751-4668.
TL English (A); Czech (B), German (B). **SL** French (C).
Memb AIIC, TAALS (pres).

* VAN REIGERSBERG, STEPHANIE R 6957 Duncraig Ct, McLean, VA 22101 USA *Tel* 703-356-7294; 202-632-8916.
TL English (A); French (B), Spanish (B). **SL** Italian (C), Portuguese (C).
Affil US Dept of State. **Memb** TAALS.

VAUCHER, VIVIANE 20 chemin Petite-Boissière, CH-1208 Geneva, Switzerland *Tel* (022) 35 03 94.
TL French (A), German (A). **SL** Italian (C).
Memb AIIC.

VERBER, MARIA Geyschlägergasse 11/51, A-1150 Vienna 15, Austria *Tel* (0222) 95 41 77.
TL & SL German (A); English (B).
Accred Universitas. **Memb** AIIC.

VICARI, VERA 45 chemin de l'Etang, CH-1210 Châtelaine, Switzerland *Tel* (022) 96 10 40.
TL Italian (A); French (B). **SL** English (C), German (C).
Memb AIIC.

VILLOUTREYS, LILY DE 42 rue de Vermont, CH-1202 Geneva, Switzerland *Tel* (022) 33 46 91.
TL English (A); Russian (B). **SL** French (C).
Memb AIIC.

* VITALI, MARIA INÉS MOREDO DE Av Espana 2880 #301, Montevideo, Uruguay *Tel* 79-8024 *Cable* FRAVIT MONTEVIDEO. Correspondence: Casilla de Correo 1198, Montevideo, Uruguay.
TL English (A), Spanish (A). **SL** French (C), Italian (C), Portuguese (C).
Memb TAALS.

VOSTEEN, THOMAS R 42 Forest View Ct, Iowa City, IA 52240 USA.
TL English. **SL** French.
Memb ASI.

VRIENDT, JOAN DE 45 chemin de l'Etang, CH-1210 Châtelaine, Switzerland *Tel* (022) 96 10 40.
TL Dutch (A); English (B), French (B). **SL** Indonesian (C).
Memb AIIC.

WAL, LEONORA DE La Vigna, via di Marino Campagna 73, I-00040 Rocca di Papa, Rome, Italy *Tel* (06) 949 91 70.
TL Dutch (A), English (A). **SL** French (C), German (C), Italian (C).
Accred Univ of Sorbonne. **Memb** AIIC.

WARD, PATRICIA 73 rue de Vaugirard, F-75006 Paris, France *Tel* (1) 544 55 10, 734 55 72.
TL English (A); French (B). **SL** Italian (C).
Memb AIIC.

WATSON, HILDE 5 Elm Park Gardens #17, London SW10 9QQ, UK *Tel* (01) 352 3630.
TL English (A), German (A). **SL** French (C).
Memb AIIC.

WEALE, EDNA 24 Clavelawn Ave, GB-London SW14 8B6, UK *Tel* 876 5429.
TL & SL English (A); French (B), Spanish (B).
Memb AIIC.

WEBER, WILHELM-KARL Monterey Inst of Foreign Studies, 425 Van Buren St, Monterey, CA 93940 USA *Tel* 408-649-3113.
TL German (A); French (B). **SL** Dutch (C), English (C).
Affil Dept of Translation and Interpretation (director). **Memb** AIIC.

WEHIK, EDA Hubertusbader-Str 16, D-1 Berlin 33, West Germany *Tel* (030) 825 84 34; (0821) 823 20.

TL German (A); English (B). **SL** French (C).
Memb AIIC.

* WEIDE, URSULA 601 Four Mile Rd #327, Alexandria, VA 22305 USA *Tel* 703-683-4122. c/o N Velluet, 9 rue de Nesle, Paris 6, France *Tel* 326 8104.
TL German (A); English (B). **SL** French (C).
Memb AIIC, TAALS.

WEIGEL, INGE c/o Laurent, 32 rue Moillebeau, CH-1209 Geneva, Switzerland *Tel* 33 75 29.
TL Portuguese (A); English (B), German (B). **SL** French (C), Italian (C), Spanish (C).
Memb AIIC, São Paulo Assn of Conference Interpreters.

WEITZEL-MUDERSBACH, MICHAEL von Beedenkirchener Str 36, D-6147 Lautertal-Reichenbach, West Germany *Tel* (06254) 7667.
TL German (A); English (B). **SL** French (C).
Memb AIIC.

WESENFELDER, RALF 16 rue Louis-Dardenne, F-92170 Vanves, France *Tel* (1) 736 21 18.
TL German (A), Spanish (A); French (B). **SL** English.
Memb AIIC.

* WESTMAN, DONALD R 6406 Franklin Ave #21, Hollywood, CA 90028 USA.
TL English (A). **SL** French (C), Spanish (C).
Memb TAALS.

WILSON, BARBARA 9 Kirklee Terrace, GB-Glasgow G12 OTH, UK *Tel* (041) 357 1264.
TL English (A); French (B). **SL** German (C).
Memb AIIC.

WINKLER, EDDA Neufeldstr 139, CH-3012 Bern, Switzerland *Tel* (031) 23 05 15.
TL & SL English, German.
Memb ASTI.

WINNINGTON, G PETER Les 3-Chausseurs, CH-1411 Orzens (VD) Switzerland *Tel* (021) 81 61 21.
TL & SL English, French.
Memb ASTI.

WOLF, NELLY Litorales 67, Las Aguilas, Mexico 20, DF, Mexico *Tel* 593 4226.
TL Spanish (A). **SL** English (C), French (C), German (C).
Memb AIIC.

WORONOFF, JON c/o Lingua Language Services Ltd, 152 W 42 St #1421, New York, NY 10036 USA *Tel* 212-391-0199; 688-4337 *Cable* LINGUISTIC.
TL English (A); French (B). **SL** German (C), Spanish (C).
Memb AIIC.

WORSDALE, WILLIAM 29 quai Rouget-de-l'Isle, F-67000 Strasbourg, France *Tel* (88) 35 38 55.
TL & SL English (A); French (B).
Affil Council of Europe. **Memb** AIIC.

WORSDALE-WASSMUTH, GISELA 29 quai Rouget-de-l'Isle, F-67000 Strasbourg, France *Tel* (88) 35 38 55.
TL German (A); English (B). **SL** French (C).
Memb AIIC.

* **WUST, KLAUS** 350 Bleecker St #4-S, New York, NY 10014 USA *Tel* 212-675-7215; 703-459-4598.
TL German (A); English (B). **SL** French (C).
Memb AIIC, TAALS.

YABLONSKY, ANDREW 4 rue St-Saëns, F-75015 Paris, France *Tel* 579 20 59. 1847 19

Ave, San Francisco, CA 94122 USA *Tel* 415-661-3847.
TL English (A), Russian (A). **SL** French (C), German (C).
Memb AIIC.

ZACZEK, MARION Lercheng 23/1/12, A-1080 Vienna, Austria *Tel* (222) 43 93 75, 634 04 64.
TL & SL German (A); French (B).
Memb AIIC.

ZEVALLOS, ANITA Z 130 East End Ave, New York, NY 10028 USA *Tel* 212-535-8760.
TL Spanish. **SL** English, French.
Memb ASI.

ZILBERBERG, LOUIS-JACQUES 31 Platts Lane, GB-London NW3 7NN, UK *Tel* (01) 794 94 15; 935 40 61.

TL French (A); English (B). **SL** Russian (C), Spanish (C).
Memb AIIC.

ZINK, HELGA Sollingergasse 8/4, A-Vienna, Austria *Tel* 36 55 144.
TL German (A); Spanish (B). **SL** English (C), French (C).
Memb AIIC.

ZUBER DE TOMAS, URSULA Queralt 4, E-Barcelona 17, Spain *Tel* 93 248 20 96.
TL German (A); French (B). **SL** English (C), Spanish (C).
Accred ESIT. **Memb** AIIC.

ZUCKERMAN, LEDA 78 rue Beaubourg, F-75003 Paris, France *Tel* 887 68 88, 326 54 52.
TL English (A); French (B). **SL** Spanish (C).
Affil ESIT. **Memb** AIIC.

Conference Interpreters —Classified by Language

Target language (language *into which* a translation is made) appears in boldface caps; source language (language *from which* a translation is made) appears in upper and lowercase boldface. Conference interpreters are entered in alphabetical order under their specific target/source languages followed by the standard two-letter state abbreviation or abbreviated country name to identify regional accessibility. Pleast note that, in this classification, interpreters have been classified in the following manner: (1) target language for members of ASI and ASTI; (2) target language (A) only for members of AIIC and TAALS. An asterisk preceding a name identifies an interpreter as a conference translator also.

Into ARABIC from:

English

Abou-Zahr, O (Switz)
Douek, R I (Fr)
Hamad, S (Egypt)
Lotfi, R L (Switz)
Mostafa, S (Can)

French

Abou-Zahr, O (Switz)
Douek, R I (Fr)
Hamad, S (Egypt)
Lotfi, R L (Switz)
Mostafa, S (Can)

Into BULGARIAN from:

English

Milev, G (Bul)

Russian

Milev, G (Bul)

Into CATALAN from:

English

Muller de Abadal, C (Sp)
Sole-Leris, A (It)

French

Muller de Abadal, C (Sp)
Sole-Leris, A (It)

German

Sole-Leris, A (It)

Italian

Sole-Leris, A (It)

Spanish

Muller de Abadal, C (Sp)
Sole-Leris, A (It)

Into CHINESE from:

English

Sethi, R (China)

French

Sethi, R (China)

Into CZECH from:

English

Baburkova, D (Czech)

French

Kelis, J (Czech)

German

Baburkova, D (Czech)
Kelis, J (Czech)

Slovak

Kelis, J (Czech)

Into DANISH from:

English

Anslev, A A (Den)
Binzer, J J (Den)
Erichsen, B (Den)
Thygesen, J C (Lux)

French

Erichsen, B (Den)
Thygesen, J C (Lux)

German

Anslev, A A (Den)
Binzer, J J (Den)
Thygesen, J C (Lux)

Norwegian

Anslev, A A (Den)
Binzer, J J (Den)
Thygesen, J C (Lux)

Swedish

Anslev, A A (Den)
Binzer, J J (Den)
Thygesen, J C (Lux)

Into DUTCH from:

English

Cambien, R (Bel)
Dolder, L (Bel)
Herschberg, H (Neth)
Horspool, M (UK)
Methorst, H W (Neth)
Mulder-Berry, W (Can)
Muller-Vierin, G (Neth)
Schwarz, E (Neth)
*Selo-Fralin, M (NY)
Slivko-Smesman, D (Bel)
Thier, A (Bel)
Vriendt, J de (Switz)
Wal, L de (It)

French

Cambien, R (Bel)
Dolder, L (Bel)
Geuzendau, A (Bel)
Herschberg, H (Neth)
Horspool, M (UK)
Methorst, H W (Neth)

Mulder-Berry, W (Can)
Muller-Vierin, G (Neth)
Schwarz, E (Neth)
*Selo-Fralin, M (NY)
Slivko-Smesman, D (Bel)
Thier, A (It)
Vriendt, J de (Switz)
Wal, L de (It)

German

Cambien, R (Bel)
Dolder, L (Bel)
Geuzendau, A (Bel)
Herschberg, H (Neth)
Horspool, M (UK)
Methorst, H W (Neth)
Mulder-Berry, W (Can)
Muller-Vierin, G (Neth)
Schwarz, E (Neth)
*Selo-Fralin, M (NY)
Slivko-Smesman, D (Bel)
Wal, L de (It)

Hebrew

Herschberg, H (Neth)

Indonesian

Vriendt, J de (Switz)

Italian

Dolder, L (Bel)
Wal, L de (It)

Portuguese

Dolder, L (Bel)

Spanish

Dolder, L (Bel)
*Selo-Fralin, M (NY)

Yiddish

Herschberg, H (Neth)

Into ENGLISH from:

Arabic

Abdel Sayed, S (Egypt)
Makarius, R (Fr)

Catalan

Sole-Leris, A (It)

Chinese

Sethi, R (China)

Czech

*Valyiova, L (NY)

Danish

Bertelsen, S (Fr)
Binzer, J J (Den)
Gillman, R (Den)
Schalit, R (Bel)

Dutch

Berger, E (Switz)
Heymans, J (Fr)
Horspool, M (UK)
*McMillan, E N (DC)
Rosshandler, L (Can)
Rutgers-Sollberger, V (MD)
Wal, L de (It)

French

Abdel Sayed, S (Egypt)
Allain, J-P (Switz)
Anderson, V (UK)
Ayers, LH (Can)
Back-Sole, R (Ger)
Baer-Naggar, M (NY)
*Bayo, I N (Guat)
Beck, J (Bel)
Belisle, E (VA)
*Bellagamba, M C (Pan)
Berger, E (Switz)
Bernstein, A (Fr)
Bertelsen, S (Fr)
Biass, C (It)
Biegel-Hartzell, S (Switz)
Boero, R (Urug)
Bokownew, J (Fr)
Borovski, A (Ger)
Bosman-Delzons, P-A (Neth)
Bouladon, V (Switz)
Bourdelet-Goffinet, A (Fr)
Bourgeois, D (Can)
Bouyges, Claude (Can)
*Bowen, D (VA)
Bros-Brann, E (Fr)
Buckley, P (Switz)
Burnet, D (Fr)
Caplan, F (UK)
Cardenas, M E (NY)
Carter, I (UK)
Carter, P (UK)
Cavanna, S (Sw)
Chennault, C L (Switz)
Childs, B (UK)
Cole-Egan, H (Can)
Coray, F (Switz)
Corsini-Passi, C (It)
Cory-James, A (Bel)
Cote, M (Can)
Coulter, H L (DC)
Cru, A R (Switz)
Dechamps, P (Bel)
Desbonnet, E (NY)
Duttweiler-Bilaney, A (Switz)
Dyner, R (NY)
Edwards, N (UK)
Esobar-Budge, M T (Chile)
Fagan, T (CA)
Faillace-Gindre, L (Sp)
Falcon-Pickering, J (VA)
Farrell, P (It)
Fievet, P (Fr)
Fischbourne, L (Bel)
Fischer, M (Col)
Foster, P (Switz)
Fradier, M (Fr)
Frank, W (Fr)
Gain, M (Fr)
Galvan, A (DC)
Geldart, G (Switz)
Giannini, A (Fr)
Gillman, R (Den)
Giossan, I (Can)
Glemet, R (Switz)
*Gómez, B (Mex)
González, A (NY)
Gren, N de (Switz)
Griffith, J (Fr)
Griffiths, J (Fr)
Gross, J-P (UK)
*Gutierrez-Suarez, E E de (Mex)
*Harway, M (DC)
Haszard, J (VI)
Heymans, J (Fr)

Horine, R (Switz)
Horn, M C (NY)
Horn, P L (OH)
Horowitz, D (Can)
Horspool, M (UK)
*Howard, E (NY)
Howard-Neumark, M (Isr)
Hunter C (Switz)
Jaggers, B (Fr)
Jaggers, C (Fr)
Jones, I P (Lux)
Kendrew, P (Bel)
Khan, E B (Eth)
Koch-Elles, A-M (Fr)
Konopka, J (Switz)
Konopka, S (Switz)
Kunte, A (India)
Labrada, E B (VA)
Lachow-Budeev, V (MD)
Lafforest, J de (UK)
Lamon, F (Fr)
Lewis-Bonaccorsi, E (PA)
Lindemann, H A (Switz)
Lipcovich, T (Can)
Longley, P E (UK)
Lund, H (UK)
McFarlane, M (Fr)
*McMillan, E N (DC)
Magee, R A (VA)
Major, J (Fr)
Makarius, R (Fr)
Malot, J (Fr)
Märkl-Jaenisch, B (Ger)
Marle, I van (Fr, It)
Marquez, A (Ven)
Mattern, N (Bel)
*Mertvagos, C (NY)
Meurice, P (Can)
Meyer, A (Fr)
Michaeli, B (Isr)
Michel, M Brooks (FL)
Minns, P (Fr)
Mongwa, T (Cam)
Montalte, D de (Fr)
*Morayta, I de (Mex)
Moriarty-Edmonds, F (UK)
Neaman, O (Switz)
Oliver, J (Switz)
Ouimet, C L (Can)
Parra-Idreos, V (Sp)
Patton, S (Fr)
Picard, A L (NY)
Pidgeon, D M (Switz)
Pinsonnaux Mejias, J (Can)
Pratt-Hiridjee, N (Can)
Quigley, P (Fr)
Ramsay, M (Bel)
Reigersberg, F van (VA)
Reis Leal, M A (Port)
Remedois, S (Port)
Richter-Wilde, E (Can)
Rocha, N (CA)
*Roditi, E H (Fr)
Rodriguez, E B de (Ven)
Rohatyn, J (NY)
Rosshandler, L (Can)
Rothermann, H F Broch de (NY)
Rühl, M (Fr)
Rutgers-Sollberger, V (MD)
Rutherford, A (Bel)
Schalit, R (Bel)
Scherman, L (UK)
Schwabecher, B D (Switz)
Selo-Fralin, M (NY)
Sethi, R (China)

*Sierra, A D (MD)
Sieveking, A (Switz)
Simha, E R (Switz)
Simmons, P (Switz)
Simon, B (MD)
Sole-Leris, A (It)
Steudemann, I (Switz)
Steurs, S (Bel)
Swetye, I (CT)
Taylor, N (UK)
Tempini, J (It)
Templeton, J (It)
Terra, D de (UK)
Thiery, C (Fr)
Tolnay, C (Switz)
Tolstoy, P (Fr)
Treidell, F C (Fr)
Umansky, E (Fr)
Valk, W (Fr)
*Valyiova, L (NY)
*Van Reigersberg, S R (VA)
Villoutreys, L de (Switz)
Vitali, M I M de (Urug)
Vosteen, T R (IA)
Wal, L de (It)
Ward, P (Fr)
Watson, H (UK)
Weale, E (UK)
*Westman, D R (CA)
Wilson, B (UK)
Winnington, G P (Switz)
Woronoff, J (NY)
Worsdale, W (Fr)
Yablonsky, A (Fr)
Zuckerman, L (Fr)

German

Allain, J-P (Switz)
Anderson, E E (UK)
Back-Sole, R (Ger)
*Bayo, I N (Guat)
*Bennaton, A (Guat)
Berger, E (Switz)
Bernstein, A (Fr)
Biegel-Hartzell, S (Switz)
Binzer, J J (Den)
Bokownew, J (Fr)
Borchardt, M (NY)
Bros-Brann, E (Fr)
Burnet, D (Fr)
Caplan, F (UK)
Cole-Egan, H (Can)
Coray, F (Switz)
Desrosiers, E F (VA)
Duttweiler-Bilaney, A (Switz)
Fievet, P (Fr)
Fishbourne, L (Bel)
Foster, P (Switz)
Frank, W (Fr)
Gain, M (Fr)
Gren, N de (Switz)
Griffith, J (Fr)
Gross, J-P (UK)
Horine, R (Switz)
Horowitz, D (Can)
Horspool, M (UK)
Hunter, C (Switz)
Kendrew, P (Bel)
Kolmer, H (Aust)
Konopka, J (Switz)
Konopka, S (Switz)
La Bonte, J C (Ger)
Lindemann, H A (Switz)
Lipcovich, T (Can)
Lund, H (UK)

*McMillan, E N (DC)
Märkl-Jaenisch, B (Ger)
Marle, I van (Fr, It)
Marlow, V (UK)
Mattern, N (Bel)
*Mertvagos, C (NY)
Minns, P (Fr)
Oliver, J (Switz)
Patton, S (Fr)
Richter-Wilde, E (Can)
*Roditi, E H (Fr)
Rosshandler, L (Can)
Rothermann, H F Broch de (NY)
Rutgers-Sollberger, V (MD)
Schwabecher, B D (Switz)
Selo-Fralin, M (NY)
Sieber, I (Switz)
Simha, E R (Switz)
Simmons, P (Switz)
Sole-Leris, A (It)
Spitz, R (UK)
Steudemann, I (Switz)
Stevens, E S (Switz)
Thiess, H E (DC)
Tolnay, C (Switz)
Treidell, F C (Fr)
*Tunik, G (DC)
Valk, W (Fr)
*Valyiova, L (NY)
Verber, M (Aust)
Wal, L de (It)
Watson, H (UK)
Wilson, B (UK)
Winkler, E (Switz)
Woronoff, J (NY)
Yablonsky, A (Fr)

Greek

Simha, E R (Switz)

Hebrew

Horowitz, D (Can)
Michaeli, B (Isr)
Shimoni, M (Isr)

Italian

Anderson, E E (UK)
Back-Sole R (Ger)
Baer-Naggar, M (NY)
Beck, J (Bel)
*Bellagamba, M C (Pan)
Bertelsen, S (Fr)
Buckley, P (Switz)
Cavanna, Serge (Sw)
Corsini-Passi, C (It)
Fagan, T (CA)
Faillace, L (Sp)
Falcon-Pickering, J (VA)
Farrell, P (It)
Giannini, A (Fr)
Lewis-Bonaccorsi, E (PA)
Major, J (Fr)
Marle, I van (Fr, It)
*Mertvagos, C (NY)
Moriarty-Edmonds, F (UK)
Quigley, P (Fr)
Reis Leal, M A (Port)
*Roditi, E H (Fr)
Schalit, R (Bel)
Schwabecher, B D (Switz)
Simmons, P (Switz)
Sole-Leris, A (It)
Tempini, J (It)
Templeton, J (It)
Treidell, F C (Fr)

*Van Reigersberg, S R (VA)
Vitali, M I M de (Urug)
Wal, L de (It)
Ward, P (Fr)

Japan

Komatsu, T (Japan)
Matsuo, K (Japan)
Muramatsu, M (Japan)
Saito, Y (DC)
Shiomi, K (NY)
Shirai, C R (VA)

Marathi

Kunte, A (India)

Norwegian

Binzer, J J (Den)

Pinyin

Mongwa, T (Cam)

Polish

Desbonnet, E (NY)

Portuguese

Allain, J-P (Switz)
*Bellagamba, M C (Pan)
Boero, R (Urug)
Corsini-Passi, C (It)
Desrosiers, E F (VA)
Docal, S (DC)
Escobar-Budge, M T (Chile)
Fagan, T (CA)
Falcon-Pickering, J (VA)
Galvan, A (DC)
*Gómez, B (Mex)
*Gómez, J F de (Pan)
*Guierrez-Suarez, E E de (Mex)
*Holmes, T (DC)
*Howard, E (NY)
Infante, A (DC)
Labrada, E B (VA)
McFarlane, M (Fr)
*McMillan, E N (DC)
Marquez, A (Ven)
Michel, M Brooks (FL)
*Morayta, I de (Mex)
Overman, G (PA)
Reigersberg, F van (VA)
Reis Leal, M A (Port)
Remedois, S (Port)
*Roditi, E H (Fr)
Rodriguez, E B de (Ven)
Simon, B (MD)
*Urquiaga, H C (Peru)
*Van Reigersberg, S R (VA)
*Vitali, M I M de (Urug)

Rumanian

Iarovici, E (Rum)

Russian

Ayers, H (Can)
Bernstein, A (Fr)
Borovski, A (Ger)
Carter, I (UK)
Coulter, H L (DC)
Desbonnet, E (NY)
Gren, N de (Switz)
*Holmes, T (DC)
Hunter, C (Switz)
*Martin, N (DC)
*Mertvagos, C (NY)
Tolstoy, P (Fr)

*Tunik, G (DC)
Villoutreys, L de (Switz)
Yablonsky, A (Fr)

Spanish

Allain, J-P (Switz)
Anderson, V (UK)
*Bayo, I N (Guat)
Belisle, E (VA)
*Bellagamba, M C (Pan)
*Bennaton, A (Guat)
Bernstein, A (Fr)
Bertelsen, S (Fr)
Biass, C (It)
Boero, R (Urug)
Bouladon, V (Switz)
*Bowen, D (Switz)
Buckley, P (Switz)
Calixto, N (NY)
Cavanna, Serge (Sw)
Chennault, C L (Switz)
Childs, B (UK)
Coya, F (Switz)
Desrosiers, E F (VA)
Docal, S (DC)
Edwards, N (UK)
Escobar-Budge, M T (Chile)
Fagan, T (CA)
Faillace-Gindre, L (Sp)
Falcon-Pickering, J (VA)
Fievet, P (Fr)
Fischer, M (Col)
Galvan, A (DC)
Geldart, G (Switz)
Giossan, I (Can)
Glemet, R (Switz)
*Gómez, B (Mex)
*Gómez, J F de (Pan)
González, A (NY)
Gren, N de (Switz)
*Gutierrez-Suarez, E E de (Mex)
Haszard, J (VI)
Horine, R (Switz)
*Howard, E (NY)
Infante, A (DC)
Jones, I P (Lux)
Koch-Elles, A-M (Fr)
Labrada, E B (VA)
Lachow-Budeev, V (MD)
Lamon, F (Fr)
Lipcovich, T (Can)
McFarlane, M (Fr)
*McMillan, E N (DC)
Magee, R A (VA)
Marquez, A (Ven)
*Martin, N (DC)
Mayer, B H (Mex)
Michel, M Brooks (FL)
*Morayta, I de (Mex)
Oliver, J (Switz)
Overman, G (PA)
Parra-Idreos, V (Sp)
Pidgeon, D M (Switz)
Pinsonnaux Mejias, J (Can)
Pratt-Hiridjee, N (Can)
Reigersberg, F van (VA)
Reis Leal, M A (Port)
Remedios, S (Port)
Rocha, N (CA)
*Roditi, E H (Fr)
Rodriguez, E B de (Ven)
Rodriguez, M (Mex)
Rohatyn, J (NY)
Rosshandler, L (Can)
Rutgers-Sollberger, V (MD)

Schluckbier, N (Peru)
Selo-Fralin, M (NY)
*Sierra, A. D (MD)
Sieveking, A (Switz)
Simha, E R (Switz)
Simmons, P (Switz)
Simon, B (MD)
Sole-Leris, A (It)
Steurs, S (Bel)
Swetye, I (CT)
Tempini, J (It)
Terra, D de (UK)
Tolnay, C (Switz)
*Urquiaga, H C (Peru)
*Van Reigersberg, S R (VA)
*Vitali, M I M de (Urug)
Weale, E (UK)
*Westman, D R (CA)
Woronoff, J (NY)
Zuckerman, L (Fr)

Swedish

Binzer, J J (Den)
Cavanna, S (Sw)

Yiddish

Horowitz, D (Can)
Michaeli, B (Isr)

Into FRENCH from:

Arabic

Hamad, S (Egypt)

Bulgarian

Milev, G (Bul)

Chinese

Sethi, R (China)

Czech

Ancelot, C (Fr)
Kelis, J (Czech)

Danish

Bertelsen, S (Fr)

Dutch

Berger, E (Switz)
Cambien, R (Bel)
Grandmaison-Orsucci, F de (Fr)
Hannard, J (Neth)
Hespel, D (Bel)
Heymans, J (Fr)
Kemmerling, M G (Fr)
Kengen, K (Bel)
Krafft, R (NY)
Methorst, H W (Neth)
Rutgers-Sollberger, V (MD)
Slivko-Smesman, D (Bel)

English

Allport, C A (Mex)
Ancelot, C (Fr)
Andronikoff, C (Fr)
Arditi, M (It)
Aridjis, N (Bel)
Back, J-H (Switz)
Baillieux F (UK)
*Barnabe, M (Urug)
Barrau, G (N Cal)
Bataille, L (Fr)
Baudon-Blanchet, M (Thai)
Berger, E (Switz)

Bernstein, A (Fr)
Bertelsen, S (Fr)
Biass, C (It)
Blondeau, S (UK)
Bo Bramsen, M (Den)
Bolomey, M (NY)
Bosman-Delzons, P-A (Neth)
Bourdelet-Goffinet, A (Fr)
Bourgeois, D (Can)
Bouyges, Claude (Can)
*Bowen, M (VA)
Boyde, B (UK)
Cambien, R (Bel)
Canin Lamielle, E (Fr)
Chabert, V (Fr)
Chalandon, M (Fr)
Chenais-Monjol, A (Fr)
Chevassus, J (Sen)
Chlepner, N (Fr)
Clarens, J de (Fr)
Clavel, M M (Fr)
Cory-James, A (Bel)
Cote, M (Can)
Cru, A R (Switz)
Curtis, M (Fr)
Cusumano, C (Aust)
Dana, M-J (Can)
Dechamps, P (Bel)
Decoster-Berry, A (Fr)
Delli Zotti, M (Bel)
Delpeut de Lemos, F (It)
Doble-Gesseney, M (Switz)
Ducroux, C (Switz)
Ducroux, M (Switz)
Du Jardin, J-L (It) ·
Dunand, G (Switz)
Dyner, R (NY)
Falcon-Pickering, J (VA)
Farcot, M-C (Fr)
Feret-Gain, C (Fr)
*Ferrua, P (OR)
*Fishkin, M (VA)
Folch, S (Mex)
Forster-Turpin, F (UK)
Fournier-Lluhi, S (Mex)
Gautier, M (MD)
Giannini, A (Fr)
Girot, M (Fr)
Grandmaison-Orsucci, F de (Fr)
Gross, J-P (UK)
Grossetête-Villeroux, M-T (Fr)
Hamad, S (Egypt)
Hannard, J (Neth)
*Harway, M (DC)
Herzenstein, G (It)
Hespel, D (Bel)
Heymans, J (Fr)
Heysch, D (Fr)
Horn, M C (NY)
Horn, P L (OH)
Howard-Neumark, M (Isr)
Iacovella, Y (Fr)
Jaggers, B (Fr)
Jaggers, C (Fr)
Karwinsky, N (Brazil)
Katz, J-D (Thai)
Katz, W (Fr)
Keiser, W (Bel)
Keller, B de (Fr)
Kemmerling, M G (Fr)
Kengen, K (Bel)
Khan, E B (Eth)
Kieffer, N (Indo)
Koch-Elles, A-M (Fr)
Konopka, J (Switz)

Konopka, S (Switz)
Krafft, R (NY)
Krakowsky, B (CA)
Kraushaar-Franquet, N (Can)
Krivocheine, N (UK)
Kunte, A (India)
Lafforest, J de (UK)
*Lamon, F (Fr)
Landa, M-T (It)
Lanz, A-N (UK)
Larrauri, A A (Fr)
*Lateiner de Bry, J (NJ)
Laurent, M-C (Bel)
Lederer, M (Fr)'
Leising, R (Switz)
Lewis-Bonaccorsi, E (PA)
Lindemann, H A (Switz)
Longley, P E (UK)
Luciani, B (Can)
Macherez, E (NY)
Maffre-Mallet, E (Fr)
Magee, R A (VA)
Malot, J (Fr)
Märkl-Jaenisch, B (Ger)
Meister, E (Switz)
Meral, F (Switz)
Methorst, H W (Neth)
Meurice, P (Can)
Meyer, A (Fr)
Milev, G (Bul)
Minder-Magaloff, W (Switz)
Mongwa, T (Cam)
Montalte, D de (Fr)
Neaman, O (Switz)
Nercessian, M (Fr)
Neuprez, J (Switz)
Noverraz-Dieulangard, J (Fr)
Ouimet, C L (Can)
Pegna, V (It)
Picard, A L (NY)
Pinhas, R (Fr)
Pinsonnaux Mejias, J (Can)
Ponette, B (VA)
Porret, D (Switz)
Ramsay, M (Bel)
Ras-Allard, M (CT)
Reichenbach-Desquand, S (Fr)
Repellin, A (Ger)
Ringler, S (Bel)
Rocha, A (Fr)
Roditi, E H (Fr)
Rohr, E von (Switz)
Rothermann, H F Broch de (NY)
Rühl, M (Fr)
Rutgers-Sollberger, V (MD)
Rutherford, A (Bel)
Salzmann, V H (Switz)
Schaefer-Bazelli, G (Switz)
Schai, D A (Switz)
Scherman, L (UK)
Schwabecher, B D (Switz)
Seleskovitch, D (Fr)
Sethi, R (China)
Siegenthaler, F (NY)
Simond, J (Switz)
Skuncke, M-F (Switz)
Slivko-Smesman, D (Bel)
Steudemann, I (Switz)
Steurs, S (Bel)
Stjernvall, N de (Switz)
Syrpis, V (UK)
Taylor, N (UK)
Tempé, J (Fr)
Tempini, J (It)
Thiery, C (Fr)

Toledano-Sabbatucci, E (Bel)
Tranier, P (NY)
Treidell, F C (Fr)
Udovicki, D F Y (NY)
Umansky, E (Fr)
Umansky, J (Fr)
Weale, E (UK)
Winnington, G P (Switz)
Worsdale, W (Fr)
Zilberberg, L-J (UK)

Finnish

Stjernvall, N de (Switz)

German

Ancelot, C (Fr)
Aridjis, N (Bel)
Back, J-H (Switz)
Baillieux, F (UK)
Berger, E (Switz)
Bernstein, A (Fr)
Borchardt, M (NY)
*Bowen, M (VA)
Boyde, B (UK)
Cambien, R (Bel)
Chabert, V (Fr)
Delli Zotti, M (Bel)
Doble-Gesseney, M (Switz)
Dunand, G (Switz)
Grandmaison-Orsucci, F de (Fr)
Gross, J-P (UK)
Heidelberger, B (Lux)
Hespel, D (Bel)
Heysch, D (Fr)
Karwinsky, N (Brazil)
Katz, W (Fr)
Keiser, W (Bel)
Kelis, J (Czech)
Kengen, K (Bel)
Kieffer, N (Indo)
Konopka, J (Switz)
Konopka, S (Switz)
Kramer-Meyn, M-H (Ger)
Lederer, M (Fr)
Leising, R (Switz)
Lindemann, H A (Switz)
Maffre-Mallet, E (Fr)
Märkl-Jaenisch, B (Ger)
Martin-Prevel, R (Bel)
Meister, E (Switz)
Methorst, H W (Neth)
Müller, U F (Ger)
Pelichet, H (Switz)
Repellin, A (Ger)
Roditi, E H (Fr)
Rohr, E von (Switz)
Rothermann, H F Broch de (NY)
Rutgers-Sollberger, V (MD)
Schaefer-Bazelli, G (Switz)
Schai, D A (Switz)
Schwabecher, B D (Switz)
Seleskovitch, D (Fr)
Siegenthaler, F (NY)
Slivko-Smesman, D (Bel)
Steudemann, I (Switz)
Tempé, J (Fr)
Treidell, F C (Fr)
Umansky, J (Fr)
Vaucher, V (Switz)
Zaczek, M (Aust)

Greek

Aridjis, N (Bel)
Syrpis, V (UK)

Italian

Arditi, M (It)
*Barnabe, M (Urug)
Bertelsen, S (Fr)
*Bowen, M (VA)
Chenais-Monjol, A (Fr)
Chlepner, N (Fr)
Delli Zotti, M (Bel)
Delpeut de Lemos, F (It)
Du Jardin, J-L (It)
Dunand, G (Switz)
Falcon-Pickering, J (VA)
*Ferrua, P (OR)
Giannini, A (Fr)
Heidelberger, B (Lux)
Herzenstein, G (It)
Iacovella, Y (Fr)
Keiser, W (Bel)
Kemmerling, M G (Fr)
Larrauri, A A (Fr)
*Lateiner de Bry, J (NJ)
Laurent, M-C (Bel)
Lewis-Bonaccorsi, E (PA)
Martin-Prevel, R (Bel)
Pegna, V (It)
Ponette, B (VA)
Roditi, E H (Fr)
Schaefer-Bazelli, G (Switz)
Schwabecher, B D (Switz)
Tempini, J (It)
Toledano-Sabbatucci, E (Bel)
Treidell, F C (Fr)
Udovicki, D F Y (NY)
Vaucher, V (Switz)

Marathi

Kunte, A (India)

Pinyin

Mongwa, T (Cam)

Polish

Skuncke, M-F (Switz)

Portuguese

*Barnabe, M (Urug)
Blondeau, S (UK)
Delpeut de Lemos, F (It)
Dunand, G (Switz)
Falcon-Pickering, J (VA)
*Ferrua, P (OR)
Gautier, M (MD)
Karwinsky, N (Brazil)
Krakowsky, B (CA)
Ponette, B (VA)
Ras-Allard, M (CT)
Rocha, A (Fr)
Roditi, E H (Fr)
Udovicki, D F Y (NY)

Russian

Andronikoff, C (Fr)
Bernstein, A (Fr)
Dana, M-J (Can)
Doble-Gesseney, M (Switz)
Keller, B de (Fr)
Krivocheine, N (UK)
Macherez, E (NY)
Milev, G (Bul)
Minder-Magaloff, W (Switz)
Nercessian, M (Fr)
Salzmann, V H (Switz)
Siegenthaler, F (NY)
Stjernvall, N de (Switz)

Umansky, J (Fr)
Zilberberg, L-J (UK)

Serbo-Croatian

Seleskovitch, D (Fr)
Udovicki, D F Y (NY)

Slovak

Kelis, J (Czech)

Spanish

Allport, C A (Mex)
Back, J-H (Switz)
Barnabe, M (Urug)
Bataille, L (Fr)
Bernstein, A (Fr)
Bertelsen, S (Fr)
Biass, C (It)
Blondeau, S (UK)
Bolomey, M (NY)
Canin Lamielle, E (Fr)
Chalandon, M (Fr)
Chlepner, N (Fr)
Clarens, J de (Fr)
Clavel, M M (Fr)
Cournier-Lluhi, S (Mex)
Cusumano, Caroll (Aust)
Delpeut de Lemos, F (It)
Ducroux, C (Switz)
Ducroux, M (Switz)
Du Jardin, J-L (It)
Dunand, G (Switz)
Falcon-Pickering, J (VA)
*Ferrua, P (OR)
*Fishkin, M (VA)
Folch, S (Mex)
Forster-Turpin, F (UK)
Gautier, M (MD)
Girot, M (Fr)
Grossetête-Villeroux, M-T (Fr)
Henchoz Stefanovich, A (Mex)
Karwinsky, N (Brazil)
Katz, J-D (Thai)
Katz, W (Fr)
Koch-Elles, A-M (Fr)
Krafft, R (NY)
Krakowsky, B (CA)
*Lamon, F (Fr)
Landa, M-T (It)
Lanz, A-N (UK)
Larrauri, A A (Fr)
*Lateiner de Bry, J (NJ)
Leising, R (Switz)
Luciani, B (Can)
Macherez, E (NY)
Magee, R A (VA)
Meister, E (Switz)
Meral, F (Switz)
Neuprez, J (Switz)
Noverraz-Dieulangard, J (Fr)
Pinhas, R (Fr)
Pinsonnaux Mejias, J (Can)
Ponette, B (VA)
Porret, D (Switz)
Ras-Allard, M (CT)
Reichenbach-Desquand, S (Fr)
Ringler, S (Bel)
Rocha, A (Fr)
Roditi, E H (Fr)
Rutgers-Sollberger, V (MD)
Schaefer-Bazelli, G (Switz)
Siegenthaler, F (NY)
Simond, Y (Switz)
Steurs, S (Bel)

Syrpis, V (UK)
Tempini, J (It)
Toledano-Sabbatucci, E (Bel)
Tranier, P (NY)
Tulian, M (Ven)
Udovicki, D F Y (NY)
Weale, E (UK)
Zilberberg, L-J (UK)

Swedish

Stjernvall, N de (Switz)

Into GERMAN from:

Czech

Emde Boas, M (Neth)
Kelis, J (Czech)

Danish

Aaberg-Davids, H (Den)

Dutch

Diehl, E (Switz)
Emde Boas, M (Neth)
Kengen, K (Bel)
Lehmann, R (Ger)
Rautenberg, W (Ger)
Rosshandler, L (Can)
Rutgers-Sollberger, V (MD)
Weber, W-K (CA)

English

Aaberg-Davids, H (Den)
Band, K (UK)
Bock-Michel, G (Ger)
*Borst, K (Ger)
Bouverat, C (Ger)
*Bowen, M (VA)
Brissa-Benckert, K (Switz)
Chabert, V (Fr)
Cuny-Franz, J K (Fr)
Dejean Le Feal, K (Fr)
Dellmann, R (IA)
Denis-Flock, H (Fr)
Diephaus-Altenkirch, O (Ger)
Doempke, B (Bel)
Drowski, J (Fr)
Durkop, G (Fr)
Emde Boas, M (Neth)
Eustace-Werkner, K (Ire)
Fievet, P (Fr)
Frank, W (Fr)
Freichels, B (Ger)
Freudenstein, K (Ger)
Friese, R (Ger)
Fritsch, G (Fr)
Fuchs-Vidotto, L (Ger)
Gallant-Bauer, C (Can)
Gärtner, K (Switz)
Glemser, H (Fr)
Goehring, H (Ger)
Graeber, C (Bel)
Hass-Huerni, B S (Switz)
Horak, R (Aust)
*Hutchinson, I (OH)
Jumpfelt, W (Ger)
Karara-Rohn, S (Switz)
Katz, W (Fr)
Keiser, W (Bel)
Kengen, K (Bel)
Khan-Gmur, A (Switz)
Kikel, I (Fr)
Klebes, H (Fr)
Klebes, M-L (Fr)

Klose, R K (Sw)
Koch, R (Aust)
Kolmer, H (Aust)
Konopka, J (Switz)
Konopka, S (Switz)
*Konuk, E R (VA)
Koschitzky, B von (Ger)
Kurz, I (Aust)
Kusterer, H (Ger)
La Bonte, J C (Ger)
Laden, S von der (Ger)
Lehmann, R (Ger)
Lenfert, W D (Fr)
Lindemann, H A (Switz)
*Marcuse, G (DC)
Märkl-Jaenisch, B (Ger)
Marlow, V (UK)
Melero, F (Bel)
Meng-Gubler, A (Switz)
Müller-Holdinghausen, G (Ger)
Neuenschwander-Hess, B (Switz)
Nouari, U (Fr)
Orglmeister, E I (Brazil)
Osterholz-Leblond, B (Can)
Oswald, S (Bel)
Paneth, E (UK)
Rautenberg, W (Ger)
Reinert, D (Bel)
Roos, I (Switz)
Rosshandler, L (Can)
Rothermann, H F Broch de (NY)
Russell-Augustin, I (Fr)
Rutgers-Sollberger, V (MD)
Schaefer-Bazelli, G (Switz)
Scharfenberger, A (Switz)
Schimmel-Biggs, E (Ger)
Schirmer, U (Ger)
Schütz, I (Ger)
Schwabecher, B D (Switz)
Schwamberger, K (Fr)
Seydel-Rehers, V (Ger)
Spitz, R (UK)
Steudemann, I (Switz)
Tempé, J (Fr)
Thiess, H E (DC)
Verber, M (Aust)
Watson, H (UK)
Weber, W-K (CA)
Wehik, E (Ger)
*Weide, U (VA)
Weitzel-Mudersbach, M von (Ger)
Wesenfelder, R (Fr)
Winkler, E (Switz)
Worsdale-Wassmuth, G (Fr)
*Wust, K (NY)
Zink, H (Aust)
Zuber de Tomas, U (Sp)

Finnish

Roos, I (Switz)

French

Aaberg-Davids, H (Den)
Bock-Michel, G (Ger)
*Borst, K (Ger)
Bouverat, C (Ger)
*Bowen, M (VA)
Brissa-Benckert, K (Switz)
Buhler, Hanns Hermann (Aust)
Chabert, V (Fr)
Cuny-Franz, J K (Fr)
Dejean Le Feal, K (Fr)
Denis-Flock, H (Fr)
Diehl, E (Switz)
Diephaus-Altenkirch, O (Ger)

Doempke, B (Bel)
Drowski, J (Fr)
Durkop, G (Fr)
Emde Boas, M (Neth)
Eustace-Werkner, K (Ire)
Fievet, P (Fr)
Frank, W (Fr)
Freichels, B (Ger)
Freudenstein, K (Ger)
Fritsch, G (Fr)
Fuchs-Vidotto, L (Ger)
Gallant-Bauer, C (Can)
Gärtner, K (Switz)
Glemser, H (Fr)
Goehring, H (Ger)
Goischke, U (Ger)
Graeber, C (Bel)
Hass-Huerni, B S (Switz)
Horak, R (Aust)
*Hutchinson, I (OH)
Jumpfelt, W (Ger)
Karara-Rohn, S (Switz)
Katz, W (Fr)
Keiser, W (Bel)
Kelis, J (Czech)
Kengen, K (Bel)
Khan-Gmur, A (Switz)
Kikel, I (Fr)
Klebes, H (Fr)
Klebes, M-L (Fr)
Koch, R (Aust)
Konopka, J (Switz)
Konopka, S (Switz)
Koschitzky, B von (Ger)
Kramer-Meyn, M-H (Ger)
Kusterer, H (Ger)
Laden, S von der (Ger)
Lenfert, W D (Fr)
Lindemann, H A (Switz)
Märkl-Jaenisch, B (Ger)
Melero, F (Bel)
Meng-Gubler, A (Switz)
Müller, U F (Ger)
Müller-Holdinghausen, G (Ger)
Neuenschwander-Hess, B (Switz)
Nouari, U (Fr)
Osterholz-Leblond, B (Can)
Oswald, S (Bel)
Paneth, E (UK)
Pelichet, H (Switz)
Rautenberg, W (Ger)
Reinert, D (Bel)
Roos, I (Switz)
Rosshandler, L (Can)
Rothermann, H F Broch de (NY)
Rubini-Heilmann, I (It)
Russell-Augustin, I (Fr)
Rutgers-Sollberger, V (MD)
Schaefer-Bazelli, G (Switz)
Scharfenberger, A (Switz)
Schimmel-Biggs, E (Ger)
Schwabecher, B D (Switz)
Schwamberger, K (Fr)
Steudemann, I (Switz)
Tempé, J (Fr)
Tigges, I (It)
Vaucher, V (Switz)
Watson, H (UK)
Weber, W-K (CA)
Wehik, E (Ger)
*Weide, U (VA)
Weitzel-Mudersbach, M von (Ger)
Wesenfelder, R (Fr)
Worsdale-Wassmuth, G (Fr)
*Wust, K (NY)

Zaczek, M (Aust)
Zink, H (Aust)
Zuber de Tomas, U (Sp)

Hebrew

Koch, R (Aust)

Italian

Bouverat, C (Ger)
*Bowen, M (VA)
Brissa-Benckert, K (Switz)
Diephaus-Altenkirch, O (Ger)
Drowski, J (Fr)
Durkop, G (Fr)
Emde Boas, M (Neth)
Eustace-Werkner, K (Ire)
Fuchs-Vidotto, L (Ger)
Horak, R (Aust)
Keiser, W (Bel)
Koch, R (Aust)
Koschitzky, B von (Ger)
Melero, F (Bel)
Meng-Gubler, A (Switz)
Orglmeister, E I (Brazil)
Osterholz-Leblond, B (Can)
Oswald, S (Bel)
Rautenberg, W (Ger)
Reinert, D (Bel)
Roos, I (Switz)
Rubini-Heilmann, I (It)
Schaefer-Bazelli, G (Switz)
Schütz, I (Ger)
Schwabecher, B D (Switz)
Tigges, I (It)
Vaucher, V (Switz)

Portuguese

Freudenstein, K (Ger)
Orglmeister, E I (Brazil)

Russian

Brissia-Benckert, K (Switz)
Khan-Gmur, A (Switz)
Koy, M (Ger)
*Marcuse, G (DC)
Roos, I (Switz)

Slovak

Kelis, J (Czech)

Spanish

Durkop, G (Fr)
Eustace-Werkner, K (Ire)
Fievet, P (Fr)
Goehring, H (Ger)
Katz, W (Fr)
Khan-Gmur, A (Switz)
Klose, R K (Sw)
*Konuk, E R (VA)
Lehmann, R (Ger)
Melero, F (Bel)
Orglmeister, E I (Brazil)
Rautenberg, W (Ger)
Reinert, D (Bel)
Rosshandler, L (Can)
Rutgers-Sollberger, V (MD)
Schaefer-Bazelli, G (Switz)
Schirmer, U (Ger)
Seydel-Rehers, V (Ger)
Wesenfelder, R (Fr)
Zink, H (Aust)
Zuber de Tomas, U (Sp)

Swedish

Klose, R K (Sw)
Roos, I (Switz)

Into GREEK from:

English

Lefcaditi, A M (Gr)

French

Lefcaditi, A M (Gr)

German

Lefcaditi, A M (Gr)

Into HEBREW from:

English

Frost, B (Isr)
Koch, R (Aust)
Michaeli, B (Isr)

French

Frost, B (Isr)
Koch, R (Aust)
Michaeli, B (Isr)

German

Frost, B (Isr)
Koch, R (Aust)

Italian

Koch, R (Aust)

Yiddish

Michaeli, B (Isr)

Into HUNGARIAN from:

Danish

Pandy, C de (Sw)

English

Pandy, C de (Sw)

French

Pandy, C de (Sw)

German

Pandy, C de (Sw)

Norwegian

Pandy, C de (Sw)

Swedish

Pandy, C de (Sw)

Into ITALIAN from:

Dutch

Abate-Krahe, I (Bel)

English

Ambroso Ruberl, L (It)
Arditi, M (It)
Back-Sole, R (Ger)
Benedek, M (Fr)
Biass-Malucelli, M-P (Switz)
Boyce, C (UK)
Camici, G (Fr)
Campagnola, M (Fr)
Cavanna, S (Switz)
Corsini-Passi, C (It)
Erba-Sain, G (It)
Fedrighini, D (It)
*Ferrua, P (OR)
Fuchs-Vidotto, L (Ger)

Herzenstein, G (It)
Koch, R (Aust)
*Lewis-Bonaccorsi, E (PA)
Lombrassa-D'Oro, P (It)
Marle, I van (Fr, It)
Moggio, L (It)
Monterisi, D (Fr)
Negroni Coucke, M R (Bel)
Pansini, F (Lux)
Pedroni, S (Fr)
Pegna, V (It)
Perkhofer, E (It)
Reinert, D (Bel)
Schmitt-Arno, F (Bel)
Schwabecher, B D (Switz)
Tempini, J (It)
Thellung-Fontana, A (It)
Toledano-Sabbatucci, E (Bel)
Trevisan-Csergo, C (UK)
Vicari, V (Switz)

French

Abate-Krahe, I (Bel)
Ambroso Ruberl, L (It)
Arditi, M (It)
Back-Sole, R (Ger)
Benedek, M (Fr)
Biass-Malucelli, M-P (Switz)
Boyce, C (UK)
Camici, G (Fr)
Campagnola, M (Fr)
Cavanna, S (Sw)
Choi, M (Switz)
Corsini-Passi, C (It)
Credazzi Salvi, M (It)
Erba-Sain, G (It)
Fedrighini, D (It)
*Ferrua, P (OR)
Fuchs-Vidotto, L (Ger)
Herzenstein, G (It)
Koch, R (Aust)
Lewis-Bonaccorsi, E (PA)
Lombrassa-D'Oro, P (It)
Marle, I van (Fr, It)
Moggio, L (It)
Monterisi, D (Fr)
Muller, U (Lux)
Negroni Coucke, M R (Bel)
Pansini, F (Lux)
Pedroni, S (Fr)
Pegna, V (It)
Perkhofer, E (It)
Raso, G (Urug)
Reinert, D (Bel)
Romanini-Roda, I (It)
Rossi-Valsecchi, F (Bel)
*Saxon-Forti, A (NY)
Schmitt-Arno, F (Bel)
Schwabecher, B D (Switz)
Tempini, J (It)
Thellung-Fontana, A (It)
Toledano-Sabbatucci, E (Bel)
Trevisan-Csergo, C (UK)
Vicari, V (Switz)

German

Abate-Krahe, I (Bel)
Back-Sole, R (Ger)
Benedek, M (Fr)
Campagnola, M (Fr)
Choi, M (Switz)
Fuchs-Vidotto, L (Ger)
Koch, R (Aust)
Marle, I van (Fr, It)
Moggio, L (It)

Muller, U (Lux)
Pedroni, S (Fr)
Perkhofer, E (It)
Reinert, D (Bel)
Romanini-Roda, I (It)
Rossi-Valsecchi, F (Bel)
Schmitt-Arno, F (Bel)
Schwabecher, B D (Switz)
Trevisan-Csergo, C (UK)
Vicari, V (Switz)

Hebrew

Koch, R (Aust)

Portuguese

Corsini-Passi, C (It)
*Ferrua, P (OR)
Romanini Roda, I (It)

Spanish

Cavanna, S (Switz)
*Ferrua, P (OR)
Monterisi, D (Fr)
Pansini, F (Lux)
Perkhofer, E (It)
Raso, G (Urug)
Reinert, D (Bel)
Tempini, J (It)
Toledano-Sabbatucci, E (Bel)
Trevisan-Csergo, C (UK)

Swedish

Cavanna, S (Sw)

Into JAPANESE from:

English

Blauenstein, R (Switz)
Komatsu, T (Japan)
Matsuo, K (Japan)
Muramatsu, M (Japan)
Saito, Y (DC)
Shiomi, K (NY)
Shirai, C R (VA)

French

Blauenstein, R (Switz)

Into MARATHI from:

English

Kunte, A (India)

French

Kunte, A (India)

Into PINYIN from:

English

Mongwa, T (Cam)

French

Mongwa, T (Cam)

Into POLISH from:

English

Dobosz, I (Switz)

French

Dobosz, I (Switz)

Russian

Dobosz, I (Switz)

Into PORTUGUESE from:

English

Delpeut de Lemos, F (It)
Docal, S (DC)
Drapier, A I (MD)
Meyer, L (DC)
Mizne, S (Brazil)
Orglmeister, E I (Brazil)
Overman, G (PA)
Reis Leal, M A (Port)
Remedios, S (Port)
Weigel, I (Switz)

French

Delpeut de Lemos, F (It)
Mizne, S (Brazil)
Reis Leal, M A (Port)
Remedios, S (Port)
Weigel, I (Switz)

German

Mizne, S (Brazil)
Orglmeister, E I (Brazil)
Weigel, I (Switz)

Italian

Delpeut de Lemos, F (It)
Orglmeister, E I (Brazil)
Reis Leal, M A (Port)
Weigel, I (Switz)

Spanish

Calixto, N (NY)
Delpeut de Lemos, F (It)
Docal, S (DC)
Drapier, A I (MD)
Meyer, L (DC)
Mizne, S (Brazil)
Orglmeister, E I (Brazil)
Overman, G (PA)
Reis Leal, M A (Port)
Remedios, S (Port)
Weigel, I (Switz)

Into RUSSIAN from:

English

Anderson, T (NJ)
Andronikoff, C (Fr)
Bernstein, A (Fr)
Cerebrog, J (NY)
Deruguine, T (Fr)
Holmes, T (DC)
Illin-Borck, B (Sp)
Keller, B de (Fr)
Kiriloff, N (Can)
Krivocheine, N (UK)
*Lukianoff, B (CT)
*Martin, N (DC)
*Mertvagos, C (NY)
Nurock, E (Switz)
Petroff, A (Switz)
Roos, I (Switz)
Stjernvall, N de (Switz)
Tolstoy, P (Fr)
*Tunik, G (DC)
Yablonsky, A (Fr)

Finnish

Roos, I (Switz)
Stjernvall, N de (Switz)

French

Anderson, T (NJ)
Andronikoff, C (Fr)
Bernstein, A (Fr)
Cerebrog, J (NY)
Deruguine, T (Fr)
Illin-Borck, B (Sp)
Keller, B de (Fr)
Kiriloff, N (Can)
Krivocheine, N (UK)
*Mertvagos, C (NY)
Nurock, E (Switz)
Petroff, A (Switz)
Roos, I (Switz)
Stjernvall, N de (Switz)
Tolstoy, P (Fr)
Yablonsky, A (Fr)

German

Bernstein, A (Fr)
Deruguine, T (Fr)
Kiriloff, N (Can)
Koy, M (Ger)
*Lukianoff, B (CT)
*Mertvagos, C (NY)
Nurock, E (Switz)
Petroff, A (Switz)
Roos, I (Switz)
*Tunik, G (DC)
Yablonsky, A (Fr)

Hebrew

Nurock, E (Switz)

Italian

*Lukianoff, B (CT)
*Mertvagos, C (NY)
Roos, I (Switz)

Portuguese

Holmes, T (DC)

Spanish

Bernstein, A (Fr)
Cerebrog, J (NY)
Illin-Borck, B (Sp)
*Martin, N (DC)

Swedish

Roos, I (Switz)
Stjernvall, N de (Switz)

Into SERBO-CROATIAN from:

English

Udovicki, D F Y (NY)

French

Udovicki, D F Y (NY)

Italian

Udovicki, D F Y (NY)

Portuguese

Udovicki, D F Y (NY)

Spanish

Udovicki, D F Y (NY)

Into SLOVAK from:

Czech

Kelis, J (Czech)

French

Kelis, J (Czech)

German

Kelis, J (Czech)

Into SPANISH from:

Catalan

Muller de Abadal, C (Sp)
Sole-Leris, A (It)
Valero-Bovet, M (Switz)

Chinese

Juan, M de (Sp)

Dutch

Rosshandler, L (Can)

English

*Adelo, A S (NM)
*Alarcon, S M (Mex)
Allain, J-P (Switz)
Andresco, I (Switz)
Arditi, S (Isr)
*Barbajosa, A (Mex)
*Barnabe, M (Urug)
Bayo, I N (Guat)
Belcher, M (FL)
*Bellagamba, M C (Pan)
*Bennaton, A (Guat)
Bertone, L E (Fr)
Boero, R (Urug)
Botero-Browning, S (N Hebr)
Brauenstein, A (Ger)
Brook, M-C (Hong Kong)
Buenoia, M T (MD)
Campos, F (VA)
*Cardoso, P (Switz)
Cogliati, B E (Arg)
Daguerre-Massieu, C (Can)
De La Vega, M I (Col)
Desrosiers, E F (VA)
Diez, A (NY)
Duran, R (Mex)
Durkop, G (Fr)
Escobar-Budge, M T (Chile)
Etchegorry, A M (Switz)
Fagan, T (CA)
Falcon-Pickering, J (VA)
Fernandez de Cordoba, D (Pan)
Fischer, M (Col)
*Gáler, R (NY)
Galvan, A (DC)
García-Landa, M (Bel)
*Garrido, O (DC)
Gómez, J F de (Pan)
Gómez de Silva, G (NY)
*Gutierrez-Suarez, E E de (Mex)
Guzman-Pabon, M T (MD)
Hare, C (Fr)
*Howard, E (NY)
Infante, A (DC)
Juan, M de (Sp)
Kahane, E (UK)
Koch-Elles, A-M (Fr)
Krakowsky, B (CA)
Labrada, E B (VA)
Lachow-Budeev, V (MD)
Lamon, F (Fr)
Landa M-T (It)
Larrauri, A A (Fr)
Lipcovich, T (Can)
Marquez, A (Ven)
Martinez-Smith, M (Fr)

Martorani, S (NY)
Mayer, B H (Mex)
Montecino, M (DC)
*Morayta, I de (Mex)
Muller de Abadal, C (Sp)
*Nedelcovic, B (VA)
Ofri, N (Switz)
Pansini, F (Lux)
Pinkney, M (UK)
Posewitz, R (Switz)
*Ramler-Vaisberg, M (Ven)
Ras, M (NY)
Reigersberg, F van (VA)
*Rivas, I de (Col)
Rodriguez, E B de (Ven)
Rodriguez, M (Mex)
Rodriguez-Delgado, R (Sp)
Rosshandler, L (Can)
Ruckhaus, K (Ven)
*Sagasti-Hochhausler, E (VA)
Schluckbier, N (Peru)
Serrano, G (Switz)
*Sierra, A D (MD)
Simon, B (MD)
Sole-Leris, B (It)
Steurs, S (Bel)
Tell, B G-C de (Can)
Tempini, J (It)
Torrents Dels Prats, A (Switz)
Tovar, A R (Mex)
*Urquiaga, H C (Peru)
*Valdivia-Mendoza, L (Switz)
Valero-Bovet, M (Switz)
*Vitali, M I M de (Urug)
Weale, E (UK)
Wesenfelder, R (Fr)
Wolf, N (Mex)
Zevallos, A Z (NY)

French

*Alarcón, S M (Mex)
Allain, J-P (Switz)
Andresco, I (Switz)
Arditi, S (Isr)
*Barbajosa, A (Mex)
*Barnabe, M (Urug)
*Bayo, I N (Guat)
Belcher, M (FL)
*Bellagamba, M C (Pan)
Bertone, L E (Fr)
Boero, R (Urug)
Botero-Browning, S (N Hebr)
Brook, M-C (Hong Kong)
Buenoia, M T (MD)
Cardenas, M E (NY)
*Cardoso, P (Switz)
Cogliati, B E (Arg)
Daguerre-Massieu, C (Can)
De La Vega, M I (Col)
Diez, A (NY)
Duran, R (Mex)
Durkop, G (Fr)
Escobar-Budge, M T (Chile)
Etchegorry, A M (Switz)
Fagan, T (CA)
Falcon-Pickering, J (VA)
Fischer, M (Col)
Fishkin, M (VA)
*Gáler, R (NY)
Galvan, A (DC)
García-Landa, M (Bel)
Gitai, S (Isr)
Gómez de Silva, G (NY)
*Gutierrez-Suarez, E E de (Mex)
Hare, C (Fr)
Henchoz Stefanovich, A (Mex)

*Howard, E (NY)
Juan, M de (Sp)
Kahane, E (UK)
Koch-Elles, A-M (Fr)
Krakowsky, B (CA)
Labrada, E B (VA)
Lachow-Budeev, V (MD)
Lamon, F (Fr)
Landa M-T (It)
Larrauri, A A (Fr)
Lipcovich, T (Can)
Marquez, A (Ven)
Martinez-Smith, M (Fr)
Martorani, S (NY)
Massieu, J (Can)
*Morayta, I de (Mex)
Muller de Abadal, C (Sp)
Ofri, N (Switz)
Pansini, F (Lux)
Pinkney, M (UK)
Posewitz, R (Switz)
*Ramler-Vaisberg, M (Ven)
Ras, M (NY)
Reigersberg, F van (VA)
*Rivas, I de (Col)
Rodriguez, E B de (Ven)
Rodriguez-Delgado, R (Sp)
Rosshandler, L (Can)
Ruckhaus, K (Ven)
Serrano, G (Switz)
*Sierra, A D (MD)
Simon, B (MD)
Sole-Leris, A (It)
Steurs, S (Bel)
Tell, B (Can)
Tempini, J (It)
Torrents Del Prats, A (Switz)
Tovar, A R (Mex)
Tulian, M (Ven)
*Valdivia-Mensoza, L (Switz)
Valero-Bovet, M (Switz)
*Vitali, M I M de (Urug)
Weale, E (UK)

Wesenfelder, R (Fr)
Wolf, N (Mex)
Zevallos, A Z (NY)

German
Allain, J-P (Switz)
*Bayo, I N (Guat)
*Bennaton, A (Guat)
Braunstein, A (Ger)
Desrosiers, E F (VA)
Durkop, G (Fr)
García-Landa, M (Bel)
Lipcovich, T (Can)
Posewitz, R (Switz)
*Ramler-Vaisberg, M (Ven)
Rosshandler, L (Can)
*Sagasti-Hockhausler, E (VA)
Sole-Leris, A (It)
Wesenfelder, R (Fr)
Wolf, N (Mex)

Hebrew
Arditi, S (Isr)
Gitai, S (Isr)
Ofri, N (Switz)

Italian
*Adelo, A S (NM)
*Barnabe, M (Urug)
*Bellagamba, M C (Pan)
Campos, F (VA)
Cogliati, B E (Arg)
Durkop, G (Fr)
Fagan, T (CA)
Falcon-Pickering, J (VA)
García-Landa, M (Bel)
Gómez de Silva, G (NY)
Larrauri, A A (Fr)
Martorani, S (NY)
*Nedelcovic, B (VA)
Pansini, F (Lux)
Ras, M (NY)

Rodriguez-Delgado, R (Sp)
Serrano, G (Switz)
Sole-Leris, A (It)
Tempini, J (It)
Vitali, M I M de (Urug)

Portuguese
*Adelo, A S (NM)
Allain, J-P (Switz)
*Barnabe, M (Urug)
Belcher, Marila (FL)
*Bellagamba, M C (Pan)
Bertone, L E (Fr)
Boero, R (Urug)
Campos, F (VA)
*Cardoso, P (Switz)
Cogliati, B E (Arg)
De La Vega, M I (Col)
Desrosiers, E F (VA)
Escobar-Budge, M T (Chile)
Etchegorry, A M (Switz)
Fagan, T (CA)
Falcon-Pickering, J (VA)
Galvan, A (DC)
*Garrido, O (DC)
*Gómez, J F de (Pan)
*Gutierrez-Suarez, E E de (Mex)
*Howard, E (NY)
Infante, A (DC)
Krakowsky, B (CA)
Labrada, E B (VA)
Marquez, A (Ven)
*Migone, R (Arg)
*Morayta, I de (Mex)
*Nedelcovic, B (VA)
Ras, M (NY)
Reigersberg, F van (VA)
Rodriguez, E B de (Ven)
*Sagasti-Hochhausler, E (VA)
Simon, B (MD)
*Urquiaga, H C (Peru)
*Vitali, M I M de (Urug)

Russian
Andresco, I (Switz)
Torrents Del Prats, A (Switz)

Serbo-croatian
*Nedelcovic, B (VA)

Yiddish
Arditi, S (Isr)
Ofri, N (Switz)

Into SWEDISH from:
Danish
Levy, M (Sw)
Pandy, C de (Sw)

English
Levy, M (Sw)
Pandy, C de (Sw)

French
Pandy, C de (Sw)

German
Levy, M (S)
Pandy, C de (Sw)

Hungarian
Pandy, C de (Sw)

Norwegian
Levy, M (Sw)
Pandy, C de (Sw)

Into TURKISH from:
English
Akbelen, H (Tur)

French
Akbelen, H (Tur)

8

Translators' & Interpreters' Market Place

The following listings, arranged alphabetically by country, identify some (1) governmental and intergovernmental agencies; (2) national and international associations, societies, institutes, and organizations; (3) private enterprises in commerce, industry, and technology; (4) publishers of translations journals (i.e., journals devoted exclusively to translated texts that originally appeared in another language) throughout the world that are known to employ translators and/or interpreters on their staffs, or to use their services regularly or periodically on a free-lance basis, or who have reason to depend on translation and/or interpretation to one degree or another, owing to the nature of their activities.

Argentina

ASOCIACIÓN INTERAMERICANA DE ESCRITORES, *see* Inter-American Association of Writers

ASOCIACIÓN INTERNACIONAL DE LECTURA
Talcahuano 1040 Of. 111, 1013 Buenos Aires.
Latin American office of International Reading Association, USA.

INTER-AMERICAN ASSOCIATION OF WRITERS (Asociación Interamericana de Escritores)
Casilia de Correo 4852, Humberto 1, #431, Buenos Aires.
Publications *Hoja Informativa; Biblioteca Interamericana.*

Australia

BIBLIOGRAPHICAL SOCIETY OF AUSTRALIA AND NEW ZEALAND (BSANZ)
English, Monash Univ, Clayton, Victoria 3186.
Publications *Bulletin of BSANZ.*

Austria

AGENCE INTERNATIONALE DE L'ENERGIE ATOMIQUE (AIEA), *see* International Atomic Energy Agency (IAEA).

INTERNATIONAL ATOMIC ENERGY AGENCY (IAEA) (Agence International de L'Energie Atomique, AIEA)
Kaerntnerring 11, Postfach 590, A-1011 Vienna *Tel* 524511 *Telex* 012645 *Cable* Inatom Vienna *Founded* 1957.

INTERNATIONAL COMMUNITY OF BOOKSELLERS' ASSOCIATIONS (ICBA)
Grünangersgasse 4, A-1010 Vienna.

INTERNATIONAL INFORMATION CENTER FOR TERMINOLOGY (INFOTERM)
Österreichisches Normungsinstitut (Austrian Standards Inst), Leopoldsgasse 4, A-1021 Vienna *Dir* Helmut Felber *Founded* 1971.
Sponsored by UNESCO within the framework of the UNISIST program, INFOTERM works in liaison with the Technical Committee 37 "Terminology: Principles and Coordination" of the International Organization for Standardization (ISO), and is engaged in compiling an International Bibliography of Standardized Vocabularies (forthcoming).
For individual Terminological Data Banks, see: Terminology Bank of the University of Montreal (Canada); French Association for Standardization (France); Institute for Applied Linguistics (German Dem Rep); Federal Office of Languages (German Fed Rep); Siemens AG (German Fed Rep); Commission of European Committees (Luxembourg); South African Institute of Translators (S Africa); Center of Technical Terminology (Sweden); All-Union Research Institute (USSR); National Bureau of Standards (USA).

INTERNATIONAL INSTITUTE FOR CHILDREN'S LITERATURE AND READING RESEARCH, UNESCO CATEGORY C
Fuhrmannsgasse 18A, A-1080 Vienna *Tel* 433543 *Dir* Richard Bemberger.
Employs one translator for English, occasionally uses the services of free-lance translators/interpreters, with basic target and source languages English and German.
Publications *Bookbird; Jugend and Buch; PA-Kontakte.*

ORGANISATION DES NATIONS UNIES POUR LE DÉVELOPPEMENT INDUSTRIEL (ONUDI), *see* United Nations Industrial Development Organization (UNIDO)

UNITED NATIONS INDUSTRIAL DEVELOPMENT ORGANIZATION (UNIDO) (Organisation des Nations Unies pour le Développement Industriel ONUDI)
Felderhaus, Rathausplatz 2, A-1010 Vienna *Tel* 43 500 *Telex* 75612 *Cable* ONIDO.

Belgium

ASSOCIATION EUROPÉENNE DES ÉDITEURS D'ANNUAIRES, *see* European Association of Directory Publishers

ASSOCIATION EUROPÉENNE DES ÉDITEURS DE PUBLICATIONS POUR LA JEUNESSE, *see* European Association of Publishers of Publications for Young People, EUROPRESS-JUNIOR

BUREAU MARCEL VAN DIJK, S A—INGÉNIEURS-CONSEILS EN MÉTHODES DE DIRECTION
Av Louise, 409, Bte 1, B-1050 Brussels *Tel* (02) 648 66 97.

CENTER FOR AFRICAN ECONOMIC AND SOCIAL DOCUMENTATION (Centre de Documentation économique et sociale africaine, CEDESA)
7 place Royale, B-1000 Brussels.
Publications *Bibliographical Enquiries* (documentary monographs).

CENTRE DE DOCUMENTATION ÉCONOMIQUE ET SOCIALE AFRICAINE (CEDESA), *see* Center for African Economic and Social Documentation

CENTRE INTERNATIONAL DE DOCUMENTATION ÉCONOMIQUE ET SOCIALE AFRICAINE (CIDESA), *see* International Centre for African Economic and Social Documentation

CENTRE TECHNIQUE AUDIO-VISUEL INTERNATIONAL, *see* International Audio-Visual Technical Center

CINÉMATHÈQUE SCIENTIFIQUE INTERNATIONALE, *see* International Scientific Film Library

COMMISSION DES COMMUNAUTÉS EUROPÉENNES (CCE), *see* European Economic Community (EEC)

COMMISSION OF THE EUROPEAN COMMUNITIES (EC)
B-Brussels.

The Commission is one of five institutions comprising the European Community—the Council of Ministers, Economic and Social Committee (Brussels), European Parliament (Luxembourg and Strasbourg), and Court of Justice (Luxembourg). Although each institution has its own language department, the Commission is by far the most important in terms of language activities, with a total staff of around 800 translators, of whom 550 are in Brussels and the remainder in Luxembourg. In Brussels there is a division for each of the six Community languages: Danish, Dutch, English, French, German, and Italian. The impending addition of English as an official language led to a rapid growth in its use even before the United Kingdom's membership in 1973, since a vast body of Community treaties, regulations, and legal documents had to be translated into English with great speed and accuracy. Translators in the English division have no interpreting duties (which come under a separate directorate) and translate only into their native language.

A ratio of one reviser for two translators is the general aim, based on the principle that a reviser can normally handle twice as many pages per day as a translator. All translations are revised before leaving the division in order to guarantee accuracy and to provide the translator with the necessary feedback for training purposes. With an average monthly work load of around 7,000 pages, the English division is broken up into seven specialized groups of ten or so members with a senior adviser in charge of each. In the French division of the Community languages, the main accent is on French, which is the language in which the vast majority of documents are drawn up. Though many on the staff know non-Community languages, documents which cannot be handled within the division are usually sent out to free-lancers, most located in Belgium.

Translator qualifications and recruitment translators are normally required to have a degree from a recognized university, not necessarily in modern languages. Two Community languages are required in addition to the mother tongue. Recruitment for assistant translators is by public examinations, held as needs arise and advertised in the *Official Journal of the European Communities*. The examination includes the translation into English and summarization of test pieces in the foreign language, and is followed by an oral examination and interview designed to probe the candidates' knowledge of the Community and of current affairs, as well as to ascertain their psychological aptitude for the job.

All new translators are first assigned to one of the so-called specialized groups. Upon successful completion of the probationary period, the translator may request transfer to a more specialized group, such as those dealing with energy or monetary matters, where he can learn the associated terminology and jargon and gradually widen his knowledge of the chosen field. Promotion prospects depend largely on merit but also depend on such factors as age and seniority.

CONSEIL DE COOPÉRATION DOUANIÈRE (CCD)
40 rue Washington, B-1050 Brussels *Tel* 648 80 90, 648 81 50 *Cable* CUSCOOPCO.

EUROCONTROL (EURO)
72 rue de la Loi, B-1040 Brussels *Tel* (02) 513 83 00 *Telex* Eurocontrolbru 21173.

EUROPEAN ASSOCIATION OF DIRECTORY PUBLISHERS (Association Européenne des Editeurs d'Annuaires)
42 rue Antoine Dansaert, B-1000 Brussels *Tel* 512 44 99 *Pres* George Henderson *Secy Gen* Jean L Lerat.

Does not have a permanent staff of translators/interpreters, but utilizes the services of free-lancers in French, English, German, and Italian, especially for its codes of ethics and practices.

EUROPEAN ASSOCIATION OF PUBLISHERS OF PUBLICATIONS FOR YOUNG PEOPLE (EUROPRESS-JUNIOR) (Association Européenne des Editeurs de Publications pour la Jeunesse)
99 av de la Brabançonne, B-1040 Brussels *Tel* (02) 341276.

EUROPEAN ECONOMIC COMMUNITY (EEC) (Commission des Communautés Européennes, CCE)
200 rue de la Loi (Complexe Berlaymont), B-1040 Brussels *Tel* 735 00 40, 735 80 40 *Telex* 21877 *Cable* COMEUR.

FÉDÉRATION INTERNATIONALE DES ARCHIVES DU FILM, *see* International Federation of Film Archives

GROUPE DES ÉDITEURS DE LIVRES DE LA CEE (ECC Book Publishers Group)
111 av du Parc, B-1060 Brussels *Tel* (02) 538 21 67.

INTERNATIONAL ACADEMIC UNION (Union Académique Internationale)
Palais des Académies, 1 rue Ducale, B-1000 Brussels *Admin Secy* M Leroy.

Publications *Corpus Vasorum Antiquorum; Catalogue des Manuscrits alchimiques; Oeuvres de Grotius; Dictionnaire du Latin médiéval; Tabula Imperii Romani et Forma Orbis Romani; Documents historiques inédits concernant le Japon; Corpus Philosophorum Medii Aevi; Etudes Islamiques; Monumenta Musicae Byzantinae; Catalogus translationum et commentariorum; Dictionnaires assyriens; Corpus Vitrearum; Dictionnaire Pâli; Corpus des Troubadours; Corpus des Antiquités précolombiennes; Oeuvres d'Érasme; Fontes Historiae Africanae; Civilisations de l'Asie Centrale; Sylloge Nummorum Graecorum; Corpus Inscriptionum Iranicarum; Lexique Iconographique; Lexique de Codicologie; Corpus Constitutionnel; Atlas Linguarum Europae;* Répertoires de l'art.

INTERNATIONAL AUDIO-VISUAL TECHNICAL CENTER (Centre Technique Audio-Visuel International)
Foundation-Lamoriniérestr 236, B-2000 Antwerp.

Publications *Bibliographical References; Studies & Reports.*

INTERNATIONAL CENTRE FOR AFRICAN SOCIAL AND ÉCONOMIC DOCUMENTATION (Centre International de Documentation Économique et Sociale Africaine, CIDESA)
7 place Royale, B-Brussels 1 *Secy Gen* J B Cuyvers.

Publications Bulletin of information on current research on human sciences concerning Africa (in both English and French).

INTERNATIONAL FEDERATION OF FILM ARCHIVES (Fédération Internationale des Archives du Film)
74 galerie Ravenstein, B-1000 Brussels *Tel* (02) 511 13 90.

INTERNATIONAL SCIENTIFIC FILM LIBRARY (Cinémathèque Scientifique Internationale)
31 rue Vautier, B-1040 Brussels.

Publications *Catalogue of Films Deposited.*

INTERNATIONAL UNION OF RADIO SCIENCE (Union Radio-Scientifique Internationale, URSI)
81 rue de Nieuwenhove, B-1180 Brussels.

Publications *Proceedings of General Assemblies of URSI; Information Bulletin; Review of Radio Science; International Reference Ionosphere.*

NORTH ATLANTIC TREATY ORGANIZATION (NATO)
B-1110 Brussels *Tel* 241 00 40/44 00/44 90 *Telex* 23867.

SUPREME HEADQUARTERS OF ALLIED POWERS, EUROPE (SHAPE)
B-7010 Mons *Tel* (065) 4 44 47.

UNION ACADÉMIQUE INTERNATIONALE, *see* International Academic Union

UNION OF INTERNATIONAL ASSOCIATIONS
1 rue aux Laines, B-1000 Brussels.

Publications *Yearbook of International Organizations* (English and French editions); *Directory of Periodicals Published by International Organizations; International Associations* (monthly). "International Congress Science" series, volume 9 E of which is *Practical Guide for Users of Conference Language Services* (excluding interpretation) by the International Association of Conference Translators in English & French editions.

UNION RADIO-SCIENTIFIQUE INTERNATIONALE (URSI), *see* International Union of Radio Science

Cameroon

REGIONAL CENTER FOR THE PROMOTION OF THE BOOK IN AFRICA
BP 1646 Yaoundé.

Permanent staff of translators who conduct the regular work of translation in the Center. In the event of simultaneous conferences for any of the several international conferences that it organizes within the framework of its program of activities, the Center hires the services of free-lance translators and interpreters who work within other services in Cameroon. Translations are made from French and into English and vice versa. All legal and important documents are translated into English or French, the working languages of the Center.

Publications *Bulletin of Information.*

Canada

CANADIAN BUREAU FOR TRANSLATIONS
Dept of the Secy of State, Ottawa, ON K1A OX3 *VP for Langs* Walter Kent, Jr.

The Bureau of Translations is responsible for translating parliamentary reports, documents, debates, bills, acts, proceedings, and correspondence from English into French and vice versa. It provides interpretation of French and English in the House of Commons and Senate, and for all government departments and agencies as required. The Multilingual Division of the Bureau is also responsible for the translation of material from and into other languages and the Multilingual Interpretation Section handles interpretation in connection with international visits and conferences.

The Bureau employs well over 1000 staff translators and interpreters as well as an army of free-lance translators. Preference is given in free-lance assignments to residents of Canada.

INTERNATIONAL CIVIL AVIATION ORGANIZATION (ICAO) (Organisation de l'Aviation Civile International, OACI)
International Aviation Bldg, 1080 Univ St, Montreal, PQ *Tel* 514-866-2551 *Cable* ICAO.

INTERNATIONAL FICTION ASSOCIATION
Univ of New Brunswick, Fredericton, NB.

Publications *The International Fiction Review* (biannual).

INTERNATIONAL UNION OF GEODESY AND GEOPHYSICS (IUGG) (Union Géodésique et Géophysique Internationale)
Geophysics Laboratory, Univ of Toronto, Toronto 5, ON.

Publications *IUGG Chronicle* (bimonthly); *IUGG Monographs; Proceedings of Assemblies.*

INTERNATIONAL UNION OF GEOLOGICAL SCIENCES (IUGS) (Union Internationale des Sciences Géologiques)
Geological Survey of Canada, 601 Booth St, Ottawa, ON K1A OE8.

Publications *Episodes* (newsletter).

ORGANISATION DE L'AVIATION CIVILE INTERNATIONALE (OACI), *see* International Civil Aviation Organization (ICAO)

TERMINOLOGY BANK OF QUEBEC (Banque de Terminologie de Québec) Office
for French Language, Cité Parlementaire (Edifice G), Quebec, PQ.

TERMINOQ is the name of the system which provides terminological information service, translation aid, and preparation of different lists of terms in the areas of science, technology, economy in English and French (occasionally German, Italian, Latin).

TERMINOLOGY BANK OF THE UNIVERSITY OF MONTREAL (Banque de terminologie de l'Université de Montréal)
Montreal 101, PQ.

TERMIUM, as the system is known, provides translation aid, terminological information service, and preparation of different lists of terms used in science, technology, and economics in German, English, French, Latin.

UNION GÉODÉSIQUE ET GÉOPHYSIQUE INTERNATIONALE, *see* International Union of Geodesy and Geophysics (IUGG)

UNION INTERNATIONALE DES SCIENCES GÉOLOGIQUES, *see* International Union of Geological Sciences (IUGS)

Chile

CÁMARA LATINOAMERICANA DEL LIBRO (CIAL) *see* Latin-American Book Association

LATIN-AMERICAN BOOK ASSOCIATION (Cámara Latinoamericana del Libro, CIAL)
Rafael Cañas 16, Dp 1, Santiago *Tel* 40055.

Colombia

CENTRO REGIONAL PARA EL FOMENTO DEL LIBRO EN AMÉRICA LATINA (CERLAL) *see* Regional Center for Encouragement of Books in Latin America

REGIONAL CENTER FOR ENCOURAGEMENT OF BOOKS IN LATIN AMERICA (Centro Regional para el Fomento del Libro en América Latina, CERLAL)
Calle 70 No 9-52, Apdo Aereo 17438, Bogotá.

Costa Rica

ASOCIACIÓN INTERAMERICANA DE BIBLIOTECARIOS Y DOCUMENTALISTAS AGRICOLAS (AIBDA), *see* Inter-American Association of Agricultural Librarians and Documentalists

INTER-AMERICAN ASSOCIATION OF AGRICULTURAL LIBRARIANS AND DOCUMENTALISTS (Asociación Interamericana de Bibliotecarios y Documentalistas Agricolas, AIBDA)
Centro Interamericano de Documentación e Información Agrícola (CIDIA), Turrialba *Tel* 56-01-22 *Telex* CR 2144 IICA *Cable* IICA SANJOSE *Pres* Fernando Monge *Vice-Pres* Yone Chastinet *Exec Secy* Ana María Paz de Erickson.

Does not have a permanent staff of translators or interpreters, but employs simultaneous interpretation services available at host countries for the triennial Inter-American meetings. Translations of all documents and papers published by AIBDA is carried out by the Executive Secretary. Target language is Spanish, source languages usually English and Portuguese.

Publications *Bibliográfia Agricola; Boletín Informativo; Boletín Especial.*

Denmark

INTERNATIONAL UNION OF PREHISTORIC AND PROTOHISTORIC SCIENCES (Union Internationale des Sciences Préhistoriques et Protohistoriques)
Mosegaard, Højbjerg *Secy Gen* O Klindt-Jensen.

Publications *Inventaria Archaeologica; Archaeologia Urbium.*

UNION INTERNATIONALE DES SCIENCES PRÉHISTORIQUES ET PROTOHISTORIQUES, *see* International Union of Prehistoric and Protohistoric Sciences

Egypt

AFRO-ASIAN WRITERS' PERMANENT BUREAU
104 Kasr el-Aini St, Cairo.

Publications *Lotus* (magazine of Afro-Asian writing in English, French, and Arabic); *Afro-Asian Literature Series.*

ARAB REGIONAL BRANCH OF THE INTERNATIONAL COUNCIL ON ARCHIVES
The National Library, Midan Ahmed Maher, Bab El-Khalq, Cairo.

ASSOCIATION OF ARAB UNIVERSITIES
Scientific Computation Ctr, Tharwat St, Orman Post Office, Giza.

Publications *Bulletin* (biannual); *Proceedings of Seminars.*

LEAGUE OF ARAB STATES (LAS) (Ligue des États Arabes)
Midan Al Tahir, Cairo *Tel* 811 960, 890.

LIGUE DES ÉTATS ARABES, *see* League of Arab States (LAS)

Ethiopia

CONGRÈS INTERNATIONAL DES AFRICANISTES, *see* International Congress of Africanists

INTERNATIONAL CONGRESS OF AFRICANISTS (Congrès International des Africanistes)
Haile Selassie Univ, Addis Ababa.
Publications *Proceedings of the Third International Congress of Africanists* (in English and French).

France

ASSOCIATION DES ÉCRIVAINS D'EXPRESSION FRANÇAISE DE LA MER ET DE L'OUTRE-MER, *see* Association of Writers in French in France and Abroad

ASSOCIATION FRANÇAISE DE NORMALISATION (AFNOR), *see* French Association for Standardization

ASSOCIATION INTERNATIONALE DE BIBLIOPHILIE
Bibliothèque nationale, 58 rue de Richelieu, F-75084 Paris.
Publications *Le Bulletin du Bibliophile* (quarterly).

ASSOCIATION INTERNATIONALE DE LITTÉRATURE COMPARÉE, *see* International Comparative Literature Association

ASSOCIATION INTERNATIONALE D'EDITEURS DE LINGUISTIQUE APPLIQUÉE (AIDELA), *see* International Association of Applied Linguistics Publishers

ASSOCIATION INTERNATIONALE DES CRITIQUES LITTÉRAIRES, *see* International Association of Literary Critics

ASSOCIATION INTERNATIONALE DES DOCUMENTALISTES ET TECHNICIENS DE L'INFORMATION (AID), *see* International Association of Documentalists and Information Officers

ASSOCIATION INTERNATIONALE POUR LA LECTURE
54 rue de Varenne, F-75007 Paris *Tel* 222-7171.
European office of International Reading Association, USA.

ASSOCIATION OF WRITERS IN FRENCH IN FRANCE AND ABROAD (Association des Écrivains d'Expression Française de la Mer et de l'Outre-Mer
41 rue de la Bienfaisance, F-75008 Paris.

CENTRE INTERNATIONAL DE DOCUMENTATION CLASSIQUE
14 rue Paul Deroulede, Bois Colombe.
Publications *Bulletin des Sommaires des 700 Periodiques Mondiaux et des Livres Reçus a la Bibliotheque du Centre.*

COMITÉ INTERNATIONAL DES SCIENCES HISTORIQUES, *see* International Committee of Historical Sciences

COMITÉ INTERNATIONAL D'HISTOIRE DE L'ART (CIHA), *see* International Committee on the History of Art

COMITÉ INTERNATIONAL POUR LA DOCUMENTATION DES SCIENCES SOCIALES, *see* International Committee for Social Science Documentation

CONFÉDÉRATION INTERNATIONALE DES SOCIÉTÉS D'AUTEURS ET COMPOSITEURS, *see* International Confederation of Societies of Authors and Composers

CONSEIL INTERNATIONAL DE LA MUSIQUE, *see* International Music Council (IMC)

CONSEIL INTERNATIONAL DE LA PHILOSOPHIE ET DES SCIENCES HUMAINES, *see* International Council for Philosophy and Humanistic Studies (ICPHS)

CONSEIL INTERNATIONAL DES ARCHIVES, *see* International Council on Archives

CONSEIL INTERNATIONAL DES UNIONS SCIENTIFIQUES, *see* International Council of Scientific Unions (ICSU)

COUNCIL OF EUROPE
Palais de l'Europe, F-67006 Strasbourg Cedex.

EUROPEAN SPACE AGENCY
114 av Charles de Gaulle, F-92522, Neuilly-sur-Seine.
Publications Reports, bulletins, notes, memoranda.

FRENCH ASSOCIATION FOR STANDARDIZATION (AFNOR) (Association française de normalisation)
Tour Europe, F-92080 Paris.
The system NORMATERM provides a terminological information service and preparation of different lists of standardized terms for French standards, ISO recommendations and standards of IEC recommendations in English and French.

INTERGOVERNMENTAL COPYRIGHT COMMITTEE
Copyright Div, UNESCO, Place de Fontenoy, F-75700 Paris.

INTERNATIONAL ASSOCIATION OF APPLIED LINGUISTICS PUBLISHERS (Association Internationale d'Éditeurs de Linguistique Appliquée, AIDELA)
9 av des Vosges, F-67000 Strasbourg.

INTERNATIONAL ASSOCIATION OF DOCUMENTALISTS AND INFORMATION OFFICERS (Association internationale des Documentalistes et Techniciens de l'Information, AID)
74 rue des Saint-Pères, F-75007 Paris.

INTERNATIONAL ASSOCIATION OF LITERARY CRITICS (Association Internationale des Critiques Littéraires)
38 rue du Faubourg-St-Jacques, F-75014 Paris *Pres* M R André.
No permanent staff of translators/interpreters, but their services used on a free-lance basis. Target language: French. Source languages: English, German, Rumanian.
Publications *Revue.*

INTERNATIONAL ASSOCIATION OF UNIVERSITIES (IAU)
1 rue Miollis, F-75732 Paris Cedex 15.
Publications *IAU Bulletin* (text in English and French; H M R Keyes and G Daillant, eds).

INTERNATIONAL COMMITTEE FOR SOCIAL SCIENCE DOCUMENTATION (Comité international pour la documentation des sciences sociales)
27 rue Saint-Guillaume, F-Paris 7e *Secy Gen* Jean Meyriat.
Publications Bibliographies; directories; *International Political Science Abstracts.*

INTERNATIONAL COMMITTEE OF HISTORICAL SCIENCES (Comité international des Sciences historiques)
270 blvd Raspail, F-75014 Paris *Secy Gen* Michel François.
Publications Bibliographies; Congress Reports; *Bulletin d'Information.*

INTERNATIONAL COMMITTEE ON THE HISTORY OF ART (Comité international d'histoire de l'art, CIHA)
Institut d'Art et d'Archéologie, 3 rue Michelet, F-75006 Paris.
Publications *Bulletin du CIHA; Corpus international des vitraux du Moyen Age; Repertoire d'Art et d'Archéologie* (quarterly).

INTERNATIONAL COMPARATIVE LITERATURE ASSOCIATION (Association Internationale de littérature comparée)
Institut de littératures modernes comparées, 17 rue de la Sorbonne, F-Paris 5e.

INTERNATIONAL CONFEDERATION OF SOCIETIES OF AUTHORS AND COMPOSERS (Confédération Internationale des Sociétés D'Auteurs et Compositeurs)
11 rue Keppler, F-75116 Paris.
Publications *Interauteurs.*

INTERNATIONAL COUNCIL FOR PHILOSOPHY AND HUMANISTIC STUDIES (ICPHS) (Conseil International de la Philosophie et des Sciences Humaines)
Maison de L'UNESCO, 1 rue Miollis, F-75732 Paris Cedex 15.
Publications *Bulletin of Information* (biennial): *Diogenes* (quarterly).

INTERNATIONAL COUNCIL OF SCIENTIFIC UNIONS (ICSU) (Conseil International des Unions Scientifiques)
51 blvd de Montmorency, F-75016 Paris.
Publications *ICSU Year Book; ICSU Bulletin.*

INTERNATIONAL COUNCIL ON ARCHIVES (Conseil International des Archives)
60 rue des France-Bourgeois, F-75003 Paris.
Publications *Archivum; ADPA/Archives and Automation; Bulletin of the Microfilm Committee; Bulletin of the ICA.*

INTERNATIONAL INSTITUTE FOR EDUCATIONAL PLANNING (IIEP)
7-9 rue Eugène-Delacroix, F-75016 Paris *Tel* (01) 504 28 22. *Founded* 1963.
An international center financed by UNESCO and by voluntary contributions from individual member states for advanced training and research in educational planning.
Publications Economics of education, costs and financing, administration and management of education, manpower and employment, educational technology, etc.

INTERNATIONAL MUSIC COUNCIL (IMC) (Conseil International de la Musique)
UNESCO, 1 rue Miollis, F-75732 Paris Cedex 15.
Publications *The World of Music* (quarterly).

INTERNATIONAL SOCIETY OF LIBRARIES AND MUSEUMS FOR THE PERFORMING ARTS (Société internationale des Bibliothèques-Musées des Arts du Spectacle, SIBMAS)
1 rue de Sully, F-75004 Paris *Tel* 277 4421.
Publications *L'Information du Spectacle; Bibliothèques et Musées des Arts du Spectacle dans le Monde.*

INTERNATIONAL UNION FOR ORIENTAL AND ASIAN STUDIES (Union Internationale des Etudes Orientales et Asiatiques)
77 quai du Port-au-Fouarre, F-94100 Saint-Maur *Secy Gen* L. Bazin.
Publications bibliographies, dictionaries, linguistic atlases.

INTERNATIONAL UNION OF BIOLOGICAL SCIENCES (Union Internationale des Sciences Biologiques)
51 blvd de Montmorency, F-75016 Paris.

MINISTÈRE DES AFFAIRES ÉTRANGÈRES *See* Ministry of Foreign Affairs

MINISTRY OF FOREIGN AFFAIRS (Ministère des Affaires Étrangères)
23 rue La Perouse, F-75016 Paris *Tel* 553 52 00.

ORGANISATION DE COOPÉRATION ET DE DÉVELOPPEMENT ÉCONOMIQUES (OCDE), *see* Organization for Economic Co-operation and Development (OECD)

ORGANIZATION FOR ECONOMIC CO-OPERATION AND DEVELOPMENT (OECD) (Organisation de Coopération et de Développement Économiques, OCDE)
2 rue André Pascal, F-75775 Paris *Tel* 524 82 00 *Telex* 62160 *Cable* DEVELOPECONOMIE.

SOCIÉTÉ INTERNATIONALE DES BIBLIOTHÈQUES-MUSÉES DES ARTS DU SPECTACLE (SIBMAS), *see* International Society of Libraries and Museums for the Performing Arts

UNION INTERNATIONALE DES ÉTUDES ORIENTALES ET ASIATIQUES, *see* International Union for Oriental and Asian Studies

UNION INTERNATIONALE DES SCIENCES BIOLOGIQUES, *see* International Union of Biological Sciences

UNITED NATIONS EDUCATIONAL, SCIENTIFIC AND CULTURAL ORGANIZATION (UNESCO)
7 place de Fontenoy, F-75700 Paris *Tel* (01) 5571610 *Cable* UNESCO Paris *Telex* 204461 Paris *Chief, Interpretation Div* Paul Tolstoy
Ten permanent interpreters plus free-lance interpreters work in the languages of the organization (Arabic, Chinese, English, French, Russian, Spanish) and in the areas of education, culture, reference, communications, general & social science, scientific maps, periodicals. UNESCO observes the AIIC code of ethics and practices, since about 80 percent of the interpreters employed are members of AIIC.
Publications Eight periodicals and three series in the fields of social science, mass communications, and statistics, and numerous titles intended for specialists in the fields of libraries, culture & art, international exchange, etc., including two important updated volumes: *Bibliography of interlingual scientific and technical dictionaries* (5th ed, 1961, 250 pp); *Bibliography of monolingual scientific and technical glossaries* by E Wüster, 2 vols (1955–59, 219 pp & 146 pp).
Index translationum (Translation Index), is an international bibliographical catalog of translated books published each year based on information received from member states of UNESCO, including a relatively small number of translations published in earlier years not previously listed in the *Index*. The bibliographies, arranged by countries in French alphabetical order, are presented under the ten major headings of the Universal Decimal Classification system (UDC).
Acknowledgment is made at the beginning of each bibliography to the organization which provided the information. In many cases this work necessitates the transliteration of titles of works, names of translators, and other essential information into Latin characters. The alphabetical list of principal authors, at the end of each volume, provides serial numbers referring to the translations included.
Preceding the author index is a statistical chart giving the number of entries in each bibliography by categories. These figures have

only an indicative value because of the different criteria applied in the various countries to define a book and because of the fact that a single entry can cover a series of volumes representing, for example, the complete works of an author.
The ISO (International Organization for Standardization) system for transliterating Cyrillic alphabets is employed generally throughout the *Index* to obtain uniformity in the spelling of the names of authors. The transliteration of other languages using yet other alphabets is not yet based on uniform international systems. Examples of the different systems followed by specialists in the various countries who prepare the biographical data are found in the *Index*.
The most recent *Index* examined at the New York Public Library, Vol. 26 (1976), contains a listing of 46,976 translated books published in 1973 in 61 member states.

Germany, West (Federal Republic)

ASSOCIATION INTERNATIONALE DES BIBLIOTHÈQUES DE DROIT, *see* International Association of Law Libraries (IALL)

BUNDESMINISTERIUM DER FINANZEN (BMF), *see* Ministry of Finance

BUNDESMINISTERIUM DER VERTEIDIGUNG (BMVg), *see* Ministry of Defense

DEUTSCHE GESELLSCHAFT FÜR OSTEUROPAKUNDE
Deutsche Verlagsanstalt GmbH, Neckarstrasse 121, Postfach 209, D-7000 Stuttgart.
Publications *International Bulletin for Research on Law in Eastern Europe* (text in English, German, and French).

FEDERAL OFFICE OF LANGUAGES (Bundessprachenamt)
Horbeller Strasse, D-503 Hürth (Cologne).
The Terminology data bank offers translation aid and preparation of different lists of terms in science and technology in German, English, French, Russian.

INSTITUTE FOR APPLIED LINGUISTICS AND DATA PROCESSING CENTER (Institut für Angewandte Sprachwissenschaft und Rechenzentrum)
Technical University Dresden, Mommsenstr 13, 8027-Dresden.
Elektronisches Wörterbuch der Fachsprachen (EWF) (Electronic Vocabulary of Technical languages) is the system which provides translation aid and preparation of different lists of terms in the fields of electrical technology, electronics, chemistry, hydraulics, and pneumatics in German, English, French, Russian.

INTERNATIONAL ASSOCIATION OF LAW LIBRARIES (IALL) (Association Internationale des Bibliothèques de Droit)

D-355 Marburg/Lahn, Savignyhaus, Universi-
tätsstr 6.
Publications *International Journal of Law
Libraries; IALL Newsletter.*

**INTERNATIONAL GEOGRAPHICAL
UNION (IGU) (Union Géographique Inter-
nationale)**
Geographisches Institut II der Universität
Freiburg, Werderring 4, D-78 Freiburg im
Breisgau.
Publications *IGU Bulletin* (biannual).

**INTERNATIONAL LEAGUE OF ANTI-
QUARIAN BOOKSELLERS**
Poststr 14-16, D-2000 Hamburg 36 *Tel* 343236.

**INTERNATIONAL STUDY GROUP OF
RESTORERS OF ARCHIVES, LIBRAR-
IES, AND GEOGRAPHIC REPRODUC-
TIONS**
Postfach 540, 355 Marburg.
Publications *"IADA-Mitteilungen,"* in *Mal-
technik.*

**INTERNATIONAL UNION OF ANTHRO-
POLOGICAL AND ETHNOLOGICAL
SCIENCES (Union Internationale des Sci-
ences Anthropologiques et Ethnologiques)**
Freie Universität Berlin, Berlin *Secy Gen* L
Krader.

**INTERNATIONAL YOUTH LIBRARY (In-
ternationale Jugendbibliothek)**
Kaulbachstr 11a, D-8000 Munich 22.
Publications *International Youth Library;
Prize Book Catalogue; The Best of the Best.*

**INTERNATIONALE JUGENDBIBLI-
OTHEK,** *see* International Youth Library

**MINISTRY OF DEFENSE (Bundesminis-
terium der Verteidigung, BMVg)**
Ermekeilstrasse 27, D-53 Bonn *Tel* (02221)
122.

**MINISTRY OF FINANCE (Bundesminis-
terium der Finanzen, BMF)**
Rheindorferstrasse 108, D-53 Bonn, *Tel*
(02221) 791.

SIEMENS A G
Sprachendienst (Language Service), Hof-
mannstr 51, D-8000 Munich.
Terminologie-Erfassungs- und Auswer-
tungs-Methode (TEAM) (Terminology Evaluation and Acquisition Method) provides translation aid, preparation of different lists of
terms, and production of terminological vocabularies (Digiset) in German, English, Dutch,
French, Spanish, Italian, Portuguese, Russian.

**UNESCO INSTITUTE FOR EDUCATION
(UIE)**
Feldbrunnenstr 70 D-2000 Hamburg 13.
Founded in 1951 as a research center for international cooperative projects in the relation
of lifelong education to national systems of
education, to school curricula, to basic education, teacher training, evaluation, and research.
Publications Over 120 titles and *International Review of Education* (quarterly).

**UNION GÉOGRAPHIQUE INTER-
NATIONALE,** *see* International Geographical Union (IGU)

**UNION INTERNATIONALE DES SCI-
ENCES ANTHROPOLOGIQUES ET
ETHNOLOGIQUES,** *see* International
Union of Anthropological and Ethnological
Sciences

Ghana

**ASSOCIATION OF AFRICAN UNIVER-
SITIES**
PO Box 5744, Accra.
Publications *Bulletin* (biannual); *Creating
the African University; List of Staff Vacancies in
African Universities.*

**UNION DES ÉCRIVAINS NEGRO-AFRI-
CAINS,** *see* Union of Writers of the African
Peoples

**UNION OF WRITERS OF THE AFRICAN
PEOPLES (Union des Écrivains Negro-Af-
ricains)**
Ghana Assn of Writers, PO Box 4414, Accra.
Publications *African World Alternatives.*

Israel

**ASSOCIATION INTERNATIONALE
POUR L'HISTOIRE DES RELIGIONS,**
see International Association for the History
of Religions

**INTERNATIONAL ASSOCIATION FOR
THE HISTORY OF RELIGIONS (Associ-
ation internationale pour l'Histoire des Reli-
gions)**
Hebrew Univ of Jerusalem, Jerusalem *Secy
Gen* Z Werblowsky.

Italy

**ªUREAU INTERGOUVERNEMENTAL
POUR L'INFORMATIQUE—CENTRE
INTERNATIONAL DE CALCUL,** *see* In-
tergovernmental Bureau for Informatics—
International Computation Center (IBI—
ICC)

**FOOD AND AGRICULTURE ORGANI-
ZATION OF THE UNITED NATIONS
(FAO)**
Vie delle Terme di Caracalla, I-00100 Rome
Tel (06) 5797.
The FAO is concerned with the areas of agriculture, the world food situation, economics
& statistics, fisheries, forestry & forest products, nutrition, legislation, educational materials on what the FAO describes as a "world intelligence service on production, price, and
trade that covers almost every commodity used
to feed, clothe, and house people throughout
the world."

Publications Monographs, periodicals, official records of the work of FAO, yearbooks,
and annuals.

**INTERGOVERNMENTAL BUREAU FOR
INFORMATICS—INTERNATIONAL
COMPUTATION CENTER (IBI—ICC)
(Bureau Intergouvernemental pour
L'Informatique—Centre International de
Calcul)**
CP 10253, Viale della Civilta del Lavoro 23,
EUR, I-00144, *Dir* F A Bernasconi.
Publications *International Directory of Com-
puter and Information System Services*
(monthly newsletter).

**LEAGUE OF EUROPEAN RESEARCH LI-
BRARIES (Ligue des Bibliothèques Europé-
ennes de Recherche, LIBER)**
The Library, European Univ Inst, Badia Fieso-
lana, Florence.
Publications *LIBER Bulletin.*

**LIGUE DES BIBLIOTHÈQUES EUROPÉ-
ENNES DE RECHERCHE (LIBER),** *see*
League of European Research Libraries

Japan

**THE CENTER FOR JAPANESE SOCIAL
& POLITICAL STUDIES**
2-8-8 Nishinogawa, Komae-shi, Tokyo 201 *Tel*
(03) 489-2175.
A nonprofit organization that conducts a variety of activities within the fields of the social
sciences and political science.
Publications *The Japan Interpreter.*

**JAPAN CENTER FOR INTERNATIONAL
EXCHANGE (JCIE)**
9-17 Minami Azabu 4-chome, Minato-ku, Tokyo *Tel* 446-7781 *Cable* JAPACENEX Tokyo
A nonprofit organization devoted to translation and research in the social sciences, and
specializing in international exchange and education.
Publications *The Japanese Interpreter,* a
quarterly journal published to acquaint English-speaking readers with current Japanese
thinking on social, political, and economic issues, both domestic and international. *Ed*
Kano Tsutomu *Contrib Eds* Frank Baldwin
(Tsukuba Univ), W K Cummings (Univ of
Chicago), Peter Grilli, T J Pempel (Cornell
Univ), David Plath (Univ of Illinois), J A A
Stockwin (Australian National Univ).

Kuwait

**ARAB UNIVERSITY LIBRARY ASSOCI-
ATION**
Kuwait Univ, P.O. Box 5969, Kuwait.

Luxembourg

PARLEMENT EUROPÉEN
Centre Européen, Kirchberg, Luxembourg *Tel*
479 41.

Malaysia

ASSOCIATION OF SOUTH-EAST ASIAN PUBLISHERS (ASEAP)
Kuala Lumpur.

Mexico

ASOCIACIÓN LATINOAMERICANA DE ESCUELAS DE BIBLIOTECOLOGÍA Y CIENCIAS DE LA INFORMACIÓN (ALEBCI), *see* Latin American Association of Schools of Library and Information Science

LATIN AMERICAN ASSOCIATION OF SCHOOLS OF LIBRARY AND INFORMATION SCIENCE (Asociación Latinoamericana de Escuelas de Bibliotecología y Ciencias de la Información, ALEBCI)
Colegio de Bibliotecología, Universidad Nacional Autónoma de México, México 20, DF.
Publications *ALEBCI Boletin Informativo.*

The Netherlands

ASSOCIATION INTERNATIONALE DES BIBLIOTHÉCAIRES ET DOCUMENTALISTES AGRICOLES, *see* International Association of Agricultural Librarians and Documentalists (IAALD)

ASSOCIATION INTERNATIONALE DES BIBLIOTHÈQUES D'UNIVERSITÉS POLYTECHNIQUES, *see* International Association of Technological University Libraries (AITUL)

COMITÉ INTERNATIONAL PERMANENT DES LINGUISTES, *see* Permanent International Committee of Linguists

CONSEIL INTERNATIONAL DES ASSOCIATIONS DE BIBLIOTHÈQUES DE THÉOLOGIE, *see* International Council of Theological Library Associations

COUR INTERNATIONALE DE JUSTICE *see* International Court of Justice

FÉDÉRATION INTERNATIONALE DE DOCUMENTATION, *see* International Federation for Documentation

FÉDÉRATION INTERNATIONALE DES ASSOCIATIONS DE BIBLIOTHÉCAIRES ET DES BIBLIOTHÈQUES, *see* International Federation of Library Associations and Institutions (IFLA)

INSTITUT INTERNATIONAL DE STATISTIQUE, *see* International Statistical Institute

INTERNATIONAL ASSOCIATION OF AGRICULTURAL LIBRARIANS AND DOCUMENTALISTS (IAALD) (Associa-tion Internationale des Bibliothécaires et Documentalistes Agricoles)
Hullerpad 14, NL-Lunteren 6160.
Publications *IAALD Quarterly Bulletin* (text in English, French, German, or Spanish; G De Bruyn, ed).

INTERNATIONAL ASSOCIATION OF TECHNOLOGICAL UNIVERSITY LIBRARIES (IATUL) (Association Internationale des Bibliothèques d'Universités Polytechniques) c/o Bibliotheek Technische Hogeschool Twente, Campus Drienerlo, Postbus 217, Enschede.
Publications *IATUL Proceedings.*

INTERNATIONAL COUNCIL OF THEOLOGICAL LIBRARY ASSOCIATIONS (Conseil International des Associations de Bibliothèques de Théologie)
Faber Str 7, NL-6800 Nijmegen.

INTERNATIONAL COURT OF JUSTICE (Cour Internationale de Justice)
Palais de la Paix, NL-The Hague *Tel* 92 44 41 *Cable* INTERCOURT LA HAYE.

INTERNATIONAL FEDERATION FOR DOCUMENTATION (Fédération internationale de documentation)
PO Box 30115, 2500 GC, NL-The Hague.
Does not have a permanent staff of translators/interpreters, but utilizes services of freelancers for translations into and from English and French.
Publications *FID News Bulletin; International Forum on Information and Documentation; R & D Projects in Documentation and Librarianship; FID Directory; Annual Report; Extensions and Corrections to the UDC;* also Proceedings of Congresses and Seminars, UDC editions in several languages, Studies on Information Science, Manuals, Bibliographies and Directories.

INTERNATIONAL FEDERATION OF LIBRARY ASSOCIATIONS AND INSTITUTIONS (IFLA) (Fédération Internationale des Associations de Bibliothécaires et des Bibliothèques)
Netherlands Congress Bldg, Churchillplein 10, NL-The Hague *Tel* (070) 547231 *Telex* 31700 NECON *Secy Gen* Margreet Wijnstroom.
IFLA does not have a permanent staff of interpreters, but avails itself of the services of a team of young librarians who act as simultaneous interpreters during the annual conferences. The team (16–20) works from and into English, French, German, Russian. Only official documents are issued in English and French, most other IFLA documents, journals, etc, in English only. The *IFLA Journal* abstracts material in three languages. Papers for conferences are accepted in English, French, German, or Russian. Officers of sections in which these papers are presented usually seek translations in the country of the target language.
Publications *IFLA Journal* (including *IFLA News*); *Annual; Directory.*

INTERNATIONAL GROUP OF SCIENTIFIC, TECHNICAL, AND MEDICAL PUBLISHERS (STM)
Keizergracht 462, NL-1016 GE Amsterdam.

INTERNATIONAL STATISTICAL INSTITUTE (Institut International de Statistique)
Prinses Beatrixlaan 428, NL-Voorburg.
Publications Glossaries, bibliographies, journals.

INTERNATIONAL TRANSLATIONS CENTER (ITC)
101 Doelenstraat, NL-2611 NS Delft *Tel* (015) 142242; 142423 *Telex* 31673 ITC NL *Ed* D van Bergeijk.
Publications *Journals in Translation,* a guide to journals containing translations, jointly with the British Library Lending Division, Boston Spa, UK. Most of the translations are into English, and the journal lists cover-to-cover translations, full translations of particular journals from which all articles have been translated, and journals containing selected articles. Omitted from this bibliography are journals published simultaneously in two or more languages, with the exception of a few, where one of the languages is Russian or Japanese. Also omitted are journals that contain only abstracts/synopses of articles which appeared originally in another language. The publication contains a Keyword Index and an Original Title Index and a COMfiche version is available from the Instituto de Información y Documentación en Ciencia y Tecnologia, the Spanish participant in the network.

PERMANENT INTERNATIONAL COMMITTEE OF LINGUISTS (Comité International Permanent des Linguistes)
Stationsplein 10 (910A), Leiden *Secy Gen* E M Uhlenbeck.
Publications *Linguistic Bibliography.*

New Zealand

INTERNATIONAL SOCIETY FOR MUSIC EDUCATION (ISME)
The School of Music, The Univ of Canterbury, Christchurch 1.
Publications *ISME Year Book; Reports of ISME Conferences and Seminars.*

Nigeria

STANDING CONFERENCE OF AFRICAN UNIVERSITY LIBRARIES (SCAUL)
PO Box 48, Univ of Lagos Post Office, Akoka, Yaba, Lagos.
Utilizes the services of free-lance translators/interpreters regularly for its conferences, the proceedings of which are published in English and French.
Publications *Conference Proceedings; SCAUL Newsletter* (E Bejide Bankole, ed).

Senegal

ASSOCIATION INTERNATIONALE POUR LE DÉVELOPPEMENT DE LA DOCUMENTATION, DES BIBLIOTHÈQUES, ET DES ARCHIVES EN

AFRIQUE, *see* International Association for the Development of Documentation, Libraries, and Archives in Africa

INSTITUT AFRICAIN DE DÉVELOPPEMENT ÉCONOMIQUE ET DE PLANIFICATION (IDEP)
BP 3186, Dakar *Tel* 225 77, 268 39.

INTERNATIONAL ASSOCIATION FOR THE DEVELOPMENT OF DOCUMENTATION, LIBRARIES, AND ARCHIVES IN AFRICA (Association Internationale pour le Développement de la Documentation, des Bibliothèques, et des Archives en Afrique)
BP 375, Dakar *Tel* 34139.

South Africa

THE SOUTH AFRICAN INSTITUTE OF TRANSLATORS
PO Box 3593, Pretoria 0001.
The terminology data bank provides translation aid, preparation of different lists of terms, and production of terminological vocabularies in the fields of science, technology, economics in German, English, Afrikaans, French, Russian.

Sweden

CENTER OF TECHNICAL TERMINOLOGY (TNC) (Tekniska nomenclaturcentralen)
Liljeholmsvägen 32, Box 43041, S-10072 Stockholm.
TERMDOK provides preparation of different lists of terms and production of terminological vocabularies in the areas of science, technology, and economics in German, English, Danish, Norwegian, Swedish, French, Russian, Japanese, Finnish.

Switzerland

ACCORD GÉNÉRAL SUR LES TARIFS, *see* General Agreement on Tariffs and Trade (GATT)

ASSOCIATION DES BIBLIOTHÈQUES INTERNATIONALES, *see* Association of International Libraries

ASSOCIATION EUROPÉENNE DE LIBRE-ÉCHANGE (AELE) *see* European Free Trade Association (EFTA)

ASSOCIATION FOR THE PROMOTION OF THE INTERNATIONAL CIRCULATION OF THE PRESS (Association pour la Promotion de la Press)
Beethovenstrasse 20, CH-8002 Zurich.

ASSOCIATION OF INTERNATIONAL LIBRARIES (Association des Bibliothèques Internationales)
Library, United Nations, CH-1211 Geneva.
Publications *Newsletter.*

ASSOCIATION POUR LA PROMOTION DE LA PRESS, *see* Association for the Promotion of the International Circulation of the Press

BUREAU INTERNATIONALE DU TRAVAIL, *see* International Labour Organisation '(ILO)

COMITÉ INTERNATIONAL DE LA CROIX-ROUGE (CICR) *see* International Red Cross Committee

CONSEIL DES ORGANISATIONS INTERNATIONALES DES SCIENCES MEDICALES, *see* Council for International Organizations of Medical Sciences (CIOMS)

COUNCIL FOR INTERNATIONAL ORGANIZATIONS OF MEDICAL SCIENCES (CIOMS) (Conseil des organisations internationales des Sciences medicales)
c/o WHO, ave Appia, CH-1211 Geneva 27.
Publications *Calendar of International and Regional Congresses* (annual); *Proceedings of Symposia; International Nomenclature of Diseases.*

EUROPEAN ASSOCIATION OF MANUFACTURERS AND DISTRIBUTORS OF EDUCATIONAL MATERIALS (EURODIDAC)
Jägerstr 5, CH-4058 Basel.

EUROPEAN BROADCASTING UNION (EBU)
Ancienne Rte 17, CP 193, CH-1211 Geneva 20.

EUROPEAN FREE TRADE ASSOCIATION (EFTA) (Association Européene de Libre-Échange, AELE)
9-11, rue de Varembé, Ch-1211 Geneva 20 *Tel* 022 34 90 00 *Telex* 22 660 EFTA CH.

EUROPEAN ORGANIZATION FOR NUCLEAR RESEARCH (CERN) (Organisation européenne pour la recherche nucléaire)
CH-1211 Geneva 23.
Publications *CERN Courier* (in English & French); *Annual Report; Technical Notebooks; A Look at CERN.*

FÉDÉRATION INTERNATIONALE DES ASSOCIATIONS D'ÉTUDES CLASSIQUES, *see* International Federation of the Societies of Classical Studies

FÉDÉRATION INTERNATIONALE DES SOCIÉTIÉS DE PHILOSOPHIE (FISP), *see* International Federation of Philosophical Societies

GENERAL AGREEMENT ON TARIFFS AND TRADE (GATT) (Accord Général sur les Tarifs)
Interim Commission for the International Trade Organization, 154 rue de Lausanne, CH-1202 Geneva *Tel* (022) 31 02 32 *Cable* INCITO.

INTERNATIONAL ASTRONOMICAL UNION (Union astronomique internationale)
Observatoire de Geneve, CH-1290 Sauverny (GE) *Gen Sec* Edith A Müller.
Publications *Transactions of the International Astronomical Union and Symposia Organized by the IAU.*

INTERNATIONAL BOARD ON BOOKS FOR YOUNG PEOPLE (IBBY)
Leonhardsgraben 38a, CH-4051 Basel *Pres* Kund-Eigil Hauberg-Tychsen (Denmark) *Vice Pres* Shigeo Watanabe (Japan) Regina Yolanda Werneck (Brazil) *Secy* Leena Maissen.
An international, cross-disciplinary organization interested in promoting greater understanding through children's books, the distribution of literature for children of high literary and artistic standards, and encouraging the establishment of national and international libraries and the continuing education of those involved with children and children's literature. The US National Section of IBBY is composed of members of the Association of Library Service to Children (ALSC) of the American Library Association and members of the Children's Book Council (CBC).
IBBY promotes International Children's Book Year, observed each year throughout the world on April 2, Hans Christian Andersen's birthdate; biennial Congresses focusing on a particular aspect of children's literature; biennial Honor List, including translators of children's books (see Sec 3, International).
Publications *20 Years of IBBY; Congress Reports; International Guide to Sources of Information about Children's Literature* (contains a listing of IBBY National Sections in approximately 40 countries, and organizations providing information or services relating to children's literature); *Bookbird* (quarterly publication-of-record, containing criticism, reviews, and news about children's literature).

INTERNATIONAL FEDERATION OF PHILOSOPHICAL SOCIETIES (Fédération internationale des Sociétiés de Philosophie, FISP)
Universitat Bern, Institut für exacte Wissenschaften, Sidlersstr 5, CH-3012 Berne *Secy Gen* André Mercier.
Publications *Proceedings of the International Congresses of Philosophy; An International Bibliography of Philosophy; Chroniques de Philosophie.*

INTERNATIONAL FEDERATION OF THE SOCIETIES OF CLASSICAL STUDIES (Fédération internationale des Associations d'Études classiques)
c/o F Paschoud, 26 rue de Vermont, CH-1202 Geneva.

Publications *L'Année philologique; Fasti Archeologici; Thesaurus Linguae Latinae; Lustrum;* other bibliographies, dictionaries, reference works.

INTERNATIONAL LABOUR ORGANISATION (ILO) (Bureau Internationale du Travail)

ILO Publications, 4 rte des Morillons, CH-1211 Geneva 22 *Tel* (022) 996 111.

Branch offices are located at 87-91 New Bond St, London W1Y 9LA, UK; 1750 New York Ave NW, Washington, DC 20006 USA.

Publications Fall into main categories such as international exchange of factual information, analysis of trends in social affairs, the results of ILO research, comparative studies as a basis for international cooperation in solving economic and social problems, etc. Over 1200 titles in print: studies, monographs, handbooks, periodicals, reports on conditions and practices in different countries.

INTERNATIONAL MUSICOLOGICAL SOCIETY

CP 588, CH-4001 Basel *Secy Gen* Rudolf Hausler.

Publications: *Acta Musicologica; Documenta Musicologica; Catalogus Musicus; RILM; RIDIM.*

INTERNATIONAL ORGANIZATION FOR STANDARDIZATION (ISO) (Organisation internationale de Normalisation)

1 rue de Varembe, CP 56, CH-1211 Geneva 20.

Publications *International Standards Series:* ISO/R 1087-1969. *Vocabulary of terminology.* ISO/R 919-1969. *Guide for the Preparation of Classified Vocabularies.* ISO/R 704-1968. *Naming principles.* ISO/R 860-1968. *International Unification of Concepts and Terms.* ISO/R 1149-1969. *Layout of Multilingual Classified Vocabularies.* ISO/R 639-1967. *Symbols for Languages, Countries, and Authorities.* ISO 1951-1973. *Lexicographical Symbols.*

INTERNATIONAL PUBLISHERS ASSOCIATION

3 ave de Miremont, CH-1206 Geneva.

INTERNATIONAL RED CROSS COMMITTEE (Comité International de la Croix-Rouge, CICR)

17 ave de la Paix, CH-1211 Geneva *Tel* 34 60 01 *Telex* 22269.

INTERNATIONAL SOCIETY FOR BUSINESS EDUCATION

Chemin de la Croix, CH-1052 le Mont-Sur-Lausanne.

Publications *International Review for Business Education* (text in English, French, German, Italian, and Spanish; Felix Schmid, ed).

INTERNATIONAL TELECOMMUNICATION UNION (ITU) (Union Internationale des Télécommunications, UIT)

Place des Nations, CH-1211 Geneva 20 *Tel* (022) 34 60 21; International 41 22 34 60 21 *Telex* 23 000 *Cable* Burinterna Geneva.

Permanent staff of translators, of which eight are in the French section, five in English, and 12 in Spanish. During conference periods, as well as for their preparation, this team may be reinforced by short-term recruitment of freelance translators. The majority of incoming texts are received in the three working languages, English, French, and Spanish. However, the abilities of the translators are not limited to these and translations can be made for a wide variety of the more widely used languages (Russian, Arabic, German, Swedish, etc). A great proportion of translation in ITU is of a technical nature and consequently one of the requirements for filling permanent posts is that candidates have some experience in this field of work, preferably within a national telecommunications administration.

Interpreters are employed only on a short-term free-lance basis as required for meetings and conferences. For certain important conferences, interpretation will be provided in Russian, Chinese, and Arabic.

Publications *Central Library List of Recent Acquisitions* (text in English, French, and Spanish; A G el-Zanati, ed); *Operational Bulletin* (editions in English, French, and Spanish).

INTERNATIONAL TRADE CENTER, UNCTAD-GATT (ITC)

Villa le Bocage, Palais des Nations, CH-1211 Geneva 10.

Publications *International Trade Forum* (editions in English, French, and Spanish; J Goertz, ed).

INTERNATIONAL UNION FOR HEALTH EDUCATION

3 rue Viollier, CH-1207 Geneva.

Publications *International Journal of Health Education* (editions in English, Spanish, French, and German; Annette Le Meitour-Kaplun, ed).

ORGANISATION EUROPÉENNE POUR LA RECHERCHE NUCLÉAIRE, see European Organization for Nuclear Research (CERN)

ORGANISATION INTERNATIONALE DE NORMALISATION, see International Organization for Standardization (ISO)

ORGANISATION MÉTÉOROLOGIQUE MONDIALE, see World Meteorological Organization (WMO)

ORGANISATION MONDIALE DE LA PROPRIÉTÉ INTELLECTUELLE (OMPI), see World Intellectual Property Organization (WIPO)

ORGANISATION MONDIALE DE LA SANTÉ (OMS), see World Health Organization (WHO)

UNION ASTRONOMIQUE INTERNATIONALE, see International Astronomical Union

UNION INTERNATIONALE DES TÉLÉCOMMUNICATIONS (UIT), see International Telecommunication Union (ITU)

UNION POSTALE UNIVERSELLE, see Universal Postal Union (UPU)

UNITED NATIONS ORGANIZATION (UNO)

Palais des Nations, CH-1211 Geneva *Tel* (022) 34 60 11; 31 02 11 *Telex* 22212, 22344 *Cable* UNATIONS.

See also United Nations, USA

UNIVERSAL POSTAL UNION (UPU) (Union Postale Universelle)

Weltpoststrasse 4, CH-Berne *Tel* (4131) 43 22 11 *Telex* 32 842 UPU CH *Cable* UPU Berne.

Although the only official language of the UPU is French, other languages are used at meetings and for documents and publications. The member countries have formed language groups which employ permanent translators who work either at the Union Headquarters in Berne or at regional centers. The UPU uses both free-lance translators and interpreters for French, Arabic, English, Russian, Spanish.

WORLD HEALTH ORGANIZATION (WHO) (Organisation Mondiale de la Santé, OMS)

20 ave Appia, CH-1211 Geneva 27 *Tel* (022) 34 60 61 *Telex* 27821 *Cable* UNISANTE.

Publications Designed to convey information relating to the various aspects of medicine and public health.

WORLD INTELLECTUAL PROPERTY ORGANIZATION (WIPO) (Organisation Mondiale de la Propriété Intellectuelle, OMPI)

32 Chemin des Colombettes, CH-1211 Geneva 20.

Publications *Le Droit d'Auteur; Copyright; La Propiedad Intelectual.*

WORLD METEOROLOGICAL ORGANIZATION (WMO) (Organisation Météorologique Mondiale)

41 ave Giuseppe-Motta, CP 5, CH-1211 Geneva 20 *Tel* 34 64 00 *Telex* 23 260 *Cable* METEOMOND GENEVA *Chief, Lang Branch* L Colson.

Founded in 1951, when it took over the work of the 73-year-old International Meteorological Association and became an agency of the UN, WMO employs a permanent staff of translators/interpreters and utilizes the services of free-lancers regularly, with conditions of employment, examinations, etc—the same as for other international civil servants. Main target and source languages: English, French, German, Spanish, Russian.

Publications Records and reports of congresses, cloud atlases, manuals on nomenclature, weather reporting, and guides to regulations and instrumentation.

Thailand

UNITED NATIONS ECONOMIC AND SOCIAL COMMISSION FOR ASIA AND THE PACIFIC (UN ESCAP)

Sala Santitham, Bangkok 2 *Tel* 2829-161, 171, 181.

Union of Soviet Socialist Republics

ALL-UNION RESEARCH INSTITUTE FOR ENGINEERING INFORMATION (Vsesoyuznyi Nauchno-Issledovatel'skii Institut Tekhnicheskoi Informatsii, Klassifikatsii i Kodirovaniya, VNIIKI)
Ul Scuseva 4, Moscow K-1.

The Terminology Bank of the Automated System for the Terminological Information Service (SBT ACITO) provides terminological information service and preparation of different lists of standardized terms in the fields of Terminology of the State Standards (GOST), ISO-Recommendations and Standards, IEC-Recommendations, CMEA Standards, other foreign standards.

Languages include German, English, French, and Russian with a projected language registration of Rumanian, Bulgarian, Czech, Polish.

United Kingdom

ASLIB
3 Belgrave Sq, London SW1X 8PL, UK *Tel* (01) 235 5050 *Telex* 23667 *Dir-Gen* Basil Saunders. *Conference Dept* Barbara Hobbs.'

An association of technical translation and informatics groups for promoting the effective management and use of information in industry and commerce, central and local government, educations and the professions. Since the translation of technical documents is costly and time-consuming—and this is particularly true if the same document is translated more than once because individual organizations commissioning translations are unaware of each other's activity—the service Aslib offers is designed to save members' time and money and to increase the effectiveness of their translating effort by providing a central index to translations which have been made.

Since 1951 Aslib has maintained an index to English translations of articles in all languages and numerous subject fields with emphasis on science and technology, including entries listed in the past in *Translations register-index, Transatom Bulletin, USAEC Translations List,* and *World Transindex* (see Sec 6, Journals). It also recommends suitable translators with linguistic proficiency in given subject fields.

The proceedings of their 1978 "Translating and the Computer" seminar will be published by North-Holland, 335 Jan van Galenstraat, PO Box 103, NL-1000 AC Amsterdam, the Netherlands.

ASSOCIATION INTERNATIONALE DES BIBLIOTHÉCAIRES ET DOCUMENTA-LISTES AGRICOLES, *see* International Association of Agricultural Librarians and Documentalists (IAALD)

ASSOCIATION INTERNATIONALE DES ÉTUDES ET RECHERCHES SUR L'INFORMATION, *see* International Association for Mass Communication Research

ASSOCIATION OF LIBRARIES OF JUDAICA AND HEBRAICA IN EUROPE
Jews' College Library, 11 Montagu Pl, London W1, UK
Publications Occasional newsletter.

BIODETERIORATION INFORMATION CENTER
Biological Sciences, Univ of Aston, 80 Colehill St, Birmingham B4 7PF, UK.
Publications *International Biodeterioration Bulletin* (editions in English, French, German, and Spanish; T A Oxley, H O W Eggins, eds).

THE BRITISH LIBRARY LENDING DIVISION
Wetherby, Yorkshire.

The former National Lending Library for Science and Technology began in 1959 to sponsor the cover-to-cover translation into English of specific Russian journals with scientific or technological content. The initial program covered 17 titles, but some of these are no longer translated, some are now translated selectively (non-technical or low-interest material being excluded), and some are now covered by translation journals based on more than one original journal. Other titles and languages have been taken into the program.

The Lending Division is now responsible for the overall financial control of the program, but the translating, technical editing, production, and marketing of the journals are the responsibility of various Research Associations, learned societies, and commercial publishers. The English-language titles are listed below together with details about each one. Each journal is available on subscription only from the address shown; none is available from the British Library.

Publications *Automatic Welding* (Welding Inst, Abington Hall, Abington, Cambridge CB1 6AL, UK); *International Polymer Science and Technology* (RAPRA, Shawbury, Shrewsbury, Salop SY4 4NR, UK); *Machines and Tooling; Russian Engineering Journal* (PERA, Melton Mowbray, Leics LE13 OPB, UK); *Russian Chemical Reviews; Russian Journal of Inorganic Chemistry; Russian Journal of Physical Chemistry* (The Chemical Society, Distribution Ctr, Blackhorse Rd, Letchworth, Herts SG6 1HN, UK); *Russian Mathematical Surveys* (London Mathematical Society, Macmillan Journals, Brunel Rd, Basingstoke, Hants RG21 2XS, UK); *Steel in the USSR* (Metals Society, 1 Carlton Terrace, London SW1Y 5DB, UK); *Thermal Engineering* (Building Services Research and Information Association, Pergamon Press, Headington Hall, Oxford OX3 OBW, UK); *Welding Production* (Welding Institute, Abington Hall, Abington, Cambridge CB1 6 AL, UK).

FÉDÉRATION INTERNATIONALE DES HÔPITAUX, *see* International Hospital Federation

FÉDÉRATION INTERNATIONALE DES LANGUES ET LITTÉRATURES MODERNES, *see* International Federation of Modern Languages and Literatures

INTER-GOVERNMENTAL MARITIME CONSULTATIVE ORGANIZATION (IMCO) (Organisation Intergouvernementale Consultative de la Navigation Maritime)
101-104 Piccadilly, London W1V OAE, UK *Tel* (01) 499 9040 *Telex* 23588 *Cable* INMARCOR-LONDON W1.

Within the Conference Division of IMCO there are at present four translation sections (English, French, Russian, and Spanish), which constitute probably the most important noncommercial units in the world specializing solely in the translation of maritime texts of a technical nature: international conventions, resolutions, recommendations, etc. Subjects include: ship design and construction; stability, load-lines and container transport; tonnage measurement; navigation and traffic separation; maritime radio & satellite communications; safety, live-saving appliances & fire-fighting; search and rescue at sea; transport of dangerous goods and special cargoes; novel marine craft, prevention & control of marine pollution; international maritime law and administration.

In the specific case of the Spanish translation section, in view of the fact that most technical maritime texts originate in English, a systematic effort is made, with the cooperation of Spanish-speaking member countries, to establish an acceptable uniform standard Spanish terminology in the above-mentioned fields in order to obviate differences in usage that have developed historically both within and between Spain and Latin America.

INTERNATIONAL ASSOCIATION FOR MASS COMMUNICATION RESEARCH (Association internationale des études et recherches sur l'information)
Ctr for Mass Communication Research, Univ of Leicester, 104 Regent Rd, Leicester Le1 7LT, UK *Tel* (0533) 28437 *Pres* James D Halloran *Secy* Emil Dusiska.

No permanent staff of translators or interpreters, but the association does use the services of free-lance translators and interpreters on occasion for biennial international conferences and general assemblies where simultaneous translators are required for a whole week. These take place in various countries. Major languages: French and German, occasionally Italian, Spanish, and East European languages. Target language is mainly English, sometimes French.

INTERNATIONAL ASSOCIATION OF AGRICULTURAL LIBRARIANS AND DOCUMENTALISTS (IAALD) (Association Internationale des Bibliothécaires et Documentalistes Agricoles)
Library Ministry of Agriculture, Fisheries & Food, Central Veterinary Laboratory, New Haw, Weybridge, Surrey, KT15 3NB, UK
Publications *Quarterly Bulletin; Current Agricultural Serials; Primer for Agricultural Libraries.*

INTERNATIONAL COFFEE ORGANIZATION (ICO)
22 Berners St, GB-London W1P 4DD *Tel* 580 8590 *Telex* 267659 *Cable* INTERCAFE.

INTERNATIONAL FEDERATION OF MODERN LANGUAGES AND LITERA- TURES (Fédération internationale des Langues et Littératures Modernes)
St Catharine's College, Cambridge, UK
Publications *Répertoire chronologique des Littératures modernes; Act of the Triennial Congresses.*

INTERNATIONAL HOSPITAL FEDERA- TION (Fédération internationale des Hôpitaux)
126 Albert St, GB-London NW1 7NF.
Publications *World Hospitals* (quarterly in English with French and Spanish supplements).

INTERNATIONAL UNION OF PURE AND APPLIED CHEMISTRY (IUPAC) (Union internationale de Chimie pure et appliquée)
Bank Court Chambers, 2-3 Pound Way, Cowley Ctr, Oxford OX4 3YF, UK *Tel* (0865) 770125, 772834.
Publications *Pure and Applied Chemistry* (One vol of 12 issues each year); *Information Bulletin.*

ORGANISATION INTERGOUVERNE- MENTALE CONSULTATIVE DE LA NAVIGATION MARITIME, *see* Inter-Governmental Maritime Consultative Organization (IMCO)

UNION DE L'EUROPE OCCIDENTALE (UEO), *see* Western European Union (WEU)

UNION INTERNATIONALE DE CHIMIE PURE ET APPLIQUÉE, *see* International Union of Pure and Applied Chemistry (IUPAC)

WESTERN EUROPEAN UNION (WEU) (Union de L'Europe Occidentale, UEO)
9 Grosvenor Pl, GB-London SW1 7HL, UK *Tel* 235 5351 *Cable* EURUNI-KNIGHTS.

United States of America

AMERICAN ACADEMY OF ARTS AND SCIENCES
Survey of Translation Needs, 165 Allandale St, Jamaica Plain Sta, Boston, MA 02130 *Tel* 617-522-2400 *Dir* Harriet Ritvo.
Conducted a "Survey of Translation Needs in the History of Architecture," made possible by a grant from the National Endowment for the Humanities and designed to explore a single aspect of the larger problem of translation: to select texts for translation from foreign languages into English and to arrange for the translation and publication of source materials in uncommon languages, classic works of scholarship, recent scholarship in uncommon languages, and general histories. A steering committee is to be established, probably under the auspices of the Society for Architectural Historians, to consider these issues further and to enlist the help of appropriate specialists.

AMERICAN INSTITUTE OF CHEMICAL ENGINEERS
345 E 47 St, New York, NY 10017 *Tel* 212-644-8025.
Publications *International Chemical Engineering* (quarterly journal of translations from USSR, Eastern Europe, Asia, and Japan; Renate U Churchill, ed).

AMERICAN METEOROLOGICAL SO- CIETY (AMS)
45 Beacon St, Boston, MA 02108.
Compiles and publishes abstracts covering all fields of environmental science and astrophysics: glaciology, hydrology, physical oceanography, radio astronomy, geophysics, geomagnetism, etc. Also produces machine-readable tapes of its publications for the National Oceanographic and Atmospheric Agency (NOAA). The latest detailed data indicate the use of foreign periodicals from 125–130 countries in about 40 languages and from over 1000 serials. The majority of items abstracted come from 10–12 countries in six to eight languages: Russian, German, French, Japanese, Spanish, Italian, and some Hungarian, Polish, and Dutch.
Publications *AMS Bulletin; Meteorological and Geoastrophysical Abstracts (MGA).*

ASSOCIATION OF CARIBBEAN UNI- VERSITY AND RESEARCH LIBRAR- IES (ACURIL)
Box S, Univ Sta, San Juan, PR 00931 *Pres* Maritza Eustatia *Gen Secy* Oneida R Ortiz.
Translations for publications done by Publications Committee, those for Council or Committee meetings by members. Simultaneous interpretation and translation used for annual conferences in Spanish and English, at times in French.
Publications *ACURIL Newsletter.*

ASSOCIATION OF SCIENTIFIC INFOR- MATION
Dissemination Centers, PO Box 8105, Athens, GA 30601
Publications *ASIDIC Newsletter.*

BANQUE INTERNATIONALE POUR LA RECONSTRUCTION ET LE DÉVEL- OPPEMENT (BIRD), *see* World Bank

BUREAU OF ECONOMIC ANALYSIS
Foreign Demographic Analysis Div, US Dept of Commerce, 14 & K Sts NW, Washington, DC 20235 *Tel* 202-655-4000.

CENTER FOR INTER-AMERICAN RE- LATIONS
680 Park Ave, New York, NY 10021 *Tel* 212-249-8950.
Publications *Review* (English language journal devoted to Latin American & Caribbean literature and art).

COLD REGIONS BIBLIOGRAPHY PROJECT
Science and Technology Div, Library of Congress, Washington, DC 20540 *Tel* 201-426-5668 *Dir* Geza T Thoronyi.

DEFENSE INTELLIGENCE AGENCY
Translations Branch of the Central Reference Div, Arlington Hall, Arlington, VA 22212.

DOMESTIC AND INTERNATIONAL BUSINESS ADMINISTRATION (DIBA)
US Dept of Commerce, 14 St bet E St & Constitution Ave, Washington, DC 20001 *Tel* 202-377-2000.
Assists the US export business community in expanding its international business through (1) reports on each foreign country's economic and marketing conditions, trading regulations; (2) export statistics of the world's leading exporting countries to most of the world's importing countries by individual products, based on original foreign country statistical sources; (3) dissemination of trade leads to US exporters and assisting foreign buyers in contacting appropriate US firms; (4) organization of the participation of US exporters in overseas trade events. DIBA utilizes a multitude of foreign language resources, both oral and written, in promoting US products in printed matter in many languages.

ECONOMIC DEVELOPMENT ADMINIS- TRATION (EDA)
Dept of Commerce, 14 St bet E St & Constitution Ave NW, Washington, DC 20001 *Tel* 202-377-2000.
Distinct from the Office of Minority Business Enterprise, which works entirely in English, the EDA helps finance projects in "rural business" among large minorities speaking foreign languages. It also deals with Indian tribes in the Southwest.

ENVIRONMENTAL PROTECTION AGENCY (EPA)
Translations Service, Yorktown Bldg #340, Research Triangle Park, NC 27711.

FONDS MONÉTAIRE INTERNATIONAL (FMI), *see* International Monetary Fund (IMF)

INFORMATION & RESEARCH MAN- AGEMENT
39 Mine St, New Brunswick, NJ 08901 *Tel* 201-828-1242.
Publications *IRM Reports.*

INTER-AMERICAN COMMISSION OF HUMAN RIGHTS
Organization of American States (OAS), 1725 I St NW, Washington, DC 20006 *Tel* 202-331-1010.

INTER-AMERICAN COMMISSION OF WOMEN
Organization of American States (OAS), 1735 I St NW, Washington, DC 20006 *Tel* 202-331-1010.

INTER-AMERICAN DEFENSE BOARD
Organization of American States (OAS), 2600 16 St NW, Washington, DC 20009 *Tel* 202-308-1605.

INTER-AMERICAN INSTITUTE OF AGRICULTURAL SCIENCES

Organization of American States (OAS), 1725 I St NW, Washington, DC 20006 *Tel* 202-331-1010.

INTER-AMERICAN NUCLEAR ENERGY COMMISSION

Organization of American States (OAS), 1735 I St NW, Washington, DC 20006 *Tel* 202-331-1010.

INTER-AMERICAN STATISTICAL UNIT

Organization of American States (OAS), 1725 I St NW, Washington, DC 20006 *Tel* 202-331-1010.

INTERNATIONAL ASSOCIATION OF ORIENTALIST LIBRARIANS

c/o Bronwen Solyom, Asian Studies Program, Univ of Hawaii at Manoa, 1890 East-West Rd, Honolulu, Hawaii 96822.

INTERNATIONAL ASSOCIATION OF SCHOOL LIBRARIANSHIP

Western Michigan Univ, Kalamazoo, MI 49008.

Publications *Newsletter of the IASL* (quarterly); *Conference Proceedings*.

INTERNATIONAL INSTITUTE OF IBEROAMERICAN LITERATURE

1312 CL, Univ of Pittsburgh, PA 15260.

Publications *Revista Iberoamericana; Memorias*.

INTERNATIONAL MONETARY FUND (IMF) (Fonds Monétaire International, FMI)

Washington, DC 20431 *Tel* 202-393-6362 *Cable* INTERFUND.

Publications *International Financial Statistics* (editions in English, French, and Spanish; Earl Hicks, ed).

INTERNATIONAL READING ASSOCIATION

800 Barksdale Rd, PO Box 8139, Newark, DE 19711 *Pres* Dorothy S Strickland, Kean College *Vice Pres* Roger Farr, Indiana Univ *Exec Dir* Ralph C Staiger.

Does not have a permanent staff of translators/interpreters, but utilizes interpreters from those available in cities or nearby places where international meetings are held. Permanent staff includes a number of bilingual and trilingual members who utilize their knowledge for small translation jobs (letters, reports, etc.), but not for the translation of books. Free-lance simultaneous interpreters used in world congresses. Source and target languages: English, French, Spanish, German, and Japanese.

Maintains a European office in Paris (Association International pour la Lecture) and a Latin American office in Buenos Aires (Asociación Internacional Lectura).

Publications a Spanish-language journal on reading in Latin America planned for the future.

INTERNATIONAL TELECOMMUNICATIONS SATELLITE CONSORTIUM (INTELSAT)

950 L'Enfant Plaza S, SW, Washington, DC 20024 *Tel* 202-554-6410.

LANGUAGE AND LANGUAGE BEHAVIOR ABSTRACTS

PO Box 2206, San Diego, CA 92122.

A multidisciplinary quarterly reference work providing access to the world literature. Each issue includes approximately 1500 English abstracts from 1000 publications in 32 languages and 25 disciplines: anthropology, applied linguistics, audiology, clinical psychology, communication sciences, education, gerontology, laryngology, linguistics, neurology, otology, pediatrics, pharmacology, philosophy, phonetics, physiology, psychiatry, psycholinguistics, psychology, rhetoric, semiotics, sociolinguistics, sociology, speech, speech pathology.

Cumulative author, subject, book, and periodical indices available to Volumes I–V (1967–1971).

MARITIME ADMINISTRATION

US Dept of Commerce, 15 & E Sts NW, Washington, DC 20235 *Tel* 202-377-200.

Office of International Activities maintains on its staff employees who gather information on foreign shipping costs and who must know the local languages in Rome, Brussels, Rio de Janeiro, Tokyo, and London. The agency also takes part in international conferences on shipping, and maintains Russian interpreters on its staff for this purpose.

NATIONAL AERONAUTICS AND SPACE ADMINISTRATION (NASA)

Scientific and Technical Information Div, NANA KSS-1, Washington, DC 20546.

Practically no translation work done in-house, but contracted out to translation agencies, with some work being channeled through JPRS to free-lance translators. All contractors must follow a strict format provided by the agency: they must provide a suitable abstract, cover page, title page, three xerographic copies, and pay all incidental charges. NASA, in return, pays a variety of rates per 1000 words of text, specifying different rates for "rush," "standard," and "economy" translations. It also differentiates between rates for technical and nontechnical material.

NATIONAL BUREAU OF STANDARDS

Terminology Data Bank, Standards Information Service (SIS), US Dept of Commerce, Gaithersburg, MD 20760 *Mailing Address* Bldg 225 #B162, Washington, DC 20234 *Tel* 301-921-2587 *Mgr* William Slattery *Foreign Standards Specialist* Cheryl Wise.

Coordinates US and foreign scientific and industrial standards of all kinds through cooperation with international bodies. Conducts between 30 and 40 percent of its work in French, German, and Russian (correspondence and technical documents). As a member of several international organizations—International Organization for Legal Metrology, International Organization for Standardization (ISO), Inter-

national Information Center for Terminology (INFOTERM) and others—it translates into English their publications which appear in French.

The Standards Information Service (SIS) is a terminological information service with KWIC Index.

NATIONAL INSTITUTES OF HEALTH (NIH)

Translations Section, 9000 Rockville Pike, Bethesda, MD 20014.

Translations contracts are awarded through the NIH Procurement Office, which solicits bids by language from a list of many languages submitted by the Translations Section.

NATIONAL OCEANIC AND ATMOSPHERIC ADMINISTRATION (NOAA)

US Dept of Commerce, NMFS, 3300 Whitehaven St NW, Washington, DC 20007 *Tel* 202-655-4000.

NOAA depends on the Language Services Branch, Office of International Fisheries (a part of NOAA's National Marine Fisheries Service) for its translation services. At regular intervals it issues the following publications: "Received or Planned Current Foreign Fisheries, Oceanographic and Atmospheric Translations," listing documents of interest to scientists, researchers, administrators, businessmen, and industry; "Survey of Foreign Fisheries, Oceanographic and Atmospheric Literature," containing full translations, summaries, or abstracts of foreign articles; "Translated Tables of Contents of Current Foreign Fisheries, Oceanographic and Atmospheric Publications."

NATIONAL TECHNICAL INFORMATION SERVICE (NTIS)

US Dept of Commerce, 425 13 St NW, Washington, DC 20004 *Tel* 202-724-3374. Orders to: NTIS, 5285 Port Royal Rd, Springfield, VA 22151.

NTIS is the sales agent for numerous government technical documents in photocopy form and administers the National Science Foundation's program to obtain translations of scientific literature by the expenditure abroad of Public Law 480 funds accumulated in foreign currencies. Translations, most of them not commercially available, are mainly from Russian, French, and German.

Publications *Translations of People's Republic of China Press,* published in three series: daily survey of newspapers, magazine selections, and background briefs. Translations by US Consulate General in Hong Kong.

ORGANIZATION OF AMERICAN STATES (OAS)

17 & Constitution Ave NW, Washington, DC 20006.

An international intergovernmental organization for Latin American countries and the United States with 25 member states employing four official languages: Spanish (18), English (5), French (1), Portuguese (1).

Like the United Nations, the OAS has its own staff of translators and interpreters, and the division is composed of four language units (one for each official language) and an interpreting unit. Although there are about 25 translators in the units, the OAS also engages free-lance translators and conference interpreters. The interpreting unit has 10 staff interpreters. The OAS does not hire escort interpreters. In general, the OAS adopts the pay rates of the US Department of State, which usually serve as guidelines for the Washington, DC, metropolitan area.

Translators and interpreters are required to pass an aptitude test, regardless of the nature of their appointment, permanent or temporary. The organization has a training program for in-house trainees only, who must also pass an aptitude test. Because the OAS maintains high-quality standards of both translation and interpretation, its aptitude tests are difficult.

Publications *OAS Chronicle* (editions in English and Spanish); *OAS Directory* (editions in English, French, Spanish, and Portuguese); *Inter-American Review of Bibliography* (text in English, Portuguese, and Spanish; Armando Correia Pacheco, ed).

PAN AMERICAN HEALTH ORGANIZATION (PAHO)
Computerized Linguistic Ctr, 525 23 & Virginia Aves NW, Washington, DC 20037 *Tel* 202-223-4700.

REGIONAL INFORMATION & COMMUNICATION EXCHANGE
Fondren Library, Rice Univ, Houston, TX 77001 *Tel* 713-528-3553 *Telex* 910-881-3766.
Publications *Regional Information & Communications Exchange Newsletter.*

SOCIETY FOR INTERNATIONAL DEVELOPMENT
1346 Connecticut Ave NW, Washington, DC 20036.
Publications *Survey of International Development* (French edition: *Aperçu sur le Developpement International;* Spanish edition: *Commentarios Sobre el Desarrollo Internacional).*

TRANSLATION RESEARCH INSTITUTE
5914 Pulaski Ave, Philadelphia, PA 91944 *Dir* Charles Parsons.
Publications *Russian–English Dictionary of Suppositional Names* by Dov B Lederman; *Russian–English Dictionary of . . . ost' Words* by Charles Parsons; *Russian–English Index to Scientific Apparatus Nomenclature* by James F Shipp; *RETX (Russian–English Translators Exchange* (see Sec 6, Journals).

UNITED NATIONS (UN)
New York, NY 10017 *Tel* 212-754-6487 *Cable* UNATIONS.

US ARMY COLD REGIONS LABORATORY
Corps of Engineers, PO Box 282, Hanover, NH 03755 *Tel* 603-643-3280.
Publications *Sendout.*

US ARMY FOREIGN SCIENCE AND TECHNOLOGY CENTER (FSTC)
Foreign Language Research Branch, 220 Seventh St NE, Charlottesville, VA 22901.

US BUREAU OF THE CENSUS
Dept of Commerce, Washington, DC 20233 *Tel* 202-655-4000.

The Bureau provides "Overseas Consultation and Technical Services," advising foreign governments in the developing countries on establishing statistical programs covering demographics, industry, agriculture, and economics. A portion of this work is done in Spanish and Portuguese, some in Arabic or French. For the regular decennial census in 1980, the Bureau plans to use bilingual enumerators on a local basis, to provide a telephone answering service in several languages, and to publish a booklet translating common questions about the Census into many languages. The Census of Puerto Rico is taken entirely in Spanish.

US DEPARTMENT OF ENERGY (DOE)
Washington, DC 20545.

US DEPARTMENT OF STATE
Language Services Div, 320 21 St NE, Washington, DC 20002 *Tel* 202-632-0580.

The Division consists of a Translating Branch and an Interpreting Branch, with in-house linguists in each. It also maintains its own list of cleared contract interpreters and translators who have passed the Division's test.

US JOINT PUBLICATIONS RESEARCH SERVICE (JPRS)
1000 N Glebe Rd, Arlington, VA 22201. Orders to: National Technical Information Service (NTIS), Springfield, VA 22161.

Established in 1957 by the Central Intelligence Agency (CIA) and maintained until 1973 as part of the US Dept of Commerce, the JPRS is the only Federal office or agency founded for the express purpose of (1) servicing translation requests of various Federal agencies; (2) assigning translations directly to free-lance translators in the US; (3) tapping the translator capabilities of a large group of American citizens; and (4) providing systematic translation of materials on economics, industry, trade, and services, and on natural and labor resources. It is one of the largest translation services in the country.

Starting with one office in New York in 1957, it added another in Washington, DC, later that year, and established a West Coast office in San Francisco in 1960. In 1961 the administration of the Service was transferred to the Office of Technical Services of the US Dept of Commerce.

JPRS receives requests from a wide variety of Federal agencies, contracts with free-lance translators qualified in many subject fields, and publishes thousands of pages of translations or of research in the form of abstracts per year. It also initiates translations in various fields as part of its information-gathering programs.

Publications *Translations on Japan* (1975, irreg, 1–2 per month); *Translations on Latin America* (1967, irreg, 3–4 per week); *Translations on Law of the Sea* (irreg, 1–2 per month); *Translations on Mongolia* (irreg, 4–6 per year); *Translations on Eastern Europe: Economic and Industrial Affairs* (1968, irreg, 10–14 per month); *Translations on Eastern Europe: Political, Sociological, and Military Affairs* (1968, irreg, 10–14 per month); *Translations on Eastern Europe: Scientific Affairs* (1968, irreg, 2–4 per month); *Translations on Environmental Quality* (1973, irreg, 2–3 per month); *Translations on Near East and North Africa* (irreg, 10–14 per month); *Translations on North Korea* (1966, irreg, 4–5 per month); *Translations and Reprints from the Original Sources of European History* (irreg, Univ of Pennsylvania Vol 6 no 2); *Translations on South and East Asia* (irreg, 5–6 per month); *Translations on Subsaharan Africa* (irreg, 9–12 per month); *Translations on Telecommunications Policy* (irreg); *Translations on USSR Economic Affairs* (1969, irreg, 9–12 per month); *Translations on USSR Industrial Affairs* (1969, irreg, 5–7 per month); *Translations on USSR Military Affairs* (irreg, 9–10 per month); *Translations on USSR Resources* (1969, irreg, 6–8 per month); *Translations on USSR Political and Sociological Affairs* (1969, irreg, 10–12 per month); *Translations on USSR Science and Technology: Biomedical Sciences* (1976, irreg, 4–6 per month); *Translations on USSR Science and Technology: Physical Sciences and Technology* (irreg, 4–6 per month); *Translations on USSR Trade and Services* (1973, irreg, 10–12 per month); *Translations on Vietnam* (1966, irreg, 2–3 per week); *Translations on Western Europe* (1968, irreg, 3–4 per week).

US PATENT AND TRADEMARK OFFICE
Dept of Commerce, 2021 Jefferson Davis Hwy, Arlington, VA 22202 *Tel* 703-557-3158.

Although foreign patent holders must apply for corresponding US patents in English, the Office translates the original patents into English from the following languages: German, French, Japanese, Italian, Russian, the Scandinavian group, Spanish, Portuguese, Czech, and Chinese. These translations are then included in a monthly accessions list with summaries.

US TRAVEL SERVICE (USTS)
Dept of Commerce, 14 St bet E St and Constitution Ave NW, Washington, DC 20001 *Tel* 202-377-2000.

USTS personnel, stationed at its offices in France, Germany, Japan, Mexico, and Quebec, Canada, must have a reasonable degree of fluency in the local language in order to deal with local government officials and others on travel questions. All translations of USTS printed matter are done overseas.

WORLD BANK (Banque Internationale pour la Reconstruction et le Développement, BIRD)
1818 H St NW, Washington, DC 20433 *Tel* 202-477-4222.

YIVO INSTITUTE FOR JEWISH RESEARCH
1048 Fifth Ave, New York, NY 10028.
Publications *News of the YIVO* (text in English and Yiddish).

Index